less is more

content
dictates form

god is in
the details

content
dictates
form

less
is
more

content
dictates
form

god is in
the details

less is more

less
is
more

god is in
the details

content
dictates
form

Finishing
the Hat

Stephen Sondheim

Finishing the Hat

Collected Lyrics (1954-1981)
with Attendant Comments,
Principles, Heresies,
Grudges, Whines
and Anecdotes

Alfred A. Knopf 🐕 New York 2010

This Is a Borzoi Book
Published by Alfred A. Knopf

Copyright © 2010 by Stephen Sondheim

All rights reserved. Published in the United States by Alfred A. Knopf,
a division of Random House, Inc., New York, and in Canada
by Random House of Canada Limited, Toronto.

www.aaknopf.com

Knopf, Borzoi Books, and the colophon are registered trademarks
of Random House, Inc.

Library of Congress Cataloging-in-Publication Data
Sondheim, Stephen.
[Songs. Selections. Texts]
Finishing the hat : collected lyrics (1954–1981) with attendant comments,
principles, heresies, grudges, whines and anecdotes /
by Stephen Sondheim.—1st ed.
p. cm.
ISBN 978-0-679-43907-3
Includes bibliographical references and index.
1. Musicals—Excerpts—Librettos.   2. Songs—Texts.   I. Title.
ML54.6.S69S66 2010
782.1'40268—dc22   2010011056

Manufactured in the United States of America
First Edition

To my unsung collaborators

Julius J. Epstein

Arthur Laurents

Burt Shevelove

Larry Gelbart

George Furth

James Goldman

John Weidman

Hugh Wheeler

James Lapine

"I collabor him and he collabors me."
— GEORGE FURTH, *Merrily We Roll Along*

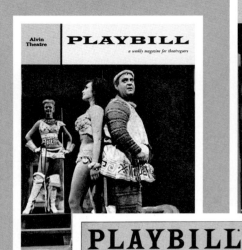

Contents

At a rehearsal for Sweeney Todd

Note to the Reader

In the lyrics that follow, I have often omitted the dialogue interwoven into them, for reasons of length. Dialogue is included only when necessary to understand the content and flow of the song.

Also, sprinkled throughout the book are thumbnail observations about the men and woman (yes, just one) who by general consensus comprise the Pantheon of Great Lyricists in the English-speaking musical theater. I have not included any living examples, for reasons explained in the Introduction, nor have I expounded on those who didn't write steadily for the theater, such as Johnny Mercer, Leo Robin, Carolyn Leigh, Howard Dietz, John LaTouche, Meredith Willson, DuBose Heyward, and others. I only wish they'd written more, because sometimes what they wrote was wonderful and would be worth commenting on. In particular, I have omitted assessments of Betty Comden and Adolph Green, and of Fred Ebb, because they are not dead to me—their loss is too recent, and they were friends.

There are some minor discrepancies between the lyrics printed herein and those printed in other sources because, apart from the occasional misprint, I sometimes change my mind about word choices after first, or even second, publication. The ones in this book can be considered definitive. Until I change my mind.

Cast of Characters

(In order of appearance)

Most of the lyricists and composers referred to in the following pages hail from musicals written before the 1980s. For those readers to whom some of these writers may be unfamiliar, let me offer this glossary of names and musical-theater credits (a number of them were playwrights, poets and novelists as well), accompanied by some of their more well-known shows (in italics) and theater songs (in quotation marks), thus avoiding the bumpy intrusions of having to identify them as they pop up in the commentaries.

Oscar Hammerstein II (1895–1960)
lyricist, librettist, occasional co-librettist
Show Boat; Oklahoma!; Carousel; The King and I
"Ol' Man River," "All the Things You Are,"
"Some Enchanted Evening"

Richard Rodgers (1902–1979)
composer, occasional lyricist
On Your Toes; The Boys from Syracuse; South Pacific; The Sound of Music
"My Funny Valentine," "Bewitched, Bewildered,"
"If I Loved You"

Jerome Kern (1885–1945)
composer
Sunny; Show Boat; Music in the Air
"Ol' Man River," "Smoke Gets in Your Eyes,"
"All the Things You Are"

Phyllis McGinley (1905–1978)
poet and occasional lyricist
Small Wonder

Noël Coward (1899–1973)
composer, lyricist, librettist, playwright, actor, director, etc.
Bitter Sweet; Conversation Piece; Tonight at 8:30
"Mad About the Boy," "I'll See You Again,"
"Mad Dogs and Englishmen"

Lorenz Hart (1895–1943)
lyricist, occasional co-librettist
A Connecticut Yankee; Babes in Arms; Pal Joey
"Blue Moon," "Where or When," "My Funny Valentine"

Alfred Newman (1901–1970)
film composer
Street Scene (film); *The Song of Bernadette* (film); *The Greatest Story Ever Told* (film)

Maxwell Anderson (1888–1959)
lyricist and librettist, although best known as a playwright
Knickerbocker Holiday; Lost in the Stars
"September Song," "Lost in the Stars"

Truman Capote (1924–1984)
lyricist, librettist, although best known as a novelist and short-story writer
House of Flowers

Anthony Burgess (1917–1993)
lyricist, librettist, although best known as a novelist
Cyrano de Bergerac; Dr. Faustus (opera)

Langston Hughes (1902–1967)
lyricist/librettist, although best known as a poet
Street Scene (contributed lyrics); *Simply Heavenly*

DuBose Heyward (1885–1940)
lyricist, librettist, playwright
Porgy and Bess (co-lyricist)
"Summertime," "My Man's Gone Now,"
"I Loves You, Porgy"

Richard Wilbur (b. 1921)
lyricist, although best known as a poet
Candide
"Glitter and Be Gay," "Make Our Garden Grow"

W. H. Auden (1907–1973)
lyricist, librettist, co-librettist, although best known
as a poet
The Rake's Progress

John Kander (b. 1927)
composer
A Family Affair; Chicago; Kiss of the Spider Woman
"Cabaret," "All That Jazz," "New York, New York"

Fred Ebb (1928–2004)
lyricist
Flora, the Red Menace; Cabaret; And the World Goes 'Round
"Willkommen," "Home," "Razzle Dazzle"

Jerry Bock (b. 1928)
composer, lyricist
Fiorello!; Fiddler on the Roof; The Rothschilds
"If I Were a Rich Man," "When Did I Fall in Love,"
"She Loves Me"

Sheldon Harnick (b. 1924)
lyricist
Tenderloin; The Apple Tree; She Loves Me
"Politics and Poker," "Matchmaker, Matchmaker,"
"Sunrise, Sunset"

Charles Strouse (b. 1928)
composer, occasional lyricist
Bye, Bye, Birdie; Golden Boy; Annie
"A Lot of Livin' to Do," "Once Upon a Time,"
"I Want to Be with You"

Lee Adams (b. 1924)
lyricist
*Applause; All American; It's A Bird . . . It's A Plane . . .
It's Superman*
"Put On A Happy Face," "You've Got Possibilities,"
"Welcome to the Theatre"

Irving Berlin (1888–1989)
lyricist, composer
As Thousands Cheer; This Is the Army; Annie Get Your Gun
"Alexander's Ragtime Band," "(We're Having a) Heat
Wave," "There's No Business Like Show Business"

Ira Gershwin (1896–1983)
lyricist, co-lyricist
Lady, Be Good; Funny Face; Lady in the Dark
"Embraceable You," "The Man I Love," "'S Wonderful"

Cole Porter (1891–1964)
lyricist, composer
Anything Goes; DuBarry Was a Lady; Kiss Me Kate
"Night and Day," "I Get a Kick Out of You,"
"Begin the Beguine"

George Gershwin (1898–1937)
composer
Girl Crazy; Of Thee I Sing; Porgy and Bess
"I Got Rhythm," "Summertime," "Love Is Sweeping
the Country"

Frank Loesser (1910–1969)
lyricist, composer
Where's Charley?; Guys and Dolls; The Most Happy Fella
"Once in Love with Amy," "Luck, Be a Lady,"
"Standing on the Corner"

Dorothy Fields (1905–1974)
lyricist, co-librettist
Blackbirds of 1928; A Tree Grows in Brooklyn; Sweet Charity
"I Can't Give You Anything But Love," "Make the Man
Love Me," "Big Spender"

Leonard Bernstein (1918–1990)
composer, occasional lyricist
On the Town; West Side Story; Candide
"New York, New York," "Maria," "Make Our
Garden Grow"

Craig Carnelia (b. 1949)
lyricist, composer
*Working; Is There Life After High School?;
Sweet Smell of Success*
"Just a Housewife," "The Kid Inside," "Fran and Janie"

E. Y. Harburg (1896–1981)
lyricist, co-librettist
Walk a Little Faster; Life Begins at 8:40; Finian's Rainbow
"Fun To Be Fooled," "Down With Love,"
"How Are Things in Glocca Morra?"

Kurt Weill (1900–1950)
composer
The Threepenny Opera; Lady in the Dark;
One Touch of Venus
"Ballad of Mack the Knife," "Speak Low," "September
Song"

Lionel Bart (1930–1999)
lyricist, composer
Lock Up Your Daughters; Oliver!
"Food, Glorious Food," "Oliver!," "As Long As He
Needs Me"

Alan Jay Lerner (1918–1986)
lyricist, librettist
Brigadoon; My Fair Lady; On a Clear Day You
Can See Forever
"I Could Have Danced All Night," "If Ever I Would Leave
You," "On a Clear Day You Can See Forever"

Frederick Loewe (1901–1988)
composer
Brigadoon; My Fair Lady; Camelot
"Almost Like Being in Love," "Wouldn't It Be Loverly?,"
"Camelot"

Leo Robin (1900–1984)
lyricist
By the Way; Hello Yourself; Gentlemen Prefer Blondes
"Thanks for the Memory," "Louise," "Diamonds Are a
Girl's Best Friend"

Jule Styne (1905–1994)
composer
High Button Shoes; Gypsy; Funny Girl
"I Still Get Jealous," "Everything's Coming Up Roses,"
"People"

Sammy Cahn (1913–1993)
lyricist, occasional composer
High Button Shoes; Skyscraper; Walking Happy
"Bei Mir Bist Du Schoen," "Time After Time,"
"Come Fly with Me"

Betty Comden (1917–2006) and
Adolph Green (1914–2002)
co-lyricists and co-librettists
On the Town; Bells Are Ringing; Hallelujah, Baby!
"New York, New York," "Some Other Time,"
"Long Before I Knew You"

Nacio Herb Brown (1896–1964)
composer
Singin' in the Rain (film); *Take a Chance*
"Singin' in the Rain," "All I Do Is Dream of You,"
"You Are My Lucky Star"

Ray Henderson (1896–1970)
composer, occasional lyricist
George White's Scandals; Good News; Follow Thru
"Bye Bye Blackbird," "I'm Sitting on Top of the World,"
"You're the Cream in My Coffee"

Harold Arlen (1905–1986)
composer, occasional lyricist
Bloomer Girl; St. Louis Woman; House of Flowers
"The Eagle and Me," "Any Place I Hang My Hat is
Home," "A Sleepin' Bee"

Cy Coleman (1929–2004)
composer
Sweet Charity; On the Twentieth Century; Barnum
"I've Got Your Number," "Big Spender," "If My Friends
Could See Me Now"

Morton Gould (1913–1996)
composer
Billion Dollar Baby; Arms and the Girl
"Bad Timing," "Nothin' for Nothin'," "A Cow, A Plough
and a Frau"

Jimmy McHugh (1894–1969)
composer
Blackbirds of 1928; Hello, Daddy; As the Girls Go
"I Can't Give You Anything But Love," "On the Sunny Side of the Street," "I'm in the Mood for Love"

Anne Caldwell (1867–1936)
lyricist, librettist
Criss Cross; Stepping Stones; Good Morning, Dearie

Carolyn Leigh (1926–1983)
lyricist
Peter Pan; Little Me; How Now, Dow Jones
"I Won't Grow Up," "On the Other Side of the Tracks," "Real Live Girl"

Sigmund Romberg (1887–1951)
composer
The Student Prince; The Desert Song; Up in Central Park
"Softly, as in a Morning Sunrise," "Lover, Come Back to Me," "April Snow"

Burton Lane (1912–1997)
composer
Hold on to Your Hats; Finian's Rainbow; On a Clear Day You Can See Forever
"The World Is in My Arms," "Old Devil Moon," "Come Back to Me"

Arthur Schwartz (1900–1984)
composer, occasional lyricist and librettist
The Band Wagon; At Home Abroad; A Tree Grows in Brooklyn
"Dancing in the Dark," "By Myself," "I Guess I'll Have to Change My Plan"

Otto Harbach (1873–1963)
lyricist, librettist
Rose Marie; The Desert Song; Roberta
"Smoke Gets in Your Eyes," "Indian Love Call," "Yesterdays"

Buddy DeSylva (1895–1950)
lyricist, composer, librettist
Good News; Take a Chance; Du Barry Was a Lady
"I'll Say She Does," "The Best Things in Life Are Free," "Life Is Just a Bowl of Cherries"

Lew Brown (1893–1958)
lyricist, occasional composer
Good News; Hold Everything!; Flying High
"Don't Sit Under the Apple Tree," "Button Up Your Overcoat," "You're the Cream in My Coffee"

Arthur Freed (1894–1973)
lyricist, composer
"Singin' in the Rain," "I've Got a Feelin' You're Foolin'," "Broadway Rhythm"

Howard Dietz (1896–1983)
lyricist
The Little Show; At Home Abroad; The Band Wagon
"Dancing in the Dark," "You and the Night and the Music," "Haunted Heart"

W. S. Gilbert (1836–1911)
lyricist, librettist
H.M.S. Pinafore; The Pirates of Penzance; The Mikado
"I'm Called Little Buttercup," "I Am the Very Model of a Modern Major-General," "The Flowers That Bloom in the Spring"

At the piano

Preface

There are only three principles necessary for a lyric writer, all of them familiar truisms. They were not immediately apparent to me when I started writing, but have come into focus via Oscar Hammerstein's tutoring, Strunk and White's huge little book *The Elements of Style* and my own sixty-some years of practicing the craft. I have not always been skilled or diligent enough to follow them as faithfully as I would like, but they underlie everything I've ever written. In no particular order, and to be written in stone:

Content Dictates Form

Less Is More

God Is in the Details

all in the service of

Clarity

without which nothing else matters.

If a lyric writer observes this mantra rigorously, he can turn out a respectable lyric. If he also has a feeling for music and rhythm, a sense of theater and something to say, he can turn out an interesting one. If in addition he has qualities such as humor, style, imagination and the numerous other gifts every writer could use, he might even turn out a good one, and with an understanding composer and a stimulating book writer, the sky's the limit.

Explication and examples will follow, especially in the chapters on *Pacific Overtures, Merrily We Roll Along* and *Assassins*.

At work

Introduction

This book is a contradiction in terms. Theater lyrics are not written to be read but to be sung, and sung as parts of a larger structure: musical comedy, musical play, revue—"musical" will suffice. Furthermore, almost all of the lyrics in these pages were written not just to be sung but to be sung in particular musicals by individual characters in specific situations. A printed collection of them, bereft of their dramatic circumstances and the music which gives them life, is a dubious proposition. Lyrics,* even poetic ones, are not poems. Poems are written to be read, silently or aloud, not sung. Some lyrics, awash with florid imagery, present themselves as poetry, but music only underscores (yes) the self-consciousness of the effort. In theatrical fact, it is usually the plainer and flatter lyric that soars poetically when infused with music. Oscar Hammerstein II's

> *Oh, what a beautiful mornin',*
> *Oh, what a beautiful day.*
> *I got a beautiful feelin'*
> *Ev'rythin's goin' my way!*

is much more evocative than this couplet from his "All the Things You Are":

> *You are the promised kiss of springtime*
> *That makes the lonely winter seem long.*

The first, buoyed by Richard Rodgers's airy music, sounds as profoundly simple (especially if you ignore the dialect) as something by Robert Frost. The second sounds even more overripe than it is in print, given Jerome Kern's setting, which merely by being music—

and beautiful music, unfortunately—makes the extravagance of the words bathetic.

Poetry is an art of concision, lyrics of expansion. Poems depend on packed images, on resonance and juxtaposition, on density. Every reader absorbs a poem at his** own pace, inflecting it with his own rhythms, stresses and tone. The tempo is dictated less by what the poet intends than by the reader's comprehension. All of us, as we read poetry (prose, too), slow down, speed up, even stop to reread when overwhelmed by the extravagance of the images or confused by the grammatical eccentricities. The poet may guide us with punctuation and layout and seduce us with the subtle abutment of words and sounds, but it is we who supply the musical treatment.†

Poetry can be set to music gracefully, as Franz Schubert and a long line of others have proved, but the music benefits more from the poem which gives it structure than the poem does from the music, which often distorts not only the poet's phrasing but also the language itself, clipping syllables short or extending them into near-unintelligibility. Music straitjackets a poem and prevents it from breathing on its own, whereas it liberates a lyric. Poetry doesn't need music; lyrics do.

---

*GROUND RULE 1: In this book the word "lyrics" denotes musical-theater lyrics, unless otherwise specified.

**GROUND RULE 2: Rather than hacking my way through a jungle of convoluted syntax every time I want to refer to people of both genders, by "he" and "his" and other assorted masculine pronouns I mean "she" and "her" as well, unless I'm referring to a particular person.

†NOËL COWARD, a writer whose lyrics I cordially but intensely dislike, summed up the problem succinctly in his Introduction to his own book of lyrics: "Unless the reader happens to know the tune to which the lyric has been set, his eye is liable to be bewildered by what appears to be a complete departure from the written rhythm to which his ear has subconsciously become accustomed. . . . In many instances, the words and rhythms he reads, divorced from the melody line that holds them together, may appear to be suddenly erratic, inept or even nonsensical."

Lyrics are not light verse, either. Light verse doesn't demand music because it supplies its own. All those emphatic rhythms, ringing rhymes, repeated refrains: the poem sings as it's being read. Browning's "The Pied Piper of Hamelin" percolates with unwritten music so strong that I would guess everybody reads it at the same trotting pace. In fact light verse, like "serious" poetry,* is diminished by being set to music. Music either thuddingly underlines the dum-de-dum rhythms or willfully deforms them, trying to disguise the very singsong quality that gives the verse its character. This is why "The Pied Piper" has never been set well: take away the singsong and you destroy the poem, keep it in the music and you bore the listener mercilessly with rhythmic repetition. Music tends to hammer light verse into monotony or shatter its grace. It would seem easy to set Dorothy Parker's famous "Comment" to music:

> *Oh, life is a glorious cycle of song,*
> *A medley of extemporanea;*
> *And love is a thing that can never go wrong;*
> *And I am Marie of Roumania.*

The trouble is that she's already done it. The jauntiness of the rhythm perfectly balances the wry self-pity of the words. Music doesn't understate, that's not its job: its job is to emphasize and support the words or, as in opera, dominate them. Thus any accompaniment, whether light or lyrical, is likely either to turn Parker's irony into a joke or to drown it in sentimentality. Light verse is complete unto itself. Lyrics by definition lack something; if they don't, they're probably not good lyrics.

When it comes to theater songs, the composer is in charge. Performers can color a lyric with phrasing and rubato (rhythmic fluidity), but it's the melody which dictates the lyric's rhythms and pauses and inflections, the accompaniment which sets the pace and tone. These specific choices control our emotional response, just as a movie director's camera controls it by restricting our point of view, forcing us to look at the details he wants us to notice. For the songwriter, it's a matter of what phrase, what word, he wants us to focus on; for the director, what face, what gesture. An actor singing "Oh, what a beautiful mornin' " might want to emphasize "beautiful," but Rodgers forces him to emphasize "mornin' " by setting the word on the strongest beat in the measure and the highest note in the melody. Song stylists—club singers, recording artists, jazz vocalists and the like— often take liberties with lyric phrasings and tempos, but the music restricts their choices. This is not always a good thing: The unlucky lady who has to sing "Seven to midnight I *hear* drums" from Rodgers and Hart's "Ten Cents a Dance" is forced to sing "*hear* drums" no matter how she squirms. The same holds true for anyone singing "It Never Entered My Mind" in the same team's *Higher and Higher;* she has to make "And order orange *juice* for one," sound natural.** The songwriter sets the emphasis, for good or for ill.

Another thing about music is that it isn't explicit. Play a recording of Debussy's *La Mer* for someone who hasn't heard it and ask what it brings to mind. The reply will seldom be "The sea!," although in Music Appreciation courses that's what is taught. True enough, over the years certain orchestral sounds have come to be associated with specific emotions, especially in the movies (saxophones for sexiness, bassoons for clumsiness, flutes for happiness), just as certain instrumental themes resonate immediately from repeated exposure: Alfred Newman's title music from *Street Scene* evokes New York, just as "Dixie" evokes the South and "La Marseillaise," France. Still, music is abstract and its function in song is to fulfill what it accompanies; poems are fulfilled all by themselves. Under spoken text, music is background, atmosphere and mood and nothing more. In song, music

---

*GROUND RULE 3: To some, there is a chasm between "light" and "serious"; to me they differ only in style, not in substance. I put Phyllis McGinley right up there with Keats and Shelley.

**GROUND RULE 4: Mis-stressing is a cardinal sin, and as an occasional sinner myself, it drives me crazy. More on this subject later.

is an equal partner. Hammerstein, like all good lyricists, not only understood but counted on the power of music to glorify the understatement of his language, a collaborative surrender which poets who write for musical theater tend to underestimate or resist. Professional lyricists recognize music's capacity not only to make a lyric vibrate, but also to smother it to death. If a lyric is too full of itself, as in "All the Things You Are," music can make it muddy or grandiose. The lyrics of Maxwell Anderson, Truman Capote, Anthony Burgess and Langston Hughes, to name some of the most prominent crossover poets, fall into this trap. Their lyrics convey the aura of a royal visit: they announce the presence of the writer. When the stories deal with exotic times or cultures, as in Burgess's lyrics for *Cyrano* and Capote's for *House of Flowers,* the self-consciousness can be acceptable, but when the characters are supposed to be speaking in the vernacular, as in Hughes's *Street Scene* and Anderson's *Lost in the Stars,* the lyrics become faintly but persistently ludicrous.

It's the music that does them in. Poets tend to be poor lyricists because their verse has its own inner music and doesn't make allowance for the real thing. The two great exceptions are DuBose Heyward's lyrics in *Porgy and Bess* and Richard Wilbur's in *Candide.* Their work bespeaks an understanding not only of how music operates with words, but of how words operate in drama. They know how to combine the density of poetry with the openness of lyrics and still not intrude their own selves into the characters. I hasten to add that intrusion is a problem for non-poet lyricists as well. To cite a favorite example of my own, from *West Side Story:* "It's alarming / How charming / I feel," sings Maria, a lower-class Puerto Rican girl who has been brought up on street argot and whose brother is a gang leader, but who suddenly sings the smoothly rhymed and coyly elegant phrases of a character from a Noël Coward operetta because the lyricist wants to show off his rhyming skills.

In opera, density is less of a problem because text occupies a back seat. Usually, the lyrics matter minimally except when necessary to carry the plot forward, and most operas have very little plot to carry—traditionally, the drama is supposed to be carried by the music. The

lyrics by W. H. Auden and Chester Kallman for *The Rake's Progress* read gracefully and sing unintelligibly, not only because Stravinsky distorts them but because they're too packed for the listener to comprehend in the time allotted for hearing them. If poetry is the art of saying a lot in a little, lyric-writing is the art of finding the right balance between saying too much and not enough. Bad lyrics can be either so packed that they become impenetrable or so loose that they're uninteresting.

Most lyrics written in my generation and the generations before me do not make for good reading.* Nostalgists for what is popularly termed the Golden Age of Musicals (1925–1960), who appreciate how good many of the songs were and ignore how terrible most of the shows were, might disagree; but even they, I hope, would have to admit that prior to the late 1930s lyrics tended to be generalized and gooey ("You Are Love"— Hammerstein),** arch and gooey ("I'll Follow My Secret Heart"—Coward), strenuously effortful ("Lover, when I'm near you / And I hear you / Speak my name, / Softly, in

---

*GROUND RULE 5: With few exceptions, I won't be dealing with the work of living writers, for reasons I'll explain at the end of this Introduction.

**GROUND RULE 6: Despite his influence on my life, Oscar Hammerstein II is not my idol. For those who know that he was an artistic father to me as well as a personal substitute for a real one during my teen years, this disapproving heresy, and others to follow, may come as something of a seismic shock. But the truth is that in Hammerstein's shows, for all their revolutionary impact, the characters are not much more than collections of characteristics—verbal tics and quirks, like Southern accents or bad grammar, which individualize a character only the way a black hat signifies a villain— and his lyrics reflect that naïveté. Refining his innovations was left to my generation, and a lot of us went at it with a will. Songwriters like Kander and Ebb, Bock and Harnick, Strouse and Adams—we all explored the new territory with playwrights who happily accepted the notion that musicals could be more than constructs of block comedy scenes and novelty songs leavened by the occasional ballad, or lightly cynical cartoon shows like *Of Thee I Sing* and *Pal Joey.* Thus *Cabaret, She Loves Me, West Side Story,* etc.

my ear you / Breathe a flame"—Hart), convoluted ("Into Heaven I'm hurled"—Ira Gershwin) or at best unadorned and repetitious ("I'll be loving you always / With a love that's true always"—Irving Berlin), all of them perfectly satisfactory for theater songs of the time, but uninteresting or wince-making on the page.

The curious thing is that it was Hart, Berlin, Cole Porter and their contemporaries who ushered in a colloquial revolution; they instilled the way we actually speak into the formalized artifice of theater songwriting. But it was Hammerstein, experimenting with the dramatic equivalent of this in *Show Boat* (1927), who made the first serious attempt to focus on unique feelings of individual characters in specific situations through the lens of a realistic, although period, vernacular—and all in a show which dealt with taboo subjects such as racial prejudice and miscegenation. The attempt was important, even if the results, by today's standards, were fairly generic. Ironically, *Show Boat* was so startlingly different for its time that, despite its success, it didn't have much immediate effect on other writers. They were too comfortable with traditional musical comedy to think in terms of creating songs to fit characters because there *were* no characters in musical comedy, only personalities. It wasn't until *Oklahoma!* (1943) that Hammerstein's influence flowered.

The one great pre-*Oklahoma!* exception, of course, was *Porgy and Bess*. DuBose Heyward's lyrics* and George

Gershwin's music completely individualized characters for the first time in Broadway musical history. If the show had been presented in an opera house, perhaps it mightn't now seem to have been such an extraordinary event. In its time, as a commercially presented musical, few noticed how subtly and elegantly written the piece was, least of all the critics, who generally panned it. This was because the characters were so much more powerful than their predecessors (including the shallow, romanticized figures in *Show Boat*) and because Heyward didn't come out of a songwriter's tradition but out of a poet-playwright's, much like Lorenzo Da Ponte, who was Mozart's librettist, and Hugo von Hofmannsthal, who was Strauss's. Unlike Anderson, Capote and the other poet-playwrights who wrote musicals, Heyward understood the difference between character and characteristics; the lyrics sounded like heightened natural speech rather than self-advertised "poetry."

With *Oklahoma!*, though, Hammerstein fired the shot heard round the musical-theater world. The show was such a gigantic financial triumph that other writers not only noticed, they took notes. They scrambled to get on board, and before long "musical comedy" morphed into "musical play," a development that has turned out to be a mixed blessing. Even today, a lot of people (including critics) deplore the loss of what they see as the light-hearted silliness of the old musicals. For songwriters and playwrights, however, involving an audience in a story with singing characters who are more than skin deep is much more interesting work. Rodgers and Hammerstein spoiled musical theater for the rest of us sloggers in the field—or saved it, depending on your point of view.

Even the lyrics in the enlightened post-*Oklahoma!* era, however, tend in print to seem simple and threadbare, homiletic or tortuously clever. A number of lyrics by Cole Porter and E. Y. Harburg come to life on the page because of their formal brilliance; a few others, particularly those of Frank Loesser and Dorothy Fields, read easily because of their unforced conversational energy. Still, most have nowhere near as much effect as when they're accompanied by their indispensable musical partner and performed by singers who know what

---

*GROUND RULE 7: As far as I'm concerned, the lyrics in *Porgy and Bess* are the work of DuBose Heyward, who also wrote the libretto. Although Ira Gershwin is usually credited exclusively with them, most were written by Heyward, certainly all of the distinguished ones, a few exceptions being co-credited to both writers. The contributions of Ira Gershwin alone are easily distinguished by their firmly traditional, generalized stance: for example, "It Ain't Necessarily So," a self-consciously rhymed lyric that could just as easily be sung by Crown as by Sportin' Life. Moreover, nowhere else in Gershwin's work is there a trace of the poetic use of language in *Porgy*. I make the distinction between the two lyricists not to denigrate Ira Gershwin but because I think Heyward's lyrics are the high-water mark in musical theater.

they're doing. The vast majority lie dead on the page until sung, at which point they spring instantaneously to life (some of them, anyway).

Why a book of lyrics, then? Especially theater lyrics, which are a fringe enthusiasm at best, considering their tiny impact on what is currently coming out of people's earphones or the bar down the block or the car blasting by. The lyrics of contemporary popular song, of rock and rap and country, are the ones which reflect the immediacy of our world, much as theater songs did in the first half of the twentieth century. They are the sociologist's totems, and studies of them have resulted in an inundation of essays and books, not to mention college courses. Live theater itself is at most an ancillary part of American culture these days. Ever since the advent of movies and television, theatergoing has increasingly become either a dutiful activity for a dwindling, aging audience or an occasional festive night out, the purchase of hard-to-get tickets being its greatest pleasure. Broadway theater, formerly the fount of new American plays, has for many years been focused predominantly on musicals, chiefly two kinds: stolid solemn uplift equipped with impressive lumbering spectacle, and elaborate concerts of familiar pop songs threaded along a story line, a genre familiarly known as the "jukebox musical," which the critic Stephen Holden has characterized as "karaoke hell." (As I write this, a third kind has recently overrun the theater like kudzu: the self-referential "metamusical," which makes fun of its betters by imitating their clichés while drawing attention to what it's doing, thus justifying its lack of originality without the risk of criticism.) Off-Broadway and regional musicals are numerous and often adventurous, but even they are only part of a cottage industry with fewer new cottages and more refurbished ones every season.

Happily, schools still persist in putting on plays. Performing live theater still seems to be fun for young people. Nevertheless, rock concerts are their theater of choice, and even that territory is succumbing in popularity to more passive forms: movies, television and the Internet. I used to think that the need for live theater would never die; I fear I was wrong.

So once again, why collect these lyrics and make this book? Because a publisher asked me to; because it offered me the opportunity to append these comments on a craft I know a great deal about; because most of the lyrics are conversational and therefore stand the chance of being an entertaining read; but mostly because I think the explication of any craft, when articulated by an experienced practitioner, can be not only intriguing but also valuable, no matter what particularity the reader may be attracted to. For example, I don't cook, nor do I want to, but I read cooking columns with intense and explicit interest. The technical details echo those which challenge a songwriter: timing, balance, form, surface versus substance, and all the rest of it. They resonate for me even though I have no desire to braise, parboil or sauté. Similarly, I hope, the specific techniques of lyric-writing will enlighten the cook who reads these pages. Choices, decisions and mistakes in every attempt to make something that wasn't there before are essentially the same, and exploring one set of them, I like to believe, may cast light on another.

Since most of the lyrics which follow belong in the mouths of particular characters in particular situations, characters who are only partly knowable without the context of the dialogue and actions in their stories, I've included synopses to introduce each show and each song. These are shadows, however, not substance. With few exceptions, every lyric in this collection is prompted by the beginning, middle or end of a culmination of incidents before it, incidents of which the reader is likely to be unaware. For example, "In Buddy's Eyes" (from *Follies*) loses much of its tone and all of its subtext when disconnected from the placid surface of its music and the scenes and dialogue which have preceded it. How can we know what Sally means or what she's trying not to say, without knowing Sally? It's as if we were asked to know Hamlet from his soliloquies alone, for what are solo songs but musicalized soliloquies, encapsulated moments even when addressed to other characters? Lyrics without the scenes from which they sprout, at least the ones in this book, are just as incomplete as lyrics without music.

Some songs, of course, are small scenes in themselves. I've been asked many times why I don't write the books for my own musicals, since I treat lyrics as short plays whenever I can. The key word in that sentence is "short." I'm by nature a playwright, but without the necessary basic skill: the ability to tell a story that holds an audience's attention for more than a few minutes. Writing plays is, in my view, the most difficult of the literary arts. A play has to be as packed and formally controlled as a sonnet, but roomy enough to let the actors and the stagecraft in. Packed but loose, like a good lyric. Poets rarely have to deal with plot; novelists never have to deal with actors. A playwright has to deal with both and still make the result immediate enough to grip an audience for, on the average, two and a half hours. (That usually includes an intermission, where he loses them for fifteen minutes and has to woo them back.) I like to think I can hold their interest with short forms: playlets which are called songs. The longest I've written is the opening number of *Into the Woods,* a mere twelve-minute sequence, and that includes a good deal of dialogue. I'm in awe of good playwrights, even when I don't like the plays, and ever since the day I started working with my first professional collaborator and learned what went into the craft of playwriting, I have never tried to do it alone.

Actually, I've wanted to set these observations in print for years. I like to pontificate as much as anyone who thinks he knows what he's talking about, but I've done it only when being interviewed or when arguing with other songwriters. My reluctance to write them down, apart from the universal writer's reluctance to write anything down, is two-pronged. To begin with, lyrics are such a small and specialized art form that they hardly seem worth lengthy public comment. Moreover, why not let them speak (sing) for themselves? Examining songs like the ones in these pages in light of how swiftly stencils change in popular art is not only a stroll down Memory Lane, it smacks of archeology. The counterargument in both cases is the same: any art, no matter how small, is a form of teaching, and for me teaching is a sacred profession. My intellectual life, and to some extent my per-

sonal one as well, was guided and changed by teachers: Lucille Pollock, a Latin teacher in ninth grade; Robert Barrow, professor of music at Williams College; and Milton Babbitt, with whom I studied composition after graduating from college. Not to mention my immediate mentor, Oscar Hammerstein, and every other collaborator I've worked with. Reading about how someone else practices a craft, no matter how individual or arcane—designing roller coasters, managing hedge funds, harvesting salt—if it's detailed, clear and the writer is passionate about his pursuit, can be not just mesmerizing but enlightening. It is the best kind of teaching. In my case, writing lyrics for the theater is such a craft and I would like to pass my knowledge of it on, just as Oscar passed his on to me.

There is, however, a third reluctance: How can you comment critically on someone's work without hurting the writer whose work you're dissecting? My answer is cowardly but simple: criticize only the dead. I have never believed in "*de mortuis nil nisi bonum*"; speaking ill exclusively of the dead seems to me the gentlemanly thing to do. The subject cannot be personally hurt, and his reputation is unlikely to be affected by anything you say, whereas publicly passing judgment on living writers is both hurtful and stifling—I speak from experience, as someone who has been disdained both by journalists and by many of my songwriting elders and contemporaries as well. Don't look in these pages for critical opinions of the work of anybody but myself and those who can no longer defend themselves—but who also cannot be upset by anything I have to say. As for my own lyrics, I hope to be able to point out their virtues as well as their flaws. Self-deprecation is easy, self-praise has a bad reputation and is hard for a nice upper-middle-class boy like me who was brought up not to boast.

What you *can* look for, when helpful, are plot, scene and character descriptions, mixed in with a few anecdotes, to help place each lyric in its appropriate setting, both theatrical and real. They're no substitute for the music, but they may give the lyric a bit more life. What you shouldn't look for is much gossip—I can promise a little, but not a cornucopia. Gossip depends on memory, and now that I've waited so long to set things down on paper, I don't trust it. Fully aware of the distortions that even yesterday's memory can engender, I've checked the anecdotes and histories accompanying the songs with whoever is alive and still compos mentis.

So now, as Portnoy's psychiatrist said, vee may perhaps to begin, yes?

As Maxie Schwartz in the PBS production of June Moon *(1974)*

With Leonard Bernstein in the Jefferson Hotel, Washington, D.C., during the tryout of West Side Story

Rhyme and Its Reasons

The immediate distinguishing difference between lyrics and dialogue is the conscious use of rhyme. There are many varieties: true rhymes, near rhymes, visual rhymes, regional rhymes, assonance, consonance, run-on, identities—as many types as academic taxonomy will allow. The most effective kind for a story-telling theater song is the first, so in what follows, when I say "rhyme," I mean "true rhyme."

A *true* (or *perfect*) rhyme consists of two words or phrases whose final accented syllables sound alike except for the consonant sounds which precede them. The accent can be on the last syllable (*home/roam, convey/dismay*), which is called a masculine rhyme, or on the penultimate syllable (*never/forever*), which is called a feminine rhyme, perhaps because the fall-off after the accent gives it a bit of added grace. The accent can even be on an earlier syllable (*rational/national, simulator/stimulator*), but the sounds which follow must be the same while the accented consonants must be different.*

An *identity* matches not only the final syllables but also the consonants that introduce them (*motion/promotion*). What distinguishes a rhyme from an identity is the accented syllable: "mustache" rhymes with "just ash" if the accents are on "must" and "just"; if the accents are on "–ache" and "ash," they're identities.

A *near* (*false*) rhyme comes in two flavors, *assonance* and *consonance*. In *assonance* the vowel sounds are alike, the subsequent consonants different (*home/alone,*

together/forever). *Consonance* is the reverse: the consonant sounds are alike, but the accented vowels are different (*buddy/body*)—this is sometimes called a *slant* rhyme.

There is nothing "wrong" with near rhymes: two generations of listeners brought up on pop and rock songs have gotten so accustomed to approximate rhyming that they neither care nor notice if the rhymes are perfect or not. To their ears, near rhymes are not only acceptable, but preferable; as in all popular art, familiarity breeds content (accent on the second syllable). In fact, pop listeners are suspicious of perfect rhymes, associating neatness with a stifling traditionalism and sloppy rhyming with emotional directness and the defiance of restrictions. Here is the rationale for that view, as offered by one of pop music's most successful lyricists, whom I shall discreetly refrain from naming and refer to imaginatively as X. X ventured out of pop into musical theater once—and with a hit show, I might add. Shortly before the show opened on Broadway, a television interviewer commented to X that "some theater critics might get picky about the fact that your rhymes are not always 'true' ones. How do you feel about that?" X replied:

> I hate all true rhymes. I think they only allow you a certain limited range. . . . I'm not a great believer in perfect rhymes. I'm just a believer in feelings that come across. If the craft gets in the way of the feelings, then I'll take the feelings any day. I don't sit with a rhyming dictionary. And I don't look for big words to be clever. To me, they take away from the medium I'm most comfortable with, which is Today . . .

Allowing for X's dismissal of every first-rate lyricist from Berlin to Hammerstein as having a limited range, X is nevertheless not the only songwriter to voice this defense

---

* Regional accents can confuse the issue. To me, a native New Yorker, "dawn" rhymes with "lawn" and "gone" with "on." When I worked with Leonard Bernstein, who was born near Boston, he insisted, to my horror, that all four words rhymed with each other. For a musical version of "The Boston Strangler," that might have been acceptable. For a show about New York street gangs, it was not.

of laziness; I reprint it simply because it's the most articulate one that I've come across. The notion that good rhymes and the expression of emotion are contradictory qualities, that neatness equals lifelessness is, to borrow a disapproving phrase from my old counterpoint text, "the refuge of the destitute." Claiming that true rhyme is the enemy of substance is the sustaining excuse of lyricists who are unable to rhyme well with any consistency.

"If the craft gets in the way of the feelings, then I'll take the feelings any day." The point which X overlooks is that the craft is supposed to *serve* the feeling. A good lyric should not only have something to say but a way of saying it as clearly and forcefully as possible—and that involves rhyming cleanly. A perfect rhyme can make a mediocre line bright and a good one brilliant. A near rhyme only dampens the impact.

"I don't sit with a rhyming dictionary." The implication is that using a rhyming dictionary is somehow a cheat, as if the only words which are genuine in feeling and expression are those you can think of without any outside assistance. The fact is that lyric writers who don't use a rhyming dictionary have, to use X's phrase, "a limited range": It's easy to think of rhymes for "love," there being so few, but who can think of all the useful rhymes for "day" without using a rhyming dictionary?

"And I don't look for big words to be clever." What are "big words" for this lyricist, those over three syllables?

And are they used to be "clever" or to be precise and nuanced, to let the language's variety flower and fulfill itself? The idea that "big" words are cobwebbed and stultifying (to use a word that X would probably disapprove of) is another line of defense for the tell-it-like-it-is songwriters, dooming them to tell it like everybody else does. Oscar Hammerstein wrote simple lyrics with "feelings that come across" and every rhyme he used was a perfect one or an identity. But then, he wrote for the theater and, more tellingly, he worked hard. Craig Carnelia, a first-rate composer-lyricist, put it exactly:

> **True rhyming is a necessity in the theater, as a guide for the ear to know what it has just heard. Our language is so complex and difficult, and there are so many similar words and sounds that mean different things, that it's confusing enough without using near rhymes that only acquaint the ear with a vowel. . . . [A near rhyme is] not useful to the primary purpose of a lyric, which is to be heard, and it teaches the ear to not trust or to disregard a lyric, to not listen, to simply let the music wash over you.**

There is something about the conscious use of form in any art that says to the customer, "This is worth saying." Without form the idea, the intention and, most important, the *effect,* no matter how small in ambition, becomes flaccid; as the old Communist dictum proclaims, "If it isn't art, it isn't propaganda." The more random and imprecise, the more writing becomes blather, a letter to the editor. God knows the woods are full of blather, and God knows a lot of people enjoy it, partly because listeners today have even lazier ears than those of my generation: pop music has encouraged them to welcome vagueness and fuzziness, to exalt the poetic yearnings of random images. There are wonderful lines in pop lyrics, but they tend to be isolated from what surrounds them. They are rarely part of a dramatic progression; the meaning of their succession doesn't matter as much as their individual impact, and therefore the rhyming—the glue that holds the song together—is less important than it would be in a theater song. Pop songs may have many values, including the immediacy of feeling that X refers to, but specificity of language, a sine qua non of good writing, isn't one of them.

All rhymes, even the farthest afield of the near ones (*home/dope*), draw attention to the rhymed word; if you don't want it to be spotlighted, you'd better not rhyme it. A perfect rhyme snaps the word, and with it the thought, vigorously into place, rendering it easily intelligible; a near rhyme blurs it. A word like "together" leads the ear to expect a rhyme like "weather" or "feather." When the ear hears "forever," it has to pause a split second to bring the word into focus. Like a note that's a bit off pitch, a false rhyme doesn't destroy the meaning, but it weakens it. An identity makes the word clear, but blunts the line's snap because the accented sound is not a fresh one. And both identities and false rhymes are death on wit. Take, for example, the Dorothy Parker verse I mentioned in the Introduction, but substitute an identity for the rhyme:

> *Oh, life is a glorious cycle of song,*
> *A revel that verges on mania;*
> *And love is a thing that can never go wrong;*
> *And I am Marie of Roumania.*

Or try it with a near rhyme:

> *Oh, life is a glorious cycle of song,*
> *An endless euphoric fantasia;*
> *And love is a thing that can never go wrong;*
> *And I am Marie of Roumania.*

Close, but no cigar; in each case, the punch line lands with a muffled thud. Jokes work best with perfect rhymes.* Emotional statements are sometimes effective using identities, because the repetition of the sound parallels the intensity of the feeling; it's a technique particularly favored by Hammerstein ("Younger than springtime am I / Gayer than laughter am I"). I've never come across a near rhyme that works better than a perfect one would.

There are, of course, numerous reasons to rhyme apart from emphasizing a word, chief among them being the sheer pleasure of verbal playfulness, such as the use of inner rhymes and trick rhymes (and alliterative self-referential phrases like "rhyme and its reasons"), especially as practiced by the rare likes of E. Y. Harburg and Cole Porter. (More of that in the following pages.) There are reasons not to rhyme, too—not only not to rhyme but to keep the consonant and vowel sounds as different from each other as possible. In fact, songs without rhymes, whose lines end with sounds completely unlike each other, can invigorate the nonrhymed words more than approximate rhymes. (More of that later, too.)

Using near rhymes is like juggling clumsily: it can be fun to watch and it *is* juggling, but it's nowhere near as much pleasure for an audience as seeing all the balls—or in the case of the best lyricists, knives, lit torches and swords—being kept aloft with grace and precision. In the theater, true rhyme works best on every level, and since this is a book about theater lyrics, that's what the word "rhyme" will mean.

---

*Curiously enough, rhymes whose endings are spelled differently (for example, "rougher/suffer") are more interesting than those which are spelled the same ("rougher/tougher"), not only to the eye but to the ear, perhaps because the brain subliminally sees them in print and is therefore more surprised when they come along. "Weary" and "bleary" are a less effective pair than "weary" and "eerie" or even "weary" and "leery," not to mention "weary" and "hara-kiri."

Finishing
the Hat

JANUARY 21 – MARCH 26, 2000

BOOK **JULIUS J. EPSTEIN**
STEPHEN SONDHEIM MUSIC & LYRICS

SATURDAY NIGHT

A MUSICAL COMEDY

Based on the play *Front Porch in Flatbush* by Julius J. Epstein & Philip G. Epstein

WITH **Andrea Burns, David Campbell,
Donald Corren, Natascia A. Diaz,
Christopher Fitzgerald, Kirk McDonald,
Michael Pemberton, Joey Sorge,
Clarke Thorell, Rachel Ulanet,
Frank Vlastnik, Lauren Ward,
Michael Benjamin Washington,
David A. White, Greg Zola**

ORCHESTRATIONS **Jonathan Tunick**
MUSICAL DIRECTION **Rob Fisher**
SETS **Derek McLane**
COSTUMES **Catherine Zuber**
LIGHTS **Donald Holder**
SOUND **Scott Lehrer**
PRESS **Richard Kornberg & Associates**
CASTING **Johnson-Liff Associates, Tara Rubin**
MUSIC COORDINATOR **Seymour Red Press**
ASSOCIATE DIRECTOR **Rob Ashford**
PRODUCTION STAGE MANAGER **Karen Moore**
STAGE MANAGER **Karen Evanouskas**

DIRECTOR / CHOREOGRAPHER
KATHLEEN MARSHALL

Saturday Night is made possible, in part, by the generous support
of The Hale Matthews Foundation & The Blanche and Irving Laurie Foundation.
Baldwin Piano is the official piano of Second Stage Theatre.

1. Saturday Night (1954)

Book by Julius J. Epstein
Based on the play Front Porch in Flatbush
  by Julius J. and Philip G. Epstein

The Notion

Brooklyn in the spring of 1929. A group of working-class boys in their late teens and early twenties, on the advice of their charismatic but misguided leader Gene, a runner on Wall Street, pools their money in an effort to make a killing in the stock market. After comic and romantic complications, they fail, having learned that getting rich quick is harder than it seems.

General Comment

I met Oscar Hammerstein II and his family when I was eleven years old. He became a surrogate father to me for the next five years, and it was because of my teenage admiration for him that I became a songwriter. Oscar was my professional guide and mentor until the day he died, when I was thirty and he was sixty-five. After reading my adolescent lyrics, he suggested a set of four writing exercises for me: adapt a good play as a musical, adapt a flawed play as a musical, adapt another form, such as a novel or a short story, into a musical and,

finally, write a musical entirely of my own devising. I did just that, beginning with George S. Kaufman and Marc Connelly's *Beggar on Horseback* and plowing my way through Maxwell Anderson's *High Tor* and P. L. Travers's *Mary Poppins* stories, arriving eventually at *Climb High,* a four-hour summation of my views on life, ambition, morality, theater and art, with a passing swipe at love. Kaufman gave me permission to have *Beggar on Horseback* (which I retitled *All That Glitters*) performed in college* (Williams): my first "serious" work performed in front of an audience, and a surprisingly happy experience. Anderson denied me the chance to let *High Tor* be seen because he was planning to adapt it himself with Kurt Weill. *Mary Poppins* remains unfinished—I couldn't figure out how to make disparate episodes hang together dramatically, even though they involved the same characters (neither could Disney). Years later, though, I had another crack at the form with *Company.* As for *Climb High,* I didn't finish it until after I'd graduated. I had high and foolish hopes for a production of it on Broadway, but fortunately I had to abandon them in order to earn a living writing a television series called *Topper,* based on the comic ghost stories by Thorne Smith.

The scores for these four musicals, whatever their shortcomings (and they consisted mostly of shortcomings), provided me with a portfolio of songs to use as audition material and led me to my first experience as a professional songwriter: a collaboration with an experienced, much-awarded screenwriter and occasional playwright named Julius J. Epstein. He and his twin brother, Philip, who had recently died, had written a play called *Front Porch in Flatbush;* it was now, in 1952, to be turned into a musical, produced by Lemuel Ayers, one of Broadway's most admired set designers and the co-producer of *Kiss Me, Kate.* The job had been turned down by no less than Frank Loesser, but Ayers had heard some of my apprentice work and thought it worth taking

---

*I didn't know the man, but I sent him my adaptation of the script, complete with lyrics, in a spring binder, which cost about $2.00, no small sum to me. He sent me back the script and a note granting me permission to do the show. It was written on a piece of embossed personal stationery, which was a thrill for me even though I was startled to see that he'd torn off the bottom half of the sheet—for economic purposes, I assume, since he also kept the binder.

"Class"

a chance on a young writer. I wrote three songs on spec for a hundred dollars and got the assignment.*

Saturday Night was in the traditional Rodgers and Hammerstein form, except for one novel notion: there was no chorus. *Front Porch in Flatbush* had a company of twenty-five, *Saturday Night* only fifteen, but every member of the cast was a distinct character. I don't recall having seen a Broadway musical before it which didn't employ the generic backup bodies and voices known as the chorus: Policemen in Scene One, Diplomats in Scene Three, Reporters in Scene Six, etc. *Saturday Night* turned out, unintentionally, to be a chamber musical in an age when there was no such commercial thing. We didn't recognize it at the time, because in 1952 nobody was taking musicals seriously enough to label them "chamber," "concept," "metamusical" or anything like.

Even as a born-and-bred New Yorker, I could not have been more unsuited for the piece. I was upper-middle-class Manhattan, Julie's characters were working-class Brooklyn. I had never even *been* to Brooklyn except for the occasional Dodgers game, and New York's boroughs were then, as they are now, exotically different from each other. Still, I was taken with the script and ambitious enough to be excited by the opportunity, and I remembered William Faulkner's dictum: a writer needs three things, experience, observation and imagination, any two of which, at times any one of which, can supply the lack of the others. Observation and imagination, check; experience, no. I soon discovered that I had a gift for one particular form of observation: mimicry. Not just mimicry of character (I'd been an actor in college), but mimicry of dialogue. I was able to imitate the Jewish Brooklynese of the Epstein brothers as if I'd been born in Greenpoint. Subsequently, I found I could just as enthusiastically imitate the disparate styles of collaborators as distinct from one another as Arthur Laurents, James Goldman, Hugh Wheeler, George Furth, John Weidman and James Lapine. The only style I had trouble with was the deceptively elegant surface that Burt Shevelove and Larry Gelbart concocted for *A Funny Thing Happened on the Way to the Forum,* as will become crucially clear a few chapters hence. Mimicry is a fortunate talent, and essential if a collaborative piece is meant to sound like the work of a single writer, as it should.

*I auditioned at Lem's apartment for Epstein's agents, the hottest pair in New York theater circles: Audrey Wood and her husband, William Liebling. Liebling fell asleep during the opening number, which was not an encouragement to me, but Wood kindly kept trying to waken him by tapping her foot surreptitiously under the sole of the shoe on his crossed leg while I warbled on. He finally blurred his eyes open after the third song, pondered a moment and, seeing the look on his wife's face, gave his approval, much to Lem's relief.

ACT ONE

Early spring of 1929. The front porch of Gene's house in Flatbush, Brooklyn, about seven o'clock on a Saturday night.

Dino, a boy of nineteen, is playing ragtime on an upright piano. Artie and Ray, both slightly older, are seated on the sofa, Artie with a ukulele, which he occasionally strums. Ray is peering earnestly at an open newspaper. Another boy, Ted, can be glimpsed in the living room, phone in hand, trying to get a date with a girl.

Saturday Night

RAY
He's gonna get the axe from huh*—
What would ya say to seein' a
Pitcha?
How does the combination of
Johnny Mack Brown and Bessie Love
Hitcha?

(Ted returns to the porch, dejectedly)

DINO
The moon's like a million-watt electric
    light—
It shines up the city as it climbs.
And I gotta spend another Saturday
    night
Alone with the *Sunday Times*.

TED
Moonlight on Flatbush Avenue,
That's what I call a lovely view . . .

DINO
So what can you do
On a Saturday night—alone?

RAY
Who needs a view
On a Saturday night—alone?

ARTIE
If it's a Saturday night
And you are single,
You sit with a paper and fight

_____
*Brooklynese—"her" without the final "r" sound.

The urge to mingle.

DINO
And home is a place
Where you gotta go back—alone.

TED
Home is a place
Where the future looks black—alone.

RAY
I like the *Sunday Times* all right,
But not in bed . . .

ALL
Alive and alone on a Saturday night
Is dead.

RAY
(Looking at the newspaper)
Here's a revival of "Ben Huh,"
Goes on at nine-fifteen at the
Cushman.

ARTIE
So when I got my mind on sex,
Who gives a damn for Francis X.
Bushman?

ALL
The moon's like an overloaded Moxie
    sign,
It shines at you friendly and bright.
I got my buddies and my buddies are
    fine—
But not on a Saturday night!

RAY
Johnny Mack Brown and Bessie
    Love . . .

ALL
Love, love, love, love,
Love, love, love, love . . .

So what can you do
On a Saturday night—alone?
Who needs a view
On a Saturday night—alone?
If it's a Saturday night
And you are single,
You sit with a paper and fight
The urge to mingle.

And home is a place
Where you gotta go back—alone.
Home is a place

Where the future looks black—alone.

Things'd be different any other night
    instead,
But we're on our own
On a Saturday night,
With no one to phone
On a Saturday night,
And when you're alone
On a Saturday night,
You might as well be dead!

Finding appropriate rhymes that haven't been used before is one of the few pleasures of lyric writing, an occupation consisting chiefly of tedious list-making and frustration. However, characters who speak in dialects and accents, or with vocal oddities like a cold or a lisp, can offer possibilities. Thus, mindful of the fact that Frank Loesser had been the producer's first choice to write the show and imagining what he might have done with Brooklyn accents (well, stage Brooklyn accents), "picture" and "hit you" become "pitcha" and "hitcha" and the short article "a," a virtually impossible word to rhyme properly, can rhyme with "huh," the Flatbush version of "her." In the song "Manhattan," Lorenz Hart used Brooklynese to justify "spoil/goil" and Hammerstein took advantage of the New England setting in *Carousel* for "stickler/pertickler," a unique, if somewhat coy, rhyme. A character with a lisp opens the door to rhyming the traditionally unrhymeable "month." But only onth. After that, it loses its surprise.

Nevertheless, there are plenty of fresh rhymes still to be found. The problem is one of appropriateness: the situation has to justify the rhyme. I once rhymed "Let Papa sit" with "opposite" (perhaps others have, but at the time it was virgin to me) because I had a scene involving a mother seating her family at a dinner table. The most satisfying rhyme for a lyricist is one which has been lying around in plain sight for years before the right situation allows it to be picked up. "Uppity" and "cup o' tea" need a British milieu and probably a song about the class system before a lyricist can play with it—which is exactly what Lionel Bart did in *Oliver!* and E. Y. Harburg did more acutely in a show called *Darling of the Day*. Wouldn't it be nice to find a situation where you could rhyme "cryptic" with "diptych" or "Ochi chornya" with "California"? Somebody has probably already done so, I hope.

Gene, the charismatic leader of the group, enters from the living room, dressed in evening clothes, eager for his weekly Saturday night journey across the Brooklyn Bridge to Manhattan. His friends both admire and scoff at him.

Class

GENE

The bridge is my rainbow,
The bridge is my friend,

And it's got a pot o' gold at the other
    end.
Not a pot o' gold
You can buy or sell—
It's the Plaza Hotel.

I'm crossing the rainbow,
I'm taking a ride
To a razzle-dazzle world on the other
    side.
Very special world:
Gotta have a pass
Called "class."

A man can be
A runner by day,
But socially
What counts is the way
He looks.
That's what I mean by "class."

I've got two suits,
Just two to my name.
I've got just two suits
But both of 'em came

From Brooks.
That's what I mean by "class!"

"Class" is when you're wrapped in
    Harris tweed
And always look impeccable in what
    you're wrapped in.
"Class" is when you demonstrate your
    breeding,
Like, for instance, when you call a
    waiter "Captain."*

---

*"Class," along with other songs in *Saturday Night*, is a treasure trove of lyricists' sins. This quatrain contains the first of many. SIN 1: VERBOSITY. For me, the hardest sin to avoid. A passage like this exhausts the listener more than it does the singer. Unless a character is hyperarticulate for a reason (panic, defensiveness, exuberance, etc.), cleverly rhymed logorrheic patter draws attention to the lyricist, not the character.

FRANK LOESSER
The Idea Man

You'd think that for my initial professional outing the first lyricist I'd imitate on the way to finding my own voice would be Oscar Hammerstein II, but as most of the lyrics for *Saturday Night* indicate, my model turned out to be Frank Loesser. This was an unconscious choice, although it may have been influenced by my knowing that Loesser had turned *Saturday Night* down when Lemuel Ayers appropriately enough had offered it to him. More likely, it's because I knew and admired his work, especially the urban songs, like those in *Guys and Dolls*. Loesser, along with his predecessors Dorothy Fields and Irving Berlin, was a master of conversational lyrics, though with a difference: he tailored his lyrics to the individual characters at hand, whereas Berlin wasn't interested in character and Fields's lyrics were mostly reflections of herself, rueful and amused ("I Can't Give You Any-thing But Love"). When they were characters he could understand in-stinctively, urban or raffish or both, as in *Guys and Dolls*

and *How to Succeed in Business Without Really Trying,* Loesser was able to perform the rare trick of sounding modestly conversational and brilliantly dextrous at the same time, a skill only Fields and occasionally Berlin possessed before him. Like them, he concealed the artifice behind the art; he could bury and reveal his virtuosity simultaneously.

Moreover, the characters in *Saturday Night* had a quintessentially New York Jewish wisecrack flavor, which describes Loesser's lyrics at their relaxed best. When Loesser gets fanciful, as in folktale-style pieces like *Greenwillow* and the movie *Hans Christian Andersen,* or tries to infiltrate exotic climes and cultures like that of Italian farmers in the Napa Valley (*The Most Happy Fella*), the results are less convincing and sometimes embarrassing, especially when he waxes "poetic" à la Hammerstein ("Warm all over / Warm all over / Gone are all the clouds that used to swarm all over").

Loesser was one of the very few lyricists who were genuinely funny.

The lyrics of Gershwin and Hart received appreciative smiles and sometimes even chuckles, but not the kind of hearty laughter that songs like "Adelaide's Lament" got. Even Porter, Harburg and Berlin got laughs only occasionally. The reason for this can in part be attributed to Loesser's blossoming when musicals were becoming more grounded in character after the *Oklahoma!* revolution. The character was funny, as in "Adelaide's Lament," then the lyric didn't have to generate guffaws entirely on its own. And if the situation was funny as well, the lyric didn't have to do anything at all except emphasize it (listen to "I Believe in You" in *How to Succeed in Business Without Really Trying*).

Most impressive to me are the ideas behind Loesser's songs. The concepts of "Make a Miracle" from *Where's Charley?* and "Fugue for Tinhorns" from *Guys and Dolls,* among many others, are so strong that the lyrics need not be brilliant in execution: they can ride on their notions alone and bring the house down. Which they did, and still do.

This is why
A room is a "flat."
You don't say "tie,"
You call it "cravat."
Say you drink from a "tumbler"
Instead of a glass.
That's the mark of someone who has
What I call "class."

The beautiful people
Who live out there
Have savoir-faire—
That's "class" in French.
The beautiful people
Who live with grace
On Sutton Place
Wear robes and peignoirs
And purchase Renoirs.

The beautiful people
Are *my* people—it's them I belong with!
Now tell me, what's wrong with
That?

HANK
The beautiful people
Are not for you.
Their blood is blue,
They're out of your class.
Be yourself, Gene, be yourself.

(Joined by others)

Be yourself, Gene, be yourself . . .

*(They keep singing the line underneath
the following)*

GENE
I'd like to own a Rolls-Royce,
A Braque, a Dufy,**

All things expensive and choice
And rare.***
I've got the friends that I need
To share them with me,
But I need the things to share.

Some people live out their lives
And don't give a damn.
They buy things on the install-****
Ment plan.

That's not for me—I don't want
To be what I am,
I want to be what I can!

The beautiful people get up at noon
And spend all their time having fun.
They better make way, 'cause pretty
    soon
The four hundred will be four
    hundred and one!

TED
When asked, "*Quelle heure?*"
By Mrs. Dupont,
You say to her,*****
"Why, naturellement,
Ma'mselle."
That's what he means by "class."

ARTIE
If I were near
The Deb of the Week,
I'd say, "My dear,
I think you look chic
As hell."
Is that what you mean by "class"?

GENE
Could you tell the Astors that your
    great-

Great-great grandmother
Came over with the pilgrims?

CELESTE
No, but I could tell them Uncle Nate
Came over with a man who knows
The man who founded
    Milgrim's.******

GENE
Ten-buck tips,
Havana cigars,
Cross-country trips
In high-powered cars.
"Captain, bring me a brandy
And a large demitasse!"
Week nights I'm a Brooklyn boy,
But on Saturday night
I've got class!

Apart from its exemplary transgressions, this song is interesting because it's a type that became increasingly prominent after the Rodgers and Hammerstein revolution. Once *Oklahoma!* had made character and story, rather than personality and diversion, the major concern of musicals, characters, especially the central ones, suddenly were required to express their needs and wishes early on in the evening in order to establish themselves. Thus was born the "I am" or "I want" song, usually the second number in the show, which expresses the defining desire of the protagonist and prefigures the progression of the story, songs such as "Twin Soliloquies" (I want) and "A Cockeyed Optimist" (I am) in *South Pacific* or "Something's

---

SINS 2 AND 2A: TWO FOR THE PRICE OF ONE: first, substituting rhyme for character. It's possible, though just barely, that Gene, with his limited education, knows about Renoirs and peignoirs and Rolls-Royces from the magazines, but Braque and Dufy? I doubt it. Second, sonic ambiguity: "A Braque, a Dufy," set legato as it is, comes across as "A Brockadoofee," which sounds like nothing so much as a scat phrase. By the time the ear has figured out what is actually being sung, the singer is in the middle of the next line and the listener has to waste his concentration on catching up.

***SIN 3: REDUNDANT ADJECTIVAL PADDING:** using a series of synonyms to fill out a line because there's not enough to say. "Expensive *and* choice *and* rare?"

****SIN 4: ARCHITECTURAL LAZINESS.** The pattern of this section, as exemplified by the verse above ("I'd like to own . . .") establishes a rhyme between the first and third lines (Royce/choice) which is not echoed here (lives/stall). I was probably writing too quickly and didn't notice it at the time. On occasion (a rare one) it's useful to break a lyric pattern, but patterns are what form is about, and most of

the time this particular Sin comes from not noticing or, more likely, not wanting to be bothered.

*****SIN 5: INCONSISTENCY.** In the opening number, "her" was pronounced "huh" to rhyme with "a." Suddenly now, "her" is pronounced properly, in order to rhyme with the slightly mispronounced (ie., Brooklynized) "heure." How convenient for the lyricist, unless Ted is more literate than his friends— and there is no indication in the dialogue that such is the case.

******SIN 6: STRAINED JOKE.** No exegesis necessary.

Coming" (I want) in *West Side Story* and "Some People" (both) in *Gypsy*. This inheritance from Rodgers and Hammerstein disappeared in the musicals of the late 1960s, as less direct forms of playwriting appeared. And not a moment too soon.

Gene goes to the Plaza Hotel in Manhattan, as he does every Saturday night, trying to crash a debutantes' party. From the ballroom we hear a dance band with a vocalist.

Love's a Bond

VOCALIST

I'm smart as a fox
With bonds and with stocks;
I've cornered wheat, alfalfa and rye.
But now I'm tired of
That hue and cry.
Consolidated Love
Is all I buy.

When put to the test,
I like to invest,
But I won't be a great financier.
Love's the stock I like,
It's free and clear,
And it'll be blue chip
If you chip
In with me, my dear.

Love's a bond that's pure.
Its dividends are sure.
This bond, if you get it,
Is stable and yet it
Will grow if you let it
Mature.

And darling, have you heard?
The market's spiraling like a bird!
As A.T.& T. will
Go up and up, we will,
For this new love of ours
Is gilt-edged preferred.

This lyric, even though it's a pastiche, or maybe *because* it's a pastiche, is the most fully realized in the show and the only one without Sin.

Gene is frustrated in his attempts to get past the ballroom attendant. In an anteroom, he meets a flirty Southern coquette named Helene. He persuades her to dance with him to the music coming from inside the ballroom on the grounds that it would be cozy and private, away from all the other debutantes. As they waltz, Helene sings, in a coy Southern belle accent.

Isn't It?

This is nice, isn't it?
Ah mean, the music.
This is nice, isn't it?
Ah mean, the band.

Don't you think
We make natural partners?
Ah mean, like food and drink,
Or supply and demand?

We're so right, aren't we?
Ah mean, for dancing.
Hold me tight, cling to me—
Ah mean, mah hand!

Ah feel fine!
Ah'm aglow with a Sunday shine!
Could ah be fallin' in—?
Ah mean to say—
Well, anyway,
Isn't it grand?

The boys take their dates to see Stella Dallas, on the strict understanding that everyone chip in. Outside the movie house, the boys argue and the girls, gazing at the movie posters, dream.

In the Movies

RAY
I paid sixty cents for the cab.

HANK
Ray paid sixty cents for the cab.

ARTIE
Sixty cents for the *cab*?

DINO
Sixty cents for the *cab*?

ARTIE
The meter only said forty cents!

RAY
Well, what about the tip?
Twenty cents for the tip!

HANK
Big spender!

ARTIE
Big shot!

DINO
Big tipper!

HANK
I paid fifty cents for the hat check,
Fifty cents for the hat check.

ARTIE
I didn't wear any hat!

DINO
I didn't wear any hat!

ARTIE
So we don't have to pay for the hat
    check!

HANK
So what about the gum?
Thirty cents for the gum!
You guys chewed the gum,
So pay me for the gum!

DINO
I paid—!

RAY
I paid—!

HANK
And don't forget the Hershey bars!

MILDRED
Stella Dallas had her dreams.
She would see her daughter dwell
In stately homes and palaces.
Stella went to all extremes,

Till finally a wealthy fella
Showed at Stella Dallas's.

CELESTE

Stella worked it pretty well,
But in the last analysis,
Though Stella's daughter got the
     swell,
All Stella got was calluses.

MILDRED, CELESTE

It just goes to show that even though
Your family tree is bare,
You still can wind up the intended of
A well-to-do millionaire.

MILDRED

It's so true!
It's so real!
It has such universal appeal . . .

CELESTE

And it proves Mr. Samuel Goldwyn
Is nobody's schlemiel.

If a person treads the path of sin
So her daughter can eat quail,
In the movies she's a heroine,
But in Brooklyn she'd go to jail.
In the movies, life is finer,
Life is cleaner.
But in Brooklyn, it's a minor
Misdemeanor.

In the movies, when a girl has come
From the wrong side of the tracks,
In a week she has a wealthy chum
Who can buy her presents at Saks.
You can start with a bagel
And end up with Conrad Nagel
On the screen,
But in life you wind up
Right behind a
Pillar in the mezzanine.

Feed the plot to the fish;
Life is not like the movies make it
     seem.
Still, we've got Dorothy Gish—
We can lean back
And settle for the dream.

ARTIE

I paid three bucks for the doll.

HANK

That's a personal present.

RAY

Mildred's *your* date!

DINO

Mildred's *your* date!

ARTIE

Mildred's our collective date.
We all agreed to split her.

HANK

A personal gift don't count, though.

ARTIE

Split three bucks four ways:
You and me and Ray and Dino—

RAY

It only cost two for all that we know!

MILDRED

Look what's coming:
Valentino!
Valentino . . .

CELESTE

Vilma Banky . . .

CELESTE, MILDRED

Lots of sand and
Hanky-panky . . .

MILDRED

(Wailing, Arab-style)
Ahhhhhhh!
Wearing a purple turban,
Panting, he holds his hand out.
He crushes her lips, she shivers and
     sighs—

CELESTE

But wait till she tries
Picking the sand out.

MILDRED

Ahhhhhhhhhhhhhhhhhhh!

CELESTE

Hey, wake up there,
Theda Bara,
You're a long way
From the Sahara . . .

In the movies, you get carried off
By a sheik dressed in silk robes.
On a sand dune built for two, you lie
While he gaily kisses your lobes.

Then he murmurs, "Come, I bid you,
To my tent" yet.
But in Brooklyn, he says, "Did you
Pay the rent yet?"

When a girl needs male
     companionship,
On the screen she can keep cool;
She just slouches and extends a hip
While she whispers, "Kiss me, my
     fool!"
It's a movie tradition,
But when I'm in that position,
I get cramps.
So I fold my tent and
Pay the rent and
Leave the vamping to the vamps.

CELESTE, MILDRED

If you must
Be like them,
And you're just
Getting up a head of steam,
Never trust
MGM.
Keep your hips in
And settle for the dream.

One of my favorite lyric writers is Dorothy Fields. My enthusiasm may be compounded by the fact that my father had introduced her to her future husband, his closest friend, and I grew up knowing her as Aunt Dorothy. I didn't know she was a songwriter till I was in my teens, but when I'd written *Saturday Night* Dad thought it might be a useful idea for me to play the score for her. I did so, and when I came to the line "But in life you wind up / Right behind a / Pillar in the mezzanine," she complimented me on the word "pillar" because the sound of the initial "p" filled out the rhyme with "wind up." It made me feel like a professional. And it may not be a coincidence that the flavor of "In the Movies" is more like a lyric of hers than any I've written. It lacks her skillful appearance of effortlessness, of course, although I like to think she wouldn't have minded signing her name to "But in Brooklyn, / It's a minor / Misdemeanor."

Back in Brooklyn, Bobby, the youngest of the group, boasts fraudulently to his sexually innocent buddies that he's been having an affair with a married woman and demonstrates how to prepare for a make-out session, demonstrating with each object as he mentions it.

Exhibit A

BOBBY

Every little pillow has its use.
Take it from a *connoissoor.*
I'm the boy who coined the word
    "seduce,"
Not some lousy *amachoor.*
Every little thing has its function
In conjunction
With *amour.*
Take it from a boy who's had
Rendezvoos galoor.

To impress, to appeal,
Use finesse, be genteel.

Exhibit A:
A couch must be sprayed with
The fragrance of new pine,
And soon all vertical things'll be
    supine.
A woman'll feel at ease
As long as she's smelling trees
In bloom.

Exhibit B:
A door ain't a door till
You close it and lock it.
She can't get out if the key's in your
    pocket,
And nobody else but you can get in—

    (Pausing suggestively)

The room.

Exhibit C:
Music, if it's slow and smooth,
Hath charms to soothe
The savage guest.
Get her stretched out
And let rhythm do the rest.
That fascinating rhythm . . .

Exhibit D:
A cushion is just like

A girl when it's fluffed up.
Girls and cushions are
Meant to be roughed up,
But never, never pawed!

To appeal, to impress,
Be genteel, use finesse
With the shyest and daintiest
Creature on earth—a broad.

Exhibit E:
A flask is for girls who
May have their suspicions.
A shot will help 'em forget
    inhibitions.
The shot'll become a cup,
And finally it'll be
"Bottoms up!"

Exhibit F:
A hammock is drafty,
A place to catch cold in.
But just remember that silence is
    golden,
And hammocks are better than sofas
    or swings:
No springs.

Exhibit G:
Lights make a room cheerier,
But I prefer
The lights that fail,
'Cause with no lights
You can talk to her in Braille.
That's what they mean
When they say love is blind . . .

Exhibit H:
A girl is a thing which is made
Out of glass and lace.
So you must take care
When you're setting up shop.
If you want to come out on top,
Then put every prop in its proper
    place.
Just checking:

    (Checking the objects)

A-B-C-D-E-F-G-H-I-
Rest my case!

This lyric contains a small example of the most pervasive Sin of all in theatrical lyric-writing: mis-stressing. In the Exhibit C section of the song, the phrase "stretched out" should be accented on the word "out," but the downbeat is on "stretched." Result: "*stretched* out" instead of the natural "stretched *out*." As Bobby would say, this is the mark of the amachoor. It is also the mark of the careless professional: Lorenz Hart was a major and habitual sinner in this respect.

Helene, now revealed not as a debutante but as a Brooklyn girl, née Helen, who also was trying to crash the ball, has tracked Gene down and come to see him. He puts a record on the porch phonograph and they start to dance.

A Moment with You

VOCALIST

It took Wilbur Wright
Years to learn to build something
    that flew,
But my heart took flight
In no time
By spending a moment with you.

It took Fred Astaire*
Years to learn to tap out that tattoo,
But I danced on air
In no time
By spending a moment with you!

The look in your eyes was a pleasure,
My personal treasure
Was in it.
J. P. Morgan works weekends,
I got rich in a minute!

It took Sigmund Freud*
Years to learn what makes people
    feel blue.

---

*ANOTHER SIN SURFACES IN THIS LYRIC: ANACHRONISMS. In 1928 Fred Astaire was neither a star nor a soloist, merely half of Fred and Adele Astaire, a moderately well-known dance team, one of many. Furthermore, Sigmund Freud was not yet a household name. They would hardly belong in a popular song of the period in the way Wilbur Wright would. But appropriate three-syllable names were scarce.

But I'm overjoyed:
I avoid being low
Just by spending a moment with you!

VOCALIST
It took Wilbur
Wright
He worked
every night—
Years to learn
to build
Something that
flew,

But my heart
took flight
In no time
By spending
A moment
with you.

It took Fred
Astaire

Years to learn to
Tap out that
tattoo,

But I danced
on air
In no time
By spending
A moment
with you.

HELEN, GENE
It took Wilbur
Wright—

Learn to build
Something that
flew,
Until he turned
blue!

But my heart was
light
In no time
By spending
A moment with
you.

It took Fred
Astaire—
And he's pretty
fair!
Learn to
Tap out that
tattoo,
That rhythmic
tattoo!

But I danced on
air
In no time
By spending
A moment with
you.

HELEN, GENE, VOCALIST
The look in your eyes was a pleasure,
My personal treasure
Was in it.
J. P. Morgan works weekends,
I got rich in a minute!

HELEN, GENE
It took Sigmund
Freud

Years to learn
what makes
People feel
Blue.

VOCALIST
It took Mister
Freud—
He got quite
annoyed!
Learn what makes

People feel—
Unhappy and
blue.

But I'm

Overjoyed:

I avoid being low
Just by spending
A moment
with you!

But I'm no more
in a void,
My cares are
destroyed.
I avoid being low
Just by spending
A moment with
you!

Helen and Gene kiss, but the record has a crack in it and the Vocalist continues repetitively.

VOCALIST
A moment with you . . .
A moment with you . . .
A moment with—
A moment with—
A moment with—
A moment with—

Gene kicks the phonograph stand and the needle scratches to the end of the record.

HELEN, GENE
You!

The gang has pooled all their money in order to invest in a stock called Montana Chemical, a fact which Hank has kept secret from Celeste. The music echoes a ticker tape as the gang reads the week's newspapers to see how the market is faring.

Montana Chem. (2000)

(MONDAY)

DINO
Railroads up . . .

RAY
Electrics up . . .

DINO
Currencies, utilities—

RAY
Commodities—

BOTH
Up!
Montana Chem.—

DINO
(*Moving his finger down the page*)
—Down a point and a half.

(*Their smiles fade; Dino turns to Ray reassuringly*)

Look, Gene says wait until tomorrow.
Gene says tomorrow we'll laugh.
Gene says we're in a boom.
Tomorrow, zoom—
Right off of the graph!

(TUESDAY)

ARTIE
U.S. Steel is up three points,
Consolidated Edison five.

TED
Tobacco—?

ARTIE
Climbed.
Oil as well.
Up four and seven-eighths for
Tel & Tel.

TED
Montana Chem.—?

ARTIE
Montana Chem.—

TED, ARTIE
—Fell.

But Gene says the market's mediocre,
Gene says tomorrow's a cinch.
Gene says he heard it from some joker
Who's the nephew of a broker
Down at Merrill Lynch.

(WEDNESDAY)

(*Celeste has the paper*)

CELESTE
Bootleg war . . .
Skirts are getting higher . . .

HANK
Good.
Could I see the financial page—?

CELESTE
Al Smith says Hoover is a liar . . .

HANK

Big surprise.
Honey, the financial page—

CELESTE

Let's see . . .

(Moving her finger down the page)

Bonds are up . . .

HANK

Montana Chem.—?

CELESTE

I'm getting to it.
Stocks are up
All along the line . . .

HANK

Montana Chem.—?

CELESTE

Montana Chem. down a little—

HANK

Down a little?
What's a little?

CELESTE

Nine.

HANK

But Gene said—

CELESTE

I know what Gene said, and it breaks my heart.

(Pats his head)

Thank God you didn't listen to him . . .

(THURSDAY)

(All the boys are onstage, reading)

BOYS

Corn went up,
Wheat went up,
Everything, you name it, on the street went up.
Montana Chem. did not go up—
But it didn't go down!

ARTIE

First time!

OTHERS

Right!

BOYS

And Gene says,
Wait until tomorrow night,
The stock is going out of sight!

(FRIDAY)

BOYS

Wait until tomorrow . . .
Wait until tomorrow . . .
Gene says, wait until tomorrow . . .

"Montana Chem." was added to the score when the show finally received its first professional performance in New York City in 2000.

Helen and Gene declare their love for each other.

So Many People

HELEN

I said the man for me
Must have a castle.
A man of means he'd be,
A man of fame.
And then I met a man who hadn't any,
Without a penny
To his name.

I had to go and fall
For so much less than*
What I had planned from all
The magazines.

---

*Another prevalent Sin among song-writers: mismatching music and lyric. In this case, the melodic line pauses after "less than" but the lyric phrase doesn't. Thus there is a needless hesitation before "What I had planned." Spoken sentences break themselves into phrased chunks, and conversational lyrics should reflect the phrasing of the music or they sound unnatural. You don't want a (pause) sentence like this to (pause) sit on the (pause) music like this. At least you shouldn't.

I should be good and sore,
What am I happy for?
I guess the man means more
Than the means.

So many people in the world,
And what can they do?
They'll never know love
Like my love for you.
So many people laugh
At what they don't know—
Well, that's their concern.
If just a few, say half
A million or so,
Could see us, they'd learn.

So many people in the world
Don't know what they've missed.
They'd never believe
Such joy could exist.
And if they tell us
It's a thing we'll outgrow,
They're jealous
As they can be,
That with so many people in the world,
You love me!

The gang, joined by various dates and girlfriends, celebrates Gene and Helen's engagement.

One Wonderful Day

CELESTE

One wonderful day,
Wonderful things can happen
In a wonderful way!
Wonderful girl meets wonderful boy.
What a wonderful chance to start a life
Full of wonder and joy!

One wonderful day,
Somebody wonderful sweeps
All your worries away!
If the feeling's mutual,
Then the future will
Burst into song,
And it's one wonderful day all year long!

ARTIE

Let's have a party!

DINO

Congratulations!

RAY

I wish you luck and prosperity!

HANK

I wish you hearty felicitations!

FLORENCE

I wish that someone would marry me.

BOBBY

Don't do it, Gene.
Don't do it, Gene.
Love with a spouse is a household
    routine.
Then, when you're through,
What can you do?
Can't send a dame home
Who lives in the same home
As you!

One horrible day,
You will wake up to find
You're in a horrible way.
You will be married, you will be caught.
Every day you'll come home
And she'll be there—
What a horrible thought!

One night on a swing
May make a casual affair a permanent
    thing.
If you can't keep casual,
Then she has you all
Ready to hook,
And it's one horrible day—
I can't look.

My married dame
Says, "It's a shame,
But sex, if it's lawful,
Is awfully tame."
Husbands I've known
Say, "Live alone.
Wives are abhorrent
Except when they aren't
Your own."

CELESTE

Pay no attention
To Mr. Smarty,
He's full of beans and banana oil.
He'll throw a wrench in
This lovely party,
So just ignore him, don't let him spoil
This glorious—

BOBBY

Terrible—

CELESTE

Victorious—

BOBBY

Unbearable—

CELESTE

Uproarious—

BOBBY

Irreparable—

CELESTE

Uxorious—*

BOBBY
(Giving up)

Occasion!

ALL

One wonderful day,
Wonderful things can happen
In a wonderful way!
Wonderful girl meets wonderful boy.
What a wonderful chance to start
A life full of wonder and joy!

One wonderful day,
Somebody wonderful sweeps
All your worries away!
If the feeling's mutual,
Then the future will
Burst into song
And it's one wonderful day,
One marvelous day,
One beautiful day,
One glorious day,**
One wonderful day all year long!

ACT TWO

The front porch. Seven o'clock Saturday night, a week later. The gang is sitting around as usual.

Saturday Night

(reprise)

DINO

I know a dame in Richmond Hill.

RAY

Yeah, but will she—?

DINO

She will.
She's what I'd call a well-built beast.

RAY
(*Suggestively*)

Has she got two—?

DINO

At least.

TED

When you are by your lonesome,
All you can do is phone some
Broad who says she's already got a
    date.

DINO

Wish that I knew a girlie
Who'd like to retire early
And get up late.

---

*TWO MORE SINS REAR THEIR UGLY HEADS HERE, first in the adjective war between Celeste and Bobby: substituting rhyme for thought, which is far worse than substituting rhyme for character if for no other reason than that it's more noticeable. And here you get substituting rhyme for character as well: "Uxorious"— what has Celeste been reading?

** THE SECOND OF THOSE TWO SINS IS PROBABLY THE MOST COMMON OF ALL: adjectival padding. "Wonderful," "marvelous," "beautiful" and "glo-rious" were the most overworked songwriters' words in the Golden Age, their syllabic equivalence making them handy in replacing one another for variety. When they were used individually to convey something specific (as in, once again, "Oh, What a Beautiful Mornin'") they could have real impact. But when they came in packets of two or more, as they often did, their generalized meanings flattened the emotional tone. Hammerstein was careful to repeat "beautiful" instead of replacing it in each line with one of its sister anodynes.

RAY
Who wants to scare up a poker game?

ARTIE
I wanna scare up a dame.

DINO
Call up a dame
And invite her to see
A show . . .

TED
Call up a dame
And her answer'll be—
No go!

ARTIE
What's the result of the trouble
You took to reach her?
A single man at a double
Lousy feature.

RAY
Midnight ahead
And the hay to be hit—alone.

ARTIE
You made your bed,
So you're lyin' in it—alone.

DINO
Sunday, the day of rest
Should be a welcome sight—

ALL
But who needs a rest
After resting all Saturday night?

*Celeste and Hank, the only married cou-
ple in the group, are sitting on the porch.
Hank is reminiscing romantically.*

I Remember That

HANK
I have a memory for small details.
I have a memory that never fails.
I can remember names, dates and
    places,
And even faces of people whose faces
I don't want to know.

I know the date of the Parthenon,
But there's a date that I'm hazy on:
That was the date we had, I
    remember,
In early September—
Or was it November?—
Three years ago.
Up to a certain point my mind is
    clear,
Every detail of that date, that fateful
    year.

I arrived at seven;
I stopped along the way
To buy a big bouquet
For you—
I remember that.

In a French-type restaurant,
Run by a guy named Jake,
We had a sirloin steak
For two—
I remember that.

I remember we sat out in Prospect
    Park
In the glow of moonlight.
After that we went back to your house
And danced till dawn.

I was pouring coffee,
You lit a cigarette.
From then on I forget
What I said, what I did and where I
    was at.

For I'd fallen in love with you,
I remember I'd fallen in love with
    you,
That's the one thing I do remember,
I remember that.

CELESTE
Up to a point your mind is clear, no
    doubt,
But I can remember some things that
    you left out:

I was dressed at seven,
But you arrived at eight.
And you were never late
Again—
I remember that.

Since you'd bought me flowers,
You couldn't pay the check.

You were a nervous wreck
By then—
I remember that.

I remember we sat in the park
In the glow of a policeman's
    flashlight.
After that we went back to my house
And sat some more.

You were pouring coffee
All over my new dress.
From then on, I confess,
I forget what I said and where I was at.

But I did fall in love with you,
I remember I did fall in love with you,
That's the one thing I do remember,
I remember that.

Most of the people who read this book
will know a song by Alan Jay Lerner
and Frederick Loewe in *Gigi* called
"I Remember It Well." It was a duet
between Honoré (Maurice Chevalier)
and Madame Alvarez (Hermione Gingold) and sprang from the same notion
as "I Remember That": a couple reminiscing about their first date, he inac-
curately. I hasten to add that *Saturday
Night* was written in 1954 and *Gigi* appeared in 1958, although I may have
cribbed the idea unconsciously, as
Lerner had apparently written a version of his song with Kurt Weill for a
show called *Love Life* in 1948, a show
which I saw. The differences between
the musical approaches reflect the
differences in character and tone.
Honoré and Madame Alvarez are
middle-aged ex-lovers and politely
hesitant in declaring their fondness for
each other, so Loewe's tune is a bittersweet hesitation waltz, textured with
fits and starts; Hank and Celeste are
young and flip, so the tune is casual,
set to an easy, strolling rhythm.

The differences in the lyrics illus-
trate even more clearly how character
determines approach. Lerner alter-
nates the statements of his characters
and their corrections of each other,
and the rejoinders are gentle, as befits
two romantically tentative people. In
Saturday Night, Hank is openly trying

I HAVE A MEMORY FOR SMALL DETAILS,

I HAVE A MEMORY THAT NEVER FAILS;

I CAN REMEMBER NAMES, DATES, AND PLACES,

 AND EVEN FACES OF PEOPLE WHOSE FACES

  I DON'T WANT TO KNOW.

I KNOW THE DATE OF THE PARTHENON,

BUT THERE'S A DATE THAT I'M HAZY ON -

 THAT WAS THE DATE WE HAD, I REMEMBER,

  IN EARLY SEPTEMBER -

  OR WAS IT NOVEMBER? -

   THREE YEARS AGO.

Up to a certain point my mind is clear

~~I CAN REMEMBER DETAILS, LIKE WHAT YOU WORE,~~

Every detail of that date that fateful year,   *disappear*

~~THREE YEARS AGO THIS SEPTEMB - OR WAS IT FOUR?~~

WELL, ANYWAY,

~~WHAT I CAN BEST TO I DO REMEMBER~~ — *You were a new blue dress.*

I ARRIVED AT SEVEN,

dressed in   *I STOPPED ALONG THE WAY*   *wearing*

wearing blue   ~~AND YOU WERE DRESSED IN WHITE.~~ — *And you were ~~dressed~~ in blue*

You said the   *TO BUY A BIG BOUQUET*   *You told me that the dress*

~~I'D BROUGHT A BUNCH OF BRIGHT~~   *was new.*

dress was new   *FOR YOU*

that day   ~~BLUE FLOWERS~~ - I REMEMBER THAT.

                  IN FRENCH-TYPE   *I had brought you flowers.*

The evening sky ~~IN~~ A ~~QUIET~~ RESTAURANT, *There was a small café,*

was bright   ~~THE OWNER'S NAME WAS SAKE~~

with stars   ~~WE WINED AND DINED AND TALKED~~

                  ~~WE HAD A SIRLOIN STEAK~~

                  ~~AND LATER ON WE WALKED~~

                  FOR TWO

                  FOR HOURS - I REMEMBER THAT.

                       OUT IN PROSPECT

I REMEMBER ~~WE SAT ON A BENCH~~ IN THE PARK IN THE GLOW OF MOONLIGHT.

~~AFTER THAT, IT BEGAN TO RAIN, SO I TOOK YOU HOME.~~   *Hon-DAWN,*

                  WE WENT BACK TO ~~YOUR~~ HOUSE AND TALKED TILL

I REMEMBER CLEARLY

~~I WAS POURING COFFEE;~~   I WAS POURING COFFEE

      YOUR

~~I LIT A CIGARETTE.~~   YOU LIT A CIGARETTE;

FROM THEN ON, I FORGET

WHAT I SAID, WHAT I DID, AND WHERE I WAS AT.

FOR I'D FALLEN IN LOVE WITH YOU,

I REMEMBER I'D FALLEN IN LOVE WITH YOU,

THAT'S THE ONE THING I DO REMEMBER - I REMEMBER THAT.

In a crowded restaurant,
We had to wait a while
                while

I'd brought you roses
bright bright,
white and red.

Up to a point, your mind is clear, no doubt.
But I can remember some things that you've left out.

For instance:

starved

I WAS DRESSED AT SEVEN,

BUT YOU ARRIVED AT ~~NINE~~ EIGHT;

AND YOU WERE NEVER LATE

~~WE DIDN'T WINE AND DINE~~

AGAIN

~~TILL TEN~~ - I REMEMBER THAT.

We had to stand in line wait on

No, not after that

SINCE YOU'D BOUGHT ME FLOWERS,

I made sure of that

YOU COULDN'T PAY THE CHECK;

I can vouch for that

you were

~~I WAS~~ A NERVOUS WRECK

you got it in the neck ourself once more

BY THEN - I REMEMBER THAT.

WE SAT

I REMEMBER ~~THE BENCH~~ IN THE PARK IN THE GLOW OF A POLICEMAN'S

FLASHLIGHT,

AFTER, WE WENT BACK TO ~~M.Y~~ HOUSE AND SAT SOME MORE

~~AND THE DRENCHING I GOT~~ WITH THE RAIN DRIPPING OFF YOUR HAT.

YOU WERE POURING COFFEE

ALL OVER MY NEW DRESS.

FROM THEN ON, I CONFESS,

I FORGET WHAT I SAID AND WHERE I WAS AT,

BUT I DID FALL IN LOVE WITH YOU -

I REMEMBER I DID FALL IN LOVE WITH YOU -

THAT'S THE ONE THI NG I DO REMEMBER - I REMEMBER THAT.

I arrived at seven,   I arrived at seven

~~But we went out at eight~~   +I stopped along the way

I'd brought a small bouquet   ~~I'd bought~~ a big bouquet

And you were wearing na -   For you -

vy blue.

In a crowded restaurant   In a little restaurant -

We had to wait on line   The owner's name was Jake -

To wait with you was fine   We had a sirloin steak

With me -   For two.

ALAN JAY LERNER
No There There

Lerner is one of the more highly praised lyricists in the American musical theater, largely due to the successes of *Brigadoon, My Fair Lady* and *Camelot,* but if I had to describe the central quality of his lyrics in a single word, I'd call them pleasant, an adjective which does not connote much enthusiasm. They are almost always smooth and tasteful (virtues particularly inappropriate to *Paint Your Wagon,* his musical about miners and pioneers in the nineteenth century). They flirt with sophistication but remain at heart polite, if not genteel: they lack energy and flavor and passion. Compared with the songs of everyone else in the Pantheon from Hammerstein to Harburg to Hart, they miss the one thing that would distinguish them: personality. What they do have more than occasionally is grace, a quality not to be dismissed or unappreciated, but by itself unfulfilling.

I have never been exhilarated by a Lerner lyric except for "A Hymn to Him" in *My Fair Lady,* which scintillated me in a way that the rest of the songs did for most people, and which is only slightly spoiled by its wink-wink title. Nor have I ever laughed at or been moved by a Lerner lyric the way I have by many of his less well-known peers (see below); at most I've smiled or sighed sympathetically. My reaction to his work is similar to the one I have to W. S. Gilbert's. More important, Lerner's lyrics are not as natty as they strut to be. For example, there's an appearance of high gloss on *My Fair Lady*'s lyrics, but take Henry Higgins' claim in "I'm an Ordinary Man" that "I'd be equally as willing / For a dentist to be drilling / Than to ever let a woman in my life," a syntactical train wreck, especially noticeable coming from a professor of English so meticulous about the language that the plot depends on it. Then there's "bother me" and "rather

be" in "On the Street Where You Live" from the same show, an imperfect rhyme in a score which because of its subject demands impeccability. These may seem like niggles, but since with Lerner the surface is the substance, the tiniest flaws in the gloss stand out.

Lerner's suave gentility was ill-suited not only to the Old West sensibility of *Paint Your Wagon,** it deadened the sexual insistence of his version of *Lolita* and smoothed out the raunchy Italian edges of *Carmelina,* the story of which many years later turned into *Mamma Mia!,* which is even less raunchy and Italian. (The lesson to be learned from this is that Lerner took his subject seriously, whereas the authors of *Mamma Mia!* couldn't have cared less: one show fulfilled its goal, the other did not—an important difference between a disaster and a success.) And when he tried to muscle in on Harburg's territory (verbal ingenuity) he came up with cringe-makers like this from "The Seven Deadly Virtues" in *Camelot:*

> You'll never find a virtue
> Unstatusing my quo
> Or making my Be-elzebubble burst.

Lerner found his perfect match in the Shaw of *Pygmalion,* but I don't think he'd have done so well adapting *Saint Joan.* With Lerner suave gentility was the default mode, and when he tried to apply it to another sociopolitical comedy, he unfortunately settled on a Shavian imitation: *Idiot's Delight,* a didactic play by Robert E. Sherwood that was like a heavy-handed riff on *Major*

Barbara.* The musical was called *Dance a Little Closer* and Lerner, like Sherwood, wasn't nimble enough to capture Shaw's tone. More significantly, there was no personal point of view to the show. Throughout his career, Lerner kept trying to find a persona, from political thinker (*1600 Pennsylvania Avenue, Dance a Little Closer*) to whimsical fantasist (*On a Clear Day You Can See Forever*) to chronicler of Americana (*Love Life, 1600 Pennsylvania Avenue*), but he was a chameleon of one color.

For me he belongs among the lower deities in the Pantheon: lyricists who are skilled, sometimes spectacularly so, but have no discernible stamp of style or personality. They include such first-rate songwriters as Howard Dietz ("By Myself"), Leo Robin ("Diamonds Are a Girl's Best Friend"), John La Touche ("Lazy Afternoon") as well as a sizable company of others. Some of them didn't write enough songs to establish a style, some of them had a style but didn't write enough shows (Johnny Mercer, DuBose Heyward), some of them came too soon in the theater game to thrive on character and plot the way the post–Rodgers and Hammerstein generation did, and some of them were simply generic craftsmen, admirable but indistinguishable from each other.

It's hard to comment on or even write about Alan Jay Lerner because his work is so professional and uninteresting when compared to that of the other major theater lyricists. Critical of Hart and Gershwin though I am (as you'll find out further on), I would rather live with the second-best of their songs than the best of Lerner's. Having said all this, I must report that I saw the second preview of *My Fair Lady* in New Haven and the eventual product in New York, and it's the most entertaining musical I've ever seen (exclusive of my own, of course).

---

*Just the way that Hammerstein, comfortable in the West, was unsuited to Shaw—he and Rodgers had, in fact, turned *Pygmalion* down long before Lerner picked it up.

to be romantic and Celeste is clear-eyed in her assessment of him, so their conversation consists of two monologues, his a rosy-eyed set of remembrances and hers a fond but tart set of contradictions. The relationship between Honoré and Madame Alvarez is left unresolved, whereas Hank and Celeste neatly sum up their feelings for each other. Neatness for the young people, ambiguity for the old. The songs could not be more similar, or more different.

Gene is in trouble with both the law and his friends and is suicidal. Helen tries to give him courage.

I'm All for You

HELEN
I'm all for you,
Whatever happens,
My dreams are yours to share.
Sometimes, it's true,
My words are bitter,
But that's because I care.

If I get mad
When I think you're wrong,
Maybe I am wrong, too.
But good or bad,
Everything I do
Is all for love of you.

Gene is about to go to jail. The gang rallies around him.

It's That Kind of a Neighborhood

DINO
It's that kind of a neighborhood—

ALL
That kind of a neighborhood!

DINO
Share and share alike—

HANK
That's the way to be!

ARTIE, RAY
(To each other)
I share with you—

BOBBY
I share with me.

ALL
It's that kind of a neighborhood,
That kind of a neighborhood!

HANK
We never, never kick a fellow when he's down—

TED
Unless, of course, he comes from out of town.

DINO
All of us are for brotherhood—

BOYS
For brotherhood!

RAY
All of us are for motherhood—

GIRLS
For motherhood!

HANK, TED
All of us are for each and every other hood—

ALL
Other hood!

ARTIE
All of us are for hoods.

ALL
It's that kind of a neighborhood,
That kind of a neighborhood.

(Chorale style)

Fair Brooklyn,
Pride of the port of New York!
There's a friendly golf course with greens,

And a friendly hash house with beans.
There's a friendly clink whence
Come juvenile delinquents,
But they were born in Queens.

Fair Brooklyn—
Look at the cop on the beat.
As he does his job, he takes pride
(And a little graft on the side).
His badge has luster—
When he says "Move on, buster!"
You feel all teary-eyed.

We love the homes of Brooklyn,
The dives of Brooklyn,
The streets of Brooklyn,

BOBBY
The wives of Brooklyn . . .

ALL
We're proud of every thoroughfare
In this borough, fair
Brooklyn!
The pride of,
The thorn in the side of
New York!

It's that kind of a neighborhood,
That kind of a neighborhood.

MILDRED
A hope in every heart.

CELESTE
A means to every end.

RAY
A dame on every corner,
Waiting for a friend.

ALL
It's that kind of a neighborhood,
That kind of a neighborhood.

ARTIE
We respect the law, but let us make it plain,
If chicanery is called for, we'll chicane.

HANK
Being part of a civilized community,
We believe in a democratic unity,
Where everyone has an equal opportunity—

In the movies, life is finer, life is cleaner.
But in Brooklyn, it's a minor misdemeanor.
In the movies, she is noble, she is regal.
But in real life, what is noble is illegal!
In the movies, life's a riot, life's a bubble.
But in real life, if you try it, you're in trouble.

STELLA DALLAS HAD ~~A~~ DREAMS –
  SHE WOULD SEE HER DAUGHTER DWELL
  IN STATELY HOMES AND PALACES.
STELLA ~~~~~~~~~~~~~~~~~~~ WENT TO ALL EXTREMES
AND FINALLY ~~NEVER LED~~ A WEALTHY FELLA
SHOWED ~~A CARD TO~~ STELLA DALLAS'S.
  STELLA ~~WORKED AND SLAVED LIKE HELL~~ WORKED IT PRETTY WELL,
  BUT IN THE LAST ANALYSIS,
THOUGH STELLA'S DAUGHTER GOT THE SWELL
A ~~LAND~~ STELLA GOT ~~THE~~ CALLUSES.
It just goes to show that ~~~~~~~~~~~~~~~~~~~~ family tree is bare,
~~SUFFERING IS NOBLE, SUFFERING IS CLEAN,~~
~~SUFFERING IS FUN – WHEN IT'S ON THE SCREEN.~~
~~A girl can wind up the intended of a wealthy millionaire~~
  IF A ~~~~~~~~ GIRL TREADS THE PATH OF SIN
  ~~TO PROVIDE FOR HER OLD MUM,~~ SO HER DAUGHTER CAN EAT QUAIL
  IN THE MOVIES SHE'S A HEROINE,
  BUT IN ~~~~~~~~~~~ SHE'D ~~BE IN JAIL.~~
THE THIRTEENTH PRECINCT
  DOESN'T GO FOR
  HANKY-PANKY –
NOT UNLESS YOU'RE
CLARA BOW OR
VILMA BANKY.
  IN THE ~~MOVIES, WHEN~~ A PERSON ~~HAILS~~
  FROM THE WRONG SIDE OF THE TRACKS,
  ~~WITHIN HOURS~~ SHE IS EATING SNAILS
  AND EXCHANGING PRESENTS AT SAKS.
  YOU CAN START WITH A BAGEL
  AND END UP WITH CONRAD NAGEL
  ON THE SCREEN,
  BUT IN LIFE YOU WIND UP
  RIGHT BEHIND A
  PILLAR IN THE MEZZANINE.

~~LIFE'S A POT~~ FEED THE PLOT
~~FULL OF FISH;~~ TO THE FISH;
LIFE IS NOT
~~WHAT THE MOVIES MAKE IT SEEM.~~ WHAT THE MOVIES MAKE IT SEEM.
STILL WE'VE GOT
DOROTHY GISH –
~~AND~~ WE CAN LEAN BACK AND SETTLE FOR THE DREAM.

  IN THE MOVIES, ~~'NEATH A DESERT SKY,~~ when you meet a guy,
  ~~YOU'RE A SHEIK'S WIFE IN~~ SILK ROBES. He's a sheik dressed in
  ON A SAND DUNE BUILT FOR TWO, YOU LIE
  WHILE HE ~~SOFTLY KISSES~~ YOUR LOBES. FIERCELY NIBBLES
  THEN HE MURMURS, "COME, I BID YOU,
  IN MY TENT YET."
  BUT IN REAL LIFE, HE SAYS, "DID YOU
  PAY THE RENT YET?"
  WHEN A GIRL NEEDS MALE COMPANIONSHIP
  ON THE SCREEN, ALL THE MEN DROOL.
  SHE JUST SLOUCHES AND EXTENDS HER HIP
  WHILE SHE WHISPERS, "KISS ME, MY FOOL!"
  IT'S A MOVIE TRADITION,
  BUT WHEN I'M IN THAT POSITION,
  I GET CRAMPS.
  SO I FOLD MY TENT
  AND PAY THE RENT
  AND LEAVE THE VAMPING TO THE VAMPS.

  IF YOU MUST BE LIKE THEM,
  AND YOU'RE JUST GETTING UP A HEAD OF STEAM,
  NEVER TRUST MGM –
  KEEP YOUR HIPS IN AND SETTLE FOR THE DREAM.

[Handwritten marginalia:] financial wizard / blizzard / sold her soul / noble, brave & crooked / you steel / THE POLICE FORCE / FIRST REEL / BY IN THE THIRD REEL / If she starts / and go on to / In the movies, when a girl has come / In a week, she has a wealthy ... who sends her presents at Saks / BETTER / A sheik wearing / you get kidnapped by ... when you meet a guy / She can keep cool

UP WITH CON-RAD NAG-EL ON THE SCREEN. BUT IN

LIFE YOU WIND UP RIGHT BE—HIND A PIL-LAR IN THE MEZ-ZA—

NINE. FEED THE PLOT TO THE

FISH, LIFE IS NOT WHAT THE MOV-IES MAKE IT SEEM. STILL WE'VE

DINO

—To hide your friends from the cops.

ALL

It's that kind of a neighborhood,
Our kind of a neighborhood.
We're proud of our neighborhood,
Even if the world doesn't approve.
And besides,
Who can afford to move?

*Gene is about to go to jail, but only for a
short while, this being a musical comedy.
He bids a temporary farewell to Helen, as
his friends cheer them on.*

What More Do I Need?

GENE

Once I hated this city,
Now it can't get me down.
Slushy, humid and gritty,
What a pretty
Town!
What, thought I, could be duller,
More depressing, less gay?
Now my favorite color
Is gray!

A wall of rain as it turns to sleet,
The lack of sun
On a one-
Way street.
I love the grime
All the time,
And what more do I need?

HELEN

My window pane has a lovely view:
An inch of sky
And a fly
Or two.
Why, I can see
Half a tree,
And what more do I need?

GENE

The dust is thick and it's galling.

HELEN

It simply can't be excused.

GENE

In winter, even the falling
Snow looks used.

HELEN

My window pane may not give much
    light,
But I see you,
So the view
Is bright.

BOTH

If I can love you,
I'll pay the dirt no heed.
With your love, what more do I need?

DINO

Someone's shouting for quiet.

ARTIE

Someone's starting a brawl.

RAY, DINO, TED

Down the block there's a riot—

HELEN

And I'll buy it
All.

CELESTE

Listen now, I'm ecstatic.

HANK

Hold me close and keep still.

MILDRED

Hear the lovely pneumatic
Drill!

GENE

A subway train thunders through the
    Bronx.

HELEN

A taxi horn
On the corner
Honks.

GENE, HELEN

But I adore
Every roar,
And what more
Do I need?

HELEN

I hear a crane making street repairs.

GENE

A two-ton child
Running wild
Upstairs.

HELEN

Steam pipes bang—

GENE

Sirens clang—

BOTH

And what more do I need?

POLICEMEN

The neighbors yell in the summer.

HANK, CELESTE

The landlord yells in the fall.

BOYS

So loud you can't hear the plumber
Pound the wall.

HELEN, GENE

An aeroplane* roars across the bay,
But I can hear
You as clear
As day.
You said you love me,
Above the sound and speed!
With your love, what more do I need?

Our producer, Lemuel Ayers, planned
the production of *Saturday Night* for
1955, but, unbeknownst to anyone except his wife, he was suffering from

---

*ONE LAST SIN, SMALL AND
INFREQUENT BUT A SIN NONE-
THELESS: Adding needed syllables, as
in "aeroplane." I justified (to myself) the
pronunciation on the grounds that this
is the way the word was still being
spelled in the twenties. Even if it weren't
such a flimsy excuse, each syllable has
equal musical value, so that we hear a
long "o" instead of a short one: air-o-
plane instead of air-uh-plane, as it's pronounced in real life. On the other hand,
I'm pleased with the inner rhymes in
"The lack of <u>sun</u> on a <u>one</u>-way street"
and similarly placed ones throughout
the lyric; they lend speed and focus,
which is what inner rhymes do best.

---

leukemia. He died that year. We had raised about half of the $300,000 budget and his widow wanted to move ahead with the show, but she was too inexperienced to handle it and the production died as well. It had a brief resuscitation when Jule Styne wanted to produce it in 1960, with Bob Fosse directing, choreographing and playing Gene. It wasn't until we started casting that I realized I didn't want to return to old work, and I scuttled the project. It finally came to light in 1997, when a small theater in London presented it; shortly thereafter, it was produced in Chicago and then off-Broadway in New York. But the show had served its purpose long before: it provided me with a set of songs that could be deemed professional and that I could use to announce my presence on the musical-theater scene.

One of my announcements took place at E. Y. Harburg's apartment. I had been invited to an informal dinner there by Harold Arlen, whom I knew slightly as a result of our being co-godfathers of the same child. He knew I was a songwriter and thought I might be interested in hobnobbing not only with him and Harburg, but also Burton Lane and other eminences. I was thrilled, and I came prepared. Anticipating that I would be called on to display my wares, I spent the day practicing "Saturday Night," "Isn't It?" and "One Wonderful Day"— a suite as carefully calibrated as a three-movement symphony: a charming foot-tapper, a humorous waltz and a rousing finale.

Sure enough, during coffee, Lane got up and played requests, followed by Arlen doing the same (sometimes joined by Harburg), and then Harburg quieted the room to announce the presence of a talented young man, one Stephen Sondheim. I blushed appropriately, went to the piano and launched into my program. I charmed them, then tickled them, then knocked them out, all according to plan. After much applause and admiration, I sat down, outwardly modest but preening away inside, and found myself next to Arlen, a soft-spoken, reserved man. "Don't be afraid not to write a blockbuster," he gently murmured. And I thought of his "A Sleeping Bee" in *House of Flowers* (lyrics by Arlen and Truman Capote), a mesmerizing song and moment, quietly arrived at and quietly gone. Harold taught me a lesson I've never forgotten: It's extremely satisfying to wow an audience, but to try to do it persistently carries an air of desperation.

In any event, *Saturday Night* provided me with credentials, and I was ready for my Broadway debut, which turned out to be both less and more than I had expected.

"A Moment with You"

West Side Story

A New Musical

2. West Side Story (1957)

Book by Arthur Laurents
Music by Leonard Bernstein

The Notion

Romeo and Juliet transposed to New York City, 1957. The Montagues and Capulets are two gangs, the Jets (white) and the Sharks (Puerto Rican). The lovers are Tony (Romeo), a former member of the Jets, and Maria (Juliet), the sister of Bernardo (Paris), leader of the Sharks. Riff (Mercutio) is the leader of the Jets and Tony's best friend. .

General Comments

For most people *West Side Story* is about racial prejudice and urban violence, but what it's really about is theater: musical theater, to be more precise. It's about the blending of book, music, lyrics and, most important, dance into the seamless telling of a story. It was not the first serious attempt to incorporate dance as an essential part of a commercial musical instead of its traditional function as diversion or ornamentation. That privilege belongs to *Oklahoma!,* where Agnes de Mille's choreography individualized characters and even reflected an emotional crisis in the heroine's mind, inaugurating the first "dream" ballet, a notion which both invigorated and infected Broadway shows for decades to come,* including

---

*Dance had been used by George Balanchine in *On Your Toes* as part of the plot but not as a metaphor.

ing *West Side Story,* whose Act Two dream ballet not only recapitulates in the lovers' minds the traumatizing events of Act One, but also makes (or rather, pounds home) a point about prejudice and togetherness, largely through an ethereally presented song which explains it to the audience. Jerome Robbins's staging of the show carried de Mille's idea even further: some songs and passages were formally choreographed, but there were also set pieces like "Prologue" and "The Rumble," which consisted of choreographed natural movement rather than formal choreography. In Jerry's hands, dance was an integral part of the creative collaboration, not just an occasional dividend, though the show has enough of those, too: numbers like "America" and "Gee, Officer Krupke," which serve to remind the audience that this is an entertainment, not a sociological treatise. Part of what *West Side Story* was about was collaboration. It certainly was for me.

At George School in Pennsylvania, which I had attended in my teens, I'd collaborated with two classmates on the book and lyrics of a show cleverly titled *By George*. Again, later on with my roommate at Williams College in the last half of our freshman year (1947) we'd written a campus satire cleverly titled *Phinney's Rainbow,* that being the year when *Finian's Rainbow* was first produced on Broadway and the president of Williams was James Phinney Baxter. Later, professionally, I had collaborated with Julie Epstein on *Saturday Night,* but it had been a telephone collaboration for the most part, my job being to musicalize scenes already in the play, his being to tidy up the holes and condense the characters to an affordable cast size. Collaboration with Bernstein, Laurents and Robbins was another matter entirely. To begin with, not only was I for the first time writing lyrics to someone else's music, the someone else was a legend verging on myth, whose score for *On the Town,* from the

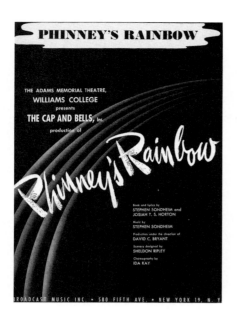

PHINNEY'S RAINBOW

THE ADAMS MEMORIAL THEATRE,
WILLIAMS COLLEGE
presents
THE CAP AND BELLS, Inc.
production of

Phinney's Rainbow

Book and Lyrics by
STEPHEN SONDHEIM and
JOSIAH T. S. HORTON

Music by
STEPHEN SONDHEIM

Production under the direction of
DAVID C. BRYANT

Scenery designed by
SHELDON RIPLEY

Choreography by
IDA KAY

BROADCAST MUSIC INC. • 580 FIFTH AVE. • NEW YORK 19, N. Y.

Phinney's Rainbow

Synopsis of Scenes

Act I

1. A dormitory. Three rooms.
2. A path leading to the Haymaker Monument.
3. The Haymaker Monument.
4. The bedroom of the Alumnum.
5. The Outer Office of the Alumnum.
6. The Interior of the Dim Dinner.
7. The Inner Office (Conference Room) of the Alumnum.

Act II

1. The goat room of the Dogma Nu Fraternity House.
2. The Interior of the Dim Dinner.
3. A dormitory room.
4. The living-room of the Dogma Nu Fraternity House.
5. The bedroom of the Alumnum.
6. A campus walk.
7. The Haymaker Monument.

Time: The present.

Place: Swindlehurst Prep School for Boys.

Musical Numbers

Act I

Scene 1
1. Opening Number .... *Muscles, Killer, DumDum, Errol, Tyrone, Clifton, Louis, Cecil, Humphrey*
2. "Strength Through Sex" .... *Nine Boys*

Scene 3
3. "Strength Through Sex" .... *Muscles, Errol, Louis and Chorus*

Scene 4
4. Alumnum's Song .... *Alumnum*

Scene 5
5. Alma Mater .... *Alumnum, J. A., Secretaries, Students*
6. "How Do I Know?" .... *Yolanda*
   Dance .... *Bourne and White*
7. "We're Gonna Have a Meeting" .... *Professors Pillie, Marrow, C'attlagarrea, Lunt, Schumaker, Dean Books, Alumnum*

Scene 6
8. "The Dim Dinner" .... *Len, Ray, Bill*
9. "I Opened a Book" .... *John and Yolanda*

Scene 7
10. Faculty Song .... *Six Professors*
11. "Ave Alumnum" .... *Six Professors*
12. Professors' Reports .... *Six Professors*
13. Finaletto .... *Entire Company*

Act II

Scene 1
14. "Dogma Nu" .... *Tyrone and Boys' Chorus*

Scene 2
15. Reprise: "The Dim Dinner" .... *Len, Ray, Bill*
16. "Gwendolyn" and "Yolanda" .... *Alumnum and John*

Scene 3
17. "The Q-Ladies' Waltz" .... *Daphne, Petunia, Colette, Frou-Frou*

Scene 4
18. Fumblington Girls' Song .... *Olga, Salome and Chorus of Fumblington Girls*
19. "Phinney's Rainbow" .... *Olga and Chorus of Girls and Boys*
    Tap Dance .... *Utley and Turpin*

Scene 5
20. Lullaby .... *Hedwige*
21. Dream Ballet .... *Q-Ladies, Hedwige, Alumnum, J. A., Professors, Fumblington Girls, Secretaries*

Scene 6
22. Reprise: "Q-Ladies' Waltz" .... *Q-Ladies*
23. "Still Got My Heart" .... *John and Yolanda*

Scene 7
24. Finale .... *Entire Company*

Piano Accompanists:
Gerald F. O'Brien, Stephen Sondheim

---

moment I'd heard it sizzling out of the orchestra pit when I was fourteen, had given me that rush of excitement you rarely get from musicals: a fresh, individual and complex sound, a new kind of music.

My audition for Lenny had not been auspicious. I had been sent to him by Arthur, who had heard my songs for *Saturday Night* and liked the lyrics. Arthur and Lenny and Jerry were looking for a lyric writer for their musical version of *Romeo and Juliet,* someone to perhaps replace Betty Comden and Adolph Green, who were supposed to supply the lyrics but who were embroiled in a movie contract. I arrived at the vast Bernstein apartment with my portfolio and was ushered into Lenny's small, dark studio—he liked to work with as little visual distraction as possible, so chose to use not only the smallest of the fourteen rooms but also the only one that looked out on an airshaft. I played him a few songs from *Saturday Night.* He listened intently, then asked me, "Have you got something more poetic?" I had indeed, but I told him no, I had only conversational lyrics to offer. I had no intention of bringing my early overripe work to light—lyrics from my apprentice shows, when I was imitating Oscar and his penchant for nature imagery, none of which I felt or even believed (but many of which I suspect Lenny would have loved). It had been Oscar himself who told me I should write what I felt, not what I thought he did, and my lyrical take on things was strictly contemporary and vernacular. Lenny shrugged politely and said he'd let me know within a week whether or not Comden and Green would be available to work on the show.

I left with mixed feelings: I wanted to be asked to the party, I just didn't want to go. The fact was, and still is, that I enjoy writing music much more than lyrics, and even though *Saturday Night* seemed as if it were dead in the water, I was planning other projects. I had the good sense to discuss all this with Oscar and it was he who

persuaded me that if I was offered the job, I should leap at it. The show had an interesting idea, he said, and here was a chance to work with three of the most gifted and experienced men in music and theater; my desire to compose could be satisfied at any time. When Lenny phoned a week later and invited me to join the crew, I duly leapt.

I have only two regrets about that decision. First, it tagged and then dogged me with the label "lyricist," so that when my music finally popped into the open two shows and five years later, I was dismissed by some as an overly ambitious pretender who should stick to his own side of the street. (The label has persisted to this day, though with less intensity.) The second regret was that many of the lyrics in *West Side Story* suffer from a self-conscious effort to be what Lenny deemed "poetic." I had originally been hired to be a co-lyricist with him, and I knew from the start that I was getting into a collaboration with someone whose idea of poetic lyric writing was the antithesis of mine—but Oscar had given me such confidence that I naïvely thought I could prevail. The collaboration was a delight in every way except for the lyrical result. Lenny was supportive but insistent, and I was just insecure enough to accede and present him with lines like "Today the world was just an address" and "I have a love," these sung by street kids on the pavements of New York City. He especially liked "Tonight there will be no morning star": granted, Tony is supposed to be a dreamy character, but it's unlikely he's even seen a morning star (you don't see stars in Manhattan except at the Planetarium), much less that he would be inclined to use it as an image. Lenny kept encouraging me to come up with these maunderings, but by the time we got around to writing "Something's Coming" late in rehearsals, I had rebuilt enough confidence over two years of collaboration to insist on the kind of imagery I thought Tony should be using—baseball, for example, rather than the night sky over Manhattan.

Here is a lyric Lenny wrote for the tune that became "I Have a Love":

MARIA

Once in your life,
Only once in your life,
Comes a flash of fire and light.
And there stands your love,
The harvest of your years . . .

Maria is talking entirely in imagery, and very articulately. Now look at Arthur's approach to her dialogue: Here she is (with Tony) when they meet at the dance.

TONY

You're not thinking I'm someone else?

MARIA

I know you are not.

TONY

Or that we've met before?

MARIA

I know we have not.

TONY

I felt, I *knew* something never before was going to happen, had to happen. But this is . . .

MARIA

My hands are so cold.

(Taking them in his)

Yours, too.

(Moving his hands to her face)

So warm.

TONY

Yours, too.

MARIA

But of course. They are the same.

TONY

It's so much to believe. You're not joking me?

MARIA

I have not yet learned to joke that way. I think now I never will.

By sticking to language that is formal and elliptical and awkward, and by avoiding images, Arthur makes the dialogue poetic rather than "poetic." I imitated his technique as often as I could, resisting Lenny's instinct to enrich the lyrics. Here's the way I set the same passage that Lenny set:

MARIA

I have a love,
And it's all that I have.
Right or wrong, what else can I do?
I love him, I'm his,
And everything he is . . .

Lenny liked the use of the word "love" as a generalized noun, the way he had used it in his lyric, much the way

"Cool" (1957)

With Leonard Bernstein (ca. 1965)

it had been used as a staple of Romantic poetry (I think he felt it gave the sentiment a noble size), so I dutifully wrote the first line and then scrambled to overcome its depersonalized quality and its overtone of Importance. I hoped the simplicity of the language, set against the gorgeous passion of the music, would serve as a corrective. It almost worked, but when I hear it today, I wish it were in a foreign language in an opera. It still sounds like the writer, not the character. In the words of Else Lasker-Schüler, "A true poet does not say 'azure,' a true poet says 'blue.' " I hasten to make clear: the collaboration with Lenny was never for a moment less than exhilarating, it was frustrating only because we had two different approaches to the same goal. It was fueled by his galvanic energy and, like the collaborations with Arthur and Jerry, it was an education.

From Lenny I learned to approach theater music more freely and less squarely. I had been brought up to think of Broadway songs in terms of four- and eight-bar phrases, as Berlin and Porter and Rodgers and Kern— even Gershwin—did. Lenny taught me by example to ignore the math. Four bars may be expected, but do you really need them all? How about three bars? And why have the same number of beats in every bar? How about varying the meter? I was used to this in contemporary concert music, but I had never experienced it on Broadway until *On the Town* had exploded on me. It may not seem much of a revelation today, but back in 1955 such liberty-taking was radical on Broadway. There were other musical things that I learned from Lenny by osmosis, but the largest lesson was the one I took from both his art and his life: namely, that the only chances worth taking

are big ones. All the mistakes he made, if indeed they were mistakes, were huge—he never fell off the lowest rung of the ladder.

If Lenny was theatrically enthusiastic in our collaboration (he vibrated on the brink of shouting "Eureka!" whenever he invented a melodic surprise or heard a "poetic" lyric he liked), Arthur was enthusiastic but measured. Working with him was so easy and rewarding that we continued doing so through four musicals as well as two plays of his for which I wrote background music. Sadly, it ended with our falling off the lowest rung of the ladder: a show called *Do I Hear a Waltz?*, but more of that later. Unlike Julie Epstein, Arthur let me into his mind as he wrote, and by the osmosis of collaboration, I began to distinguish more completely than I had with Oscar the difference between a scene and something that seems like a scene but isn't. (The difference has mostly to do with subtext, but, again, more about that later—in the next chapter, in fact.) I also learned from him something about economy. The most remarkable feature of his book for *West Side Story* is how spare it is, how much plot he covers in how brief a time—necessarily brief, because there is so much singing and dancing in the show.

Of all the things I gleaned from working with Arthur, the most pointed was an awed respect for the book writer. The book writer of a musical is rarely acknowledged as being a playwright; moreover, he is often the first target of the unhappy reviewer who, having semienjoyed a show, will state, "The delightful songs and sparkling performances don't quite compensate for the clumsy book of (*fill in hapless playwright's name*) . . . ," ignoring the fact that the delightful songs and sparkling performances spring from characters and situations the book writer has invented. The most valuable asset a theater songwriter can have, apart from talent, is a good book writer. In fact, with a good book writer, the songwriter doesn't need much talent, as has been proven more than once. The book writer is the source from which the songwriter—in this particular case, me—takes character, diction, tone and style, and sometimes dialogue. Certainly, I often make suggestions and offer ideas to my collaborators, but the building blocks are theirs and my contributions depend on them. This is neither modesty nor largesse.

The collaboration with Jerry was more difficult for Arthur and Lenny than for me, there having been a long and tangled association among them. For me it was easy: Arthur was my spokesman and protector, since we agreed about everything, diplomatically as well as artistically. Jerry was well known for his sullen and vicious attacks. I was the victim of one during the Washington tryout, a dramatic occasion which concerned the cutting of a song called "Like Everybody Else" (see below), but I also had a number of less virulent if equally uncomfortable moments with him, the most memorable of which occurred when he heard "Maria" for the first time. It was I who had to play it for him, Lenny having gone out of town, and when I'd finished, Jerry's only comment was "What's Tony doing?" A bit baffled, I replied, "He's singing about this girl he's just met." Jerry shook his head impatiently. "No, what's he doing onstage?" "Well, it's a sort of internal monologue." "I know that," he grumbled, "but what's he doing?" "Well, he's on his way to her house and just singing about her. Maybe the set's changing?" "Okay, you stage it," he snapped. I was speechless. Weren't musicals full of love songs that had no action attached? Yes, they were, but what Jerry was telling me in his uniquely hostile way was that when you write a song for the theater, you should have the staging in mind. If it's a static song with no one else in the scene, and it's in the sort of show that's trying to tell a compelling story, there had better be either some stage action or some development in the lyric to keep things moving forward. It's up to the songwriter to plan it, to give the director a springboard from which to spring. Ever since that tense little conversation, I stage in my mind every song I write. I can tell the director exactly where I think the character should be facing, when he should be moving, what is happening physically as well as emotionally, and I write many of these stage directions in the printed lyric. The director can throw my ideas out, and often does, but at least he has a blueprint to work from. Any time I'm hit with the frequent director's complaint, "What do you expect me to do there?," I have an answer.

West Side Story also exposed me to another, less reliable, kind of collaborator: the producer. A month before rehearsals were to begin, Cheryl Crawford, who had held the option on our show for more than a year and who was a lady with a distinguished record of producing plays by Clifford Odets and Tennessee Williams and musicals such as *Brigadoon* and *Paint Your Wagon,* suddenly decided to drop us, on the grounds that the script hadn't sufficiently explored the causes of juvenile delinquency. She announced it to us casually in her office one afternoon in May, disregarding the fact that rehearsals were to begin in July and that we wouldn't be able to postpone them since Lenny was obligated to take charge of the New York Philharmonic Orchestra in September, and in Israel, meaning he would then be lost to us forever. Stunned and discouraged, we left Cheryl's office to regroup over a drink at the nearest watering hole, which turned out to be the cocktail lounge at the legendarily theatrical Algonquin Hotel, only to suffer another blow: the management refused us entry because Arthur wasn't wearing a tie. Even more discouraged, we repaired to the hotel next door, the Iroquois, a far less fancy Indian reservation where we were permitted to enter and where Arthur proceeded to place a phone call from a telephone booth to Roger Stevens, Cheryl's co-producer, who was traveling in Europe. Roger reaffirmed his faith in the show and told Arthur not to worry. But

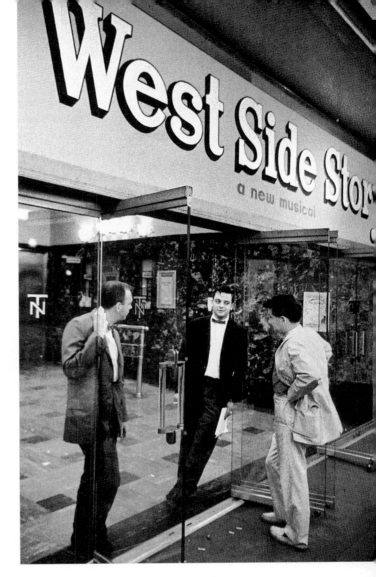

Between Harold Prince and Leonard Bernstein, Washington, D.C. (1957)

Roger was primarily a fund-raiser, not a producer, not someone who could make and effect executive decisions about casting and stage management and set and costume design, who could supervise the advertising and arrange the booking and cope with the unions—all the grubby chores a producer has to attend to, and attend to well. For all his good will and financial acumen, we still needed a producer and it would be difficult, if not impossible, to find one on such short notice who was free, competent and willing to take a chance with a show as daring and idiosyncratic as *West Side Story.*

Gloomily, I trudged home, certain that my Broadway debut was now postponed indefinitely. No sooner had I entered my apartment, however, when the phone rang. It was my good friend, the newly successful producer Harold Prince (*The Pajama Game, Damn Yankees*), calling me from Boston to sigh about the trouble he was having with his latest show, *New Girl In Town.* Like a good friend, I patiently listened till he was finished and when, as good friends do, he then asked me how I was, I told him that *West Side Story* had just gone down the drain and that my life was over. The timing could not have been more perfect. Eager to find something new to concentrate on while *New Girl in Town* was running its course for good or for ill, Hal suggested that I send him and his partner, Robert Griffith, a copy of our script. Ironically, I had wanted them to produce the show two years earlier, but my collaborators had refused to take a chance on such fledgling producers; this time desperation changed their minds. The script went off post haste and a day later Hal called me in a state of extravagant excitement to say that he and Bobby would come down to New York in the middle of their tryout to hear the score, which they did. They enthusiastically agreed to produce the show, adding, however, that they would give it no thought until *New Girl in Town* had opened. No

matter how excited, they said, they would concentrate on only one show at a time—an indication of what good producers they were.

Most of all, what I learned from the collaboration on *West Side Story* is how much I need a collaborator. Even if I were a skilled playwright (and there's no literary profession more elusive), I wouldn't write my own librettos. I have to work <u>with</u> someone, someone who can help me out of writing holes, someone to feed me suggestions when my invention flags, someone I can feed in return. To be part of a collaboration is to be part of a family, and for me—the only child of constantly working and mostly absent parents, a kid who grew up without any sense of family—every new show provides me with one. It may be a temporary family, but it always gives me a solid sense of belonging to something outside of myself.

The "Jet Song" (1957)

ACT ONE

After a series of street encounters with the Sharks, the Jets assert themselves, led by Riff.

Jet Song

RIFF
When you're a Jet,
You're a Jet all the way
From your first cigarette
To your last dyin' day.

When you're a Jet,
If the spit hits the fan,
You got brothers around,
You're a family man.

You're never alone,
You're never disconnected.
You're home with your own—
When company's expected,
You're well protected!

Then you are set
With a capital J,
Which you'll never forget
Till they cart you away.
When you're a Jet,
You stay
A Jet!

ACTION, BABY JOHN
When you're a Jet,
You're the top cat in town,
You're the gold-medal kid
With the heavyweight crown!

A-RAB, ACTION, BIG DEAL
When you're a Jet
You're the swingin'est thing.
Little boy, you're a man;
Little man, you're a king!

ALL
The Jets are in gear,
Our cylinders are clickin'!
The Sharks'll steer clear,
'Cause every Puerto Rican
'S a lousy chicken!

Here come the Jets
Like a bat out of hell—
Someone gets in our way,
Someone don't feel so well!

Here come the Jets!
Little world, step aside,
Better go underground,
Better run, better hide!

We're drawin' the line,
So keep your noses hidden!
We're hangin' a sign
Says "Visitors Forbidden,"
And we ain't kiddin'!

Here come the Jets—
Yeah! And we're gonna beat
Every last buggin' gang
On the whole buggin' street!

On the whole—!
Ever—!
Mother—!
Lovin'—!
Street!

This was completely different from our first attempt at an opening number. The original version, below, was a combination of dialogue (some of which I've omitted) and song, set in a clubhouse where the Jets are simply fooling around, reading comic books, playing games, doing push-ups, waiting for Riff to arrive. The talk centers on space travel, which was a major topic of conversation in 1957. Music is constant.

Opening (The Clubhouse)
(cut)

BABY JOHN
How long does it take
To reach the moonarooney?

ACTION
Huh?

BABY JOHN
To reach the moonarooney.

ACTION
I dunno.
Five days . . .

BABY JOHN
Wait till Riff gets here. He'll know all about it.

MOUTHPIECE
Where *is* Riff?

DIESEL
Getting sweet and shined up,
Got a chicklet lined up.

OTHERS (ad lib)
You know Riff . . . Always dresses the sweetest . . . Sweeter than God . . .

BABY JOHN
We all of us do.
The Jets dress the neatest.

ALL
Oh, when the Jets fall in
At the Tuesday dance,
We'll be the sweetest dressin' gang in
    pants!
And when those chicks dig us
At the Crystal Cave,
They're gonna give, gonna give
Like they never gave!

(They dance together—a little wild. Riff enters.)

RIFF
(almost whispered)
Hey.
Cool.
Easy.
Sweet . . .
At ease, Jets.

BABY JOHN
Hey, Riff—how long does it take to reach the moon?

DIESEL
I told him—three days.

RIFF
One day,
Buddy boy.

Kachung, up!
Tsavoom, land!
Just one little day to reach the
    moonarooney!

GANG
Crazy, daddy-o!

RIFF
It's spinnin' fast,
Terrible fast, buddy boys.

ALL
Fast!

RIFF
No time, man,
Accelerate—
The jet's all set and the moon won't
    wait.

DIESEL
Geez, before you start, you're late.

RIFF
Stations, rocketmen!

GANG
Commander!

RIFF
Pressure!

GANG
Comin' up!

RIFF
Combustion!

GANG
Comin' up!

GANG
Ejection!

GANG
Comin' up!

RIFF
Seatbelts!

GANG
Comin' up!

RIFF
Forceps!

GANG
Comin' up!

RIFF
Blast off!

GANG
Blast off! Go!

RIFF
Frackadatrack!

GANG
Frabbajabba!

RIFF
Frackadatrack, frackadatrack!
Roger Wilco!

GANG
Roger Wilco!

BABY JOHN
I forgot my gravity belt!

RIFF
Soon we'll be on the yellow moon!

ACTION
Kill the thing from the Black Lagoon!

MOUTHPIECE
Back on earth by this afternoon!

SOME
Up to the moon,
Gonna bomb it.
Up like a comet,
Burnin' the stars!

ALL
Up to the moon,
Got a mission.
Nuclear fission,
Blow it to Mars!

ACTION
Space suit—
Cashmere.

MOUTHPIECE
Side vents
Up to here.

ALL
Ca-razy, daddy-o!

ACTION
Lead pants,
No cuff.

MOUTHPIECE
Tapered
Just enough.

RIFF
Land ho!

ALL
Land ho!
Down we go!

RIFF
Frackadatrack, frabajabba!

GANG
Frabbajabba!

RIFF
Frackadatrack, frackadatrack!
Roger Wilco!

GANG
Roger Wilco!

BABY JOHN
Look, moon maidens!

RIFF
See that babe, what a sexy one!

ACTION
She must weigh 'bout a half a ton!

MOUTHPIECE
Nothin' on but a rocket gun!

ALL
Down to the moon,
Mild and mellow.
Down to the yellow,
Down to the mellow,
Down to the yellow—

BABY JOHN
Look out for the crater!

ALL
Voom!

(They all sit down hard)

Hello, moon!

BABY JOHN
Wow!

MOUTHPIECE
That was the greatest.

DIESEL
Nah, the greatest day was the day we went to the South Pole.

ACTION
Nah, when we stinkbombed every store on the block with a even number . . .

RIFF
Buddy boys, they're all the greatest.

My greatest day
Was the day I was born
And the day I was eight
And the day I was five.
Also the day
When I first blew a horn,
When I first stayed out late,
When I first learned to drive.

Yesterday was great—
Had a date,
Had a ball.
Day before was great—
Didn't have a date at all!

My greatest day
Is today
And tomorrow
And also the day after that
And the day after the day after
The day after that!

BABY JOHN
My greatest day
Was that great day when we
Went and snuck into six
Different movies for free.

DIESEL
How 'bout the day
When we made all that mess
With the mice we let loose
On the Bronx Park Express?

SNOWBOY
Hallowe'en was great,
With those wild cigarettes!

BABY JOHN
May the twelfth was great.

ALL
Huh?

BABY JOHN
That's the day I joined the Jets!

ALL
Our greatest day
Was the day that we beat
Every last buggin' gang
On the whole buggin' street!
On the whole—
Ever—
Mother—
Lovin'—
Street!

Finding a language for the Jets was one of Arthur's larger problems. He knew that yesterday's slang ages quicker than you can say Jack Robinson and that the average span of a musical from writing to production was, even then, two years, so that whatever shards of contemporary argot he could use would be hopelessly out of date by the time the show opened. What he came up with was a hybrid slang, a mixture of tough and naïve, of both invented and actual jargon: "Fracka-datrack," "Frabbajabba" and "Riga-tigatum" intertwined with jazz-inflected words like "cool" and "daddy-o," alongside expressions of gang loyalty like "Womb to tomb—sperm to worm." The style may now seem quaint, especially in light of the open and frequent use of four-letter words on the stage today, but it only occasionally sounds dated. "Cool" still has currency, "daddy-o" does not. Moreover, Arthur made Riff a sort of Space Commander, dividing his troops into "Acemen," "Rocketmen" and such. The kidlike aspect of this and of the language is what I was trying to convey in the gang's banter and in the trip to the moon. As for the naïveté, Lenny wanted me to concentrate on Riff's free-spiritedness, and the music he wrote for "My Greatest Day" couldn't have reflected it better: if you sing the opening lines to the tune of the "Jet Song," you'll see what I mean. (The music for the release is different.)

It took us the better part of a month to work out the song, but when we presented it to Jerry, his reaction was to say that he could introduce the Jets (and the Sharks) better in dance—that is, set up the gang's feeling that the neighborhood was their territory alone. And he was right, as he usually was (theatrically). Lenny exported some of the music to "The Dance at the Gym" ("Oh, when the Jets fall in at the Tuesday dance . . .") and expanded the rest (the banter and the trip to the moon) into what is now known as "Prologue." Once we'd abandoned the clubhouse idea, opting for choreography that would simmer with violence, we needed a song to end the first scene, a war cry from the Jets addressed to Riff, their leader. This was the result:

Mix! *(cut)*

JETS
Mix!
Make a mess of 'em!
Pay the Puerto Ricans back,
Make a mess of 'em!
If you let us take a crack,
There'll be less of 'em,
There'll be less of 'em.

Mix!
If you only say the word,
We can cut 'em up!
Go ahead and say the word,
And we'll shut 'em up!
We can shut 'em up!

Spics!
Every one of 'em's chicken, chicken!
Fix 'em!
Give the suckers a lickin'!
If those brown little bums are lookin'
   for kicks,

Every brown little greasy son-of-a-
    Puerto Rican
Gets a kisser full of bricks!

Make a mess of 'em,
Make the sonsabitches pay,
Make a mess of 'em.
When the smoke has cleared away,
There'll be less of 'em,
There'll be less of 'em.
Mix!

Riff, we've been spoilin',
Our motor needs an oilin',
Our radiator's boilin'!

Riff, let's get goin',
Our Dynaflow is flowin',
Our safety valves are blowin'!
Give 'em the gun, give 'em the gun,
    give 'em the gun!
We'll make 'em run, we'll make 'em
    run, we'll make 'em run!

Spics!
Make a mess of 'em,
Make the sonsabitches pay,
Make a mess of 'em.
When the smoke has cleared away,
There'll be less of 'em,

Less and less of 'em,
Less of 'em . . .
Mix!

A mixture of right and wrong rhyme
choices. Right: the heavy use of hard
consonants like "k" and "p," which
have anger and determination behind
them. Wrong: the heavy use of soft
consonants like "s" and "n," which
make the Jets sound more like a
hissing radiator than a gang on the
warpath. (Although the song never
saw the light of day, Lenny used the
music for the second movement of the
Chichester Psalms, which he wrote
in 1964. The text was in Latin, which
was, I have to say, a considerable improvement.) "Mix!" pleased nobody
but Lenny, so I took the "My Greatest
Day" section of our first Opening
and rewrote it as the "Jet Song."
    We wrote the following in
Washington, the first stop on our
out-of-town tryout, in response to
a complaint from some of our production collaborators that the "Jet
Song" was not menacing enough.
Thus:

With Leonard Bernstein and Jerome Robbins (1957)

This Turf Is Ours (cut)

JETS

This turf is ours!
Drew a big white line
With a "keep out" sign,
And they crossed it.

This turf is ours!
Gotta hold our ground
Or we'll turn around
And we've lost it!

We're stakin' a claim,
The boundaries are set out!
The foreigners came—
Well, now they're gonna get out!

We know the score,
We fought before—
And this is war!

So let 'em leave us alone
And get a turf of their own.
This turf is ours!

This turf is ours!
Got a long-term lease
And no lousy greasers
Will break it!

This turf is ours!
And we're gonna fry
Anyone who's trying
To take it!

You're gonna get hurt,
Or else you're gonna beat it!
Stay off of our dirt,
Or else you'll have to eat it!

So listen, world,
And listen clear:
Stay out of here!
Go home and leave us alone,
Go get a turf of your own.
This turf is ours!

RIFF

C'mon, Jets! Straighten up!
We're on a spot!
Time to get hot!
Buddy boys, it's only a little dot—
It may be small,
But it's all
We got.

JETS

It's our beat!
It's our street!
It's our turf!

RIFF

East to the Avenue—

JETS

The ever-lovin' Avenue!

RIFF

And west to the Drive—

JETS

The ever-mother-lovin' Drive!

RIFF

South to the parkin' lot—

JETS

The cotton-pickin' parkin' lot!

RIFF

And north to the Five and Ten.

JETS

A-men, A-men!

RIFF

C'mon, Jets! Straighten up!

JETS

Crazy, Daddy-o,

RIFF

You ready?

JETS

Daddy-o,

RIFF

You hear me?

JETS

Daddy-o,

RIFF

You with me?

JETS

Daddy-o,

RIFF

The word's out!

ALL

The word's out!
This turf is ours!

"This Turf Is Ours" proved too harsh for our cohorts, however, and the "Jet Song" was reinstated.

Riff meets Tony and asks him to rejoin the gang for the forthcoming rumble. Tony reluctantly agrees, but says he wants to leave the Jets for good and get on with his life, that he senses something important is about to happen to him.

Something's Coming

TONY

Could be . . .
Who knows? . . .
There's something due any day—
I will know right away,
Soon as it shows.
It may come cannonballing down
    through the sky,
Gleam in its eye,
Bright as a rose.
Who knows?

It's only just out of reach,
Down the block, on a beach,
Under a tree.
I got a feeling there's a miracle due,
Gonna come true,
Coming to me!

Could it be? Yes, it could.
Something's coming, something good,
If I can wait.
Something's coming, I don't know
    what it is,
But it is
Gonna be great!

With a click, with a shock,
Phone'll jingle, door'll knock,
Open the latch.
Something's coming, don't know
    when, but it's soon.
Catch the moon,
One-handed catch!

Around the corner,
Or whistling down the river,
Come on, deliver
To me!

Will it be? Yes, it will.
Maybe just by holding still,
It'll be there.
Come on, something, come on in,
    don't be shy,
Meet a guy,
Pull up a chair!

The air
Is humming,
And something great is coming!

Who knows?
It's only just out of reach,
Down the block, on a beach,
Maybe tonight . . .

Some of the images here may seem "poetic" in the way I deplore, but I would claim that they are the expression of an inarticulate, excited young man. They are not measured, they are not "written."

OSCAR HAMMERSTEIN II
Upward Nobility

Hammerstein is usually thought of as the Norman Rockwell of lyricists: earthy, optimistic, sometimes ponderously bucolic, a proponent of small-town American values, a purveyor of generosity and kindness toward the world and his fellow humans and of empathy with their small sufferings and dreams. Like Rockwell, he has been both underestimated (for his craft) and overestimated (for his philosophy). The more apt comparison would be to Eugene O'Neill. That may seem a bizarre linking—the cozy lyricist with the mighty playwright— but they have more in common than immediately meets the eye (and ear). Both use language which often aspires to poetry but is usually more earthbound than earthy and tends to veer off into preachment, in contrast to their theatrical imaginations, which soar. They are both experimental playwrights with things to say profound enough to override their literary limitations.

Hammerstein once commented to me that some of Irving Berlin's ballads were built on melodies that are symphonic in their granite-like simplicity. He might have been talking about his own work, which at its best ("Ol' Man River," "Oh, What a Beautiful Mornin'," and so on) makes quibbling about it essentially irrelevant. Of course, a consequence of his naked plain-spokenness (low on rhymes and wordplay) is that quibbles are easy to come by, which is one reason his lyrics are held in such disdain by people who prefer the sophisticated lightheartedness of Rodgers's other partner, Lorenz Hart. Hammerstein's work is full of life, but not liveliness; he is easy to make fun of because he's so earnest. Since elsewhere in this book I have many critical things to say about Hart (along with a few others in the Pantheon), and despite the fact that Oscar taught me virtually everything I know about lyric writing, I feel obligated to list some of my own quibbles, poking fun along the way, such as:

Redundancy. Not repetition, as in "Younger Than Springtime," where repeating "are you" increases the intensity ("Younger than springtime are you / Softer than starlight are you"), but redundancy as in "Allegro" ("Brisk, lively, / Merry and bright! / Allegro!"). Brisk, lively, merry *and* bright? *And* Allegro? It sounds like a thesaurus entry. Or as in "A Cock-eyed Optimist" (*South Pacific*) when Nellie Forbush claims that "I could say life is just a bowl of Jell-O / And appear more intelligent and smart." As opposed to intelligent and dumb? A lot of songwriters fill in empty spaces in the music with reiteration, but there's a fervent lack of surprise in Hammerstein's thoughts, made manifest by his need to spell things out with plodding insistence, as in "Who can explain it? / Who can tell you why?" from "Some Enchanted Evening" (*South Pacific* again) or this from "You've Got to Be Carefully Taught" (*South Pacific* yet again): "You've got to be taught before it's too late, / Before you are six or seven or eight," a statement which always makes me want to ask, "What about five or nine or thirteen?"

"Softer than starlight" brings up the matter of Oscar's imagery, so much of which is celestial, seasonal or ornithological. Moon, stars, dew and their reflections, along with anything featuring feathers and wings, were basic fodder for most popular songwriters of Oscar's period, although no one persisted with those images as long or as enthusiastically as he did. In addition to the omnipresence of "dream" in his songs (a pervasive all-purpose evocative word in lyrics of the period), what these images did was lend a prettified and lofty air to them, particularly the ballads, and also made his characters generic. He was writing in a style held over from his *Desert Song* days, attributable to the influence of Otto Harbach, the preeminent lyricist of American operetta in the 1920s.

Just as Hammerstein was my mentor, so was Harbach his. Harbach, twenty-two years Hammerstein's senior, wrote both book and lyrics for a number of successful shows, on some of which (*The Desert Song, Rose-Marie*) he invited young Hammerstein to collaborate. This was both good and bad: good in that Hammerstein learned his craft from a professional; bad in that the flowery affectation of operetta lyrics was something Hammerstein subsequently could never entirely shake. That quality is what makes so much of his work feel old-fashioned and sugary today— an ironic consequence, since it was he who was responsible in the post-*Oklahoma!* era for songs and characters becoming increasingly more "realistic." The fact is he was at his most poetic when he was at his least "poetic."

The corollary (or perhaps the cause) of that is the problem of diction, with which Hammerstein felt comfortable in period pieces like *Oklahoma!, Carousel* and *The King and I,* but with which he had trouble in contemporary shows such as *Allegro* and *South Pacific.* What is a character like Nellie Forbush, a self-professed "corny as Kansas in August" girl doing singing "I'm bromidic and bright / As a moon-happy night / Pouring light on the dew" (in "I'm in Love with a Wonderful Guy")? More to the point, what is she doing even with a word such as "bromidic"? Moreover, like a lot of other Broadway songwriters, Hammerstein sometimes gets carried away by "pretty" words and images instead of accurate ones. In "A Cockeyed Optimist," Nellie sings, "When the sky is a bright canary yellow / I forget every cloud I've ever seen." When is a sky a bright canary yellow? As far as I know, only in the eye of a hurricane. If the sky were a bright canary yellow, I'd run to the nearest storm cellar. And even if such a sky exists, how often would Nellie see it? She may be a cockeyed optimist, but not very often.

Hammerstein's signature imagery features birds and their activities— all kinds of birds, although their activities are pretty much confined to flying and singing. Larks, to pick just one species, fill his songs: "A lark'll wake up in the medder," "The sweet, silver song of a lark," "A lark that is learning to pray." (And while we're at it, how can you tell a lark that is just learning to pray from one that's actually praying? Wait a minute—a lark praying? What are we talking about?) There are other sorts populating his lyrics as well, like "A hawk / Making lazy circles in the sky," "Where the brown birds fly / Through a pale blue sky," "Every whippoorwill / Is selling me a bill," and then of course there are birds in general, as in "I touch your hand, / And my arms grow strong, / Like a pair of birds / That burst with song," a line I have never understood. It's not only the birds themselves who give flight to his fancy, however, it's also what they do. They fly—and, on occasion, float. There is at least one song (and sometimes as many as four) in each of the scores Hammerstein wrote with Rodgers as well as in most, if not all, of the shows he wrote before Rodgers, that involves images of floating or flying or both: "Out of my dreams and into your arms / I long to fly," "Down the aisle you float," "Only to fly as day / Flies from moonlight," "You fly down the street / On the chance that you'll meet," and so on.

If this seems like heavy-duty nitpicking, it's a result of Oscar's teaching me to examine every word in a lyric with fierce care, because there are so few of them in a song (unless it's written by W. S. Gilbert or Noël Coward or a number of contemporary pop songwriters, who seldom use one word when twelve will do). Each one is valuable, and had better be invaluable. But again, these are quibbles. Hammerstein rarely has the colloquial ease of Berlin, the sophistication of Porter, the humor of Hart and Gershwin, the inventiveness of Harburg or the grace of Fields, but his lyrics are sui generis, and when they are at their best they are more than heartfelt and passionate, they are monumental. They have a weight that the lyrics of his contemporaries (with the exception of DuBose Heyward) do not, just as O'Neill's plays have a weight that no other American playwright can claim. The flaws in Oscar's lyrics are more apparent than in those of the others because he is speaking deeply from himself through his characters and therefore has no persona to hide behind. He is exposed, sentimental warts and all, every minute and in every word, especially in the songs he wrote with Kern and Rodgers. In the end, it's not the sentimentality but the monumentality that matters. Few lyrics can match "Soliloquy" or "What's the Use of Wond'rin'?" for digging into the heart of what a theater song can be.

Tony meets Maria at the dance. They exchange a few words, dance together and fall in love. Afterward, Tony makes his way to Maria's apartment.

Maria

TONY

Maria . . .
The most beautiful sound I ever
    heard.

VOICES

Maria, Maria, Maria, Maria . . .

TONY

All the beautiful sounds of the world
    in a single word . . .

VOICES

Maria, Maria, Maria, Maria . . .

TONY

Maria!
I've just met a girl named Maria,
And suddenly that name
Will never be the same
To me.

Maria!
I've just kissed a girl named Maria,
And suddenly I've found
How wonderful a sound
Can be.

Maria!
Say it loud and there's music
    playing—
Say it soft and it's almost like
    praying—
Maria . . .
I'll never stop saying
Maria!

The most beautiful sound I ever
    heard—
Maria.

The problem here was how to write a love song for two people who have just met. They have exchanged exactly ten lines, but they have encountered each other in a surreal, dreamlike dance sequence, so that the audience believes that they have an intimate, even mystical, connection. Nevertheless, when the gymnasium set dissolves into the street outside Maria's house and Tony is back in reality, he has to sing something real. He knows nothing about the girl except that her name is Maria and that she is Puerto Rican and therefore "the enemy," so what can he rapturously sing about? The only subject I could think of was her name.

There was another reason for this solution, if a coy one. Originally, Tony was to have been a blond Polish Catholic, in order to contrast him as much as possible with the Puerto Ricans. This gave the name "Maria" a religious resonance, which I pushed with the line "Say it soft and it's almost like praying." Of course, once we eventually withdrew the Polish-Catholic connection, the line made little sense and merely contributed a kind of overall wetness to the lyric—a wetness, I regret to say, which persists throughout all the romantic lyrics in the show, but which appealed to my collaborators and which may very well have contributed to the score's popularity. The lyric, significantly, was one which Oscar Hammerstein particularly liked; when I first played the song for him and his wife, Dorothy, she came across the room and kissed me on behalf of both of them.

Tonight, tonight
There's only you tonight (and every other night)

Tonight, tonight
And every other night
There'll be you, only you, always you.

Tonight, tonight
And every other night   There's only you tonight
The only thing I see will be you.   There's nothing I can see b

Tonight, tonight
You're part of me tonight
What you think, what you say, what you do.

There's something strange tonight
There's no one else but us, you and I
There's no one it can see, only you.   *in the world*

A miracle took place (is here)   taking place
A miracle('s) in sight
A miracle is happening here (now)

There's no one else in sight
And the moon doesn't move in the sky
There's a sun & a moon in the sky

The miracle for me that is true   *has come*

BALCONY SCENE ("TONIGHT")

TONY

Tonight, tonight
Is not like any night;
Tonight there will be no morning star.
Tonight, tonight,
We own the world tonight
And for us, stars will stop where they are.

MARIA

Today, all day I had the feeling
A miracle would happen;
I know now I was right.
It's you, it's you,
The miracle I knew would come true
Tonight.

TONY

What are you?
Tell me everything you are, Maria.
Are you shy, are you quick?
Tell me what you like to do.
Who and what are you?
Tell me!

MARIA

I like summer and people and dancing.
I like rain late at night and I love you!

TONY

Tell me, tell me...

MARIA

What are you?
You don't have to speak a word.
Everything you are I love!

TONY

All I know is that you are my love!

MARIA

It's happened, it's happened,
I've waited for you.
I love you, I love you, I love you.

TONY

I want you, I want you,
I've waited for you.
I need you, I need you, I love you.

MARIA

I'm alive, I'm awake for the first time.
I'm a brand-new Maria tonight!...

Maria comes out of her apartment and onto the fire escape outside. In a transposition of the Balcony Scene from Romeo and Juliet, *Tony climbs up to join her.*

Tonight

MARIA
Only you, you're the only thing I'll
    see, forever.
In my eyes, in my words and in
    everything I do,
Nothing else but you,
Ever!

TONY
And there's nothing for me but Maria,
Every sight that I see is Maria.

MARIA
Tony, Tony . . .

TONY
Always you, every thought I'll ever
    know,
Everywhere I go,
You'll be!

MARIA
All the world is only you and me!

Tonight, tonight,
It all began tonight,
I saw you and the world went away.
Tonight, tonight,
There's only you tonight,
What you are, what you do, what
    you say!

TONY
Today, all day I had the feeling
A miracle would happen—
I know now I was right.
For here you are,
And what was just a world is a star
Tonight!

BOTH
Tonight, tonight,
The world is full of light,
With suns and moons all over the
    place.

Tonight, tonight,
The world is wild and bright,
Going mad, shooting sparks into
    space.

Today, the world was just an address,
A place for me to live in,
No better than all right,
But here you are
And what was just a world is a star
Tonight!

Goodnight, goodnight,
Sleep well and when you dream,
Dream of me
Tonight.

The song we first wrote for this scene was "One Hand, One Heart." As the score developed, it came to seem too settled and stately for a first declaration of passion, and when we wrote the "Quintet" (see below), we realized that the sections for Tony and Maria in that piece could be developed into a more turbulent and spontaneous moment, and so we did. As with the opening number, I had a language problem: how to combine the artificial jive talk that Arthur had invented for Tony and the Jets with the style he had adopted for Maria and the Sharks— elegant and polite, rather like a literal translation from the Spanish—so that the lovers could sing in duet. Hence the formality of the lyric, and its lapses into "poetry."

Always frugal, we found a place for "One Hand, One Heart" later in the score.

In an alley outside the apartment building, the Sharks and their girlfriends assemble. One of the girls, Rosalia, is homesick for her native land. Anita is not.

America

ROSALIA
Puerto Rico,
You lovely island,

Island of tropical breezes.
Always the pineapples growing,
Always the coffee blossoms
    blowing . . .

ANITA
Puerto Rico,
You ugly island,
Island of tropic diseases.
Always the hurricanes blowing,
Always the population growing,
And the money owing,
And the babies crying,
And the bullets flying . . .

I like the island Manhattan—
Smoke on your pipe and put that in!

ANITA, GIRLS
I like to be in America,
O.K. by me in America,
Everything free in America—
For a small fee in America.

ROSALIA
I like the city of San Juan—

ANITA
I know a boat you can get on.

ROSALIA
Hundreds of flowers in full bloom—

ANITA
Hundreds of people in each room.

ANITA, OTHERS
Automobile in America,
Chromium steel in America,
Wire-spoke wheel in America—
Very big deal in America.

ROSALIA
I'll drive a Buick through San Juan.

ANITA
If there's a road you can drive on.

ROSALIA
I'll give my cousins a free ride—

ANITA
How you get all of them inside?

ANITA, OTHERS
Immigrant goes to America,
Many "hellos" in America!

Nobody knows in America
Puerto Rico's in America.

ROSALIA
When I will go back to San Juan—

ANITA
When you will shut up and get gone?

ROSALIA
I'll give them new washing machine.

ANITA
What have they got there to keep
    clean?

ANITA, OTHERS
I like the shores of America,
Comfort is yours in America.
Knobs on the doors in America,
Wall-to-wall floors in America.

ROSALIA
I'll bring a T.V. to San Juan—

ANITA
If there's a current to turn on.

ROSALIA
Everyone there will give big cheer!

ANITA
Everyone there will have moved here!

Rehearsal, the author at the piano

Some lines of this lyric are respectably sharp and crisp, but some melt in the mouth as gracelessly as peanut butter and are impossible to comprehend, such as "For a small fee in America," which smashes the "l"s and the "f"s together, making it sound like "For a smafee." Using quadruple rhymes and very short lines in order to punch up the jokes (because it was essentially one joke with variations, as the repeated rhyme of "San Juan" and "on" demonstrates) proved to be an insuperable task much of the time. The reason was that I had underestimated the speed of the music, which turned the collision of consonants into major crashes. The music in this instance came before the pile-ups: Lenny had returned from a vacation in Puerto Rico, fired up, he told me, by a dance rhythm he had heard called *hua-*

pango, which seemed a perfect choice for the song, and was. What I didn't know at the time was that he had written the tune years earlier for an unproduced ballet called "Conch Town."

"America" was intended to be an argument between Bernardo and Anita, partly to enrich their relationship by adding some contention to it, since Arthur had no time in the libretto to explore it, but Jerry insisted that the song be for girls only, as it was his only chance for a full-out all-female dance number in the show. The character of Rosalia was invented to take Bernardo's point of view. When the movie was made four years later, Jerry agreed to have the number danced by both the men and the women and to revert to the original lyric, which went like this:

America
(film version)

ANITA
Puerto Rico,
My heart's devotion—
Let it sink back in the ocean.
Always the hurricanes blowing,
Always the population growing,
And the money owing,
And the sunlight streaming,
And the natives steaming.

I like the island Manhattan—
Smoke on your pipe and put that in!

GIRLS
I like to be in America,
O.K. by me in America,
Everything free in America—

BERNARDO
For a small fee in America.

ANITA
Buying on credit is so nice.

BERNARDO
One look at us and they charge twice.

CONSUELO
I'll have my own washing machine.

CHINO
What will you have, though, to keep clean?

ANITA
Skyscrapers bloom in America.

ANOTHER GIRL
Cadillacs zoom in America.

ANOTHER GIRL
Industry boom in America.

BOYS
Twelve in a room in America.

ANITA
Lots of new housing with more space.

BERNARDO
Lots of doors slamming in our face.

ANITA
I'll get a terrace apart*ment*.

BERNARDO
Better get rid of your *accent*.

ANITA, THREE GIRLS
Life can be bright in America,
If you can fight in America.
Life is all right in America,
If you're all-white in America.

ANITA, CONSUELO
Here you are free and you have pride.

BERNARDO
Long as you stay on your own side.

ANITA
Free to be anything you choose.

ALL BOYS
Free to wait tables and shine shoes.

BERNARDO
Everywhere grime in America,
Organized crime in America,
Terrible time in America.

ANITA
You forget I'm in America.

BERNARDO
I think I go back to San Juan.

ANITA
I know a boat you can get on.

BERNARDO
Everyone there will give big cheer!

ANITA
Everyone there will have moved here.

This lyric is sharper and easier to understand than the version I came up with for Jerry, maybe because I resented having to change it, but more likely because it's rooted in real character conflict rather than in an artificial argument consisting of punch lines set up by an ad hoc straight man (woman, in this case). In fact, because Rosalia is a nonentity, the stage version makes Anita something of a smartass.

Some people did understand the lyric clearly. Shortly after the show opened, I received a letter from Dr. Howard Rusk, founder of the Rusk Institute, complaining that I had maligned Puerto Rico in the verse, that in fact the island had a very low incidence of tropical disease. I'm sure his outrage was justified, but I wasn't about to sacrifice the line that sets the tone for the whole lyric.

Toward the end of rehearsals, Jerry felt that there should be some light or comic relief in the first act, and suggested that there might be a song for the three misfits in the Jets: A-rab, who was the shortest; Baby John, who was the youngest; and Anybodys, who was the only girl in the gang. Here it is:

Like Everybody Else
(cut)

A-RAB
"Knock off, get lost."

A-RAB, BABY JOHN
"Go knit a shawl."

A-RAB, BABY JOHN, ANYBODYS
"Move, hit the road."

ANYBODYS
"Little lady, that's all!"

That's all I ever hear—
And I believe it, too.
Buddy boys, I'm with you.

Girls ain't good for anything,
Swearing or smoking or spitting or anything,
No good for nothing but wiggling and giggling around.

Girls are good for kickin' out,
Screamin' and flirtin' and certain to chicken out.
Some should be clobbered, the rest of 'em oughta be drowned.

Now take me—
I ain't like any other girl on earth,
Don'tcha see?
I'm an accident of birth!
It's revoltin' . . .

I ain't like the other girls,
Drooly and sticky and icky like other girls.
I swear and *I* smoke, and *I* inhale—
Why can't I be male,
Like everybody else?

(To Baby John)

"Scram, little boy,
Go home to bed."

ANYBODYS, BABY JOHN
"Back to your crib."

BABY JOHN
"Get your diapers, drop dead!"

That's all I ever hear,
But I don't have no choice,
Buddy boys, it's my voice!

Kids ain't good for anything,
Shaving or driving or necking or
    anything,
No good for nothing but sounding
    like girls when they speak.

Kids are good for staring at,
No good for swearing but real good
    for swearing at.
Nobody listens to no one who swears
    with a squeak.

I say "Hell"
And no one ever even looks around.
When I yell,
Only dogs can hear the sound!
Hell and dammit . . .

I ain't like the other kids,
Yappy and snoopy and poopy like
    other kids.
I been to Night Court and I been
    rolled—
Why can't I be old,
Like everybody else?

                ANYBODYS
                (To A-rab)
"Listen, you shrimp,
You ain't no prize."

        ANYBODYS, A-RAB
"Shorty, get out—

                A-RAB
—of that hole and get wise."

That's all I ever hear.
So tell me how to grow,
Buddy boys, you don't know . . .

Shrimps ain't good for anything,
Watching parades or the movies or
    anything.
I should get refunds for all of the
    scenes that I miss.

Shrimps ain't good for you-know-
    what,
Only a pygmy can dig me for you-
    know-what.
No broad respects you who has to
    bend down for a kiss.

I seem rude,
I don't get up for any chick in town.
I ain't rude,
I'm just taller sitting down.
It's repulsive . . .

Shrimps ain't good for anything,
Watching parades or the movies or
    anything,
No good for nothing but crawling and
    stalling around.

                BABY JOHN
                (Overlapping)
Kids ain't good for anything,
Shaving or driving or necking or
    anything,
No good for nothing but drooping
    and pooping around.

                ANYBODYS
                (Overlapping)
Girls ain't good for anything,
Swearing or smoking or spitting or
    anything.
I swear and I smoke, and I inhale—

                ALL
Why can't I be—

                A-RAB
Big?

                BABY JOHN
Old?

                ANYBODYS
Male?

                ALL
Like everybody else!

This song worked charmingly in rehearsal, but one evening after a run-
through in Washington, Arthur gave
an eloquent speech to the effect that
the number, charming as it was, would
tip the first act into traditional musical
comedy and betray the show's integrity. Lenny was convinced, which
did not please Jerry, and when I con-
curred, Jerry turned on me with the
famous Robbins fury (being the
youngest of the group, I was the easy
whipping boy), snarling that if the

lyric had half the wit of (and here he
named a lyric writer whose work he
knew I found feeble), the show might
be in better shape. Public humiliation,
even among friends, is something I
don't take well; I was paralyzed from
making any contribution for days afterward. Happily, Lenny and Arthur
prevailed. It wasn't a bad song, but it
was a wrong one.

*The Jets wait in Doc's drugstore for a war
council with the Sharks. Riff tries to de-
fuse the mounting tension and keep the
gang together.*

Cool

                RIFF
Boy, boy, crazy boy,
Get cool, boy.
Gotta rocket
In your pocket,
Keep coolly cool, boy.

Don't get hot,
'Cause, man, you got
Some high times ahead.
Take it slow,
And Daddy-o,
You can live it up and die in bed.

Boy, boy, crazy boy,
Stay loose, boy.
Breeze it, buzz it,
Easy does it,
Turn off the juice, boy.

Go, man, go,
But not like a yoyo schoolboy.
Just play it cool, boy,
Real cool.

*Tony meets Maria at the bridal shop
where she works. They imagine and perform their own wedding ceremony.*

One Hand, One Heart

TONY

Make of our hands one hand,
Make of our hearts one heart,
Make of our vows one last vow:
Only death will part us now.

MARIA

Make of our lives one life,
Day after day, one life.

BOTH

Now it begins, now we start:
One hand, one heart.
Even death won't part us now.

Make of our lives one life,
Day after day, one life.
Now it begins, now we start:
One hand, one heart.
Even death won't part us now.

This was an expansion of a song that had been written to a lyric by John Latouche for *Candide*, which began:

One
Hand,
One
Heart.
Your
Hand,
My
Heart.

Lenny had written only one note for each bar, so each word lay there, heavy and detached from the word that followed. It was like a sequence of anchors. As I wrote at the time:

One
Word,
One
Bar.
My
Word,
Your
Bar.

That was my effort to dissuade him humorously from restricting me to so few words. As in "Somewhere," the tune hamstrings the lyricist by virtually precluding the use of any two-syllable words, which sound ridiculous when stretched out so slowly. But Lenny was very fond of the melody and wanted to use it for the Balcony Scene, so I asked him merely to give me a couple of extra quarter-notes per bar, which didn't change the melodic outline. The paucity of notes did have one virtue: it made me write simply. A little *too* simply, but still . . .

The gangs ready themselves for the rumble, Tony and Maria prepare to see each other, and Anita anticipates her date afterward with Bernardo.

"Tonight" Quintet

JETS

The Jets are gonna have their day
Tonight.

SHARKS

The Sharks are gonna have their way
Tonight.

JETS

The Puerto Ricans grumble,
"Fair fight."
But if they start a rumble,
We'll rumble 'em right.

SHARKS

We're gonna hand 'em a surprise
Tonight.

JETS

We're gonna cut 'em down to size
Tonight.

SHARKS

We said, "O.K., no rumpus,
No tricks."
But just in case they jump us,
We're ready to mix,
Tonight!

ALL

We're gonna rock it tonight,
We're gonna jazz it up and have us
    a ball.

They're gonna get it tonight.
The more they turn it on, the harder
    they'll fall.

JETS

Well, they began it!

SHARKS

Well, they began it!

ALL

And we're the ones to stop 'em once
    and for all,
Tonight!

ANITA

Anita's gonna get her kicks
Tonight.
We'll have our private little mix
Tonight.
He'll walk in hot and tired,
So what?
Don't matter if he's tired,
As long as he's hot*
Tonight.

TONY

Tonight, tonight
Won't be just any night,
Tonight there will be no morning star.
Tonight, tonight,
I'll see my love tonight.
And for us, stars will stop where
    they are.

Today
The minutes seem like hours,
The hours go so slowly,
And still the sky is light.
Oh, moon, grow bright,
And make this endless day endless
    night.

---

* As recently as fifty years ago, this line struck the film studio that made *West Side Story* as too risqué for the unprotected public, so I had to change it, which I did in my best inoffensive style:

> He'll walk in hot and tired,
> Poor dear.
> Don't matter if he's tired,
> As long as he's near.

Even Oscar might have winced.

The sun sits in my window
And mocks me with its light

Tonight is when,
I'll see my girl love again
As we kiss meet
If we please, stars will freeze where they are.

Tonight, tonight   Today the minutes go so slowly
I'll see my love tonight   And hour after hour
When we kiss, ———   The sun is still in sight

Today the minutes drag creep crawl   The moon has risen early
The moon is in the my window   It sits outside my window
But still the sky is light   and still the sky is light

Today the minutes go so slowly,   The minutes hours last forever
The minutes must seem be passing like hours,   It seems I wait forever
And But still the sky is light.   Today can't last forever

Oh moon, be swift
And let us have the gift of tonight.

Oh sun, make day
and let the moon turn day into
Oh moon, make endless day endless night

Oh moon, turn burn bright white   Oh sun, turn white
And make ———

Just look around & will be there

The Jets are comin' out on top
We're gonna watch Bernardo drop
fix him up Old Ice is gonna make him drop
Just land those punches where they hurt
We'll are Bernardo eatin' dirt

CS - JETS ON THE MOVE TOWARDS RUMBLE AREA

SUGGESTED VERSION	ORIGINAL VERSION

RIFF (To Ice)
(We're countin' on you to be there)
~~Tonight~~
You're gonna win it fair and square
Tonight
And will be right behind you there
Tony bt

~~ICE~~
~~The~~ Puerto Rican punk'll
~~Go down~~

~~ACTION (excitedly)~~
~~And when he hollers Uncle~~
~~We'll tear up the town~~

~~RIFF~~
~~The Jets are comin' for you~~

ICE
All right

ACTION
We're gonna have us a ball

Tonight

ICE
Easy, freezy

Cooly, cool

~~RIFF~~
~~We'll stop 'em once and for all~~

ALL
Tonight

RIFF (To Tony)
~~I'm counting on you to be there~~
~~Tonight~~
~~When Diesel wins it fair and square~~
~~Tonight~~

That Puerto Rican punk'll
Go down

And when he's hollered Uncle
We'll tear up the town

RIFF ~~with you~~
~~So I can count on you, boys~~
We'll be in back of you, boy
~~TONY~~ ICE
~~All~~ right

RIFF you're   flatter him good
~~We're~~ gonna ~~have us a ball~~
~~TONY~~ ICE
~~All~~ right

~~Womb to tomb~~ 1 - 2 - 3

RIFF
~~Sperm to worm!~~ 1 - 2 - 3
And then we'll
~~our games~~ have us a ball
~~I'll see you there about eight..~~

TONY
Tonight...

RIFF'S first line "I'm counting on you to be there" doesn't work at all
since ICE is walking right beside him.

Ask Sou Y: when pierced?
        Jerry's no.
        P. 39 of "America" scene

Bernardo's gettin' good and hurt gonna lose his shirt
Old Ice'll have him eatin' dirt
(CR57022)

RIFF
(To Tony)
I'm counting on you to be there
Tonight.
When Diesel wins it fair and square
Tonight.
That Puerto Rican punk'll
Go down.
And when he's hollered "Uncle,"
We'll tear up the town
Tonight!

(The following passages are sung
simultaneously)

MARIA
Tonight, tonight
Won't be just any night . . .

RIFF
So I can count on you, boy?

TONY
All right.

RIFF
We're gonna have us a ball.

TONY
All right.
Womb to tomb!

RIFF
Sperm to worm!
I'll see you there about eight.

TONY
Tonight . . .

BERNARDO, SHARKS
We're gonna rock it tonight!

ANITA
Tonight . . .

BERNARDO, SHARKS
We're gonna jazz it tonight.
They're gonna get it tonight.
They began it, they began it,
And we're the ones
To stop 'em once and for all!
The Sharks are gonna have their way,
The Sharks are gonna have their day,
We're gonna rock it tonight!
Tonight!

ANITA
Tonight, late tonight,
Late tonight,
We're gonna mix it tonight.
Anita's gonna have her day,
Anita's gonna have her day,
Bernardo's gonna have his way
Tonight.
Tonight, this very night,
We're gonna rock it tonight,
Tonight!

RIFF, JETS
They began it!
They began it!
We'll stop 'em once and for all!
The Jets are gonna have their day,
The Jets are gonna have their way,
We're gonna rock it tonight,
Tonight!

MARIA
Tonight there will be no morning star.
Tonight, tonight, I'll see my love
    tonight
And for us, stars will stop where
    they are.

TONY, MARIA
Today the minutes seem like hours,
The hours go so slowly,
And still the sky is light.
Oh, moon, grow bright,
And make this endless day endless
    night,
Tonight!

This "Quintet" is actually a quartet,
since both Maria and Tony sing the
same melodic line, but once we'd ex-
tracted their tune and expanded it for
the Balcony Scene, it seemed needless
to fool around with the form, and the
mistaken title became a minor matter
of nomenclature. The most instructive
aspect of the piece for me was that we
wrote it to occur *before* the scene in
the bridal shop, since we felt that Tony
would never agree to rumble after
he'd "married" Maria. Jerry, however,
refused to listen to the logic and insisted that the number should occur
after the bridal-shop scene. Even
Arthur couldn't get him to come
around; Jerry just folded his arms,
shut his eyes and shook his head at
every argument. That was his customary manifestation of adamant stub-
bornness whenever he couldn't
articulate his reasons; it happened
frequently, as verbal articulation
was Jerry's enemy, and he became
a fortress of refusal whenever he
glimpsed a lucid argument on the
horizon. We did get him to agree to
two run-throughs of the show, one
with the "Quintet" before the bridal
shop and one after it and, as you might
guess, Jerry turned out to be right. The
plot logic may not have made much
sense, but the show flowed better. That
was when I learned that there is a significant difference between logical
truth and theatrical truth.

*The rumble takes place, during which
Bernardo kills Riff, and Tony, in revenge,
kills Bernardo.*

ACT TWO

*Maria, unaware of what has happened
at the rumble, is in her apartment with
her friends Rosalia and Consuelo, happily
getting dressed to meet Tony.*

I Feel Pretty

MARIA
I feel pretty,
Oh, so pretty,
I feel pretty and witty and bright,
And I pity
Any girl who isn't me tonight.

I feel charming,
Oh, so charming,
It's alarming how charming I feel,
And so pretty
That I hardly can believe I'm real.

See the pretty girl in that mirror there,
Who can that attractive girl be?
Such a pretty face,

Such a pretty dress,
Such a pretty smile,
Such a pretty me!

I feel stunning
And entrancing,
Feel like running
And dancing
For joy,
For I'm loved by a pretty wonderful
        boy!

ROSALIA, CONSUELO
Have you met my good friend Maria,
The craziest girl on the block?
You'll know her the minute you see her.
She's the one who is in an advanced
        state of shock.

She thinks she's in love.
She thinks she's in Spain.
She isn't in love,
She's merely insane.

It must be the heat,
Or some rare disease,
Or too much to eat,
Or maybe it's fleas.

Keep away from her—
Send for Chino!
This is not the Mar—
Ia we know!

Modest and pure,
Polite and refined,
Well-bred and mature,
And out of her mind!

MARIA
I feel pretty,
Oh, so pretty
That the city should give me its key.
A committee
Should be organized to honor me.

I feel dizzy,
I feel sunny,
I feel fizzy and funny and fine,*

---

*SIN: Using alliteration to dress up rep-
etition of thought and conceal lack of
substance. The phrase "funny and fine"
showed up, to better advantage, in
"Small World" in *Gypsy.*

And so pretty,
Miss America can just resign.

See the pretty girl in that mirror there!

ROSALIA, CONSUELO
What mirror, where?

MARIA
Who can that attractive girl be?

ROSALIA, CONSUELO
Which? What? Where? Who?

MARIA
Such a pretty face,
Such a pretty dress,
Such a pretty smile,
Such a pretty me!

ALL
I feel stunning
And entrancing,
Feel like running and dancing for joy,
For I'm loved
By a pretty wonderful boy!

Having spent a year on the score
rhyming "way/day," "alone/own,"
"tonight/light/bright" and the like in
order to be faithful to the characters'
inarticulateness, and knowing that
West Side Story was to be my first professional exposure, I was hungry for
any opportunity to show off with inner
rhymes and trick rhymes. "I Feel
Pretty," being a playful song to contrast dramatically with the melodrama
which was to follow, seemed to be the
ideal chance. To this misguided end,
the original lyric included the following interlude, which was subsequently
cut, fortuitously, for length:

ROSALIA, CONSUELO
Put on your mantilla, Maria,
And put silver combs in your hair.
A touch of perfume from Sevilla—
There won't be a
Prettier
Girl anywhere!

You stroll down the street,
The toast of Madrid,
And most of Madrid
Falls down at your feet.

Those cheers are for you—
The Plaza is full.
When they kill the bull,
The ears are for you!

Every matador that adores you
Cries ecstatically,
"I am yours!" You
Drive them insane,
They swoon and they drop—
The entire pop-
Ulation of Spain!

It was Sheldon Harnick, an expert
lyricist and an old friend, who after
hearing the song at a run-through
shortly before we left for our out-of-
town tryout gently pointed out to me
that perhaps lines like "It's alarming
how charming I feel," words like
"stunning" and phrases like "an advanced state of shock" might not belong in the mouths of Maria and her
friends. I had been aware myself of
this, and that the play on words in
"pretty wonderful boy" drew attention
to the lyric writer rather than the
character, but I had hoped no one
would notice anything but the cleverness of it. I was wrong. In an advanced
state of shock, I quickly rewrote the
lyric to make it simpler and more in
keeping with the way Maria and the
girls expressed themselves in the rest
of the score, but my collaborators
would have none of it—they liked it
the way it was. And is. I have blushed
ever since.

*In a ballet, Tony and Maria, along with
the Jets and the Sharks, dream of getting
away from the turmoil of their lives. An
offstage voice sings as they dance.*

There's a place for us,
Somewhere a place for us.
Peace and quiet and open air
Wait for us, somewhere.

There's a time for us,
Some day a time for us,
Time together with time to spare,
Time to learn, time to care.

Some day,
Somewhere,
We'll find a new way of living,
We'll find a way of forgiving.
Somewhere,
Somewhere . . .

There's a place for us,
A time and place for us.
Hold my hand and we're halfway
    there.
Hold my hand and I'll take you there
Some day,
Somehow,
Somewhere!

As with "One Hand, One Heart," this was a melody that was dear to Lenny, one that he had tried to find a use for in other shows and instrumental pieces and, like "One Hand, One Heart," hell for a lyricist to set, particularly the opening motif, with its rhapsodic upward leap on the second note. What word is worthy of such a climax at the beginning of the thought? I couldn't, and didn't, solve the problem. In fact, the most unimportant word in the opening line ("a") is the one that gets the most important note. Burt Shevelove was fond of referring to this song as the "a" song. But then, he was a lyricist.

"Somewhere" was also the occasion of a dramatic confrontation in Washington. During the orchestra readings of the score, Jerry had objected to the way Sid Ramin and Irwin Kostal had orchestrated the song—under Lenny's supervision and with his approval. When Jerry realized during the dress rehearsal that Lenny had no intention of changing it, he simply stopped everything, walked down the aisle to the orchestra pit and proceeded to dictate the alterations he wanted directly to the conductor and the musicians. I had witnessed the arrogance of directors before, watching Agnes de Mille in operation on *Allegro*, but not on this scale. I turned in my seat to get Lenny's reaction, but he was nowhere to be seen. I left the theater and, on a hunch, looked around for the nearest bar; sure enough, there he was in a booth, glumly staring at shots of Scotch lined up on the table in front of him. Despite the global awe and respect he enjoyed, it turned out that he couldn't stand confrontation any more than I could, particularly with Jerry Robbins, who intimidated everyone he ever worked with, except for Arthur Laurents and Jule Styne. It may be one of the reasons Lenny was so loved. And Jerry so hated.

The Jets, on the run from the rumble, stop to regroup and mockingly assess the authorities who interfere with their lives.

Gee, Officer Krupke

ACTION
Dear kindly Sergeant Krupke,
You gotta understand:
It's just our bringin' upke
That gets us outta hand.
Our mothers all are junkies,
Our fathers all are drunks.

ALL
Golly Moses, natcherly we're punks!

Gee, Officer Krupke, we're very upset:
We never had the love that every
   child oughta get.
We ain't no delinquents,
We're misunderstood.
Deep down inside us there is good!

ACTION
There is good!

ALL
There is good, there is good,
There is untapped good.
Like inside, the worst of us is good.

SNOWBOY
That's a touchin' good story.

ACTION
Lemme tell it to the world!

SNOWBOY
Just tell it to the judge.

ACTION
Dear kindly Judge, your Honor,
My parents treat me rough.
With all their marijuana,
They won't give me a puff.
They didn't wanna have me,
But somehow I was had.
Leapin' lizards, that's why I'm
   so bad!

DIESEL
Right!
Officer Krupke, you're really a square.
This boy don't need a judge, he needs
   a [sic] analyst's care.
It's just his neurosis that oughta be
   curbed.
He's psychologically disturbed!

ACTION
I'm disturbed!

ALL
We're disturbed, we're disturbed,
We're the most disturbed.
Like we're psychologically
   disturbed.

DIESEL
In the opinion of this court, this child is depraved on account he ain't had a normal home.

ACTION
Hey, I'm depraved on account I'm deprived!

DIESEL
So take him to a head shrinker.

ACTION
My father is a bastard,
My ma's an S.O.B.

My grandpa's always plastered,
My grandma pushes tea.*

My sister wears a mustache,
My brother wears a dress.
Goodness gracious, that's why I'm a
   mess!

A-RAB
Yes!
Officer Krupke, you're really a slob.
This boy don't need a doctor, just a
   good honest job.
Society's played him a terrible trick,
And sociologically he's sick!

ACTION
I am sick!

ALL
We are sick, we are sick,
We are sick, sick, sick,
Like we're sociologically sick!

A-RAB
In my opinion, this child don't need to have his head shrunk at all. Juvenile delinquency is purely a social disease.

ACTION
Hey, I got a social disease!

A-RAB
So take him to a social worker!

ACTION
Dear kindly social worker,
They say go earn a buck,
Like be a soda jerker,
Which means like be a schmuck.
It's not I'm anti-social,
I'm only anti-work.
Gloryosky, that's why I'm a jerk!

BABY JOHN
Eek!
Officer Krupke, you've done it again.

---

* Once again, United Artists flinched and asked for a rewrite. Here it is:

My daddy beats my mommy,
My mommy clobbers me,
My grandpa is a Commie,
My grandma pushes tea,

This boy don't need a job, he needs a
    year in the pen.
It ain't just a question of misunder-
    stood—
Deep down inside him he's no good!

ACTION
I'm no good!

ALL
We're no good, we're no good,
We're no earthly good,
Like the best of us is no damn good!

DIESEL
The trouble is he's crazy.

A-RAB
The trouble is he drinks.

BABY JOHN
The trouble is he's lazy.

DIESEL
The trouble is he stinks.

A-RAB
The trouble is he's growing.

BABY JOHN
The trouble is he's grown!

ALL
Krupke, we got troubles of our own!

Gee, Officer Krupke,
We're down on our knees,
'Cause no one wants a fella with a
    social disease.
Gee, Officer Krupke,
What are we to do?
Gee, Officer Krupke—
Krup you!

This was the only song we wrote
where the music in its entirety came
first. It had been a song in *Candide*
called "Where Does It Get You in the
End?" and had the right vaudeville
feeling for the moment, although the
moment was something I had severe
doubts about: it was hard for me to
believe that a gang on the run from
being accessories to a double murder
would stop on the street to indulge in
a sustained comic sneer. My collaborators disagreed, on the traditional theatrical grounds that, as the drunken
Porter in *Macbeth* exemplifies, comedy in the midst of melodrama makes
the comedy more comic and the melodrama more melodramatic. I grumpily
acceded, not least because I realized,
once I'd thought of the title, that the
song would afford me the opportunity
of being the first lyricist to use a serious four-letter obscenity in a Broadway musical. The ice had been broken
by Tennessee Williams in *Cat on a Hot
Tin Roof* when Big Daddy boomed
out, "Bullshit!" That was the expletive
heard round the world—prior to it,
nothing but "hell" and "damn" had
ever sullied the American commercial
stage. But such language had never
been heard in a musical, and here was
my chance to make my mark by having a loud choral "Fuck you!" as the
punch line of a song. All was well until
we played it for the producers, at least
one of whom blanched visibly. We
were also informed by Columbia
Records, the company set to record
the album, that it could never be
shipped over state lines because of the
obscenity laws, which would significantly limit sales, to say the least. I was
in despair until Lenny came up with
"Krup you!," which may be the best
lyric line in the show and which was
actually an improvement, since it fitted
the kidlike nature of the Jets better
than the harsher and more realistic
expletive.

I ran into the same problem, inadvertently, in the recording studio.
Goddard Lieberson, the producer of
the album, informed me on the spot
that the word "schmuck" would have
to be changed for the same reason.
To his surprise, I confessed that I
had no idea the word was obscene. I
thought it was simply a vulgarity to
describe someone both stupid and obnoxious, not an obscenity that could
prevent the recording from being dis-
tributed. It was a rhyming word, so it
involved writing a new couplet, and I
had about an hour before the song was
scheduled to be recorded. I came up
with this:

Dear kindly social worker,
They say go earn some dough,
Like be a soda jerker—
Which means like be a schmo.

For the movie I improved it a bit:

Dear kindly social worker,
They tell me, "Get a job."
Like be a soda jerker,
Which means like be a slob.

I wrote a number of other verses and
choruses on the way to the final result.
At one stage, Action sang the first chorus solo:

ACTION
Gee, Officer Krupke,
I'm not playin' games.
My parents are the culprits—I can
    give you their names.
I'm not a delinquent
I'm misunderstood,
'Cause in the worst of us there's good.
There is good, there is good,
There is untapped good.
Even in the worst of us there's
    good . . .

Later, he sang:

ACTION
I'm sensitive by nature,
I'm delicate and shy.
When people say "I hate ya"
I always start to cry.
I'm ever so artistic,
An orchid in a slum—
Goodness gracious,
That's why I'm a bum!

PSYCHOLOGIST (A-RAB)
Check!
Officer Krupke,
Be kind to the kid.
It's just he's got a crazy mixed-up
Sort of an id.
He needs self-expression,
It mustn't be curbed—
He's psychologically disturbed.

ACTION
I'm disturbed!

ALL

We're disturbed, we're disturbed
Ever so disturbed,
Like we're psychologically disturbed!

Here are the authority figures gathered together.

JUDGE

This boy don't need correction,
The trouble's in his dome.

PSYCHOLOGIST

He don't need no injection,
The trouble's in his home.

SOCIAL WORKER

He don't need social welfare,
The trouble's in his glands.

ALL THREE

Sufferin' catfish—
Get him off our hands!

And for the finale:

ALL

Society don't love us,
We just don't seem to fit.
Society don't love us,
So how can we love it?
Society don't love us,
We read it in the press—
Sufferin' catfish,
That's why we're a mess!

As for the inappropriateness of the moment, I suggested to Jerry and Arthur that we switch this song with "Cool." The playfulness of "Krupke" belonged in the first act, I argued, whereas "Cool" was precisely the kind of song that they'd sing in their second act state of tension. Jerry was persuaded to try it in Washington, but found that the way the scenery had been planned ("Krupke" on a shallow stage, "Cool" on a full one), prevented him from doing it. When the show was sold to the movies, however, he did indeed switch them. I'm no longer sure if it was for the better or not, and ever since then I've been haunted by the

feeling that I shouldn't have opened my mouth.

Anita rails at Maria for having fallen in love with Tony. Maria responds.

A Boy Like That
I Have a Love

ANITA

A boy like that who'd kill your
      brother,
Forget that boy and find another,
One of your own kind.
Stick to your own kind!

A boy like that will give you sorrow.
You'll meet another boy tomorrow,
One of your own kind.
Stick to your own kind!

A boy who kills cannot love,
A boy who kills has no heart.
And he's the boy who gets your love
And gets your heart!
Very smart, Maria, very smart!

A boy like that wants one thing only,
And when he's done he'll leave you
      lonely.
He'll murder your love; he murdered
      mine.
Just wait and see,
Just wait, Maria,
Just wait and see!

MARIA

Oh, no, Anita, no,
Anita, no!
It isn't true, not for me,
It's true for you, not for me.
I hear your words,
And in my head
I know they're smart,
But my heart, Anita,
But my heart

Knows they're wrong
And my heart
Is too strong,
For I belong
To him alone, to him alone.

One thing I know:
I am his,
I don't care what he is.
I don't know why it's so,
I don't want to know!

Oh, no, Anita, no, you should know
      better!
You were in love, or so you said.
You should know better . . .

I have a love, and it's all that I have.
Right or wrong, what else can I do?
I love him, I'm his,
And everything he is
I am, too.

I have a love, and it's all that I need,
Right or wrong, and he needs me,
      too.
I love him, we're one.
There's nothing to be done,
Not a thing I can do
But hold him, hold him forever,
Be with him now, tomorrow
And all of my life!

BOTH

When love comes so strong,
There is no right or wrong,
Your love is your life.

In contrast to "Gee, Officer Krupke," Anita's chorus of "A Boy Like That" is the only occasion when I wrote a lyric first and Lenny set it exactly the way it was handed to him: it was late in our collaboration and I felt confident enough to do such a thing. In fact, looking back at all the *West Side Story* lyrics now, I become aware of how my growing confidence over the two years of writing the show allowed me to improve my work; the later lyrics, like "Something's Coming," "Gee, Officer Krupke" and "Like Everybody Else," have a relaxed tone which is markedly less self-conscious than the earlier ones. Perhaps that was the most important thing the show did for me. Despite my mixed feelings about what I contributed to it, it was—along with *Allegro*—the show which shaped my professional life.

"The Dance at the Gym"

ETHEL
MERMAN
in
GYPSY
a new musical

3. Gypsy (1959)

*Book by Arthur Laurents (suggested by
    the memoirs of Gypsy Rose Lee)*
Music by Jule Styne

The Notion

Gypsy Rose Lee was the burlesque queen who put the
"tease" in striptease. Although the show is called *Gypsy,*
the central character is her relentlessly driven mother,
Rose, who during Gypsy's childhood is determined to
make Gypsy's younger sister, June, into a vaudeville star.
The chronicle of Rose, Louise (Gypsy's real name) and
June covers a period of approximately ten years.

General Comments

Gypsy is the show where I came of age—lyrically, at
any rate. From Hammerstein and *Saturday Night* I had
learned my craft and from *West Side Story* I had acquired
the confidence to use it without apology. I no longer felt
I had to imitate other writers or to follow instructions
from collaborators; my apprenticeship was over. I felt
like an equal, not least because *Gypsy* was a musical
whose characters were types familiar to me, whose
diction I could imitate with natural ease and whose
backgrounds I could relate to.

Before Rodgers and Hammerstein popularized musicals with compelling stories and people with at least two
dimensions to them, the characters in Broadway shows
hadn't been characters so much as collections of characteristics, the kinds who could be described with one adjective and one noun: the shy hero, the aggressive vamp,
the wisecracking friend, the stodgy parent, and so on. As

a consequence, the songs they sang reflected only the
outlook of the songwriters or the personalities of the
performers. Cole Porter's characters were all aspects of
Cole Porter, or at least his public image: the worldly
cosmopolitan with an aching heart. Lorenz Hart's were,
like him, the wryer, New York version of same. Noël
Coward's were unfailingly brittle and condescending
or operetta-sentimental, E. Y. Harburg's whimsical and
innocent-seeming; indeed, all the leading lyricists of the
day from Ira Gershwin to Dorothy Fields had a strong
personal style that transcended whatever story they
chose to tell. The performing list included Ethel Merman
(brash), Libby Holman (sultry) and Sophie Tucker
(raunchy), along with Bob Hope, Jimmy Durante and
a dozen others with distinct and individual profiles,
personal as well as physical.

After the shattering success of *Oklahoma!,* however,
librettists began to produce narratives with some dramatic weight, and lyricists had more interesting characters to write for. The characters in *Saturday Night* and
West Side Story may not have had much depth or complexity (in *Saturday Night,* one is ambitious, one is
boastful, one is naïve, one is pretentious, etc.; in *West
Side Story* one is angry, one is yearning, one is resentful,
etc.), but they had enough individual flavor so that they
didn't have to sound like me. *Gypsy* was my first chance
to write lyrics for characters of considerable complexity.
Arthur Laurents's people were more dimensional than
any who had ever appeared in musicals before (if you
discount *Porgy and Bess* as an opera) and as he started
to shape them, I suggested that, given their substance,
Gypsy might be more satisfying as a straight play; after
all, no matter how subtly written, songs can't character-
ize with the same depth that extended dialogue can.
Music can evoke and sustain an atmosphere and elicit
an emotional response quickly and lastingly, but Shakespeare's *Othello* is more interesting than Verdi's, and

Sandra Church and Ethel Merman in the final scene of Gypsy

Higgins and Eliza are more layered and surprising in *Pygmalion* than they are in *My Fair Lady* (which, I hasten to add, is one of the most enjoyable musicals I ever saw). Arthur's response to my suggestion was one of patient dismissal: he was drawing his characters in broad strokes, he said—if he'd wanted to put them in a play, they would have had much more variety and many more shadings. Rose and Louise were certainly richer characters than those in *West Side Story* because he had room to write twice as much dialogue, but they belonged in a musical; he was writing them to be artificial enough to sing.

Best of all for both Arthur and me, Rose was that dramatist's dream, the self-deluded protagonist who comes to a tragic/triumphant end. When an audience knows more than the character does, every line of dialogue and lyric has an edge. It's the principle of suspense, as Alfred Hitchcock was fond of pointing out: if we know there's a time bomb hidden under the dinner table and the diners don't, it makes all the dinner conversation, no matter how trivial, riveting. Self-delusion is at the heart of plays from *Oedipus Rex* to *Death of a Salesman* via *Othello* and *A Streetcar Named Desire.* Knowing something the character doesn't gives audiences the superior feeling of omniscience and helps to maintain their interest in the story; they wait in suspended anticipation of the inevitable moment when the character will be forced to face the truth. They think: I get it, why doesn't he? If they care enough about him, every moment of the evening is freighted, and when he finally does get it, it's both devastating and satisfying. Self-delusion, moreover,

gives the actor a subtext to play that can flavor every moment; actors can only be grateful to have a song in which they sing "Everything's so white" while sitting in a blue set. Rose is the classroom example of self-delusion, a showbiz Oedipus.

This particular Oedipus, however, was to be played by Ethel Merman, which made the challenge of writing the character doubly tricky, but that was why I had taken the job in the first place. Originally, Arthur, Jerry and the producers had asked me to write the music as well as the lyrics for the show—but Ethel was reluctant to take a chance on an unknown composer and suggested Jule Styne. Arthur tried to persuade me to write lyrics only, but after *West Side Story* I was afraid of being pigeon-holed forever as a lyricist (a fear which proved to be well founded), so I refused. It was Oscar who convinced me otherwise. He thought it would be valuable for me to learn how to write for a star, a specific and predictable personality who makes an audience feel as if they are greeting an old friend. Once again he was right: my experience with *Gypsy* prepared me for a future which involved writing for the likes of Phil Silvers (whom Burt Shevelove, Larry Gelbart and I had in mind when we were writing *A Funny Thing Happened on the Way to the Forum*), Zero Mostel (who actually did it), Angela Lansbury, Elaine Stritch and others who will surface in these pages. What pushed me over the edge to say yes, however, was the knowledge that the role of Rose would offer Ethel and us authors a chance to startle that audience, to blindside those expectations. Not only would we be writing for Rose, we would be writing for Rose as played by a flamboyant performer with a blazingly recognizable persona that audiences came specifically to see— a genuine Broadway star personality who, we all hoped, could act.

There was some reason to doubt this, apart from the bright, cheerful, loud sameness of all her performances. It can be exemplified by an incident which occurred long after *Gypsy,* during the 1966 revival of *Annie Get Your Gun.* After a performance one night, Ethel summoned Jerry Orbach, one of the supporting players, to her dressing room in a state of some agitation. "What were you doing during my speech in the boat scene?" she demanded. "Nothing, Miss Merman," Jerry said, baffled. "Yes, you were, you were doing *something*," she insisted, "I saw you out of the corner of my eye." "I was only reacting to your speech," he replied, still baffled. "Look," she snapped, "you don't react to my lines, I don't react to yours, okay?" Which brings me to the subject of performers.

When I'd first started to work with Arthur on *West Side Story,* he suggested that I accompany him to a session at the Actors Studio. I did, and sat there in shock and awe, not to say embarrassment, watching actors read scenes and then submit themselves to the criticism, often personal, of their fellow actors and, eventually, of their grand panjandrum, Lee Strasberg (who, as demonstration of his status, had a chair-boy following him to support him wherever he chose to land). What struck me most was how seriously the actors took themselves, hyperanalyzing both their lives and their craft. When we left, the cries of "subtext" and "sense memory" ringing in my ears, I commented to Arthur that a lot of what went on seemed to me to be self-indulgent and pretentious, and I asked him why he had brought me there. "You've got to know the instruments you're working with," he explained, in a tone somewhere between scorn and admiration for them. Suddenly everything I'd witnessed seemed, if no less silly, much more focused: I began to understand something about what actors require. Just as a composer shouldn't write for the piano without knowing something about how to play it, so a playwright (and by implication a lyric writer) shouldn't write for the musical theater without understanding acting from an actor's point of view. Writing for actors, you have to ask yourself: How do they approach a role? How do they see themselves? How, in fact, do they *think*? Not every actor uses the Stanislavsky techniques on which the Actors Studio is based, but that afternoon was an invaluable, if unsettling, experience.

As for subtext, it was a word that had only recently come into vogue, largely due to the Studio's influence.

Arthur, both in his own writing and in his frequent tirades on the dire state of the American theater, emphasized to me the importance of it: often what is not being said, the counterpoint underneath a scene, is what keeps the scene alive. Counterpoint, being a musical idea, is exactly what a composer can supply. This means, however, that you have to have something worth not saying. Those two lessons—the idea of the actor as an instrument, and the uses of subtext—informed nearly everything I wrote after that session at the Studio. One of the things that still astonishes me after all these years is the extent to which talented performers can bring songs to life—even songs good enough not to need much help—if you only leave them some space, some interstices to fill.

A word about *Gypsy*'s music: if Arthur supplied the character, Jule Styne supplied the atmosphere of both the milieu and of musical theater itself. Just as Lenny had caught the sounds of the city in *West Side Story* with jazzy, dissonant, "modern" music, Jule's score was redolent not only of vaudeville and burlesque but of the old-fashioned, straightforward, character-driven musical play, the model that Hammerstein had pioneered, of which *Gypsy* was one of the last examples and probably the best. That era was soon coming to an end, to be replaced by rock-pop sensibilities and the experimentation of the 1960s playwrights.

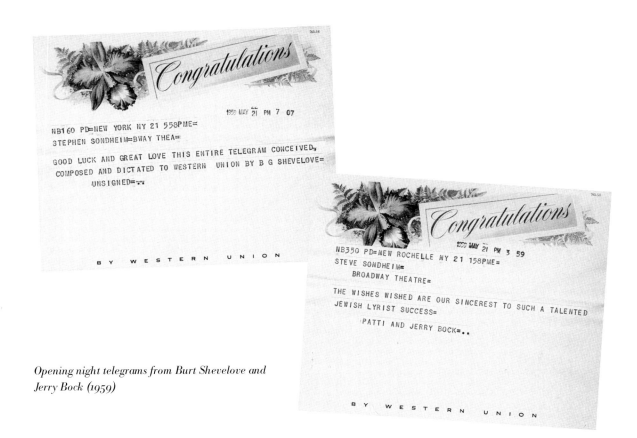

Opening night telegrams from Burt Shevelove and Jerry Bock (1959)

The stage of a vaudeville house in the 1920s. Auditions are being held for Uncle Jocko's Kiddie Show. Baby June and her sister, Louise, sing and dance.

May We Entertain You

JUNE
May we entertain you?

LOUISE
May we see you smile?

JUNE
I will do some kicks.

LOUISE
I will do some tricks.

JUNE
I'll tell you a story.

LOUISE
I'll dance when she's done.

BOTH
By the time we're through
Entertaining you,
You'll have a barrel of fun!

More about this song later.

At home the sisters' mother, Rose, tries to wheedle money from her father in order to get herself and her daughters out of a miserable lower-middle-class existence and to promote a vaudeville career for June, the younger of the two.

Some People

ROSE
Anybody that stays home is dead! If I die, it won't be from sittin'! It'll be from fightin' to get up and get out!

Some people can get a thrill
Knitting sweaters and sitting still—
That's okay for some people
Who don't know they're alive.

Some people can thrive and bloom,
Living life in a living room.
That's perfect for some people
Of one hundred and five!

But I
At least gotta try.
When I think of
All the sights that I gotta see yet,
All the places I gotta play,
All the things that I gotta be yet,
Come on, Poppa, whaddaya say?

Some people can be content,
Playing bingo and paying rent—
That's peachy for some people,
For some
Hum-
Drum
People to be,
But some people ain't me!

I had a dream,
A wonderful dream, Poppa,
All about June and the Orpheum
    Circuit—
Give me a chance and I know I can
    work it.

I had a dream,
Just as real as can be, Poppa.
There I was in Mr. Orpheum's office,
And he was saying to me:

"Rose!
Get yourself some new
    orchestrations,
New routines and red velvet curtains,
Get a feathered hat for the Baby,
Photographs in front of the theatre,
Get an agent—and in jig time
You'll be being booked in the big
    time!"

Oh, what a dream,
A wonderful dream, Poppa.
And all that I need
Is eighty-eight bucks, Poppa.
That's what he said, Poppa,
Only eighty-eight bucks, Poppa . . .

POP
You ain't gettin' eighty-eight cents from me, Rose!

ROSE
Then I'll get it some place else—but I'll get it and get my kids *out!*

Some people say, "Rose, sit tight—
Sweep all morning and sleep all
    night."
That's what you get from people
Who got nothing to give.*

Some people can sit around,
Under glass till they're underground.
That's perfect for some people
Who don't know how to live!*

Goodbye
To blueberry pie!
Good riddance to all the socials I had
    to go to,
All the lodges I had to play,
All the Shriners I said hello to—
Hey, L.A., I'm coming your way!

Some people sit on their butts,
Got the dream—yeah, but not the
    guts!
That's living for some people,
For some
Hum-
Drum
People, I suppose.
Well, they can stay and rot—
But not
Rose!

I suspect that the profusion of inner rhymes here is due less to character than to the exuberance I felt at being

---

*These quatrains were cut for reasons mentioned in the commentary.

You want —
everybody wants that
Want v want v want

I've worked my fingers to the bone, Papa.
And I've had to do it all alone, Papa.

Just a mother & her children
Fatherless
Innocent & unprotected
Kankakee to Chillicothe
Out against the world together
No, don't think (they'd) object
Oh, no not that I'm complaining
But my
Those two girls are something special
They deserve a little better —
Papa, do it for them —
Don't do it for me, but do it for them.
They're not run of the mill —
Papa, last night
I had a dream —
A wonderful dream, Papa
All about June (and Louise) and the Orpheum Circuit —
Give us a chance and I know we can work it —
'Cause I had a dream —
Just As real as can be, Papa.
Cause There I was in Mr. Orpheum's office,
With telephones ringing
And headliners famous celebrities
But Mr. Orpheum shut them off looked at me, waved them away
Looked only at me, Papa — and he said:

Anything that other kids can do,
June can do on point.

released from two years of *West Side Story*'s "right/night/fight" rhyming. Although inner rhyming exudes cleverness unless it's very subtle (and Rose is not verbally clever), here the interior rhymes don't announce themselves; in fact, most listeners probably don't even notice them. What does matter, however, is the awkward cue to the song.

Lead-ins to songs are the trickiest things to get right in a musical, along with buttons (the endings which cue applause). Transitions are tough enough to accomplish in straight plays; getting gracefully from one thought to another within a speech or one tone to another in a scene often requires a lot of delicate sweat work. Unlike novels, plays happily have handy tools known as actors, who can smooth out the bumps. With a song, however, performers are stuck with whatever the songwriter hands them. If the transition from speaking to singing is too abrupt, it will seem awkward; if overprepared with underscoring, it will be predictable and boring, a signboard proclaiming the arrival of the song from a mile away. In the case of "Some People," Rose has just finished an impassioned speech to her father (interrupted with a sting chord from the orchestra, announcing "SONG COMING!") which ends with her shouting at the top of her lungs, at which point she then begins singing on the lowest note in her register. I didn't realize the anticlimactic thud of this cue until the show was in its Philadelphia tryout and I heard the song accompanied by an orchestra, rather than just a rehearsal piano, which allows the imagination to dismiss flaws.

Lowering her voice at the peak of passion is something neither Rose nor Merman would ever do. Either the music or the lyric, preferably both, had to start on a higher note. The obvious solution was to write a verse which would bring both her voice and her emotion down enough to start the song at a believable level. I had wanted to begin it in the middle of her passion, going instantaneously from

speaking to singing, catching the audience unprepared (surprise is the lifeblood of the theater, a thought I'll expand on later). The abrupt contrast between high and low made it impossible, however. Cutting the first two quatrains and beginning with the release, which starts loud and high ("Goodbye to blueberry pie! . . .") accomplished this at the start of the second chorus; it allowed Rose to shout the words ". . . get my kids out!" at her father and pick up singing at the same emotional peak. There was no way to do this at the top of the song without a traditional verse, which Jule and I duly wrote, and which I can no longer remember or find. In it Rose told Poppa to go to hell, but Ethel refused to sing it because, she claimed, her fans would never forgive her for cursing her father. And there the cue to the song sits. Rose didn't care what people thought of her; Merman did.

Rose meets Herbie, an unmarried man who sells candy to vaudeville houses. She sees in him a good prospect as an agent for her kids' act and flirts with him.

Small World

R O S E
Funny, you're a stranger who's come
    here,
Come from another town.
Funny, I'm a stranger myself here—
Small world, isn't it?

Funny, you're a man who goes travel-
    ing,
Rather than settling down.
Funny, 'cause I'd love to go
    traveling—
Small world, isn't it?

We have so much in common,
It's a phenomenon.
We could pool our resources
By joining forces
From now on.

Lucky, you're a man who likes
    children—
That's an important sign.
Lucky, I'm a woman with children—
Small world, isn't it?
Funny, isn't it?
Small and funny and fine.

The young Louise and Baby June eavesdrop from high up behind one of the flats on the stage. They are no dopes.

Momma's Talkin' Soft (cut)

BABY JUNE, LOUISE
Momma's talkin' soft,
Momma's got a plan.
Momma's eyes are wide,
Momma's seen a man.

Momma's blushin' pink,
Fluffin' up her hair.
Momma has a smile—
And when she has a smile,
No one else has a prayer.

Momma's talkin' low,
Momma's gonna win.
Momma's movin' slow,
Momma's movin' in.

Bet when Momma's done,
Not a soul survives.
Momma's talkin' soft,
Everybody run for your lives.

We scrapped this song during the Philadelphia tryout, partly because the little girl who played Louise was afraid of heights and cried every time she had to get up on a ladder to peer over the flats, but chiefly because the show was long. My only regret about the cut is that I had used fragments of it in the climactic number of the show, "Rose's Turn," as you'll see, and their resonance was lost.

Baby June performs her act, which Rose has written, accompanied by four kids (including Louise) dressed as newsboys.

Baby June and Her Newsboys

NEWSBOYS
Extra! Extra! Hey, look at the head-
    line!
Historical news is being made!
Extra! Extra! They're drawing a red
    line
Around the biggest scoop of the
    decade!
A barrel of charm, a fabulous thrill!
The biggest little headline in
    vaudeville:
Presenting,
In person,
That three-foot-three bundle of
    dynamite,
Baby June!

JUNE
    Hello, everybody! My name is June.
    What's yours?

Let me entertain you,
Let me make you smile.
Let me do a few tricks,
Some old and then some new tricks,
I'm very versatile!
And if you're real good,
I'll make you feel good—
I want your spirits to climb.
So let me entertain you,
And we'll have a real good time,
Yes, sir!
We'll have a real good time!

The original version of June's act was
slightly more on the nose:

Mother's Day (cut)

JUNE
Don't take your mother for granted—
Mothers don't grow on trees.
You love and respect her,
So never neglect her,
Which is why I'm reminding you,
    please:

Send a dozen gardenias to your
    mother.
Tomorrow's Mother's Day.
You can never replace her with
    another,
No matter what they say.

Give her the earth,
That's what she's worth.
Give her a little something—
She gave you birth.

And by this time next year,
She may not be here,
Make every day Mother's Day!

A second version of the song specifically accommodated Jerry's notion
that the kids should be dressed as
newsboys:

NEWSBOYS
When a newsboy sells his papers—

LOUISE
Papers—

NEWSBOYS
And his working day is done—

LOUISE
Is done.

NEWSBOYS
He needs that something extra—

LOUISE
Extra—

ALL
That extra bit of fun.

LOUISE
I call my girl upon the phone,
And after we confer—

ALL
We meet somewhere on old Broad-
    way.
And as we stroll up old Broadway,
It's then I say to her:

Let's go to the movies,
Let's go to the show.

Let's make hanky panky
Along with Vilma Banky
And lovely Clara Bow.

With Milton Sills there,
We'll know some thrills there,
But we will steal every scene.

So let's go to the movies,
But let's not watch the screen, no, sir!
We won't watch the screen.

Jule Styne and I were not only a
generation apart, we were different
species, coming as we did from different musical-theater traditions, he the
spontaneous "tunesmith," as he called
himself, and I the austere revolutionary. We'd known each other only
slightly, at parties, but we quickly and
firmly cemented ourselves as a team
by tackling a vaudeville number first.
The day we started working together,
Jule handed me thirteen trunk tunes.*
I murmured that it might be a good
idea to write everything fresh for the
characters at hand. Two of the tunes,
however, were written in vaudeville
style and, not being expressions of
character, would be usable for the
kids' numbers; one of them was the
"Cow Song" (see below), which served
to introduce us to one another as collaborators.
    Robbins wanted *Gypsy* to encom-
pass all of vaudeville. To this end, he
auditioned dog acts, jugglers, whistlers,
double-jointed acrobats, everything
possible to use between book scenes.
In the face of Arthur's fierce and righteous objections, the plan was scuttled,
but in exploring its possibilities along
the way, Jerry and I also discussed
what the first vaudeville number
should be about. I whined to him that
the hardest kind of lyric to come up
with is a lyric with no specific situation, the kind which has so many pos-

---

* The term refers to the imaginary trunk of
unused songs accumulated over a lifetime of
writing them, most—but not all—unused for
good reason, and therefore dangerous to
unpack.

sibilities that there is no basis for choosing one. He glared at me impatiently and said, "Just say what it's about." "Like what?" I challenged. "I don't know. Something along the lines of 'Let us entertain you.'" How like a nonwriter, I thought to myself: blunt and flavorless. But I wrote it down in front of him so that he'd think I was taking him seriously. I decided that I could best avoid the problem by concentrating on the book songs (that is, the dramatic, character-driven ones), which I told myself were far more important than the pastiche routines. Eventually, though, I had to face it. "Eventually" took place on a train to Manchester, England, where *West Side Story* was warming up on its way to London. It was December, we were due to go into rehearsal with *Gypsy* in February, and Jerry was pressuring me to turn my attention to the vaudevilles, especially the opening and, even more important, the one that *Gypsy* would sing for her first striptease in a burlesque house. Rattling along in the shabby elegance of a British Railways compartment, I dragged out my vaudeville and burlesque notes, wishing I had only one song to write instead of two, and my wish came true. I saw that Jerry's phrase could, with a simple change of pronoun, serve as a refrain for both Baby June's bright-eyed vaudeville solo and grown-up Louise's sultry burlesque come-on. Score one for the blunt and flavorless.

It isn't the only time in my writing life that a casual *ad hoc* phrase has given rise to a song. It indeed took me a long while to realize the aptness of Jerry's suggestion, but sometimes a phrase will take blossom immediately.

For example, one day when I was searching for a refrain line that would establish Rose's personality in her first song, I was walking down Park Avenue with Arthur (between Fifty-seventh Street and Fifty-eighth—I remember the exact spot vividly) and in the middle of our discussion of it, he said, "Rose thinks anyone who doesn't want to get out of Seattle is insane. She can't understand how some people—" He never got to finish the sentence. I muttered a quick good-bye to him and triumphantly ran home to my pencil and pad.* The lyric was an easy write.

Years pass. The kids have grown up, even if the act has not. They are teenagers, all living with Rose and Herbie in a cheap rooming house. It is Louise's birthday (she is about fourteen years old) and they are celebrating with Chinese food, when Herbie enters excitedly with a Mr. Goldstone, a booker for the Orpheum circuit. The act has been booked into the big time. After Rose recovers from the shock, she excitedly plies Mr. Goldstone with food.

Have an Egg Roll, Mr. Goldstone

ROSE
Have an egg roll, Mr. Goldstone,
Have a napkin, have a chopstick,
   have a chair!
Have a sparerib, Mr. Goldstone—
Any sparerib that I can spare,
I'd be glad to share!

Have a dish, have a fork,
Have a fish, have a pork,

Put your feet up, feel at home.
Have a smoke, have a Coke,
Would you like to hear a joke?
I'll have June recite a poem!

Have a litchi, Mr. Goldstone,
Tell me any little thing that I can do.
Ginger-peachy Mr. Goldstone,
Have a kumquat—have two!
Everybody give a cheer,
Santa Claus is sittin' here—
Mr. Goldstone, I love you!

(Hysterical with excitement)

Have a Goldstone, Mr. Egg Roll,
Tell me any little thing that I can do.
Have some fried rice, Mr. Soy Sauce,
Have a cookie, have a few!
What's the matter, Mr. G?
Have another pot of tea!
Mr. Goldstone, I love you!

There are good stones and bad stones,
And curbstones and Gladstones,
And touchstones and such stones as
   them.
There are big stones and small stones,
And grindstones and gallstones,
But Goldstone is a gem!

There are milestones, there are
   millstones,
There's a cherry, there's a yellow,
There's a blue!
But we don't want any old stone,
Only Goldstone
Will do!

ALL
Moonstone, sunstone,
We all scream for one stone:
Mervyn Goldstone, we love you!
Goldstone!

---

* For those like me who are curious about a writer's habits: the pencils I write with are Blackwings, a brand formerly made by Eberhard Faber but alas no longer. Their motto, printed proudly on the shaft, is "Half the Pressure, Twice the Speed," and they live up to that promise. They utilize very soft lead, which makes them not only easy to write with (although extremely smudgy) but also encourages the user to waste time repeatedly sharpening them, since they wear out in min-

utes. They also have removable erasers which, when dried out, can be reversed to resume their softness and which are flat, preventing the pencil from rolling off a table. The pad I write on is a yellow legal pad with thirty-two lines, allowing alternate words to be written above one another without either crowding or wasting the space. These pads are hard to find, as most legal pads come with fewer or more lined spaces. Having been warned by Burt Shevelove, a stationery afi-

cionado, that stationery supplies are frequently discontinued, I had the good sense to stock up on them as well as the Blackwings before they disappeared, and now have a lifetime supply.

Some people write sitting at a desk, some standing at one; I write lying down on a couch (except when I'm at the piano), for the obvious reason that it allows me to fall asleep whenever I encounter difficulties, which is often.

This is a boilerplate example of the "list" song at its most egregious. A list song is just that: one idea illustrated by a list of examples. If either the idea is worth expressing or the examples are witty enough or have a cumulative effect, the list song can be one of the glories of musical theater, as witness Cole Porter's "Let's Do It," "You're the Top" and "Let's Not Talk About Love," among others. Porter was the supreme master of the form, although lovers of W. S. Gilbert might disagree. Then there are Howard Dietz's equally exhilarating "Rhode Island Is Famous for You" and Harburg's "Napoleon," two of the most inventive. List songs are comparatively easy to write, because they don't require developing ideas, but if the song has little to say and the songwriter doesn't keep filling the list with witty or surprising examples, the result is an increasingly monotonous waste of time, like Porter's "Nobody's Chasing Me" or "There Must Be Someone for Me." (Porter was also the supreme master of the boring list song, especially late in his life.) At their best, list songs are endlessly inventive, at their worst merely endless.

In this example, once Rose has offered Mr. Goldstone an egg roll, the joke is over, the joke being that Rose is notoriously stingy even with the kids in her act: her sudden generosity gets a big isn't-that-just-like-Rose roar of recognition from the audience. I was well aware of the thinness of the song as I was writing it, but some kind of celebratory number was called for in order to emphasize Louise's feeling of loneliness with "Little Lamb," the contrasting song which followed (and which was designed to interrupt "Mr. Goldstone" rather than follow it). I tried to build some interest into the lyric by tracking Rose's increasing hysteria, but it stubbornly remained one joke stuffed with wordplay to distract the listener. I love wordplay, but when there's nothing behind it, when its function is to prolong a tiny idea, it becomes masturbatory. "Exhibit A," "Gee, Officer Krupke" and even "America," for all their flaws, are effective list songs, but "Have an Egg Roll, Mr. Goldstone" sweats with effort. We couldn't even find an ending for it, since there was no place for the song to go, so we were stuck with the group shouting "Goldstone!" the way choruses used to shout "Yeow!" to button high-spirited dance numbers in most of the musicals of the forties, fifties and sixties (and even today). Nevertheless, it set up "Little Lamb" exactly as we'd hoped.

Louise loves animals and Rose has given her a pet lamb as a birthday present. Away from the celebration, alone in another room and surrounded by her animals, both live and stuffed, she sings to them.

Little Lamb

LOUISE
Little lamb, little lamb,
My birthday is here at last.
Little lamb, little lamb,
A birthday goes by so fast.

Little bear, little bear,
You sit on my right, right there.
Little hen, little hen,
What game should we play, and when?

Little cat, little cat,
Ah, why do you look so blue?
Did somebody paint you like that,
Or is it your birthday too?

Little fish, little fish,
Do you think I'll get my wish?
Little lamb, little lamb,
I wonder how old I am.
I wonder how old I am . . .
Little lamb.

A Chinese restaurant. Rose is concentrating on June's upcoming audition for T. T. Grantziger, a high-powered impresario. Herbie is upset at Rose's refusal to commit herself to marrying him and mutters that if he ever gives vent to his frustration it may result in his leaving her. She replies, in song.

You'll Never Get Away from Me

ROSE
You'll never get away from me.
You can climb the tallest tree,
I'll be there somehow.

True, you could say, "Hey, here's your hat,"
But a little thing like that
Couldn't stop me now.

I couldn't get away from you,
Even if you told me to,
So go on and try!

Just try,
And you're gonna see
How you're gonna not at all get away
from me!

HERBIE
Rose, I love you,
But don't count your chickens.

ROSE
Come dance with me.

HERBIE
I warn you
That I'm no Boy Scout.

ROSE
Relax awhile—come dance with me.

HERBIE
So don't think
That I'm easy pickin's—

ROSE
The music's so nice—

HERBIE
Rose!
'Cause I just may
Some day
Pick up and pack out.

ROSE
Oh no, you won't,
No, not a chance.
No argument,
Shut up and dance.

(As they dance)

You'll never get away from me,
You can climb the tallest tree,
I'll be there somehow.

True, you could say "Hey, here's your
    hat,"
But a little thing like that
Couldn't stop me now.

BOTH
I couldn't get away from you,
Even if I wanted to—

ROSE
Well, go on and try!
Just try—

HERBIE
Ah, Rose!

ROSE
And you're gonna see—

HERBIE
Ah, Rose!

ROSE
How you're gonna not at all
Get away from me!

On the day that Jule and I first met, when he handed me a number of trunk tunes and I murmured that it might be a good idea to start fresh, I made one exception. For the few years preceding, whenever I'd been invited to show-business parties, Jule Styne had been a constant and welcome presence because, like Gershwin before him, nothing delighted him more than settling himself at a piano and playing songs in the background. Unlike Gershwin, he played not only his own songs but those of his peers: a rare trait among theater composers, many of whom have a very small repertoire of their competitors' work. One tune of his own that Jule would sometimes play, and that I would often request, was called "Why Did I Have To Wait So Long?" It had been written for an unproduced movie and had an unfinished lyric (by Sammy Cahn). I said to him that if there was any trunk

tune to be used, that's the one I'd like, should there be a proper place for it in the story. Sure enough, the Chinese Restaurant scene offered the right moment for a jaunty romantic ballad, which it was. At my request, Jule got Sammy Cahn's permission to use the tune with a different title. Mine was "You'll Never Get Away From Me."

At the opening-night party, a college friend of mine who was a theater-song buff burbled to me how much he had enjoyed my rewrite of Jule's "I'm in Pursuit of Happiness." What do you mean? I asked, perplexed. "From *Ruggles of Red Gap*, the TV musical he wrote with Leo Robin," he replied, clearly perplexed at my perplexity. "The song that Michael Redgrave sang." With a completed lyric? I said. "Oh, yeah. But yours was even better." Why I never heard from Leo Robin (he didn't die until twenty-five years later) I'll never know. Perhaps Jule heard. Perhaps Leo Robin's lawyers were asleep, thank God. The interesting question is: why didn't Jule tell me he'd used the song? He was a fertile composer, as was Lenny, but they both did a lot of recycling. And generally for the better.

Rose auditions the act, now called Dainty June and Her Farm Boys, for T. T. Grantziger at the Palace Theater.

Dainty June and Her Farm Boys

FARM BOYS
Extra! Extra! Hey, look at the
    headline!
Historical news is being made!
Extra! Extra! They're drawing a red
    line
Around the biggest scoop of the
    decade!

A barrel of charm, a fabulous thrill!
The biggest little headline in
    vaudeville!
Presenting, in person, that five-foot-
    two bundle of dynamite: Dainty
    June!

JUNE
Hello, everybody! My name is June!
    What's yours?

I have a moo cow,
A new cow,
A true cow
Named Caroline.

COW
Moo moo moo moo . . .

JUNE
She's an extra special friend of mine.

COW
Moo moo moo moo . . .

JUNE
I like everything about her fine.

COW
Moo moo moo moo!

JUNE
She likes to moo in the moonlight
When the moody moon appears.
And when she moos in the
    moonlight,
Gosh, it's moosic to my ears—
She's so moosical!

She loves a man cow,
A tan cow
Who can cow
Her with a glance.
When he winks at her she starts to
    dance,
It's what grown-ups call a real romance.

But if we moved to the city
Or we settled by the shore,
She'd make the mooooooove,
'Cause she loves me more!

FARM BOYS
Broadway, Broadway! We've missed
    it so!
We're leaving soon,
And taking June
To star her in a show!

Bright lights! White lights!
Rhythm and romance!
The train is late,
So while we wait,
We're gonna do a little dance.

(Which they do)

JUNE
Broadway, Broadway! How great
   you are!
I'll leave the farm
With all its charm
To be a Broadway star!

Bright lights! White lights!
Where the neons glow!
My bag is packed,
I've got my act.
So all aboard, come on, let's go!

In the first version of the show, Rose, in a foul temper because Grantziger wants only June and not the whole act, exits the stage to argue with him, leaving Herbie behind. Herbie sings, meditatively:

Nice She Ain't (cut)

HERBIE
Her manner's charming,
But nice she ain't.
Her smile's disarming,
But nice she ain't.

She's a dame with more love to give
   than she pretends,
And a heart that's too warm to be
   refused.
Every place that she goes, she makes a
   million friends.
That lady has friends that she ain't
   even used.

Well, I'm no bargain, and she's no
   saint,
But, oh, so nice—she ain't.

He then repeats the chorus, ending on a sweeter note:

HERBIE
Well, I'm no bargain—I've no
   complaint,
'Cause mine, all mine she is.

The song was cut, primarily for reasons of time (one of *Gypsy's* constant problems was overlength) and because Herbie's feelings didn't seem worth the attention when the audience's concentration was on Rose and the two girls.

In the office, Grantziger's secretary offers Rose a contract for June to study acting, providing that Rose stays away. Rose does not take too kindly to this, causes a scene and exits to argue it with Grantziger himself, leaving the girls alone to lament their fate.

If Momma Was Married

LOUISE
If Momma was married, we'd live in a
   house,
As private as private can be:
Just Momma, three ducks, five
   canaries, a mouse,
Two monkeys, one father, six turtles
   and me . . .
If Momma was married.

JUNE
If Momma was married I'd jump in
   the air
And give all my toe shoes to you.
I'd get all these hair ribbons out of my
   hair,
And once and for all, I'd get Momma
   out too . . .
If Momma was married.

LOUISE
Momma, get out your white dress!
You've done it before—
Without much success.

BOTH
Momma, God speed and God bless,
We're not keeping score—
What's one more or less?

Oh, Momma, say yes,
And waltz down the aisle while
   you may.

LOUISE
I'll gladly support you,
I'll even escort you—

JUNE
And I'll gladly give you away.

BOTH
Oh, Momma, get married today!

JUNE
If Momma was married,
There wouldn't be any more
"Let me entertain you,
Let me make you smile.
I will do some kicks—"

LOUISE
"I will do some tricks."

JUNE
"Sing out, Louise!"

LOUISE
"Smile, baby!"

BOTH
Momma, please take our advice!

LOUISE
We aren't the Lunts.

JUNE
I'm not Fanny Brice.

BOTH
Momma, we'll buy you the rice,
If only this once
You wouldn't think twice!

It could be so nice,
If Momma got married to stay.

LOUISE
But Momma gets married—

JUNE
And—

LOUISE
Married—

JUNE
And—

LOUISE
Married—

BOTH

BOTH

And never gets carried away.
Oh, Momma,
Oh, Momma,
Oh, Momma, get married today!

In an alley outside a theater where the act is playing, Tulsa, one of the Farm Boys, is practicing a solo act, as Louise watches.

All I Need Is the Girl

TULSA

Once my clothes were shabby,
Tailors called me "Cabbie,"
So I took a vow,
Said, "This bum'll
Be Beau Brummel."

Now I'm smooth and snappy,
Now my tailor's happy.
I'm the cat's meow,
My wardrobe is a wow:
Paris silk, Harris tweed—
There's only one thing I need.

Got my tweed pressed,
Got my best vest,
All I need now is the girl!

Got my striped tie,
Got my hopes high,
Got the time and the place, and I got
    rhythm,
Now all I need's the girl to go
    with 'em.

If she'll
Just appear, we'll
Take this big town for a whirl.

And if she'll say,
"My darling, I'm yours," I'll throw
    away
My striped tie and my best-pressed
    tweed.
All I really need
Is the girl!

At the train station, as the act is about to pack off to another town, Rose learns that June has eloped with Tulsa and that the boys are leaving the act. Undaunted, de- spite *Herbie's and Louise's pleas to give up show business and live an ordinary life, she shifts her ambition from one daughter to the next and defiantly determines to make Louise a star.*

Everything's Coming Up Roses

ROSE

I had a dream,
A dream about you baby!
It's gonna come true, baby!
They think that we're through,
But, baby—

You'll be swell, you'll be great,
Gonna have the whole world on a
    plate!
Starting here, starting now,
Honey, everything's coming up roses!

Clear the decks, clear the tracks,
You've got nothing to do but relax!
Blow a kiss, take a bow—
Honey, everything's coming up roses!

Now's your inning,
Stand the world on its ear!
Set it spinning,
That'll be just the beginning!

Curtain up, light the lights,
You got nothing to hit but the
    heights!
You'll be swell,
You'll be great,
I can tell—
Just you wait!
That lucky star I talk about is due!
Honey, everything's coming up roses
For me and for you!

You can do it,
All you need is a hand.
We can do it—
Momma is gonna see to it!

Curtain up, light the lights,
We got nothing to hit but the heights!
I can tell,
Wait and see.
There's the bell,
Follow me.
And nothing's gonna stop us till we're
    through!

Honey,
Everything's coming up roses and
    daffodils,
Everything's coming up sunshine and
    Santa Claus,
Everything's gonna be bright lights
    and lollipops,
Everything's coming up roses for me
    and for you!

Ethel Merman was one of the two premier leading ladies of musical theater at the time of *Gypsy*, Mary Martin (*South Pacific, The Sound of Music*) being the other. They were polar opposites as personalities: Ethel blatant and brassy, Martin sly and sugary. Unsurprisingly, Martin appealed more to the public; there were many audiences who stayed away from Merman, put off by her blunt delivery, which they mistook for vulgarity. This, however, was precisely the quality Arthur wanted for Rose: obnoxious indomitability, an unstoppable confidence, a total absence of self-censorship. The problem was that Ethel had been brought up in farce musicals as a low comedienne (an expert one, I hasten to add) and had never been tested as an actress. We had no reason to believe she could do anything but bray her way through a show. I decided therefore to utilize that quality for the railroad scene and suggested to Jule that we write her a typical Merman number, a trumpeting fanfare of a song such as "Blow, Gabriel, Blow," the Cole Porter showstopper from *Anything Goes*—something she could easily sing while the performers playing Herbie and Louise, being actors first and singers second, could express the horror of the moment. Ethel would have nothing to do but be Ethel. Thus, the one-tone lyric of "Roses," which repeats a single idea unremittingly, the images derived from childhood and show business, the only references Rose is capable of making. As it happened, Ethel turned out to be a better actress than we'd anticipated, limited in range

I got an announcement to make (to the world)   Look ahead
                                                      (Like I said)

Clear the stage   light
Curtain up,   hit the lights   (just the brights)   Clear the aisles

We got nothin' to hit but the heights
Startin' here
Take a bow - startin' now,   Happy days happy nights

(Honey,) everything's comin' up roses!

You + me - we'll be great   giving   Now we're back on the track

Gonna have us the world on a plate

You + me - wait + see!

Honey, everything's comin' up roses!

Hold the phone - hit the brake

Got a little announcement to make

                                   Clear the decks, clear the tracks
                                        You
                                   We got nothin' to do but relax!

Clear the tracks, just and relax   Blow a kiss, take a bow

Honey - everything's coming up roses!

                                   You can do it,

                                   All you need is a hand

                                   We can do it

I can tell - wait + see!   Mama is gonna see to it.

There's the bell - follow me!   Will be swell, will be great

And Nothing's gonna stop us till we're through!   Gonna have us the world on a plate

Take the good with the good

Stand the world on its ear

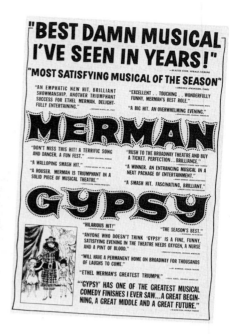

Ethel Merman as Rose

but capable of shadings and variety and with, of course, impeccable timing. She was able to tap into the reserve of anger that fuels every comedian, high or low.

It took me a week of sporadic thinking and jotting to come up with a title for the song, a phrase that could serve as a refrain. The difficulty was to find a way to say "Things are going to be better than ever" without being flatly colloquial on the one hand or fancifully imagistic (à la *West Side Story*) on the other. I was proud of the solution, and especially so when I picked up the *New York Times* one morning in 1968 and read the first sentence in the leading editorial: "Everything is not coming up roses in Vietnam." I had passed a phrase into the language.

Interestingly, the phrase almost never saw the light of day, because when I sang it for Jerry late one night during the Manchester tryout of *West Side Story* he complained, with the characteristic sullenness he assumed whenever he felt someone was trying to put something over on him, "But her *name* is Rose." As Arthur and I ex-

changed weary glances and suppressed our giggles, he continued, "I mean, everything's coming up Rose's *what?*" I promised him fervently that if anyone else was ever confused by the coincidence of "Rose" and "rose" that I'd find another title. No one did, and I was able to retain my triumph.

ACT TWO

Rose finds herself stranded in a southwestern desert, rehearsing Louise's act, which is like June's, complete with an American flag finish, but which now includes a troupe of six teenage girls, none with any discernible talent. She tries to teach them show business basics.

Smile, Girls (cut)

ROSE
What you must keep in mind as the
    act curtains part
Is the primary law of theatrical art:

Smile, girls,
And you'll lay 'em in the aisle, girls.
If you smile, girls,
They'll die on the spot.

Smile, girls.
Drive 'em crazy with your youth, girls.
Flash a tooth, girls,
Show 'em everything you've got—
Which ain't an awful lot.

Smile, girls,
Or we're never gonna work, girls.
Just a smirk, girls,
Might well save the day.
Get style, girls,
And the customers will stay.

So smile, Agnes,
Smile, Dolores,
Smile, Thelma,
Smile, Whateveryournameis,
Smile, Edna,
Smile, Marjorie May . . .

Smile, girls,
Make 'em think you're being clever.
But whatever
Happens,
Smile,
No matter what.

When the scenery smacks you, smile.
When a stagehand attacks you, smile.
When they boo in the gallery, smile.
When I don't pay your salary, smile.
When the comedy's dying, smile.
When Dolores is crying, smile.
When tomatoes are flying—duck.
But smile.

(The girls attempt to do splits)

Smile, girls.
It only hurts a little while, girls.
If you smile, girls,
It's sure to go away.

Get style, girls,
Even if you have to ham it,
But dammit,
Smile, Agnes,
Smile, Dolores,
Smile, Thelma,
Smile, Whateveryournameis—
Smile, Edna,
Smile, Marjorie May . . .

Smile, girls,
And when the act begins to sag,
Drag out the flag—
And smile!

This song was added in Philadelphia because Jerry felt that Ethel didn't have enough solo material in the second act. It went in for one performance and went out immediately—the show was long enough.

Rose, Louise and Herbie sing about camaraderie in order to keep up their spirits.

Together Wherever We Go

ROSE
Wherever we go,
Whatever we do,
We're gonna go through
It together.

We may not go far,
But sure as a star,

Wherever we are,
It's together!

Wherever I go, I know he goes.
Wherever I go, I know she goes.
No fits, no fights, no feuds and no
    egos—
Amigos,
Together!

Through thick and through thin,
All out or all in,
And whether it's win, place or show,
With you for me and me for you,
We'll muddle through,
Whatever we do,
Together wherever we go!

ALL
Wherever we go,
Whatever we do,
We're gonna go through
It together.

ROSE
Wherever we sleep—

LOUISE
If prices are steep—

HERBIE
We'll always sleep cheap-
Er together.

ROSE
Whatever the boat I row, you row—

HERBIE
A duo!

ROSE
Whatever the row I hoe, you hoe—

LOUISE
A trio!

ROSE
And any IOU I owe, you owe—

HERBIE
Who, me owe?
No, you owe!

LOUISE
No, we owe—

ALL
Together!
We all take the bow,

ROSE
Including the cow,

ALL
Though business is lou-
Sy and slow.

ROSE
With Herbie's vim, Louise's verve—

HERBIE, LOUISE
Now all we need is someone with
    nerve . . .

ROSE
Together—

HERBIE, LOUISE
Together—

ROSE
Wherever—

HERBIE, LOUISE
Wherever—

ALL
Together wherever we go!

ROSE
If I start to dance,

HERBIE, LOUISE
We both start to dance,

ALL
And sometimes by chance
We're together.

ROSE
If I sing B flat: Ohhhh—

LOUISE
We both sing B flat: Ohhhh—

HERBIE
We all can be flat: Ohhhh—

ALL
Together!

HERBIE
Whatever the trick, we can do it!

I

The (road may be) going is slow ~seem~
But ~this you should~ know ~one thing I~
Wherever we go, it's together

Wherever we go
We'll never feel low ?
As long as we know it's together
We haven't gone
We may ~not~ go far
But sure as a star
Whatever we are, it's together

Whatever we do, it's together
Wherever I go, I know he goes.
Wherever I go, I know she goes.
No fits, no fights, no feuds
~No jealousies, no~ fights + no egos,
Amigos
Together!
Through thick or through thin
All out or all in
And whether it's win, place or show
~Its~ you for me ~with~
And me for you
We'll muddle through
However
Whatever we do,
Together wherever we go.

LOUISE

With teamwork we're bound to get
   through it!

ROSE

There really isn't anything to it—
You do it.

(They attempt a trick, using pie plates)

I knew it—

(It fails)

ALL

We blew it—
Together!

We go in a group,
We tour in a troupe,
We land in the soup,
But we know:
The things we do, we do by threes,
A perfect team—

*(Rose and Herbie start to exit Stage Left,
Louise Stage Right)*

ROSE

No, this way, Louise!
Together—

HERBIE, LOUISE

Wherever—

ALL

Together wherever we go!

Jule and I had written half a dozen
songs when one day Ethel called us
to say that her friend Cole Porter
was deeply depressed and might be
cheered up if we played him the score.
We happily agreed, and a few evenings
later we were invited along with Ethel
to his Waldorf-Astoria Towers apartment. He had had both legs ampu-
tated, the result of many operations
resulting from a riding accident he
had suffered in the 1930s, and was indeed, as he had once written for Ethel,
"down in the depths on the 90th
floor."

    After dinner, Jule and I played and
sang what we had written, and when I
got to the word "Amigos" in the first

release of "Together, Wherever We
Go," I heard a gasp of delight in the
corner of the room. Mr. Porter had
been caught by surprise: he hadn't anticipated the quadruple rhyme. Needless to say, surprising a pro is one of the
greatest joys a writer can experience,
and this pro not only was a master of
surprising rhymes, he often sprinkled
his lyrics with foreign words and
phrases as markers of his cosmopolitan
style. Any time I need an ego boost, I
conjure up that gasp; it may well be
the high point of my lyric-writing life.

*Her act having been booked into a bur-
lesque house, Louise gets advice about it
from three strippers: Mazeppa, who uses
a bugle, Electra, who switches on lights
attached to strategic parts of her costume,
and Tessie Tura, who bumps and grinds
while dancing like a ballerina. Louise listens attentively: what she learns here is
what transforms her into Gypsy Rose Lee.*

You Gotta Get a Gimmick

MAZEPPA

You can pull all the stops out
Till they call the cops out,
Grind your behind till you're banned,
But you gotta get a gimmick
If you wanna get a hand.

You can sacrifice your sacro
Workin' in the back row,
Bump in a dump till you're dead.
Kid, you gotta get a gimmick
If you wanna get ahead.

You can (*bump!*), you can (*bump!*),
You can (*bump!*) (*bump!*) (*bump!*)—
That's how burlesque was born.
So I (*bump!*) and I (*bump!*)
And I (*bump!*) (*bump!*) (*bump!*)—
But I do it with a horn!

Once I was a schlepper,
Now I'm Miss Mazeppa
With my Revolution in Dance.
You gotta have a gimmick
If you wanna have a chance!

ELECTRA

She can (*bump!*), she can (*bump!*),
She can (*bump!*) (*bump!*) (*bump!*)—
They'll never make her rich.
Me, I (*bump!*), and I (*bump!*),
And I (*bump!*) (*bump!*) (*bump!*)—
But I do it with a switch!

I'm electrifying,
And I'm not even trying.
I never have to sweat to get paid.
'Cause if you got a gimmick,
Gypsy girl, you've got it made!

TESSIE

All them (*bump!*)s, and them (*bump!*)s
And them (*bump!*) (*bump!*) (*bump!*)
Ain't gonna spell success.
Me, I (*bump!*), and I (*bump!*)
And I (*bump!*) (*bump!*) (*bump!*)—
But I do it with finesse!

Dressy Tessie Tura
Is so much more demurer
Than all them other ladies, because
You gotta get a gimmick
If you wanna get applause!

ALL

Do somethin' special.
Anything that's fresh'll
Earn you a big fat cigar.
You're more than just a mimic
When you got a gimmick—
Take a look how different we are!

(They all do exactly the same moves)

ELECTRA

If you wanna make it,
Twinkle while you shake it.*

TESSIE

If you wanna grind it,
Wait till you've refined it.

MAZEPPA

If you wanna bump it,
Bump it with a trumpet!

---

* The original line, which I like better, was
"Shake it till you break it," but Jerry wanted
me to draw attention to the costume. This is
what we call a compromise.

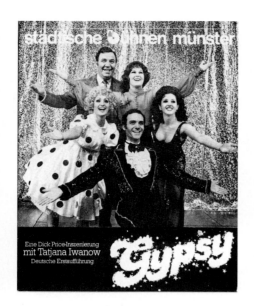

Again, the length of the show required ruthless cutting, and this moment was accomplished more economically by a couple of halting lines in a brief reprise of "Small World."

In a musical montage of time passing, Louise becomes the burlesque star Gypsy Rose Lee. The montage climaxes with an elaborate Christmas pageant at Minsky's, filled with scantily dressed chorus girls singing as a dulcet choir.

Three Wishes for Christmas
(cut)

BURLESQUE GIRLS
If I had three wishes for Christmas,
I'd make my first wish for a tree.
I'd make my second for a gift from
    someone,

A remembrance from one
Who is dear to me.

I'd make my third for a snowball,
And if my three wishes came true,
On Christmas night
I would light
My tree,
The snow falling silently,
And open my Christmas present from
    you—
If I had you.

This was another song dropped because of the show's length. Besides, satirical silliness or, more accurately, camp (show girls with shrill voices singing sentimental lyrics) has for me a short shelf life.

Rose, rejected by her daughter with a cry of "Momma, you have got to let go of me!," realizes the futility of her dreams and explodes into fantasy.

ALL
Get yourself a gimmick
And you, too,
Can be a star!

Herbie finally decides he can't live with Rose any longer. In Louise's dressing room, he announces that he is leaving her and exits. She angrily yells after him, "You go to hell!" and then sings to herself.

Who Needs Him? (cut)

ROSE
Who needs him?
One up, one down.
This show's been running for years—
It should have closed out of town.
One day it's on, one day it's through,
And I got twenty better things to do.

Who needs him?
Not me—oh, no!
There will be others to come,
Sure, and others to go.
They're passing phases,
They can go to blazes!

Who needs them?
Who needs it?
Who needs him?
Who?

"Everything's Coming Up Roses"

Rose's Turn

ROSE

With what I have in me, I could've been better than ANY OF YOU! What I got in me—what I been holding down inside of me—if I ever let it out, there wouldn't be signs big enough! There wouldn't be lights bright enough!

(The orchestra plays a chord)

Here she is, boys!

(And another)

Here she is, world!

(And another)

Here's Rose!!

Curtain up!
Light the lights!

Play it, boys!

You either got it,
Or you ain't—
And, boys, I got it!
You like it?

ORCHESTRA

Yeah!

ROSE

Well, I got it!

Some people got it and make it pay,
Some people can't even give it away!
This people's got it,
And this people's spreadin' it around.
You either have it—
Or you've had it.

Hello, everybody! My name's Rose.
What's yours?

(Strutting like a stripper)

How d'ya like them egg rolls, Mr.
Goldstone?

Hold your hats and Hallelujah,
Momma's gonna show it to ya!

Momma's talkin' loud,
Momma's doin' fine!
Momma's gettin' hot,
Momma's goin' strong,
Momma's movin' on!
Momma's all alone,
Momma doesn't care,
Momma's lettin' loose,
Momma's got the stuff,
Momma's lettin' go—

(Stammering)

M-M-Momma—

(Again)

M-M-Momma—

(Recovering)

Momma's got the stuff,
Momma's gotta move,
Momma's gotta go—
M-Momma—
M-Momma's—
Momma's gotta let go!

Why did I do it? What did it get me?
Scrapbooks full of me in the
     background.
Give 'em love and what does it
     get you?
What does it get you?
One quick look as each of 'em
     leaves you!
All your life and what does it get you?
Thanks a lot, and out with the
     garbage!
They take bows and you're battin' zero!

I had a dream—
I dreamed it for you, June.
It wasn't for me, Herbie.
And if it wasn't for me,
Then where would you be,
Miss Gypsy Rose Lee?!

Well, someone tell me, when is it my
     turn?
Don't I get a dream for myself?
Startin' now, it's gonna be my turn!
Gangway, world, get off of my run-
     way!
Startin' now, I bat a thousand!
This time, boys, I'm takin' the
     bows and

Everything's coming up Rose!
Everything's coming up roses!
Everything's coming up roses
This time for me!
For me!
For me!
For me!
For me!
FOR ME!!

If the "Amigos" moment with Cole Porter was the high point of my lyric-writing life, the making of "Rose's Turn" remains the high point of my theatrical life—at least the life I had imagined it would be from the movies, as in the scene from *Lady Be Good* in which Ann Sothern and Robert Young compose the title song in two minutes of excited improvisation, or the scene from *The Saxon Charm*, in which Robert Montgomery transforms Audrey Totter instantaneously from a vapid singer into a cabaret star, or in any number of other Hollywood moments of creative inspiration (usually taking place at nighttime and in the empty darkness of a theater or a nightclub). My moment came about as follows:

Rose's climactic breakdown was originally to be a surreal ballet, in which Rose would be confronted by all the people in her life (how Jerry intended to use Ethel Merman in a ballet is something we'll never know, I'm sorry to say). One week into rehearsals, Jerry suddenly announced that he didn't have time to choreograph the ballet; it would have to be a song, and Jule and I should meet with him at the end of the day to discuss it. As it happened, Jule had a social engagement that evening, so I went to meet with Jerry alone.

At that point, we were rehearsing in a small theater on the top floor of the New Amsterdam Theatre on Forty-second Street. This theater had been the location of Florenz Ziegfeld's *Midnight Frolic*, an informal extravaganza held every now and then after the *Follies* itself, involving many of the *Follies* performers strutting their stuff in front of an invited champagne-guzzling audience of society nobs and friends of the producer. By 1959 this theater was

Someone tell me when is it my turn.

Don't I get a dream for myself —

Momma's gotta dream for herself — From

Someone tell me why did I do it

I got more in this little finger

Me w/ it   my

Change the billing — Mama's through

now

OK

Gangway, children I'm lettin' you now

Hang the others — I'm for me now

you'll see now

Mama's talkin' loud   This time

Mama's doin' fine   Everything's comin' up R this time for me

Mama's gettin' hot

Mama's goin' strong   This is   This is me, boys!
                                   Now it's me, boys! Now it's my turn,
Mama's movin' on   Slap   pink   you'll see, boys
                                   Hit me with the blue and when I turn

Mama's all alone   Hold your hats, boys! Hallelya!

Mama doesn't care   Hit the floods, I'm throwin' it to ya

Mama's lettin' loose out   loose   Bustin' loose gonna bust

Mama's got the stuff   in a thousand

Mama's lettin' go   This time out I'm takin' the bows +

Mama ... Mama's ...

Mama's gettin' hot   Hit me with the special +

Mama's got the stuff

Mama's gotta move   (give)

Mama's gotta go ..

Mama's ...

Mama has gotta let go now .

"What'd I do it for? That's all I want to know."

Why'd I do it? what did it get me?

Scrapbooks fall on me in the background   one rotten cow's head

Give 'em love + what does it get you?   Blink your eyes + somebody's
One long look at somebody leavin' — (walkin') One quick look as each of 'em
Thanks a lot and out with the garbage   leaves you
Get your life + what does it get you?
They take bows while you're battin' zero.

I had a dream — I dreamed it for you, Baby,   June
It wasn't for me,   Herbie
I made it come true, Baby. (It wasn't for me.)
(And)
And if it wasn't for me, then where would you be (Baby?) Miss Gypsy Rose Lee.

And it wasn't for me!

No someone tell me — when is it my turn.   all you gotta do is just ask me
                                           I got more in this little finger
Mama's special, Mama's someone

a shabby shell of its former self, but it had a ratty auditorium and a usable stage, and the atmosphere suited *Gypsy* well. I met Jerry around seven o'clock. The setting was excessively theatrical: everyone had gone home and there was no light in the auditorium except, on the stage, a ghost light (a single exposed bulb on a stand). It was like every shimmering nighttime rehearsal scene I'd ever loved in the movies.

I suggested to Jerry that since he had wanted all the people in the story to collide in a ballet, perhaps if Rose's breakdown were to be sung rather than danced it could comprise fragments of all the songs associated with her and the people in her life: the songs we'd heard all evening, colliding in an extended surreal medley consisting of fragments of the score. He asked me to improvise what I meant. I don't like improvising in front of other people, but sitting at a piano in a deserted, ghost-lit auditorium with a man I considered a genius was too glamorous to resist. As I pounded out variations on the burlesque music, Jerry clambered onto the stage and started to move back and forth across it like a stripper, but a clumsy one: like Rose doing a strip. That was the beginning of three exhilarating hours of musical and choreographic improvisation, as we shaped and constructed the number to be a summary of the score.* I even improvised lyrics, something which was anathema to me. By the time we finished, "Rose's Turn" was outlined and ready for detail work. I brought it to Jule the next morning with some trepidation but a blast of enthusiasm, and we filled it out within the day.

When we played the song for Ethel at rehearsal, she received it with some uncertainty. "It's sorta more an aria than a song," she commented doubtfully, halfway between a question and

---

* As I noted earlier, one of the songs I built it on, "Momma's Talkin' Soft," was cut in Philadelphia, but I couldn't remove the section without collapsing the whole number. So there it remains, with the audience missing the reference. And I regret to say that it doesn't matter.

a complaint. I assured her that it was merely a collage of songs that she had either sung or heard during the course of the show. That seemed to calm her, but there was one detail that bothered her: the stammer on the word "Momma" at the moment of Rose's breakdown. She wanted to know whether the third syllable (M-M-*Momma*) should be on the downbeat or the upbeat. I explained that it was like a moment I had seen (actually, one I had stolen) in *A Streetcar Named Desire* when Blanche Du Bois started to crack up, and that it didn't matter where the beat was, that the stammer was a sort of mental seizure arising from the line which preceded it ("Momma's lettin' go") because that line reminded her of Louise's last jab at her ("Momma, you have got to let go of me!"). I assured Ethel that we had devised a "safety bar"—a bar that an orchestra can repeat until the singer is ready to resume singing—so that from night to night she could stammer any way she liked: murmured, explosive, sluggish, hysterical, lots of quick "M"s, a few slow ones, whatever—the conductor would catch her for "Momma's gotta let go!" Ethel nodded thoughtfully while we waited to see whether or not she understood and accepted the explanation. She concentrated mightily for a moment. "Yeah, but does it come in on the downbeat or the upbeat?" she asked.

Despite her misgivings, Ethel triumphed. Not only did she perform the song with vigor and passion, the audience was treated to the spectacle of Ethel Merman, the loud, frozen ("Call me Miss Bird's Eye," she reputedly said to Irving Berlin, referring to the rigid reliability of her performance once she had set it), low comedienne, singing an "aria," and they responded accordingly—or rather, they wanted to. I had persuaded Jule to end the number on a high, dissonant chord of eerie violin harmonics: a woman having a nervous breakdown would not wind up on a triumphant tonic chord. In the name of purity, I killed the hand.

When Oscar came to Philadelphia to see the show, I thought he would be

proud of me for it: I had followed his teachings and made the song fit the psychological situation rather than pander to the audience. To my chagrined astonishment, he urged me to let the number come to a show-stopping climax and allow Ethel to have her deserved thunderous ovation. When I protested that a big finish didn't suit the character's meltdown, he made the same point Jerry had made with the "Quintet" in *West Side Story:* sometimes a theatrical truth takes precedence over a logical one. If we didn't let an audience express its enthusiasm for the performer at the end of the song, he insisted, they would sit there in a distracted state, unconsciously waiting for the curtain call when they could tell Ethel how terrific she was. As a result, he argued, the audience wouldn't be (and wasn't) listening to the scene which followed, a three-minute resolution between Rose and Louise that reconciled them and made the most affecting point of the play: namely, that all children eventually become their parents. Gently chastened, I gave up and we affixed a big ending and a tonic chord to the song, Ethel got an enormous ovation and the audience listened to the last scene in rapt silence. Lesson learned. (Many years later, Arthur improved on Oscar's injunction and figured out a way for us to eat our cake and have it, too. He kept Rose bowing through the applause and continuing even after it died, indicating that the ovation was all in her mind.)

Despite my frustration at not being allowed to write the music, as well as a small series of unpleasant clashes during the tryout and the New York previews, *Gypsy* was a joy to create and to help ferry to the stage. It took only four months to write, which may be the chief reason for its spontaneity and vitality. I've seen mistaken productions of the show (including those directed by the show's author) that make it seem contrived or cartoonish, but never does it seem tired. Like *Citizen Kane*, arrogant though the comparison may be, there's not a moment in *Gypsy* that isn't entertaining.

ZERO MOSTEL

IN

A FUNNY THING
HAPPENED ON THE WAY TO THE FORUM

America's Funniest Musical

4. A Funny Thing Happened on the Way to the Forum (1962)

Book by Burt Shevelove and Larry Gelbart

Based on plays by Titus Maccius Plautus

The Notion

The time: Two hundred years before the Christian era, on a day in spring. The place: A street in Rome in front of the houses of Lycus, a venal brothel-keeper; Senex, a lecherous patrician; and Erronius, a befuddled old man. The plot revolves around the efforts of Pseudolus, a conniving slave, to gain his freedom by solving his young master's love life, and the complications that ensue.

General Comments

A Funny Thing Happened on the Way to the Forum was to be the first Broadway show that featured my own music attached to my own lyrics. Burt Shevelove, Larry Gelbart and I had written it over the course of four years and it had gone through two major producers, two major directors and one major star by the time we were ready to go into rehearsal. I should have been feeling exhilarated at the prospect. Instead, I felt a rapidly burgeoning panic, which I attributed to hysteria from the excitement of finally launching myself as a composer, but I didn't trust such an easy explanation. I wanted reassurance, so I turned to my playwright friend James Goldman and asked him to take a look at the script and listen to the songs. After reading it, he praised its brilliance; after hearing the score, he was equally enthusiastic. I started to glow in relief, when he added, "The problem is that they don't go together."

I had been trained by Oscar Hammerstein to think of a song as a one-act play which either intensifies a moment or moves the story forward. The song can have a sense of urging the show ahead even when it doesn't actually propel the plot: the principle is that the character singing undergoes an emotional change or expresses a feeling so powerful that it leads to an action. (The "Soliloquy" from *Carousel,* for example, accomplishes both these purposes.) Prodded by my academic musical training as well as by Oscar, I had become accustomed to thinking of songs as being structured in sonata form: statement, development and recapitulation. For Oscar it was first act, second act, third act. He tried to avoid writing lyrics that confined themselves to one idea, the traditional practice of virtually every lyricist in the theater and the standard function of songs before he came along and revolutionized the way writers thought about musicals. *Show Boat* hadn't convinced them, but once *Oklahoma!, Carousel* and *South Pacific* had become enormous hits, most songwriters converted. The success of those shows was not entirely beneficial, however. As Larry Gelbart put it in his Introduction to the published libretto of *Forum,* "Broadway, in its development of musical comedy, had improved the quality of the former at the expense of a good deal of the latter." The playfulness of musicals had been dampened by Oscar and his imitators and here I was, a convert myself, confronted with a musical that was nothing if not playful.

Forum required exactly the reverse of what Oscar had taught me to do. It was a farce: a play with broadly drawn characters who find themselves in uncomfortable situations which, when seemingly solved, lead to further and more uncomfortable situations. As in every play, the situations arise from character, but the characters in a farce, like those in traditional musical comedy, are one-dimensional (Hammerstein upped the ante to two) one adjective–one noun personalities: the conniving slave, the lecherous husband, the braggart warrior. It is the clash among these personalities that keeps the plot boiling. The problem is that one-dimensional characters do not give rise to songs that move like Oscar's one-act plays, nor do they allow for the subtext and resonance that Arthur Laurents had taught me to appreciate; they generate songs which, like the characters who sing them, deal with only one idea at a time and play with it. To use a graceful phrase of Burt's, such songs "savor the moment." This had been the function of songs in Roman comedy and remained so for the better part of two thousand years afterward. "Savoring the moment" describes most Broadway theater songs prior to *Oklahoma!* Cole Porter, Lorenz Hart, Ira Gershwin and their contemporaries (as well as their predecessors) wrote lyrics that presented one idea, toyed with rather than developed. "Let's Not Talk About Love" and "I Wish I Were in Love Again," two of the best examples, contain notions ripe for exploration that remain unplumbed because back then exploration was not the modus operandi of the musical stage. But it was the modus operandi I felt comfortable with and the lyrics of *Forum* remain the most difficult set I've ever had to write.

At the time, I complained incessantly to Burt that although I had loved many of the savor-the-moment songs in the old shows and had written my fair share for *Saturday Night, West Side Story* and *Gypsy,* trying to write an entire score of them was cramping my tutored style. I grumbled that *Forum* would be better off as a play than a musical—a suspicious echo of my similar suggestion to Arthur about *Gypsy.* Burt replied that if it were just a play, it would be relentlessly and unrelievedly funny and the audience, unable to recover between gasps of laughter, would soon become restless for a breathing space. The few of Plautus's plays which survive probably didn't last more than an hour, but even so, they included songs which served as necessary respites from the unremitting farcical push. I had to write one-joke songs, so I picked spots for them where the situations would supply substance: songs like "Impossible" and the drag version of "Lovely," which were dramatically static but theatrically funny. My mistake was that in trying to unlearn everything Oscar had taught me and write static songs which were nothing more than playful, I felt I had to justify them with cleverness, by juggling with words, leaning on rhymes, puns, alliteration and all the other boilerplate devices of light verse. I made the subtle, though thankfully not fatal, error of being witty instead of comic. Most of the score ended up as salon songs, lapidary and self-conscious, focusing attention on the songwriter rather than the characters. What I didn't appreciate properly was the robustness of the book Burt and Larry had written: low farce clothed in elegant language. I was deceived by the details of the dialogue, by aphoristic lines like "I meant yes, it just came out no" or comically

poetic phrases like "clump of myrrh," as in "Hide the girl behind that clump of myrrh." I appropriated their style without appreciating its substance.

Although I do think that the book of *Forum* is the tightest, most satisfyingly plotted and gracefully written farce I've ever encountered* (*pace* lovers of Molière and Feydeau), I don't think that farces can be transformed into musicals without damage—at least, not good musicals. The tighter the plotting the better the farce, but the better the farce the more the songs interrupt the flow and pace. Farces are express trains; musicals are locals. Savoring moments can be effective while a farce is gathering steam, but deadly once the train gets going. That's why the songs in *Forum* are bunched together in the first half of the first act, where there is more exposition than action, and then become scarcer and scarcer, until eventually in the last twenty minutes before the Finale there are no songs at all. Those twenty minutes comprise one long frenetic chase in which all the characters are on the run; for one of them to stop even an instant and sing a song would dampen the moment and kill the momentum. Farcical musicals such as *The Boys from Syracuse* and *Where's Charley?* have songs sprinkled throughout, but they don't attempt to maintain the tension of a true farce; they pause for diversions. Even though it's based on *Charley's Aunt,* one of the most durable farces in the English language, the intention of *Where's Charley?* is to be amiable and jolly, not tense and hysterical and threatening, which is what a serious farce should be. The stakes are lower in shows of that kind, shows that wear the trappings of farce but are actually traditional musical comedies with farcical moments. Farcical operas stand a better chance of maintaining the necessary tightness because the music is continuous, but is Puccini's *Gianni Schicchi* one tenth as funny as *Forum* or any play by Goldoni? Whatever the case, Jim Goldman was right, and even if I had realized all these things back then when he made his observation, I wouldn't have had time to do anything about it. As it was, I took a deep breath and just plunged ahead with the songs, but the sad fact is that the book and the score didn't go together, and they still don't.

Oddly enough, *Forum* fit into my *Allegro* legacy perfectly: in its own modest way, it was experimental. Dispensing with the visual and aural variety of Broadway musicals—singing and dancing choruses, scenic opulence, panoplies of costumes—*Forum* was a piece with

---

* And for good reason. Burt and Larry approached the piece with the utmost seriousness of intention. As Larry wrote in his aforementioned Introduction: "We would preserve the classic unities of time, place and action. We would have no anachronisms or sly references to today. We would use Plautus' characters, but we would have to invent a plot (the original plots are negligible) to accommodate all the characters we wanted to use."

a small cast, one set, and, except for a brief drag interlude, one costume per character. It was experimental in
another way as well: it was the birth of the theatrical
process that has come to be known as workshopping.

When Burt had first suggested the plays of Plautus as
the basis for a musical, I floated the notion to Jerome
Robbins, who I thought would be the ideal director, as
evidenced by the antic and poetic humor that made his
hilarious dances like *The Concert* and the Keystone Kops
ballet in *High Button Shoes* such airborne delights. We the
authors, along with Hal Prince, the producer, wanted
him desperately. Jerry accepted with enthusiasm, but he
was a slippery fellow, allergic to any kind of calendar
commitment. He hemmed and hawed and finally suggested that since he had a number of questions about
both the script and the unfinished score, it might be a
good idea to assemble a group of actors and have them
read through the show while I played and sang whatever
songs I had written.

This was a startling and seemingly needless idea at the
time. In the early 1960s the process of making a Broadway musical was usually, as it had always been, a simple
chronological one: first you wrote it, then a producer
decided to produce it, then it was cast, then it was rehearsed and then it was presented to the public in an out-
of-town tryout. In other words, no one tested it, no one
knew what the animal was until the first day of rehearsal
made it come alive. Nor was there any need to—after all,

conventional wisdom had it, there would be plenty of
time to fix the show during rehearsals and subsequently
in New Haven or Boston or Philadelphia or Washington
or any combination thereof. But there never really was.
The hours and days it took to write, rehearse, stage and
orchestrate new scenes and songs and then incorporate
them into the show were never sufficient, what with the
vagaries of union restrictions, the difficulties of putting in
and taking out new dialogue and numbers every few
days, along with other, unforeseen, problems. By the time
most of the shows in what is referred to as the Golden
Age of Musicals (ca. 1925–1960) opened in New York,
the first act of each was far better than the second because
there hadn't been time enough to fix the second. Producers and writers accepted this as a necessary evil, and
Jerry's notion of assembling a group of actors to read an
unfinished piece, especially ones who might not eventually be cast, would have struck them as a waste of time
and money. Nevertheless, to indulge him, Hal rented a
large room with a piano, and the actors and I fumbled
our way through the show to a small audience: Hal, Burt,
Larry, Jerry and a smattering of Hal's office staff.

The reading, of course, turned out to be a revelation.
Unadorned by scenery and costumes, unrehearsed, sung
(by me) with no refinement and only approximate pitch,
the show was stripped naked, plain for all of us to see at
both its best and worst, as well as the dangerous territory
in between. In the usual course of events, this would

never have been possible, even on the first day of rehearsal, for by then many of the adornments would have already been inflexibly in place: the cast would have been chosen, the sets and costumes in the process of being built, the orchestrators already at work. But in that large, empty room we could see the show for what it was; the scenes and songs that worked were greeted with enthusiastic guffaws (actors and authors are great audiences), the ones that didn't with pained glances, the in-between with tolerant smiles. So much that had to be rewritten or filled out or cut down was suddenly clear. And, best of all, it was still malleable. The rawness of this ad hoc reading, this unprotected headlong plunge into the unknown, and most of all the knowledge that there was time to fix things before going into rehearsal, gave us all a burst of energy and confidence that eventually made the show as good as it turned out to be. What we had effectively done was to save ourselves large amounts of time that would have been spent fixing the show in the customary rushed, exhausted late-night ambience of out-of-town hotel rooms.

The notion worked so well that years later, when Hal was getting ready to produce and direct *Company*, he and I decided to repeat the experience. Once George Furth, the book writer, had written a few scenes and I had written the first songs, we held readings of the script and score, no matter how unfinished, every couple of months or so, tracking the show as it grew and changed, until rehearsals began. It was not always with a cluster of professional actor-singers but sometimes with Hal alone reading all the dialogue while I sang and played, again just for ourselves and occasionally the design team, the casting director and Hal's office personnel. Each reading saved days, even weeks, which would have been used up during the tryout, questioning and solving and fixing, and never with enough time.

After *Company*, Hal and I repeated the process with *Follies* and *A Little Night Music*, as well as all our subsequent shows, and over time other producers and directors started to recognize its value. Before long, every gestating musical held readings, which unfortunately burgeoned into "workshops," rapidly progressing from the simplicity of actors sitting around a table with scripts they had barely had time to read and a composer singing solo at a piano to elaborately staged and choreographed semi-productions with skeletal sets and suggestions of costumes, complete with a small band and a large invited audience. What had begun as a learning experience for the authors became transmogrified into a thinly disguised backers' audition. Workshops today have turned into events with performances that are scheduled to run for as long as two weeks, not so that the authors can discover the weaknesses and strengths of their work but so that the producers can raise production money and start the highly desired (and overrated) anticipation known as "buzz." In truth, the workshop notion is most valuable only when it is used for the creators' education. Workshops with carefully chosen full-sized casts, staged to entertain deep-pocketed strangers, are virtually worthless, certainly nowhere near as instructive as a performance with one person reading and one person (or two, if it's a team) playing and singing through the show. I'm pained to say that I speak from experience.

As anyone with a penchant for irony might expect, Jerry Robbins, having inadvertently launched a major development in the history of preparing a Broadway musical, hemmed and hawed and eventually decided not to direct the show anyway. That chore was taken up by George Abbott, the grand master of Broadway comedy, musical and otherwise, but it was not the end of Jerry's flirtation with *Forum*. Thank God.

ACT ONE

Prologus, the deliverer of the Prologue, addresses the audience.

Comedy Tonight

PROLOGUS
Something familiar,
Something peculiar,
Something for everyone—a comedy tonight!
Something appealing,
Something appalling,
Something for everyone—a comedy tonight!

Nothing with kings,
Nothing with crowns,
Bring on the lovers, liars and clowns.

Old situations,
New complications,
Nothing portentous or polite.
Tragedy tomorrow,
Comedy tonight!

(The Proteans [three male performers who play numerous parts during the show] enter)

PROLOGUS
Something convulsive,
Something repulsive,
Something for everyone—a comedy tonight!

Something esthetic,

PROTEANS
Something frenetic,

PROLOGUS
Something for everyone—a comedy tonight!

PROTEANS
Nothing with gods,
Nothing with fate.

PROLOGUS
Weighty affairs will just have to wait.

PROTEANS
Nothing that's formal,

PROLOGUS
Nothing that's normal,

ALL
No recitations to recite!
Open up the curtain—
Comedy tonight!

PROLOGUS
Something erratic,
Something dramatic,
Something for everyone—a comedy tonight!

Frenzy and frolic,
Strictly symbolic,
Something for everyone—a comedy tonight!

(The entire Company enters)

ALL
Something familiar,
Something peculiar,
Something for everybody—comedy tonight!

Something that's gaudy,
Something that's bawdy,
Something for everybawdy—comedy tonight!

Nothing that's grim,
Nothing that's Greek,

PROLOGUS
(Referring to a tall, buxom young woman)
She plays Medea later this week.

ALL
Stunning surprises,
Cunning disguises,
Hundreds of actors out of sight!

(Variously)

Pantaloons and tunics,
Courtesans and eunuchs,
Funerals and chases,
Baritones and basses,
Panderers,
Philanderers,
Cupidity,
Timidity,
Mistakes,
Fakes,

Rhymes,
Mimes,
Tumblers,
Grumblers,
Fumblers,
Bumblers,

ALL
No royal curse,
No Trojan horse,
And a happy ending, of course!

Goodness and badness,
Man in his madness,
This time it all turns out all right—
Tragedy tomorrow,
Comedy tonight!

Oscar Hammerstein had emphasized to me repeatedly that opening numbers could make or break a musical. Their job, he said, was to introduce the story and perhaps the characters in an entertaining way and, more important, to lay down the ground rules for the audience, establishing a tone and telling them what kind of show to expect. He claimed once that if the opening number of a musical was the right one, the performers could read from a telephone directory for half an hour and the audience would still have a good time. He might have been referring to "Comedy Tonight,": like the telephone directory, the lyric is a list, albeit a shorter one and better rhymed. Moreover, interspersed among the verses were hilarious Shevelove-Gelbart gobbets of expository information delivered directly to the audience by Prologus and illustrated by the dancing Proteans. It was also one of the most brilliantly inventive and the most hilariously staged opening numbers in the history of musical comedy.

Tellingly, "Comedy Tonight" took a long while and a circuitous path to arrive at. The opening number I had originally written had, I thought, fulfilled Oscar's prescription: a blunt announcement of our intentions to present a low comedy but in mock-Classic language, relaxed enough to put an audience at their ease while still including a sting of irony at the end. This was it:

write
right
slight
bite
light
oversight
polite
delight it
everying
Nothing

Nothing

attend us, tremendous   begin
Give us attention   Lone
Masters, receive us   none
go, begone   spectate

We have decided on

Nothing that's woebegone

Nothing, that's ponderous   greetings
welcome

Smoky disguises   Playgoers,

sudden surprises   Herewith presenting

something for everybody, a   Pleased to announce to you

Comedy tonight.   Bring on
Here come the clowns

Nothing with
No wails of sorrow
Sorrow
That's for tomorrow   liars, lovers & clowns
We have decided on   Bring on the (hero, villain) (players) (clowns, etc.)!
We have prepared for you   Play the play.   Playgoers, smile with us
We are about
we have come out to do   chorus   a while with us
We have resolved to do
We're here to offer you   Greeks did before us

Virgins and lechers   Old situations |Nothing momentous

Tragedy next Monday   Corpses on stretchers   New complications |Nothing portentous

Comedy tonight   Servants and masters, plagues & disasters

Lepers and pirates   Constant commotions
Famine and fire   Trances
All you desire, It's   Curses & potions
Passions
Trances & lovers, Frauds & deceivers

What plots we borrow   Grecians and Persians   Incest and laughter
Go back to them   Dancing
Will you back to the   Naked diversions   Arson thereafter

Greeks   misery
Man in his madness   faces

Who good enough for th Funerals and fires   embraces

Greek   Lechers and liars   chases

Tragedy next week   away with passions
off with princes take out the
away   taunts & crowns
Take out the kings,   go & clowns
Pillars & arches   Care &   hand us downs
Throne

Hornpipes & marches   Bring on the liars, the lovers & clowns

deus ex machina

What plots we borrow, deal not with sorrow
only with foolish delight
Nothing symbolic   Nothing of sorrow, what plots we borrow

spectators   Deal with surprise
Playgoers, welcome,   Tragedy tomorrow
Gentlemen and ladies,   delight

A comedy tonight!

tender   angelic   enraptured
alluring   adorning   impassioned
attractive

④ Brian   Passions and fevers   Young men eloping
   & ??   ~~Fakers,~~   Old men still hoping
             ~~Frauds~~ and Deceivers

   Presly   Something romantic   True love in trouble
                                                      Fakers

            Portents
⑤ — Ruth: Statues   ~~Potions~~ and erotic   Something with frolic
             ~~Potions~~ and potions,   3:   clearly   for frolic
            Constant commotions   )   ~~Nothing symbolic~~
              Violent emotions   )   patrician
                 devotion

                                             Ghosts
                                             Soothsayers
⑥ Jack: Servants and masters,   white gowns   town
             Plagues and disasters,   night gowns   boars

                                             parchments with writing

                                             Fits of hysterics clerics

⑦ Ruth
Barley & Girls: Nothing ~~with~~ fate that's grim
                  Nothing that's Greek
                  see us in
                  We're doing Clytemnestra next week.   Oedipus Rex will start in a week.
                                                        comic techniques
                  Something exotic,
                  Something erotic,

                  night tomorrow
                  Sophocles on Monday, Plautus tonight!
⑧ Davy: Virgins and eunuchs   ]
             togas and   ]
             ~~All wearing~~ tunics   ]   perversion
             Grecians and Persians   excursion
             Davy   aspersions
             ~~Making~~ diversions
             ──
             Oedipus tomorrow
             A Funny Home tonight,

Invocation (cut)

PROLOGUS, COMPANY
(Looking heavenward)

Gods of the theater, smile on us.
You who sit up there stern in judg-
    ment, smile on us.
You who look down on actors (and
    who doesn't?),
Bless our little company and smile
    on us.
Think not about deep concerns,
Think not about dark dilemmas.
We offer you rites and revels,
Smile on us for a while.

(Looking out to the audience)

Gods of the theater, smile on us.
You who sit out there stern in judg-
    ment, smile on us.
Think not about deep concerns,
Think not about dark dilemmas.
We offer you rites and revels,
Bless our play and smile.

Forget war, forget woe,
Forget matters weighty and great.
Allow matters weighty to wait
For a while.
For this moment, this brief time,
Frown on reason, smile on rhyme.

Forget pomp, forget show,
Forget laurels, helmets and crowns.
Receive lovers, liars and clowns
For a while.
For this moment, this brief span,
Celebrate the state of man.

Forget war, forget woe,
Forget greed and vengeance and sin,
And let mime and mockery in
For a while.

Gods of the theater, smile on us.
Gods of the theater, bless our efforts,
    smile on us.
We offer you rites and revels,
Grace and beauty,
Joy and laughter,
Sly disguises,
Wild confusions,
Happy endings.

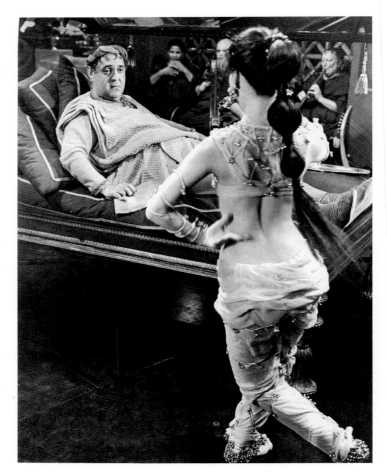

Zero Mostel as Pseudolus in the movie (1966)

If we please you, bless our play,
Smile our way.
Smile this moment, then at length
Go, and with a new-found strength:

Resume war, resume woe,
Resume matters weighty and great.
Resume man's impossible state,
But now smile.

For this moment,
This brief stay,
Bless these players,
Bless this play!

I thought that this song combined everything, and so did George Abbott, our director. He had only one objection: the music. He found it "not hummable enough" to draw the audience in. I must admit that the music was Hollywood-barbaric, a hybrid of ancient modalities and Broadway pizzazz, and probably sounded a bit harsh to him, but it was by no means startlingly dissonant. Nevertheless, Mr. Abbott, as he was deferentially known, was a Broadway legend, famous not only as a writer-director but also as a "play doctor," the miracle worker who lays his hands on an out-of-town show in trouble and transforms it from an embarrassing failure into a scintillating hit. I was a neophyte composer, eager to cooperate and learn from a legendary master who was a hero of my hero Jerry Robbins and, in his own field Jerry's equal, at least by reputation. So I wrote a song hummable enough, I hoped, to appeal to both him and the audience:

Love Is in the Air (cut)

PROLOGUS, PROTEANS

Love is in the air,
Quite clearly.
People everywhere
Act queerly.
Some are hasty, some are halting,
Some are simply somersaulting.
Love is going around.

Anyone exposed
Can catch it.
Keep your window closed
And latch it.
Leave your house and lose your
 reason,
This is the contagious season.
Love is going around.

It's spreading each minute
Throughout the whole vicinit-
Y. Step out and you're in it.
With all the fun involved,
Who can stay uninvolved?

Love is in the air
This morning.
Bachelors beware,
Fair warning!
If you start to feel a tingle
And you like remaining single,
Stay home, don't take a breath;
You could catch your death,
'Cause love is around.

"Love Is in the Air" was deemed hummable enough and we opened with it in New Haven, where the show was received with scathing reviews from the critics and indifference from the audiences. We couldn't understand why; every night Burt, Larry, George, Hal and I would huddle in the back of the house, baffled at the long silences punctuated by mild and tiny spurts of laughter which greeted what we thought were screamingly funny scenes and lines. Even George Abbott, the theater's most accomplished play doctor, murmured, "I don't know—I guess we'll have to call in George Abbott."

We didn't call in George Abbott, but in Washington, in our final week before coming to New York, at my suggestion and with George's approval, we did call in Jerry, or rather recalled him. He was an obvious and appropriate choice: we knew that he liked the material and that he worshipped George, and we figured that his guilty conscience for having scuttled the project in the first place would make it difficult for him to refuse. He agreed to come, and his first piece of advice was to change the opening number. It was indeed hummable, he said, and breezy and charming and welcoming and the audience enjoyed it, and it killed everything that followed. It misled them into expecting a light, not a low, comedy, something gracefully filigreed rather than elegantly vulgar. It was Oscar's lesson all over again: Tell the audience what the show is about— in this instance not breezy and charming, but blatant and straightforward. I muttered with barely concealed exasperation that that was precisely what I *had* written the first time around, but George had rejected it. To which Jerry replied, with no attempt to conceal *his* exasperation, that I should stop complaining and get busy writing another song which accomplished the same thing, but one that George could hum. He added, with his customary contentiousness, "Don't write any jokes, Steve. Let me do the jokes." And with his uproarious and inventive staging,* that's exactly what he did. The result, "Comedy Tonight," which I wrote over the weekend, changed what had been a catastrophe in New Haven and Washington into a three-year hit on Broadway. Oscar hadn't been exaggerating. I had always put his notion of "make or break" with the opening number down to instructional exaggeration. The out-of-town tryout of *Forum* showed me how wrong I was.

---

* Jerry not only staged "Comedy Tonight" but the Act Two Chase, as well as enough other significant bits and pieces to transform the show from a sparkling show on paper into a sparkling show onstage.

Pseudolus is the personal slave of Hero, a young man who has fallen in love at first sight with a courtesan in the house next door, owned and operated by Marcus Lycus, a procurer. Hero's patrician parents, Senex and Domina, are leaving for the country. Domina, an overbearing wife to her husband and overprotective mother to her son, bids farewell to Hero and to the household slave, Hysterium.

Farewell† (cut)

DOMINA

Farewell, beloved son.
Farewell, devoted slave.
Farewell, ancestral home.
Farewell, my Rome.

Farewell, you temples and basilicae,
More rich than Athens or Pompeii.
Though country life be more idyllic, I
Could never long stay away-ee.‡

Farewell, responsive son.
Farewell, respectful slave.
Farewell, resplendent Rome.
Farewell, my home.
Farewell.

Farewell, inestimable domicile.
Farewell, domestic work of art.
Although I journey far, I promise I'll
Keep every portico,
Every pediment,
Every plinth in my heart—
I start.

*(She leaves reluctantly, only to reappear
a moment later at the other side
of the stage)*

---

† This song was written for the 1971 production in Los Angeles for Nancy Walker, whom we wanted desperately to play Domina and who wanted desperately to have another solo in addition to her Act Two number, "That Dirty Old Man."
‡ Not content to let this pronunciation joke die with limited-engagement Los Angeles audiences, I used a variation of it many years later in *Road Show*.

Farewell, angelic son.
Farewell, efficient slave.
Farewell, exquisite Rome.
Farewell, my home.
Farewell!

Could anyone conceive a view
More beautiful than this and these?
One look before I take my leave
   of you:

(To Hysterium)

So scrub my atrium, leave it stainless.
Wash my architrave when it's rainless,
Keep my progeny chaste and brain-
   less.
Please, no tears,
My frieze, my dears . . .

Farewell, beloved son.
Farewell, devoted slave.
Farewell, ancestral home.
Farewell, my Rome,
Farewell.

(She leaves again and reappears almost
   immediately)

DOMINA

Farewell!

Left alone onstage, Hero takes the audience into his confidence.

Love, I Hear

HERO

Now that we're alone,
May I tell you
I've been feeling very strange?
Either something's in the air
Or else a change
Is happening in me.

I think I know the cause.
I hope I know the cause.
From everything I've heard,
There's only one cause it can be . . .

Love, I hear,
Makes you sigh a lot.
Also, love, I hear,
Leaves you weak.

Love, I hear,
Makes you blush
And turns you ashen.
You try to speak with passion
And squeak—

(Which he does)

I hear.

Love, they say,
Makes you pine away,
But you pine away
With an idiotic grin.

I pine, I blush, I squeak, I squawk.
Today I woke too weak to walk.*
What's love, I hear,
I feel—I fear—
I'm in.

(Sighs)

See what I mean?
Da-da-da-da-da-da-da . . .
(I hum a lot too.)

I'm dazed, I'm pale, I'm sick, I'm sore,
I've never felt so well before!
What's love, I hear,
I feel, I fear,
I know I am—I'm sure—I mean—
I hope—I trust—
I pray I must
Be in!

Forgive me if I shout.
Forgive me if I crow.
I've only just found out
And, well, I thought you ought to
   know.

**This song had originally been planned
for Hero to sing to Philia, the courtesan
of his affections, as she stood on her bal-**

---

* Opportunities to use alliteration, where the
initial consonants of each word are alike,
simultaneously with consonance, where the
final consonants are alike, are rare, which is
what makes them effective. My first version of
this line was "I woke too weak to walk to
work," which I thought was pretty dazzling,
until Burt pointed out that the sons of patri-
cians in ancient Rome didn't work.

---

cony, but we decided that direct address
to the audience would be fresher. And it
was. Here, though, is the first attempt:

The Window Across the Way (cut)

There are stars every night through
   my window,
But I stare at the window across
   the way.
There are stars coming right through
   my window,
But there's you in the window across
   the way.

I'm aware
Of the moon,
But I never see it,
And my prayer
Is that soon
Some day

I'll be there, close to you,
Staring out at a lovely view
Of a newly deserted window
Across the way.

*Pseudolus, a wily conniver, suggests to
Hero that he, Pseudolus, will spirit Philia
away from the House of Lycus and into
Hero's arms if Hero will grant him his
freedom. Hero agrees.*

Free

PSEUDOLUS

Oh, what a word!
Oh, what a word!
   Say it again.

HERO

Free.

PSEUDOLUS

I've often thought,
I've often dreamed
How it would be . . .
And yet I never thought I'd be . . .
   Once more.

HERO

Free!

PSEUDOLUS

But when you come to think of such
    things—
A man should have the rights that all
    others—
Can you imagine what it will be like
    when I am—?
Can you see me!

Can you see me as a Roman with my
    head unbowed?
Sing it good and loud—

HERO

Free!

PSEUDOLUS

Like a Roman, having rights, and like
    a Roman, proud!
Can you see me?

HERO

I can see you!

PSEUDOLUS

Can you see me as a voter fighting
    graft and vice?
Sing it soft and nice—

HERO

Free.

PSEUDOLUS

Why, I'll be so conscientious that I
    may vote twice!
Can you see me? Can you see me?

When I'm free to be whatever I want
    to be,
Think what wonders I'll accomplish
    then!
When the master that I serve is me
    and just me,
Can you see me being equal with my
    countrymen?
Can you see me being Pseudolus the
    citizen?
Can you see me being—give it to me
    once again—!

HERO

Free!

PSEUDOLUS

That's it!

HERO

Free!

PSEUDOLUS

Yes!

HERO

Fr—

PSEUDOLUS

(Clapping his hand over Hero's mouth)

Now, not so fast, I didn't think . . .
The way I am, I have a roof, three
    meals a day,
And I don't have to pay a thing.

I'm just a slave and everything's free.
If I were free, then nothing would be
    free.
And if I'm beaten now and then,
What does it matter?

HERO

(Whispers seductively)

Free . . .

PSEUDOLUS

(Galvanized)

Can you see me?

Can you see me as a poet writing
    poetry?
All my verse will be—

HERO

Free!

PSEUDOLUS

A museum will have me pickled for
    posterity!
Can you see me?

HERO

I can see you!

PSEUDOLUS

Can you see me as a lover, one of
    great renown,
Women falling down?

HERO

Free?

PSEUDOLUS

No, but I'll buy the House of Lycus
    for my house in town!
Can you see me? Can't you see me?

Be you anything from king to baker of
    cakes,
You're a vegetable unless you're free!
It's a little word but oh, the difference
    it makes:

It's the necessary essence of
    democracy,
It's the thing that every slave should
    have the right to be,
And I soon will have the right to buy
    a slave for me!
Can you see him?
Well, I'll free him!

When a Pseudolus can move, the
    universe shakes,
But I'll never move until I'm free!
Such a little word but oh, the differ-
    ence it makes:

I'll be Pseudolus the founder of a
    family,
I'll be Pseudolus the pillar of society,
I'll be Pseudolus the man if I can
    only be—

HERO

Free!

PSEUDOLUS

Sing it!

HERO

Free!

PSEUDOLUS

Spell it!

HERO

F-R-double—

PSEUDOLUS

No, the long way!

HERO

F! R! E! E!

BOTH

Free!!!

When *Forum* was to be made into a movie in 1966, I thought it would be fun to write a more pointed version of the song, one which focused on the limitlessness of Pseudolus's imagination and ambitions, and one which would take advantage of the camera's ability to switch locations quickly.

Free (cut from film version)

PSEUDOLUS
Oh, what a word!
Oh, what a word!

Say it again.

HERO
Free.

PSEUDOLUS
I've often thought,
I've often dreamed
How it would be . . .
And yet I never thought I'd be . . .

Once more.

HERO
Free!

PSEUDOLUS
Imagine all the things I might do,
A man of my ambition and talents.
There isn't any limit, master, once you free me!
Can you see me?!

(First Fantasy: Pseudolus with "FREE" monogrammed on his toga, the camera pulling back to reveal it also monogrammed on dinnerware, towels, chairs, the whole room, while Pseudolus and Hero are heard as voice-overs)

PSEUDOLUS (V.O.)
Can you see me as a gentleman of property,
When I get to be—

HERO (V.O.)
Free!

PSEUDOLUS
I'll have monograms on everything the eye can see!

HERO
I can see you!

PSEUDOLUS
Can you see me?!

(Second Fantasy: Pseudolus swanning around at the baths)

Can you see me at the baths with the aristocrats
Every moment that's—

HERO
Free!

PSEUDOLUS
Sweating freely with philosophers and diplomats—
Can you see me?

HERO
No, it's steamy.

(Back in reality)

PSEUDOLUS
Can you see me as a man of culture and taste,
Owning every work of art in sight?
So aesthetic that there's not a moment to waste:

(Third Fantasy: Pseudolus in his study; Pseudolus fondling a sculpture; Pseudolus listening to a salon concert of beautiful women plucking lyres; Pseudolus exchanging Socratic dialogues with scholars; Pseudolus painfully scratching the word "Free" on a tablet)

PSEUDOLUS (V.O.)
At my house I'll have a concert going day and night,
Intellectual discussions till the early light.
While I'm at it, I may even learn to read and write
When I'm—

HERO (V.O.)
Free!

PSEUDOLUS (V.O.)
That's it!

(Back in reality)

HERO
Free!

PSEUDOLUS
Yes!

HERO
Fr—

PSEUDOLUS
(Clapping his hand over Hero's mouth)

Now, not so fast, I didn't think . . .
The way I am, I have a roof, three meals a day,
And I don't have to pay a thing.

I'm just a slave and everything's free.
If I were free, then nothing would be free.
And if I'm beaten now and then,
What does it matter?

HERO
(Whispers seductively)
Free . . .

PSEUDOLUS
(Galvanized)
Can you see me?!

(Fourth Fantasy: Pseudolus reading his poems aloud in the Forum; Pseudolus directing one of his plays in an amphitheater; a statue of Pseudolus on the outside of the Colosseum)

PSEUDOLUS (V.O.)
Can you see me as the author of a trilogy?
All my verse will be—

HERO (V.O.)
Free!

PSEUDOLUS (V.O.)
They'll be carving me in marble for posterity!
Can you see me?

HERO (V.O.)
I can see you!

(*Fifth Fantasy: Pseudolus delivering an oration and getting a wild ovation in the Senate*)

PSEUDOLUS (V.O.)
Can you see me at the Senate intro-
    ducing laws
For my favorite cause:

HERO (V.O.)
Free!

PSEUDOLUS (V.O.)
Getting thunderous applause for
    every minor clause!
Can you see me?
It's so dreamy!

(*Back in reality*)

PSEUDOLUS
When a Pseudolus can move, the
    Universe shakes,
And the time for it to shake is here!

Such a little word but oh, the
    difference it makes:

(*Sixth Fantasy: Pseudolus being crowned as Emperor; Pseudolus on a palace balcony, surrounded by his ministers, waving to thousands of citizens gathered below*)

PSEUDOLUS (V.O.)
I will probably be Emperor within the
    year,
The inevitable climax of a great
    career.
As my citizens surround me, I can
    hear them cheer:

(*The ministers—conspirators all—stab him to death as the citizens below raise their fists and scream.*)

CITIZENS, CONSPIRATORS
FREE!!!

PSEUDOLUS
(*Dying*)
Sing it!

CITIZENS, CONSPIRATORS
FREE!

(*Back in reality*)

PSEUDOLUS
(*Still "dying"*)
Spell it!

HERO
F-R-double—

PSEUDOLUS
No, the long way . . .

HERO
F-R-E-E-

(*Pseudolus is revivified*)

BOTH
Freeeeeeeeee!

This was my first opportunity to design a song directly for the screen, and I grabbed at it with both hands. I had

"Funeral Sequence"

been a movie buff all my life and had made a number of home movies, reveling in the editing process. Richard Lester, the director of the *Forum* movie, had already demonstrated his virtuoso editing skills in his Beatles film *A Hard Day's Night* and assured me that what I had done would work perfectly, but he never shot the sequence, although in the finished print there's a curiously clumsy cut at the place where I'd cued the song, which makes me think that it was at least planned. Rereading it now, I wish he had. I didn't get the chance to design another for twenty-five years, when I wrote two sequences for the movie of *A Little Night Music*, one of which was filmed the way I wrote it, one of which was not.

Pseudolus persuades Marcus Lycus that he has come into a large sum of money, has bought his freedom and is in the market for, as he puts it, "a lifetime companion." Lycus is happy to present his wares, one by one, as Pseudolus and Hero look for Philia, in vain.

The House of Marcus Lycus (cut)

LYCUS
There is merchandise for every need
At the house of Marcus Lycus.
All the merchandise is guaranteed
At the house of Marcus Lycus.
For a sense of sensuality
Or an opulence thereof,
Patronize the house of Marcus Lycus,
Merchant of love.

Behold . . . Tintinabula. Out of the East, with a face like an idol . . . the arms of a willow tree . . . and the pelvis of a camel.

Hot-blooded, cool-headed, warm-hearted, sly,
Light-footed, dark-featured, dim-witted, shy.
Only recently arrived from Greece,
Likes her love experimental.

Every inch of her a masterpiece—
High standards, low rental . . .

(Tintinabula dances; Pseudolus rejects her)

May I present Panacea. To make her available to you, I outbid the King of Nubia. Panacea, with a face that holds a thousand promises, and a body that stands behind each promise.

Uncanny, unnerving, unblemished, untaught,
Unstinting, unswerving, unselfish, unbought.
Here's potential that is still untapped,
Here are fires still unstarted.
Here are raptures that are still unwrapped,
Whole sections uncharted . . .

There's potential that is still untapped
At the House of Marcus Lycus.
There are raptures that are still unwrapped
At the House of Marcus Lycus,
'Neath the cherry-blossom and the quince
And the cooing of the dove,
At the House of Marcus Lycus,
Prince of Love.

(Panacea dances; Pseudolus rejects her)

Then may I present Gymnasia. A giant stage on which a thousand dramas can be played.

Expansive, explosive, exquisite and excruciating,
Exceeding exciting, exhausting but exhilarating.
Wait until the day she's fully grown,
She'll be useful on safari.
You could purchase her for shade alone
And never be sorry . . .

(Gymnasia dances; Pseudolus rejects her)

Then consider the Geminae. A matched pair. Either one a divinely assembled woman, together an infinite number of mathematical possibilities.

A banquet, a bargain, laid end to end.
A lifetime's provisions—invite a friend.
Feast until you're fully satisfied,
Gorge on gorgeousness compounded.
Face the future side by side by side,
Completely surrounded . . .

(The Geminae—twins—dance; Pseudolus rejects them)

You may feast until you're satisfied
At the House of Marcus Lycus.
Face the future side by side by side
At the House of Marcus Lycus.

COURTESANS
For a sense of sensuality
And a plethora thereof:

LYCUS
One is ecstasy,
One is mystery,
One is six foot three,
Two is company—

LYCUS, COURTESANS
At the House of Marcus Lycus,
Merchant of Love!

We all liked this lyric, but the consensus was that the moment would be better served by a series of dances. All that remained of it finally was the first eight lines.

Philia, a virgin, has been sold to a Captain of the Army, who is shortly arriving to claim her, but Pseudolus manages a ruse to bring her and Hero together for a brief while, while he goes off to the harbor to hire a boat that will take them away before the Captain arrives. Left alone with Hero, Philia admits to being uneducated. She has been taught "beauty and grace and nothing more."

Lovely

PHILIA

I'm lovely,
All I am is lovely,
Lovely is the one thing I can do.

Winsome,
What I am is winsome,
Radiant as in some
Dream come true.

Oh, isn't it a shame?
I can neither sew, nor cook,
Nor read or write my name.

But I'm happy,
Merely being lovely,
For it's one thing I can give to you.

HERO

You're lovely,
Absolutely lovely,
Who'd believe the loveliness of you?

Winsome,
Sweet and warm and winsome,
Radiant as in some
Dream come true.

PHILIA

True.

HERO

Now Venus would seem tame.
Helen and her thousand ships
Would have to die of shame.

BOTH

And I'm happy,
Happy that I'm (you're) lovely,
For there's one thing loveliness
   can do:
It's a gift for me to share with you.

**In the first version of the script, an-
other song in this spot emphasized
Hero's bashfulness and Philia's air-
headedness at greater length.**

Your Eyes Are Blue
(cut)

HERO

Once upon a time,
It happened there lived a boy
Who loved a girl . . .
Your eyes are blue . . .

And every single night
He'd see her across the way.
I'd want to say—
He'd want to say,
"Your eyes are blue
And I love you!"

But never had they spoken,
Never had he dared.
Beautiful as she was,
I was—*he* was
Scared.

Then suddenly one day
He met her, and he could see
Her eyes were blue
As they could be.
What did he do?
Well . . .
You tell me.

(Encouraging her)

Once upon a time—

PHILIA

Let *me* try:
"There lived a boy . . ."

HERO
(Coaching her)
"Who loved a girl . . ."

PHILIA

"Whose eyes were—

(Thinking hard)

Blue!"

And every single night
She'd see him across the way.
She hoped he'd say,
"Your eyes are blue
And I love you!"
And yet she knew

There was a wall between them,
Built around his heart.
This was their dilemma,
Keeping them a-
Part,
When suddenly one day
She met him.
He looked so tall.

HERO

He felt so small.

PHILIA

What did he do
To break the wall?

HERO
(Simultaneously)
What could he do
To break the wall?

(They kiss)

BOTH

And that was all.

*Hysterium, outraged at Pseudolus's
maneuverings, threatens to go to the
country and tell Hero's parents of the
elopement. Pseudolus cautions him to
think it over.*

I Do Like You (cut)

PSEUDOLUS	HYSTERIUM
Friend,	Oh, today it's
Good	"Friend" . . .
Friend and true,	Yes,
I worship	It's always
You.	"Friend"
	When you need a
	Friend.
I want to do,	
Want to be	
Like my	
Friend.	"Friend, friend,
	friend,
Do	Friend, friend . . ."
What you must.	That's
I'm	What I in-
Happy just	Tend.
Being	Well, goodbye, old
A copy of the one	Friend . . .
I Trust.	

PSEUDOLUS

I like to do like you like to do,
'Cause I like you.
You do a deed,
I follow your lead,
'Cause I like you.

You climb a tree,
I climb with you.
You give a smile,
I smile.
You take a journey,
I'm with you!
Whatever you'll do,
I'll.

No one is perfect,
You have your flaws,
But I don't care.
I have the flaws
That you have because
I want to share.

You're all the things
I most admire,
All I aspire
To.
I do like you
Because I do like you.

PSEUDOLUS	HYSTERIUM
	Friend,
And the best you	You've touched me
Have.	So.
Yes,	I didn't
I thought I	Know
Would.	Such deep
No, you never	devotion
Do.	Existed, and
	Friend,
Deeper than you	I'd rather
Think.	Die
You don't have to	Than say good-
Die.	Bye.
I know how you	Friend, just as
Feel.	Soon as I get back,
	I'll cry.

*(Hysterium starts off; Pseudolus holds
him back)*

PSEUDOLUS

I like to do like you like to do,
That's how I feel.
You ruin me, and I ruin you,
You're my ideal.

We each have had a fling or two
Nobody knows but we.
You tell a little thing or two,
I tell a thing or three.

You keep a secret, I keep a secret,
Like I should.
You tell a secret, I tell a secret
Twice as good.

Since you're the model I take after,
That's what I'd have to
Do.
I have to do like you like,
Only because I do like
You.

(Hysterium gives up)

Reciprocation in the end
Is why a friend
Is true.

How could I ever doubt you,
Knowing so much about you?
I do like you,
And still I do like you.

"I Do Like You" never got past the
early rehearsal stage, for reasons too
dimly buried to remember.

*Philia, a maddeningly moral girl, is reluc-
tant to leave and break her vow to marry
the Captain, even though she loves Hero.
Pseudolus tries to persuade her through
sheer salesmanship.*

Pretty Little Picture

PSEUDOLUS

In the Tiber there sits a boat,
Gently dipping its bow,
Trim and tidy and built to float.
Pretty little picture?
Now,

Put a boy on the starboard side,
Leaning out at the rail.
Next to him put a blushing bride,

Slim and slender and starry-eyed.
Down below put a tiny bed.

The sun gets pale,
The sea gets red,
And off they sail
On the first high tide,
The boat and the bed
And the boy and the bride!

It's a pretty little picture,
Oh, my!
Pretty little picture,
How true!
Pretty little picture,
Which I,
Pseudolittleus, give to you!

Feel the roll of the playful waves,
See the sails as they swell.
Hear the whips on the galley slaves—
Pretty little picture?
Well,

Let it carry your cares away,
Out of sight, out of mind,
Past the buoy and through the bay—
Soon there's nothing but sea and
     spray.
Night descends and the moon's aglow.
Your arms entwined,
You steal below,
And far behind
At the edge of day,
The bong of the bell of the buoy in
     the bay,
And the boat and the boy
And the bride are away!

It's a pretty little picture to share,
As the little boat sails to sea.
Take a little trip free as air,
Have a little freedom on me!

HERO, PHILIA

No worries,
No bothers,
No captains,
No fathers!

PSEUDOLUS

In the ocean an island waits,
Smooth and sandy and pink.
Filled with lemons and nuts and
     dates.
Pretty little picture?
Think:

Pretty Little Picture

(Pseudolus, Hero, Philia)

CHAPPELL PROF.

pristine   In the ocean an island waits   verdant & peopleless lush   spices
                   Smooth & sandy & pink   ginger
undiscovered - unknown   All bananas & nuts & dates   lemons
populated by birds alone   Filled w/

                           virgin   I love virgins
         In the sea sits a ~~island~~ isle   Virgin isle
         Smooth & sandy & pink   and
                                       Oh, I love pink
         ~~Costy you nothing to live in style~~
         ~~~~~~

         Pretty little picture → Think —
              but cottage   cypress
     A   In a house made of mango trees   Every morning a gentle breeze
ore   B   Seashells ~~dotting~~ over the door   Tiptoes up to the door
     A   Boy and bride live a life of ease   Then the lovers can live w/ ease
     A   Boy & bride can play
        Doing nothing but what they please
        ~~Every~~ ~~time it~~ ~~~~ and every night when
ear   C   ~~Night descends and~~ the stars appear

     B C

     B-i   The sun gets low and the moon gets high

        As they sink in the sand, not a soul do they spy
        Not a sight but
        ~~the sand and~~ the sea and the stars and the sky

        And the sound of a soft little satisfied sigh

        In a cottage of cypress trees   Made of cypress trees
        Seashells ~~dotting~~ over the door   Seashells dot the door

        Boy & bride live a life of ease   Live a life of ease
        Doing nothing but what they please   Do whatever we please

        There surrounded by cypress trees
        While

        There's nothing more to see or hear
        ~~But~~ just the shore where the lovers lie
salt   The sand and the sea and the stars and the sky
        And the sound of a soft little satisfied sigh

twain

surf   sand

whips   asleep   sound of the   sea
wind   assort   sleep   dia   stars
waves   assault   swan
under weigh   assure   sled in the sky   sails   swain
               assumes   sound of a sigh   slaves
               astir   sun in the sky   lights   ship (shape)
               astray   sky   sex   slip
In the little bed fast asleep   spry   sun   shore
                                       slip   sky
                                               soft
                           sout there to spy smile   start
Through the little porthole you peep   style   stir
                                              slow
                                              sup
                                      share   sip   occurred
                                      shore   sign   spanned
                                      shy   son   stand
                                      she   salt   strand
                                      sure   say   speck
                                                       spot
                                                       spit
                    the sun goes down   spat
                                               spill
And Far behind at the edge of day   spoil   space
The bong of the bell of the buoy in the bay   sport   speak
But   spread spark
And the bed and the boy & the bride are away   spurt   speed
                                                       spill
                                                       spend
                                                       spice
                                        Past
                                        Pass the harbor, lights, busy
Set your [sail] course toward the setting sun   seven hills, bread

every night
                              come on
                              appear
             the stars   stole out
But down below not a word's said
Down below full speed ahead
For the boat and the boy & the bride and the bed

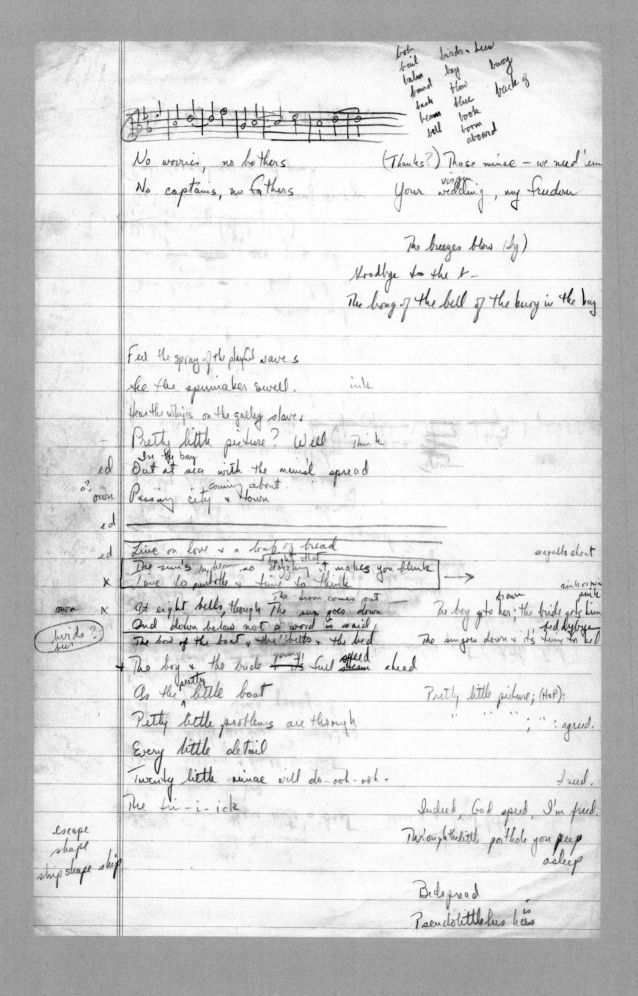

bob   birds a-bow
bail   bay   buoy
balm
board   blow
bask   blue   back of
beam   book
bell   boom
           aboard

No worries, no bothers   (Thanks?) Those minae — we need 'em

No captains, no fathers   Your wedding, my freedom
                                      virgin

                                 The breezes blow (by)

                              Goodbye to the ×—

                              The bong of the bell of the buoy in the bay

Feel the spray of the playful waves

See the spinnaker swell.   ink

Hear the whips on the galley slaves

Pretty little picture? Well think —

ed   Out at sea with the mainsal spread
          In the bay
own   Passing city × town
              coming about

ed

ed   Live on love & a loaf of bread   seagulls shout

×   The sun's daydream so dazzling it makes you blink →

×   Time to ... & time to think

own × At eight bells, though The sun goes down   The boy gets her; the bride gets him
                       The moon comes out
      And down below not a word is said,   The singers down & it's time to bed
                                                         feddybye
      The bow of the boat & the butts & the bed

+   The boy & the bride it's full speed ahead

      As the pretty little boat   Pretty little picture; (H&P):

      Pretty little problems are through   " " " ; " " ; agreed.

      Every little detail

      Twenty little minae will do-ooh-ooh.   Agreed.

      The tri-i-ick   Indeed, God speed, I'm freed.

escape   Through the little porthole you peep
shape   asleep
strip shape ship

                              Bedspread

                              Pseudolittlehis his

PSEUDOLUS (cont'd)
In a cottage of cypress trees,
Seashells dotting the door,
Boy and bride live a life of ease,
Doing nothing but what they please.
Every night when the stars appear,
There's nothing more
To see or hear,
There's just the shore
Where the lovers lie,
The sand and the sea and the stars
 and the sky,
And the sound of a soft little satisfied
 sigh . . .

ALL
All your (our) petty little problems
 will cease,
And your (our) little blessings will
 flow.
And your (our) little family increase.
Pretty little picture?

PSEUDOLUS
No, no!
Pretty little masterpiece!

ALL
Pretty little picture!

The actor we had always had in mind for Pseudolus was Phil Silvers, a comedian who had built his persona as a fast-talking conniver, a standard figure in comedy from Scapino to Harold Hill to Sergeant Bilko, the television character that made Silvers famous. All of them were direct descendants of Plautus's invention. I wrote "Pretty Little Picture" to take advantage of Silvers's fast-talking, mercurial quality, polishing the lyric on and off over a period of two years to make it trip off the tongue as lightly as possible. I wanted it to be brilliant, in the true meaning of the word: not merely glittering, but dazzling. I wanted it to reflect not only Pseudolus's verbal nimbleness, but my own. Maybe because of the years of earnestness spent in writing the lyrics for *West Side Story* and *Gypsy*, I wanted it above all

to be playful, in the spirit of Cole Porter and E. Y. Harburg.

In converting audiences to be drawn in by substance rather than style, Hammerstein effectively anesthetized their delight in lyrics for lyrics' sake. Where once the anticipation of hearing scintillating, clever songs had been a prime reason to go to a Broadway musical, it was now the prospect of hearing an interesting story featuring compelling characters. Scintillating, clever songs would just get in the way, even if sung by scintillating, clever characters—they would hold up the action. Much as I was an acolyte of Oscar's, he was never a pyrotechnic lyricist, and I was a fan of the best of that breed: Porter and Harburg especially, but also Irving Berlin and Howard Dietz, and to a lesser extent Ira Gershwin and Lorenz Hart. There were many others, of course, but those were the ones whose work commanded the field. And *Forum* seemed like the perfect chance to practice

---

E. Y. HARBURG
Word Drunk

Harburg, Porter and Berlin were the most brilliant technicians of the Golden Age, Berlin the modest one, painstakingly concealing his technique, Porter the more ostentatious, showing it off with all his pyrotechnic sparkle. Harburg was the maverick, pointedly socio-political and heavily whimsical. He leaned toward social protest ("Brother, Can You Spare a Dime?," "When the Idle Poor Become the Idle Rich") and was often preoccupied with linguistic playfulness that at its best was charming and inventive ("When I'm Not Near the Girl I Love" from *Finian's Rainbow*) and at its worst cutesy and clotted— "twee," as the British call it ("Something Sort of Grandish" from the same show).

Brilliant as some of the songs in *Finian's Rainbow* and *Bloomer Girl* are, Harburg's most consistently superb lyrics were written for the movies *Cabin in the Sky* and *The Wizard of Oz*, because despite the occasional solid naturalistic lyric like "Brother, Can You Spare a Dime?", Harburg was at his best when the subject matter suited his fanciful style. He was so at home with fantasies and satires that he could immerse himself in a miscalculation like *Flahooley*, a gooey morality play which brought out the most twee in him ("The Springtime Cometh"), and so ill at ease with conventional "reality" that he could write a set of undistinguished lyrics like those for *Darling of the Day*, an imitation

of *My Fair Lady*. Harburg was as uncomfortable writing about nineteenth-century Britishers as I would be writing about leprechauns. In his attraction to whimsy, he shows a yearning to be a poet, but he's not, he's a versifier. He traffics in wistfulness, in pretty but conventional imagery, in the vagaries and curiosities of the English language (gorgeously), but never in the indirect, vast resonance of poetry. He was born to write lyrics.

One of my favorite lyric lines comes from a song of his, as does one of my favorite couplets, both in the same show (*Bloomer Girl*) and both for the same reason: they each conjure up an ethos. In the first instance it is that of a black man in a Southern prison, in the second that of a repressive middle-class New England community, both instances taking place in the late nineteenth century. The line is from the song "The Eagle and Me":

> *Ever since the day*
> *When the world was an onion . . .*

The couplet is from "Sunday in Cicero Falls":

> *Even the rabbits*
> *Inhibit their habits*
> *On Sunday in Cicero Falls.*

Lyrics don't come any better than that.

Lunt-Fontanne Theatre
PLAYBILL
A FUNNY THING
HAPPENED ON THE WAY TO THE FORUM

Phil Silvers as Pseudolus (1971 revival)

their art, a farce being the ideal atmosphere for cleverness, for list songs, for word-juggling: for playfulness.

I was wrong, and "Pretty Little Picture" crystallizes the mistake—brilliantly, I regret to say. It is filled with the tricks of the trade: puns, jokes, word distortions and, above all, alliteration (even in the title, where the two "P"s are on the strong beats), all of it for the necessary glitter. It is emblematic of Jim Goldman's comment about the mismatch of script and lyrics: the song is clever, not funny. It never got laughs—only, at best, smiles of appreciation for the songwriter's ingenuity, just like a lot of songs by Porter and Harburg, which didn't make you laugh so much as smile in admiration of the craftsmanship and in the contentment of having understood the sophisticated observations. Their lyrics flattered the audience, me included, and I loved them (the good ones) and still do.

But if "Pretty Little Picture" isn't funny, neither is the situation, and therein lies the problem. The moment is not worth "savoring," not in the context of moving the story along, no matter how silly it is. I learned a difficult lesson from *Forum*: funny and clever are two very different things. "Adelaide's Lament" is funny; "You're the Top" is clever. It's better (and harder) to be funny than to be clever; *Forum* needed funny songs, and there were only two that got laughs rather than smiles, apart from "Comedy Tonight," which brought the house down because of its staging: "Impossible" and the reprise of "Lovely," more about which below. The reason is that they relied less on wordplay than on character and situation. Burt referred to *Forum* as a "scenario for vaudevillians" and one of the triumphs of the script, for all the intricacy of its plotting, is that the performers seem to be making it up as they go along. There are almost no jokes—everything depends on who and why and when more than on how.

In contemporary musical theater, writing with verbal dexterity often leads to accusations of "too clever by half." Playing with words for the sheer pleasure of it is now considered elitist and trivial, even though playful doesn't mean trivial any more than solemn means serious. In the heyday of Porter and Harburg, cleverness was something to be enjoyed and treasured. I wasn't around in those apparently halcyon times, but I miss them, and the ironic truth is that "Pretty Little Picture," wrong as it is for *Forum*, is one of my favorite lyrics.

Pseudolus hides Philia in Senex's house while he figures out a way to persuade her to leave. Meanwhile, Senex returns from the country unexpectedly and Pseudolus introduces Philia to him as a new housemaid. Senex is much taken with her and, as she exits back into the house, he sings his approval, encouraged by Pseudolus.

Everybody Ought to Have a Maid

SENEX
Everybody ought to have a maid.

PSEUDOLUS
Everybody ought to have a maid.

SENEX
Everybody ought to have a working
girl,
Everybody ought to have a lurking
girl,
To putter around the house.

Everybody ought to have a maid.

PSEUDOLUS
Everybody ought to have a maid.

SENEX
Everybody ought to have a menial,
Consistently congenial,
And quieter than a mouse.

Oh! Oh!
Wouldn't she be delicious,
Tidying up the dishes,*
Neat as a pin?
Oh! Oh!
Wouldn't she be delightful,
Sweeping out, sleeping in?

Everybody ought to have a maid.

PSEUDOLUS
Everybody ought to have a maid.

SENEX
Someone whom you hire
When you're short of help
To offer you the sort of help
You never get from a spouse,
Fluttering up the stairway,
Shuttering up the windows,
Cluttering up the bedroom,
Buttering up the master,
Puttering all around the house!

Oh! Oh!
Wouldn't she be delicious,
Tidying up the dishes,
Neat as a pin?
Oh! Oh!
Wouldn't she be delightful,
Sweeping out, sleeping in?

Everybody ought to have a maid,
Someone who, when fetching you
your slipper, will

* Not a perfect rhyme, but I make no claims to impeccability.

Be winsome as a whippoorwill
And graceful as a grouse,
Skittering down the hallway,
Flittering through the parlor,
Tittering in the pantry,
Littering up the bedroom,
Puttering all around the house!

*(Hysterium enters. Pseudolus whispers to
him, apprising him of the situation.)*

HYSTERIUM
A maid?

PSEUDOLUS
A maid.

SENEX
A maid.

ALL
A maid!

Everybody ought to have a maid.
Everybody ought to have a serving
 girl,
A loyal and unswerving girl
Who's quieter than a mouse.

Oh! Oh!

HYSTERIUM
Think of her at the dustbin,
'Specially when she's just been
Traipsing about.

ALL
Oh! Oh!
Wouldn't she be delightful,

HYSTERIUM
Living in . . .

SENEX
Giving out . . .

ALL
Everybody ought to have a maid,
Tidily collecting bits of paper 'n'
 strings,
Appealing in her apron strings,
Beguiling in her blouse!

HYSTERIUM
Pattering through the attic,

SENEX
Chattering in the cellar,

PSEUDOLUS
Clattering in the kitchen,

SENEX
Flattering in the bedroom,

ALL
Puttering all around the house,
The house! The house!

*(Lycus enters. Hysterium whispers the
information to him.)*

LYCUS
A maid?

HYSTERIUM
A maid.

PSEUDOLUS
A maid.

SENEX
A maid!

ALL
Everybody ought to have a maid,
Someone who's efficient and reliable,
Obedient and pliable
And quieter than a mouse.

Oh! Oh!
Wouldn't she be so nimble,
Fiddling with her thimble,
Mending a gown?
Oh! Oh!
Wouldn't she be delightful,

LYCUS
Cleaning up . . .

SENEX
Leaning down!

ALL
Everybody ought to have a maid,
Someone who'll be busy as a bumble-
 bee
And, even if you grumble, be
As graceful as a grouse!

LYCUS
Wriggling in the anteroom,

HYSTERIUM
Jiggling in the living room,

PSEUDOLUS
Giggling in the dining room,

SENEX
Wiggling in the other rooms,

ALL
Puttering all around the house!
The house! The house! The house!

Although this is nothing but a list
song, it is rooted in plot and in the differences between the attitudes of the
four leading characters, so it doesn't
seem merely to mark time the way
"Pretty Little Picture" does.

*Hysterium, living up to his name, is hys-
terically alarmed at what Pseudolus is
doing, but is forced to play along. Pseudolus tells him to keep calm, and he
attempts to do so.*

I'm Calm

HYSTERIUM
I'm calm, I'm calm,
I'm perfectly calm,
I'm utterly under control.
I haven't a worry,
Where others would hurry,
I stroll.

(He tries to walk casually, to no avail.)

I'm calm, I'm cool,
A gibbering fool
Is something I never become.
When thunder is rumbling
And others are crumbling,
I hum.

*(He tries to hum, but it turns into a
suppressed scream)*

I must think calm, comforting things:
Butterfly wings,
Emerald rings.

Or a murmuring brook,
Murmuring, murmuring,
  murmuring . . .
Look!

*(He holds out his hand to show how
steady it is, but it soon begins to tremble)*

I'm calm, I'm calm,
I haven't a qualm,
I'm utterly under control.
Let nothing confuse me—
Or faze me—

(He yawns ostentatiously)

Excuse me . . .
I'm calm,
Oh, so calm,
Oh, so—

SENEX
(From inside the house)
Hysterium!

(Hysterium resumes his hysteria)*

HYSTERIUM
I'm calm, I'm calm,
I'm perfectly calm,
Indifferent to tensions and shocks.
Unruffled and ready,
My nerves are as steady
As rocks.

(He starts twitching uncontrollably)

I'm calm, controlled,
So cool that I'm cold,
Aloofer than any giraffe.
When something's the matter,
Where others would chatter,
I laugh.

*(He tries an amused laugh,
  but it turns manic)**

I must breathe deep,
Ever so deep,
Think about sheep
Going to sleep,
Stop and count up to ten:

———————————————

* The chorus between asterisks was cut during the out-of-town tryout.

———————————————

One, two, three, four, five, six,
Seven, eight, nine—

(Completely calm)
When

You need aplomb
And want to be calm
'Cause life is a horrible dream,
Just count up to ten
Very slowly and then—
One, two, three, four, five, six,
Seven, eight, nine—

SENEX
(From inside the house)
Hysterium!

HYSTERIUM
—Scream!

(Which he does, and runs into the house)

*Senex and Hero, father and son, see each
other eyeing Philia.*

Impossible

SENEX
Why did he look at her that way?

HERO
Why did he look at her that way?

BOTH
Must be my imagination . . .

SENEX
She's a lovely blooming flower,
He's just a sprout . . .
Impossible!

HERO
She's a lovely blooming flower,
He's all worn out . . .
Impossible!

SENEX
Just a fledgling in the nest . . .

HERO
Just a man who needs a rest . . .

SENEX
He's a beamish boy at best . . .

HERO
Poor old fellow . . .

SENEX
He's a child and love's a test
He's too young to pass . . .
Impassable!

HERO
He has asthma, gout, a wife,
Lumbago and gas . . .
Irascible!

SENEX
Romping in the nursery . . .

HERO
He looks tired . . .

SENEX
Son, sit on your father's knee.

HERO
Father, you can lean on me.

BOTH
Him?
Im-
Possible!

HERO
But why did she wave at him that
  way?

SENEX
Why did she wave at him that way?

BOTH
Could there be an explanation?

HERO
Women often want a father,
She may want mine . . .
It's possible!

SENEX
He's a handsome lad of twenty,
I'm thirty-nine . . .

(Convincing the audience)

It's possible!

HERO
Older men know so much more . . .

SENEX

In a way I'm forty-four . . .

HERO

Next to him, I'll seem a bore . . .

SENEX

All right, fifty!

HERO

Then again, he is my father,
I ought to trust—
Impossible!

SENEX

Then again, with love at my age
Sometimes it's just
Impossible!

HERO

With a girl I'm ill at ease . . .

SENEX

I don't feel well . . .

HERO

Sir, about those birds and bees . . .

SENEX

Son, a glass of water, please . . .

BOTH

The situation's fraught,
Fraughter than I thought,
With horrible,
Impossible
Possibilities!

This song, in contrast to "Pretty Little Picture," exemplifies the difference between funny and clever. It's funny because the situation and the attitudes of the characters are funny. Senex's lying about his age is more theatrically satisfying than all the alliteration in the world. The important thing to note is that it gives the actors something to play rather than recite.

Miles (pronounced ME-lays) Gloriosus, a braggart warrior, arrives to claim Philia from Lycus. At this point, however, for plot purposes too convoluted to go into, Pseudolus is pretending to be Lycus.

Bring Me My Bride

MILES

My bride! My bride!
I've come to claim my bride,
Come tenderly to crush her against
my side!
Let haste be made,
I cannot be delayed!
There are lands to conquer,
Cities to loot
And people to degrade!

SOLDIERS

Look at those arms!
Look at that chest!
Look at them!

MILES

Not to mention the rest!
Even I am impressed!

My bride! My bride!
Come bring to me my bride!
My lust for her no longer can be
denied!
Convey the news,
I have no time to lose!
There are towns to plunder,
Temples to burn,
And women to abuse!

SOLDIERS

Look at that foot!
Look at that heel!
Mark the magnificent muscles of
steel!

MILES

I am my ideal!

I, Miles Gloriosus,
I, slaughterer of thousands,
I, oppressor of the meek,
Subduer of the weak,
Degrader of the Greek,
Destroyer of the Turk,
Must hurry back to work!

MILES	**PSEUDOLUS, COURTESANS**
I, Miles Gloriosus,	Him, Miles Gloriosus!

SOLDIERS

A man among men—

MILES	**PSEUDOLUS, GIRLS**
I, paragon of virtues!	Him, paragon of virtues,

SOLDIERS

With sword and with pen!

MILES

I, in war the most admired,
In wit the most inspired,
In love the most desired,
In dress the best displayed,
I am a parade!

SOLDIERS

Look at those eyes,
Cunning and keen!
Look at the size of those thighs,
Like a mighty machine!

PSEUDOLUS

Those are the mightiest thighs
That I ever have theen!
I mean . . .

MILES

My bride! My bride!
Inform my lucky bride:
The fabled arms of Miles are open
wide!
Make haste! Make haste!
I have no time to waste!
There are shrines I should be
sacking,
Ribs I should be cracking,
Eyes to gouge and booty to divide!
Bring me my bride!

SOLDIERS

Bring him his bride!

ALL

Bring him his bride!

"I am a parade" is the only direct quotation from Plautus in the show, and a good one it is. The original version of the song was more pointed, but Burt felt that it was *too* pointed, that there should be no satirical or political edge to any of the songs, since the show was to be strictly a domestic farce and not a commentary. But here it is:

There's Something About a War (cut)

SOLDIERS
One-two, one-two!

MILES
We not only fought but we won, too!

SOLDIERS
One-two, one-two!
Left-right, left-right!

MILES
There's none of the enemy left, right?

SOLDIERS
(Becoming confused)
Right! Left-right, left-left-uh-right!

MILES
Halt!

I don't know how to say it,
But there's something about a war.
Mere words cannot convey it,
But there's something about a war.
It's noisy and it's crowded
And you have to stand in line,
But there's something about a war
That's divine!

You march until you're bleary,
But there's something about a war.
The company is dreary,
But there's something about a war.
Your fingernails get broken
And the food is often vile,
But there's something about a war
Makes you smile.

The rain may rust your armor,
Your straps may be too tight,
But decapitate a farmer
And your heart feels light!

There's something about a war,
Something about a war,
Something about a war
That makes this little old world all
    right.

SOLDIERS
Oh, it's tread, tread, tread
Through the mud, mud, mud
And it's shed, shed, shed
All the blood, blood—

THIRD SOLDIER
Yich!

ALL
There's something about a war.

SOLDIERS
Oh, it's plunge, plunge, plunge
Through the dust, dust, dust
And it's lunge, lunge, lunge
And it's thrust, thrust—

THIRD SOLDIER
(Shuddering)
Oooh!

ALL
There's something about a war.

You know it isn't massacres and
    laughter all day long,
Still there's something about a war
That's like a song!

A warrior's work is never done,
He never can get a rest.
There always are lands to overrun
And people to be oppressed.

There's always a town to pillage,
A city to be laid waste.
There's always a little village
Entirely to be erased.

And citadels to sack, of course,
And temples to attack, of course,
Children to annihilate,
Priestesses to violate,
Houses to destroy—hey!
Women to enjoy—hey!
Statues to deface—hey!
Mothers to debase—hey!
Virgins to assault—hey!

MILES
Halt, hey!

ALL
Oh, it's hurry, hurry, hurry,
But there's something about a war.
It's worry after worry,
But there's something about a war.
It isn't all the drama and heroics it
    may seem,
But there's something about a war
That's a scream!

There's never time for reading,
Yet there's something about a war.
The elephants keep breeding,
But there's something about a war.
You frequently feel lonely when the
    enemy has gone,
Still there's something about a war
That goes on . . . and on . . .
    and on . . .

You sulk when someone's suing
For temporary truce,
Then another war starts brewing
And soon breaks loose!
There's something about a war,
Something about a war,
Something about a war—!

It isn't just the glory or
The groaning or the gorier
Details that cause a warrior
To smirk.
It's the knowledge that he'll never be
    out of work!

ACT TWO

Domina, Senex's formidable wife, returns from the country, suspicious of her husband's absence. She sings to Hysterium, her feelings alternating instantaneously between yearning and fury.

That Dirty Old Man

DOMINA
For over thirty years,
I've cried myself to sleep,
Assailed by doubts and fears
So great the gods themselves would
    weep!
The moment I am gone,
I wonder where he'll go.
In all your simple honesty,
You can't begin to know . . .
Ohhhhhh . . .

I want him,
I need him.
Where is he?
That dirty old man is here somewhere,

Cavorting with someone young and
    fair,
Disporting in every shameless whim,
Just wait till I get my hands on him—!

I'll hold him,
Enfold him,
Where is he?
That dirty old man, where can he be?
Profaning our vows for all to see,
Complaining how he's misunderstood,
Abusing me (if he only would!) . . .

Oh, love,
Sweet love,
Why hide?
You vermin, you worm, you villain!
Come face,
Embrace
Your bride!
Wherever he is, I know he's still an
Angel.

My angel!
Where is he,
That dirty old man divine?
I love him,
I love him!
That lecherous, lewd, lascivious,
Loathsome, lying, lazy,
Dirty old man of mine!

Like "Impossible," this song has the
advantage of being a character song,
but it's not inventive enough. Once
the comic notion of rapidly alternating
passions has been presented, I seem to
have found nothing to do with it but
repeat it. This accounts for the lame
use of alliteration at the end. Unlike
the alliterations in "Pretty Little Picture," which came in unexpected sequences, this one is right out of the
thesaurus—the writer's presence over-
shadows the character's. In many
songs, including more than a few of
my own, alliteration is used because
the lyric has too little to say and the
language has to be gussied up in an attempt to keep the listener interested.
"That Dirty Old Man" is not a total
loss, but what laughs it gets come from
the physical comedy of Domina's man-
handling Hysterium, whom she alternately embraces and shakes as a
stand-in for her husband.

*Hero and Philia are resigned to her hav-
ing to go off with Miles Gloriosus. She
tries to cheer him up.*

That'll Show Him

PHILIA
Let the captain wed me and woo me,
I shall play my part.
Let him make his mad passion to me,
You will have my heart.
He can have the body he paid for,
Nothing but the body he paid for,
When he has the body he paid for,
Our revenge will start!

When I kiss him,
I'll be kissing you,
So I'll kiss him morning and night—!
That'll show him!

When I hold him,
I'll be holding you,
So I'll hold him ten times as tight—!
That'll show him, too!

I shall coo, and tenderly stroke his
    hair.
Wish that you were there—
You'd enjoy it!

When it's evening
And we're in our tent for two,
I'll sit on his knee,
Get to know him
Intimately—
That'll show him
How much I really love you!

In an early version of the show, the situation is more complicated. Philia,
torn between her duty and her love,
decides to pray to the gods for guid-
ance; since she believes that the gods
always answer in echoes, Pseudolus
tells Hero that he will hide on the roof
and answer her prayers in such a way
as to persuade her to decide in favor
of love; at the last moment, however,
Pseudolus is knocked unconscious and
Hero has to fill in as the god. The
scheme works, until Hero gets tripped
up at the end of the song.

Echo Song (cut)

PHILIA
Tell me—

HERO
(Tell me . . .)

PHILIA
Dare I ask it?

HERO
(Ask it . . .)

PHILIA
Should I love him?

HERO
(Love him!)

PHILIA
Shall I leave with him?

HERO
(Leave with him, leave with him!)

PHILIA
Tell me—

HERO
(Tell me . . .)

PHILIA
Should I leave right now?

HERO
(Right now!)

PHILIA
I hear my heart say,
"Let him live with me!"

HERO
(Live with me, live with me!)

PHILIA
Should I hear my heart and go?

HERO
(Go! Go!)

PHILIA
Or should I, worthy, wait here
Till I meet my fate here?
Tell me, tell me, I must know.

HERO
(No, no, no . . .)

PHILIA
Tell me—

HERO
(Tell me . . .)

PHILIA
Should I hold him?

HERO
(Hold him!)

PHILIA
Or forget him—

HERO
(Get him!)

PHILIA
And forgo my love?

HERO
(Go, my love! Go, my love!)

PHILIA
Thank you!

HERO
(Thank you!)

PHILIA
I believe, now!

HERO
(Leave now!)

PHILIA
I must hurry—

HERO
(Hurry!)

PHILIA
So I'll say goodbye.

HERO
(Say goodbye, say goodbye!)

PHILIA
Only one more question, please . . .

HERO
(Please! Please!)

PHILIA
Does he want me?

HERO
(Does he!)

PHILIA
Would he miss me?

HERO
(Would he!)

PHILIA
Must I pay the debt I owe?

HERO
(Oh . . . Oh . . .)

PHILIA
Or may I go with Hero,
My beloved Hero?
Tell me yes, so I may know.

HERO
(Ye—N—Y-N-Yes!)

The echo poem was a form that I had
never come across, but it was a particular favorite of Burt's, and he persuaded me to use it. It turned out to be
heavier on cleverness than enjoyment
and was replaced in New Haven by
"That'll Show Him."

*Pseudolus has to persuade Hysterium to
dress as Philia and pretend to be dead.
Hysterium is embarrassed at being in
drag. Pseudolus reassures him.*

Lovely (reprise)

PSEUDOLUS
You're lovely,
Absolutely lovely,
Who'd believe the loveliness of you?

Perfect,
Sweet and warm and winsome,
Radiant as in some
Dream come true.

Now
Venus will seem tame.

Helen and her thousand ships
Will have to die of shame.

You're so lovely,
Frighteningly lovely,
That the world will never seem the
same!

(*Hysterium begins to become convinced*)

HYSTERIUM
I'm lovely,
Absolutely lovely,
Who'd believe the loveliness of me?

Perfect,
Sweet and warm and winsome,
Radiant as in some
Dream come true . . .

I'm so lovely,

PSEUDOLUS
Literally lovely—

BOTH
That the world will never seem the
same—

PSEUDOLUS
You're so lovely—

BOTH
That the world will never seem the
same!

In the days when Broadway shows were
a primary source of popular music, it
was important to play the potential hit
ballad as many times as possible during
the course of the evening: ideally, once
in the Overture, two choruses (at least)
in Act One, another orchestral statement in the Entr'acte, and then as a
reprise in Act Two. But once again
Hammerstein spoiled it for the rest of
us: if the songs were to be develop-
ments in the progression of a story, how
could they be repeated later on? They
had to reflect the changes in character
and plot. They could never again be
simply plugs for Hit Parade appeal, especially after the 1950s when theater
songs had increasingly little to do with
popularity, anyway. Generally, this

meant that reprises would have to reflect past action, usually in a fragmentary and melancholy way toward the end of the show, when the hero and heroine were either separated or sad or both, before they could get together once more and sing a final, full-throated happy reprise. Oscar solved it ingeniously at the end of the *first* act of *South Pacific*, where he reprised virtually every song heard so far, partly by having the hero and heroine make fun of them. "Lovely" presents another solution: the song reprised with new lyrics, reflecting the changes in character and plot. The reprise offered me the chance to use it not only as an echo of the past, but as an instant of change in itself. The lyric may look bland, but on the stage it brought the house down, partly because it was about character and situation but also because in the midst of a farce there occurred a sudden and weird emotional moment: Hysterium, initially reluctant at having to get into drag, begins halfway through the song, and clearly for the first time in his life, to feel attractive. As with the best of Chaplin, this humanity peeking through the silliness made for radiant comedy.

Miles, presented with the dead body of Philia (Hysterium in drag), demands a funeral.

Funeral Sequence

MILES
Sound the flute,
Blow the horn,
Pluck the lute,
Forward, mourn!

All Crete was at her feet,
All Thrace was in her thrall,
All Sparta loved her sweetness and
　　gall . . .

PSEUDOLUS　　MOURNERS
And Spain . . .　　All Crete was at
　　　　　　　her feet,
　　　　　　　All Thrace was in
　　　　　　　her thrall,

MILES
And Greece . . .　　Oh, why should
　　　　　　　such a blossom
　　　　　　　fall?

PSEUDOLUS
And Egypt . . .

MILES
And Syria . . .

PSEUDOLUS
And Mesopotamia . . .

MILES
Speak the spells,
Chant the charms,
Toll the bells . . .

PSEUDOLUS
(To Hysterium)
Fold the arms.

MILES
Strew the soil,
Strum the lyre,
Spread the oil,
Build the pyre! . . .

All Crete was at her feet,
But I shall weep no more.
I'll find my consolation, as before,
Among the simple pleasures of war!

Erronius, Senex's other neighbor, a befuddled old man, has been searching many years for his long-lost son and daughter. He returns to Rome and stumbles over Hysterium who, due to plot convolutions, wears a ring inscribed with a gaggle of geese, which is Erronius's family crest.

The Gaggle of Geese

(cut)

ERRONIUS
The ring! The ring!
He's wearing the ring!
The ring with the gaggle of geese!

It's proof! You see?
There only are three!
They're worn by my children and me!

The family crest, the gaggle of geese,
The ring with the galloping gaggle of
　　geese!

The gods above
Have answered my call!
Release every dove
From Carthage to Gaul!
Light welcoming fires,
Let trumpets and lyres
Proclaim it to one and to all:
This is my son!

The gaggle of geese, the gaggle of
　　geese,
It *is* the gaggle of geese,
For years I've sought the gaggle of
　　geese,
And here is the gaggle of geese
At last, the gaggle of geese!

The gaggle of geese, the gaggle of
　　geese!
It's not a covey of quails,
It's not a flight of nightingales,
It isn't a school of whales,
It must be a gaggle of geese!

Sing paeans of jubilation
In celebration!
Send runners with torches burning
To mark my son's returning!

The gaggle of geese, the gaggle of
　　geese!
Ring out . . . the gaggle . . . the
　　bells . . . the geese . . .
My son . . . the gaggle . . . is home
　　again
With the gaggle . . . he wears . . .

My heart has joy,
My mind has peace.
I've found my boy
With the gaggle of—look!
The gaggle of—see!
The gaggle of—yes!
The gaggle of—this!
The gaggle of—there!

(Speaking, music underneath)

Hysterium, why are you sitting
　　around?
It isn't enough that my son has been
　　found!

My daughter, my daughter, yes, where
   is my daughter?
And why is my boy lying down on
   the ground?
Do something at once! He's obviously
Completely exhausted from searching
   for me.

Go get a physician!
No, stay with him here and *I'll* get a
   physician—
No, first I will seek that sayer of sooth,
He'll certainly know where my
   daughter must be!
My son being here, she ought to be
   near,
Not here, but where?
Nearby, but where?
He'll know . . .
I go . . .
Goodbye . . .
Hello.
My beautiful boy!

(Sings)

The family crest
Was put to the test
And half of my quest
Is done!
I have at long last
Found my long lost
Son!

This song never even got into rehearsal. I wrote it because Erronius
was the only major character with no
song of his own. I neglected to take
into account that this late in the show,
with the farcical complications piling
up at warp speed, the last thing the
audience wanted was a new song. Too
bad, as it would have been a minor
tour de force for the actor.

*As in all farces, the complications finally
get resolved.*

Finale

PSEUDOLUS
Lovers divided
Get coincided,
Something for everyone—

HERO, PHILIA
A comedy tonight!

PSEUDOLUS
Father and Mother
Get one another—

DOMINA
Something for everyone—

SENEX
A tragedy tonight!

MILES
I get the twins,
They get the best.

ERRONIUS
I get a family—

HYSTERIUM
I get a rest.

SOLDIERS
We get a few girls—

LYCUS
I'll get some new girls—

PSEUDOLUS
I get the thing I want to be:
Free!

ALL
Free! Free! Free! Free! Free!

Nothing for kings,
Nothing for crowns,
Something for lovers, liars and
   clowns!

What is the moral?
Must be a moral.
Here is the moral, wrong or right:

PSEUDOLUS
Morals tomorrow—

ALL
Comedy tonight!

*A Funny Thing Happened on the Way
to the Forum* was a bittersweet experience for me. The sweet was all in the
writing, in the excitement of getting
back to composing music and in the
sheer pleasure of spending so much
time in the company of Burt Shevelove and Larry Gelbart, two of the funniest *and* wittiest men I've ever had
the privilege of knowing. The bitter
was the show's out-of-town tryout,
where it was met with sneering reviews and dwindling audiences (at
one Washington matinee we played
to barely more than 50 people in a
1,600-seat house). Any producer less
courageous than Hal Prince would
have felt justified in closing such a
disaster before it contaminated New
York. Worse yet, the show's problems
caused tensions among Burt and Larry
and me that took months to resolve.

    When we opened on Broadway
the bitter began to outweigh the
sweet two to one: the reception was
ecstatic—for everything but the songs.
Shortly thereafter, *Forum* was nomi-
nated for eight Tony Awards (and won
six), the only major category missing
being Best Score. As I sat at home
licking my wounds and watching
everyone receive their silver disks and
thank one another profusely on national television, I had nothing to con-
sole myself with but the knowledge
that the show was a huge success and
I would make some money. It was, in
fact, the biggest hit (in its Broadway
run) that I've ever been connected
with.* And success healed things between my collaborators and me, as
success often does. Moreover, the collaboration turning sour under tryout
pressure had one hidden benefit: it
prepared me for my experience on the
next show, which unfortunately didn't
have the compensation of being a hit;
it was a failure of the most flamboyant
order, and my first.

---

* One further, and deeply satisfying, compensation was a note from Frank Loesser praising
the score and sympathizing with me by comparing its critical reception to the similar one
accorded him on *Where's Charley?*, his first
Broadway show.

Zero Mostel as Pseudolus

5. Anyone Can Whistle (1964)

Book by Arthur Laurents

The Notion

A fanciful story about a small economically depressed American town whose venal Mayoress gets the bright idea of arranging a fake miracle to attract tourists. The tourists arrive, but they become intermixed with the inmates of the local Cookie Jar, a rest home for non-conformists. Farcical complications ensue.

General Comments

Arthur Laurents and I shared a fondness for whimsy, and *Anyone Can Whistle* was an attempt at sociopolitical satire in a free-wheeling form. It might generously be considered one of the first absurdist (with commercial intentions) musicals. Certainly, it exhibits both the strengths and the dangers of the genre: imagination and cleverness which too often, instead of enriching each other, draw attention to themselves. I once found myself on an airplane sitting next to the playwright Peter Shaffer, a man I'd met only briefly, and was startled and delighted to hear him speak enthusiastically about being among the very few who had seen the original production, which ran for thirteen performances. "It was among the most brilliant and original theater pieces I've ever been to . . . ," he was saying, adding as I started to preen, "as well as one of the most irritating." He singled out the ending of the first act, with its condescension toward the audience, as helping to explain the hostility of both press and public. He was right: Arthur and I had written the piece as if we were the two smartest kids in the class (in the back row, of course), wittily making fun of the teacher as well as our fellow students, demonstrating how far ahead of the established wisdom we

were; Peter, with his generous but unerring eagle eye, had spotted it.

The show suffered a number of indignities during the pre-Broadway tour in Philadelphia, among them the heart attack of Henry Lascoe, our chief supporting player, followed a few days later by one of the dancers falling into the orchestra pit, causing the concussion of a string player, who was then hospitalized and died within the week. Moreover, Angela Lansbury was so insecure onstage, and unhappy with her performance, that we considered replacing her. Ironically, it soon became apparent that it had been Lascoe, an old pro if ever there was one, who had made her feel like an amateur. The minute his much less confident understudy took over, she felt free to blossom, which she spectacularly did. None of those problems, however, can be blamed for the failure of the show. The fault was not in our stars but in ourselves. Still, *Anyone Can Whistle* was a perfectly respectable attempt to present something unconventional in the commercial musical theater. We were lucky to get it produced at all. It took me thirty-three backers' auditions to raise the money—a longer run than the show.

Anyone Can Whistle was my first collaboration with a writer who also functioned as director. Arthur had directed a bit before (notably *I Can Get It for You Wholesale*, the musical which brought Barbra Streisand her first public acclaim), but the pressures of rewriting and simultaneously keeping control of the company morale in the face of humiliating Philadelphia reviews and hostile Philadelphia audiences proved too much for him. Aplomb was not one of Arthur's chief virtues, and his tirades could be heard as far as Scranton. Exacerbating his edginess was his manifest dislike of one leading lady (Lee Remick) in favor of the other (Angela Lansbury), which severely disrupted the cast's equilibrium. This was hardly the worst tryout experience I've ever had—*Forum* wins that prize, hands down—but it was not a happy one, and recounting it raises the subject of writers who

think they're directors and vice versa.

David Merrick, the most successful entrepreneur of the 1960s, wanted to produce *Anyone Can Whistle*, but only on the condition that Arthur not direct it. He claimed, astutely, that authors, especially authors of musicals, shouldn't direct the initial productions of their own works. Without a director to argue with, egoistic self-indulgence might color everything, he claimed. A couple of examples, such as Noël Coward's then-recent *The Girl Who Came to Supper* and Arthur's subsequent *Nick & Nora*, prove his point.* It's true that throughout the first half of the twentieth century, plays and the more frivolous musicals had often been staged by their authors, among them: George S. Kaufman, George Kelly, George Abbott and a host of others not named George, from David Belasco to Moss Hart and beyond. By the 1950s, though, what had been a writers' theater had become a directors' theater virtually overnight. This was largely due to the prestige and power of Elia Kazan, who not only was supremely gifted but also had the good fortune to direct the two most important plays of the era, *A Streetcar Named Desire* and *Death of a Salesman*. His influence on the writing of those plays was well publicized, and soon advertisements were carrying Kazan's name over the title and the author's underneath.

It didn't take long before directors began to consider themselves as important as the playwrights. The spearhead of this cause in musical theater was Jerome Robbins, who spurned over-the-title billing but insisted instead on having a box drawn around his name and who was once glimpsed in London armed with calipers, measuring his name on a poster of *West Side Story* to be sure that its size matched that of the names of the authors, as his contract stipulated. Not only did his prominent boxed credit read "Entire Production Directed and Choreographed by Jerome Robbins," he also insisted on an additional notice directly under the title: "Based on a Conception of Jerome Robbins."

In today's musical theater, there are two kinds of directors: those who are writers and those who want to be, or, more ominously, think they are. The latter ache to be considered creators instead of mere interpreters. They feel that simply bringing the authors' work to the stage is a secondary profession—and they're right. They yearn for posterity, because does anyone today know who directed *Show Boat,* or, for that matter, *Oklahoma!*?† Not to mention *Hamlet*. To this end, many of them have a clause in their contracts demanding that "Originally directed by _____" be printed along with the authors' names on posters and programs for every future production, professional or amateur, regardless of whether any aspects of their interpretations are used or not, and no matter who actually directs it.

Theater writers used to create their plays and musicals and present them to a director, whose job was to realize the authors' inventions as deftly as possible, perhaps adding inventions of his own. Nowadays musicals, and even plays, are often "developed" by writers in meetings with directors. This can be needlessly time-consuming and frustrating, but it makes the directors happy, even though it usually results in a compromised work. A good director can be a good editor and can even spark ideas that explode in a writer's head: I have often left Hal Prince's office suffused with excitement, eager to get to the piano and the legal pad to explore what has come up in discussion. But for specifics and detail, for shape and tone, for the actual creation, I depend on the book writer, the collaborator who makes something out of nothing. The best directors have a fine sense of theatricality, but unless they're writers, their approach to structure and story is usually secondary to their focus on mise-en-scène. And unless they've been actors, their way of dealing with performers tends to emphasize whatever is immediately effective. It's not a coincidence that good directors of musicals generally do not make good directors of plays, and vice versa, much as good dramaturgs generally make poor directors.

Good directors welcome being interpretive artists rather than creative ones, and so do good theater songwriters. Like the director, the songwriter's job is to enhance the playwright's work, to explore the characters and intensify the situations. Unlike the director, a songwriter is indeed making something out of nothing, but not entirely; his inventions depend on the man who made the first something out of the first nothing. Songwriters are halfway between creator and interpreter.

The blessing of a writer serving as his own director is that one vision emerges, there being no outsider to contradict him. The curse, inevitably, is that the vision may turn out to be myopic, there being no outsider to contradict him. So it was with *Anyone Can Whistle*. There was no one to challenge Arthur and me but ourselves. We had the courage, but not the perspective.

In *All About Eve* Joseph L. Mankiewicz, referring to actors, said "It's about time the piano stopped thinking it wrote the concerto." The same goes for the conductor.

---

* The single exception to this truism is James Lapine, who handles both departments with equal skill.

† Zeke Colvan and Oscar Hammerstein II; Rouben Mamoulian.

ACT ONE

The show takes place in a small American town which is a financial and physical ruin because it manufactured a product that never wore out. From her late husband, Cora Hoover Hooper, a flirtatious and demanding woman of a certain age, has inherited not only the now-closed factory but also the mayoralty of her bankrupt town and the animosity of the townspeople—all of which does little to help her solve the immediate problem of how to pay the town's bills without dipping into her own pocketbook, stuffed as it is with the total assets of the place.

The action begins in the town square. Cora makes her entrance carried Cleopatra-like on a litter by four Pageboys who act as her personal chorus. She steps down with great hauteur even as the townspeople snarl, boo and throw things at her. Unperturbed, she addresses the audience.

Me and My Town

CORA
Everyone hates me, yes, yes,
Being the Mayoress, yes.
All of the peasants
Throw rocks in my presence,
Which causes me nervous
    distress, yes.

(Wailing)
Ooooooooh . . .

Me and my town, battered about.
Everyone in it would like to get out.
Me and my town,
We just want to be loved.

Stores are for rent, theaters are dark.
Grass on the sidewalks, but not in the
    park.
Me and my town,
We just want to be loved!

The people are starving,
So they sleep the day through.
My poor little people,
What can they do?

TOWNSPEOPLE
Boo!

CORA
Who asked you?

Come on the train, come on the bus,
Somebody please buy a ticket to us.
Hurry on down,
We need a little renown.
Love me,
Love my town!
Ooohhh-oooooohhhhh-
    ooooooooooohhhhhhhhh!

(The music suddenly becomes cheerful and lively)

PAGEBOYS
Hi there, Cora, what's new?

CORA
The bank went bust and I'm feeling
    blue.

PAGEBOYS
And who took over the bankruptcy?

CORA
Me, boys, me!

PAGEBOYS
Si, si!

CORA
Me, boys, me!

PAGEBOYS
Tell us, Cora, how you are.

CORA
I just got back from the reservoir.

PAGEBOYS
And what's the state of the water
    supply?

CORA
Dry, boys, dry!

PAGEBOYS
My, my!

CORA
Dry, boys, dry!

PAGEBOYS
Ay, ay!

CORA
A lady has responsibilities—

PAGEBOYS
Responsibilities—

CORA
And civic pride.

PAGEBOYS
Civic pride!

CORA
Well, I look around and what do
    I see?
I see no crops.

PAGEBOYS
No crops.

CORA
I see no business.

PAGEBOYS
No business.

CORA
To the North, to the South,
Only hoof-and-mouth!
To the East, to the West,
No Community Chest!

CORA, PAGEBOYS
I see a terrible depression all over the
    town.
Oh, a terrible depression,
Yes, a terrible depression.

CORA
What a terrible depression,
And I'm so depressed
I can hardly talk on the phone.
I feel all alone.

CORA, PAGEBOYS
But a lady has responsibilities—

PAGEBOYS
Responsibilities—

CORA
To all my Poor! Starving!
Cold! Miserable!
Dirty! Dreary! Depressing!
Peasants!

ALL
Peasants! Ugh!

Me & my town, bothered about

Everyone in it would like to get out

What have we done? Me & my town.

Everyone hates us - it's getting us down.

Why do the peasants hate me

why do
Everyone hates this town, yes   my   so

Everyone puts us down, yes

here
Everyone hates me & my town

Sweet little town, cozy & clean

is getting us down, yes

all of them
Why do they hate it
How can they hate it

all of them place
Everyone hates me as much as the town

Look at my town - isn't it sweet

Hating their mayor & hating their town
despising
His own
How can I cope -
Why do they hate it & me

Being despised is getting me down

even
more.

I have a town, falling apart

growth
oath

Everyone in it despises us both

My town's in trouble - yes, yes.

is total
This town is in a mess, yes

So is the mayoress, yes

All of the peasants
Throng around

Everyone hates it, yes

Will hiss in my presence
their
Also the mayoress

They feel that
In short   As long as the town is a mess, yes.

Because
which
It causes us nervous distress, yes

I am the mayoress, yes

Everyone in it

My town's - mess, yes.

Would leave in a minute
to
Except they have no place to go, no

FIXES

Blessed be the
Thank you for _the grace_

Blessed be the
Thank you for the boon

we   we all
Can all afford   Can will afford

I am unhappy   Heavy the burden
deep in despair   Everyone hates me, yes, yes
                                       'cause still I'm
                                       Being the mayoress, yes
                                       Governing peasants

Nobody knows us and nobody cares   Who _lives_ in my presence
Nobody cares _that_ we're falling apart   It's better than nothing, I guess, yes,
                                       Is not my idea of success, yes
                                       But _oo lookout_ —

The giggle are prayers   Hello Cora how are you
        and no one say too.   The bank went bust + I'm feeling
                                                                    blue.

Guess what, boys

Guess what else

CORA
But a lady has responsibilities—

PAGEBOYS
Responsibilities—

CORA
To try to be
Popular with the populace.

PAGEBOYS
She's unpopular with the populace!

CORA, PAGEBOYS
Unpopular with the populace,
Unpopular with the populace . . .

CORA
Last week a flood, this week a
    drought,
Even the locusts want to get out,
But me and my town, we never
    pout,*
We just want to be loved!

PAGEBOYS
A friendship is lovely
And a courtship sublime,
But give her a township—

CORA
Township—
Every time!

CORA, PAGEBOYS
What'll we do,
Me and my town?
Gotta do something or we're gonna
    drown!
Give me my coat,
Give me my crown,
Give me, give me your vote
And hurry on down!

CORA
Show me how much you think of me!

ALL
Love me,
Love my town!

---

* For some forgotten reason, on the original
cast album I changed these lines to:

    Everyone here hates me at length,
    Probably lynch me if they had the
      strength,
    But me and my town, me and my town . . .

This was my first attempt to use musical comedy pastiche as a means of characterization. I had used it in *Saturday Night* and *Gypsy* as a way of setting time and place, but here it was an attempt to convey Cora's heartlessness through the use of a slick, jazzy show-biz style exemplified by Kay Thompson and the Williams Brothers, a mid-century act that used intricate and polished song arrangements which were nothing more (nor less) than enormously entertaining and rhythmically exhilarating. Jazzy show-biz became the musical language for Cora and her cohorts throughout, in contrast to the more personal musical language of the other characters. Much of the time Cora sang, she was accompanied vocally and physically by the four Pageboys.

Cora's cronies comprise the Town Council: Comptroller Schub, Treasurer Cooley and Police Chief Magruder. Schub announces that he has a plan to restore the town's economic prosperity. Indeed, a short while later, Baby Joan Schroeder, the town's child mystic,† in one of her frequent trances, approaches a large rock outcropping in the local park and begins to lick it. After a moment, a fountain of water spurts forth.

Miracle Song

MRS. SCHROEDER
It's a sign! It's a sign!

CORA
And it's mine!

SCHROEDER
It's a shrine! It's a shrine!

---

† For those interested in an author's psychic eccentricities, it might be worth noting that Arthur Laurents invented a character called Baby John in *West Side Story*, a character called Baby June in *Gypsy* and a character called Baby Joan in *Anyone Can Whistle*, prompting one to ask, "Whatever happened to Baby Jane?"

CORA
And it's mine!
It's a gold mine!
And it's all mine!

TOWNSPEOPLE
(Simultaneously)
It's a sign!
It's a shrine!
See it shine!

CORA
And it's holier than thine!

(During the following, pilgrims start arriving)

TOWNSPEOPLE
There's water in a lake,
Water in a river,
Water in the deep blue sea.
But water in a rock—Lord! That's a
    miracle!

CORA, COOLEY
Who's got the miracle? We!

TOWNSPEOPLE
There's water that you part,
Water that you walk on,
Water that you turn to wine!
But water from a rock—Lord, what a
    miracle!
This is a miracle that's divine,
Truly divine!

CORA
Really divine!

CORA, COOLEY, SCHROEDER
The Lord said, "Let there be water,"
The Lord said, "Turn on the font!"
The Lord said, "Let there be pilgrims,
And let them all think whatever they
    want."

TOWNSPEOPLE
Blessed be the child,
Blessed be the tourist,
Blessed is its own reward.

COOLEY
Water is a boon,
We'll soon
Be in clover!

CORA
Better issue stock,
My rock
Runneth over!

ALL
Glory Hallelu,
You finally came through,
And thank you, Lord!
Our faith is restored!
Thank you, Lord!

CORA
Come, all ye pilgrims!

TOWNSPEOPLE, PILGRIMS
Hail the miracle!

CORA
See ye the wondrous sight!

TOWNSPEOPLE, PILGRIMS
Hail the miracle, praise the miracle!

CORA
Take ye the bus tonight.

TOWNSPEOPLE, PILGRIMS
There's a miracle that's happening
In this town!

CORA
If you want to see a miracle, then
    hurry on down!

COOLEY
Come all ye pilgrims!

TOWNSPEOPLE, PILGRIMS
Hail the miracle!

COOLEY
Hear ye the joyful bells!

TOWNSPEOPLE, PILGRIMS
Hail the miracle!

COOLEY
Fill ye the new motels!

TOWNSPEOPLE, PILGRIMS
It's a miracle that's going to change
    your life!

COOLEY
Come along and see the miracle
And bring the wife!

"Miracle Song" with Angela Lansbury as Cora

TOWNSPEOPLE, PILGRIMS
There's a miracle that's happening
In this town,
And you'll never have to worry
If you hurry on down.
There's a miracle that's going
To change your life,
Come along and see the miracle
And bring the wife!

CORA
Are you looking for hope?

TOWNSPEOPLE, PILGRIMS
Looking for hope . . .

CORA
Hoping for an answer?

TOWNSPEOPLE, PILGRIMS
Hoping for an answer . . .

CORA
New life.

TOWNSPEOPLE, PILGRIMS
New life . . .

CORA
True happiness.

TOWNSPEOPLE, PILGRIMS
True happiness . . .

CORA
Come.

PILGRIMS
Help . . .

CORA
Come and take the waters
For a modest fee.

Come and take the waters
And feel new.
Come and take the waters
And with luck you'll be
Anything whatever, except you.

PILGRIMS
Comfort . . .

TOWNSPEOPLE, PILGRIMS
Come and take the waters
With humility.
Come and take the waters
And feel new.

CORA
Come and take the waters,
And with luck you'll be
Happy and successful!

TOWNSPEOPLE, PILGRIMS
Happy and successful!

CORA
Liked and loved and beautiful and
    perfect!

TOWNSPEOPLE, PILGRIMS
Beautiful and perfect!

CORA
Healthy, rich, handsome,
    independent,
Wise, adjusted and secure and
    athletic!

PILGRIMS
Rainbow . . . Rainbow . . . Rainbow
    . . . Rainbow!
RAINBOW!!!

ALL
The Lord said, "Let there be water!"
The Lord said, "Turn on the font!"
Lord said, "Let ye be what ye want!"
Our troubles are over!
Our troubles are over,
Praise the Lord!

Look upon the gift
And lift
Up your chin now!

CORA, COOLEY
Look upon the boom,
No room
At the inn now!

ALL
Glory Hallelu,
Our problems are through,
And thank you, Lord!
Thank you, Lord!

Tourists pile in from all corners of the world and prosperity seems just around the corner. What is really around the corner, though, is Police Chief Magruder, pumping water into the rock from inside of it.

The Lame, The Halt and The Blind (cut)

This song—the promotion of the miracle over a period of time—was cut before rehearsals because, in one of our few spasms of clear-eyed assessment, we could see that we were amusing ourselves for far too long with repeating the same satirical point, and had better get back to the story.

COOLEY
Step up! Step up!
Step right up!

MAGRUDER
(Simultaneously)
Buy your blessings, get your tickets!
Cures confusion, croup and rickets!
Count your blessings, get your
    tickets!

SCHUB
(Simultaneously)
Only one blessing per pilgrim per
    ticket,
One blessing per pilgrim per
    ticket . . .

ALL THREE
All for the lame, the halt and the
    blind,
And anyone out of their mind.
The lame shall saunter, the halt
    shall run,
The blind shall look on the light of
    the sun—
It's holy, it's healthy, it's easy, it's fun!

(Separately, as before)

Step up! Step up! Step right up!
Count your blessings, get your
    tickets!

MAGRUDER
(To Cooley)
Get the blessings, count the
    tickets . . .

ALL THREE
Blest be the deaf, the dumb and the
    sick,
And anything else you can pick.
The deaf shall hear and the dumb
    shall speak,
The sick shall find all the succor they
    seek.
Minority groups get a discount this
    week!

(Separately, as before)

Step up! Step up! Step right up!
Count your blessings, get your
    tickets!

MAGRUDER
(To Cooley)
Count the suckers, find the
    blessings . . .

ALL THREE
Come slake your spiritual thirst,
Get kissed, get blessed,
Get fully immersed,
Get dry, get dressed.
Put God to the test,
But do it fast:
The first shall be first
And the last shall be last!
Step up! Step up! Step right up!
Get your tickets, buy your
    candles! . . .

Come all ye frail, ye fierce and ye
    pure,
And any who aren't too sure.
The frail shall fight and the fierce
    be fey,
The pure shall throw inhibitions
    away.
If not—well, we're sorry, you still
    have to pay:
You can't expect miracles every day!

Step up! Step up! Pay now, pray later!
Buy your tickets, light your candles!
Count your blessings, take the
    waters!
One blessing per pilgrim per ticket!
Only one blessing per pilgrim per
    ticket!
And a little child shall lead you . . .

PILGRIMS

Happy . . .

ALL

Amen.

Only one institution in town is profitable: the Cookie Jar, a sanitarium for social misfits. A large platoon of these "Cookies," pleasantly dressed and blandly smiling, shows up for the now-famous water cure. They are shepherded by Nurse Fay Apple, an outspoken young woman and clearly a disbeliever in the "miracle." The Cookies sing their brief anthem.

COOKIES

I'm like the bluebird.
I should worry, I should care.
I should be a millionaire.
I'm like the bluebird . . .

Schub and Cooley immediately realize the effect that a sizable group of non-cures will have on business, and refuse to sell tickets to the Cookies. Fay delivers an impassioned monologue, accusing them and the Mayoress of venality and fraud. While everyone's attention has been on her, the Cookies have intermingled with the "sane" pilgrims, from whom they are now indistinguishable. Fay refuses to identify her patients and Schub orders her arrest, but she escapes to the top of a hill and addresses the Cookies in song.

There Won't Be Trumpets (cut)

FAY

Those smug little men
With their smug little schemes,
They forgot one thing:
The play isn't over by a long shot yet!

There are heroes in the world,
Princes and heroes in the world,
And one of them will save us!
Wait and see!
Wait and see!

There won't be trumpets or bolts of
    fire
To say he's coming,
No Roman candles, no angels' choir,
No sound of distant drumming.

He may not be the cavalier,
Tall and graceful, fair and strong.
Doesn't matter,
Just as long as he comes along!

But not with trumpets or lightning
    flashing
Or shining armor.
He may be daring, he may be
    dashing,
Or maybe he's a farmer.

We can wait—what's another day?
He has lots of hills to climb.
And a hero doesn't come
Till the nick of time!

Don't look for trumpets or whistles
    tooting
To guarantee him.
There won't be trumpets, but sure as
    shooting,
You'll know him when you see him!

Don't know when, don't know
    where,
And I can't even say that I care!
All I know is, the minute you turn
And he's suddenly there,
You won't need trumpets!
There are no trumpets!
Who needs trumpets?

In the first version of this song, the word "hero" was the stanchion on which the song was built, but no matter how majestic I made the music, the result was weaker than I wanted it to be. The breathy "h" and the soft "r" belie what the word is supposed to convey. "Trumpets" is a word that sounds like what it means. (The verse in the second version, herewith, is the same.)

A Hero Is Coming
(cut)

FAY
(To Schub and Cooley)

A hero is coming.
You won't know him by his white
    Charger,
But he'll be the kind of knight
That we need.
A hero is coming.
No, you won't hear any band
    Playing,
But he's gonna take a stand
And succeed!

(To the Cookies)

Never fear,
He'll be here in time.
Heroes don't appear
Till the nick of time.

(Referring to Schub and Cooley)

Who are they?
Let them plot and plan.
Let them have their day
And their way
While they can,

(To Schub and Cooley)

'Cause a hero is coming,
Coming quietly with no
Trumpets,
But he'll be here any mo-
Ment, so fly, boys,
Fly!
You won't know him by his bright
Armor,
But there'll be a funny light
In his eye, boys!

Stars won't burst,
Mountains will not crash,
Thunder won't come first
And no lightning will flash.
Oh, maybe an aura—
One tiny glow—
Maybe the faintest drums.

But a hero is coming,
That much I know,
And we're not gonna do a thing till he
comes!

In the event, neither version made it into the show. "There Won't Be Trumpets" was cut just before the Broadway opening, for two reasons: first, Lee Remick, who played Fay, delivered the virtuoso monologue which preceded it so effectively and got such a huge hand that the song became an anticlimax; second, the show was overlong, not least because it was in three acts (the last such musical, I believe). Arthur and I tried to reduce it to two by eliminating one intermission and thus, with the addition of cutting the song, saving ourselves twenty minutes in toto. But we were overwhelmed by the technical problems of costume and set changes that such a rearrangement caused and were forced to revert to three acts, trimming what we could, including "There Won't Be Trumpets." We were able to diminish the running time by fifteen minutes, which improved the show enormously. But not enough.

Dr. Detmold, chief psychiatrist at the Cookie Jar, comes to the town square to meet his new assistant. He is unable to help Schub sort the Cookies from the pilgrims because, as he says, he wouldn't recognize them unless they were lying down on a couch. He urges Cora and the Council to wait for the new colleague he is expecting and leaves. Soon enough an energetic young man named J. Bowden Hapgood appears, looking for Dr. Detmold and the Cookie Jar. Cora, relieved at the arrival of professional help, asks Hapgood if he can identify the Cookies. Easily, says Hapgood, simply by applying "the principles of logic."

The scene which follows was my first substantial attempt at combining song, musicalized dialogue and action into a unified whole, a technique I refined in later shows, particularly the ones I wrote with James Lapine. As you read the following, remember that music is continuous and carefully timed to the dialogue. The lyrics are sometimes spoken and sometimes sung.

Simple

HAPGOOD
Grass is green,
Sky is blue,
False is false
And true is true.
Who is who?
You are you, I'm me!
Simple? Simple? Simple?
Simple as A-B-C.
Simple as one-two-three.

SCHUB
But who on that line is what?

HAPGOOD
One is one,
Two is two,
Who is what
And which is who?
No one's always
What they seem to be.

CORA
(A crack at Schub)
That's certainly true.

HAPGOOD
Simple? Simple?
Simple as A-B-C.
Simple as one-two-three.

(To a man on the line)

For example you, sir, with the manly good looks. Would you come forward please, Mr. Hapgood?

SCHUB
I thought you were Hapgood.

HAPGOOD
Calling the patient by my name, he identifies with me immediately, we have an instant transference and thereby save five years of psychoanalysis.

CORA
Brilliant! What happens if I call you Hoover Hooper?

HAPGOOD
Shall we dance? No, we have. Now then, Mr. Hapgood—

GEORGE
Call me Happy, Sir. Or George.

HAPGOOD
All right, Georgie.

GEORGE
Thank you, George.

HAPGOOD
Thank you. Now when we were a child, that is, when you were a child, a boy—you were a boy?

GEORGE
I was a manly little fellow, sir.

HAPGOOD
Then I'm sure there was a saying you learned that you have used ever since to govern your life. A motto, a watchcry.

GEORGE
A watchcry. Yes, sir.

"I am the master of my fate
And the captain of my soul!"

HAPGOOD
Good, Hapgood.
Now then:

(In rhythm)

Married?

GEORGE
Yes, sir.

HAPGOOD
Two children?

GEORGE
Yes, sir.

HAPGOOD
Two TV sets?

GEORGE
Yes, sir.

HAPGOOD
Two martinis?

GEORGE
Yes, sir.

HAPGOOD
Bank on Friday?

GEORGE
Yes, sir.

HAPGOOD
Golf on Saturday?

GEORGE
Yes, sir.

HAPGOOD
Church on Sunday?

GEORGE
Yes, sir.

HAPGOOD
Do you vote?

GEORGE
Yes, sir.

Only for the man who wins.
Only for the man who wins.
Only for the man who—

HAPGOOD
All right. Headaches?

GEORGE
No, sir.

HAPGOOD
Backaches?

GEORGE
No, sir.

HAPGOOD
Heartaches?

GEORGE
No, sir.

HAPGOOD
(No longer in rhythm)

Thank you, Hapgood. Group A.
Over there, please.

SCHUB
What's group A?

CORA
Obviously mad as a hatter.

SCHUB
Magruder! Place that Cookie under
arrest.

HAPGOOD
Just a moment. George—do you
ever wonder whether you're real?

GEORGE
No, sir. I know I'm not.

HAPGOOD
Group One. Over there, please.

Grass is green,
Sky is blue,
Safe is sane and tried is true.
You be you
And me to some degree.
Simple? Simple? Simple as A-B-C,
Simple as one-two-three.

CORA
Well, is he safe or sane, Doctor?
Darling.

SCHUB
Safe is sane.

HAPGOOD
Not always.

The opposite of safe is out.
The opposite of out is in.
So anyone who's safe is "in."

GEORGE
That I've always been!

CORA
Shh!

The opposite of safe is out,
The opposite of out is in.
So anyone who's out is "in."

HAPGOOD
Right!
That's how groups begin!

CORA, OTHERS
When you're in, you win!

HAPGOOD
Simple? Simple? Simple?
Simple as A-B-C.

CORA, OTHERS
Simple! Simple! Simple!

HAPGOOD
Simple as do you like me?

CORA
I do indeed like you. The
question is—

SCHUB
The question is—

(To a man who has been sneaking over to
George)

Just a moment there—

MAN IN LINE
"I am the master of my fate
And the captain of my soul."

But my name isn't George, Doctor.

HAPGOOD
What is it?

MAN
Hapgood.

HAPGOOD
Group A. Over there, please.

SCHUB
What is this?

CORA
I don't know, but it's brilliant!

SCHUB
But which group is what?

HAPGOOD
It's very simple.

Grass is green,
Sky is blue,
A is one group, One is, too.
One is One or one is A, you see . . .

CORA
Grass is green,
Sky is blue,
One is one and
A is two.

SCHUB
No, A is One and
One is, too.

CORA   COOLEY
No, one and one   No, One is green,
Is always two   A is blue.
To me!   One can be
I don't agree!   In A, you see.
A is you and   A is crazy!
Me!   Maybe . . .

MAGRUDER   SCHUB
No, A is green,
One is blue!   No, One is One,
A is "out" and   A is one group,
One is "in"!   Too.
I agree.   See?

WOMAN IN LINE
Aaaaaaaaaaaaaaaa—

(Joined by a man in the line)

—a woman's place is in the home,
A woman's place is in the house.
And home is where you hang
    your hat,
And that is where you hang your
    spouse.

HAPGOOD
Dear Mr. and Mrs. Hapgood.

JUNE
Oh, we're not married, Doctor. He's
June and I'm John. I mean, she's
John and he's June.

JOHN
June and John are engaged.

JUNE
John's my secretary.

JOHN
June used to be my secretary but his
corporation went bust.

JUNE
And her syndicate took over.

HAPGOOD
Well, it would all be in the family if
you got married.

JOHN
But John can't support June.

JUNE
Every cent John makes goes to pay
for June's dinners.

HAPGOOD
Why doesn't June give John a raise?

JUNE
He's not worth it.

HAPGOOD
I see. And neither of you wants John
to stay home and do the housekeep-
ing because—

HAPGOOD, JUNE, JOHN
A woman's place is in the home,
A woman's place is on the shelf.
And home is where he hangs her hat,
And that is where she hangs himself.

CORA, SCHUB
Group—

HAPGOOD
(To June)

A.

SCHUB
Magruder!

HAPGOOD
(To John)

One.

*(As Hapgood divides everyone into two
groups, they sing various watchcries
simultaneously)*

SCHUB
Now wait! Are they all Cookies? If
you could produce someone who is
sane, present company excluded, of
course—

*(Martin, an African-American, steps
forward)*

HAPGOOD
Ah—good lad, Hapgood. Watchcry!

MARTIN
You can't judge a book by its cover.
You can't judge a book by its cover.

You can't judge a book
By how literate it look,
No, you can't judge a book by its
    cubber.

HAPGOOD
Occupation?

MARTIN
Going to schools, riding in buses,
eating in restaurants.

HAPGOOD
Isn't that line of work getting rather
easy?

MARTIN
Not for me. I'm Jewish . . . Group A,
would you say?

HAPGOOD
Group One's more fun.

MARTIN
Crazy.

CORA
Group A . . .

SCHUB
Group One . . .

CORA
It's maddening!

SCHUB
What's the difference between them?

HAPGOOD
It's obvious:

The opposite of dark is bright,
The opposite of bright is dumb,
So anything that's dark is dumb—

MARTIN
But they sure can hum.
The opposite of dark is bright,
The opposite of bright is dumb.

HAPGOOD, MARTIN,
TWO OTHER MEN
So anything that's dark is dumb.

HAPGOOD, TWO MEN
That's the rule of thumb.

MARTIN
Depends where you're from.

HAPGOOD
Simple? Simple? Simple? Simple as
    A-B-C.
Simple as NAACP . . .

MAN
I get the point, Comptroller
Hapgood.

SCHUB
Oh, shut up and get in group A.

CORA
Who's that?

SCHUB
My brother-in-law.

CORA
But he's not a pilgrim . . . and he's
not a Cookie—Hapgood . . .

HAPGOOD
Who is what?
Which is who?
That is that, and how are you?
I feel fine, what else is new?

CORA
What was he doing on the line?

SCHUB
Oh, every fool wants a miracle.
Hapgood—

CORA
Who is on that line?

SCHUB
Doctor, you are not doing what we
want you to!

CORA
You're right! Look here, Hapgood—
darling—

Grass is green,
Sky is blue,
I'd join any group with you.
Schub's a boob, and you belong
    to me!
Simple? Simple? Simple?
Simple as one-two-three,
One-two-three,
One-two-three . . .

PILGRIMS, COOKIES
(Simultaneously, waltzing)
Doctor, what group am I in?
. . . Where do I belong? . . .
Where am I? . . . Tell me where I
go . . . Where do I fit? . . .

SCHUB
Get back! Your Honor! Cora! He's
taking over! They're turning to him!
Stop it! Doctor—Group A: Cookies?
Or Group One: Cookies? The truth
now. Which—is—what?

HAPGOOD
Watchcry!

GROUP A
(Simultaneously)
"I am the master of my fate and—"
"A woman's place is in the—"
"If at first you don't succeed—"

HAPGOOD
Rub your stomachs!
Goo-ood. Goo-ood.
Watchcry!

GROUP ONE
(Simultaneously)
"I am the master of my fate and—"
"A woman's place is in the—"
"Beauty is only skin—"

HAPGOOD
Pat your heads. Hello, hello . . .
Goo-ood . . . Hello. Hello . . .
Reverse! Good. Hello. Hello.
That's goo-ood, goo-ood.
Goo-ood, Comptroller.

SCHUB
Dammit!

CORA
I adore games!

HAPGOOD
Watchcry!

CORA
Hello.

SCHUB
He's boring from within!

HAPGOOD
Watchcry!

SCHUB
Communist!

HAPGOOD
You would say that.

The opposite of left is right,
The opposite of right is wrong,
So anyone who's left is wrong, right?

CROWD
Goo-ood! Goo-ood!

HAPGOOD
Hello!

CROWD
Hello!

HAPGOOD
Simple? Simple? Simple?
Simple as you tell me.
Simple as one-two-three
Cheers for the Red, White and
    Blue . . .

Watchcry!

MAGRUDER
Look here: I'm the Chief of—

HAPGOOD
Watchcry!

MAGRUDER
"Ours not to reason why,
Ours but to do or die."
Sergeant Magruder reporting, sir.

HAPGOOD
Occupation?

MAGRUDER
Fighting the enemy.

HAPGOOD
What enemy?

MAGRUDER
What year?

HAPGOOD
Yesterday:

MAGRUDER
The Germans: Heil!

HAPGOOD
The day before:

MAGRUDER
The Germans: Heil!

HAPGOOD
Today:

MAGRUDER
The Germans: Hail!

HAPGOOD
Tomorrow:

MAGRUDER
Hail!
Heil!
Hail? . . . Heil? . . . Hail?

HAPGOOD
Group A.

MAGRUDER
Heil?

HAPGOOD
Group One.

MAGRUDER
Hail?

COOLEY
You're just making him seem crazy,
but he's twisted. I mean—he's been
twisted.

HAPGOOD
Grass is blue,
Sky is green,
Change of time is change of scene.
What you meant is what you mean!
Watchcry!

COOLEY
Hallelujah!

Now listen, Brother—

HAPGOOD
Occupation?

COOLEY
Preacher—er, Treasurer.

HAPGOOD
Oh, you were a preacher, Hapgood.

COOLEY
I'm a treasurer, Cooley—I mean—

HAPGOOD
They threw you out of your pulpit—

COOLEY
Brother!

HAPGOOD
Because you were crazy!

COOLEY
Because I believed!

HAPGOOD
In being treasurer.

COOLEY
In God, and they only believed in
religion.

HAPGOOD
And that made you crazy, Hapgood.

COOLEY
I am not crazy, Cooley!

HAPGOOD
No, you're Crazy Hapgood.

COOLEY
I am not Cooley, I mean I am not
crazy, I'm Hapgood!

HAPGOOD
Are you sure?

COOLEY
I am completely Schub!

SCHUB
He's crazy!

HAPGOOD
Thank you. Group A: Watchcry!

*(Group A responds with their watchcries;
Hapgood turns to Group One)*

Watchcry!

*(They respond similarly; Hapgood turns
to Schub)*

Watchcry!

SCHUB
I don't have one, Cooley!

HAPGOOD
Aha!

SCHUB
Hapgood, we are going to end all
this right here and now, my dear
Treasurer, I mean Doctor, dammit!
Right now! which group is—

HAPGOOD
Two questions.

SCHUB
One answer.

HAPGOOD
Just two little questions, Schub, and
you'll know which group is what.
Where does most of your money go?

SCHUB
I hardly—

HAPGOOD
Where does most of your money go,
Hapgood?

SCHUB
In taxes.

HAPGOOD
(To the Groups)
Goo-ood . . .

(To Schub)

What do you think of someone who
makes a product and doesn't use it?

SCHUB
He's crazy.

HAPGOOD
(To the Groups)
Hello, hello . . .

(To Schub)

Most of your money goes to the government in taxes. What does the

government do with most of the money? Makes bombs.

(To the Groups)

Reverse! Goo-ood . . . Hello, hello . . .

(To Schub)

But you say to make a product and not use it is crazy. Isn't that what you said, Comptroller Cooley? And doesn't that make you crazy for letting them waste your money, Treasurer Schub?

(To the Groups)

Reverse!

(To Schub)

But perhaps the government is making bombs because it means to use the product. Which means everyone will be killed, Hapgood. Including you, Schub.

(To the Groups)

Both together now!

(To Schub)

Which means you are paying most of your money to have yourself killed. Which means, my dear Doctor Comptroller Mayor Schub, you are the maddest of all! Watchcry!

SCHUB
Help!!

HAPGOOD
Watchcry!

CORA
Brilliant!

HAPGOOD
Watchcry!

GROUPS
Grass is green.
Sky is blue.
The opposite of left is right.
The opposite of right is wrong.

Simple? Simple? Simple?
Simple as A-B-three,
Simple as one-two-C,
As grass is green,
As sky is blue,
As simple as the opposite of left is
      right
Is wrong is right is A is One
Is A is One Hello! Hello!
Goo-ood! Goo-ood!
A is One! One is A!
Grass is who is opposite of what is
Green is safe is opposite of dark is
Opposite of simple which is
Watchcry! Watchcry! Watchcry!
      Watchcry!
Who is what? Which is who?
Who is what? Which is who?
Who is what? WHICH is WHO is
      WHO?

HAPGOOD
You are all mad.

(Rows of theater seats appear onstage and the cast sits in them, becoming an audience, fanning themselves with their programs and laughing and applauding the real audience as the curtain falls)

This last conceit exemplifies what Peter Shaffer meant by our condescension toward the audience. The first act has a glib, smug tone that is sometimes funny and often clever, but more often irritatingly arch. There's a very thin line between smart and smart-ass, and we overstepped it. The second and third acts were a better mix of satire and feeling.

ACT TWO

Group A and Group One parade through the town, each proclaiming its collective sanity and superiority, both of them endorsing Hapgood for Mayor.

The A-1 March

GROUP A
Hooray for A,
The Group that's well-adjusted,
Everyone can be trusted
In Group A.

GROUP ONE
Have fun with One,
The Group that's not neurotic,
Everyone's patriotic
In Group One.

BOTH
Dignity, integrity, and so on,
We haven't much to go on,
Still we go on.
We've a platform strong enough to
      grow on.

GROUP A
Whenever they cheer, we're incensed!

GROUP ONE
Whatever they're for, we're against!

Hooray for Hapgood,
Hapgood can be trusted,
Friend of the well-adjusted
In Group A!

GROUP ONE
Hooray for Hapgood,
Hapgood's patriotic,
Friend of the un-neurotic
In Group One!

BOTH
Hapgood has no answers or
      suggestions,
Only a lot of questions—
We like questions!
What's the use of answers or
      suggestions?
As long as we're told where to go,
There isn't a thing we need to know!

The celebration is momentarily interrupted by the arrival of a Lady from Lourdes—provocative dress, rhinestone slippers, dark glasses, flame-red wig and heavy French accent—who has been sent, she says, to test the miraculous waters. It is clearly Fay in disguise. She meets and flirts with Hapgood.

Rehearsals

Come Play Wiz Me

FAY
Docteur, docteur, vous êtes charmant.

HAPGOOD
Mademoiselle, vous aussi.

FAY
You like my hair, yes? My lips, yes?
Ze sway
Of my—how you say?—
Of my hips, yes?
You wish to play wiz me?
Okay wiz me.
Come out and play wiz me.

HAPGOOD
Mademoiselle, vous êtes jolie.

FAY
Docteur, docteur, si gentil.

You like my style, yes? My brand, yes?
Ze lay
Of my—how you say?—
Of my land, yes?
You wish to pray wiz me?
To stray wiz me?
Come out and play wiz me.

HAPGOOD
Mademoiselle, vous êtes timide.

FAY
Docteur, docteur, you're so right.
I like your—how you say—
Imperturbable perspicacity.
It isn't how you say, it's what you see!

We have ze lark, yes? Ze fling, yes?
Ze play
Is ze—how you say?—
Is ze thing, yes?
If you will play wiz me,
Mon cheri,
Though we may not agree
Today,
In time,
Mais oui,
We may.

(They dance)

Docteur, docteur,
Ze English it fails me.
Ah, but, *docteur,*
You're good for what ails me.

HAPGOOD
I like your hair—

FAY
Yes?

HAPGOOD
Your lips—

FAY
Yes?

HAPGOOD
Ze sway
Of your—how you say?—
Of your hips—

FAY
Yes?

HAPGOOD
Come up and play wiz me.

FAY
Come out and play wiz me.

BOTH
Come on and play wiz me.

FAY
Docteur, docteur, let's play *docteur . . .*

HAPGOOD
Mademoiselle, you're not well!
But I like your style—

FAY
Yes?

HAPGOOD
Your brand—

FAY
Yes?

HAPGOOD
Ze lay
Of your—*qu'est-ce que c'est?*—
Of your land—

FAY
Yes?

HAPGOOD
Come up and play wiz me.

FAY
Come out and play wiz me.

BOTH
Come on and play wiz me!

HAPGOOD
Mademoiselle, doctor's orders . . .

FAY
You're ze *docteur,* I'm impatient . . .

HAPGOOD
I like your—how you say?—
Unmistakable authenticity.
It isn't how you say, it's what I see!

FAY
We have ze lark—yes? Ze fling—yes?
Ze play
Is ze—how you say?—
Is ze thing—yes?

FAY, HAPGOOD
Come on and play wiz me,
Mon ami,
Come have your way wiz me
Today!
You play
Wiz me—

HAPGOOD
My way—

FAY
Maybe—

HAPGOOD
Bébé—

FAY
Mais oui!

BOTH
We play!

Their flirtation heats up and they find themselves in a bedroom of the local hotel, starting to make love. As the moment becomes more torrid, the Lady from Lourdes removes her wig and identifies herself as Nurse Apple, shaped by order and control. Wistfully, she ruminates.

Anyone Can Whistle

FAY

Anyone can whistle,
That's what they say—
Easy.
Anyone can whistle,
Any old day—
Easy.

It's all so simple:
Relax, let go, let fly.
So someone tell me why
Can't I?

I can dance a tango,
I can read Greek—
Easy.
I can slay a dragon
Any old week—
Easy.

What's hard is simple,
What's natural comes hard.
Maybe you could show me
How to let go,
Lower my guard,
Learn to be free.
Maybe if you whistle,
Whistle for me.

Ever since I first performed this song at a benefit concert in 1973, musical-theater rhapsodists have appropriated it as my personal statement. As the emcee of a recent concert introduced it with dramatic inaccuracy, "'Anyone Can Whistle' is the only song that Stephen Sondheim has publicly acknowledged to be autobiographical." He is one of many who fall into the trap of ascribing the character of the art to the character of the artist. Just as some movie fans thought Cary Grant must have been as unflappably suave as his public persona or assumed Edward G. Robinson to be a tough uneducated thug rather than the worldly art collector he actually was, so some musical-theater lovers think of Irving Berlin as an artless super-American and Oscar Hammerstein as a good-hearted hayseed. Labels make the labeler feel comfortable and simplify the complications which might blur any image, reducing the personalities to familiar packages which shorten the distance between the dreamer and the dream. To believe that "Anyone Can Whistle" is my credo is to believe that I'm the prototypical Repressed Intellectual and that explains everything about me. Perhaps being tagged with a cliché shouldn't bother me, but it does, and to my chagrin I realize it means that I care more about how I'm perceived than I wish I did. I'd like to think this concern hasn't affected my work, but I wouldn't be surprised if it has.

Back in the town square, Cora wonders why it's Hapgood who's being carried around by both Groups on her litter.

A Parade in Town

GROUP A
Hooray for Hapgood,
Hapgood can be trusted,
Friend of the well-adjusted
In Group A!

GROUP ONE
Hooray for Hapgood,
Play a part with Hapgood,
Miracles start with Hapgood,
Gladden your heart with Hapgood!

BOTH
Join the parade with Hapgood!
No one's afraid with Hapgood!
Follow your star with Hapgood!
Know who you are with Hapgood!
Throw in your lot for Hapgood!
Everyone's hot for Hapgood!

CORA
Hi! . . . Hey! . . . Wait! . . . Voters . . .

I see flags, I hear bells,
There's a parade in town.
I see crowds, I hear yells,
There's a parade in town!

I hear drums in the air,
I see clowns in the square,
I see marchers marching,
Tossing hats at the sky.

"Anyone Can Whistle" with Lee Remick as Fay

Did you hear? Did you see?
Is a parade in town?
Are there drums without me?
Is a parade in town?

Well, they're out of step, the flutes are
     squeaky,
The banners are frayed.
Any parade in town without me
Must be a second-class parade!
So! . . . Ha! . . .

BOTH GROUPS
Hapgood has no answers or
     suggestions,
Only a lot of questions.
We like questions!
What's the use of answers or
     suggestions?
As long as we're told where to go,
There isn't a thing we need to know.

CORA
Did you hear? Did you see?
Was a parade in town?

Anyone Can Whistle *recording session*

But then she wouldn't be a cartoon of venality and narcissism. What would make Cora sing such a song? What would be the reason for the song?

A very, very long pause followed. Then:

LANSBURY

Besides, Fay has five songs and Cora has only four.

As good a reason to write a song as any, I say—hence, "A Parade in Town." And Angela was happy, or at least till we got to Philadelphia.

In Hapgood's bedroom, he urges Fay to forget her inhibitions and responsibilities and set the Cookies free by tearing up their hospital records. He confesses that he is not a doctor at all, merely a new patient for the Cookie Jar, a former statistician who thought he could prove anything with numbers and logic. He grabs one of the records and starts to tear it up. Fay yells, "Don't!"

Were there drums without me?
Was a parade in town?
'Cause I'm dressed at last, at my best,
And my banners are high.
Tell me, while I was getting ready,
Did a parade go by?

After we had been in rehearsal for a week, Angela Lansbury, who was playing Cora, called me in a state of some agitation to ask if we could meet, which we immediately did. No sooner had she sat down than my worst fears were confirmed: She wanted to leave the show. Cora, she had discovered, was more a cartoon than a character, and she didn't know how to play a cartoon. I murmured diplomatically that being the discerning and intelligent actress she was (and is), she surely must have recognized that fact when she agreed to play the part. The following is not a verbatim transcription of the conversation which followed, but it's a respectable approximation.

SONDHEIM

All the characters, even the slightly more developed romantic leads, are exaggerations—the whole show is a cartoon.

LANSBURY

But there's no emotion for me to play.

SONDHEIM

Isn't greediness an emotion?

LANSBURY

A warm emotion, I mean. Couldn't Cora have a song with genuine feeling?

Everybody Says Don't

HAPGOOD
Everybody says don't,
Everybody says don't,
Everybody says don't, it isn't right,
Don't, it isn't nice!

Everybody says don't,
Everybody says don't,
Everybody says don't walk on the
     grass,
Don't disturb the peace,
Don't skate on the ice.

Well, I say
Do!
I say

Walk on the grass, it was meant to
    feel!
I say
Sail!
Tilt at the windmill,
And if you fail, you fail.

Everybody says don't,
Everybody says don't,
Everybody says don't get out of line.
When they say that, then,
Lady, that's a sign:
Nine times out of ten,
Lady, you are doing just fine!

Make just a ripple.
Come on, be brave.
This time a ripple,
Next time a wave.
Sometimes you have to start small,
Climbing the tiniest wall,
Maybe you're going to fall,
But it's better than not starting at all!

Everybody says no,
Everybody says stop,
Everybody says mustn't rock the boat,
Mustn't touch a thing.

Everybody says don't,
Everybody says wait,
Everybody says can't fight City Hall,
Can't upset the cart,
Can't laugh at the King!

Well, I say,
Try!
I say,
Laugh at the kings or they'll make
    you cry.

Lose your
Poise.
Fall if you have to,
But, lady, make a noise!

Everybody says don't.
Everybody says can't.
Everybody says wait around for
    miracles,
That's the way the world is made.

I insist on miracles, if *you* do them!
Miracles—nothing to them!
I say don't—
Don't be afraid!

(Fay agrees to free herself from her
inhibitions by freeing the Cookies. She
destroys the hospital records)

In the Introduction to this book, I
posited Ground Rule 4: Mis-stressing
is a cardinal sin. I say with pride and
sweat that I haven't committed that
particular sin often, but "if *you* do
them" is a blatant example of it, especially since it serves as the climax of
the song. The accent in the musical
phrase is on the word "if" while
clearly the word that should be accented is "you." The verbal phrase,
however, said exactly what I wanted to
say and I could find no other way of
saying it. I could have added a note at
the beginning of the melodic line to
take care of the "if" and then landed
heavily on the downbeat with "you,"
padding out the phrase with a word
such as "will" or "go" ("if *You* will do
them" or "if *You* go do them"), but
that would substitute fuzziness for suc-
cinctness. I chose the slyer coward's
path by abruptly raising the note on
the word "you," giving it a manufactured emphasis and making it sound
like an inflection rather than a mistake. This is a handy example of the
composer riding to the lyricist's rescue
(something I wish Rodgers had done
more frequently with Hart, the master
of mis-stress) and may be something
only a lyricist would notice, but I
wince every time I hear it—which, due
to the infrequency with which the
song is sung, is thankfully not very
often.

ACT THREE

Cora, Schub, Cooley and Magruder hatch
a plan to get rid of both the Lady from
Lourdes and Hapgood, who threaten their
miracle. They will turn off the fountain to
stop the Lady's investigation and blame
the failure on Hapgood, which will turn
the town against him. They pace Cora's
office, planning.

I've Got You to Lean On

SCHUB
Now why did the miracle go dry?

MAGRUDER
'Cause we turned the water off,
    is why.

CORA
Idiot!

SCHUB
Fool!

COOLEY
Oaf!

SCHUB
Moron!

CORA
Idiot!

SCHUB
Dolt!

CORA
Idiot!

SCHUB
We didn't turn it off, you see,
'Cause we didn't turn it on, not *we* . . .

MAGRUDER
Who did?

SCHUB
He did.

CORA
He did?

COOLEY
He did?

MAGRUDER
You did?

SCHUB
(Points upward)
He did!

CORA, COOLEY, MAGRUDER
(*The light dawns*)
He did!

ALL
Just what we needed, just what we
    needed!
Just what we needed, needed!

SCHUB
Now, why did he turn it off so quick?
A sign that our little town is sick.

CORA
Brilliant!

COOLEY
Clever!

MAGRUDER
Good!

CORA
(*Shoots them a look*)
Brilliant!

MAGRUDER
Brilliant!

COOLEY
Brilliant!

SCHUB
Sick people running wild, no less.
And who is responsible?

(*Smiling slowly*)

One guess.

MAGRUDER
Who?

CORA
Doctor Hapgood.

COOLEY
Doctor Hapgood.

ALL
(*Joyfully*)
Hallelujah, brother, cheers and
    acclaim!
Hallelujah, we've got someone to
    blame!
Hallelujah, praise the Lord and Amen!

CORA
Schub, you've done it again.

Whenever my world falls apart,
I never lose hope or lose heart.
Whatever the form
Of the storm
That may brew,
I've got you to lean on.

When everything's hopelessly gray,
You'll notice I'm youthfully gay!
There isn't a sing-
Le great thing
I can't do,
Not with you to lean on,
Darling you!

With you to depend on, I'll never
    quit.
There isn't a murder I couldn't
    commit.
I feel like a love-
Ly girl of
Twenty-two!
I've got you to lean on!

SCHUB
I've got you to lean on!

COOLEY
I've got you to lean on!

SCHUB
Now how do we educate the mass?

MAGRUDER
With hoses and Tommy-guns and gas.

CORA
Idiot!

SCHUB
Fool!

COOLEY
Oaf!

SCHUB
Moron!

CORA
Idiot!

SCHUB
Dolt!

CORA
IDIOT!

SCHUB
Can't tear a hero down by force.
So how do we educate—?
Of course!

MAGRUDER
How?

SCHUB
Smear him.

CORA
Smear him?

COOLEY
Smear him . . .

MAGRUDER
Spear him?

SCHUB
Smear him.

OTHERS
Smear him!
No one'll hear him!

SCHUB
Now what can we label him, my
    friends?
A phrase that the rabble
    comprehends—

COOLEY
"Religious pervert."

MAGRUDER
Brilliant!

CORA
Terrible!

MAGRUDER
Terrible!

CORA
Idiot.

SCHUB
A phrase with a little more finesse . . .
Obscene but inspiring—

Ah, yes.

MAGRUDER
Yes?

SCHUB
"Enemy of Heaven."

CORA
"—Heaven . . ."

COOLEY
"—Heaven . . ."

MAGRUDER
"—Heaven . . ."

CORA
Heaven!

MEN
Enemy of God,
Enemy of the church,
Enemy of Heaven!

CORA
I didn't hear it,
But spread it.
I never said it,
But spread it!

ALL
Hallelujah, all our problems are
    through!

Hallelujah, that's what teamwork
    can do!
Hallelujah, Brothers, pull on the oars!

CORA
Schub, my kingdom is yours!

Whenever my world turns to dust,
I've always got someone to trust.
Whatever the sort
Of support
That I need,
I've got you to lean on.

MEN
When everything's hollow and black,
You'll always have us at your back.
No matter how hollow,
We'll follow
Your lead.
And with us to lean on,
You'll succeed.

CORA
What comfort it is to have always
    known
That if they should catch me I won't
    go alone.
I'll always give credit
Where credit
Is due.
I've got you to lean on!

MEN
We've got you to lean on!

CORA
I've got *you* to lean on!

*Hapgood and Fay discover the pump
inside the rock. She wants to expose the
fake miracle. Hapgood replies that the
world will believe it's a miracle anyway,
because that's what it wants and he, Hapgood, is just going to relax on his veranda
and watch it happen. Fay rushes off in a
rage.*

See What It Gets You

FAY
Take one step
And see what it gets you,
See what it gets you,
See what it gets you!
One step up and see how it gets you
Down.

Give yourself
If somebody lets you.
See what it gets you,

Harry Guardino as Hapgood with Lee Remick

See what it gets you!
Give yourself and somebody lets you
Down.

Here's how to crawl,
Now run, lady!
Here's how to walk,
Now fly!
Here's how to feel—have fun, lady,
And a fond goodbye!

Reach out your hand
And see what it gets you,
See what it gets you,
See what it gets you!
Trouble is, whatever it gets, you
Find
That once you see,
You can't stay blind.

What do I do now,
Now that my eyes are wide?
Well, when the world goes mad,
Then they've got to be shown,
And when the hero quits,
Then you're left on your own,
And when you want things done,
You have to do them yourself alone!
And if I'm not ready, and light-
    headed,
I can't stand here dumb.
So, ready or not, here, I hope, I come!

Anyone can whistle, that's what they
    say—easy.
Anyone can whistle any old day—
    easy.
It's all so simple: relax, let go, let fly.
And someone tell me, why can't I?
Whistle at a dragon, down it'll fall—
    easy.
Whistle at a hero, trumpets and all—
    easy.
Just once I'll do it,
Just once before I die.

Lead me to the battle,
What does it take?
Over the top!
Joan at the stake!
Anyone can whistle—

(She tries to whistle, but can't quite do it)

Well, no one can say
I didn't try!

---

*In a ballet of waltzes, Cora, Schub and
Dr. Detmold, with the assistance of the
State Police, try to round up and cage the
Cookies all over town.*

The Cookie Chase

CORA
(To the troops)
On your toes!

*(They oblige. Even the Policemen are in
ballet slippers)*

CORA
Lock 'em up! Put 'em away! In the Jar!
Time to start getting the nets out!
Lock 'em up! Into the cage! Quietly!
No one must know.
Cart 'em off into the bin! Turn
    the key!
Quick, before anyone gets out!
Turn the key! Throw it away! There
    we are!
Forty-eight to go!

*(No one, including Dr. Detmold, has any
idea which people are Cookies, even as
they're being arrested)*

CORA
Are they breathing? Then they're
    Cookies.
Are they moving? Then they're
    Cookies.
Are they living? Then they're Cookies.
So get on with it! Quick, get on
    with it!
Are they human? Then they're
    Cookies.
So shut up, my dear doctor, and shut
    her up, too!

Looky, looky, here comes Cookie
Now.
Naughty Cookie, playing hooky—
That we don't allow.

*(She turns to Schub, after a number of
people have been caged)*

You take the key, my love,
I'm too exhausted to move!
Music, I must have music,
A moment's music or my head will
    burst!
I know you'll meet the test—
You've been well rehearsed.
Do your best
(Meaning do your worst),
Let me rest
And remember, *Schubchen*,
Women and children first!

*(A series of dance variations takes place,
during which more Cookies and non-
Cookies are rounded up, capped by Fay
entering as the Lady from Lourdes and
vamping Schub in a waltz while attempting to steal the key of the cage from him.)*

FAY *
You hold ze key, mon Schub,
You hold ze key of my heart.
Music,
I must have music!
We make ze music
Six o'clock ce soir.
First we dance like zis,
Zen we ooh la la.
Zen ze kiss,
Zen etcetera.
All ze bliss . . .
And remember,
Schubette,
You hold ze key to moi.

*(Failing to get the key, she reappears a
short while later, this time trying to start
a panic)*

FAY
Fire!
Hurricane!
Everyone off of ze streets!
Run for your lives, run for your lives!
Ze dam has burst!
Run for your lives, run for your lives!
Ze lion's loose!

---

* This section was cut prior to the New York
opening.

Fire, bubonic plague, air raid
    warning—
Hurry, run! Run! Run!

(Fay and Cora comfort each other)

In traditional musicals, there is a
bookmark known as the eleven-
o'clock number. Dating back to the
days when the curtain rose at eight
thirty and musicals were essentially
vehicles for star performers, the term
meant a song performed by one or
more of them just before the finale,
calculated to bring down the house. It
served as the climax of the show and
was something the audience eagerly
anticipated during the whole evening—
and it usually involved a string of en-
cores. ("Anything You Can Do" from
Annie Get Your Gun is a classic example.) Since Lee Remick and Angela
Lansbury were indeed stars and had
not appeared in a scene together before this moment, a comic confrontation between the two, dressed exactly
alike (Fay having disguised herself
as Cora in order to cause confusion),
seemed like the eleven-o'clock number to end all eleven-o'clock numbers,
even though three scenes and one
more song were still to come. Call it a
ten-thirty number. It occurred when
Cora sees Fay in action and has her
arrested.

There's Always a Woman (cut)

CORA
There's always a woman
To spoil the illusion,
The rotten banana
That ruins the bunch.
It's always a woman
Who causes confusion.
There's nothing as low as a woman . . .
We must lunch.

FAY
Love to.

CORA
Noon-ish.

FAY
Tomorrow.

CORA
Today.

FAY
My place?

CORA
(Pointedly)
Mine.

FAY
There's always a woman,
The one disappointment,
The note that goes sour
And gums up the tune.
The ant at the picnic,
The fly in the ointment.
There's nothing as low as a
    woman . . .
Ring me soon.

CORA
Love to.

FAY
'Voir.

(Tries to sneak off)

CORA
Leaving?

FAY
I thought . . .

CORA
I know.

FAY
I tried.

BOTH
It's always a woman—

CORA
The counterfeit check.

FAY
The snake in the woodpile.

CORA
The pain in the neck.

BOTH
The sand in the oyster
That isn't the pearl.
There's nothing as low as a
    woman . . .
Darling girl.

CORA
Pet.

FAY
Lamb.

CORA
Dove.

FAY
Fish.

CORA
The run in the stocking,
The snag in the zipper,
The weather in London,
The water in France.
It's always a woman,
It's Jacqueline the Ripper.
There's nothing as low as a
    woman . . .
Shall we dance?

FAY
Waltz?

CORA
Tango?

FAY
Can-can?

CORA
Rumba?

FAY
Schottische?

CORA
Gavotte?

FAY
Cha-cha?

CORA
Tap?

FAY
Bolero?

CORA

Polka?

FAY

Bridge?

CORA

Two hearts.

FAY

Three clubs.

CORA

I pass.

FAY

There's always a woman,
A crimp in the writing,
The hole in the sidewalk,
The gum on the shoe.
She almost looks human,
It must be the lighting.
Whatever it is,
It's a woman.
How are you?

CORA

Fine.

FAY

Pity.

BOTH

It's always a woman—

FAY

The hand in the till.

CORA

The five-dollar diamond.

FAY

The three-dollar bill.

BOTH

A genius for trickery
That's second to none.
There's nothing as low as a woman—
Isn't this fun!

CORA

Lovely!

FAY

Charming!

CORA

Delicious!

FAY

Stunning!

CORA

Fabulous!

FAY

Gorgeous!

BOTH

Exquisite!

CORA

A knife would be perfect.

FAY

A gun would be perfect.

CORA

It's quick and it's quiet.

FAY

At least I could try it.

CORA

I hear they do wonders—

FAY

And you can do wonders—

CORA

—With poisonous gas.

FAY

—With slivers of glass.

CORA

There's always the quarry.

FAY

There's always curare.

CORA

She'd never be found.

FAY

I have some around.

CORA

A noose is efficient—

FAY

Bamboo is efficient—

CORA

She won't make a sound.

FAY

—as long as it's ground.

BOTH

Whatever will do it,
If anything will,
There's nothing as low
As a woman—

CORA

Sneak.

FAY

Thief.

CORA

Cheat.

FAY

Crook.

CORA

Frump.

FAY

Fake.

CORA

Bore.

FAY

Bag.

CORA

Leech.

FAY

Crone.

CORA

Witch.

FAY

Ghoul.

BOTH

Police!
Shoot to kill!

**Unfortunately, although the comic
confrontation was a delight, it was a**

First day read-through

limited one, as was the audience's applause. It wasn't even a ten thirty number, more like a ten fifteen. It was quickly and prudently yanked. As for the rhyming of "woman" and "human," I have no excuse.

The Cookies are recaptured. Hapgood, renouncing his renouncement of the world, decides to reenter the human condition and tries to persuade Fay, now without her protective red wig, to join him. She can't go, she says—her Cookies need her. She gestures to him as he starts to leave.

With So Little to Be Sure Of

HAPGOOD
With so little to be sure of,
If there's anything at all,
If there's anything at all,
I'm sure of here and now and us
    together.

All I'll ever be I owe you,
If there's anything to be.
Being sure enough of you
Makes me sure enough of me.

Thanks for everything we did,
Everything that's past,
Everything that's over too fast.
None of it is wasted,
All of it will last,
Everything that's here and now and us
    together!

It was marvelous to know you,
And it isn't really through.
Crazy business this, this life we
    live in—
Don't complain about the time we're
    given.
With so little to be sure of in this
    world,
We had a moment,
A marvelous moment . . .

FAY
A marvelous moment.
A beautiful time.

I need you more than I can say.
I need you more than just today.
I guess I need you more than you
    need me,
And yet I'm happy.

All I'll ever be I owe you,
If there's anything to be.
Being sure enough of you
Made me sure enough of me.

HAPGOOD
(Simultaneously)
The more I memorize your face,
The more I never want to leave.
Come with me, Fay.

FAY
Thanks for everything we did,
Everything that's past,
Everything that's over too fast.

HAPGOOD
(Simultaneously)
There's more of love in me right now
Than all the little bits of love
I've known before.

BOTH
None of it was wasted,
All of it will last,
Everything that's here and now and us
    together!

It was marvelous to know you,
And it's never really through.
Crazy business this, this life we
    live in—
Can't complain about the time we're
    given!
With so little to be sure of in this
    world—

FAY
Hold me.
Hold me.

(Hapgood leaves. A new miracle is discovered in a neighboring town. As Cora and her cohorts rush off to take advantage of it, a new nurse takes charge of the Cookies, who march happily off to the Jar, singing.)

COOKIES
I'm like the bluebird,
I should worry, I should kick,
I should be a heretic,
I'm like the bluebird . . .

(Fay watches them go off, then for the first time in her life, whistles—for Hapgood to return. He does, and the rock spouts a fountain of rainbow-colored water)

CURTAIN

The ending of "With So Little to Be Sure Of" was problematical: the final harmony was left unresolved, which made the fading farewell of the two lovers effective but left the audience unready to applaud when they wanted to. It was the same problem I had faced with the ending of "Rose's Turn." This time I was determined to resist the false big finish, but in the isolation of my Philadelphia hotel room during the tryout I couldn't figure out how. So one evening I went down to the theater in the hope that I would get a Eureka! moment from seeing and hearing the song in its full panoply. After it finished to the usual uncertain audience reaction and while the sound of the orchestra and the emotions of the singers were still fresh in my head, I bolted from my seat in the back row (which is where I like to take notes, as it affords me the opportunity for a quick exit when an actor forgets his lines or a piece of scenery gets stuck) to try to figure out a solution. I didn't leave the theater because I wanted to be there to see the final five minutes, and I knew that the quietest place to go would be the men's room, which was down a long flight of stairs to the basement. I pushed through the door, sat down on one of the steps and held my hands over my ears to drown out the faint sounds of dialogue and music coming from the auditorium above so that I could concentrate on how to fix the cadence. As I played the music over and over in my head, I heard the door above me open and footsteps come down the stairs. They belonged to a middle-aged theatergoer on his way to relieve himself. I caught his eye as he passed and, seeing me huddled on the stair-case holding my head in my hands, he murmured sympathetically, "Got money in the show, huh, kid?"

Anyone Can Whistle was my first commercial failure and, after reading the mostly dreadful notices, I expected to feel devastated. Instead, I felt only disappointment: disappointment that the show would close almost immedi-ately and therefore that more people who might enjoy it would not have the chance to see it. I was buoyed by the realization that I had loved writing it and that I was happy with the result. Smart-ass though it may have been, *Whistle* was unconventional and inven-tive and, above all, playful. It gave me my first chance to write extended song-forms involving dialogue, as in "Sim-ple," and allowed me to use pastiche for comment on character and style, as in Cora's songs and "The Cookie Chase"—devices I continued to experiment with in subsequent shows. It was a laudable attempt to present something off-cen-ter in mainstream musical theater. It was my first direct inheritance from *Al-legro*, and like *Allegro*, it didn't work.

With Lee Remick

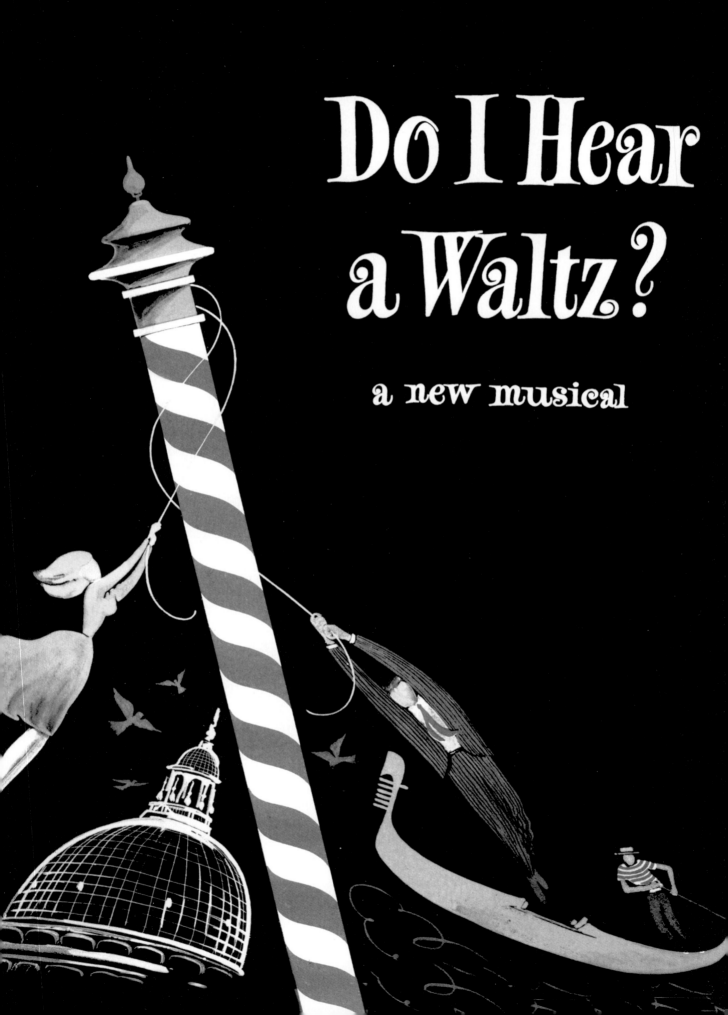

Do I Hear a Waltz?

a new musical

6. Do I Hear a Waltz? (1964)

Book by Arthur Laurents

Music by Richard Rodgers

Based on The Time of the Cuckoo *by*

   Arthur Laurents

The Notion

Leona Samish, an attractive, cheerful and repressed American secretary in her early thirties, goes on vacation to Venice, her first time abroad, falls in love with a married man and returns to America sadder but wiser.

General Comments

Just as *Anyone Can Whistle* didn't work, this show didn't either, but for the opposite reason: *Whistle* suffered from Arthur and me loving it too much, *Do I Hear a Waltz?* from our not caring about it enough. Shortly after *Gypsy* opened, Arthur had asked Oscar Hammerstein if he would be interested in making a musical of *The Time of the Cuckoo,* a play of Arthur's which had been produced in 1952 and was his first big hit. Oscar was attracted to the idea, but noted that David Lean's movie version of the story, called *Summertime* and released in 1955, was too recent, adding that if Arthur could wait a few years, it might be just the thing he and Richard Rodgers would like to write. A year later, Oscar died.

In my last meeting with him, Oscar, knowing he was dying and worried about leaving his partner bereft, urged me to consider writing a show with Rodgers, should he ever ask me. Since Oscar knew I wanted to write my own music (sadly for me, he never lived to hear any of it presented professionally), he was, in effect, asking a favor of

me. I chose to see it as a compliment, though an unwelcome one. And indeed, during the years after Oscar's death in 1960, Rodgers sent me three or four ideas, none of which interested me. Then, unfortunately, Arthur had an idea. Stinging as we were from the critical and financial failure of *Whistle* (we had labored on it for two years and because we'd waived our royalties, actually emerged $1,500 poorer than when we had begun, $1,500 being the amount we each foolishly sank into a pathetic last-minute advertisement in *The New York Times*), Arthur thought of approaching Rodgers with *Cuckoo,* this time with me as lyricist. His enticement to me was that it would be easy to write, and with Rodgers's name attached, we'd make a ton of money. I thought: Great, I can pay off my promise to Oscar and have the pleasure of working with Arthur again, but Arthur as a writer only, without the burden of his being his own director. And make a ton of money.

God knows, I had seen dozens of cautionary tales in movies and plays about self-deception, about being seduced by what's easy, by money, by fame, by expedience (mostly by money), so I was fully aware of the poison pill being offered me. The deceptive factor was that in this instance I had the justification of telling myself that I was paying my dues to Oscar, the man who had shaped so much of my life. It made me feel noble to sublimate my need to write music in order to support his forlornly abandoned partner. In addition, Mary Rodgers, Dick's daughter and a close friend of mine, kept encouraging me quietly but forcefully to collaborate with him on the grounds that I was young and upcoming and he was feeling old and out of touch. Warmed by the personal aspects of the venture and rationalizing right and left, I agreed to write the lyrics, as wrongheaded a decision as I've ever made.

To begin with, there was Rodgers the man as well as Rodgers the collaborator. He had been little more than a shadow in the background of my life as a protégé of the

Hammerstein family but, through his daughter, I had gotten to know him slightly. He had struck me as a funny, sour, difficult fellow, but I'd dealt with Jerome Robbins and come through comparatively unscathed, so I thought I could handle anything. What I hadn't taken into account was his corrosive conviction that his creative powers were failing, that the well had run dry, something Jerry never suffered from. This manifested itself in his refusal to rewrite, a stubborn ploy to cover his imagined infertility. Once he had put the music down on paper, he adamantly refused to reconsider even one note of it; he was afraid he had no other notes in reserve. This made for a fair amount of dull and repetitive music, especially in tunes like "What Do We Do? We Fly!" and "Bargaining," which were songs designed to be comic or to carry the story forward, songs which weren't geared for popularity outside the show and which he referred to as "mechanicals." The adventurous grace of the music he had written for *Oklahoma!* and *Carousel* was now rarely available to him. Unlike Lenny and even Jule, who had come from a thirty-two-bar-song tradition, Rodgers mistrusted any song whose measures didn't add up to a multiple of four, or at least two. I would bring him the sketch of a lyric on music paper with a suggested rhythmic notation attached, and he wouldn't even read it until he had counted the bars, usually by tapping on my sketch with a pencil in authoritarian skepticism; woe betide me if it turned out to be an odd number.

Songwriting collaboration is a volatile business at best, as even the hardiest partnerships, such as Gilbert and Sullivan, have proven, and my collaboration with Rodgers was far from the best. I had hoped that we could move the piece out of its conventional groove by having our heroine not sing until the last scene, when she has had her epiphany and learned something about herself through experience. The story was, after all, about a lonely, uptight (read "arid") American woman flung completely unprepared into an exotic, uninhibited (read "juicy") culture. Wouldn't it make emotional sense and be dramatically interesting, I thought, if throughout the evening the Italians sang (juicy) and she spoke (arid), and not until she had come out of her emotional confinement at the end of the story would she be able to sing. The leading lady would have only one song, but it would be a glorious aria of emotional release. The notion seemed metaphorically and theatrically right, but Rodgers would have none of it. I remembered then that the first carping reviews Rodgers had ever received during his collaboration with Hammerstein were for *Allegro,* and he had told Oscar that he would never again write an experimental show. I finally came to understand that the Rodgers and Hammerstein revolution was essentially Hammerstein's. Rodgers was an archconservative: his idea of innovation consisted of gimmicks, such as having all the action take place within the confines of a theater (*Me and Juliet*) or eliminating strings and having the orchestra wander through the show (*No Strings*)—both notions his, and both cosmetic experiments dictated not by content but by whim.

Rodgers's insecurity crossed the border into paranoia; he became convinced that Arthur and I were against him, which reinforced his resistance to our suggestions for changes and paralyzed the progress of the show, since he was also the producer. Moreover, to my surprise, he had neither interest nor understanding in how to tell a story through song, which meant that for everything except the ballads, I had to write the lyrics first. This might have seemed like a ticket to write whatever I wanted to, but because Dick refused to rewrite, every "mechanical" was stiff, set in stone the minute he put it to music. When I'd collaborated with Jule, I would often bring him part of a lyric, but only part, with notated suggestions for the rhythm and contour of the melody. I wanted him to be stimulated by it, to feel free to invent, to change what I had written but use the structure and tone that I had in mind. With Lenny, it had been constant collaboration— tunes he had written for other purposes, like "America," "One Hand, One Heart" and "Somewhere," he changed a bit to accommodate me, but, as I said earlier, only once did he set an entire lyric of mine ("A Boy Like That") and only once did I set a completed tune of his ("Gee, Officer Krupke"). Both *Gypsy* and *West Side Story* were true collaborations; *Do I Hear a Waltz?* was more like a set of assignments, either from me to Rodgers or Rodgers to me. Jule had been mercurial but secure. His well was full. He was musically so fertile that if his work suffered from anything, it was the lack of an editor; he was so eager to burst forth with something new that he would rewrite an entire song rather than just part of it, and I constantly found myself in the position of having to prevent his throwing out the baby with the bathwater. Lenny, too, when I met him, was worried that he was running out of original ideas and having to plagiarize ("Now I know this is nothing but Brahms," he would offer defensively before playing something rich and melodic, and completely Bernstein), but his ego was still gigantically intact. Rodgers, on the other hand, was in despair. He need not have been, as songs like "Take the Moment" and the show's title tune attest. But I was too young to understand the fear of superannuation. I refused to believe that a man who had written the score of *Carousel* could run dry. These days, as I age, I recognize what Rodgers and Bernstein were coping with: the smell of becoming old-fashioned, of being reduced to recycling old ideas, a feeling hard to avoid when you hear the work of newcomers, even the worst of them. Only supreme confidence keeps you writing fearlessly into old age; Jule was one of the few who had it in spades, and in exuberant spades at that.

Do I Hear a Waltz? was not a bad show, merely a dead one. It was well constructed, literate, even entertaining. It has some wit in the lyrics, some lovely music that could

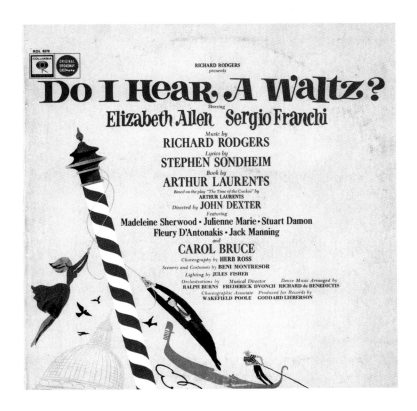

have come only from Richard Rodgers and a neatly constructed, touching libretto, but it was dead to begin with. It comes under the heading of what Mary Rodgers calls a "Why?" musical: a perfectly respectable show, based on a perfectly respectable source, that has no reason for being. (The irony of her having helped push me into writing one has not escaped me.) "Why?" musicals usually come from successful novels, movies and plays. Their authors are blinded by the attractiveness of the source material, how easily it could sing, how effectively it might be staged, which actor would be perfect for the leading role. They never question the *need* to musicalize* the piece. They never ask themselves what music will do for the story that hasn't already been accomplished by the original author. When Oscar adapted a moderately successful play called *Green Grow the Lilacs* into a musical called *Away We Go!* (later called *Oklahoma!*), he transformed a play about homosexuality and the loneliness of the early Western settlers into a paean to American pioneering and expansion. He remolded *Liliom,* a Hungarian play about Budapest lowlifes, into *Carousel,* a parable about undying love in a cozy nineteenth-century New England fishing village. "Why?" musicals can be good only if they're truly transformed or if they're the result of genuine passion for the original material, as in the case of *My Fair Lady*, one of the few examples of a good show that resembles its source almost identically (the 1938 British movie version of Shaw's *Pygmalion*). But *Do I Hear a Waltz?* is an exemplar of the "Why?" musical. It is based on a small, charming play that would have gained nothing from being musicalized, even by Puccini. The compelling reason to write a theater musical cannot be convenience or the desire to turn a quick buck. Although there may have been (especially recently) calculated and successful efforts to take popular titles and turn them into cash cows for no other reason than to make money, the venture is usually a fool's game. The biggest hits, even the most execrable ones, have generally been written by people who loved the story they were telling and how they were telling it. In the sorry case of *Do I Hear a Waltz?* that category did not include Arthur Laurents, Richard Rodgers or me. The show deserved its failure. I had learned from observing Lenny that there is nothing wrong with falling, as long as you don't fall from the lowest rung. *Do I Hear a Waltz?* was the lowest rung. Between it and *Anyone Can Whistle* I learned that the only reason to write a show is for love—just not too much of it.

---

* A hybrid word I would dearly love to avoid, but in a book this length, how many times can you say "make a musical from" or "adapt a musical of" or variations of same?

ACT ONE

Leona arrives in Venice. Having fallen into a canal, but exhilarated by the sight of the city, she sings to her nine-year-old urchin guide, Mauro.

Someone Woke Up

LEONA

Someone woke up one incredible day,
Had an idea and was prompted to say,
"Let's build a city! Where should it
        be?
How about the middle of that sea?"
Someone drew plans like a set for a
        stage,
Someone spilt colors all over the
        page.
Then they built it, cookie, you know
        why?
Just so Leona could come here and
        cry.

Some people cry at "Hellos" and
        "Farewells,"
Some people cry at nostalgia with
        bells.
Some cry at weddings, some at the
        moon,
I cry promptly Mondays at high noon.
Some people cry at Vienna or Rome.
This one is mine, cookie, this one is
        home!
Look, they even painted the damned
        sky,
Just so Leona could come here and cry.

Some people cry when they see their
        old pals.
Me, I'm a sucker for chimes and
        canals.
Look, they even painted the damned
        sky,
Just so Leona could
Come here and stand
Like a lump dripping wet
With no shoes on at noon
On a Monday—

And cry!

Trick of the trade: To intensify the emotion at the end of a song, establish an image or a set of images which can be repeated throughout the lyric, and then extend them at the climax, but unrhymed. This makes it seem as if the character's feelings are getting out of hand, since rhymes, being verbally self-conscious, imply control. It's a technique I've used often, in "Everything's Coming Up Roses" from *Gypsy*, "All Things Bright and Beautiful" from *Follies*, and others sprinkled throughout this collection.

Leona arrives at the Pensione Fioria, where she encounters Signora Fioria, the owner, as well as the other guests: Jennifer and Eddie Yaeger, a young American couple, and Mr. and Mrs. McIlhenny, an older pair. Fioria comments to them about her tourist trade.

This Week Americans

FIORIA

Last week the Germans—
You can keep the Germans.
Always cheap, the Germans,
Even on a trip.
Sweet, not the Germans,
Sweat a lot, the Germans,
Full of smiles, the Germans,
Don't expect a tip.

But this week Americans,
Open-armed Americans,
"I-am-charmed" Americans,
Welcome, welcome, welcome!
I love Americans,
The pleasure is mine.
Remember, no breakfast after half
        past nine.

Next week the English—
You should see the English.
All that tea, the English,
Thirsty, I suppose.
Good eggs, the English,
Rotten legs, the English,
All those teeth, the English,
Rows and rows and rows.
But this week Americans,

More than kind Americans,
Much maligned Americans,
Welcome, welcome, welcome!
I love Americans,
And my home is yours.
I can't be responsible, so lock your
        doors.

Then come Parisians—
Full of food, Parisians,
Always rude, Parisians,
Every one a sneak.
Perfumed Parisians,
Over-groomed Parisians,
Middle-class Parisians,
Far more cheek than chic.

But this week Americans,
Generous Americans,
Never fuss Americans,
Welcome, welcome, welcome!
Thank you, Americans, for coming to
        stay.
How charming my guests are from
        the U.S.A.!

No alcoholic Swedes,
No double-dealing Russians,
No Spaniards with their beads
And their deafening discussions.
No narcissistic Greeks,
They're worse than the Italians,
With overblown physiques
And St. Christopher medallions.
No millionaire Brazilians
Who somehow never pay.
I much prefer the millions
From the U.S.A.!

At the end of the show, when the Americans leave and are replaced by Britishers, Fioria sings a different tune—well, the same tune, but a different lyric:

Last week Americans,
Who can bear Americans?
Wash-and-wear Americans,
Charmlessly naïve.
Two-faced Americans,
Dreadful taste Americans,
Summertime Americans—
Thought they'd never leave!

But this week the Britishers,
Cultivated Britishers,
Educated Britishers,

Welcome, welcome, welcome!
Thank God for Britishers,
You're not like *them*.
And welcome till Saturday at
    three P.M.!

As the tourists assemble for cocktails at dusk, the subject of air travel comes up. Leona, fearing that she will be left alone when they all go out for the evening, tries to prolong the conversation.

What Do We Do? We Fly!

MRS. McILHENNY
Lloyd tells me, "Never go by plane."
I tell Lloyd, "Flying is insane."
We agree we would rather die.
We see a brochure
And sign for a tour,
And what do we do? We fly!

It starts the minute you check in.
Departure time is at noon.
A cup of tea and a schnecken
And, "Quick, it's leaving soon!"
One o'clock and you're at the gate;
Two o'clock and the flight's still late.
When you finally leave, it's eight.
And what do we do? We fly. Why?
What do we do? We fly!

MRS. McILHENNY   LEONA
I hate planes . . .   I agree.
Sitting three abreast . . .   You're like
                        me.
I hate planes . . .   I do, too.
Never get a rest . . .

(To Mr. McIlhenny)

I hate planes.   What about
        .   you?

MR. McILHENNY
I hate every single one.
The crossing was rough,
Which wasn't enough,
The fun hadn't yet begun.

The seat was throwing my back out,
But there I was with a book,
When suddenly there's a blackout

And everywhere I look
Is a close-up of Doris Day,
Ninety minutes of Doris Day!
There was nothing to do but pray,
And how do we go? We fly.
Why? How do we go? We fly!

MR. AND MRS. McILHENNY
I hate planes . . .

LEONA
I agree . . . (etc.) . . .

MR. AND MRS. McILHENNY
Most of all the sound.
I hate planes,
Even on the ground.
Can't stand planes . . .

LEONA
Have a drink . . .

(To Jennifer)

What do you think?

JENNIFER
I hate even more than those
The kids in the aisle
Surrounding you while
Their parents pretend to doze.

The kid I noticed the first was
The one who stood on my feet.
The kid I hated the worst was
The one who kicked my seat.
There was one on the left who bit,
There was one on the right who spit,
There was one in the back I hit!
But what did we do? We flew. Ugh!
What did we do? We flew!

McILHENNYS, JENNIFER
I hate planes . . .

LEONA
I agree . . . (etc.) . . .

McILHENNYS, JENNIFER
Never can adapt.
I hate planes.
Always feel I'm trapped.
Can't stand planes.

LEONA
I'm that way.

(To Eddie)

What do you say?

EDDIE
I hate most of all the chow.
To know what is what
Is difficult, but
I think I've discovered how:

The shiny stuff is tomatoes,
The salad lies in a group.
The curly stuff is potatoes,
The stuff that moves is soup.
Anything that is white is sweet,
Anything that is brown is meat.
Anything that is gray—don't eat!
But what do we do? We fly. Why?
What do we do? We fly!

ALL
You're zooming up like a comet,
Your ears are starting to ring.
Your neighbor's starting to vomit,
There's ice along the wing.
As you wait for your palms to dry,
You can see your whole life flash by,
And they tell you it's fun to fly!

Your chance of survival's so remote
You're far better off to cut your throat,
But who has the time to take a boat?
So what do we do? We fly!

This may seem like nothing more than a "list" song, a series of rhymed variations on a single joke, but in fact it's a nice example of subtext. The lyric appears to be, brazenly, nothing more than a series of jokes about air travel, whereas really it's about Leona's loneliness. It gives the actress something to play: the character's attempt to keep the chatter going so that she can have company as long as possible. Making it a list song was a way to emphasize the threadbare repetitiousness of the ostensible subject, which underlines Leona's desperation. At least, that was the intention: chances for humor in the songs for this show were in short supply.

Leona, left alone in the garden of the pensione, leafs through her guidebook.

Relax at the end of the day – have a drink

The Americans gave the world the cocktail hour.

Everybody talks about drinking – that's the only .
        thing wrong with drinking

Anecdotes of disasters
        What happened next?   (She prompts)
        That's incredible!
Terrible Experience(s)
                    Robbery
                    Strange man on the plane
                    Plane troubles – flying is terrible.
                        Travel by boat, never by air
                        We drove (Jennifer) is pointless
                                            (the waitress)
        F: But the important thing is here. |or she's terrified
            anyway you are here. |+ took pills + fell
                                                  |asleep
_____
I can never get used to the time change
    The tempo is different in Italy |Have another drink|

Someone Woke Up

(Reprise)

LEONA

"Churches, museums and palazzos
    to see . . .
Problems of drainage (see Sewers:
    page three) . . .
Useful addresses . . . Special
    Events . . .
Forty-seven lire is eight cents . . .
Venice is gradually sinking (see
    note) . . .
Visit the house where Lord Byron
    once wrote . . .
See the Lido after it gets dark . . .
Sit in the Piazza San Marco . . .
For shopping, the colorful
Alleys around the Rialto
Contain many charming
    boutiques . . ."

While on a shopping tour the next morning, Leona sees a beautiful eighteenth-century Venetian glass goblet and decides that she wants a pair of them. The shop owner, an attractive older man named Renato Di Rossi, says he will try to find another for her and sings to her as if he were not only himself but the goblet, too.

Someone Like You

DI ROSSI

We waited for someone,
But somehow we never
Had looked for someone like you.
Our chances were many,
But we were too clever,
We wanted someone like you.

Suddenly, the door,
Wonderful surprise!
Wonderful and more,
Before
Our eyes.

We thought that surprises
Were over forever,
And then came someone like you.

Originally, Di Rossi was more forward with his charm.

Perhaps (cut)

DI ROSSI

If you take perhaps
A ride,
And you wish perhaps
A guide,
If I might perhaps
Provide,
Let me do.

If you wish perhaps
To buy
At a price perhaps
Too high,
No one bargains
As well as I.
Let me do.

For whatever emergencies arise,
Laundry or lira rates or bath supplies,

Elizabeth Allen (Leona), Stuart Damon (Eddie), Julienne Marie (Jennifer), Carol Bruce (Fioria)

You require someone who
Can take care of these for you.

And if I, perhaps, will do,
I will do.

Until working on *Do I Hear a Waltz?*, I had dealt only with brash characters, larger than life, musical comedy–size: rowdy adolescents, showbiz juggernauts, comics in togas, cartoons. I'd found them all comparatively easy to write, but now I was faced with a character defined by that elusive quality, charm. Furthermore, Di Rossi was a foreigner, which introduced the problem of writing for someone who speaks the not-so-good English. This is easy when you're making fun of it, using mispronunciation or grammatical eccentricity. But to make Di Rossi's lyrics funny-charming rather than funny-ha-ha without falling into mawkishness was a more difficult matter, especially since the addition of swoony Italianate music was bound to sentimentalize everything it touched.

Happily, Arthur had set the styles for all the Italians in the script with vocabulary, grammar and sound different for each, so I had examples to imitate. As I said earlier, I'm a good imitator, which has proved a strength rather than a weakness in the shows I've worked on, especially considering the wide range of styles among my collaborators. Better still, I've been able to maintain my own voice while imitating theirs. With each show, I never start writing lyrics till the librettist has finished a couple of scenes. I examine and question virtually every syllable to be sure I understand his intention, and often by the time we go into rehearsal I know the script better than he does. Over the years there have actually been times when I've corrected a word in the dialogue that the playwright hasn't caught, just as there have been times during recording sessions when the playwright has questioned a lyric mistake which I've overlooked. When you're the writer, you make so many choices along the way that they tend to blur in retrospect and thus occasionally elude your ear; when later you're part of the audience, the choices have been made and you hear everything with critical clarity. You may spend so many hours choosing between "the" and "a" that, after time passes, you forget which choice you made.

Di Rossi's elegant but slightly askew English may have been eminently imitable, but giving him charm seemed to me to require a Hammerstein-like simplicity, even though I'd often found Hammerstein's pidgin English treatment of characters who misspoke the English language, such as Bloody Mary in *South Pacific* and the King in *The King and I*, cute and condescending. Again, mimicking Arthur's dialogue was the solution; only rarely did his Italians become cute. And Rodgers's music, far from sentimentalizing our exotic romantic, gave Di Rossi—just as it had done in the case of *South Pacific*'s exotic romantic, Emile de Becque—charm.

Di Rossi continues to charm Leona by giving her tips on how to bargain with Venetian shopkeepers.

With Richard Rodgers at the recording session

Bargaining

DI ROSSI
You say you aren't sure.
You look, you handle, you wonder,
     you frown.
You dwell on what is poor:
Too big, too little, too orange, too
     brown.
You tell him that you think you see a
     crack.
He tells you that it's just the old
     shellac.
You say you saw a better one in Rome
     a week before.
He says that if you did, it must have
     cost a thousand more.

You say, "Too rococo."
He says, "Shall I wrap it?"
You: "Is it real Venetian?"
He: "I can guarantee it!"
"Let me see some others, please!"
"Madame, all we have are these."
"May I use a check to pay?"
"Madame, anything you say!"
"Will you mend it?"
"We will mend it."
"Can you send it?"
"We can send it."
"Will you—?"
"Madame . . ."
"Can you—?"
"Madame . . ."
"Is it—?"
"Madame . . ."
"May I—?"
"Madame . . ."
"Let me think it over, I'll come back
     another day!"

You start to leave the shop.
He smiles, he fusses, he opens the
     door.
You start and then you stop.
You smile, you ponder, you wander
     some more.
You wander and you wait, and he the
     same.
Whoever waits the most will win the
     game.
You wander near the goblet maybe
     once or maybe twice.
You wait until it's closing time
And *then* you ask the price.

You say, "How much is it?"
He says, "Inexpensive."
You: "What is inexpensive?"
He: "Only venti mille!"
"That is twenty thousand, yes?"
"But for you I make it less."
"Will you make it una mille?"
"No, I'll make it dieci mille."
"Due mille?"
"Dieci mille!"
"Quattro mille?"
"Nove mille!"
"Cinque?"
"Otto!"
"Sette?"
"Sei!"
"Sei?"
"Sei! All right, sei!"
"Let me think it over, I'll come back
     another day!"

You start to leave again;
You go into the street.
And if he follows then,
That signals his defeat.
And that, you see, is when
The bargaining is done.
You haven't really saved a single lira,
But you've won!

I was worried about Di Rossi's charm becoming mere placidity and thought that at this point we should have a showstopper for him, something that would galvanize an audience and lead them to understand that this was not just a manicured chamber musical, but a traditional romantic one, with plenty of occasions to appreciate and vigorously applaud the performers—a song, for example, like "Where Is the Life That Late I Led?" in *Kiss Me, Kate.* Also, we wanted a more animated leading man than the similar Emile de Becque (older, sophisticated foreigner involved with younger, naïve American girl). To this end, I gave him two separate characters to play in a single lyric, one in falsetto. It would, I hoped, be a tour de force for both the actor and the character. It wasn't. It was pleasant, but it was no showstopper, and *Do I Hear a Waltz?* needed showstoppers.

That evening, Leona finds herself the only person sitting alone in the Piazza San Marco. She surveys the throng of strollers promenading, which includes Fioria and the Yaegers.

Here We Are Again

FIORIA
How sudden the fall of evening,
The soft, seductive light.
The joining of hands at evening
Anticipates the night.
Is it well with you?

JENNIFER
Young lovers come out at evening
To primp and preen and fuss.

EDDIE
Young lovers come out at evening,

BOTH
Reminding us of us.

FIORIA
Is it well with you?

JENNIFER
Lovely!

LEONA
Here we are again,
Sharing things together.
See the pretty people—
Feel the pretty weather.
We don't have to say much,
We're so much of a kind.
Isn't it a marvel
How we read each other's mind?

Here we are again.
What'll we do later?
See the pretty people—
Shall we call the waiter?
Pretty people two by two,
That's as it ought to be.
And here we are, as usual,
I and me.

JENNIFER
Look at the evening.

EDDIE
Yes, it's lovely.

JENNIFER
Beautiful evening.

EDDIE
There's a breeze.

JENNIFER
How I love evening.

EDDIE
I suppose so.

JENNIFER
Don't you love evening?

EDDIE
Honey, please!

FIORIA
Is it well with you?

LEONA
Here we are again,
Botching things together,
Gaping at the people,
Talking to the weather.
We don't have to say much
To make the job complete.
Isn't it a marvel
How we do it with our feet?

Here we are again,
Time to call the waiter.
Maybe we should ask him
What he's doing later.
Pretty people, two by two,
Do as they've always done,
And here we are, as usual,
One by one.

*(After the strollers have gone, Leona is
left alone once more)*

LEONA
Here we are again
With our friend, the waiter.
Gone the pretty people,
And it's getting later.
Pretty people, two by two,
Do as they've always done.
And here we are at home again:
One by one.

**In the following early version of
this moment, the McIlhennys and**

Di Rossi's son Vito are among the strollers. Here also, Leona refers to herself as "Cookie," which is her friendly way of addressing strangers.

Two by Two (cut)

LEONA
Ciao, cookie, ciao!
What, cookie, now?
Sit at least for a while
And smile, cookie, smile.

Two by two by two,
Everybody is two by two by two.
Everybody is him and her,
Everybody is he and she.
Everybody is arm in arm,
Two by two—
And cookie makes three.

One has none to lose.
By myself, I can say
And do what I choose.
But it's funny:
When all is said and done,
One and one make one.
Have you heard the news?
The world goes on by twos.

VITO, GIRL
How lovely is the evening.
How soft the air and bright.
One notices in the evening
The stirrings of the night.
Is it well with you?

EDDIE, JENNIFER
Beginnings of night,
How soft the air.
And anything might
Happen at night
In the square.
Is it well with you?

FIORIA, MALE COMPANION
How dangerous is the evening,
How soft the air and bright.
One notices in the evening
The stirrings of night.

(To other strollers)

Is it well with you?

MR. AND MRS. McILHENNY
Look at the evening.

MR. McILHENNY
Yes, it's lovely.

MRS. McILHENNY
Where is the camera?

MR. McILHENNY
I don't know.

MRS. McILHENNY
Isn't that Eddie?

MR. McILHENNY
No, it isn't.

MRS. McILHENNY
Where are we eating?

MR. McILHENNY
Edith—

MRS. McILHENNY
Oh . . .

BOTH
(To other strollers)
Is it well with you?

*Di Rossi comes to the pensione to ask
Leona to go with him to a concert in
the Piazza San Marco. Although partly
delighted, she suspects that his motives
may be mercenary, and parries with him,
reluctant to accept his invitation.*

Thinking

DI ROSSI
I was thinking,
All of that Puccini going to waste . . .

LEONA
I was thinking,
Coffee and Puccini isn't my taste.

DI ROSSI
I keep thinking,
Such a fine beginning,
Such a lovely evening we could
 spend . . .

LEONA
Such a fine beginning,
I keep thinking more about the end.

I was thinking,
Wonder what he's thinking,
Not what he should . . .

DI ROSSI
I was thinking,
All this heavy thinking,
This is not good.

But think of coffee cups clinking
To a duet.
We could sit drinking,
See the sun set.
What are you thinking?

LEONA
I was just thinking,
What you are thinking—
Forget!

I was thinking,
Tête-à-têtes for two
So often fall flat . . .

DI ROSSI
I was thinking,
Tête-à-têtes for one
Are flatter than that.
I am thinking,
This is very awkward.
Frankly, you prefer that I should go?

LEONA
This is very awkward—
I am thinking,
Very frankly, no.

I was thinking,
Why is it I get so easily hurt?

DI ROSSI
I was thinking,
Has she noticed yet
The spot on my shirt?

But think of two of us linking
Arms in the Square.
See the stars winking,
Feel the night air.
What are you thinking?

LEONA
I was just thinking,
What am I going to wear?

DI ROSSI
And as the sun begins sinking,
Night starts to fall . . .

LEONA
Stars appear blinking,
Gondoliers call . . .

BOTH
What am I thinking?
I should be thinking
Not what I'm thinking
At all!

Eddie, the young American, has been flirting with Fioria. They are about to go out together and have what may possibly be a sexual interlude, but they are delayed by the entrance of Fioria's maid Giovanna, who has come to arrange the cocktail settings. Giovanna's English leaves something to be desired (this becomes a plot point later) and they give her an English lesson. As they sing, they suit actions to words.

No Understand

EDDIE
This is the—?

GIOVANNA
Whiskey.

EDDIE
Whiskey. This is the—?

GIOVANNA
Ices.

EDDIE
(Lets it go)
Ices. These are the—?

GIOVANNA
Windows.

EDDIE
Glasses.

(Points to the window)

Windows.

GIOVANNA
Windows . . . Glasses . . .

FIORIA
Pouring the whiskey—

GIOVANNA
Pouring.

FIORIA
Drop in the ices—

GIOVANNA
Drop in.

FIORIA
Lifting the glasses—

GIOVANNA
Lifting.

FIORIA
(Raises her glass to Eddie)
Here's to discretion!

GIOVANNA
Non capisco.
No understand,
I no understand,
I no understand you crazy language.
Non capisco.
No understand.
I no understand you, my dear!

FIORIA
This is the—?

GIOVANNA
Fingers.

FIORIA
Fingers. This is the—?

GIOVANNA
Soldiers.

FIORIA
Shoulders.

(Indicates Eddie's body)

This is the—?

GIOVANNA
Ah, ha.

FIORIA
Body.

GIOVANNA
Bella . . .

FIORIA
Molto . . .

EDDIE
Married . . .

FIORIA
This is to stand up—

GIOVANNA
Stand up.

FIORIA
This is to turn round—

GIOVANNA
Turn round.

FIORIA
This is to go off—

GIOVANNA
Go off.

FIORIA
This is goodbye now—

GIOVANNA
(Not leaving, out of curiosity)
Non capisco.
No understand,
I no understand,
I no understand you crazy language.
Non capisco.

FIORIA
You understand?

EDDIE
Oh, I understand all too well.

FIORIA, EDDIE
Some phrases don't translate,
Others are universal.
Some you communicate
After a brief rehearsal.

FIORIA
"Good afternoon."

EDDIE
"How do you do?"

FIORIA
"You are so kind."

EDDIE
"Where's the hotel?"

FIORIA
"Send up the drinks."

EDDIE
"Bring me the bill."

FIORIA
"Gondola, please!"

GIOVANNA
Capisco!

EDDIE
You take the—?

GIOVANNA
Whiskey.

EDDIE
Whiskey.
Empty the—?

GIOVANNA
Ices.

EDDIE
Ices.
Wash out the—?

GIOVANNA
Windows.

EDDIE
Glasses.

(Points to the window again)

Windows.

GIOVANNA
Wash out?

EDDIE
Skip it!

FIORIA
Bad Giovanna,

GIOVANNA
Bad?

FIORIA
Stay in this evening.

GIOVANNA
Stay?

FIORIA
No see Alfredo.

GIOVANNA
No?

FIORIA
This is goodbye now.

GIOVANNA
Si! capisco!
Io capisco!
I understand now.
I understand you crazy language.
Ai, capisco! I understand.
Si, I understand you, my dear.

FIORIA, EDDIE
Some phrases don't translate,
Others are universal.
Some you communicate
After a brief rehearsal.

FIORIA
"Under the trees."

EDDIE
"On the lagoon."

FIORIA
"Down on the beach."

EDDIE
"Up on the roof."

FIORIA
Not in the house.

EDDIE
You name the place.

FIORIA
Gondola, please.

GIOVANNA
Capisco!

FIORIA, EDDIE
I *capisco.*

GIOVANNA
I *capisco.*

LORENZ HART
Jaunty and Careless

Lorenz Hart is the laziest of the pre-eminent lyricists, and one of the most disconcerting (the other two being Ira Gershwin and Noël Coward). When someone of mediocre gifts does his best, you may wince but you have to applaud his persistence and determination. When someone blessed with style, wit and personality coasts on glibness and attitude, you (I) want to point out that the emperor has no clothes—or, more accurately, that there may be clothes but they're cheaper than they ought to be.

Hart's pervasive laziness manifests itself in three areas: mis-stressed syllables, convoluted syntax and the sacrifice of meaning for rhyme. In 1971 I agreed to give an ad-lib talk about musicals as part of the YMHA "Lyrics and Lyricists" series. I naïvely assumed that my audience would consist of theater students and professional practitioners, and when I found that I would instead be talking to (mostly) middle-aged culture-seekers with nothing better to do on a Sunday evening and little more than mild interest in the subject, I turned with alarm to Arthur Laurents for advice on how I could organize un-structured remarks to an audience with a limited attention span for technical talk about anapests and sprung rhythm and tonic-subdominant progressions. He made the life-saving suggestion that I prepare a pack of about fifty 3 X 5 filing cards, writing on each one a Topic of Interest demanding no more than a few minutes' explication, such as "The use of inner rhymes" or "What was Ethel Merman really like?," shuffle them in front of the crowd and turn them up one at a time, dealing with each subject as it arose. Although there would be time for only fifteen or twenty, he noted, it would give me a structure while guaranteeing variety of subject and leaving me free to ramble, which is what I do best in public arenas. As it happened, one of the cards that came up was "Lorenz Hart—sloppiness" and when it did, I performed a stunt: I took the Rodgers and Hart Songbook, opened it to a (truly) random page and read the lyrics printed thereon. Since each page contained sixteen bars at most, comprising twenty to thirty words, I

was taking a chance of not being able to make my case, but sure enough in every instance—I repeated the exercise three times—there was a wrong stress, a tortuous rhyme, a non sequitur or a meaning sacrificed to effect (or to the writer's impatience). Not every page of the songbook contained an egregious clumsiness, but there were enough so that I had little fear of failing. Here are some examples:

Mis-stressed syllables, apart from the ones I cited in the Introduction to this book: "I know a movie executive / _Who's_ twice as bright" (from "Take Him" in _Pal Joey_); or "Psychoana_lysts_ are all the whirl" (from "Too Good for the Average Man" in _On Your Toes_); or "All of my future is _in_ you" (from "Lover" in _The Boys from Syracuse_). Lord knows, I've been guilty of this Sin myself—in addition to the example I pointed out in "Everybody Says Don't," there is the subtler "One thousand whims to which I _give_ in" from "You Must Meet My Wife" in _A Little Night Music_, as well as a few others. But only a few. Hart has a treasure trove.

Convoluted syntax (from "I Married an Angel" in the show of the same name): "An angel I married. / To Heaven she's carried this / Fellow with a kiss." Ira Gershwin commits this Sin even more frequently than Hart, but unlike his co-Sinner he doesn't mis-stress syllables as often.

Sacrifice of meaning for rhyme: "Your looks are laughable, / Unphotographable" (from "My Funny Valentine" in _Babes in Arms_). Unless the object of the singer's affection is a vampire, surely what Hart means is "unphotogenic." Only vampires are unphotographable, but affectionate "–enic" rhymes are hard to come by. Then there's this from "My Romance": "My romance / Doesn't need a castle rising / In Spain / Nor a dance / To a constantly surprising / Refrain." What refrain is constantly surprising? Maybe one by Alban Berg, but nothing you'd ever hear on a dance floor. Even Cole Porter's refrains were only inter-mittently surprising—if a refrain were constantly surprising, it would cease to be a refrain. And even if such a thing existed, would a dance to an occasionally surprising or even a totally unsurprising one be less romantic?

All three of these come together in the richly bad lyric for "Lover":

> _Lover, when we're dancing,_
> _Keep on glancing_
> _In my eyes_
> _Till love's own entrancing_
> _Music dies._

Love's _own_ entrancing music _dies_? Why "own"? Whose else would it be? And it dies in such a short period of time? Why? If so, it can't mean an awful lot to the lovers. And even if it lasts for the whole dance (which the lyric implies it doesn't), then what? Considering the ardor of the rest of the lyric, it doesn't make sense. The nonsense of the lyric, the convoluted syntax in the first quatrain and the emphasis on "Till" are representative of a lot of Hart's work.

Perhaps it seems easy and mean-spirited to pick apart a single lyric in such detail and it will strike some people as heresy to criticize Hart for anything at all, but the fact is that Porter and Harburg and Fields and Loesser rarely indulge in these kinds of sloppiness, and the lyricists of my generation—Sheldon Harnick, Fred Ebb, Lee Adams, Jerry Herman et al.—almost never do. We take meticulous-ness for granted, a legacy from Porter and Harburg and Fields and Loesser, not to mention Hammerstein.

Hart reveals himself more openly than any other lyricist except Hammerstein: in his case, jaunty but melancholy, forceful but vulnerable. There is a pervasive sweetness about him that comes through in even his most self-conscious work. He was verbally nimble, full of humor, and a lazy craftsman. Anyone who can write

> _Unrequited love's a bore_
> _And I've got it pretty bad,_
> _But with someone you adore,_
> _It's a pleasure to be sad._

should be ashamed to sign his name to "Lover." But as Alan Jay Lerner reported Hart's telling him: "I've got a lot of talent, kid. If I cared, I could probably have been a genius." I don't think so, but he certainly could have been better. Hart's attitude distin-guishes him as a lyricist, but attitude is not enough. You have to care.

You *capisco*?

GIOVANNA

Me *capisco*.

ALL

Si, capisco.
We capisco.
Capisco!

How many jokes and how much charm can you make from unidiomatic English? Not enough to sustain an evening, as it turned out, although the actors did have something to play and some of the jokes are good.

Leona is furious at Di Rossi when she learns that he is married and still with his wife but "lives outside," as he says. He accuses Leona of being naïvely romantic and unrealistically puritanical. He offers her his affection and an affair during the time she will be in Venice.

Take the Moment

DI ROSSI

Take the moment,
Let it happen.
Hug the moment,
Make it last.

Hold the feeling
For the moment,
Or the moment
Will have passed.

All the noises buzzing in your head,
Warning you to wait—
What for?
Don't listen!

Let it happen,
Take the moment.
Make the moment
Many moments more.

Make for us a thousand more.

ACT TWO

At the pensione that night, Jennifer, Fioria and Leona, in separate rooms, contemplate the moon.

Moon in My Window

JENNIFER

Moon in my window,
See that little dome?
By the time you reach it,
Eddie will be home.

Moon in my window,
Play this little game.
By the time he's reached me,
Things will be the same.

Moon, take charge and take pity.
Shine and change the scene.
Shine and wash the city
Clean.

Moon in my window,
Passing by that dome,
When you reach that cloud there,
He'll be home.

FIORIA

Moon in my window,
I am not impressed.
Waken other lovers,
Let me get my rest.

Moon in my window,
Make the lovers smile.
Let them have their dreamings
For this little while.

Glow, pass by, then diminish,
So romantic moon.
All adventures finish
Soon.

Moon in my window,
It is getting late.
You'll be back tomorrow—
I can wait.

LEONA

Moon in my window,
How are you so bright?

Guess I've never seen you,
Not until tonight.

Moon in my window,
Going oh so slow,
Are you giving lessons?
Thank you, but I know.

ALL

Moon, your light can be blinding,
But the night will end.
I don't need reminding,
Friend.

Moon in my window,
As you disappear,
Come again tomorrow.
I'll be here.

JENNIFER

Oh, moon!

FIORIA

Ah, moon!

LEONA

Hey, moon!

Eddie and Jennifer have a fight over his flirtation with Fioria. It's not their first. They try to reassure themselves about their marriage.

We're Gonna Be All Right

EDDIE

It may not all be bliss,
But every wound is treatable.
We won't go under,
We're gonna be all right.
Don't see how we can miss,
Our team is undefeatable.
I wouldn't wonder,
We're gonna be all right.

JENNIFER

We may have had unhappy landings,
Misunderstandings,
We're still growing.

EDDIE

Some years are bad,
We're hale and hearty,

We'll keep the party
Going.

Hey, babe, let's have a kiss—
Remember, we're unbeatable.
We're gonna blunder,
We're gonna hold on tight.
Hi-ho! We're gonna be all right.
Hey, babe, We're gonna be all right.
With love, we're gonna be all right!

The edgy banter between Eddie and Jennifer presented me with a welcome opportunity to write a typical Lorenz Hart lyric (lighthearted but acerbic, bristling with unexpected non sequiturs) for a typical pre-Hammerstein Rodgers tune. The above specimen is no such animal, but the original was. In fact, when I first presented the original to Rodgers, he gave me a smile and a hug, both gestures unusual for him, especially if you were a man. It was clear that he welcomed being back in Hart territory. Among musical-theater fans, there are frequent arguments about which constitutes the "better" Rodgers—the bounciness and throwaway quality of his Hart songs or the beauty and majesty of his best work with Hammerstein. Rodgers was acutely attuned to the tone of whichever lyricist he was writing with, and he was extremely proud of the breadth of his work with Hammerstein, but his enthusiastic reaction indicated to me that he missed the old anything-goes days of Hart. In fact, when Rodgers wrote his first music-and-lyrics score (for the show *No Strings*), he tried to combine the two styles—which unfortunately adulterated both of them.

His enthusiasm about my lyric turned to outrage overnight, however. The very next day he called for a lunch meeting with Arthur, John Dexter (our director) and me. Over a meal getting colder by the sentence, he repeatedly slapped a copy of the lyric against his wrist, as if slapping mine, and insisted that the lyric was unacceptable. Rodgers was an articulate man, but he could not (that is, would not) explain his objections, because they weren't his. They were his wife

Dorothy's. When I'd first read Arthur the lyric, Arthur had said, "You'll never get away with it—Dick will shoot you." I bet him that he was wrong, and for at least twenty-four hours I'd been right. But I'd reckoned without Dorothy. Now I could picture Dick enthusiastically showing her the lyric and her response, which must have dwarfed Krakatoa for explosiveness. She recognized the marriage I was writing about as having characteristics similar to their own (not the homosexuality alluded to—both Rodgerses were dedicated homophobes, despite Dick's closeness to his homosexual partner Lorenz Hart). Needless to say, the lyric was replaced with the bland and smooth version above. Here's the original:

We're Gonna Be All Right

(Original version)

EDDIE
Honeybunch,
Sad to say, but I have a hunch
Screen Romances went out to
    lunch—
That's no reason to pout.
Don't look bleak,
Happy endings can spring a leak.
"Ever after" can mean one week,
We're just having a drought.
Smile and sweat it out.

If we can just hang on,
We'll have compatibility.
You mustn't worry—
We're gonna be all right.
One day the ache is gone—
There's nothing like senility,
So what's your hurry?
We're gonna be all right.

Meanwhile, relax—
You take a lover,
I'll take a lover.
When that's played out,
They get the axe,
We can retire,
Sit by the fire—
Fade out!

We'll build our house upon
The rock of my virility.
We'd better scurry,
We're gonna be all night.
Oh, boy!
We're gonna be all right.

JENNIFER
I was told,
Just be faithful and never scold.
Sounded easy, so I was sold.
I've been miserable since.
I was taught
When the prince and the dragon
    fought,
That the dragon was always caught—
Now I don't even wince
When it eats the prince.

I know a perfect pair,
Their lives are at the pinnacle,
But how do we know
They're gonna be all right?
The bride is slightly square,
The groom is slightly cynical,
A little vino—
They're gonna be all right.

She aims to please,
She has a baby,
Then, though they may be
Having fine times,
When there's a *crise*,
She has another—
Now she's a mother
Nine times!

It all went wrong, but where?
Details are slightly clinical.
She's out in Reno—
The kids adored the flight.
Hi-ho!
They're gonna be all right.

EDDIE
Honeychile,
Bury everything, learn to smile.
Happy couples can stay in style
Just by practicing charm.
All is well,
Least as far as their friends can tell.
Please ignore the peculiar smell,
There's no cause for alarm.
Mildew
Will do
Harm.

Publicity photos

JENNIFER
She once was quite well read.

EDDIE
He once was intellectual.

BOTH
No one's suspicious—they're gonna
be all right.

JENNIFER
She's nice and sweet and dead,

EDDIE
He's tall and ineffectual,

BOTH
They look delicious—they're gonna
be all right.

JENNIFER
Who's on the skids?
She'll go to night school,

EDDIE
If it's the right school,
He'll permit her.

JENNIFER
They love their kids,
They love their friends, too.

EDDIE
Lately, he tends to
Hit her.

JENNIFER
Sometimes she drinks in bed,

EDDIE
Sometimes he's homosexual,

BOTH
But why be vicious?
They keep it out of sight.
Good show!
They're gonna be all right.
And so,
We're gonna be all right.
Hi-ho!
We're gonna be all right!

*Leona has always believed that when
she truly fell in love she would hear a
waltz. Alternately enchanted by Di Rossi
and mistrusting him, and thinking he
has stood her up on a date, she sees him*

*arriving at the pensione with the gift of a
garnet necklace she has longed for.*

Do I Hear a Waltz?

LEONA
Do I hear a waltz?
Very odd, but I hear a waltz.
There isn't a band
And I don't understand
It at all.

I can't hear a waltz—
Oh, my Lord, there it goes again!
Why is nobody dancing in the street?
Can't they hear the beat?

Magical, mystical miracle,
Can it be? Is it true?
Things are impossibly lyrical.
Is it me? No, it's you!

I do hear a waltz!
I see you and I hear a waltz!
It's what I've been waiting for
All my life, to hear a waltz!

Do you hear a waltz?
Oh, my dear, don't you hear a waltz?
Such lovely Blue Danubey
Music, how can you be
Still!

You *must* hear a waltz!
Even strangers are dancing now:
An old lady is waltzing in her flat,
Waltzing with her cat.

Roses are dancing with peonies.
Yes, it's true! Don't you see?
Everything's suddenly Viennese,
Can't be you! Must be me!

Do I hear a waltz?
I want more than to hear a waltz:
I want you to share it 'cause
Oh, boy, *do* I hear a waltz!
I hear a waltz!
I hear a waltz!

"Danubey / can you be." Trick rhymes
are tricky in more ways than one, as

are fancy ones like "Peonies / Viennese." On the one hand, they exude
cleverness, a quality which was not
only perfectly acceptable but welcome
for characters in the pre–Rodgers and
Hammerstein musicals, since they
were seldom characters to be taken
seriously and audiences enjoyed lyricists' showing off. When audiences
are asked to believe and get involved
with a character, however, as they are
today, the lyricist more often than not
should get out of the way. Here I justified the rhyme as an expression of
Leona's giddiness, which is one of the
functions of playful lyrics. Unlike the
self-conscious rhyming for Maria and
friends in "I Feel Pretty," which is a
similar emotional statement, Leona's
rhymes reflect a sophisticated and educated mind. Maria's joy should have
had a simpler expression.

*Leona waltzes off to a gondola with Di
Rossi. As he is bringing her home the next
morning, he asks her not to return to
America.*

Stay

DI ROSSI
I am not the dream come true,
But stay.
Not perfection, nor are you,
But stay.
Who is brilliant, who is witty?
Am I handsome? Are you pretty?
Throw the dream away,
Stay and stay and stay!

Did you wish a duke?
At least a duke you should have.
If I could have been a duke,
For you, I would have.
All the things you should have
I cannot supply you
I would give you,
I would buy you.

I am not the dream come true,
But stay.
No one is the dream come true,
But stay.

Do I hear a waltz!!   How can you be still
a wonderful   Danube   With the Danube music I hear?
mystical   can you believe
magical
miracle

                    Do I hear a waltz   I do hear a waltz
I could swear   Very strange (odd)   You are here and I hear a waltz
                    It's insane but I hear a waltz If you're here then I hear a waltz
                    There's no band but I hear a waltz Did you appear and I hear a waltz
                                                    Don't you hear the waltz

                    There isn't a
I thought I'd swear I don't see a band   Oh my God
I hear   And   Hold your hat, there it goes again
music but there is So I don't understand it at all All aboard for Vienna
Do I?   I can't hear   can you be
                    I can't be a waltz
                    There are not the Vienna woods The Blue Danube was never blue as this
                                                    Doesn't anyone hear it
                                                    why is everyone standing in a trance
                                                    why is nobody dancing   Can't be? Is it true?
In my thoughts   Hold it, look out, there it goes Can't be
                    there it comes again   Is it me?
                    When I look   Can't be
                    Every time   No, it's you
                    I see you   I do hear a waltz

                    Crocuses waltzing   is it me?
                    Roses are waltzing with peonies — can this be?
I close my eyes   everything's suddenly   Can't be me,
It's there   What's making everything Viennese
anyhow   This is the waltz I've been waiting for — can't be? Is it true?
                    Violins suddenly start to play
                    When should it suddenly start playing

                    I've waited around all my life for a waltz
Can't be?   I hear every word that you say and a waltz
Is it true?   I lost all my fella and I hear a waltz
won't be   The feeling feel when you're here a waltz
No it's you   Why hot when I look up at you a waltz
                    The feeling when I look at you a waltz
                    The minute I look up at you, there's a waltz

Here we have this special feeling,
No denying,
No concealing.
Throw the dream away,
Stay and stay and stay and stay
And stay!

Leona wants to share her happiness and gives a party at the pensione *for everyone there. They all dance, observing and gossiping about each other as they do so.*

Perfectly Lovely Couple

EDDIE
He with his radiant smile—

MRS. McILHENNY
She with her elegant style—

BOTH
They make a perfectly lovely couple.

MRS. McILHENNY
Don't they?

EDDIE
They do!

(Mr. McIlhenny takes over from Mauro and dances with Giovanna)

JENNIFER
He with his vigor and pep—

FIORIA
She with her delicate step—

BOTH
They make a perfectly lovely couple.

JENNIFER
Don't they?

FIORIA
They do!

EDDIE, JENNIFER
Hey there, you two, when's the wedding?

FIORIA
Sooner than you think!

EDDIE, JENNIFER, MRS. McILHENNY
He's all right, but she's beginning to sink.

EDDIE
Where's my drink?

(Eddie takes over from Mr. McIlhenny)

JENNIFER, MRS. McILHENNY
He lacks a certain finesse—

FIORIA
She likes it nevertheless—

JENNIFER, MRS. McILHENNY, FIORIA
They make a perfectly lovely couple,
No matter where.

JENNIFER, MRS. McILHENNY, FIORIA, MR. McILHENNY
They make a practically perfect pair.

EDDIE
He with his classical grace—

FIORIA
She with her dear little face—

BOTH
They make a perfectly lovely couple.

EDDIE
Don't they?

FIORIA
They don't.

(Eddie sweeps her off into an elaborate dance)

MR. McILHENNY
He ought to go on the stage.

JENNIFER
She dances well for her age.

BOTH
They make a perfectly lovely couple.

JENNIFER
Do they?

MR. McILHENNY
They do!

ALL
(To Di Rossi and Mrs. McIlhenny)
Hey there, you two, why so bashful?
That's no way to be!
Come on in; the music's fine and it's free!

DI ROSSI
(To Mrs. McIlhenny)
Madame?

MRS. McILHENNY
Si!

JENNIFER, FIORIA
He's such a pleasure to watch.

EDDIE, MR. McILHENNY
She's had a bottle of Scotch.

ALL
They make a perfectly lovely couple,
No matter where.
They make a practically perfect pair!

MR. McILHENNY
Me with my classical nose—

MRS. McILHENNY
Me with your feet on my toes—

BOTH
We make a perfectly lovely couple.
Don't we? We do!

EDDIE
Me with the prettiest date—

JENNIFER
Me with the mother you hate—

BOTH
We make a perfectly lovely couple,
Don't we? We do!

MR. AND MRS. McILHENNY
(To Leona and Di Rossi)
Hey there, you two, how's the weather?

LEONA
Very much okay!

McILHENNYS, YEAGERS
You two ought to get together
To stay!

DI ROSSI
And stay and stay and stay!

EDDIE, MR. MCILHENNY
She with her innocent air—

JENNIFER, MRS. MCILHENNY
He with his beautiful hair—

ALL
They make a perfectly lovely couple,
No matter where.
They make a practically perfect pair!

LEONA
Hey there, have you seen my garnets?
Aren't garnets nice?
If you're good I'll let you look at them
    twice!

(Shows them to Giovanna)

GIOVANNA
Very ice.

MEN
Me with my woozy appeal—

WOMEN
Me with the feeling I feel—

ALL
We make a perfectly drunken couple,
But I don't care!
We make a practically perfect,
Perfectly stunning,
Stunningly charming,

LEONA
Charmingly garnets—!

ALL
Perfectly lovely pair!

In a rage at what she perceives to be a financial betrayal by Di Rossi, Leona gets drunk at the party and lashes out at him, then at everybody else. In the morning, sober and humiliated, she apologizes to them all. Later, alone with Di Rossi, she begs him to give her another chance, but he sorrowfully informs her that the feeling he had for her is gone, that he is too old for all this and that she is too complicated. He tries to comfort her.

Thank You So Much

DI ROSSI
Complicated, yes,
But I do not regret it.
Sooner than you guess,
I think you may forget it.
Why resent because it could not last
    forever?
Some have longer . . . some have
    never . . .

LEONA
Friendly people, brac-
Ing air and lovely weather,
Quite a charming place
To visit altogether.
Sparkling water, soft blue sky—
Ah, why avoid it?
Altogether, I enjoyed it.*

Thank you so much,
Sir, wasn't it fun?
No reason at all to cry.
Let's keep in touch,
Sir, now that it's done,
You can't say we didn't try.

Did it go by so quickly?
Really, it seems such a crime.
But thank you so much
For something between
Ridiculous and sublime.
Thank you for such
A little but lovely time.

DI ROSSI
Thank you so much,
Ma'am, somehow I trust
We'll think of this now and then.
Please keep in touch,
I wish we were just
Beginning to meet again.

BOTH
Did it go by so quickly?
Really, it seems a crime.
But thank you so much
For something between
Ridiculous and sublime.
Thank you for such
A little but lovely time.

---

* This stanza and the stanza above it were cut before the New Haven tryout.

As I pointed out at the beginning of this book, I'm a conservative when it comes to song forms. I believe not only that perfect rhymes give greater pleasure and have more emotional effect than imperfect ones, I also believe that rhyming patterns should be consistent, and for the same reason. Consistency may seem like a stodgy substitute for imagination, but it is frequently the basis for satisfaction in art, especially in small forms like song lyrics. Sometimes breaking the pattern has a purpose, but more often than not it has its roots in laziness. Robert Browning is a hero of mine in this regard: he both rigidly maintains and dramatically breaks patterns for effectiveness: contrast "The Pied Piper of Hamelin" with "My Last Duchess." In the case of "Thank You So Much," although it looks fine in print, the mismatch between Di Rossi's reply to Leona's "much, sir / touch, sir" with the musically equivalent "much, Ma'am / touch, I" makes for an anticlimax. It wouldn't have been hard to fix, but this lyric was written at the end of a long and increasingly difficult collaboration, and I probably didn't care enough at the time.

Fussy details and contentiousness, however, were hardly the major problems with writing this song. The crucial one was that this moment in the show was the resolution for the major character, the moment in which, as in all traditional drama, the protagonist learns from her experience. It was exactly the moment in which *not* to state her self-discovery, which is what I did the first time around, as follows. Here is the original version that went into rehearsal, with Leona alone onstage:

Everybody Loves Leona

(cut)

LEONA
Everybody loves Leona,
Leona is swell.
Everybody loves Leona,
Leona can tell.

Everybody wants Leona,
Leona's the end.
She's glad to be
Everybody's dearest friend.

Bully for Leona.
Tell us more, Leona.
Everybody loves you, true.
Everybody loves you but you.

Everybody loves Leona,
She's cheerful, she's nice.
Everybody loves Leona,
She's good with advice.
Everybody wants Leona,
Leona's such fun.
She doesn't want
Everybody—please, just one.

Friendly old Leona.
Heart-of-gold Leona,

Everybody loves her, true.
Everybody loves her but . . .

    I want to go home.

A neat lyric, and what bathos is all about. It's as if Oedipus sang, "Oh God, I've married my mother and killed my father" rather than tearing his eyes out. Show, don't tell, as the old playwriting adage goes. I had to write "Everybody Loves Leona" and hear it performed before I could see that it was too bald a statement and made her sentimentally self-pitying. Leona's unhappiness expresses itself in self-deprecating humor and anger, which is why she's worth caring about and why the audience likes her. Indirection is her mode. Subtleties of character like that rarely show up in musicals; they should be taken advantage of by the lucky lyricist who gets a chance to deal with them.

Do I Hear a Waltz? was, like *Saturday Night* and subsequently *A Little Night Music*, a show that relied on charm. Unlike the other two, though, it had no inner energy, mostly because it didn't arise from a need to tell the story: that story had been told perfectly well in *The Time of the Cuckoo*. *Do I Hear a Waltz?* was well written, adequately performed and a failure in every respect. Discussing the song "Bargaining," above, I said that it was pleasant, but no showstopper. Unfortunately, that describes the whole show. That and the fact that it shouldn't have been written in the first place. It was my first and only "Why?" musical. Friendship, obligation and greed are not good enough reasons to write anything.

Final scene: Leona and Mauro

Dean Jones
Barbara Barrie
George Coe
John Cunningham
Teri Ralston
Charles Kimbrough
Donna McKechnie
Charles Braswell
Susan Browning
Steve Elmore
Beth Howland
Pamela Myers
Merle Louise
AND
Elaine Stritch

COMPANY

A MUSICAL COMEDY

MUSIC AND LYRICS BY
Stephen Sondheim

BOOK BY
George Furth

SETS & PROJECTIONS DESIGNED BY
Boris Aronson

COSTUMES BY
D. D. Ryan

LIGHTING BY
Robert Ornbo

MUSICAL DIRECTION BY
Harold Hastings

ORCHESTRATIONS BY
Jonathan Tunick

DANCE MUSIC ARRANGEMENTS BY
Wally Harper

ORIGINAL CAST ALBUM ON
Columbia Records

MUSIC PUBLISHER
Tommy Valando

MUSICAL NUMBERS STAGED BY
Michael Bennett

PRODUCTION DIRECTED BY
Harold Prince

ALVIN THEATRE
52nd Street, West of Broadway

7. Company (1970)

Book by George Furth

The Notion

A man with no emotional commitments reassesses his life on his thirty-fifth birthday by reviewing his relationships with his married acquaintances and his girlfriends. That is the entire plot.

General Comments

My taste for experiment in the commercial theater was formed early, when at the age of seventeen I was hired for twenty-five dollars a week (not a bad sum at a time when subway rides cost a nickel and orchestra seats cost $4.40) to be Oscar's assistant on the third Rodgers and Hammerstein show, *Allegro*. After the successes of *Oklahoma!* and *Carousel,* it was expected that they would deliver another homey, uplifting, straightforward piece of storytelling. But just as Hammerstein had confounded audiences with the novelty of *Oklahoma!*, so he did with *Allegro,* which for Broadway musicals was startlingly experimental in form and style. It chronicled on a bare stage the first forty years of a man's life, a Greek chorus taking the place of the conventional musical-comedy chorus, commenting on events and charting the hero's social and emotional life from his birth to his regeneration in middle age. Unfortunately, its stylistic boldness was more accomplished than its storytelling and it was both a critical and commercial failure, which made it an invaluable theater experience for me. I learned how the best intentions of gifted professionals can be blunted and blurred by egotism (Agnes de Mille, the director), intransigence (Rodgers) and the chasm between imagination and execution (Hammerstein). Cameron Mackintosh,

the astute producer of *Side by Side by Sondheim* (not to mention *The Phantom of the Opera* and *Les Misérables*), once said to me that I've spent my life trying to fix the second act of *Allegro*. The more I think about the shows I've worked on, which writing this retrospective has led me to do, the more I suspect he was right.

I had no idea *Company* would be so unsettling to public and critics alike, but then I've been similarly naïve about almost every musical I've been connected with. In each instance I've thought, "What am I worried about? It's got clear melodies, regular rhythms, drama, humor, nice orchestrations, good performers, colorful sets and costumes—what could possibly upset a lover of traditional musical comedy except for its mildly unconventional approach?" and in each instance I've been stunned by the polarized reactions of fervent admiration and ferocious rejection—not unlike the responses to *Allegro*.

Company derives from a group of eleven brief one-act plays written in the late 1960s by George Furth, an actor I'd worked with briefly (in *Hot Spot,* an ill-fated venture of 1963 to which I'd contributed a couple of songs) who had just started writing for the theater. Most of the plays concerned two people in a relationship (marriage, lovers, close friends) joined by an outsider (best friend, ex-lover, mere acquaintance) who serves as catalyst for the action. A production of seven of the plays had been scheduled and then canceled, and George asked me for advice on where to go with them next. I passed them on to Hal Prince, the best adviser I could think of. To our surprise he suggested they be turned into a musical. To George and me, the problem of merging unrelated scenes into a unified evening seemed an impossible one to solve (making the project irresistible) until we came up with the now obvious solution—to turn the different outsiders into a single person. We called him Robert, known to his friends also as Bob, Bobby, Robby and Rob-o, and soon the central theme of the evening emerged: the challenge of maintaining relationships in a society becoming increasingly depersonalized.

The form which grew out of this notion* combined the constant changes of tone and style characteristic of revues with the cohesive narrative tension of the "integrated" musical. Revues, an outgrowth of vaudeville consisting of unconnected songs, dances and comedy sketches, had been a staple of Broadway since the turn of the century, and there had even been a few revues with "themes," such as the Moss Hart/Irving Berlin *As Thousands Cheer*, in which each number and scene was related to contemporary headlines. Most other musicals, except for Hammerstein's idiosyncratic *Show Boat*, sprinkled the songs, dances and sketches into a flimsy, lighthearted plot; these were called "book" musicals. With the success of *Oklahoma!* in 1943, however, the book musical became known as the "integrated" musical, a musical which didn't merely contain songs but told a story *through* them. This form served as the dominant model for musical theater for decades and in its chronological linear state still exists, although it now has acquired, to use Lorenz Hart's phrase, "the faint aroma of performing seals." *Company* does have a story, the story of what happens inside Robert; it just doesn't have a chronological linear plot. As far as I know, prior to *Company* there had never been a plotless musical which dealt with one set of characters from start to finish. In 1970, the contradictory aspect of the experiment (a story without a plot) was cause for both enthusiasm and dismay. Audiences kept waiting for something to happen, some incident that would lead to another that would lead to another, and were baffled when nothing did. Thus was born the "concept musical," a meaningless umbrella term used to describe this new amalgam of old forms. Many shows before *Company* had "concepts," but of different sorts: not only *As Thousands Cheer*, but also *Of Thee I Sing* (cartoon satire), *The Cradle Will Rock* (bare stage agitprop), *Love Life* (history as vaudeville), *West Side Story* (choreography as the chief means of narrative), *Cabaret* (night club interludes commenting on the plot), even *Oklahoma!* (dream ballets and an individualized chorus). *Company* confused the commentators, however, and they needed to come up with a convenient label for it.

The show takes place not over a period of time, but in an instant in Robert's mind, perhaps on a psychiatrist's couch, perhaps at the moment when he comes into his apartment on his thirty-fifth birthday. The framework is a surreal surprise party for him, which opens and closes each act.[†] The scenes which take place in between are all observations which he makes about his married friends, his girlfriends and himself. And because he is the cam-

era, as in Christopher Isherwood's famous metaphor, Robert has often been accused by the show's detractors of being a cipher, a void at the heart of the piece. This view was changed significantly with John Doyle's remarkable production on Broadway in 2006. In his "concept" all of the characters played musical instruments, constituting the orchestra for the show—all, that is, except for Robert, who played only a brief kazoo solo until the end of the evening, when, accepting his vulnerability, he accompanied himself at a piano to sing "Being Alive," his orchestral friends gradually joining in to support him.[‡] The result was that perhaps for the first time in the history of the show the character moved the audience. In part, this was due to the charismatic performance of Raúl Esparza, who played Robert, but primarily it was due to Doyle's theatrical metaphor. In Hal Prince's elegant original production, the stage had been a metaphor for New York City, made spectacular by Boris Aronson's chrome-and-Plexiglas set (complete with translucent elevator); in Sam Mendes's more intimate 1996 London version, the stage had been a bare suggestion of Robert's apartment, representing his internal emptiness. In both cases, the theatrical feeling was one of removal, accurate for the character but distancing for the audience, and the show was labeled "cold" even by its admirers; Robert, despite his ultimate song, never became sufficiently alive. "Cold" is an adjective that frequently crops up in complaint about the songs I've written, both individually and in bulk, and it all began with *Company*. *Company* was my first full immersion in evening-length irony—irony not merely employed as a tone for stray individual songs like "Gee, Officer Krupke" and Cora's numbers in *Anyone Can Whistle*, but as the modus operandi of an entire score. *Company*, in fact, was the first Broadway musical whose defining quality was neither satire nor sentiment, but irony. It was an observational musical, told at a dry remove from beginning to end; in that sense, it was a descendant of *Allegro*, although *Allegro* had not a drop of irony in its heartfelt soul. Of course many plays, from Restoration comedy onward, have been purveyors of irony—Brecht built a body of work on it—and a number of musicals like *Cabaret* contained ironic moments, but *Company* was suffused with it. Most of the shows I did with Hal had this observational aspect to them, the exceptions being *Sweeney Todd* and, to a lesser extent, *A Little Night Music*, both of which, not without significance, had been suggestions of mine. The truth is that Hal was the ironist (witness *Evita* and *Lovemusik*, among others, both of which he encouraged and directed), and I the romantic (*Sunday in the Park with George* and *Passion*, for example), which is one of the reasons that our collaboration was so good. Nevertheless, "cold" has been

---

* Principle 1: Content Dictates Form.
† Or at least it did in the initial production. In subsequent ones, the party at the end of the first act was replaced by the song "Marry Me a Little."

---

‡ A notion exactly like the idea Richard Rodgers rejected for "Do I Hear a Waltz?" although Doyle arrived at it entirely on his own.

the handy earmark for my work ever since, the ostentatious literacy of some of the lyrics only compounding the felony. Continued exposure to the songs over the years seems to have instituted a thaw, but whether that's merely wishful thinking on my part or not, *Company* is a show I'm extremely happy with. It influenced musicals, for good and ill, for years afterward and continues to do so. It made a lot of grown-ups who had disdained musicals take them seriously and it not incidentally gave me my first good notices.

Writing the score for *Company* presented the same difficulty as writing the score for *Forum* but for entirely different reasons. *Forum* required songs that were essentially nothing more than punctuation and didn't advance the plot; here there was no plot to advance. More difficult still, George Furth's dialogue was sharp, fast and witty but self-sufficient; it not only didn't lead naturally into song, it virtually precluded it. The only effective approach I could come up with was quasi-Brechtian: songs which either commented on the action, like "The Little Things You Do Together," or *were* the action, like "Barcelona,"—but never *part* of the action. They had to be the opposite of what Oscar had trained me to write, even though he himself had experimented with songs of that kind in (of course) *Allegro*. I decided to hold the score together through subject matter: all the songs would deal either with marriage in one sense or another, or with New York City.

That solution led to a bigger difficulty: I knew almost nothing about the primary subject. I had never married, or even been in a long-term relationship. Of course, I hadn't known anything about 1929 Brooklyn or New York street gangs or ancient Rome either, but in those other shows, I'd had scripts to guide me and plots to animate. Here was the unknown Kingdom of Marriage and I was stuck with making enough and varied comments on it to fill an evening, since there were neither stories to tell nor characters who needed fleshing out in song. How could I write about relationships (a buzzword in the sixties) without merely reiterating the received wisdom I'd gleaned from plays and movies and sitcoms? As in the case of *Saturday Night,* I relied on Faulkner's remark about experience, observation and imagination and decided to talk to someone with experience, since I felt I could supply the observation and imagination. I asked Mary Rodgers, a songwriter herself, to tell me what she knew about marriage. (I figured it was the least she could do after steering me into *Do I Hear a Waltz?*) She had recently begun her second attempt at it and she knew enough to know what she didn't know, which made her comments fresh, personal discoveries rather than predigested truisms. I took notes—literally—as we talked. For me it may have been secondhand experience, but it was experience nonetheless, and fulfilled Faulkner's dictum enough to give me the confidence to go ahead and write the score.

With George Furth, Harold Prince and Michael Bennett

ACT ONE

*Robert, thirty-five years old and unmarried, enters his apartment and is confronted with a surprise birthday party given by his best friends, five married couples: Sarah and Harry, Peter and Susan, Jenny and David, Amy and Paul, Joanne and Larry. Strangely, they don't seem to know each other; the party has a dreamlike quality, a surreal hush. The seemingly breezy banter is slightly disjointed and detached, culminating in a toneless "Happy Birthday," after which the assemblage presents Robert with a cake, the candles of which he is unable to blow out. As everyone commiserates with him for not getting his wish, he demurs that it doesn't matter: he didn't make one.
Their voices begin to hammer at him.*

Company

JENNY
Bobby . . .

PETER
Bobby . . .

AMY
Bobby baby . . .

PAUL
Bobby bubi . . .

JOANNE
Robby . . .

SUSAN
Robert darling . . .

(Lines begin to overlap and continue to do so until Robert sings)

DAVID
Bobby, we've been trying to call
  you . . .

OTHERS
Bobby . . . Bobby . . . Bobby
  baby . . . Bobby bubi . . .

SARAH
Angel, I've got something to tell
  you . . .

OTHERS
Bob . . . Rob-o . . . Bobby,
  love . . . Bobby, honey . . .

AMY, PAUL
Bobby, we've been trying to reach you
  all day . . .

OTHERS
Bobby . . . Bobby . . . Bobby
  baby . . . Angel . . . Darling . . .

DAVID, JENNY
The kids were asking, Bobby . . .

OTHERS
Bobby . . . Robert . . . Robby . . .
  Bob-o . . .

LARRY, JOANNE
Bobby, there was something we
  wanted to say.

OTHERS
Bobby . . . Bobby bubi . . .
  Sweetheart . . . Sugar . . .

DAVID, JENNY
Your line was busy . . .

PETER
What have you been up to, kiddo?

AMY, PAUL
Bobby, Bobby, how have you been?

HARRY, SARAH
Fella . . . Sweetie . . . How have you
  been?

PETER, SUSAN
Bobby, Bobby, how have you been?

DAVID, JENNY, JOANNE,
  LARRY
Stop by on your way home . . .

AMY, PAUL
Seems like weeks since we talked to
  you . . .

HARRY, SARAH
Bobby, we've been thinking of you . . .

PETER, SUSAN
Bobby, we've been thinking of you . . .

DAVID, JENNY, JOANNE,
  LARRY
Drop by anytime . . .

AMY, PAUL
Bobby, there's a concert on
  Tuesday . . .

DAVID, JENNY
Hank and Mary get into town tomorrow . . .

PETER, SUSAN
How about some Scrabble on Sunday?

SARAH, HARRY
Why don't we all go to the beach—

JOANNE, LARRY
Bob, we're having people in Saturday
  night . . .

HARRY, SARAH
—next weekend?

OTHERS
Bobby . . . Bobby . . . Bobby baby . . .

DAVID, JENNY
Whatcha doing Thursday?

OTHERS
Bobby . . . Angel . . . Bobby bubi . . .

SARAH, HARRY
Time we got together, is Wednesday
  all right?

OTHERS
Bobby . . . Rob-o . . . Bobby,
  honey . . .

AMY, PAUL
Eight o'clock on Monday.

OTHERS
Robby darling . . . Bobby
  fella . . . Bobby baby . . .

ALL EXCEPT ROBERT
Bobby, come on over for dinner!
We'll be so glad to see you!

Betty, I've been trying to ~~reach~~ call you all day

Robert, where you been? Haven't seen you in weeks.
Robert / where have you been? It's been / weeks.
We want to see you
What's new? / Haven't talked to you /
Just called, / Wanted to see what you /
What's new? / What you been up to?
How's things? /
We were worried / / Haven't heard from you
Hank & Mary, Chuck & Helen, Bob & Jane are in town

Why don't I come over & cook you a ~~meal~~ shag yr off
Whatcha need a barber for? I'll cut your hair
Listen, baby, you're taking me out

~~Betty... Betty... Betty, Betty...~~
~~(Betty...) Betty baby, listen, Betty~~ we've been trying to reach you
Betty, baby, angel, darling, sweetie, ~~kitten~~

We haven't really talked in a while

Bobby, come on over for dinner!
Just be the three of us,
Only the three of us!
We looooove you!

ROBERT
(To the audience)

Phone rings,
Door chimes,
In comes company!
No strings,
Good times,
Room hums, company!
Late nights,
Quick bites,
Party games,
Deep talks,
Long walks,
Telephone calls.
Thoughts shared,
Souls bared,
Private names,
All those
Photos
Up on the walls,
"With love . . ."

With love filling the days,
With love seventy ways,
"To Bobby with love"
From all those
Good and crazy people, my friends,
These good and crazy people, my
    married friends!
And that's what it's all about, isn't it?
That's what it's really about,
Really about!

(His three girlfriends enter)

APRIL
Bobby . . .

KATHY
Bobby . . .

MARTA
Bobby baby . . .

PAUL
Bobby bubi . . .

JOANNE
Robby . . .

SUSAN
Robert darling . . .

SARAH
Angel, will you do me a favor?

(Lines begin to overlap, as before)

OTHERS
Bobby . . . Bobby . . .

ROBERT
Name it, Sarah.

OTHERS
Bobby baby . . . Bobby bubi . . .

PETER
Listen, pal, I'd like your opinion . . .

OTHERS
Bob . . . Rob-o . . .

ROBERT
Try me, Peter . . .

OTHERS
Bobby love . . . Bobby honey . . .

LARRY, AMY
Bobby, there's a problem, I need your
    advice . . .

OTHERS
Bobby . . . Bobby . . . Bobby
    baby . . . Angel . . . Darling . . .

APRIL, KATHY, MARTA
Just half an hour . . .

ROBERT
Amy, can I call you back tomorrow?

DAVID, JENNY
Honey, if you'd visit the kids once or
    twice . . .

OTHERS
Bobby . . . Bobby . . . Bobby
    bubi . . . Sweetheart . . . Sugar . . .

APRIL, KATHY, MARTA
What's happened to you?

ROBERT
Jenny, I could take them to the zoo on
    Friday . . .

WIVES
Bobby . . . Bobby . . . Where have you
    been?

HUSBANDS
Fella . . . kiddo . . . Where have you
    been?

APRIL, KATHY, MARTA
Bobby . . . Bobby . . . How have you
    been?

HARRY, SARAH, PETER, SUSAN
Stop by on your way home . . .

ROBERT
Susan, love, I'll make it after seven if
    I can . . .

WIVES
Bobby, dear, I don't mean to pry . . .

HUSBANDS
Bobby, we've been thinking of you!

APRIL, KATHY, MARTA
Bobby, we've been thinking of you!

PAUL, AMY, JOANNE, LARRY,
    DAVID, JENNY
Drop by anytime . . .

ROBERT
Sorry, Paul, I made a date with Larry
    and Joanne . . .

WIVES
Bobby dear, it's none of my
    business . . .

HUSBANDS
Lookit, pal, I have to work Thursday
    evening . . .

WIVES
Darling, you've been looking
    peculiar . . .

HUSBANDS
Bobby boy, you know how I hate the
    opera . . .

WIVES
Funny thing, your name came up
    only last night . . .

ROBERT
Harry . . . David . . . Kathy, I—

APRIL, KATHY, MARTA
I shouldn't say this, but—

ROBERT
April . . . Marta . . . Listen, people—

WIVES
Bobby, we've been worried, you sure
    you're all right?

HUSBANDS
Bobby . . . Bobby . . . Bobby baby . . .

APRIL, KATHY, MARTA
Did I do something wrong?

HUSBANDS
Bobby bubi, Bobby fella, Bobby,
    Bobby . . .

ALL EXCEPT ROBERT
Bobby, come on over for dinner!
We'll be so glad to see you!
Bobby, come on over for dinner!
Just be the three of us,
Only the three of us!
We looooooooooooooooove you!

ALL
Phone rings,
Door chimes,
In comes company!
No strings,
Good times,
Just chums, company!
Late nights,
Quick bites,
Party games,
Deep talks,
Long walks,
Telephone calls,
Thoughts shared,
Souls bared,
Private names,
All those
Photos
Up on the walls,
"With love . . ."

With love filling the days,
With love seventy ways,
"To Bobby with love"
From all those (these)
Good and crazy people, my (your)
    friends,
Those (These) good and crazy people,
    my (your) married friends!

And that's what it's all about, isn't it?
That's what it's really about.

That's what it's really about,
Really about!

ALL EXCEPT ROBERT
Isn't it? Isn't it? Isn't it? Isn't it?

ROBERT
(Simultaneously, with the others)
You I love and you I love and you and
    you I love
And you I love and you I love and
    you and you I love, I love you!

ALL
Company! Company!
Company! Lots of company!
Years of company!
Love is company!
Company!

Here I was again, as with *Forum*, faced
with the problem of writing an opening
number which would not only set the
theme and tone and introduce the
characters but would also, with Hal's
insistent urging, be called "Company"—
not coincidentally, the title of the
show. I knew it was an impossible
word to rhyme without tortuous attempts like "bump a knee," which
Lorenz Hart had already used and
which, like any novelty rhyme,
couldn't be used repeatedly and therefore was unworkable as part of a refrain. The solution was to rhyme as
many words in the refrain as possible
<u>except</u> for the title, and rhyme them as
frequently as possible in order to reflect the repetitive quality of Robert's
life.
    Incidentally, *"looooooooooooooooove"*
was sung on one note, and held a
lot longer than what it looks like on
paper: forty seconds, to be exact. This
was not for purposes of irony; it was
the time Michael Bennett needed to
choreograph the fourteen members of
the cast from their scattered positions
on a half-dozen stage levels into a climactic wedge downstage center in
time for the second chorus. With Boris
Aronson's help, I estimated how long
it would take for the elevator to rise
and fall and the actors to descend the
staircases, and then had to find something for them to sing that would be

intelligible for forty seconds' worth of
running down steep glassine steps,
pushing through revolving doors and
riding down in an elevator. "Love"
conquered all, just as it's supposed
to do.

*Robert visits Harry and Sarah, a fondly
competitive couple. Harry has discovered
that Sarah has been taking karate lessons
and challenges her to demonstrate her
skills. She throws him to the ground.
Joanne appears on a balcony, looks down
at the scene and addresses us.*

The Little Things You Do Together

JOANNE
It's the little things you do together,
Do together,
Do together,
That make perfect relationships.
The hobbies you pursue together,
Savings you accrue together,
Looks you misconstrue together
That make marriage a joy.
Mm-hm . . .

*(Harry challenges Sarah again, but this
time he blocks her)*

JOANNE
It's the little things you share together,
Swear together,
Wear together,
That make perfect relationships,
The concerts you enjoy together,
Neighbors you annoy together,
Children you destroy together,
That keep marriage intact.

It's not so hard to be married
When two maneuver as one.
It's not so hard to be married,
And, Jesus Christ, is it fun.

It's sharing little winks together,
Drinks together,
Kinks together,
That makes marriage a joy.
It's bargains that you shop together,
Cigarettes you stop together,

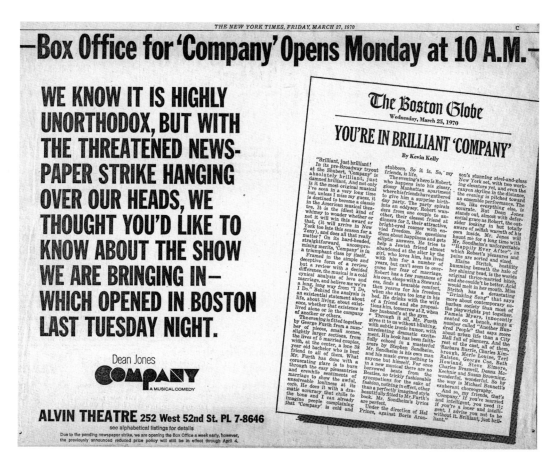

Clothing that you swap together
That make perfect relationships.
Uh-huh . . .
Mm-hm . . .

(*Harry and Sarah are soon locked in combat on the floor. The other married couples enter*)

ALL
It's not talk of God and the decade
    ahead that
Allows you to get through the worst.
It's "I do" and "You don't" and
    "Nobody said that"
And "Who brought the subject up
    first?"*

———————————————

* Here is the original quatrain:

    It's not the profound philosophic discussions
    That get you through desperate nights.
    It's not talk of God and the moon and the
    Russians,
    It's who gets to turn out the lights.

There are times when you have to sacrifice smoothness for conversational energy. This was not one of them. I should have stuck to the original.

———————————————

It's the little things,
The little little little little little things . . .

JENNY, DAVID, AMY, PAUL
The little ways you try together—

SUSAN, PETER, JOANNE,
    LARRY
Cry together—

JENNY, DAVID, AMY, PAUL
Lie together—

GROUP
That make perfect relationships.

SUSAN, PETER, JOANNE,
    LARRY
Becoming a cliché together—

JENNY, DAVID, AMY, PAUL
Growing old and gray together—

JOANNE
Withering away together—

GROUP
That makes marriage a joy.

MEN, JOANNE
It's not so hard to be married.

WOMEN
It's much the cleanest of crimes.†

MEN, JOANNE
It's not so hard to be married,

JOANNE
I've done it three or four times.

JENNY
It's people that you hate together,

PAUL, AMY
Bait together,

PETER, SUSAN
Date together,

———————————————

† This line is a meaningless embarrassment, but "times" is a hard word to rhyme in this context, and I didn't have the strength to let go of the punch line which follows. It's a common trap for lyricists: if the setup line sounds forced, it announces a zinger to come, thereby weakening the surprise when it does.

GROUP
That make marriage a joy.

DAVID
It's things like using force together,

LARRY
Shouting till you're hoarse together,

JOANNE
Getting a divorce together,

GROUP
That make perfect relationships.
Uh-huh . . .
Kiss, kiss . . .

JOANNE
Mm-hm.

The glibness of this lyric, which is by turns amusing and irritating (at least to me), is partly due to its being a list song (see "Have an Egg Roll, Mr. Goldstone"), but also due to another, subtler problem. One-idea songs like Porter's "Let's Do It" are acceptable because they are playful and clever and not Making a Point. Here, making the point over and over with the same irony renders the lyric not only monotonous but condescending. I tried to keep the touch as light as possible by sprinkling the good lines far from each other ("Children you destroy together . . . Getting a divorce together . . . Withering away together . . ."), but the tight triple-rhyme scheme necessitated silliness and vague generalities, which draw attention to the lyricist rather than the lyrics, even when they make sense (do notions like "swear together" and "bait together" really mean anything?). The lyric succumbs to sophistry because substance is too often sacrificed for rhyme.

When I began to write the score for *Company*, I realized that it was going to require comment songs like the ones in *Forum*, songs which "savor the moment," in Burt Shevelove's phrase, songs in which one idea is stated repeatedly, with variations. Thus the tightly packed rhymes, to give it some aural interest. But whereas in the title song of *Company* the tight rhymes serve to reflect the joyless repetitiveness of Robert's life, here the tone is one of easy sophistication, and more the sophistication of the lyricist than of the characters. "The Little Things" is a decent, pointed idea for a list song, but it illustrates another common snare for lyricists, the use of multiple rhymes to conceal poverty of thought—rhyming poison. Tight rhyme schemes may make for surface brilliance, but they can be as tiresome as they are elaborate.

Such observations about this perfectly respectable lyric may seem unduly harsh, but that's because it exemplifies some of the more obvious holes into which "sophisticated" lyrics can fall. Crowded and incessant rhyming is something I deplore in the work of others (Ira Gershwin, in particular), but something I'm not always able to avoid myself, I regret to say.

It would be nice to claim that the clinky xylophone-like accompaniment of "Little Things" is meant to reflect the brittle hollowness of Joanne and her fellow sophisticates, but in fact it's the result of where I wrote it: on the *Queen Mary* during my one transatlantic boat trip. I was en route to deliver the first few songs to Hal Prince, who was shooting a movie in Bavaria, and since ocean liners, like the plays and musicals I had grown up with, were on the way out, I decided to travel in the old glamorous fashion. The purser arranged for me to have a small salon room, complete with piano, so that I could work while I traveled, assuaging my guilt over such luxurious time-wasting. But the ship kept listing to starboard and I unwittingly kept sliding toward it on the piano bench, resulting in a preponderance of treble plinks. Thus is insightful art produced.

After the scene with Harry and Sarah, Robert asks Harry if he's sorry he got married. Two other husbands, Larry and David, join the answer.

Sorry-Grateful

HARRY
You're always sorry,
You're always grateful,
You're always wondering what might
   have been.
Then she walks in.

And still you're sorry,
And still you're grateful,
And still you wonder and still you
   doubt.
And she goes out.

Everything's different,
Nothing's changed,
Only maybe slightly
Rearranged.

You're sorry-grateful,
Regretful-happy.
Why look for answers where none
   occur?
You always are what you always were,
Which has nothing to do with,
All to do with her.

DAVID
You're always sorry,
You're always grateful,
You hold her, thinking, "I'm not
   alone."
You're still alone.

You don't live for her,
You do live with her,
You're scared she's starting to drift
   away—
And scared she'll stay.

LARRY
Good things get better,
Bad get worse.
Wait—I think I meant that in reverse.

HARRY, DAVID, LARRY
You're sorry-grateful,
Regretful-happy,
Why look for answers where none
   occur?
You'll always be what you always
   were,
Which has nothing to do with,
All to do with her.

IRA GERSHWIN
Rhyming Poison

Effortfulness is the defining characteristic of Gershwin's lyrics. Unlike Hart, Gershwin is conscientiously meticulous in trying to play with language and be conversational at the same time, but unlike Berlin, Loesser and Fields, to name the best of that era's other conversational writers, he makes you feel the sweat. Hart's lyrics are sloppy but freewheeling, Gershwin's are clenched. He is often undone by his passion for rhyming, for which he sacrifices both ease and syntax. Harburg and he are habitual users (sometimes overusers) of closely knit rhyme schemes and unexpected manufactured rhymes such as the former's "Riddle / indi-vid'l" and the latter's "Free 'n' easy / Viennesy." Gershwin takes the same kind of verbal delight in the language that Harburg does, deploying puns, alliteration, even mild Harburg-like word morphs ("'S Wonderful"), but his technique isn't good enough to hide the strenuousness of his applying it. As with Hart, you can almost always feel the straining for lapidary brilliance while you listen, especially when he crams the rhymes together, as in this, from the verse to "How Long Has This Been Going On?"

> *'Neath the stars,*
> *At bazaars,*
> *Often I've had to caress men.*
> *Five or ten*
> *Dollars, then*
> *I'd collect from all those yes-men.*
> *Don't be sad;*
> *I must add*
> *That they meant no more than*
> *Chessmen.*

In his insatiable need to rhyme, Gershwin surrenders sense (How often are charity bazaars conducted outdoors at night? Do women sell caresses—I thought they sold kisses, and why are the singer's customers "yes-men"?); stress ("Often *I've* had to caress men"); and syntax (by "Five or ten / Dollars, then / I'd collect . . ." he means "Then I'd collect five or ten dollars").

That last syntactical convolution comes under the heading of what might be called songwriters' syntax, the chief symptom of which is subject-object reversal (for example, "Into Heaven I'm hurled" from the song

above), a practice common in poetry, mostly pre-twentieth-century poetry, but one which both makes a contemporary conversational lyric sound anachronistic and draws attention to the lyricist. Gershwin, like Hart and Coward, frequently lapses into this convention. Harburg and Porter also use self-conscious technical formalities, but theirs are subsumed into individual styles (Harburg's being whimsy, Porter's being camp) and they rarely sacrifice gracefulness, as both Gershwin and Hart do. Only Dorothy Fields (and a bit later, Frank Loesser) was as good as Berlin in making technique unobtrusive. As I've said before, there is nothing wrong with being obtrusive: when Porter and Harburg are at their juggling best, who could ask for anything more (to quote one of Gershwin's own phrases? As long as the technique is worth displaying, ostentation is fine. Gershwin is in his element when he's writing satirical shows like *Of Thee I Sing*, where the push for far-out rhymes and wordplay is part of the fun. As with a "bad" (that is, forced) pun, the strain behind it invites you to deplore it, and therein lies its charm.

Away from his satirical bent, Gershwin shares with Fields a natural warmth and friendliness and, like her, he is at his best when he's not trying to show off, whereas Harburg and Porter are at their best when they're doing exactly that. The finest lyric Gershwin wrote, and I'm surprised that he's credited with it, is "Oh, Bess, Oh Where's My Bess?", one of the more thrilling songs in *Porgy and Bess*. Most of the lyrics for that show were the work of Heyward, who also wrote the libretto, but Gershwin wrote a few and collaborated with Heyward on two. As I noted earlier, Heyward's lyrics for *Porgy and Bess* are, as a set, the most beautiful and powerful in our musical-theater history. This is chiefly owing to the fact that although he was a poet rather than a lyricist, his verse was colloquial enough for the medium, and George Gershwin was a collaborator inventive enough to set what he wrote with minimum changes and maximum force. Heyward's lyrics—all of Act I and most of the rest—set a style that only

sparingly uses rhyme, as in "Summertime" and "My Man's Gone Now." The songs for *Porgy* which George wrote with Ira, however, were usually written music first and words second, which may account for lyrics like the over-rhymed "It Ain't Necessarily So." (Even if you accept the notion that Sportin' Life is a smooth-talker, the lyric is both too literate and too laborious.) But "Oh, Bess, Oh Where's My Bess?" is simple and impressive and moving.

A songwriter friend of mine who feels as I do about Ira Gershwin's work suggested to me a possible source for his obsession with rhyming. It's the kind of insight which smacks of ten-cent psychoanalysis but one I've come to believe is true: Ira was trying to match his brother's brilliance. It was a kind of competition, an attempt to invent and dazzle (verbally) in equal measure to his brother, not for public acclaim but for his own sense of self. Chronologically, he was the older brother, but my guess is that as a collaborator he felt like the younger. His work bespeaks a generous, warm and talented man, but his brother was a genius. There is no comparison, and he was trying to bridge the gap.

I recognize that this opinion, like my opinion of Hart, is a heresy—no two lyricists are worshipped more in the American pantheon than Gershwin and Hart—but the truth is that Gershwin is too often convoluted and Hart too often sloppy. In *Lyrics on Several Occasions,* Gershwin talks about his lyrics with an ease I miss in most of the examples. Here is one, though, which rides along with the effortless rhyming felicity he so relentlessly pursued. It's a stanza from "Let's Take a Walk Around the Block" in *Life Begins at 8:40*:

> *You're just the companion*
> *I want at Grand Canyon*
> *For throwing old blades down the*
> * rock.*
> *Whatever we have'll*
> *Go for travel—*
> *Meantime, let's walk around the*
> * block.*

Of course, he co-wrote it with E. Y. Harburg and it should have been *the* Grand Canyon, but still . . .

HARRY, LARRY

You'll always be what you always were,
Which has nothing to do with,
All to do with her.

HARRY

Nothing to do with,
All to do with her.

Robert visits David and Jenny. They smoke pot and talk about Robert's being single. He claims that he wants to get married, and that he's been dating three girls. The girls appear in limbo.

You Could Drive a Person Crazy

KATHY, MARTA, APRIL

Doo-doo-doo-doo,
Doo-doo-doo-doo,
Doo-doo-doo-doo doo-doo!

You could drive a person crazy,
You could drive a person mad.
Doo-doo-doo-doo-doo.
First you make a person hazy,
So a person could be had.
Doo-doo-doo-doo doo.

Then you leave a person dangling
    sadly
Outside your door,
Which it only makes a person gladly
Want you even more.

I could understand a person
If he said to go away.
Doo-doo-doo-doo doo.
I could understand a person
If he happened to be gay.*

_____

* The original quatrain:

> *I could understand a person*
> *If it's not a person's bag.*
> *I could understand a person*
> *If a person was a fag.*

In 1970, the word "fag" was only faintly demeaning, perfectly appropriate for the girls' annoyance without being offensive to the audience. By 1995, when the show was first revived on Broadway, it sounded not only offensive but old-fashioned, so I changed it.

_____

Doo-doo-doo-doo doo.
Boo-boo-boo-boo.

But worse 'n that,
A person that
Titillates a person and then leaves her
    flat
Is crazy,
He's a troubled person,
He's a truly crazy person
Himself!

KATHY

When a person's personality is per-
    sonable,
He shouldn't oughta sit like a lump.
It's harder than a matador coercin' a
    bull
To try to get you off of your rump.
So single and attentive and attractive
    a man
Is everything a person could wish,
But turning off a person is the act of
    a man
Who likes to pull the hooks out of
    fish.

KATHY, MARTA, APRIL

Knock, knock, is anybody there?
Knock, knock, it really isn't fair.
Knock, knock, I'm working all my
    charms.
Knock, knock, a zombie's in my arms.

All that sweet affection,
What is wrong?
Where's the loose connection?
How long, oh Lord, how long?
Bobby baby, Bobby bubi, Bobby,

You could drive a person buggy,
You could blow a person's cool.
Doo-doo-doo-doo doo.
Like you make a person feel all huggy
While you make her feel a fool.
Doo-doo-doo-doo doo.

When a person says that you've
    upset her,
That's when you're good:
You impersonate a person better
Than a zombie should.

I could understand a person
If he wasn't good in bed.
Doo-doo-doo-doo doo.

I could understand a person
If he actually was dead.
Doo-doo-doo-doo.

Exclusive you,
Elusive you,
Will any person ever get the juice of
    you?

You're crazy,
You're a lovely person,
You're a moving, deeply maladjusted,
Never to be trusted
Crazy person
Yourself!

(Spoken)

Bobby is my hobby and I'm giving
    it up!

A further word about trick rhymes (see *Do I Hear a Waltz?*) like "Coercin' a bull / Personable": Trick rhymes invest the character who sings them with a certain amount of wit, the amount depending on the frequency of the rhymes (for example, The Major General in *The Pirates of Penzance*). Also, as I pointed out before, they draw attention to their author; if they're not written with ease and grace, they drip with the lyricist's sweat. In this case I was imitating a verbally playful style—the lighthearted Andrews Sisters patter songs of the 1940s—to contrast with the acidity of what was being sung. I never would have had Kathy sing the line as an extension of her own dialogue.

Robert leaves. The five couples appear and pepper him with invitations.

Have I Got a Girl for You

JENNY

Bobby . . .

PETER

Bobby . . .

AMY

Bobby Baby . . .

PAUL

Bobby Bubi . . .

ALL BUT ROBERT

Robby . . .

SUSAN

Robert, darling . . .

ALL BUT ROBERT

Bobby, we've been trying to reach
you . . .

SARAH

Angel, I've got something to tell
you . . .

AMY & PAUL

Bobby, it's important or I wouldn't
call . . .

ALL BUT ROBERT

Whatcha doing Thursday?

SARAH & HARRY

Bobby, look, I know how you hate it,
and all . . .

ALL BUT ROBERT

But this is something special!
Bobby, come on over for dinner,
There's someone we want you to
meet.
Bobby, come on over for dinner!

HUSBANDS

This girl from the office—

WIVES

My niece from Ohio—
It'll just be the four of us—
You'll loooooooooooooooove her!

(The wives leave. The husbands corner
Robert)

LARRY

Have I got a girl for you! Wait till you
meet her!
Have I got a girl for you, boy?
Hoo, boy!
Dumb—and with a weakness for
Sazerac slings:
You give her even the fruit and she
swings.

The kind of girl you can't send
through the mails—
Call me tomorrow, I want the details!

PETER

Have I got a chick for you? Wait till
you meet her!
Have I got a chick for you, boy?
Hoo, boy!
Smart! She's into all those exotic
mystiques:
The Kama Sutra and Chinese tech-
niques—
I hear she knows more than seventy-
five—
Call me tomorrow if you're still alive!

*Originally, Larry had the last word here
and a section ensued in which the wives
had their say, as follows:*

LARRY

Dumb—and with a weakness for
Sazerac slings:
You give her even the fruit and she
swings.
But if the thing that you want is
restraint,
I'll take her out, pal,
And you can sit here with Old Paint.

(Jenny appears)

ROBERT

Your hairdo looks great.

JENNY

Thank you, Bobby.

DAVID

Your hairdo looks great.

JENNY

Well, it should—it's a wig.

(Sarah appears)

ROBERT

You're losing some weight.

SARAH

Thank you, Robert.

HARRY

You're losing some weight.

SARAH

And I look like a pig.

(Amy appears)

ROBERT

That bracelet's a smash.

AMY

Thank you, Bobby.

PAUL

That bracelet's a smash.

AMY

It's not bad for a fake.

(Joanne appears)

ROBERT

That dress has panache.

JOANNE

Thank you, Robby.

LARRY

That dress has panache.

JOANNE

Jesus, give me a break.

HUSBANDS

Whaddaya like, you like laughter
filling your days,
Somebody on your side ever more?
Whaddaya like, you like constant
showers of praise?
Then whaddaya wanna get married
for?

Look what you got now, an army of
wives.
Flirt with them and nobody will
snitch.
You're in their heads, buddy, we're in
their lives.
Listen, you fortunate son of a bitch—

(The wives take over)

SARAH

Have I got a girl for you! Wait till you
meet her!
Have I got a girl for you, Bob?
Ooh, Bob!
Chic! I never saw so much chic in
my *vie.*

I must admit that she's terribly me.
However, somehow she's terribly
    you . . .
Yes, dear, I know, but a *young* forty-
    two.

WIVES
(Overlapping)
Have I got a girl for you? Wait till you
    meet her!
Have I got a girl for you, Bob?
Ooh, Bob!

JOANNE
Perf! You've never seen so much perf
    in one broad!
You'll have to curb yourself not to
    applaud.
And all she wants is a man who's a
    man.
Tall, blonde and rich and her name is
    Joanne.

*The section was cut primarily for reasons
of length, but also because it made the
wives bitches and the husbands chumps, a
danger in a show where the women are
drawn more incisively than the men. In
its final incarnation, the song picked up
as follows:*

HUSBANDS
Have I got a girl for you? Wait till you
    meet her!
Have I got a girl for you, boy?
Hoo, boy!
Boy, to be in your shoes what I
    wouldn't give—
I mean the freedom to go out and
    live!
And as for settling down and all
    that—
Marriage may be where it's been,
But it's not where it's at.

Whaddaya like, you like coming
    home to a kiss?
Somebody with a smile at the door?
Whaddaya like, you like indescrib-
    able bliss?
Then whaddaya wanna get married
    for?

Whaddaya like, you like an excursion
    to Rome,
Suddenly taking off to explore?

Whaddaya like, you like having meals
    cooked at home?
Then whaddaya wanna get married
    for?
Whaddaya wanna get married
    for? . . .

Robert is left alone to ponder this.

Someone Is Waiting

ROBERT
Someone is waiting,
Cool as Sarah,
Easy and loving as Susan—
Jenny.
Someone is waiting,
Warm as Susan,
Frantic and touching as Amy—
Joanne.

Would I know her even if I met her?
Have I missed her? Did I let her go?
A Susan sort of Sarah,
A Jennyish Joanne—
Wait for me, I'm ready now,
I'll find you if I can!

Someone will hold me,
Soft as Jenny,
Skinny and blue-eyed as Amy—
Susan.
Someone will wake me,
Sweet as Amy,
Tender and foolish as Sarah,
Joanne.

Did I know her? Have I waited too
    long?
Maybe so, but maybe so has she,
My blue-eyed Sarah
Warm Joanne
Sweet Jenny
Loving Susan
Crazy Amy,
Wait for me,
I'll hurry.
Wait for me.
Hurry.
Wait for me . . .
Hurry . . .
Wait . . .

*Robert sits on a park bench with April,
an airline stewardess. After she leaves,
Marta comments from the sidelines.*

Another Hundred People

MARTA
Another hundred people just got off
    of the train
And came up through the ground
While another hundred people just
    got off of the bus
And are looking around
At another hundred people who got
    off of the plane
And are looking at us
Who got off of the train
And the plane and the bus
Maybe yesterday.

It's a city of strangers:
Some come to work, some to play.
A city of strangers:
Some come to stare, some to stay.
And every day
The ones who stay

Can find each other in the crowded
    streets
And the guarded parks,
By the rusty fountains and the dusty
    trees
With the battered barks.
And they walk together past the
    postered walls
With the crude remarks,

And they meet at parties through the
    friends of friends
Who they never know.
Will you pick me up, or do I meet
    you there,
Or shall we let it go?
Did you get my message, 'cause I
    looked in vain?
Can we see each other Tuesday if it
    doesn't rain?
Look, I'll call you in the morning
Or my service will explain . . .

And another hundred people just got
    off of the train.

(April is replaced by Kathy, who tells Robert that she's leaving New York to get married. Marta comments again.)

MARTA

It's a city of strangers—
Some come to work, some to play.
A city of strangers—
Some come to stare, some to stay.
And every day
Some go away . . .

Or they find each other in the
    crowded streets
And the guarded parks,
By the rusty fountains and the dusty
    trees
With the battered barks.
And they walk together past the
    postered walls
With the crude remarks,

And they meet at parties through the
    friends of friends
Who they never know.
Will you pick me up, or do I meet
    you there,
Or shall we let it go?
Did you get my message, 'cause I
    looked in vain?
Can we see each other Tuesday if it
    doesn't rain?
Look, I'll call you in the morning
Or my service will explain . . .

And another hundred people just got
    off of the train.
And another hundred people just got
    off of the train.
And another hundred people just got
    off of the train.
And another hundred people just got
    off of the train.
And another hundred people just got
    off of the train.

George Furth wrote Marta as a feisty, outspoken, quintessentially New York Jewish girl, not, one would think, a hard part to cast on Broadway. Like Kathy, she had no solo song; among Robert's girlfriends only April had her own musical moment, and even that was part of a duet. After auditioning a dozen fine unexciting possibilities, we were suddenly confronted by a recently graduated twenty-one-year-old Cincinnati Conservatory student with no stage experience named Pamela Myers, who strode in purposefully, belted out "Shy" from *Once Upon a Mattress* and broke us up laughing, then followed it with "Little Green Apples" and broke us up crying. We knew we had a "discovery" on our hands. The only problem was that she was blond, Midwestern, looked like a 4-H poster girl and was about as Jewish as the squeaky-clean MGM ingenue June Allyson, whom she distantly resembled. We held a brief but intense conference about her inappropriateness for the role. There ensued a version of that glamorous moment which I had seen in so many Hollywood movies about show business (most famously *42nd Street*), the moment I had hoped I would some day be part of, when the director picks an understudy or someone out of the chorus, the songwriters write her a great song and she becomes a star overnight. As it happened in our low-budget version, Hal turned to George and said, "Think you can rewrite Marta for this girl?" to which George eagerly nodded; Hal then swiveled to me and barked, "Can you write a song for her, kid? Give her a real spot?" I could feel the cameras turning on me as I barked back, "Of course!"

The result was "Another Hundred People," a song Marta sang in the second act. It was the only song in the score not directly concerned with interpersonal relationships and the above explains why: it was written for a performer instead of a character—which makes me no less pleased with it as a song. During rehearsals it clearly threatened to stop the show and indeed at the first preview on a Saturday night in Boston did exactly that. But the preview was also more than three hours long and we were scheduled to open to the press Tuesday, so on Sunday we cut over twenty minutes, most of them in the second act—including, reluctantly but ruthlessly, "Another Hundred People." On Monday morning, with the cast assembled in the front rows of the theater, Hal outlined the changes we'd be making over the next two days. When he finished and there was a break before the rehearsal began, I went to where Pam was sitting on the aisle in the fifth row. To my surprise she was neither tearful nor ostentatiously stoic; she was in fact so centered that I felt any condolences on my part would be condescending. Wanting to say *something*, however, I blurted melodramatically, still in my movie mode, "I'll have that song back in by tomorrow night!" Stuck in my fantasy, I returned to my hotel room, that mythical place where all shows get rewritten and magically transformed from flops into hits, and tried to figure out a way to reinstate the song with a minimum of change in the staging and lighting so that I could sell it to Hal and Michael, since they had only a few hours of rehearsal in which to rework things. The solution turned out to be simple: I combined the three separate girl-friends' scenes in the first act into one scene by having them all take place on the same park bench, and divided the song into three sections, using it to string the scenes together. Pressed as they were for time, Hal and Michael accepted the notion and the song went back into the show Tuesday night, just in time for the critics. My fantasy became reality: Even the critics who disliked the show loved Pam. It was a triumph of her attitude as much as her talent, exactly the way I had hoped: Ruby Keeler in *42nd Street*, with variations.

Robert is in Amy's kitchen. It is the morning of her wedding day, and Robert is best man. Amy has finally consented to marry Paul, with whom she has been living for two years, but she is terrified of marriage, and imagines the forthcoming ceremony.

Beth Howland as Amy with Dean Jones as Robert

Getting Married Today

CHURCH LADY
(As a choir hums)
Bless this day, pinnacle of life,
Husband joined to wife.
The heart leaps up to behold
This golden day.

PAUL
(To Amy)
Today is for Amy.
Amy, I give you the rest of my life,
To cherish and to keep you,
To honor you forever.
Today is for Amy,
My happily
Soon-to-be
Wife.

AMY
(To the audience)
Pardon me, is everybody there?
Because if everybody's there,
I want to thank you all for coming to
   the wedding.

I'd appreciate your going even more,
I mean, you must have lots of better
   things to do,
And not a word of it to Paul.
Remember Paul? You know, the man
   I'm gonna marry,
But I'm not, because I wouldn't ruin
Anyone as wonderful as he is—

But I thank you all
For the gifts and the flowers.
Thank you all,
Now it's back to the showers.
Don't tell Paul,
But I'm not getting married today.

CHURCH LADY
Bless this day, tragedy of life,
Husband yoked to wife.
The heart sinks down and feels dead
This dreadful day.

AMY
Listen, everybody,
Look, I don't know what you're
   waiting for.
A wedding, what's a wedding?
It's a prehistoric ritual

Where everybody promises fidelity
   forever,
Which is maybe the most horrifying
   word I've ever heard,
And which is followed by a
   honeymoon
Where suddenly he'll realize
He's saddled with a nut
And want to kill me, which he
   should.

So listen,
Thanks a bunch,
But I'm not getting married.
Go have lunch,
'Cause I'm not getting married.
You've been grand,
But I'm not getting married.
Don't just stand
There, I'm not getting married!
And don't tell Paul,
But I'm not getting married today.

Go!
Can't you go?
Why is no-
Body listening?

AMY (second verse - to replace "Tacky little
chapel...")

LISTEN EVERYBODY, LOOK, I
DON'T KNOW WHAT YOU'RE WAITING FOR - A
WEDDING, WHAT'S A WEDDING? IT'S A
PREHISTORIC RITUAL WHERE
EVERYBODY PROMISES ~~FIDELITY~~ FI-
DELITY FOREVER WHICH IS
MAYBE THE MOST HORRIFYING
WORD I EVER HEARD AND WHICH IS
FOLLOWED BY A HONEYMOON WHERE
SUDDENLY HE'LL REALIZE HE'S
SADDLED WITH A NUT AND WANNA
KILL ME AND HE SHOULD, SO WOULD YOU
CLEAR THE HALL.......

LISTEN, EVERYBODY, I'M A-
FRAID YOU DIDN'T HEAR, OR DO YOU
WANT TO SEE A CRAZY LADY
FALL APART IN FRONT OF YOU, IT
ISN'T ONLY PAUL WHO ~~WILL~~ (MAY) BE
RUINING HIS LIFE, YOU KNOW, WE'LL
BOTH OF US ~~ARE~~ (BE) LOSING OUR ~~XXXXXXXXXX~~ I-
DENTITIES, I TELEPHONED MY
ANALYST ABOUT IT AND HE
SAID TO SEE HIM MONDAY BUT ~~BY~~ (on)
MONDAY I'LL BE FLOATING IN THE
HUDSON WITH THE (OTHER) GARBAGE, ~~LOOKIT~~ (I'M
I'M NOT WELL, (A)   ~~JUST~~

Telephoned my analyst at
Bout it & he said to see him
Monday and I told him that by

Listen, I don't think you under-
stood, I mean it isn't only
Paul who may be ruining his life
Life oh no we both may well be
Don't you see the danger will be   [struck through] (can't)
Losing our identities I
Telephoned my analyst but
He was with a patient so he
Really couldn't talk to me He
Said he'd see me Monday but by
Monday I'll be floating in the
Hudson with the garbage and
(Pollution that's another reason)
I'm not well, so I'm not getting married
You've been sweet, but
Thanks a heap, but
Get some sleep, 'cause

Listen to me people, I don't   [to me body struck through]
Think you got the point   (understood you see)
It isn't only Paul who may be
Ruining his life I mean the   (sure)
Danger that we both may well be

Wanna see a crazy lady   (okay / or do you)
Fall apart in front of you; it
Isn't only Paul who may be
Ruining his life you know, we
Both'll be destroying our   (as we are falling)
Identities

Listen, everybody, I'm a-
Fraid you didn't hear, you see it   (I mean)
Isn't only Paul who may be   (will)
Ruining his life

___ ___ I telephoned my
Analyst about it he said   (and)
To see him come in on Monday
I'll see you   (couldn't)

but by

Monday I'll be floating in the
Hudson with the garbage look it   (and gotten)

Goodbye!
Go and cry
At another person's wake.
If you're quick,
For a kick
You could pick
Up a christening,
But please,
On my knees,
There's a human life at stake!

Listen, everybody, I'm afraid you
    didn't hear,
Or do you want to see a crazy lady
Fall apart in front of you?
It isn't only Paul who may be ruining
    his life, you know,
We'll both of us be losing our
    identities—
I telephoned my analyst about it
And he said to see him Monday,
But by Monday I'll be floating
In the Hudson with the other
    garbage.

I'm not well,
So I'm not getting married.
You've been swell,
But I'm not getting married.
Clear the hall,
'Cause I'm not getting married.
Thank you all,
But I'm not getting married.
And don't tell Paul,
But I'm not getting married today!

CHURCH LADY
Bless this bride, totally insane,
Slipping down the drain,
And bless this day in our hearts,
As it starts to rain.

PAUL	AMY
Today is for Amy.	Go, can't you go?
Amy,	Look, you know
I give you	I adore you all,
The rest of my life,	But why
	Watch me die
To cherish	Like Eliza on the
	ice?
And to keep	Look, perhaps
You,	I'll collapse
	In the apse
To honor you	Right before you
	all,
Forever,	So take
	Back the cake,

Today is for Amy,   Burn the shoes
                        and boil the
                        rice!
My happily   Look, I didn't
                        want to
Soon-to-be   have to tell you,
Wife,   But I may be
                        coming down
                        with hepatitis
                     And I think I'm
                        gonna faint,
                     So if you wanna
                        see me faint,
                     I'll do it happily,
                     But wouldn't it
                        be funnier
My adorable   To go and watch
                        a funeral?
                     So thank you for
                        the
Wife!   Twenty-seven
                        dinner plates
                        and
                     Thirty-seven
                        butter knives
                        and
                     Forty-seven
                        paper weights
                        and
                     Fifty-seven
                        candle
                        holders—

PAUL
One more thing—

AMY
I am not getting married!

CHURCH LADY, GUESTS
Amen.

PAUL
—Softly said:

AMY
But I'm not getting married!

CHURCH LADY, GUESTS
Amen.

PAUL
With this ring—

AMY
Still I'm not getting married!

CHURCH LADY, GUESTS
Amen.

PAUL
—I thee wed.

AMY
See, I'm not getting married!

CHURCH LADY, GUESTS
Amen.

PAUL	AMY
Let us pray,	Let us pray
And we are	That I'm not
Getting married	Getting
today.	married today!

OTHERS
Amen!

I wrote this song just before the show began its tryout in Boston and never had a chance to polish it properly. The patter sections may seem difficult to sing in one breath as they ought to be sung, but in fact they're calculated to alternate vowel and consonant sounds in such a way as to make them easy for the tongue, teeth and breath to articulate, at least until the end of the second section, when "which he should" muddles the fluency. Worse yet is the final section, as in " . . . he said to see him Monday, / But by Monday I'll be floating / In the Hudson with the other garbage," with its glued-together "m" sounds and its collision of "I'll," "be" and "floating," all of which require completely different mouth formations. In the best rapid patter songs, the faster you sing, the easier it is—you need less breath and the words flow trippingly off the tongue.

Another point worth making: I mentioned earlier that there were sometimes reasons not to rhyme. This is one of them. If I had rhymed the lines in the patter, it would have implied an organized control of Amy's thought processes, when in fact disorder is the essence of hysteria. Simply avoiding rhymes, however, would not have been a satisfying solution; to give unrhymed lines full value (that is, to make them interesting and funny) you have to keep the sounds of the accented words as different from each other as possible. Also, a completely unrhymed song would have been monotonous and shapeless, which is why Amy suddenly starts to rhyme with a vengeance in short, sharp, machine-gun rapidity, bespeaking another kind of dementia.

It was for these reasons that I replaced the original song, which in rehearsal sounded over-rhymed and annoyingly staccato. Here it is (show-business argot keeps popping up in the lyric because in the first version of the scene much was made of Amy's being a TV actress):

The Wedding Is Off (cut)

AMY
(After the first Choir section)
The music is swelling,
The guests are inside,
The parents are kvelling,
And look at the bride:
Beautiful gown, even at retail—
Lamp the veil, folks, notice the coif.
And another fabulous detail:
The wedding is off!*

(After the next Choir section)

The choir is singing,
The preacher's been paid,
The bells go on ringing—
I hope it's a raid.
Staggering gifts, dazzling flowers,
Picturewise, the show is a boff—
Thanks a heap, now back to the
    showers,
The wedding is off!

---

* "Off" is always a dangerous word to rhyme because, like a number of other words, its pronunciation depends on regional idiosyncrasy. New Yorkers would rhyme it with "cough" whereas Bostonians would rhyme it with "doff." I tried to have it both ways in this lyric because I liked the tone of "coif" so much. And there aren't many useful rhymes for "off," anyhow.

Hey, chaps,
You can clear the apse.
And you on the keys,
Please
Play "Taps."
Be nice,
Kindly strike the rice.
I'm cutting the act, ankling the pact,
Chickening out, and as a matter of
    fact—

CHOIR
Bless this day,
Pinnacle of life—

AMY
I know it's been rough, gang,
To come all this way.
Can't thank you enough, gang—
I wish I could stay.
Gotta cut out, due at the shrinker,
Plus I have this terrible cough—
Futurewise, the show is a stinker—

(Another Choir section, after which Amy becomes completely hysterical)

Look, who's the musician?
Is this an audition?
No, something is odd—
Will those who hear me, nod?
Look, I really don't mind it,
But who is behind it,
The Marquis de Sade?
(I'm only kidding, God!)

Look, if you enjoy public disaster,
If you like to snicker and scoff,
You can be sick forty times faster:
Go to a funeral, a funeral's groovy,
Sit through an Antonioni movie,
Look into *National Geographic*,
Watch a pedestrian killed in traffic,
But, sorry, folks—
This wedding is off!

(The last note she sings ascends until it culminates in a scream)

In the original production in 1970, Act One ended with Amy going off to marry Paul and Robert back at his surreal party, once again being presented with a birthday cake. In the current version, Robert is left alone onstage and sings:

Marry Me a Little

ROBERT
Marry me a little,
Love me just enough.
Cry, but not too often,
Play, but not too rough.
Keep a tender distance,
So we'll both be free.
That's the way it ought to be.
I'm ready!

Marry me a little,
Do it with a will.
Make a few demands
I'm able to fulfill.
Want me more than others,
Not exclusively.
That's the way it ought to be.
I'm ready!
I'm ready now!

You can be my best friend.
I can be your right arm.
We'll go through a fight or two.
No harm, no harm.
We'll look not too deep,
We'll go not too far.
We won't have to give up a thing,
We'll stay who we are.
Right?
Okay, then,
I'm ready!
I'm ready now!

Amy,
Marry me a little,
Love me just enough.
Warm and sweet and easy,
Just the simple stuff.
Keep a tender distance
So we'll both be free.
That's the way it ought to be.
I'm ready!

Marry me a little,
Body, heart and soul.
Passionate as hell,
But always in control.
Want me first and foremost,
Keep me company.
That's the way it ought to be.
I'm ready!
I'm ready now!

Oh, how gently we'll talk,
Oh, how softly we'll tread.
All the stings, the ugly things
We'll keep unsaid.
We'll build a cocoon
Of love and respect.
You promise whatever you like,
I'll never collect.
Right?
Okay, then,
I'm ready!
I'm ready now!
Someone,
I'm ready!

"Marry Me a Little" was intended to be Robert's proposal to Amy after she decides (temporarily) not to marry Paul. I was halfway through writing it when I realized I'd run into a problem that often arises in playwriting: the character who knows too much too soon. When I write a song, I try to become the character—or more accurately, I try to be the actor who has to play the character. A good actor will not let you know where a scene is going while he's playing it; he may foreshadow it but he won't give away the rest of its development or his "journey" (the grandiose word so favored by actors) in order to leave himself someplace emotionally to go during the course of the play. Similarly, if you're writing a song to be sung in the first act, even though you know the character will kill himself at the end of the second, it is a dramaturgical mistake to write a lyric which conveys that knowledge. Although I understood this principle from having worked with professional playwrights like Arthur and Burt and Larry and George, I was halfway through "Marry Me a Little" before I recognized that if Robert could articulate such thoughts aloud to someone he cared for, he would indeed have nowhere to go for the rest of the show; he would have completed his "journey." I therefore abandoned it. After the show opened, I finished the song as a favor to a friend, and in the 1995 Roundabout Theater production, at the suggestion of its director Scott Ellis, we tried it out at the end of Act One, where, because Amy has turned Bobby down, it works well as an internal monologue of despair and self-deceptive determination. It has remained there ever since.

ACT TWO

Robert is back at his birthday party, surrounded once more by his married friends.

Side by Side by Side

ROBERT
Isn't it warm,
Isn't it rosy,
Side by side by side?
Ports in a storm,
Comfy and cozy,
Side by side by side.

Everything shines.
How sweet—

ROBERT, JENNY, DAVID
Side by side—

ROBERT
By side.
Parallel lines
Who meet—

AMY, PAUL, PETER, SUSAN,
SARAH, HARRY, DAVID, JENNY
Love him,
Can't get enough of him.

ROBERT
Everyone winks,
Nobody's nosy,
Side by side by side.
You bring the drinks
And I'll bring the posy—

ROBERT, LARRY, JOANNE
Side by side—

ROBERT
By side.

One is lonely and two is boring,
Think what you can keep ignoring,
Side by side by side.

COUPLES
Never a bother,
Seven times a godfather.

ROBERT, AMY, PAUL
Year after year,
Older and older . . .

ALL
Sharing a tear,
Lending a shoulder . . .

ROBERT, PETER, SUSAN,
SARAH, HARRY
Ain't we got fun?
No strain . . .

COUPLES
Permanent sun,
No rain.
We're so crazy,
He's so sane.

Friendship forbids
Anything bitter . . .
Being the kids
As well as the sitter . . .

ROBERT
One's impossible, two is dreary,
Three is company, safe and cheery,

ALL (EXCEPT ROBERT AND
SARAH)
Side—
By side—
By side—

ROBERT
Here is the church,
Here is the steeple.
Open the doors and
See all the crazy married people!

(The following verses are broken up with dance breaks, parades, a tug-of-war and other choreographic punctuations)

COUPLES
What would we do without you?
How would we ever get through?
Who would I complain to for hours?

Who'd bring me the flowers
When I have the flu?
Who'd finish yesterday's stew?
Who'd take the kids to the zoo?

Who is so dear
And who is so deep,
And who would keep her/him
    occupied
When I want to sleep?
How would we ever get through?
What would we do without you?

What would we do without you?
How would we ever get through?
Should there be a marital squabble,
Available Bob'll
Be there with the glue.
Who could we open up to,
Secrets we keep from guess-who?

Who is so safe and who is so sound?
You never need an analyst with Bobby
    around.
How could we ever get through?
What would we do without you?

What would we do without you?
How would we ever get through?
Who sends anniversary wishes?
Who helps with the dishes
And never says boo?
Who changes subjects on cue?
Who cheers us up when we're blue?

Who is a flirt but never a threat,
Reminds us of our birthdays which
    we always forget?
How would we ever get through?
What would we do without you?

COUPLES
What would we do without you?

(Like a broken record)
How would we ever get—
How would we ever get—
How would we ever get—
How would we ever get—through?
What would we do without you?

ROBERT
Just what you usually do!

COUPLES
Right!
You who sit with us,

You who share with us,
You who fit with us,
You who bear with us,
You who, you-who, you-hoo,
You-hoo, you-hoo—!

ROBERT
Okay, now everybody—!

ALL
Isn't it warm, isn't it rosy,
Side by side . . .

(Harry does a brief dance break,
    answered by Sarah)

Ports in a storm, comfy and cozy,
Side by side . . .

(Paul does a brief dance break,
    answered by Amy)

Everything shines, how sweet,
Side by side . . .

(Larry does a brief dance break,
    answered by Joanne)

Parallel lines who meet,
Side by side.

(Robert does a brief dance break,
    answered by total silence. He stands
    stunned as the others look at him;
    after a brief pause, they continue
    singing vigorously.)

Year after year, older and older,
Side by side.
Sharing a tear and lending a shoulder,
Side by side.
Two's impossible, two is gloomy,
Give another number to me—
Side by side by side by side
By side by side by side
By side by side by side
By side by side
By side!

Robert brings April, a stewardess, to his
apartment. As he makes love to her, the
wives speculate about him.

Poor Baby

SARAH
Darling—

HARRY
Yes?

SARAH
Robert—

HARRY
What?

SARAH
I worry—

HARRY
Why?

SARAH
He's all alone.

(Harry grunts)

There's no one—

HARRY
Where?

SARAH
In his life.

HARRY
Oh.

SARAH
Robert ought to have a woman.

Poor baby, all alone,
Evening after evening by the tele-
    phone—
We're the only tenderness he's ever
    known.
Poor baby . . .

JENNY
David—

DAVID
Yes?

JENNY
Bobby—

DAVID

What?

JENNY

I worry.

DAVID

Why?

JENNY

It's such a waste.

(David grunts)

There's no one.

DAVID

Where?

JENNY

In his life.

DAVID

Oh.

JENNY

Bobby ought to have a woman.

Poor baby, sitting there,
Staring at the walls and playing
    solitaire,
Making conversation with the empty
    air—
Poor baby . . .

(They address Robert, who continues
making love to April)

SARAH

Robert . . .

JENNY

Bobby . . .

SARAH

Robert, angel . . .

JENNY

Bobby, honey . . .

SARAH

You know no one
Wants you to be happy
More than I do,
No one,
But isn't she a little bit, well,
You know . . . ?

SARAH

Face it. Why her?
Better, no one . . .

JENNY

—Wants you to be happy
More than I do.
No one, but—

SARAH, JENNY

Isn't she a little bit, well—
You know,
Face it.

SUSAN

(overlapping)
You know no one
Wants you to be happy
More than I do.

AMY, JOANNE

(overlapping)
You know no one
Wants you to be happy
More than I do,
No one, but—

ALL WOMEN

Isn't she a little bit, well—

(Overlapping)

SARAH

Dumb? Where is she from?

AMY

Tacky? Neurotic? She seems so
    dead . . .

SUSAN

Vulgar? Aggressive? Peculiar?

JENNY

Old? And cheap and—

JOANNE

Tall? She's tall enough to be your
    mother—

SARAH

She's very weird . . .

JENNY

Gross and—

SUSAN

Depressing and—

AMY

And immature . . .

JENNY

You know,
No one—

JOANNE

—Goliath . . .

ALL THE WOMEN

Poor baby,
All alone.
Throw a lonely dog a bone,
It's still a bone.
We're the only tenderness
He's ever known.
Poor baby . . .

*In the morning, April gets out of bed to
put on her uniform and leave.*

Barcelona

ROBERT

Where you going?

APRIL

Barcelona.

ROBERT

Oh . . .

APRIL

Don't get up.

ROBERT

Do you have to?

APRIL

Yes, I have to.

ROBERT

Oh . . .

APRIL

Don't get up.
Now you're angry.

ROBERT

No, I'm not.

APRIL

Yes, you are.

ROBERT

No, I'm not.
Put your things down.

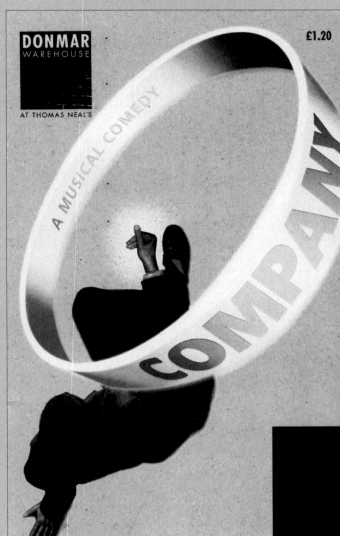

*Donmar Warehouse Production
(London, 1995)*

*Broadway revival
(2006)*

APRIL

See, you're angry.

ROBERT

No, I'm not.

APRIL

Yes, you are.

ROBERT

No, I'm not.
Put your wings down
And stay.

APRIL

I'm leaving.

ROBERT

Why?

APRIL

To go to—

ROBERT

Stay.

APRIL

I have to—

BOTH

Fly—

ROBERT

I know—

BOTH

—To Barcelona.

ROBERT

Look, you're a very special girl,
Not just overnight.
No, you're a very special girl,
And not because you're bright—

(Quickly)

Not *just* because you're bright.
You're just a very special girl, June!

APRIL

April . . .

ROBERT

April . . .

APRIL

Thank you.

ROBERT

Whatcha thinking?

APRIL

Barcelona.

ROBERT

Oh . . .

APRIL

Flight Eighteen.

ROBERT

Stay a minute.

APRIL

I would like to.

ROBERT

So—?

APRIL

Don't be mean.

ROBERT

Stay a minute.

APRIL

No, I can't.

ROBERT

Yes, you can.

APRIL

No, I can't.

ROBERT

Where you going?

APRIL

Barcelona.

ROBERT

So you said.

APRIL

And Madrid.

ROBERT

Bon voyage.

APRIL

On a Boeing.

ROBERT

Good night.

APRIL

You're angry.

ROBERT

No.

APRIL

I've got to—

ROBERT

Right.

APRIL

—Report to—

ROBERT

Go.

APRIL

That's not to
Say,
That if I had my way . . .

Oh well, I guess—okay.

ROBERT

What?

APRIL

I'll stay.

ROBERT

But . . .

(To himself, as she gets back into bed)

Oh, God.

Robert is in a night club with Joanne, who is moderately drunk. She looks around witheringly at the other women in the room, then proposes a toast.

The Ladies Who Lunch

JOANNE

Here's to the ladies who lunch—
Everybody laugh—
Lounging in their caftans and
    planning a brunch
On their own behalf.

Off to the gym,
Then to a fitting,
Claiming they're fat,

gallant

Therm stand the
  guff

graph gaff
behalf gaff
titletoff paragraph
epitaph
    on the phone
roar groan pass
jeer scream
scoff heitz
aren't they a scream
a belch a kick a gas
    a groove
      a camp
        a whale
          the best

        come
Here's to the girls who have brunch

                     fortunate   Fiddling with
Everybody laugh   idiot chattin   garrulous
       prating in a (half-potted) pointless taffeta   Talking Meeting a
Meeting in an affluent purposeless bunch   Sitting in their taffeta gowns, the whole
   Aren't they a laugh   Talking to the   bank
On their own behalf For a photograph   Hiring a staff

On some charity's behalf   Chatting with the staff

                          On their own behalf

              in a perfect school
The kids are polite

                       The ones who marry
     off at their
Kids away at schools   The strong dull men
    in their minutes   daddies
                     The ones who marry their fathers

Don't they know they're fools — Stick to the rules

I'll drink to that   Whose husbands run the city

admit hit
  bit
        Off to the   Better be Try to stay
        Fresh from the gym   fit
Do   setting trim   Having a fit
If they look They're looking grim They're staying slim   Getting a fitting
                      Rather than   Or
      Cause they're getting fat Instead of fat   Buying a hat

                                Does anyone still wear a hat

      They're looking grim   Fresh from the gym   Fresh from the gym
                                  And
      Fresh from the gym   Where they got fit   They're looking grim
           Aye   But
      Losing their fat   Rather than fat   And just as fat
And making fun Doing their bit   Do they look grim They had a fit
Of anyone   Having a fit   They had to sit   Having to sit
                Choosing the   Choosing
        wants
Who buys a hat Buying a hat   Choosing a hat   Buying a hat

Here's to the ladies who lunch –
Everybody laugh
Sitting in their taffeta gowns, planning brunch
On their own behalf.

Here's to the ~~girls~~ ladies who lunch ~~who have brunch~~
Everybody laugh
Posing in their taffeta gowns, the whole bunch
their own
For a photograph   On ~~some charity's~~ behalf

They're looking grim
Fresh from the gym
Losing their fat
Doing their bit
Having a fit
Choosing a hat,
Does anyone still wear a hat?
I'll drink to that.

Here's to the girls who stay smart
Aren't they a gas
Rushing to their classes in optical art
Praying it'll pass
                        exhausting
Another long and perfect day
Another thousand dollars
            a Pinter
A matinee perhaps a play,
      A longish
Perhaps a piece of Mahler's.
I'll drink to that.
And one for Mahler

Here's to the girls who have lunch
Everybody
Aren't they a laugh?
Sitting in their taffeta gowns, planning
                                        brunch
Chatting with the staff

Off to the gym
Then to a fitting
Thinking
Claiming they're fat
And looking grim
'Cause they've been sitting
Choosing a hat,
Does anyone still wear a hat?
I'll drink to that.

And looking grim
'Cause they've been sitting
Choosing a hat.

Does anyone still wear a hat?

I'll drink to that.

(Drinks)

Here's to the girls who stay smart—
Aren't they a gas?
Rushing to their classes in optical art,
Wishing it would pass.

Another long exhausting day,
Another thousand dollars,
A matinee, a Pinter play,
Perhaps a piece of Mahler's—
I'll drink to that.

(Drinks)

And one for Mahler.

(Drinks again)

Here's to the girls who play wife—
Aren't they too much?
Keeping house, but clutching a copy
   of *Life*
Just to keep in touch.

The ones who follow the rules
And meet themselves at the schools,
Too busy to know that they're fools—
Aren't they a gem?
I'll drink to them.
Let's all drink to them!

(Drinks)

And here's to the girls who just
   watch—
Aren't they the best?
When they get depressed, it's a bottle
   of Scotch,
Plus a little jest.

Another chance to disapprove,
Another brilliant zinger,
Another reason not to move,
Another vodka stinger—
Aaaaahhhhhh—

(A scream which degenerates into:)

I'll drink to that.

(Drinks)

So here's to the girls on the go—
Everybody tries.
Look into their eyes
And you'll see what they know:
Everybody dies.

A toast to that invincible bunch,
The dinosaurs surviving the crunch—
Let's hear it for the ladies who lunch!
Everybody rise! Rise!
Rise! Rise! Rise! Rise! Rise! Rise! Rise!

The character of Joanne was not only written for Elaine Stritch, it was based on her, or at least on her acerbic delivery of self-assessment, as exemplified by a moment George Furth had shared with her: they had entered a bar at two in the morning and Elaine, well-oiled, had murmured to the bartender in passing, "Just give me a bottle of vodka and a floor plan." It was my third attempt to write for a specific personality playing a specific character (cf. *Gypsy* and *A Funny Thing Happened on the Way to the Forum*). The song fit her perfectly, the only problem occurring when, in all innocence, she asked me what kind of pastry "a piece of Mahler's" referred to—she figured it had to be some sort of *schnecken*.

Privately, I had hoped that the number would be such a showstopper in Elaine's hands that the audience would actually get up on the "Rise!" repetitions and give her a standing ovation. It was a showstopper all right, but not quite that big. My hope was probably a holdover from my Hollywood fantasies in which on opening nights black-tied men and bejeweled women stood up at anything—much as they do nowadays, where standing ovations are a foregone conclusion, it being necessary for audiences to remind themselves that they've had a live experience by participating in it.

Disillusioned about what he thinks he's learned from observing his married friends in action, Robert sings bitterly. Urged on by their voices, what starts as a complaint becomes a prayer. The spoken interjections are written by George Furth.

Being Alive

ROBERT
Someone to hold you too close,
Someone to hurt you too deep,
Someone to sit in your chair,
To ruin your sleep . . .

PAUL
That's true, but there's more than that.

SARAH
Is that all you think there is to it?

HARRY
You've got so many reasons for not being with someone, but Robert, you haven't got one good reason for being alone.

LARRY
Come on. You're on to something, Bobby. You're on to something.

ROBERT
Someone to need you too much,
Someone to know you too well,
Someone to pull you up short
To put you through hell . . .

JOANNE
You're not a kid anymore, Robert. I don't think you'll ever be a kid again, kiddo.

PETER
Hey, buddy. Don't be afraid it won't be perfect . . . the only thing to be afraid of really is that it won't *be*!

JENNY
Don't stop now! Keep going!

ROBERT
Someone you have to let in,
Someone whose feelings you spare,
Someone who, like it or not,
Will want you to share
A little a lot . . .

SUSAN

And what does all that mean?

LARRY

Robert, how do you know so much about it when you've never been there?

HARRY

It's all much better living it than looking at it, Robert.

PETER

Add 'em up, Bobby. Add 'em up.

ROBERT

Someone to crowd you with love,
Someone to force you to care,
Someone to make you come through,
Who'll always be there,
As frightened as you
Of being alive,
Being alive, being alive, being alive.

AMY

Blow out your candles, Robert, and make a wish. *Want* something. Want *some*thing!

ROBERT

Somebody hold me too close,
Somebody hurt me too deep,
Somebody sit in my chair
And ruin my sleep
And make me aware
Of being alive, being alive.

Somebody need me too much,
Somebody know me too well,
Somebody pull me up short
And put me through hell
And give me support
For being alive.
Make me alive,
Make me alive.

Make me confused,
Mock me with praise,
Let me be used,
Vary my days.
But alone is alone, not alive.

Somebody crowd me with love,
Somebody force me to care,
Somebody let me come through,
I'll always be there
As frightened as you,

To help us survive
Being alive, being alive,
Being alive!

"Being Alive" was not the first song intended for Robert's climactic musical statement, it was the third. In an earlier version of the show, Amy reneges on her promise to marry Paul at the end of Act One, and Robert proposes to her near the end of Act Two. In that version Kathy, the girl most suited to him, has just told him she's leaving New York to get married and Robert, in his unrecognized despair, convinces himself that Amy is the girl for him. Singing, he wanders through all the rooms of his married friends, reflecting on the knowledge of married life he has accumulated throughout the evening, and ends up in Amy's kitchen, ready to propose to her. This is what he sings as he goes:

Multitudes of Amys

(cut)

ROBERT

Multitudes of Amys
Crowd the streets below;
Avenues of Amys,
Officefuls of Amys,
Everywhere I go.
Wonder what it means—
Ho-ho, I wonder what it means:
I see them waiting for the lights,
Running for the bus,
Milling in the stores,
And hailing cabs
And disappearing through revolving
    doors.

Multitudes of Amys
Everywhere I look,
Sentences of Amys,
Paragraphs of Amys
Filling every book.
Wonder if it means I've gone to
    pieces.
Every other word I speak is some-
    thing she says.

Walls hang with pictures of Amys,
Galaxies of Amys dot the night skies.
Girls pass and look at me with Amy's
    eyes.
I've seen an audience of Amys
Watch a cast of Amys act in a play.
Seems there are more of her every
    day.
What can it mean?
What can it mean?

I've caught a stadium of Amys
Standing up to cheer,
Choruses of Amys,
Symphonies of Amys
Ringing in my ear.
I know what it means—
Hey, Amy, I know what it means!
Oh, wow!
I'm ready, I'm ready, I'm ready
Now!

All that it takes is two, Amy,
Me, Amy,
You, Amy . . .
I know what it means—
Hey, Amy, I know what it means!
I'm ready, I'm ready, I'll say it:
Marry me now!

I'm sorry to say that this song never got as far as rehearsal. It's one of my favorites, but when we subsequently decided that Amy should indeed marry Paul at the end of Act One and that the Act Two scene should be cut, "Multitudes of Amys" was clearly no longer appropriate. I decided to write another kind of song for Robert instead, a hard-driving waltz, a defiant summary of what he thinks he's learned from the evening's experiences.

Happily Ever After

(cut)

ROBERT

Someone to hold you too close,
Someone to hurt you too deep,
Someone to love you too hard,
Happily ever after.

Someone to need you too much,
Someone to read you too well,
Someone to bleed you of all
The things you don't want to tell—
That's happily ever after,
Ever, ever, ever after
In Hell.

Somebody always there
Sitting in the chair
Where you want to sit—
Always, always.
Somebody always there
Wanting you to share
Just a little bit—
Always, always.

Then see the pretty girls
Smiling everywhere
From the ads and the TV set,
And why should you sweat?
What do you get?
One day of grateful for six of regret

With someone to hold you too close,
Someone to hurt you too deep,
Someone to bore you to death,
Happily ever after.

Someone you have to know well,
Someone you have to show how,
Someone you have to allow
The things you'd never allow—
That's happily ever after,
Ever, ever, ever after
Till now.

So quick,
Get a little car,
Take a little drive,
Make a little love,
See a little flick,
Do a little work,
Take a little walk,
Watch a little TV

And click!
Make a little love,
Do a little work,
Get a little drunk.
You've got one little trip,
Seventy years, spread it around!

Take your pick:
Buy a little here,
Spend a little there,
Smoke a little pot
For a little kick,
Waste a little time,
Make a little love,
Show a little feeling,
But why
Should you try?
Why not, sure, feel a little lonely
But fly,
Why not fly

With no one to hold you too close,
No one to hurt you too deep,
No one to love you too hard
Happily ever after?

No one you have to know well,
No one you have to show how,
No one you have to allow
The things you'd never allow—
That's happily ever after.
Ever, ever, ever after
For now!

Ever, ever after,
Ever, ever, ever, ever after,
Ever, ever, ever, ever, ever, ever
    after . . .

This was the song we opened with in Boston. Its bleak message was not the end of the show, however; it was followed by an epilogue in Central Park, where Robert has gone in despair instead of showing up at his birthday party. Here he meets a group of thirteen entirely different people, singly and in couples (played by the same members of the company we've seen all evening). Determined to take a step forward, he finally makes a gesture of open and needful connection to one of them, a distracted and lonely young woman. The scene was cut because the show was running much too long, and after it was gone, "Happily Ever After" seemed too much of a "downer," as Hal persistently called it. He fervently urged me to write an "up" song to replace it, but I argued that a sudden positive song, one without irony, would be unearned and pandering, not to mention monotonous, since there would be only one thing to say: namely, marriage is wonderful. Michael Bennett came up with the idea of using the same technique of interlaced spoken voices from Robert's friends that we had used in "Side by Side by Side," helping him to break through his moment of crisis. That suggested to me a song which could progress from complaint to prayer. Thus, "Being Alive."

Chekhov wrote, "If you're afraid of loneliness, don't marry." Luckily, I didn't come across that quote till long after *Company* had been produced. Chekhov said in seven words what it took George and me two years and two and a half hours to say less profoundly. If I'd read that sentence, I'm not sure we would have dared to write the show, and we might have been denied the exhilarating experience of exploring what he said for ourselves.

"The Little Things You Do Together"

8. Follies (1971)

Book by James Goldman

The Notion

The story takes place in 1971. The Weismann Theater, home to the *Weismann Follies* since 1918, is about to be torn down. Dimitri Weismann, the impresario who produced the shows, is giving a party on the stage of the theater and has invited all the living performers, along with their husbands and wives, to celebrate the nostalgia of the occasion. During the course of the party we meet them all, but the action chiefly involves two chorus girls from the 1941 *Follies,* Sally Durant and Phyllis Rogers, who were best friends then and haven't seen each other since. They are escorted by their husbands, Buddy Plummer and Benjamin Stone, who courted them when they were in the show.

General Comments

Follies, like *Company,* is virtually plotless, although it was planned as a kind of murder mystery, a who'll-do-it rather than a whodunit. Shortly after *Do I Hear a Waltz?* opened, I asked James Goldman if he would be interested in adapting his play *They Might Be Giants* into a musical. He gently refused, but offered another possibility: He had wanted for years to write a play about reunions and had recently read a squib in *The New York Times* about the thirty-fifth annual get-together party of the Ziegfeld Club, a convocation of *Follies* girls (some of them already into their eighties). I bit into the idea immediately. The notion of a reunion, where emotions and relationships buried in the past gradually resurface with the help of nostalgia and alcohol, seemed like a dramatic and, in this particular example, theatrical idea.

A party wasn't a plot, however, so we devised one. In our original scenario, each of the principals had a reason to kill one of the others: Sally, obsessed with Ben, wanting to murder him for having thrown her over in 1941; Ben, fed up with his bitter and supercilious wife, Phyllis, who refuses him a divorce, wanting her dead; Phyllis in turn, furious at Sally's rekindling her old relationship with Ben, wanting *her* out of the way; Buddy, enraged at his own weakness as well as his wife's obsession, wanting to kill either her or Ben, or even himself. Throughout the evening, the ghosts of their younger selves followed them around at the party, constantly reawakening memories and playing out scenes from the past.

The first draft of the script began with a brief moody opening, as the guests—the four principals and the other Weismann performers—arrived, shadowed spookily by their ghosts. Once the mood had been established, the plot proper began. When we read the draft over, we found that once the plot had begun, the show felt contrived and convoluted. So on the second round we extended the setting of the mood a bit longer and more elaborately, and delayed the machinations of plot until later in the evening. Once again, as we read it to ourselves, the show gripped us until the plot took over. Gradually, we realized the obvious: what was wrong with the show was the plot—the mood and atmosphere were everything, the events secondary. This epiphany was clinched when we attended the first-anniversary party of *Fiddler on the Roof,* which was held on the stage of the Imperial Theatre. After a couple of hours had gone by and the guests were getting nicely soused, I suggested to James that we sit in the orchestra and watch the activity on the stage. As we did so, one of the guests looked at his half-eaten sandwich with dismay, glanced around to find a place to deposit it and, not succeeding, dropped it into the orchestra pit. I turned to Jim and said, "There's our show." Nothing but a social gathering, people beginning in high spirits, getting drunk and increasingly emotional, performing old numbers and opening old wounds—dropping sandwiches in the orchestra pit. Nine drafts later, we were ready.

Adoring the Broadway canon as I did, the seductive aspect of the show was the opportunity to write two kinds of songs: character songs for the four principals and pastiches* for the other performers, in styles ranging from 1918 to the 1940s, the range of the Weismann shows (Ziegfeld inaugurated *his Follies* in 1908). I had used pastiches in *Saturday Night* and *Gypsy* to evoke period songs with an eyebrow raised, and in *Anyone Can Whistle* to make ironic comment on character, but here was a chance for me to pay homage without attitude to the genre I loved, the past I had known only through recordings and sheet music.

It allowed me to imitate the reigning composers and lyricists from the era between the World Wars, and I grabbed at it with all ten fingers and a rhyming dictionary. *Follies* is an orgy of pastiche. The composers: Irving Berlin, Nacio Herb Brown, Cole Porter, Ray Henderson (of DeSylva, Brown and Henderson), Richard Rodgers, Harold Arlen, Sigmund Romberg, Jerome Kern, Burton Lane, George Gershwin and Arthur Schwartz. The lyricists: Berlin, Otto Harbach, Porter, Buddy DeSylva and Lew Brown, E. Y. Harburg, Dorothy Fields, early Hammerstein, middle Hammerstein, Noël Coward, Arthur Freed, Ira Gershwin, Howard Dietz. A formidable list, to which I'll provide a scorecard (pun intended) as I canter through the songs.

What made these songwriters imitable was that most of them had a style independent of whatever show they were writing. Just as you can listen to almost any piece by Chopin without ever having heard it before and still know that it's Chopin, so it is with Arlen or Gershwin, as well as with a lyric by W. S. Gilbert or Harburg or Porter or Hart, at least the lyrics they wrote once they'd found their voices. They are as distinguishable from one another as Hemingway from Faulkner. Some of them tried to make the transition into the character-driven musicals that took over the theater after *Oklahoma!*, but no matter how hard they tried, the flavor that emerged was always that of the writer. Take Dorothy Fields, for example, one of the very best in such shows as *A Tree Grows in Brooklyn* and *Sweet Charity*: the details in any given song might refer to the specific circumstances or emotional state of the character, but the voice was always that of Dorothy Fields. The same holds true of the others of her generation, which made that part of my job easy by giving it a narrow focus. All I had to do was mimic their distinct, sharply defined, idiosyncratic voices.

What was not easy, for me as well as for Jim Goldman, was finding a way to tell a plotless story that was filled with very brief flashbacks without constantly trundling platforms holding dressing rooms, dormitories, bedrooms and other detritus of the past into and out of the stage wings. The brevity of the remembrance scenes between the mechanical rumblings would hardly enhance the misty, nostalgic mood we had in mind, so we avoided them and confined ourselves to one long flashback at the climax of the evening, a memory of the crucial and traumatic moment in the lives of our four leading characters. When we first presented the show to Hal Prince to persuade him to direct it, he asked, "Where are the flashbacks?" We explained the directorial problem—to a director, no less—and he quickly explained back that, as in a ballet, every scene could be conjured up in a pool of light. No wagons, no trundling, just lighting changes. He went so far as to suggest that we write flashback scenes on the blank facing pages of each contemporary scene (rehearsal scripts are written on one side of the page only) and to think of them as overlapping, even simultaneous. He assured us that he would take care of the scene settings. It was that assurance which allowed us to write the show as we had originally intended.

This chapter, like the show itself, deals a lot with pastiche and may be of particular interest to readers who persist in believing that the period between the World Wars was the Golden Age of Musicals. There are others who think of the Golden Age as the 1950s, but then every generation thinks the Golden Age was the previous one; my father thought the Golden Age was that of Victor Herbert and Sigmund Romberg, although he acknowledged enjoying the "modern" age of Porter, the Gershwins and Rodgers and Hart. Everybody is correct.

---

* To define the term, at least as I use it: pastiches are fond imitations, unlike parodies or satires, which make comment on the work or the style being imitated.

"Beautiful Girls"; "Who's That Woman?"; "Live, Laugh, Love"

FOLLIES

First we see, on an empty disused stage, ghostlike figures of chorines and show-girls appearing in shadows and corners. As party guests arrive amid much glad-handing and backslapping camaraderie, the figures fade, only to reappear now and then as the evening continues. Weismann has arranged for the women guests to make an entrance down the now-decrepit Grand Staircase, wearing sashes printed with the year of the show in which each appeared—shows ranging from 1918 to 1941. He has arranged for an onstage band to play the perennial introductory Follies song, sung by Roscoe, the seventy-five-year-old tenor who now introduced it.

Beautiful Girls

ROSCOE
Hats off,
Here they come, those
Beautiful girls.
That's what you've been waiting for.

Nature never fashioned
A flower so fair.
No rose can compare—
Nothing respectable
Half so delectable.

Cheer them
In their glory,
Diamonds and pearls,
Dazzling jewels by the score.

This is what beauty can be,
Beauty celestial,
The best you'll
Agree:
All for you, these beautiful girls!

ROSCOE, GUESTS
Careful,
Here's the home of
Beautiful girls,
Where your reason is undone.

Beauty can't be hindered
From taking its toll.

You may lose control.
Faced with these Loreleis,
What man can moralize?

Caution,
On your guard with
Beautiful girls,
Flawless charmers, every one.

This is how Samson was shorn:
Each in her style a
Delilah
Reborn!

Each a gem, a beautiful
Diadem of beautiful—
Welcome them, these beautiful
Girls!

A critic named Arlene Croce, in her enraged review of *Follies*, called this lyric "disgusting" in its comparison of middle-aged ladies to beasts, as evidenced by "Beauty celestial / The bestial agree." This kind of aural confusion crops up more often than you might think. When an eight-year-old Linda Rodgers, Richard's younger daughter, attended *Annie Get Your Gun* and was asked what she thought of it by her father, a producer of the show, she told him that she loved "the hurricane song." The show being hurricaneless, Rodgers asked her which song she was referring to. "Mighty Fences Are Down," she replied. (The title, for those who don't know the score, is "My Defenses Are Down.") I myself had a similar experience when I saw *Carousel* for the first time. I was startled at the daring openness of hearing Nellie, the hearty café owner, celebrating Julie Jordan's pregnancy with "Julie's Busting Out All Over." (The soprano playing the part was operetta-trained and pronounced "June is" as "June ease.") These were certainly confusions that neither Berlin nor Hammerstein could foresee, just as "bestial" was one that never occurred to me, but Linda had the excuse of being only eight years old, and in the case of "June Is Bustin' Out All Over," my confusion at least made sense. Ms. Croce's confusion makes no sense at all—if the ladies are "bestial," what are they agreeing on? Nevertheless, whether it can be attributed to willful bitchery or natural stupidity on her part, her tirade cautioned me to be careful about aural ambiguities.

Here is my first version of the opening song:

Bring on the Girls (cut)

ROSCOE
Bring on the girls,
Beautiful girls
In all their splendor.
Bring on the girls,
Beautiful girls
Who drive you wild.

They'll give you a preview
Of rapture galore.
They'll lure you, then leave you,
And still you'll beg for more.

Bring on the girls,
Beautiful girls,
The tender gender.
Beautiful girls,
Doing what girls can do.

They'll fool you, deceive you—
No matter how they grieve you,
You just must love those beautiful
girls.

Painters have tried with all of their
skill
To catch the grace
Of the feminine
Form and face.
Poets have tried, but try as they will,
They waste their time
Painting them in in-
Ternal rhyme.
Who can capture the charm sublime
Of nature's masterpieces?

Here's to the girls,
Beautiful girls
Who grace our portals.
Cheers to the girls,
Beautiful girls
Who fill our stage.

Delicious, enticing,
The *crème de la crème.*
A cakeful of icing
Cannot compare to them.

Bring on the girls,
Beautiful girls,
The true immortals.
Diamonds and pearls,
Here are the girls
For you!

They're dillies, they're dollies,
The fillies from the *Follies,*
The world's most beautiful beautiful
   girls!
Beautiful girls!
Beautiful girls!
Beautiful girls!

When I played this song for Michael Bennett, the co-director and choreographer of the show, he insisted on my writing another because, he said, he wanted to start with a clean slate: a new song rather than one that had been sitting around, gathering dust, for five years. (James and I had finished the first draft in 1966.) This seemed, and still seems, an arbitrary request, but "Beautiful Girls," the song I came up with, had the same majestic showgirl-descending-the-staircase rhythm and ambience, so I was happy with it. The only thing lost was a personal joke: the rhyme of "feminine / them in in-." It was a private elbow-in-the-ribs to Sheldon Harnick, whose work I admire enormously, especially his rhyming grace. He had written a song for a show called *The Body Beautiful* titled "Gloria," in which he rhymed "Feminine" with "A cup of tea with cream or lemon in"—a rhyme I envied. Still, meticulous rhymester though he was (and is), the "o" sound in "lemon," even when the word is pronounced as its usual "lem'n," made it an impure rhyme. I thought I would twit him in a reverent way by giving "feminine" (which, even in the sloppiest pronunciation, usually has at least a faint "i" sound on the second syllable), a perfect rhyme while at the same time pointing attention to it. I would even make a joke of what I was doing. Thus, "Painting them in in / Ternal rhyme." Since the song was omitted from the show before rehearsals began, Sheldon never heard it. I hope he's reading this book.

Now that I look at the song after all these years, I must say that it feels more authentic to the period than "Beautiful Girls." It's less sophisticated in attitude and diction. Rhymes like "Loreleis / Moralize" and "Celestial / Best you'll" belong in a Cole Porter

---

IRVING BERLIN
Deceptive Simplicity

The pastiches in *Follies* begin appropriately enough with one of Irving Berlin's "A Pretty Girl Is Like a Melody," the theme song for many of the *Ziegfeld Follies.* Berlin is a lyricist whose work I appreciate more and more the older I get. His lyrics appear to be simple, but simplicity is a complicated matter, as well as being hard to achieve without a quick slide from simple to simplistic, and Berlin's simplicity is deceptive. He might seem easy to mimic, but his lyrics are so naturally colloquial that they never constitute a distinctively recognizable style. His sentiments aren't particularly fresh or interesting, but his technique is impeccable and, apart from displaying the brilliance of that technique in such songs as "You Can't Get a Man with a Gun," he hides the creative exertion behind the art, which differentiates him from his contemporaries like Ira Gershwin and Lorenz Hart.

One reason for this is that he knows how to fuse music and lyrics into an organic, monolithic whole. This is aided, of course, by the happy coincidence of his writing his own music. As with Porter, everything feels as if it had been written simultaneously. The seeming artlessness of the music matches the seeming artlessness of the lyrics, just as the elegant self-consciousness of Porter's music matches the elegant self-consciousness of his. Berlin knows how to inflect words melodically and rhythmically so that they seem to flow organically; the listener is rarely aware of the songwriter. Not that this is a sine qua non of good songwriting; sometimes being fully aware of how hard the lyricist has worked is part of a song's delight—consider not only Porter but E. Y. Harburg and, at his infrequent best, Noël Coward, writers who can elicit responses like "How did he ever come up with that rhyme?" and other "Wow!" reactions. Ideally, that awareness shouldn't derail the listener's concentration, it should enhance the song. Berlin, in his styleless, unflashy way, exemplifies this. He has the sassiness of Hart without the carelessness, and the simplicity of Hammerstein without the sententiousness or the strenuous attempts at poetry. Every now and then he does reveal an unexpected sophistication, as in "Let's Face the Music and Dance," a song which I wouldn't have been surprised to learn that Porter had written. For me, however, Berlin's sentiments, his view of the world, I find banal; I don't love his songs the way I do some of Hammerstein's and a lot of Porter's, Fields's, Harburg's, Loesser's and others'. I only admire them—increasingly, as the years go by.

Scrupulously clear though Berlin is, I'm happy to say that he, like all of us, is capable of the unintentionally miscalculated line. One that makes me giggle is in "The Girl That I Marry" from *Annie Get Your Gun:*

> Her nails will be polished
> And in her hair
> She'll wear a gardenia
> And I'll be there.

Nesting among the follicles?

score. Not that Berlin couldn't have thought of them, just that he wouldn't have shown off in a song with such a simple purpose.

Sally sees Ben across the room and nervously presents herself to him.

Don't Look at Me

SALLY
Now, folks, we bring you
Di-rect from Phoenix,
Live and in person,
Sally Durant!
Here she is at last,
Twinkle in her eye,
Hot off the press,
Strictly a mess,
Nevertheless . . .

Hi, Ben . . .

No, don't look at me—
Please, not just yet.
Why am I here? This is crazy!
No, don't look at me—
I know that face,
You're trying to place
The name . . .
Say something, Ben, anything.

No, don't talk to me.
Ben, I forget:
What were we like? It's so hazy!
Look at these people,
Aren't they eerie?
Look at this party,
Isn't it dreary?
I'm so glad I came.*

BEN
What would you like?
What's your mood?
Sit and chat
Or go join all that
Or just get stewed?

_____

* The passage between asterisks was cut during rehearsals.

_____

204 · FOLLIES

Ought we to do
What one does,
Reminisce
About how we miss
What never was?

What would you like?
You want to go and hear the throng
Sing every ancient song
With all the lyrics wrong?

What'll we do?
I mean, apart from getting tight.
I've an idea this may be a
Long, long night.
Want to play cards?

SALLY
No, thanks.

BEN
Want to sit down?

SALLY
No, thanks.

BEN
Want to go neck?

SALLY
No, thanks.
Thanks, but no, thanks.
Twenty-five years . . .

BEN
Twenty-six.

SALLY
You know me, Ben . . .

BEN
Let's go mix.

SALLY
Aren't they darling?

BEN
Isn't it ducky?

SALLY
Aren't you perfect?

BEN
Aren't I lucky?

BOTH
I'm so glad I came.*

BEN, SALLY
So—
Just look at us . . .

SALLY
Fat . . .

BEN
Turning gray . . .

BEN, SALLY
Still playing games,
Acting crazy.

SALLY
Isn't it awful?

BEN
God, how depressing—

BEN, SALLY
Me, I'm a hundred,
You, you're a blessing—
I'm so glad I came!

BEN
What we need is a drink.

The two couples—Ben and Phyllis, Buddy and Sally—come together for the first time in thirty years to reminisce.

Waiting for the Girls Upstairs

BUDDY
(*Calling into the flies above the stage*)
Hey, up there!
Way up there!
Whaddaya say, up there?

I see it all. It's like a movie in my head that plays and plays. It isn't just the bad things I remember. It's the whole show.

Waiting around for the girls upstairs,
After the curtain came down—
Money in my pocket to spend,
"Honey, could you maybe get a friend
    for my friend?"

Boris Aronson's sketches for the set

BEN

Hearing the sound of the girls above
Dressing to go on the town—

BUDDY

Clicking heels on steel and cement—

BEN

Picking up the giggles floating down
through the vent—

BEN, BUDDY

Goddamnedest hours that I ever
spent
Were waiting for the girls upstairs.

BUDDY

Hey, up there!
Way up there!
Whaddaya say, up there?

BEN

(Pointing to a wall)
That's where the keys hung and
That's where you picked up your
mail . . .

BUDDY

I remember . . .

(To the women)

Me and Ben,
Me and Ben,
We'd come around at ten,
Me and Ben,
And hang around the wings,
Watching things
With what-the-hell-was-his-name,
You know, the old guy—?
Max! I remember!

Anyway,
There we'd stay
Until the curtain fell.
And when the curtain fell,
Then all hell broke:

Girls on the run
And scenery flying,
Doors slamming left and right—

BEN

Girls in their un-
Dies, blushing but trying
Not to duck out of sight—

BEN, BUDDY

Girls by the hun-
Dreds waving and crying,
"See you tomorrow night!"

Girls looking frazzled and girls
looking great,
Girls in a frenzy to get to a date,
Girls like a madhouse and two of
them late . . .
And who had to wait?
And wait?
And wait . . .

PHYLLIS

Waiting around for the boys
downstairs,
Stalling as long as we dare.
Which dress from my wardrobe of
two?
(One of them was borrowed and the
other was blue.)

SALLY

Holding our ground for the boys
below,
Fussing around with our hair—

PHYLLIS

Giggling, wriggling out of our tights,
Chattering and clattering down all of
those flights—

SALLY, PHYLLIS

God, I'd forgotten there ever were
nights
Of waiting for the boys downstairs.

BUDDY

You up there!

SALLY

Down in a minute!

BEN

You two up there!

PHYLLIS

Just keep your shirts on!

BEN, BUDDY

Aren't you through up there?

SALLY, PHYLLIS

Heard you the first time!

(During the following, their younger
selves appear)

BEN, BUDDY	SALLY, PHYLLIS
Look, are you coming or	
Aren't you coming 'cause	Coming, we're coming,
Look, if we're going,	Will you hold your horses,
We	We're
Got to get going 'cause	Coming, we're ready, be
Look, they won't hold us	There in a jiffy, we're
A table at ringside all	Coming, we're coming.
All night!	All right!

YOUNG SALLY

Hi.

YOUNG BEN

Girls . . .

YOUNG PHYLLIS

Ben . . .

YOUNG BUDDY

Sally . . .

YOUNG SALLY

Boy, we're beat.

YOUNG BUDDY

You look neat.

YOUNG PHYLLIS

We saw you in the wings.

YOUNG BEN

How are things?

YOUNG PHYLLIS

Did someone pass you in?

YOUNG BUDDY

Slipped a fin
To what-the-hell-was-his-name,
You know, the doorman.

YOUNG PHYLLIS

Al?

YOUNG BUDDY
No.

YOUNG SALLY
Big?

YOUNG BEN
Fat.

YOUNG PHYLLIS
Young?

YOUNG BUDDY
Bald.

YOUNG SALLY
Harry!

YOUNG BEN
Yeah.

YOUNG SALLY
Okey doaks.

YOUNG BUDDY
Come on, folks.

YOUNG PHYLLIS
And where we gonna go?

YOUNG BEN
A little joint I know.

YOUNG SALLY
What?

YOUNG BUDDY
Great new show
There.

YOUNG PHYLLIS
Hey, I thought you said
Tonight'd be Tony's—

YOUNG BUDDY
This joint is just as grand.

YOUNG SALLY
We girls got dressed for
Dancing at Tony's—

YOUNG BEN
This joint is in demand.

YOUNG SALLY, YOUNG
PHYLLIS
Ta-ta, goodbye, you'll
Find us at Tony's—

YOUNG BUDDY, YOUNG BEN
Wait till you hear the band!

GIRLS	BOYS
You told us Tony's,	
That we'd go to	I told
Tony's.	you
	Tony's?
Then Ben mentioned	I never said
Tony's—	Tony's!
Well, someone said	
Tony's.	

ALL WOMEN	ALL MEN
	When's Ben
	mentioned
	Tony's?
There's dancing at	It's ritzy at
Tony's—	Tony's—
All right, then,	All right, then,
we'll go!	we'll go!

(The younger selves vanish)

BUDDY
Waiting around for the girls upstairs,
Weren't we chuckleheads then?

BEN
Very young and very old hat—
Everybody has to go through stages
    like that.

ALL FOUR
Waiting around for the girls
    upstairs—
Thank you, but never again.
Life was fun, but oh, so intense.
Everything was possible and nothing
    made sense,
Back there when one of the major
    events
Was waiting for the girls,
Waiting for the girls,
Waiting for the girls upstairs.

The guests, in a kind of Limbo, begin performing the songs that made them famous, unheard by the others at the party. The first to take the stage is an elderly singing-dancing couple, formerly known as the Whistling Whitmans. Their act had been popular in the years immediately following World War I. They punctuate their song with rhythmic kisses.

Rain on the Roof

THE WHITMANS
Listen to the rain on the roof go
Pit-pitty-pat
Pit-pitty-pat-pitty.
Sit, kitty cat,
We won't get home for hours.

Relax and
Listen to the rain on the roof go
Plunk-planka-plink
Plunk-planka-plink-planka,
Let's have a drink
And shelter from the showers.

Rain, rain, don't go away,
Fill up the sky.
Rain through the night,
We'll stay
Cozy and dry.

Listen to the rain on the roof go
Pit-pitty-pat

(Kiss)

Plunk-a-plink

(Kiss)

Plank

(Kiss)

Pity that
It's not a hurricane.
Listen plink to the

(Kiss Kiss)

Lovely rain.

This pastiche doesn't honor a specific lyricist or composer so much as a genre: the "novelty song." Novelty songs were bouncy and catchy, often with a title which featured a repetitive gimmick ("When the Red Red Robin Comes Bob-Bob-Bobbin' Along," "Toot-Toot-Tootsie") or heavy alliteration ("Tiptoe Through the Tulips") or nonsense syllables ("Inka Dinka Doo"). I decided to use punctuated kisses.

Dry Martini   By the fire
Don't be a meanie

                                                    waterproof
Listen to the rain on the roof go   Don't be a goof   honeybunch
Pit-pitty-pat pit-pitty-pat-jitty   Don't be aloof   honey/aunt
little girl,
Honey bunch, you mustn't go home tonight

                                                        paddle
                                            give a cuddle

Pit-pitty pat, pit pitty that's pretty   Pretty pat   Pitty that
                                            Kitty-cat   itty-bitty-pretty kitty
                      ↑ look at the city
Sit, kitty-cat, the city looks pretty   hat   Kitty cat
              the weather looks pretty wet, pot.

Gloomy   at   inky plinkle
Plink plink a plunk   fat   sprinkle
Bick bick a back bick bick a back buck buck   flat   twinkle
                                                                wrinkle
Wish wish a wash   Drip drop-a-drip

Rain, rain   50
                                              rainy season on   fifty
Don't go away   Fill up the sky   sprinkly
              work up a storm   swim   40 days
Rain all night & rain all day   Rain through the night — we'd stay
Stay until another day   cozy & warm
                                dry
                                        for hours   No, sir
                take off your hat & coat   Oh, sir
                wont get   home stay just not yet, pot.
Sit, kitty cat, you can't go out tonight   Kindly hold me closer,
              pretty.
       the weather's looking gloomy.   Why, sir,   Goodbye, sir

Relax and   I, sir

                              blanket
      pluck plonk   if there's a blanket, get me Think it's so much nicer
Plunk plunk a plink
Sit   you mustn't get all wet, pot. have no idea what
We'll have a drink   until it goes away.   You don't know what for my bringing
Let's   'listen

                      Sit, kitty cat   Pit-pitty-pat (kiss)
Listen-plink-to the   Off with your hat   Tch-tch
                      listen my sweet
(kiss)(kiss) rain on the   Just think of that   Shh!

Pitty pat—   Rain

Drink up your drink

Next to sing is Solange LaFitte, a French soubrette, someone whom Weismann might have imported, much as Ziegfeld imported rising stars like Anna Held. "Cheri" was the first song I wrote for her—something she might have sung in a Paris music hall shortly after the end of World War I.

Cheri (cut)

SOLANGE
Hello, doughboy,
Welcome back from Berlin
Today!
Doughboy, no boy
Kissed me once since you've been
Away.
Now that the war is won
From the awful Hun,
Put away your gun,
We can have some fun,
And oh, boy!
Now at last we begin.
Allons, enfant, we go America,
And you will take me there to
    stay, yes?

Cheri,
Pin your medal on me,
Don't sail over the sea,
Don't go back to the U.S.A.
Without me—hey,

Cheri,
Say you haven't forgot,
Say you love me a lot.
I'm the girl from the *Rue George Cinq*!
Remember, Yank?

The mist
And the moon
And the little café—
Remember now, *mon cheri?*
We kissed,
But too soon
You were marching away.
I made a vow to wait
And you said, "Great!"

Cheri,
Now the war is *finis,*
Hail the land of the free!

Pin your medal on,
Take me back to Oregon,
Pin your medal on—
(By the way, my name's Yvonne)—
Pin your medal on
Me!

Sometimes a simple matter of casting can make a song unusable. I had thought of Solange as being about seventy years old in 1971. When Hal cast Fifi D'Orsay, a woman in her fifties, I had to replace "Cheri" with the following, which is more redolent of the late twenties and early thirties than the immediate post–World War I period:

Ah! Paris!

SOLANGE
*I have traveled over the earth
From Bombay to Venice to Perth.
I've been down to Rio
And up to Brest,
To East and West
And to all the rest.

I have seen the gardens of Kew,
And I've been to Timbuktu, too.
But when I've returned,
The thing I've learned
Is what I always knew:*

New York has neon, Berlin has bars,
But ah! Paris! [*pronounced Paree*]
Shanghai has silk and Madrid guitars,
But ah! Paris!
In Cairo you find bizarre bazaars,
In London pip-pip! you sip tea.

But when it comes to love,
None of the above
Compares, *compris?*
So if it's making love
That you're thinking of,
Ah ah ah ah ah ah ah ah ah! Paris!

---

* The stanzas between asterisks were cut, for reasons of length.

I have seen the ruins of Rome,
I've been in the igloos of Nome.
I have gone to Moscow,
It's very gay—
Well, anyway,
On the first of May!

I have seen Rangoon and Soho,
And I like them more than so-so.
But when there's a moon,
Goodbye, Rangoon.
'Allo, Montmartre, 'allo!

Peking has rickshaws, New Orleans
    jazz,
But ah! Paris!
Beirut has sunshine—that's all it has.
But ah! Paris!
Constantinople has Turkish bazz
    [baths],
And Athens that lovely debris.

Carlsbad may have a spa,
But for ooh-la-la,
You come with me!
Carlsbad is where you're cured
After you have toured
Ah ah ah ah ah
Ah ah ah ah! Paris!

"Ah! Paris!" is the first of four Cole Porter pastiches in *Follies.* This one is Porter in his I've-been-all-over-the-world mode, exemplified by such list songs as "I've a Shooting Box in Scotland." He never contributed to any of Ziegfeld's *Follies*, but his style epitomizes the world of musical-comedy sophistication between the World Wars, which is when the theoretical Weissman's *Follies* had their life.

The climax of this sequence is the appearance of Hattie Walker, a woman in her seventies.

Broadway Baby

HATTIE
I'm just a Broadway baby,
Walking off my tired feet,
Pounding Forty-second Street
To be in a show.

1

~~FOLLIES SONDHEIM~~ **FOLLIES**

They call me
Tough luck Tessie   Every Mr. Right went wrong
        seems to go
Nothing ever goes my way

my color is blue   Every sky is grim and gray   The party that they gave last night
I'm extremely blue ~~While Tessie~~ stays ← is blue

(I'm) Tough-luck Tessie

A-sleepin' in my single bed   low
All the gents I want are wed   dough
But what can I do

I'm jinxed but proper —
All of my stocks
Go down, down, down
When old man oppor —
Twenty knocks
I'm always out of town
It's Tough luck Tessie
                                                        vain
When I pray, I pray in vain   complain
Maybe if I prayed for rain   Maybe if I prayed for rain,
My sky would be blue.   my
                                   The skies would ~~turn~~ be blue

Broadway baby,
Learning how to sing and dance,
Waiting for that one big chance
To be in a show.

Gee,
I'd like to be
On some marquee,
All twinkling lights,
A spark
To pierce the dark
From Battery Park
To Washington Heights!

Someday, maybe,
All my dreams will be repaid.
Hell, I'd even play the maid
To be in a show.

Say, Mr. Producer,
I'm talking to you, sir:
I don't need a lot,
Only what I got,
Plus a tube of greasepaint and a
    follow-spot!

I'm just a Broadway baby,
Slaving at a five-and-ten,
Dreaming of the great day when
I'll be in a show.

Broadway baby,
Making rounds all afternoon,
Eating at a greasy spoon
To save on my dough.

At
My tiny flat
There's just my cat,
A bed and a chair.
Still,
I'll stick it till
I'm on a bill
All over Times Square!

Some day, maybe,
If I stick it long enough,
I may get to strut my stuff,
Working for a nice man
Like a Ziegfeld or a Weismann
In a great big
Broadway Show!

"Broadway Baby," like "Rain on the
Roof," is a genre pastiche, the genre
here being the songs of the 1920s just
before the crash, with their optimistic
dreams of upward mobility as well as
their open enthusiasm about life as
it presents itself to us Americans. If I
used any songwriters as a model here,
they were the team of Buddy DeSylva,
Lew Brown and Ray Henderson ("The
Best Things in Life Are Free," "Birth
of the Blues," "Life Is Just a Bowl of
Cherries," "Button Up Your Overcoat"). DeSylva was primarily responsible for the lyrics and his work was
usually full of earthy sugarcoating and
upbeat possibilities, threaded with
Emersonian messages about self-
determination. Happiness was in your
own backyard, these songs said, and
everybody could become a star. To see
"Broadway Baby" sung by a tough old
lady, superannuated and slightly down
on her luck, made our show's point
about surviving the past as clearly as
any moment of the evening. In fact,
the first (unfinished) version of the
song was titled "Tough Luck Tessie,"
and seventy-four-year-old Ethel
Shutta's sly, unsentimental performance appropriately saved the song
from any hint of self-pity.

*Ben and Sally find a moment alone and
Ben sings breezily about his life. The song
is interrupted by his memories of scenes
past, which Sally doesn't see.*

The Road
You Didn't Take

BEN

You're either a poet
Or you're a lover,
Or you're the famous
Benjamin Stone.

You take one road,
You try one door,
There isn't time for any more.
One's life consists of either/or.
One has regrets,
Which one forgets,
And as the years go on,

The road you didn't take
Hardly comes to mind,
Does it?
The door you didn't try,
Where could it have led?

The choice you didn't make
Never was defined,
Was it?
Dreams you didn't dare
Are dead.
Were they ever there?
Who said?
I don't remember,
I don't remember
At all . . .

*(We see a brief scene between Young Ben
and Young Buddy)*

The books I'll never read
Wouldn't change a thing,
Would they?
The girls I'll never know
I'm too tired for.

The lives I'll never lead
Couldn't make me sing,
Could they?
Could they?
Could they?

Chances that you miss,
Ignore.
Ignorance is bliss—
What's more,
You won't remember,
You won't remember
At all,
Not at all . . .

*(Another scene from the past, this one
between Young Ben and Young Phyllis)*

You yearn for the women,
Long for the money,
Envy the famous
Benjamin Stones.

You take your road,
The decades fly,
The yearnings fade, the longings die.
You learn to bid them all goodbye.
And oh, the peace,
The blessed peace . . .
At last you come to know:

COLE PORTER
Camp and Dazzle

Of all the best theater lyricists, Porter is the one whose style is most immediately recognizable. If you hear a lyric by Hammerstein that you don't know, you might think it was by Berlin; a Frank Loesser lyric might be mistaken for one by Dorothy Fields; the same holds true for Gershwin and Hart. E. Y. Harburg is the only one as immediately identifiable as Porter, and even then only at his most whimsical. It isn't just Porter's ostentatious verbal dexterity, which is shared (and imitated) by Noël Coward, nor is it the gay sensibility that surfaces in the brittle camp of his patter lyrics like "Let's Not Talk About Love" or in the overheated fervor of songs like "Begin the Beguine" and "Night and Day," also Coward trademarks. It's his unembarrassed enthusiasm for that sensibility, whether he intended to express it or not, that transforms his lyrics from hothouse to passion.

Porter is the easiest of the major lyricists to imitate because his style is so extreme in its distinction. The list songs are such a gallimaufry of pop-culture references ("You're the Top"), the salacious songs so heavy with double entendre ("But in the Morning, No"), the love songs and out-of-love songs so outrageously extravagant ("In the Still of the Night," "Down in the Depths") that they verge on, and often cross over into, camp. The unique thing about Porter, though, even at his most camp, is that the lyrics are genuinely felt. When he writes "A trip to the moon on gossamer wings" (in "Just One of Those Things"), you believe it because he believes it, just as you believe in Hammerstein's earthy optimism, no matter how ponderously bucolic. It's a line that would be laughable coming from the pen of anyone else, but followed as it is by words like "fabulous," which he emphasizes by adding a musical syllable to the equivalent word "crazy" in the first stanza (Porter was unique in his frequent use of subtle variations from stanza to stanza) and by phrases like "Goodbye, dear, and amen," the intensity of his unashamed overstatement becomes not only believable but genuinely emotional. In Porter's hands, a syntactical reversal like "My

joy delirious" from the song "So in Love" becomes an expression of ardor rather than a lazy clumsiness because of the voice behind it. Porter was too smart not to have been aware of what his writing style conveyed; what's interesting, paradoxically, is that he apparently wanted to be thought of as straight (possibly one of the reasons he married). He and Hart are the two acknowledged gay lyricists in the American pantheon, but Hart's style conceals his homosexuality, Porter's parades it.

One of the things that gives Porter's lyrics fervor is that he loves the haute monde he is satirizing. I once asked Hammerstein why he, Hammerstein, didn't write "sophisticated" musicals (I was seventeen at the time). He said, "You mean musicals about rich people in penthouses?" "Yes," I gulped, certain from his tone of voice that he was setting me up for a devastating retort which would imply my shallowness in asking such a question, but he merely responded, with a small shrug, "Because they don't interest me." That uninterest explains why his portrait of the wealthy and famous, as in *Allegro,* is embarrassingly naïve while every word Porter writes about them rings true. Rich people in penthouses are precisely what riveted Porter's attention and fired his wit; he cared about them. Hammerstein's high-life denizens describe themselves, Porter's reveal themselves in their attitude. Take the coquette who sings "My Heart Belongs to Daddy" in the 1938 *Leave It to Me!*:

> While tearing off
> A game of golf,
> I may
> Make a play
> For the caddy,
> But if I do,
> I don't follow through,
> 'Cause my heart belongs to Daddy.

Porter establishes her in eight tightly rhymed lines. She's a generic character of the period, the coy gold digger, but the attitude of the lyric gives the singer something to play. The attitude is Cole Porter's, that of the amused observer; he was always the character who sang his songs.

Technically, in both music and lyrics, no one is better than Porter and few are his equals. For one thing, he is a master of the list song, certainly the finest since, and finer than, W. S. Gilbert, whose lists are often technically adroit but rarely as interesting in concept or surprising in progression. Porter's lists at their best not only are notably brilliant in their neatness and invention ("Let's Do It"), but the tunes which support them are memorable, "You're the Top" being a supreme example. Most list songs are set to tunes that are little more than underscoring, like Coward's "Mad Dogs and Englishmen," but lesser-known Porter songs like "Let's Not Talk About Love," "Brush Up Your Shakespeare," "Friendship" and "Farming" are just as memorably melodic. Other songwriters have spun out list songs with more than serviceable tunes (for example, Howard Dietz and Arthur Schwartz's "Rhode Island Is Famous for You" and Rodgers and Hart's "I Wish I Were in Love Again"), but none as consistently as Porter.

On the other hand, anyone verbally dexterous can easily lapse into lazy glibness and Porter is no exception. "Cherry Pies Ought to Be You" (from *Out of This World*) is a feeble rewrite of "You're the Top": it has neither the verve nor the variety of its model and is merely a list of superlatives, just the way "Nobody's Chasing Me" and "They Couldn't Compare to You" are dim rewrites of earlier sparklers (all three of these redundancies are from the same show, believe it or not).

Porter's other weakness is a sniggering adolescent penchant for double entendres so blatant that they become single ones. "But in the Morning, No!" is the most egregious, but even in *Kiss Me, Kate,* a relentlessly superlative score, he can go from the wickedly sly ("You gave a new meaning to the leaning Tower of Pisa") to the grossly blunt ("If she fight like a raging boar / I have oft stuck a pig before"). That's one of the dangers of camp, of course: it can skid from giddy to vulgar in the space of an entendre.

cause you grief   shake the sky   change your life

make you cry   shake the earth

change   mean that much

mean a thing   wake the dead

even a thing

be all gold

you'll
The road you never take   didn't

Couldn't
Wouldn't   Won't life & death : matter now

The choices that you make   The world you'll never win/see

Won't   Could be rather grim   grows already
Aren't all that grim.   That's another limit.   growing dim

                  see
The world you'll never win   The choice you never make

                   they
Shouldn't cause you pain, should it   Doesn't stop your breath/don't ya
   Ben I'll never be   know
The man I could have been —

Who remembers him?

The roads you never take

Go through rocky ground

Don't they?

The choices that you make   The worlds you never see

Aren't all that grim.   could
                  Might be rather grim

           never   win   you have to you chose to
The worlds you may not see   The choices that you make

Still will be around,

Won't they?

The Ben I'll never be —

Who remembers him?

BEN (cont'd)

YOU'RE EITHER A POET
OR YOU'RE A LOVER
OR YOU'RE THE FAMOUS
BENJAMIN STONE.
YOU CHOOSE ONE ROAD,
YOU PICK ONE DOOR -
THERE ISN'T TIME FOR ANY MORE.
ONE'S LIFE CONSISTS OF EITHER/OR.

BUT YEARS GO PAST,
AND NOW AT LAST

THE ROAD YOU DIDN'T TAKE
HARDLY COMES TO MIND, DOES IT?
THE DOOR YOU DIDN'T DARE,
WHERE COULD IT HAVE LED?
THE CHOICE YOU DIDN'T MAKE
NEVER WAS DEFINED,
WAS IT?
DREAMS YOU DIDN'T AIR
ARE DEAD.
WERE THEY EVER THERE?
WHO SAID?
I DON'T REMEMBER,
I DON'T REMEMBER
AT ALL.

(handwritten margin notes: BENSON F. / TAKE / TRY; Rooms / are filled; YOU / CAN'T; YOU; THE DEAD)

(handwritten right-side notes: One has regrets / But time goes on / One regrets / And one then forgets; And / But time goes on / anew; And then one day / So one forgets / The small regrets; One has regrets / But which one forgets / And on the years go on; Try; dare / Suppose you close / Were they there or not? / Who knows? / or not; Any more.; And with time, / Of course / In due course / In a little while / And after a while; But then in time, / In time / To your delight / Surprise; forget / Have died / Are lost; forgot / they rot)

SALLY

    (speaks)

That's sad, though, isn't it, Ben? I mean, well, don't you still
want lots of things?

BEN

    (sings)

THE BOOKS I'LL NEVER READ
WOULDN'T CHANGE A THING,
WOULD THEY?
THE GIRLS I'LL NEVER KISS
I'M TOO TIRED FOR.
THE LIVES I'LL NEVER LEAD
COULDN'T MAKE ME SING,
COULD THEY? COULD THEY? COULD THEY?
ANYTHING YOU MISS,
IGNORE.
IGNORANCE IS BLISS,
AND MORE.
I DON'T REMEMBER,
I DON'T REMEMBER -

(handwritten margin notes: Chance that; You WON'T; know have; sons / tried / need; The hills I'll never climb; Forget; dropper reminisce; Thank God / My dear; Hills I'll never kiss / Too bad; touch; Memories are such / a box)

BEN (cont'd)
WHAT'S MORE

WHAT FOR?
MEMORY'S A BORE.

S: I wish we were young again.
B: ~~The young~~ To be young is to be longing.

* * * * * * *

THE ROADS YOU NEVER TAKE
GO THROUGH ROCKY GROUND,
DON'T THEY?
THE CHOICES THAT YOU MAKE
AREN'T ALL THAT GRIM.
THE WORLDS YOU NEVER SEE
STILL WILL BE AROUND,
WON'T THEY?
THE BEN I'LL NEVER BE –
WHO REMEMBERS HIM?

That was just a whim

win

I might could have been

The girls win
The ___ you never wake make
locks break

You yearn for the women,
Long for the money
Envy the famous
Benjamin Stones
The days drag on
The decades fly
The yearnings fade, the longings die
With every minute a goodbye
And oh the peace,
The blessed peace

The feelings cease
And oh, the peace

The roads you never take
Go through rocky ground,
Don't they?
The choices that you make
Aren't all that grim.

The worlds you never see
Still will be around,
Won't they?
The Ben I'll never be,
Who remembers him?

A recurrent dissonant note in the music contradicts the blitheness of what Ben is saying, which makes this song a classroom example of subtextual writing. In the interest of full disclosure, I should add that the last two lines make me glow with self-satisfaction.

A little later, it is Sally's turn to lie.

In Buddy's Eyes

SALLY

Life is slow, but it seems exciting
'Cause Buddy's there.
Gourmet cooking and letter writing,
And knowing Buddy's there.

Every morning—don't faint—
I tend the flowers.
Can you believe it?
Every weekend, I paint
For umpteen hours.

And, yes, I miss a lot
Living like a shut-in.
No, I haven't got
Cooks and cars and diamonds.
Yes, my clothes are not
Paris fashions, but in
Buddy's eyes,
I'm young, I'm beautiful.
In Buddy's eyes
I don't get older.

So life is ducky
And time goes flying,
And I'm so lucky
I feel like crying,
And . . .

(She is interrupted by the memory of a scene of her and Ben at the height of their love affair, which Ben doesn't see)

In Buddy's eyes,
I'm young, I'm beautiful.
In Buddy's eyes,
I can't get older.
I'm still the princess,
Still the prize.

In Buddy's eyes,
I'm young, I'm beautiful.
In Buddy's arms,
On Buddy's shoulder,
I won't get older,
Nothing dies.

And all I ever dreamed I'd be.
The best I ever thought of me,
Is every minute there to see
In Buddy's eyes.

Originally, this song was called "In Someone's Eyes." It had virtually the same lyric, but it also had a counterpoint from Ben:

BEN

What was I to you?
What were you to me?
Does it matter now we're older?
I don't remember you a princess.
Tell me, was I handsome,
Were you pretty then?
Were there songs we sang?
Did I make you laugh?
Did we do things
Just to do them?
I don't remember now, thank God,
And if we did,
We soon outgrew them all!
Staying out all night,
Waiting for the sun to show—
Trivial details from a thousand
   years ago.
Who remembers, remembers,
Who remembers?

Stella Deems, a hearty woman in her fifties, assembles the six now-middle-aged chorines who danced behind her in one of her numbers and persuades them to re-create it from memory. They all hold imaginary mirrors; during the song their

younger selves join the formation and dance among them as their own invisible reflections.

Who's That Woman?

STELLA

Who's that woman? I know
   her well,
All decked out head to toe.
She lives life like a carousel,
Beau after beau after beau.
Nightly, daily,
Always laughing gaily,
Seems I see her everywhere I go.
Oh—

Who's that woman?
I know I know that woman,
So clever
But ever
So sad.
Love, she said, was a fad.
The kind of love that she couldn't
   make fun of,
She'd have none of.

Who's that woman,
That cheery, weary woman
Who's dressing for yet one more
   spree?
Each day I see her pass
In my looking glass—
Lord, Lord, Lord, that woman
   is me!

SALLY, PHYLLIS, CARLOTTA,
CHRISTINE, DEE DEE,
MEREDITH

Mirror, mirror, on the wall,
Who's the saddest gal in town?
Who's been riding for a fall?
Whose Lothario let her down?
Mirror, mirror, answer me:
Who is she who plays the clown?

Is she out each night till three?
Does she laugh with too much glee?
On reflection, she'd agree.
Mirror, mirror,
Mirror, mirror,
Mirror, mirror . . .

The David Frost Show (1971)

The author with Lee Remick at a rehearsal of Follies in Concert (1985)

STELLA	DANCERS
Who's that woman?	Mirror, mirror,
I mean	on the wall,
I've seen	Who's the
	saddest gal
	in town?
That woman, who's	
joking	
But choking	
Back tears.	
All those glittering	Who's been
years,	Riding
She thought that	for a fall?
Love was a matter	Love was a
of	matter of
"Hi, there!"	"Hi,
"Kiss me!"	there!"
"Bye, there!"	"Kiss me!"
	"Bye, there!"
Who's that woman,	Mirror, mirror,
That cheery, weary	Answer me.
woman	
Who's dressing for	Who is she
yet one	who plays
More spree?	the clown?
The vision's getting	
blurred.	
Isn't that absurd?	
Lord, Lord, Lord!	Lord, Lord,
	Lord!
Lord, Lord, Lord,	Mirror,
Lord, Lord!	mirror!
That woman is me.	Mirror,
	mirror!
That woman is me,	Mirror,
	mirror!
That woman is me!	Mirror!

This pastiche is a combo platter: the lyric is an imitation of Cole Porter in his professionally weary mood ("Down in the Depths") which, because of its inherent camp, I tried to balance with music reminiscent of Richard Rodgers in his Rodgers and Hart days, spikier and less sorrowfully mellifluous than Porter's.

I had conceived the number as a routine for Stella and five older chorines as her backup, the sixth one having died. I thought it would be poignant fun to see geometric dancing patterns with an empty space in the middle, and Michael Bennett seemed to agree. Therefore I was surprised, not to say irritated, when I showed up at rehearsal one day to find him coaching Stella and all six in a perfectly conventional, geometric tap routine. When I grumbled to him that I would never have written such a banal song without the bizarre twist that accompanied and justified it, he told me that it wouldn't work and that he had come up with another idea. When I began to protest, he continued with some exasperation to point out that my notion could work if there were a dancing chorus of thirty-six or twenty-four or even sixteen making Rockette-like formations, where the hole in the patterns would register, but that with a chorus of six, the patterns were too small to make the point. I tucked my brilliant idea under my arm and quietly slunk home, while Michael went on to devise one of the most brilliantly staged numbers in Broadway history (and very Broadway it was). His idea: have the six older ladies start their routine and then be joined by the mirror-costumed ghosts of their younger, beautiful selves, true reflections of their pasts. What Michael did was to take a lightweight, semi-camp pastiche lyric and mine it for all its emotional resonances as well as its imagery. I mentioned earlier the necessity of giving a director or choreographer a specific blueprint from which to take off; Michael ignored my scenario, but it did give him the springboard for the glory he came up with. Better yet, my notion wasn't lost forever: he used it in *A Chorus Line*.

The next nostalgic solo comes from Carlotta Campion, who became a movie star after her appearance in the Follies *and who subsequently morphed into a TV personality as she slid into her late forties and her film career waned.*

Can That Boy Foxtrot! (cut)

CARLOTTA

I know this grocery clerk,
Unprepossessing.
Some think the boy's a jerk.
They have my blessing.
But when he starts to move,
He aims to please,
Which only goes to prove
That sometimes in a clerk you
Find a Hercules.
He hasn't much that's plus.
You might describe him thus:

A false alarm,
A broken arm,
An imitation Hitler and with littler
charm,
But oh, can that boy fff——oxtrot!

His mouth is mean,
He's not too clean.
What makes him look reptilian is the
brilliantine,
But oh, can that boy fff——oxtrot!

Who knows what I saw in him?
I took a chance.
Oh, yes, one more flaw in him:
He can't dance.

As dumbbells go,
He's rather slow,
And as for being saintly, even faintly,
no,
But who needs Albert Schweitzer
when the lights are low?
And oh boy, oh boy,
Can that boy fff——oxtrot!

Right now as I speak of him,
I hear those drums!
And oh, the technique of him—
He's all thumbs.

His jokes are quaint
And fairly faint,
He may be full of hokum but I've no
complaint.
He often is a bore, but on the floor he
ain't—
And oh boy, oh boy,
Can that boy fff——oxtrot!

As originally written, Carlotta was a minor character, no more important than any of the other ladies at the reunion (except for Sally and Phyllis), each of whom had one solo to sing. I thought of Carlotta as someone whose reputation had been made by a single sexy song, the way Mary Martin's was when she sang Cole Porter's "My Heart Belongs to Daddy." I wrote this song as a throwaway, something for her to sing at the party late in the evening, the theatrical notion being that she was moderately drunk, causing her to forget the lyrics now and then. And since "My Heart Belongs to Daddy" and Mary Martin were in my head, I turned again to Porter as my model, this time at his most tasteless: his penchant for the single entendre. I could have saved myself a lot of effort because, like "Cheri," this song also became a victim of casting. To play Carlotta, Hal persuaded James and me to let him hire Yvonne De Carlo, a minor movie star known more as a sexpot than as a singer, but a recognizable name to Broadway (that is, middle-aged) audiences.

We all agreed that a name that medium-big would need not merely a solo but a blockbuster solo, so I tried to expand my one-joke throwaway into a tour de force. As often happens with such misguided reasonable ideas, that way lay disaster. One unfortunate justification I had for plunging ahead was that I discovered Yvonne not only could really sing but had an extraordinary vocal range, which allowed me three distinct voices to play with: a lyric baritone, a bass baritone, and Yvonne *au naturel*. Utilizing this illusive springboard, I launched myself into the challenge and emerged with an endless, padded attempt at a showstopper, a routine which not only had the effect of removing all the sexiness from the song but elicited the most discouraging kind of applause: not a mere smattering of handclaps, just mild appreciation, encouragement that bordered on enthusiasm but never crossed the line. Here is the expansion:

(Carlotta, after the first chorus above, becomes two boys at a college dance, trying to pick her up)

CARLOTTA
(As College Boy #1)

Say, pal,
Look at the classy
Coed queen.
That gal
Wiggles her chassis
Good and mean.
Look, she's givin' us the eye,
Strictly on the sly,
Today, I think she's tryin' to vamp
    us—
See ya 'round the campus.

(As College Boy #2)

Oh, man,
Look at that hot stuff,
She is hep.
You can
Tell that she's got stuff.
See her step!
Maybe I could take a chance,
Grab her for a dance,
Make a few advances later—
See ya, alligator!

(To an imaginary Carlotta)

Hey, cutie pie,
Wanna shake it with me, cutie pie?

(As #1)

You better shut up!
Hey, Miss,
Wanna swing it with me?
I'm a cut-up!
Gimme a chance!

(Alternating between the two)

Hey, cutie—!
Hey, Miss—!
Wanna shake it up with me?
I'm a cut-up!
You better shut up!
You'll feel—
With me—
. . . as a feather and . . .

(As herself)

Whoa, boys! Whoa, boys!
Let's not fight, boys,
Being refined.
Line forms to the right, boys.
Simmer down and tell me what you
    have in mind.

(As #1)

I do the rumba,
Turkey trot,
Polka, gavotte
And tango.

(As #2)

I do the conga,
Bolero, Castle Walk
And Fandango.

(As herself)

All right, that's quite enough!
Let's see you do your stuff.

(She watches an imaginary #1 dance)

I pass . . .
Too crass . . .
You just can't foxtrot . . .

(She watches an imaginary #2 dance)

A shame . . .
Too tame . . .
You just can't foxtrot . . .

(To the audience)

Right now, as I speak of
    him . . . etc. . . .

During the show's tryout in Boston we knew the number wasn't working, but I had no idea what to substitute for it, since the character had been designed as nothing more than a sketch, and there was neither room nor necessity in the tight, bare script for Jim to flesh her out: with twenty-two musical numbers, *Follies* is possibly the shortest script ever written for a traditional song-scene-song-scene musical. Carlotta's song could be about anything, which is the worst assignment for a writer: without restrictions, choices are infinite, and an infinity of possibilities can be bewildering, if not paralyzing. Finally, in the middle of one of our daily meetings about the problem, Jim suddenly blurted out that if the character were to have any meaningful function in the show, it should be about survival. "You know, with everything she's been through, she's still around, she's still here!" As in the case of Arthur Laurents and "Some People," that was all I needed. The notion of "Everything she's been through" immediately suggested a potted social history of the U.S.A. between the Depression and the 1960s. That, I thought, might give the song some substance beyond a catalog of her ups and downs as a performer, sprinkled decoratively with rhymes of celebrities' names.

The problem was one of consistency. If all the other ladies were singing songs that had launched their careers, what was Carlotta doing singing about her own life? That would make it a "book" song, and she was not a character that merited such attention; Carlotta has a total of twelve dialogue lines in the show, so what would justify her having a seven-minute number unless it were the tour de force I hadn't been able to come up with? I never found a solution. "I'm Still Here" is a hybrid: pastiche, but not. I expected that any literal-minded listener (by which I mean me) would be confused at the mixture of intentions, and so to cover my tracks I increased the confusion by changing tone in the middle of the song. The first half is a breezy impersonal history and might be taken as a pastiche of Harburg, who often wrote sociopolitical lyrics; the second half leans toward Dorothy Fields, whose lyrics were often characterized by introspective ruefulness infused with self-deprecatory humor and eventual optimism, reflected here by the song's progression from resignation to triumph at the end. In other words, a showstopper.

I'm Still Here

CARLOTTA

Good times and bum times,
I've seen them all and, my dear,
I'm still here.
Plush velvet sometimes,
Sometimes just pretzels and beer,
But I'm here.

I've stuffed the dailies
In my shoes,
Strummed ukuleles,
Sung the blues,
Seen all my dreams disappear,
But I'm here.

I've slept in shanties,
Guest of the W.P.A.,
But I'm here.
Danced in my scanties,
Three bucks a night was the pay,
But I'm here.
I've stood on bread lines
With the best,
Watched while the headlines
Did the rest.
In the depression was I depressed?
Nowhere near.
I met a big financier
And I'm here.

I've been through Gandhi,
Windsor and Wally's affair,
And I'm here.
Amos 'n' Andy,
Mahjongg and platinum hair,
And I'm here.

I got through *Abie's
Irish Rose*,
Five Dionne babies,
Major Bowes,
Had heebie-jeebies
For Beebe's
Bathysphere.
I've lived through Brenda Frazier,
And I'm here.

I've gotten through Herbert and J.
Edgar Hoover,
Gee, that was fun and a half.
When you've been through Herbert
and J. Edgar Hoover,
Anything else is a laugh.

I've been through Reno,
I've been through Beverly Hills,
And I'm here.
Reefers and vino,
Rest cures, religion and pills,
And I'm here.

Been called a pinko
Commie tool,
Got through it stinko
By my pool.
I should have gone to an acting
school,
That seems clear.
Still, someone said, "She's sincere,"
So I'm here.

Black sable one day,
Next day it goes into hock,
But I'm here.
Top billing Monday,
Tuesday you're touring in stock,
But I'm here.

First you're another
Sloe-eyed vamp,
Then someone's mother,
Then you're camp.
Then you career
From career to career.
I'm almost through my memoirs,
And I'm here.

I've gotten through "Hey, lady, aren't
you whoozis?
Wow, what a looker you were."
Or, better yet, "Sorry, I thought you
were whoozis—
What ever happened to her?"

Good times and bum times,
I've seen them all and, my dear,
I'm still here.
Plush velvet sometimes,
Sometimes just pretzels and beer,
But I'm here.
I've run the gamut,
A to Z.
Three cheers and dammit,
C'est la vie.
I got through all of last year,
And I'm here.
Lord knows, at least I've been there,
And I'm here!
Look who's here!
I'm still here!

The true pastiche in this song is a musical one—one of my many homages throughout the years to Harold Arlen, whose music is always a thrill to hear and a pleasure to steal. His ability to extend a blues into an art song ("Stormy Weather," "Blues in the Night") without losing the simplicity of the first or the complexity of the second has always astounded me and seemed like the appropriate thing to attempt here, Carlotta being a character who would see her life as a flamboyant, torchy ballad. Besides, Arlen is one of my two favorite song composers. The other one is coming up shortly.

Arlenesque or not, "I'm Still Here" has been appropriated by performers as diverse as Lainie Kazan and Eartha Kitt, even by men (Sammy Davis, Jr., for one), who have had the lyric rewritten to personalize it and make it their own song of survival. Their lyrics may be factual but are almost always bad, so I try to stop them whenever I can. However, when it's a performer I

DOROTHY FIELDS
Wry and Dry

Dorothy Fields is the most under-rated of the major lyricists, primarily because she collaborated with so many different composers. Hart is well known because of his partnership with Rodgers, as is Hammerstein, although the latter had been moderately well known for his partnerships with Sigmund Romberg and Jerome Kern; Lerner is well known because of Loewe, Dietz because of Schwartz, Gershwin because of Gershwin. Harburg is less a household name because he kept alternating between Arlen and Lane (those two particularly, but with others as well). Dorothy Fields worked with almost everybody: Kern, Arlen, Schwartz, Romberg, Cy Coleman, Morton Gould, Jimmy McHugh. Also, she was a woman at a time when songwriters, much like directors, were predominantly male. The only woman with sustained success as a theater lyricist at that time was Anne Caldwell, who thrived in the 1910s and '20s but who is now completely forgotten, largely because her lyrics are devoid of personality and impact.

Fields's lyrics are full of both. She was the leading exponent in her generation of the truly colloquial lyricists. Berlin had used demotic language but his lyrics, while in the vernacular ("Always," for example), had a generic songwriter's formality that didn't really sound like everyday speech the way Fields's did. Songs of hers like "I Can't Give You Anything But Love," and "On the Sunny Side of the Street" resemble casual conversation—stylized with rhyme, but echoing real conversation. Hart may have injected healthy doses of colloquialism into the formal awkward self-consciousness of his predecessors' language, as Oscar insisted to me in the face of my resistance to Hart's work, but his lyrics were full of songwriters' syntax and wordplay for its own sake. It was Fields who first made Broadway song lyrics genuinely conversational. Moreover, unlike Berlin but much like Hart, her work had a consistent and distinctive attitude: wry, graceful, urban, slightly rueful, earthy. All her lyrics, no matter what characters sang them, were aspects of her. That was her legacy from growing up in Tin Pan Alley, where lyrics reflected nothing more than the songwriter's point of view. Unlike Hart, however, she took great pains to be low-key and offhand, to make the language seem "natural," with the result that she was able to show off a bit and still sound unforced, as in "He Had Refinement" from A Tree Grows in Brooklyn. This is difficult to pull off (only Frank Loesser was as good at it as she), and she did it with remarkable consistency.

Loesser is the lyricist she most resembles. He was only five years younger and didn't blossom until much later than she (Fields was twenty-two at the time of her first hit show, Blackbirds of 1928; Loesser didn't come into his own until the mid-1940s), but he must have admired her. What they have in common is, foremost, a colloquial style in which the words sit so naturally on the music that even with the repetitions of refrain lines, the tinkle of rhymes and the other small formalities of lyric writing the listener is seldom aware of the lyricist's presence: both of them hide their artifice behind their art. Another thing they share, unfortunately if rarely, is the need to dip into the "poetic," à la Hammerstein. Loesser did it in Greenwillow and The Most Happy Fella with songs like "Warm All Over" ("Gone are all the clouds that used to swarm all over"); Fields did it in Up in Central Park with, for example, "April Snow":

> There's a love as swift
> And light
> As an April snow.
> It's a shining gift,
> A bright
> Bit of touch and go . . .

Not only is the basic metaphor as suspect as Hammerstein's "When the sky is a bright canary yellow . . ." but she has uncharacteristically stuffed the brief lines with inner rhymes till the lyric bursts at its seams. It doesn't sound as if she believes a word of what she's writing, either, probably because she was constructing lyrics for an operetta, a form as far removed from her sensibilities as could be. Like Loesser (and like me in my adolescence), she was trying on Hammerstein's cloak. It was as uncomfortable a fit on her as Hammerstein's attempt at contemporary sophistication was on him (in "Marriage-Type Love" from Me and Juliet, for example). She didn't belong with a composer like Romberg, who was too schmaltzy for her. Nor was she at her best with Cy Coleman, whose music was the essence of grace and sophistication and thus better suited to Carolyn Leigh, whose lyrics were always cool. Dorothy needed someone like Kern or Arlen or McHugh—more openly emotional composers. It's a shame that she didn't form an enduring partnership with any of them.

admire and who asks me to rewrite the lyric rather than destabilize it themselves, I occasionally oblige. I'd oblige more often, except that the plethora of mercilessly brief rhymed lines in the lyric makes it a difficult job. Here are two examples of these derivatives: the first was sung by Barbra Streisand in concert (I hasten to add that the militant feminism is hers, not mine); the second, at Mike Nichols's request, by a fictional character named Doris modeled on Debbie Reynolds in his movie *Postcards from the Edge*, which was based on a book written by Reynolds's daughter, Carrie Fisher. That lyric combines the chronicles of both Reynolds and the actress who played her, Shirley MacLaine. (The original was a loose biography of Joan Crawford.)

I'm Still Here

(Barbra Streisand version)

STREISAND
Good times and bum times,
I've seen them all and, my dear,
I'm still here.
Gold statues sometimes,
Sometimes a kick in the rear—
But I'm here.

One day you're hailed for
Blazing trails,
Next day you're nailed for
Fingernails.
First it's a cheer, then a sneer—
But I'm here.

I've sung in choirs,
I've sung in cellars and bars,
And I'm here.
Clubs full of buyers,
Fancy saloons full of stars.
Then I'd hear:

"Don't tell me she de-
Signed those clothes—
Even the needy
Don't need those . . ."
"Can't cap her teeth?
She should cap her nose . . ."

"Never fear:
She'll disappear in a year . . ."
But I'm here.

They used to say,
"Talent she's got, but she screeches—
Sounds like her throat's in a sling."
So now they say,
"Talent she's got, but those
      speeches—
Why can't she shut up and sing?"

Monday the "Tony,"
Tuesday you're dough in the till—
So I'm here.
Wednesday you're "phony"
Thursday you're "over the hill."
But I'm here.

Then there's the curse of
Exposés
And, even worse, of
Overpraise.
Can't let the hisses
Or kisses
Interfere—
Who believes critics?

(Pause; shrugs)

I do.
But I'm here.

And then you hear,
"Songwriting, acting, producing—
What makes her think that she can?"
Or better yet,
"Songwriting, acting, producing—
What does she think, she's a man?"

I've been through show tunes,
I've been through funk—

(Thinks)

And it stunk—

(Thinks again, shrugs)

But I'm here.
Hit songs with no tunes,
Heavy duets with a hunk—

(Peers into audience)

Is he here?

I've kept my clothes
And kept my space.
I've kept my nose
To spite my face.
Still, once you say
You won't keep your place
Loud and clear,
Once you announce you're directing,
All you hear
Is—

(And she sailed into a chorus of "Everybody Says Don't")

I'm Still Here

(*Postcards from the Edge* version)

DORIS
Good times and bum times,
I've seen them all and, my dear,
I'm still here.
Plush velvet sometimes,
Sometimes just pretzels and beer—
But I'm here.

I've waited tables,
Smoked cigars,
Sung funny cables
To the stars,
Danced as a carton of Cheer—
And I'm here.

I've been an usher,
I've been a homecoming queen—
And I'm here.
Voted "Miss Gusher,"
Cover of *Oil* magazine—
And I'm here.

Ten years of braces,
Voice and tap,
Touring in places
Off the map,
Giving auditions on Zanuck's lap—
Never fear:
Mother drew up the contracts—
So I'm here.

I've gotten through club dates and
      guest shots and talk shows—
Gee, that was fun and a half.
When you've been through club dates
      and guest shots and talk shows,
Anything else is a laugh.

I've been through singers,
I've been through broke millionaires,
And I'm here.
Stingers with swingers,
Consciousness-raising with squares,
And I'm here.

Did my narcotics
In Key West,
Macrobiotics,
Zen and Est,
During the sixties, did I protest?
Loud and clear:
I went and burned my brassiere—
But I'm here.

Black sable one day,
Next day it goes into hock,
But I'm here.
Top billing Monday,
Tuesday you're touring in stock,
But I'm here.

First you're another
True-blue tramp,
Then someone's mother,
Then you're camp.
Then you career
From career to career.
I'm feeling transcendental—
Am I here?

The rest of this version remains pretty
much as originally written.

*As the party continues and Ben becomes
drunker, he convinces himself that his
unhappy marriage has always been shadowed by his old feelings for Sally. Moreover, Sally has always believed that her
life could be saved by running off with
Ben. In the following song, she thinks he is
singing to her, but in fact he is singing to
the young ghost of her.*

.

Too Many Mornings

BEN

Too many mornings
Waking and pretending I reach for
    you,
Thousands of mornings,

Dreaming of my girl . . .
All that time wasted,
Merely passing through,
Time I could have spent
So content
Wasting time with you.

Too many mornings
Wishing that the room might be filled
    with you,
Morning to morning,
Turning into days . . .

All the days
That I thought would never end,
All the nights
With another day to spend,
All those times
I'd look up to see
Sally standing at the door,
Sally moving to the bed,
Sally resting in my arms,
With her head against my head.

SALLY

If you don't kiss me, Ben, I think I'm
    going to die . . .

How I planned:
What I'd wear tonight and
When should I get here,
How should I find you,
Where I'd stand,
What I'd say in case you
Didn't remember,
How I'd remind you—
You remembered,
And my fears were wrong!

Was it ever real?
Did I ever love you this much?
Did we ever feel
So happy then?

BEN

It was always real . . .

SALLY

I should have worn green . . .

BEN

And I've always loved you this
    much . . .

SALLY

I wore green the last time . . .

BEN

We can always feel this happy . . .

SALLY

The time I was happy . . .

BEN, SALLY

Too many mornings
Wasted in pretending I reach for you.
How many mornings
Are there still to come?

How much time can we hope that
    there will be?
Not much time, but it's time enough
    for me,
If there's time to look up and see
Sally standing at the door,
Sally moving to the bed,
Sally resting in my (your) arms,
With your (my) head against my
    (your) head.

**In the first versions of the show, "Too
Many Mornings" occurred earlier in
the story and was preceded by a pair
of verses in which Sally, trying to be
sophisticated, and Ben, trying to be
amusing, exchange descriptions of
their lives. When the song was moved
to a later moment, these verses were
transmogrified and expanded into "In
Buddy's Eyes" and "The Road You
Didn't Take."**

Pleasant Little Kingdom (cut)

SALLY

It's a pleasant little kingdom
Full of pleasant little days.
There are charities and lectures,
And flowers to raise.
There are amateur dramatics
And evenings of bridge,
And I go to civic luncheons
When there's someone to remind me,
And I study the piano
And I never look behind me.

It's a merry little kingdom
Full of merry little chores,

And on Fridays there's a vassal
To help with the floors.
In the driveway there's a Jaguar
I shouldn't have bought,
And if on occasion
I think about you,
I eliminate the thought.

So I read a little here
And I sew a little there
And the children disappear
And the castle needs repair
And I never shed a tear
And I never turn a hair
And Ben—!

*(She breaks off, emotionally shaky, and
asks Ben about his life)*

BEN

It's a pleasant little kingdom
Full of pleasant little things,
Full of scintillating dinners
With neighboring kings.
There's a castle in the country
For weekends of rest,
And we entertain at parties
In the little time remaining,
And we're entertained by others
And it's very entertaining.

An efficient little kingdom,
The dominion of the Queen,
Where at any given moment
The ashtrays are clean.
There are many little battles
Which never are fought,
And if on occasion I think about you
It's a pleasant little thought.

So I write another book
And I head another drive
And we take a trip we took
And the dinner guests arrive
And unless you really look,
You would think we were alive,
And God help me, Sally,
I've loved you all my life!

*Buddy sees Ben and Sally embracing.
As they go off into the wings together,
he vents his fury, alternating between
thoughts of Sally and of Margie, his
mistress.*

The Right Girl

BUDDY

The right girl—yeah,
The right girl!
She makes you feel like a million
    bucks
Instead of—what?—like a rented tux.

The right girl—yeah,
The right girl!
She's with you, no matter how you
    feel,
You're not the good guy, you're not
    the heel,
You're not the dreamboat that sank—
    you're real
When you've got—yeah,
The right girl—yeah,
And I got—!

Hey, Margie, I'm back, babe.
Come help me unpack, babe.
Hey, Margie, hey, bright girl,
I'm home.

What's new, babe? You miss me?
You smell good, come kiss me.
Hey, Margie, you wanna go dancing?
I'm home.

Des Moines was rotten and the deal
    fell through.
I pushed, babe.
I'm bushed, babe.
I needed you to tell my troubles to—
The heck, babe—
Let's neck, babe.

Hey, Margie,
You wanna go dancing? You wanna go
    driving?
Or something?
Okay, babe,
Whatever you say, babe—
You wanna stay home.
You wanna stay home!

Hey, Margie, it's day, babe,
My flight goes—no, stay, babe,
You know how you cry, babe—
Stay home.

Be good now, we'll speak, babe,
It might be next week, babe—

Hey, Margie . . . Goodbye, babe . . .
I gotta go home.

The right girl—yeah,
The right girl!
She sees you're nothing and thinks
    you're king,
She knows you got other songs to sing.
You still could be—hell, well
    anything
When you got—yeah!
The right girl—
And I got . . . !

Ah, hell.

*Heidi Schiller, the oldest lady onstage,
sings in reverie the song that made her the
toast of Vienna at the beginning of the
century.*

One More Kiss

HEIDI

One more kiss before we part,
One more kiss and farewell,
Never shall we meet again,
Just a kiss and then
We break the spell.

One more kiss to melt the heart,
One more glimpse of the past . . .

(She is joined by Young Heidi)

HEIDI, YOUNG HEIDI

One more souvenir of bliss,
Knowing well that this
One must be the last.

Dreams are a sweet mistake.
All dreamers must awake.
On then with the dance,
No backward glance
Or my heart will break.
Never look back,
Never look back.

One more kiss before we part.
Not with tears or a sigh.
All things beautiful must die.
Now that our love is done,
Lover, give me one
More kiss and—goodbye.

This was the first song I wrote for *Follies*. Although I prefer to write a score in chronological order, in this case I needed to enter the world of pastiche as an act of homage rather than parody and with as much confidence as possible, and I thought that a love song in Heidi's operetta style, with its lush music and overripe lyrics, would be the easiest challenge. I chose Sigmund Romberg and Rudolf Friml, the leading operetta composers of the post–World War I period, as my target figures and Otto Harbach as my lyricist. Harbach is a largely forgotten songwriter today, but just as Hammerstein was my mentor, so was Harbach his. Harbach, twenty-two years Hammerstein's senior, wrote both book and lyrics for a number of successful operettas, many of them with Romberg as composer, on some of which (*The Desert Song*, among them, and *Rose Marie*) he invited young Hammerstein to collaborate. This was both good and bad: good, clearly, in that Hammerstein learned his craft from a professional; bad, because the flowery self-consciousness of operetta lyrics was something Hammerstein subsequently never could entirely shake. That quality is what makes so much of his work feel quaint and sugary today. Harbach's love-song lyrics, like those of his contemporaries, are filled with vague allusive images concerning moonbeams, starlight, rain, mist, springtime and other generalized reflections of nature ("Softly, as in a Morning Sunrise"), pretty to envision, easy to rhyme and ornate enough to make you blush. Or laugh.

Harbach however, had no individual style, no attitude, to provide me with a guide rail, and I floundered until I thought of the one operetta songwriter who did: Noël Coward. His music was steeped in the Friml/Romberg tradition and the lyrics to his ballads, though more smoothly written than those in the older operettas, were just as overstated, sentimental and "written," rather than experienced. They were also rife with songwriters' syntax, syntax borrowed from Romantic poetry, such as the reversal of subject and predicate (for example, "In my heart will ever lie / Just the echo of a sigh" from "I'll See You Again"). Moreover, he was still writing that kind of lyric in the 1960s, decades after operetta had died and musical-theater songs had become contemporarily conversational. Even at his most old-fashioned, though, Coward's ballads had an imitable attitude: world-weary, yearning, stultified, employing the kind of flowery language that has little to do with the way people actually speak. Coward had to find a substitute for sincerity, except when he was writing about England, at which point the sincerity turned forcefully sentimental. As soon as I had Coward in my sights, I was able to use words like "Farewell" and phrases like "Never shall we meet again" with equanimity. I even permitted myself to imitate his harmonic language, which is the kind I usually avoid like dengue fever.

Confused and defeated, Ben asks Phyllis to divorce him.

Could I Leave You?

PHYLLIS

Leave you? Leave you?
How could I leave you?
How could I go it alone?
Could I wave the years away
With a quick goodbye?
How do you wipe tears away
When your eyes are dry?

Sweetheart, lover,
Could I recover,
Give up the joys I have known?
Not to fetch your pills again
Every day at five,
Not to give those dinners for ten
Elderly men
From the U.N.—
How could I survive?

Could I leave you
And your shelves of the World's Best Books,
And the evenings of martyred looks,
Cryptic sighs,
Sullen glares from those injured eyes?
Leave the quips with a sting, jokes with a sneer,
Passionless love-making once a year?
Leave the lies ill-concealed
And the wounds never healed
And the games not worth winning
And—wait, I'm just beginning!

What, leave you, leave you,
How could I leave you?
What would I do on my own?
Putting thoughts of you aside
In the South of France,
Would I think of suicide?
Darling, shall we dance?

Could I live through the pain
On a terrace in Spain?
Would it pass?
It would pass.
Could I bury my rage
With a boy half your age
In the grass?
Bet your ass.
But I've done that already—
Or didn't you know, love?
Tell me, how could I leave
When I left long ago, love?

Could I leave you?
No, the point is, could you leave me?
Well, I guess you could leave me the house,
Leave me the flat,
Leave me the Braques and Chagalls and all that.

You could leave me the stocks for sentiment's sake
And ninety percent of the money you make,
And the rugs
And the cooks—
Darling, you keep the drugs,
Angel, you keep the books.
Honey, I'll take the grand,
Sugar, you keep the spinet
And all of our friends and—

(As he starts to leave)

Just wait a goddamned minute!

Oh,
Leave you? Leave you?
How could I leave you?
Sweetheart, I have to confess:
Could I leave you?
Yes.
Will I leave you?
Will *I* leave *you*?
Guess!

The tension among the four principals builds into an overlapping argument, augmented by their four young counterparts, until all eight reach a peak of near-hysteria. At the height of the chaos, offstage trumpets play a fanfare and the entire formerly moldy stage of the theater is transformed into a Weismann extravaganza called Loveland. White-suited Cavaliers and opulently dressed Damsels surround the principals and absorb them into their fantastical company.

Loveland

CHORUS

Time stops, hearts are young,
Only serenades are sung
In Loveland,
Where everybody lives to love.

Raindrops never rain,
Every road is Lovers' Lane
In Loveland,
Where everybody loves to live.

See that sunny sun and honeymoon,
There where seven hundred days hath
    June.

Sweetheart, take my hand,
Let us find that wondrous land
Called Loveland, Loveland,
    Loveland . . .

(Extravagantly costumed Showgirls enter one by one, each costume relating to the Cavaliers' spoken couplets)

FIRST CAVALIER

To lovers' ears a lover's voice is music,
A song that no one but a lover knows.

CHORUS

Loveland, where everybody lives to
    love.

SECOND CAVALIER

To lovers' lips, a lover's lips are
    petals,
A velvet promise budding like a rose.

CHORUS

Loveland, where everybody loves to
    live.

THIRD CAVALIER

The lover is transported by his
    rapture,
As ever heavenwards his heart
    ascends.

CHORUS

Loveland, Loveland . . .

NOËL COWARD
The Master of Blather

Most of Coward's lyrics come in two flavors: brittle and sentimental. The brittle ones are condescending, either implicitly ("I Went to a Marvelous Party") or explicitly ("Don't Put Your Daughter on the Stage, Mrs. Worthington"). The sentimental ones are florid, sometimes extending into unintentional camp ("I'll Follow My Secret Heart," "Play, Orchestra, Play"). Coward's verbal dexterity and skill at construction are evident in everything he writes, but only in some of his plays and movies does his deeply felt compassion for the lower middle class, which he escaped, come to the surface. It animates him emotionally in plays like *Fumed Oak* and *Still Life* and movies like *In Which We Serve* and *This Happy Breed*, as it rarely does in his songs.

Coward is often linked with Cole Porter, and with reason: both wrote music and lyrics, both were technically adroit, both were gay and both presented themselves as amused observers of society (mostly high). The telling difference between them is one of social status, a subject which informs the attitudes of their songs, especially the satirical ones. Both make sport of the haut monde, but Porter does it with fondness, Coward with disdain. Compare two of their lyrics which depict partygoers dishing their fellow guests: Porter's "Well, Did You Evah?" and Coward's "I Went to a Marvelous Party." Porter's consists of giggling backstairs gossip, Coward's of snickering observations about physical anomalies and sexual preferences. This difference may be a reflection of the fact that Porter was born rich and Coward poor. Porter was always part of the upper crust and felt comfortable with it; Coward was

an intruder and covered his desperation to be part of it by sneering at it. It's the difference between affection and affectation. Even Coward's jabs at being jazzy and contemporary are innately condescending when they're not simply embarrassing in their attempts to be "with it" ("Twentieth-Century Blues," "Beatnik Love Affair"). The difference in these attitudes extends even toward the audience. Porter's wit is generous to the listener as well as to his targets—unlike Coward, he's sharing his thoughts with you, not trying to make you feel a bit slow and less witty than he is. Coward wants you to feel breathless trying to catch up with him, as is evident when he sings his own patter songs, always at dispassionate breakneck speed, every word clipped as if it were topiary in order to give the impression of brilliance (his version of "Mad Dogs and Englishmen" is almost incomprehensible).

When it comes to their ballads, Coward's are no more flowery than Porter's, but they're postures; their passion is secondhand, the expression of someone trying to feel an emotion that isn't there. They're sexless. Compare "It Was Just One of Those Things" with "I'll See You Again," two songs about past love. Granted that one is a contemporary song, the other a period piece, but then all of Coward's ballads sound like period pieces, no matter what era they take place in, stuffed tightly with Victorian sentiments ("Time may lie heavy between / But what has been / Is past forgetting") and syntax ("In my heart will ever lie / Just the echo of a sigh"). On the evidence of their lyrics, it would be easy to believe that Coward was never in love and that Porter always was, if with different people. Coward's ballads can be so overripe in their effort to convey emotion that they become nonsense: "I'll follow my secret heart / Till I find love"—what does that mean? The song of Coward's often regarded as his most nakedly emotional, his personal manifesto, is "If Love Were All," largely because of the line "The most I've had is just a talent to amuse." But despite the genuinely rueful and straightforward tone with which it begins, the sentimentality and the self-conscious syntax bubble up in the release: ". . . if only / Somebody splendid really needed me, / Someone affectionate and dear, / Cares would be ended if I knew that he / Wanted to have me near." This formality is the expression not of someone in love but of someone talking about Love. Porter believes what he says, even at his most overheated, and therein lies another difference: Porter is sometimes, as he says in one of his lazier lyrics, too darn hot, but Coward,

like the public persona he cultivated, is too darn chilly. (I have no idea what he was really like—for all I know, he was as cuddly as a teddy bear.)

Another distinction between Coward and Porter is that Porter's music is notably more inventive and colorful than Coward's. It ameliorates his excesses and shortcomings, whereas Coward's exacerbates his. Contrast Porter's "Niña" with Coward's "Nina": Porter's music is tightly constructed and has some harmonic interest, and blossoms into a real tune in the release; Coward's is a rhythmically repetitious attempt to show that he can outdo Porter by making a pastiche of him in his Latin-American mode, but using more intricate rhymes and wordplay. (He even refers to this humorously in the lyric when he rhymes "who taught her to" with "Cole Porter, too"—a legitimate rhyme in British English, where "r"s are often dropped.) Neither lyric is much more than self-indulgent space-filling, but the verve of Porter's music makes the song sparkle, whereas the dullness of Coward's only points up how dry and unfunny his is. Then again I have rarely laughed at a Coward lyric, only occasionally smiled in appreciation ("Useless Useful Phrase," from *Sail Away,* being a rare exception). Coward's condescension stifles whatever exhilaration I might feel.

Defining Coward by comparing him to Porter may seem arbitrary and even unfair, but Coward himself prompted it when he wrote his own lyric to "Let's Do It" (with Porter's permission). Writing your own lyric to that song is not difficult to do— anyone with a modicum of verbal skill can invent verses to fit Porter's music and sound witty. But what's brilliant about "Let's Do It" and other Porter list songs is the idea of them, as well as the execution. Coward

merely drops names and rhymes them from chorus to chorus, which gives his version the sense of exhausted repetitiveness that marks so many of his patter songs; each of Porter's choruses deals with a different animal or geographic group, so that the lyric maintains variety and ingenuity. This is not to gainsay that Coward's verbal dexterity in his own work is impressive. He blends the lyrics in many of his patter songs so elegantly that no matter how intricately rhymed they are, they are easy to sing, and that is no small feat. Many patter songs (including some of mine) erupt in little stumbling points along the way which cause the singer trouble either with breathing or with enunciating the syllables fast enough. Coward's rarely do, and he makes the abundance of inner rhymes sound swift and natural. But most of these list songs ("Mad Dogs and Englishmen," "That Is the News," "I Went to a Marvelous Party" and others) state the same idea over and over. Restatement of jokes and ideas was something Coward never shied away from. It shows up in his dialogue, too: "Very flat, Norfolk" (*Private Lives*), "Very big, China" (*Shadow Play*)—to which it's hard to resist saying, "Very glib, Coward."

These cavils constitute another of my heresies. Coward is revered, especially in England, where he is referred to as "The Master." The awe in which he is held is due in great part to his protean talents: actor, playwright, composer, lyricist, director, salon wit. He certainly is a master craftsman and he knows what he is doing: his Introduction to his book of collected lyrics is charming, pointed and graceful and should be read by every theater songwriter. But there are other master craftsmen with more to say and more variety, sincerity and generosity in the way they say it. Much more.

FOURTH CAVALIER
The lover's heart contains a lover's
    secret,
Which only the beloved
    comprehends.

CHORUS
Loveland, Loveland . . .

FIFTH CAVALIER
Two lovers are like lovebirds in
    devotion,
If separated they must swoon and die.

CHORUS
Loveland, where everybody lives to
    love.

SIXTH CAVALIER
To lovers' eyes, a lover's eyes are
    jewels,
More radiant than the stars that light
    the sky.

CHORUS
Loveland, where everybody loves to
    live.

Lovers pine and sigh but never part,
Time is measured by a beating heart.

Bells ring, fountains splash,
Folks use kisses 'stead of cash
In Loveland, Loveland . . .
Love, Love, Loveland . . .
Love, Love, Loveland . . .
Love!

Never having seen one of the legendary *Follies*, I could only imagine the spectacle of a Ziegfeldian "Loveland" in terms of movie musicals, a territory I was familiar with but about which I'd always had mixed feelings—a blend of love, admiration and disdain, which made it ideal for the uses of pastiche. My attention focused, not surprisingly, on the MGM musicals of the late 1930s through the mid-1950s, the most revered and most accomplished of the Hollywood extravaganzas. Many of them were produced by Arthur Freed, a lyricist who had worked largely with the composer Nacio Herb Brown, turning out bland,

catchy hits like "You Are My Lucky Star" and "You Were Meant for Me." In view of the conflicts and edginess among the principals which had been evident throughout the evening, I thought this kind of song would be a suitably ironic way to introduce the sequence which was to follow. To point this up, I rewrote the Cavaliers' "Loveland" couplets for the London production, as you will see below.

The Loveland sequence (five songs) is presented as a mini-*Follies*, a set of numbers which uses pastiche to reflect both the real and the emotional lives of the principals: a sort of group nervous breakdown.

First, we see the young versions of Ben, Phyllis, Buddy and Sally as they were on their wedding days in 1942, just before the boys went off to war.

You're Gonna Love Tomorrow Love Will See Us Through

YOUNG BEN
"What will tomorrow bring?"
The pundits query.

YOUNG PHYLLIS
Will it be cheery?

YOUNG BEN
Will it be sad?

YOUNG PHYLLIS
Will it be birds in spring
Or hara-kiri?

YOUNG BEN
Don't worry, dearie.

YOUNG PHYLLIS
Don't worry, lad.

YOUNG BEN
I'll have our future
Suit your whim,
Blue chip preferred.

YOUNG PHYLLIS
Putting it in a
Synonym,
Perfect's the word.

BOTH
We're in this thing together,
Aren'tcha glad?
Each day from now will be
The best day you ever had.

YOUNG BEN
You're gonna love tomorrow.

YOUNG PHYLLIS
Mm-hm . . .

YOUNG BEN
You're gonna be with me.

YOUNG PHYLLIS
Mm-hm . . .

YOUNG BEN
You're gonna love tomorrow,
I'm giving you my personal
    guarantee.

YOUNG PHYLLIS
Say toodle-oo to sorrow.

YOUNG BEN
Mm-hm . . .

YOUNG PHYLLIS
And fare-thee-well, ennui.

YOUNG BEN
Bye-bye . . .

YOUNG PHYLLIS
You're gonna love tomorrow,
As long as your tomorrow is spent
    with me.

BOTH
Today
Was perfectly perfect, you say.
Well, don't go away,
'Cause if you think you liked today,

You're gonna *love* tomorrow.
Mm-hm . . .
You stick around and see.
Mm-hm . . .
And if you love tomorrow,

Then think of how it's gonna be:
Tomorrow's what you're gonna have a
    lifetime of
With me!

YOUNG BUDDY

Sally, dear,
Now that we're
Man and wife,
I will do
Wonders to
Make your life
Soul-stirring
And free of care.

YOUNG SALLY

If we fight
(And we might),
I'll concede.
Furthermore,
Dear, should your
Ego need
Bolstering,
I'll do my share.

YOUNG BUDDY

But though I'll try my utmost
To see you never frown—

YOUNG SALLY

And though I'll try to cut most
Of our expenses down—

YOUNG BUDDY

I've some traits, I warn you,
To which you'll have objections.

YOUNG SALLY

I, too, have a cornu-
Copia of imperfections:

I may burn the toast.

YOUNG BUDDY

Oh, well,
I may make a rotten host.

YOUNG SALLY

Do tell.

BOTH

But no matter what goes wrong,
Love will see us through
Till something better comes along.

YOUNG BUDDY

I may vex your folks.

YOUNG SALLY

Okay.
I may interrupt your jokes.

YOUNG BUDDY

You may.

BOTH

But if I come on too strong,
Love will see us through
Till something better comes along.

YOUNG BUDDY

I may play cards all night
And come home at three.

YOUNG SALLY

Just leave a light
On the porch for me.

BOTH

Well, nobody's perfect!

YOUNG SALLY

I may trump your ace.

YOUNG BUDDY

Please do.
I may clutter up the place.

YOUNG SALLY

Me, too.

BOTH

But the minute we embrace
To love's old sweet song,
Dear, that will see us through
Till something better comes along.

YOUNG SALLY

Hi.

YOUNG BEN

Girls.

YOUNG PHYLLIS

Ben.

YOUNG BUDDY

Sally . . .

*(The two songs are sung simultaneously
as a double duet)*

Because the characters were singing in
a fantasy of 1941, I decided to set this
pastiche in the style of the songwriters
who were at their peak in the late
1930s. For the verses (the introductory
sections like "What will tomorrow
bring . . ." and "Sally, dear . . .") I
chose Jerome Kern because the
melodic verve, originality and fluency of his verses have never been
equaled—including by me, although
I'm not ashamed of the attempt. And
they do sound like him. (Kern is my
other favorite composer, by the way.)
For the refrain ("You're Gonna Love
Tomorrow"), I zeroed in on the innumerable, foot-tapping, easygoing tunes
of the period like Burton Lane's "How
About You?" and Arlen's "Let's Fall in
Love."

    In the apocryphal Golden Age, al-
most every song had a verse and chorus, or "refrain," as the publishers
called it. Jerome Kern used the lovely
old-fashioned word "burthen" instead
of "refrain," which is why I publish
my songs under the aegis of Burthen
Music. Since the choruses were what
made the public buy the recordings
and sheet music, the verses were
under no obligation to be memorable
and therefore offered the songwriters
unlimited opportunities to experiment
with melody, harmony and form. The
lyrics were often characterized by the
kind of wordplay I included in my imitation: frequent trick rhymes and
inner rhymes (like "future / suit your"
and "in a / syno / nym," "synonym"
being pronounced in its colloquial
mode without the long "o") as well
as quaint words like "pundit" and
"query," words which have a charming
but distancing effect, reminding you
that you're listening to a song, not to
conversational language—conversational, perhaps, but nothing close to
everyday speech. As I've said one of
the champions of the colloquial infu-
sion into musical comedy was Lorenz
Hart. Lovers of traditional musical
theater often divide themselves into
Rodgers and Hart partisans and deni-
grators or Rodgers and Hammerstein
defenders and snipers ("The songs are
so witty!" "The songs are so shallow!"
"The songs are so moving!" "The
songs are so tedious!"); they are given

to comparing the two lyricists, who are so different as to make comparison meaningless.

As I've made clear, I am not much of a Hart fan, and my admiration of Hammerstein's work is limited, but it was Oscar himself who defended Hart to me one day after I'd made a disparaging comment about him. He claimed that it was Hart who was the pioneer in injecting demotic language into musical-comedy lyrics. Hart and his contemporaries (including Hammerstein) were sweeping away the fustiness of the operetta lyricists (including Hammerstein), which makes Oscar's observation even more generous. Compare the lyrics of his "The Desert Song" with Hart's "Mountain Greenery," both written in 1926, and the point couldn't be clearer. There are two ironies here. One is that Hammerstein never did become entirely comfortable with colloquial lyrics when they were contemporary (*Me and Juliet, Flower Drum Song*), but he could write period ones (*Show Boat, Oklahoma!*) better than anybody else. The other is that Hart's lyrics, like Ira Gershwin's, never got to the level of sounding like the way people talk; he was almost always too enamored of rhymes for the sake of rhyming, and not patient or modest enough to blend them smoothly into something that approximates real conversation, as Berlin, Fields *and* Loesser did.

The most appropriate models for the verses in this sequence's metaphorical 1941 dream-*Follies* were E. Y. Harburg and Ira Gershwin. The refrains are also meant to evoke Harburg and Gershwin, but in their affable, devil-may-care modes, by which I mean breezy toe-tappers like "Let's Take a Walk Around the Block" and "Nice Work If You Can Get It."

The discovery of a previously unused natural rhyme (as opposed to a manufactured one like "future / suit your"), a rhyme which has been just lying around for years in the language like a nugget in the dirt, can be an exhilaration, but it happens rarely. I imagine and envy the jolt of joy when whoever it was first came upon "lah-dee-dah-dee / everybody." (Actually, it may have been me, but I have a feeling I'd heard it before—in any event I used it in a song I wrote for the London production called "Ah, But Underneath.") I had a similar moment when I paired "soul-stirring" and "bolstering." The rhyme is not perfect, of course—the equal accents on "Soul" and "stir" don't quite match the heavy accent on "bol" and the lighter one on "ster," but I tried to mask that by leaping the melody up on each "-ing" to distract the ear. Imperfect it is, yes, but, as far as I know, unique, and it's been waiting all this time to be unearthed.

The original version of this double duet was a good deal more sour:

Little White House / Who Could Be Blue?

(cut)

YOUNG SALLY
We'll have a little white house
With a little white fence
Made of pickets.

YOUNG BUDDY
A house on a hill
Where, if nature consents,
We'll have crickets.

YOUNG SALLY
At the end of the day
He'll come home to his fa-
Vorite easy chair.

YOUNG BUDDY
My favorite pipe
And my favorite type
Of girl are there.

BOTH
We'll have a little pink boy,
Then a little pink girl,
Then another,
A little snub nose
And a little spit curl

Like her mother.
We'll stay home nights with the
nippers—

YOUNG SALLY
You with your pipe—

YOUNG BUDDY
The dog with my slippers—

BOTH
In our ever bright
Little white house.

YOUNG BEN
Sweetheart, I've been aware of late
You seem a trifle gloomy.
Why are you in a downcast state?
Do tell your troubles to me.
Here, kid,
Look, I brought you flowers
For your room.

Dear kid,
Brighten up your hours,
Watch them bloom.

YOUNG PHYLLIS
Sweetheart, I thank you for the gift.
You're all I need, though, for a lift.
I'm glad to say you misconstrue me.

Who,
Who could be blue,
Knowing there's you
Somewhere nearby?

When
Anyone feels your glow
Their low
Has to get high.

BOTH
So how
Could I allow
Anything now
To dim my eye?
With you,
Long as there's you with me,
The only thing blue
Is the sky.

The two songs are sung in counterpoint as a double duet, but halfway through, Young Buddy is replaced by the older Buddy, and the lyric changes.

YOUNG SALLY
At the end of the day
You'll stop off at your fa-
Vorite bar and grill,
Then come home to a spouse
In a little white house
On another hill.

BUDDY
We'll have a little fat boy
With a little weak face,
Then another:
A little tin god with a little ole case
On his mother . . .

These tunes were a more sustained
attempt to channel Kern, and I liked
them so much that I used one in the
score I wrote for Alain Resnais's movie
Stavisky. The lyrics of the verse sung
by Phyllis and Ben, with rhymes like
"gloomy / to me / misconstrue me"
and "Here, kid / Dear kid" best capture Ira Gershwin as I see him—affable
but effortful. The acrid un-Gershwin-
like turn in the last two stanzas, however, threatened to undermine the
whole *Follies* sequence by anticipating
its irony and despair, and we cut it. I
regretted losing the verbal nastiness
poised against the musical sweetness,
but I had other songs yet to write and I
made up for it in later scores.

The next Follies *fantasy is Buddy's. He
appears in a clown suit, and sings directly
to the audience.*

The God-Why-Don't-You-Love-Me Blues

BUDDY
Hello, folks, we're into the *Follies*!
First, though, folks, we'll pause for
    a mo'.
No, no, folks, you'll still get your
    jollies—
It's just I got a problem that I think
    you should know.

See, I've been very perturbed of late,
    very upset,
Very betwixt and between.
The things that I want, I don't seem
    to get.

The things that I get—you know what
    I mean?

I've got those
"God-why-don't-you-love-me-oh-
    you-do-I'll-see-you-later"
Blues,
That
"Long-as-you-ignore-me-you're-the-
    only-thing-that-matters"
Feeling,
That
"If-I'm-good-enough-for-you-you're-
    not-good-enough"
And "Thank-you-for-the-present-but-
    what's-wrong-with-it?" stuff,
Those
"Don't-come-any-closer-'cause-you-
    know-how-much-I-love-you"
Feelings,
Those
"Tell-me-that-you-love-me-oh-you-
    did-I-gotta-run-now"
Blues.

*(A chorus girl enters, playing the
fantasy Margie)*

Margie, oh, Margie!

She says she really loves me—

"MARGIE"
I love you.

BUDDY
—She says.
She says she really cares.

"MARGIE"
I care. I care.

BUDDY
She says that I'm her hero—

"MARGIE"
My hero.

BUDDY
—She says.
I'm perfect, she swears.

"MARGIE"
You're perfect, goddammit.

BUDDY
She says that if we parted—

"MARGIE"
If we parted—

BUDDY
—She says,
She says that she'd be sick.

"MARGIE"
Bleah.

BUDDY
She says she's mine forever—

"MARGIE"
Forever.

BUDDY
—She says.
I gotta get outta here quick!

"MARGIE"
Don't go! I love you!

BUDDY
I've got those
"Whisper-how-I'm-better-than-I-
    think-but-what-do-you-know?"
Blues,
That
"Why-do-you-keep-telling-me-I-
    stink-when-I-adore-you?"
Feeling,
That
"Say-I'm-all-the-world-to-you-you're-
    out-of-your-mind-
I-know-there's-someone-else-and-I-
    could-kiss-your-behind,"
Those
"You-say-I'm-terrific-but-your-taste-
    was-always-rotten"
Feelings,
Those
"Go-away-I-need-you,"
"Come-to-me-I'll-kill-you,"
"Darling-I'll-do-anything-to-keep-
    you-with-me-till-you-
Tell-me-that-you-love-me-oh-you-
    did-now-beat-it-will-you?"
Blues.

*(A chorus girl enters, playing the
fantasy Sally)*

Sally, oh, Sally! . . .
She says she loves another—

"SALLY"
Another.

BUDDY
—She says,
A fella she prefers.

"SALLY"
Furs . . . Furs . . .

BUDDY
She says that he's her idol—

"SALLY"
Idolidolidolidol . . .

BUDDY
—She says.
Ideal, she avers.

"SALLY"
You deal—"Avers"?

BUDDY
She says that anybody—*

"SALLY"
Buddy—Bleah!

BUDDY
—She says,
Would suit her more than I.

"SALLY"
Ay-yay-yay . . .

BUDDY
She says that I'm a washout—

"SALLY"
A washout!

BUDDY
—She says.
I love her so much, I could die!

"SALLY"
Get outta here!

BUDDY, "MARGIE," "SALLY"
I've got those
"God-why-don't-you-love-me-oh-
    you-do-I'll-see-you-later"

---

* Here "anybody" is pronounced to rhyme
with "muddy" in order to make the pun
word, as opposed to rhyming with "lah-dee-
dah-dee." Both pronunciations are legitimate,
but the latter sounds more classy.

Blues,
That
"Long-as-you-ignore-me-you're-the-
    only-thing-that-matters"
Feeling,
That
"If-I'm-good-enough-for-you-you're-
    not-good-enough"
And "Thank-you-for-the-present-but-
    what's-wrong-with-it?"
stuff,
Those
"Don't-come-any-closer-'cause-you-
    know-how-much-I-love-you"
Feelings,
Those
"If-you-will-then-I-can't"
"If-you-don't-then-I-gotta"
"Give-it-to-me-I-don't-want-it-if-you-
    won't-I-gotta-have-it"
High-low-wrong-right-yes-no-black-
    white
"God-why-don't-you-love-me-oh-
    you-do-I'll-see-you-later"
Blues!

This was another generic pastiche:
vaudeville music for chases and low
comics, but with a patter lyric. The
title of it probably derives from the
first time I heard the Gershwins' "The
Half of It, Dearie, Blues," but I tried
to give it the sardonic knowingness of
Lorenz Hart ("I Wish I Were in Love
Again") or Frank Loesser ("Adelaide's
Lament"). Loesser may seem too contemporary a choice for the *Follies*, but
this was a psycho-*Follies* and it called
for a tone wryer than its model. Note,
too, that the interludes use the same
technique as in the "Echo Song" in *A
Funny Thing Happened on the Way to
the Forum*, and to better effect.

*Sally appears as a torch singer, spot-
lighted in a shimmering silver gown.*

Losing My Mind

SALLY
The sun comes up,
I think about you.
The coffee cup,
I think about you.
I want you so,
It's like I'm losing my mind.

The morning ends,
I think about you.
I talk to friends,
I think about you.
And do they know
It's like I'm losing my mind?

All afternoon,
Doing every little chore,
The thought of you stays bright.
Sometimes I stand in the middle of
    the floor,
Not going left,
Not going right.

I dim the lights
And think about you,
Spend sleepless nights
To think about you.
You said you loved me,
Or were you just being kind?
Or am I losing my mind?

Musically, this was less an homage to,
than a theft of, Gershwin's "The Man
I Love," complete with near-stenciled
rhythms and harmonies. But it had a
difference: a lyric written not in the
style of his brother, but of Dorothy
Fields.

One of the pleasures of writing is
noting how a single small word can
change or intensify the emotional tone
of what is being said (or sung). For example, using the word "to" instead of
"and" in the fourth line of the last
stanza takes Sally a step further into
her obsession with Ben and offers a
nice example of the subtle powers of
the English language. As I keep saying,
God is in the details.

*Sally disappears and is replaced by Phyl-
lis, jazzy and strutting in front of a dancing chorus.*

The Story of Lucy and Jessie

PHYLLIS

Here's a little story that should make
   you cry,
About two unhappy dames.
Let us call them Lucy "X" and
   Jessie "Y,"
Which are not their real names.

Now Lucy has the purity
Along with the unsurety
That comes from being only
   twenty-one.
Jessie has maturity
And plenty of security,
Whatever you can do with them she's
   done.

Given their advantages,
You may ask why
The two ladies have such grief.
This is my belief,
In brief:

Lucy is juicy,
But terribly drab.
Jessie is dressy,
But cold as a slab.
Lucy wants to be dressy,
Jessie wants to be juicy.
Lucy wants to be Jessie,
And Jessie, Lucy.
You see,

Jessie is racy,
But hard as a rock.
Lucy is lacy,
But dull as a smock.
Jessie wants to be lacy,
Lucy wants to be Jessie.
That's the sorrowful précis,
It's very messy.

Poor, sad souls,
Itching to be switching roles.
Lucy wants to do what Jessie does,
Jessie wants to be what Lucy was.

Lucy's a lassie
You pat on the head.
Jessie is classy,
But virtually dead.
Lucy wants to be classy,

Jessie wants to be Lassie.
If Lucy and Jessie could only
   combine,
I could tell you someone
Who would finally feel just fine.

CHORUS

Now if you see Lucy "X,"
Youthful, truthful Lucy "X,"
Let her know she's better than she
   suspects.
Now if you see Jessie "Y,"
Faded, jaded Jessie "Y,"
Tell her that she's sweller than apple
   pie.
Juicy Lucy,
Dressy Jessie,
Tell them that they ought to get
   together quick,
'Cause getting it together is the whole
   trick!

Portrait of the Lyricist on Display: I tried to combine a showy dose of consonance (rhyming with similar consonants but different vowel sounds, such as "Lucy" and "lacy"), a technique frequently and flashily used by Harburg,* with the insouciant attitude of Porter when dealing with unhappy women in such songs as "The Physician" ("He did a double hurdle / When I shook my pelvic girdle / But he never said he loved me"). The song I originally wrote for this spot was all Porter, or at least I thought it was:

Uptown/Downtown

(cut)

PHYLLIS

Now this is the tale of a dame
Known as Harriet,
Who climbed to the top of the heap
   from the bottom.
A beautiful life was her aim,
And to vary it

---

* See my comments about him and his lyrics in *Bloomer Girl*.

She wanted the sun and the moon,
   and she got 'em.
She isn't the least exhausted from her
   climb,
But she does look back from time to
   time,
And the subject of this evening's quiz
Is who she was, and who she is:

Uptown, she's stepping out with a
   swell.
Downtown, she's holding hands on
   the El—
Hyphenated Harriet,
The nouveau
From New Ro-
Chelle.

Uptown, she's got the Vanderbilt
   clans.
Downtown, she's with the sidewalk
   Cézannes—
Hyphenated Harriet,
The nouveau
From New Ro-
Chelle.

She sits
At the Ritz
With her splits
Of Mumm's
And starts to pine
For a stein
With her village chums,
But with a Schlitz
In her mitts
Down in Fitz-
Roy's Bar,
She thinks of the Ritz—oh,
It's so
Schizo.

Uptown, it's Harry Winston she
   needs.
Downtown, it's strictly zircons and
   beads.
Ask her, should she be Uptown or
   Down?
She's two of the most miserable girls
   in town.

This was meant to be Porter in his bluesier "Down in the Depths" mode. The reason it was written and then replaced is a showbiz story right out of the movie *42nd Street*: it was at the request of a diva, though without the attendant drama and unpleasantness. The diva was Alexis Smith, a motion-picture star making her Broadway debut, and the request came during the second week of rehearsals. Until Hal Prince got hold of the show, the *Follies* sequence was to be a realistic enactment of *Follies* numbers by both the guests and the ghosts. Once we'd decided to make it a surreal series of nervous breakdowns, my first worry was that if I gave each of the four principals a solo, the sequence would become schematic. This was a trap that Burt Shevelove had alerted me to when we'd gone to see a show called *Top Banana*. In that show a singer named Rose Marie delivered (I use the word advisedly) a number called "I Fought Every Step of the Way," in which she compared each of her numerous marriages to a round of a prizefight. After three choruses, Burt murmured, "Do you suppose this is a ten-round or a fifteen-round fight?" It's always dangerous to let an audience see the shape of things to come. I remember seeing Rosalind Russell in *Wonderful Town* sing "One Hundred Easy Ways to Lose a Man" and thinking when she got to "Ninety-eight ways to go" that I'd be in the theater all weekend. My first solution to avoid this danger was to write a song for both Ben and Phyllis taunting each other in a tandem duet, he dancing with a line of chorus girls, she answering him with a line of boys.

The World's Full of Girls
The World's Full of Boys (cut)

BEN
The world's full of girls
Who are waiting to be kissed,
Waiting to be kissed—
Oops! There's one I missed!
The world's full of girls
And I'm making up a list,
'Cause I'm gonna kiss 'em, each and
   every one.

And when, and when
I've kissed 'em all and satisfied my yen,

GIRLS
What then?

BEN
What then?
I guess I'm gonna have to kiss 'em
   over again!

The world's full of girls
Who are virginal and pink,
Younger than you think—

(To one of them)

How about a drink?
The world's full of girls
And before I start to sink,
I am gonna kiss 'em, each and
   every one!

You, Miss—

FIRST GIRL
Me?

BEN
Yes, you with the Marilyn Monroe—

FIRST GIRL
Who? . . .

BEN
Hairdo—

FIRST GIRL
Who the fuck is Marilyn Monroe?

BEN
Yes, well then—

(To another girl)

You—
Shall we blow the joint
And go out twisting?

SECOND GIRL
Go out what?

BEN
I see your point.
Well, you then, pretty maiden,
Shall we sit and have a chat?

THIRD GIRL
I could go for that.

BEN
Good, then, pretty maiden,
Shall we hasten to my flat?

THIRD GIRL
What a pussy cat!

BEN
Now . . .

THIRD GIRL
I certainly am honored that a
   gentleman like you
Wants to take a girl like me out for a
   date
When you could probably have
   anyone at all
Like a star or a duchess.
Say, do you know Princess Grace
I mean, well, what's she really like
'Cause I gather from your book
(Although I didn't really read it)
That you know a lot of big
And important celebrities
That picture on the jacket
Doesn't really do you justice
You're more handsome in the flesh
With all that graying in your hair
But then I've always gone for
   older men
Which shouldn't hang you up
But an awful lot of older men get
   terribly uptight
Like out in public when we bump
   into friends
But if anything it's me who feels
   embarrassed
But I'm not, 'cause like I said how I'm
   honored
And so what if people think I'm being
   kept or something? . . .

*(Ben, reeling, sits down; Phyllis
   dances by)*

PHYLLIS
The world's full of boys
Who are waiting to be kissed,
Waiting to be kissed—

(To one of the boys)

Well, if you insist.
The world's full of boys

And I hardly can resist,
So I'm gonna kiss 'em, each and
    every one.

And when, and when
I've kissed 'em all and satisfied my
    yen—

BOYS
What then?

PHYLLIS
What then?
I guess I'm gonna have to kiss 'em
    over again!

The world's full of boys,
Every color, shape and kind,
Raunchy and refined—
Look at that behind!
The world's full of boys
And I'm sure you wouldn't mind
If I go and sleep with each and
    every one . . .

The musical pastiche here was of a Victor Herbert operetta galop, square and giddy, but it never went into rehearsal (although I subsequently used the tune in the operetta scene in *Stavisky*). The reason is that once we'd determined that the *Follies* sequence should be a surreal nightmare, the problem became one of finding a way to bring everything back to reality. It wasn't until the second week of rehearsals that I got the notion of Ben's breakdown as the means of reversion (see "Live, Laugh, Love" below), which necessitated my giving him a solo, rendering competition between him and Phyllis useless.

My next thought was to team Sally and Phyllis in a song, which would have the added advantage of giving our two co-stars the proverbial eleven o'clock number. The solution I came up with was "Losing My Mind." It was to be a languorous production number with the two women both yearning after Ben, singing of their obsession to a chorus of Bens: every member of the cast, male and female, dressed as Ben, the two women wandering among them. My collaborators were happy

with this idea, but Alexis called me after hearing the song and asked to see me. I knew there was some kind of problem and I feared the worst, but, as with Angela Lansbury and *Anyone Can Whistle*, there was no need to. Alexis calmly and modestly explained that she wasn't much of a singer or even a dancer but that she had great legs and would like to show them off. She went on to emphasize that Dorothy Collins, who played Sally and was a real singer, would be better off with "Losing My Mind" as a solo, and if I could write a number that would allow her (Alexis) to sing a bit and dance a bit and strut a lot, everybody, especially she, would be the better for it. She was so reasonable that I immediately acceded and batted out "Uptown/Downtown." But Michael Bennett wanted something more uptempo and rhythmically charged. Thus, eventually, "The Story of Lucy and Jessie," and everyone went home happy.

Finally, it is Ben's turn.

Live, Laugh, Love

CHORUS
Here he comes,
Mister Whiz!
Sound the drums,
Here he is!

Raconteur,
Bon Vivant—
Tell us, sir,
What we want
To know:
The modus operandi
A dandy
Should use
When he is feeling low.

BEN
When the winds are blowing—

CHORUS
Yes?

BEN
That's the time to smile.

CHORUS
Oh?

BEN
Learn how to laugh,
Learn how to love,
Learn how to live,
That's my style.

When the rent is owing—

CHORUS
Yes?

BEN
What's the use of tears?

CHORUS
Oh?

BEN
I'd rather laugh,
I'd rather love,
I'd rather live
In arrears.

Some fellows sweat
To get
To be millionaires,
Some have a sport
They're devotees of.
Some like to be the champs
At saving postage stamps.
Me, I like to live,
Me, I like to laugh,
Me, I like to love!

Some like to sink
And think
In their easy chairs
Of all the things
They've risen above.
Some like to be profound
By reading Proust and Pound.
Me, I like to live,
Me, I like to laugh,
Me, I like to love!

Success is swell and success is sweet,
But every height has a drop.
The less achievement, the less defeat.
What's the point of shovin'
Your way to the top?

To get their names in print   sheer dint   to corner coconuts

Some strive to make a mint   politics   To join the social ruts

                                                     cuts

                                                     break their fool behinds

      fellows

Some people ache to make like Napoleons

               sit +

So they can buzz to summon the staff

Some break their ass amassing simoleons

They chart their lives like charting a graph

names   downs
callgrams   diagrams
telegrams
monograms   shows

Some break their asses passing their bar exams

Then chart their lives like charting a ...

                          lining up

So they can chart their lives like a graph

Lay out

careers
then such around

                                              cuts

                                  Some guys could flunt their slats

                                  To do a

                                  One day they're diplomats

Some get a charge enlarging their monograms

                                  good

                                  Nice going

                                         congrats

Some get a boot from shooting off callgrams

On ringing doorbells to summon the staff

Or on the intercom with the staff   Or being diplomats

hotshots   crackpots
climbers   beavers   with
beavers   Some climbers get their kicks   One day they're diplomats
crackpots   From social   Nice going

          Pursuing playing politics   Well, bully a congres's

devotee
enthusiasts

simoleons
Napoleons
have a ball

ache to make the business
have a gun
an itch
get their rocks off
kicks

real rich collect
acs amass
to pass
pound feels
play away
but   guts to play
break their butts
ocean to seem

like to
fellows
gents any   and
Some people sweat to get to be millionaires   Some people like to bike & get exercise

have   followers
Some like a thing they're champions of   Some like to scan the planets above

The dollar's what they're followers of

or
Some have a sport they're devotees of   Observing things that curve on a graph
To   they've his
I find I've got a mind like a sieve

like to   sink think   easy
Some fellows quit, set on their rocking chairs
To of all
And think of things
To think of things they're risen above   What is the thing they've risen above

Some like to be profound   They prize the   they're rising above

By reading Proust & Pound

They're lives
run   charting
They chart their lives like lines on a graph

Or ringing bells
They like to
sit
Success is thrilling success is sweet   So they can buzz to summon the staff

their
But every height has a drop   Or on the intercom with the staff

The less achievement,   the less defeat

football bats

fellows die   to try   diplomats
Some people sweat to get to be President   Stock Exchange
a million bucks
breaks but
Some grind their ass amassing their stocks & bonds   stacks of stocks
to pass in   capital
in passing their bar exams   properties
in   and celebrity   & such
for class for their law degrees   socialite types
with notables famous folk   men of arts
Some get their kicks from   their income tax   break their backs

like to screw around observing
charting
Some spend their lives in front of a graph

Some like to hire & fire a staff

Some   strive to rival Napoleon

score
Some spend their lives with wives by the bushelful

as
Some like to sit like little Napoleons

play the Nation's

Live 'n' laugh 'n' love 'n'
You're never a flop.

So when the walls are crumbling—

CHORUS
Yes?

BEN
Don't give up the ship.

CHORUS
No.

BEN
Learn how to laugh,
Learn how to love,
Learn how to live,
That's my tip!

When I hear the rumbling—

CHORUS
Yes?

BEN
Do I lose my grip?

BEN & CHORUS
No!

BEN
I have to laugh,
I have to love,
I have to live,
That's my trip!

Some get a boot
From shoot-
Ing off cablegrams,
Or buzzing bells
To summon the staff.
Some climbers get their kicks
From social politics.
Me, I like to love,
Me, I like to . . .

(He forgets his lyrics briefly)

Some break their asses
Passing their bar exams,
Lay out their lives
Like lines on a graph . . .

(He stumbles)

One day they're diplomats—
Well, bully and congrats!

Me, I like to love,
Me, I . . .

(He blanks again)

Me, I like—
Me, I love—
Me . . .
I don't love me!

*(He breaks down completely, as does
the Follies)*

The homage here is not to any particular songwriter, but to a performer:
Fred Astaire. This kind of easygoing
number was written for him by everyone from Berlin ("Isn't It a Lovely
Day?") to Kern/Fields ("Never Gonna
Dance") to the Gershwins ("[I've Got]
Beginner's Luck") to Arthur Schwartz
and Howard Dietz ("By Myself"), and
it seemed appropriate here because
Astaire's persona is the way Ben sees
himself. The smoothness in that kind
of song made the rupture in his self-
assured suavity telling; to have given
him an up-tempo piece like "I Got
Rhythm" or a slow lament like
"What'll I Do" would have anticipated
the breakdown. The Pirandello effect
fooled the audience completely: they
thought it was the actor (John
McMartin—whose performance, incidentally, was as thrilling as any I've
ever seen in the musical theater)
rather than the character who had forgotten his lyrics, thereby blurring the
line between theater and reality just
as Ben had. And that's how we got the
character back from his fantasy to his
life.
   As the show progressed from its
original concept, a number of songs
fell by the wayside, songs which I liked
but which had to be sacrificed in order
to clarify, tighten or adjust the tone
and plotting of the piece. For example,
in the original script, the climactic
Follies sequence began as a show organized by Sally for her and her fellow
performers to perform in front of the
men at the party, utilizing props and
costumes from trunks in the cellar.
The show within the show quickly dis-
integrated, however, as the four prin-

cipals fell into a mutual memory of the
crucial incident in their young lives
thirty years earlier, when Phyllis and
Buddy had discovered Ben and Sally
making love in Weismann's office at
the top of the theater. This was the
song that cued it.

*As the activity of the women preparing
the show goes on in slow motion around
them, Ben, under the delusion that he still
loves Sally, offers her a bouquet of paper
flowers.*

All Things Bright and Beautiful (cut)

BEN
Here, kid—
Look, I brought you flowers:
Green, red, blue.
All things
Permanent and perfect for you,
   kid, you.

I mean all things bright and beautiful,
Everything forever—yours, kid,
Everything forever all come true.

SALLY
All things bright and beautiful,
Everything forever all come true . . .

BEN
Wait, kid—
Every minute flowers:
Night, noon, day.
Trust me,
Anything you want, you just say,
   kid, say.

You'll have all things bright and
   beautiful,
Everything forever—ask me,
Everything forever every day.

SALLY
All things bright and beautiful . . .
Ben, can we go to Paris?

BEN
Of course we can go to Paris.

SALLY
Ben, can we go to London?

BEN
Or London or Rio, you name it . . .

SALLY
All things bright and beautiful—
Ben, I get so excited
I hardly can breathe . . .

Let them laugh.
Just don't leave me.
I'm all right,
Just don't leave me again.

BEN
Let them laugh.
I won't leave you.
I won't leave,
Never ever again . . .

SALLY
(Simultaneously)
Ben, we'll be together
Tomorrow.
Ben, we'll be together
On Monday.

BOTH
And we'll be together
Tomorrow and
Monday and
April and
Christmas and

Look, love,
Everything is flowers—

BEN
Red—

SALLY
White—

BEN
Pink—

SALLY
Green—

BOTH
Blue.

Soon, love,
Everywhere I look will be you,
    love, you!

And that's all things bright and
    beautiful,
Everything forever—ours, kid,
Everything we never did, we'll do!

And we'll be together tomorrow.
And we'll be together on Monday,
And we'll be together in April
And Christmas
And next year
And always . . .

**Another cut moment, which occurred
earlier in the show:**

*Buddy tries to soften Sally's resolve to
leave him by charming her into dancing
with him. The scene took place in a dressing room, which had a pianola.*

That Old Piano Roll
(cut)

BUDDY
Listen to that old piano roll play.
When I hear that old piano roll play,
I just gotta dance,
And what I mean is dance with you.

Doesn't matter what I'm doin' or
    where—
When that ragtime rhythm tickles
    the air,
I go in a trance.
I only wanna dance
With you.

Baby, baby,
Come on along,
Come on and dance,
And maybe
By the time you get a load o'
That super-syncopated coda

You'll say "I think that old piano roll's
    nice."
Then we'll play that old piano roll
    twice.
Come on, take a chance—
I only wanna dance
With you.

There's a honky-tonk down the street,
Nothin' more than a dive.
They got somethin', though, can't be
    beat,
Somethin' really alive:
They got this player piano,
It's nothin' but a piano,
Yeah-bo, but what a piano—
The only tune that it has is jazz!
It's just a mini-piano.
A tiny, tinny piano,
But folks from every city, town and
    ghetto
Adore that ad lib allegretto,

Just listen to that old piano roll play!
I could hear that old piano all day.
I just wanna dance,
And what I mean is dance
With you.

Makes no difference, sunny weather
    or rain.
When that ragtime rhythm reaches
    my brain,
I know in advance
I'm gonna wanna dance
With you.

Baby, baby,
Kick out the blues,
Kick off your shoes,
And maybe
That sympathetic syncopation'll
Prove to be so inspirational

We won't let that old piano roll stop.
We'll keep droppin' nickels in till we
    drop.
I don't want romance,
I only wanna dance
With—
I just wanna—
I just gotta—
I just wanna—
Dance!

*In the earlier versions of the show, Sally
responded to Ben's rejection of her in a
wistful, seductive way, drawing on his
guilt.*

It Wasn't Meant to Happen (cut)

SALLY

Well, my dear,
Too bad,
It wasn't meant to happen.
No harm done—
How sad.
It wasn't meant to happen.

We had our little moment—
No, don't,
Don't worry for me.
I worry for you, dear.

I want you to be
Happy . . .
Happy . . .

So, my dear,
Good night.
It wasn't meant to happen.
Pleasant dreams . . .
I'll write . . .
It wasn't meant to happen.

The candle wick was wet,
The Champagne was flat,
The timing was wrong.
A little regret
And that's that—
I'll get along.

We'll both get along,
She said, as she exited, smiling.
No, I mean it's a shame,
But there's no one to blame.

And we've got to be strong,
She said, as she thought of
    tomorrow—
No, it would have been fun,
But it's over and done.
Now I really must run.

Well, my dear,
Take care.
It wasn't meant to happen.
Yes, I know—
Unfair.
It wasn't meant to happen,
I guess . . .
God bless . . .
It seems—

Sweet dreams.
Good try . . .

Goodbye . . .

In 1987, Cameron Mackintosh produced a revival of *Follies* in London. He asked for some changes in the script and score. I was reluctantly happy to comply, my only serious balk being at his request that I cut "The Road You Didn't Take." He felt it gave away Ben's despair too soon, and to my surprise James agreed with him. When I probed James's reasoning, it turned out that as the show had come into focus, he had begun to feel that the story concentrated too much on Ben at the expense of the other three principal characters and that it should not be Ben and Ben alone who had the nervous breakdown which shattered the illusionary *Follies* sequence and brought the principals back to reality. Nor was this the only change that Cameron and James suggested, and although I had been happy with the show the way it was, I saw no reason not to try new things, knowing we could always revert to the original (which eventually we did). The net result was four new songs.

Ben and Phyllis try to reconcile their differences and plan for their future.

Country House

PHYLLIS

How about a country house?

BEN

Fine.

PHYLLIS

You want to get a country house?

BEN

If you like.

PHYLLIS

What would *you* like?

BEN

No, a country house would be fine.

PHYLLIS

Would you like one?

BEN

Sure, if that would make you happy.

PHYLLIS
(*Dead*)

Swell.

BEN

Whatever makes you happy—

PHYLLIS

Yes.
Well . . .

BEN
(*Trying to work up enthusiasm*)

Why not?
We'll get a country house.
What kind?

PHYLLIS

Kind?

BEN

Whatever kind you have in mind.

PHYLLIS

You choose.

BEN

Look, it's *your* idea, a country
    house—

PHYLLIS

Oh, forget it.

BEN

—and a good one.

PHYLLIS

Oh.

BEN

If that's what makes you happy.

PHYLLIS
(*Wry*)

Happy . . .

BEN

Comparatively happy.

(*They smile at each other*)

BOTH
All right, where?

BEN
I don't care.

PHYLLIS
That's not fair.

BEN
Well, then, somewhere in the
woods—

PHYLLIS
(Simultaneously)
Somewhere by the sea—

(A beat)

BEN
By the sea, then.

PHYLLIS
Don't agree just to agree.

BEN
Look, it's all the same to me.

PHYLLIS
Yes, I know.

BEN
Meaning—?

PHYLLIS
Oh, let it go.

BOTH
Look, as long as we're together . . .

(Silence, as music continues under; they
fidget a bit)

BEN
How about a trip abroad?

PHYLLIS
Let's.

BEN
We haven't had a trip abroad in years.

PHYLLIS
Not for ages.

BEN
Take a ship abroad, get away—

PHYLLIS
Just the two of us.

BEN
A chance to be together.

PHYLLIS
That's the point.

BOTH
As long as it's together.

PHYLLIS
It's what we need, a trip abroad.

BEN
Where to?

PHYLLIS
(Shrugs)
To?

BEN
To London, Paris—?

PHYLLIS
Somewhere new.

BEN
Up to you.

PHYLLIS
'Round the world.

BEN
No, really.

PHYLLIS
'Round the world won't do?

BEN
(A touch impatient)
Where?

PHYLLIS
Let's not get into that one again.

BEN
(Overlapping, pulling back)
If that would make you happy—
No, really. Fine,
If that would make you happy.

PHYLLIS
(Nods, simultaneously)
"If that would make me happy."

(Their eyes meet; she smiles)

It just might.

BOTH
All right, when?

PHYLLIS
Name the day.

BEN
Just not May.

PHYLLIS
Why?

BEN
The meeting in Atlanta.

(Phyllis nods)

June? July?

PHYLLIS
No, that's my benefit for ANTA.

BEN
So—?

PHYLLIS
So—?

BEN
It's enough to lend your name.

PHYLLIS
And you couldn't do the same?

BEN
It's my board—

PHYLLIS
Oh, dear Lord—

BEN
—and they can't be ignored.

PHYLLIS
No, and you can't afford
To be bored with your board,
Can you?

(Pause)

BEN
So much for travel.

(Silence, music underneath; much
fidgeting)

PHYLLIS
How about a friendly shrink?

BEN
What?

PHYLLIS
You want to see a friendly shrink?

BEN
Why me?

PHYLLIS
Us.

BEN
I think
I'd rather have another drink—

(He waves to a passing waiter)

PHYLLIS
Okay, your turn.

BEN
But if that would make you happy . . .

(Smiles)

PHYLLIS
What?

BEN
Joke:
If a shrink would make you
    happy . . .

PHYLLIS
(Nods)
Nice joke.

*(They fidget a bit while the orchestra
vamps)**

How about a St. Bernard?

BEN
What?

PHYLLIS
We could adopt a St. Bernard.

BEN
In New York?
Are you serious, a St. Bernard?

---

* A vamp is a repeated rhythmic accompaniment.

PHYLLIS
Or a child.

BEN
Ah, the child.

*(Pause; music stops; silence for a
moment)*

PHYLLIS
It's not too late, and it—

BEN
(Simultaneously)
I can remember a time when—

*(They each stop and politely wait for the
other to continue; another moment of
silence; music resumes)*

BOTH
All right, why?

PHYLLIS
Why not?

BEN
Why now?
Why not then?

PHYLLIS
We need something we can share.

BEN
We need air.

PHYLLIS
We need something—!

BEN
We need something if it's real.

PHYLLIS
Maybe saying what we feel?

BEN
It's a deal.

PHYLLIS
For a change.

BEN
You go first.

PHYLLIS
After you.

(Brief pause)

BEN
I've got nothing to conceal,
So there's nothing to reveal.

PHYLLIS
Good. We're all set there, then.

*(Pause; these stops and starts recur until
the end of the song, as their enthusiasm
flags and dies)*

BEN
I could take a few days off . . .

(Phyllis smiles at him halfheartedly)

PHYLLIS
Maybe we could take a suite at the
    Waldorf . . .

BEN
Mm . . .

PHYLLIS
Just the two of us . . .
Second honeymoon . . .

(Pause)

BEN
(Smiling, but unable to resist)
Should be better than the first.

(Pause)

PHYLLIS
(Smiling, but not happy)
There are times when you can be a
    louse.

(Long pause)

BEN
The hell, let's get a house.

For reasons which I've forgotten, I
rewrote "Loveland" for the London
production. There were only four
Showgirls in this version, and each
one carried a shepherd's crook with
a letter of the alphabet on it.

Loveland (London version)

ROSCOE, COMPANY
Take the highway of happiness
Through the state of bliss,
Till you come to the country called
Loveland.

Every mile is a honeymoon,
Every step a kiss,
In the country that people call
Loveland.

Loveland,
Where love decides the path you take,
Where hearts can stay forever young
And never break.

Every day is a miracle,
Every night much more,
Every morning more lyrical
Than the one before.

Loveland,
Where sunny skies abound above,
Where everybody loves to live
And lives to love!

*(The first Showgirl enters, carrying
the letter "L")*

ROSCOE
L
Is for the Long Long road ahead
That leads all lovers
To the landscape of their dreams.

COMPANY
Loveland! Loveland!

*{The second Showgirl enters, carrying
the letter "O")*

ROSCOE
O
Is for the Overwhelming Optimism
Only lovers know,
Or so it seems.

COMPANY
Loveland! Loveland!

*(The third Showgirl enters, carrying
the letter "V")*

ROSCOE
V
Is for the Various Vicissitudes
They'll weather,
Because it's also for the Vow
They made together.

COMPANY
Loveland! Loveland!

*(The fourth Showgirl enters, carrying
the letter "E")*

ROSCOE
E
Is for the Endless Expectations
Lovers elevate so often
To extremes.

COMPANY
Loveland! Loveland!

ROSCOE, COMPANY
Loveland, where sunny skies abound
    above,
Where everybody loves to live
And lives to love!

*When Phyllis appears in the Love-
land sequence, she is in her boudoir,
surrounded by servants, who help her
undress and prepare her for a bubble
bath.*

Ah, But Underneath

PHYLLIS
Never judge a book by its cover—
The thing that counts is what's
    inside.
Never judge a lady by her lover—
It isn't a reliable guide.

The lady may decide her obligations
Are merely to reflect his
    expectations.
If his idea of ecstasy
'S to see what he expects to see—
Well, ignorance is bliss,
But think of what he'll miss . . .

(She gives her coat to a servant)

She was smart, tart,
Dry as a martini—
Ah, but underneath . . .

(She takes something else off)

She was all heart,
Something by Puccini—
Ah, but underneath . . .

(She takes something else off)

In the depths of her interior
Were fears she was inferior
And something even eerier,
But no one dared to query her
Superior
Exterior.

(She continues stripping throughout)

She was chic, sleek,
Anything in fashion—
That was just a shell.
Take a close peek,
You could see the passion—
That was one as well.

To conclude,
You'd
Soon discover
The secret of her
Ap—

(She peels off something)

—peal
Was the wonder
Which lay underneath—

(She teases the audience)

Which she wasn't about to reveal.

SERVANTS
She was sly, wry,
Cool or coy or candid—

PHYLLIS
That was her liability,
The curse of versatility . . .

SERVANTS
Smart, shy,
Whatever was demanded—

PHYLLIS
She'd only allow a man to see
Enough to fan his fantasy . . .

BOYS
She made compliance
Into a science,
One of the giants—

PHYLLIS
Loud or lewd or lah-dee-dah-dee,
Everything to everybody . . .

As changeable as a chameleon,
With all that entails,
But nobody saw what was really un-
Derneath all the veils.

*(She steps behind a towel, gets into the
tub. She bathes a moment, her body
masked by Soap Bubble Girls)*

She was grand, bland,
Brave or brisk or brittle,
Anything required.
Both concerned and
Strictly noncommittal—
And a little tired.

She was deftly deferential,
Or so they wrote on her wreath.
No one ever glimpsed her

*(Bump!—the "bubbles" bumping
with her)*

Potential,
But when stripped—

(Bump!)

Down to the essential—
Mind you, this is—

(Bump, bump!)

Confidential—
Way down underneath . . .

*(She is now completely covered
by the towel)*

SERVANTS
She was—!

*(They whip the towel away, revealing
empty space in a spotlight; the spotlight
does a few stripper steps)*

She was—!

(A few more steps by the spotlight)

She was—

PHYLLIS
*(Appearing at the edge of the
proscenium)*
Sometimes when the wrappings fall,
There's nothing underneath at all.

(She blows the spot out)

*In the final number, Ben appears in front
of the show curtain.*

Make the Most
of Your Music

BEN
*(To the music of Tchaikovsky and Grieg
piano concertos)*
How
Do you come
Out of numbingly humble beginnings
And get to be me?
How
Do a few
Little doodly-doodles
Turn into a beautiful symphony?

Can you make what is merely so-so
Into something big league?
Take a tip from a virtuoso
(Me, Tchaikovsky and Grieg):

What you do is construct yourself
By the way you conduct yourself.
You don't have to disclose yourself—
Compose yourself.

*(The show curtain rises, revealing a
huge, surrealistic grand piano, the keys
of which act as steps for Ben to climb)*

Find your tune,
Set your key,
Claire de lune
It may never be,
But make the most of the music
That is yours.

If your range
Isn't great,
You can change
It, just modulate.

Make the most of the music
That is yours,
Till it soars!

Compose.
Add to your theme till it grows.
Nothing extreme:
Say, a note of disdain
Here and there—
Gives the refrain
A certain flair.

Compose!
Add to the gleam
Till it glows,
Gathering steam
With a note of success—
Flaunt your talents.
A note of distress,
Though, to stress the balance—

Compose!
Don't lose the pace of your bass notes.
And when you have to erase notes,
Replace them with grace notes,

Like a note of wit
To give it style,
A note of glitter,
A note of guile,
A note of tact,
A note of friction,
A note of fact
In amongst the fiction,
And to counteract
Any contradiction,
A note or two of complete
     conviction—

BEN, CHORUS
Compose! Compose! Compose!

BEN
Luscious harp,
Soft high-hat—
If you're sharp,
Then you won't fall flat.
Make the most of the music that is
     yours!

Give it sweep,
Add a fill,
Give the people
A great big trill.
Make the most of your music till
It soars—
Till it scores!

BEN, CHORUS

Compose!
Blending the highs
With the lows,
Just so it rises:
An up-tune,
Upbeat,
Long as it keeps climbing!
Upscale,
Upstreet,
Everything is timing!

Find the blend,
Set the beat,
Keep ascending—
Don't compete,
Compose!

Comes the day
Pretty soon

When you may
Have to trust your tune.
Make the most of your music
And who knows?
You may even get to like
What you compose!

*(The number ends with Ben reaching the
highest step, but the key sticks, and out
from the bowels of the piano come Sally,
Phyllis and Buddy to help him. Chaos
ensues, and the show ends as in the
New York version.)*

Although none of the new songs was
much of an improvement—"Country
House" was too harsh a style for the
score (it would have been better suited

to *Company*), "Loveland" was unnecessary and "Make the Most of
Your Music" was too elaborate and
expensive to stage easily—"Ah, But Underneath" has proven useful as a substitute for "The Story of Lucy and
Jessie" in subsequent productions
where the woman who plays Phyllis is
more a singer than a dancer. It would
be easy to say that otherwise I wasted
my time writing these songs, but that
wouldn't be entirely true: there is always value in trying different things.
The axiom that "If it isn't broke, don't
fix it" is a valuable truism in the theater, but *Follies* is a show that's a bit
crippled by its size, ambition and mysteriousness and thus always worth the
effort of experimentation—if only it
were produced more often.

*Dorothy Collins and Gene Nelson as Sally and Buddy in the original Broadway
production*

*Opposite: Daniel Massey as Benjamin Stone in "Make the Most of Your
Music" (London, 1987)*

A Little Night Music

music and lyrics by
Stephen Sondheim

REVELATION MUSIC PUBLISHING CORP. & RILTING MUSIC, INC.
A Tommy Valando Publication

9. A Little Night Music (1973)

Book by Hugh Wheeler

Suggested by the film Smiles of a Summer Night
by Ingmar Bergman

The Notion

The place and time: a town in Sweden at the turn of the twentieth century. Fredrik Egerman, a prosperous, widowed lawyer in his early forties with a twenty-year-old son, Henrik, has been married for almost a year to an eighteen-year-old girl, Anne, whom he has known since she was a child. Due to her shyness, he has not been able to consummate the marriage. Desiree Armfeldt, an actress and his ex-lover, arrives in town to appear in a play. When she and Fredrik meet again, the old flame is rekindled, but she has a married lover, Count Carl-Magnus Malcolm, whose wife Charlotte's sister once went to school with Anne. Romantic complications ensue during a weekend party at the country estate of Madame Armfeldt, Desiree's imperious, wealthy ex-courtesan of a mother, involving also Desiree's teenage daughter, Fredrika, and Petra, the Egermans' flirtatious maid, to whom Henrik and Frid, Madame Armfeldt's butler, are both attracted.

General Comments

In 1964, shortly after Hal Prince's triumphant switch from producer to producer-director with *She Loves Me,* he and I decided that we'd like to do a romantic musical, something flowing and operetta-like. We were attracted by the idea of adapting *L'Invitation au Château,* a play by Jean Anouilh, which, in a translation by Christopher Fry

under the title *Ring Round the Moon,* had been a hit in London and New York. In our naïve self-assurance, we assumed that Anouilh would jump at the chance, but to our dismay, he said he would be interested only if Leonard Bernstein wrote the music. Or at least so his agent, a crafty fish by the name of Dr. Jan van Loewen, said he said. I licked my wounds and abandoned the wish, but a few years later, with our collective prestige having burgeoned a bit, Hal and I tried again. Again, the answer from the good doctor was an even more dismissive "No." Having assumed there would be no obstacle, Hal had invited Hugh Wheeler, a British playwright whose work we admired and a man whom we knew and liked, to write the book. After Anouilh's refusal, we scrambled to find a similar piece to adapt. Hal and Hugh, avid and knowledgeable readers both, scratched their memories for a story that would be, like Anouilh's play, an elegant high comedy which observed the Greek unities of time and situation (the action of *Ring Round the Moon* occurs entirely during a weekend at a country estate). I, not being much of a reader—I'm a slow one and I lack patience, not a winning combination—searched my memory for movies and plays that I had seen, and came up with two possibilities: Jean Renoir's *The Rules of the Game* and Ingmar Bergman's *Smiles of a Summer Night.* Renoir's film is on almost every critic's ten-best list; apostate that I am, I've always found it heavy-handed in its satirical commentary on the French social system. Tragic farce is almost always held in high esteem by cineastes—the label dignifies an approach to an art form which, they worry, is too often thought of as little more than popular entertainment. *The Rules of the Game* is the most respected example of this genre, but for my money *Smiles of a Summer Night* is more deserving of the accolade; it's a subtler story, one in which the apparent tragedy is comically averted, but the submerged one not. Happily, Hugh and Hal agreed with

me and we wrote Bergman for permission to adapt his piece. He granted us the rights, withholding only the title,* a restriction that I welcomed, since I already had a title I wanted to use: *A Little Night Music*. I'd hoped to use it once before, for a television show I'd written with James Goldman, but it had been shouted down (that show eventually was called *Evening Primrose,* the name of the story from which it was adapted).

My favorite musical form has always been that of Theme and Variations, and here, I thought, would be the perfect occasion on which to work out such a structure in both musical and theatrical terms. (Rachmaninoff's *Rhapsody on a Theme of Paganini* is for me the apotheosis of the form, which may be the reason his presence pops up so often in the score.) The plot concerns Desiree's attempts to regain Fredrik; she has arranged for her mother to invite him and his family for a weekend in the country in order to fan the flames of their old affair, only to have her plans derailed by the unexpected arrival of Count Malcolm and Charlotte. I thought: what if her plan doesn't result in a happy resolution (as in the film) but an unhappy one, and what if she screams in frustration at its failure, prompting her mother, a Norn-like figure who repeatedly plays solitaire, to redeal the cards, causing the weekend to start all over again? What if the first deal works out as a farce (characters falling in love with the wrong partners), the second one as a genuine tragedy which results in Henrik's suicide (ending the first act) and the third as a romantic comedy, in which everyone would be properly paired off and Desiree would be left alone with Fredrik? And instead of restating the theme at the end, as often happens in the classic form, I would leave something emotionally unresolved, calling for a coda, in which Desiree has to make a straightforward commitment to the man she has manipulated. I thought the show could be about the danger, and inevitable failure, of trying to maneuver people emotionally.

Hugh, however, was not a man given to what-ifs; his work had always been linear and direct, not fanciful. He tried to write the libretto I had in mind, but his heart

wasn't in it. Hal told him to go off on his annual vacation trip to St. Kitts in the West Indies and write the show his way, without input from me. Hugh replied that I would find it boring and literal, but Hal insisted he give it a shot, which he did, and which I read on his return. Hugh was right: I found it boring and literal. Not only that, but he'd taken all the darkness out of it, leaving a graceful but fluffily light comedy version of Bergman's movie. I was about to abnegate, when I received a visit from my real-life Muse, a lady who over the years has supplied me not only with good advice (mostly), but with words, phrases and ideas that casually tumble from her mouth and that I mine for gold. On this occasion, she pointed out that, despite its not being what I had wanted, this project was more than "fluff" and that a score for it would let me show off; I could let loose with verbal dazzle and technical prowess, something I had been able to demonstrate only sporadically before. So I did, and I showed off, and everyone was impressed. I should add that Hal had once described the show as being "whipped cream with knives," but he was more interested in the whipped cream and I was more interested in the knives. I kept my interest up by figuring out how to fulfill my original notion of Theme and Variations.

The solution turned out not to be a dramaturgical but a musical one. Back in the days when I was confident that we would get the rights to *Ring Round the Moon,* I had written an instrumental waltz in the manner of Maurice Ravel, the quintessential French composer, both to set the style for the score and to have something which would demonstrate to M. Anouilh my worthiness and sensitivity to the milieu. At the time it proved to be for naught, but fifteen years later it became the seminal idea of the *Night Music* score: even though Hugh had maintained the film's Swedish setting, the feeling of his adaptation was more Anouilh, or even Pinero, than it was Bergman. A score of waltz variations would be appropriate, and would supply a structural thread that could help cohere a disparate group of songs.

The scores of most musicals have always been collections of songs held together somewhat, if at all, by the composer's and lyricist's styles. A Rodgers and Hammerstein score coheres only through the consistency of their approach; the same holds true for a score by Porter or the Gershwins or any of the other songwriters with strongly distinctive styles. Bernstein liked to claim that *West Side Story* was not just a collection of songs, that it was a score composed out of the tritone (the musical interval that

Margaret Hamilton as Madame Armfeldt (1974 U.S. tour)

---

* He allowed us one exception: when the show was produced in Vienna, he permitted us to use *Das Lächeln einer Sommernacht,* thus saving us the embarrassment of the literal translation *Eine Kleine Nachtmusik,* the title of Mozart's beloved chamber piece, which would have been both misleading and disappointing to a Mozart-loving audience.

comprises the first two notes in the Jets' whistle as well as the first two notes of "Maria"), but in fact many of the tunes came from unused music in his other shows, and in most of the songs melodic tritones are either incidental or, as in "America" and "I Feel Pretty," nonexistent. What holds the score together is Bernstein's personal stamp. It's not as if he (or Rodgers or others) couldn't come up with a cohesive structure, it's simply that a musical doesn't require it. There is so much dialogue in most musicals that a through-composed score, one in which the musical pieces relate to each other, all in the service of a larger musical architecture (as in opera), would be a fool's errand. The most that a composer of musicals can hope to do is write a group of songs which, as in a song cycle, bear a resemblance to each other in melodic, harmonic and verbal ways. The term "through-composed" has been misused by critics and pretentious composers of musicals for decades now to describe shows which are through-*sung* but have no compositional plan whatsoever. Occasionally there is a feeble attempt to make the score appear to have a shape, hinted at by a couple of leit-motifs and reprises, but without development of musical material, merely with bald statements. Calling a show that does little more than dispense with dialogue "through-composed" gives the critic an appearance of musical knowledge* and the composer cachet. The vogue of slapping together a group of songs and calling

them a through-composed musical seems to be passing now, as new vogues succeed it, but every day of the year somebody somewhere is writing one and trying to elevate it by labeling it an "opera," rock or otherwise.

In any event, for someone who loves the perennial puzzle of trying to make a score into something more than a string of numbers, the idea of a Theme and Variations in which the Theme was a metric one seemed workable. An evening of waltzes alone would soon become monotonous, but variations on the basic three-beat meter could supply plenty of variety: polonaises, mazurkas, sarabands, gigues and more are all versions of triple meter, or of duple meters subdivided into six or twelve beats—enough so that even with a relentless succession of threes throughout the evening I should be able to avoid repetitiousness.[†] I think I did, and in the course of writing them, I got to like the show enormously, not least because of Hugh's supple and surprisingly ageless libretto. Whenever I have to go to see it (major revivals, school productions, some friend's granddaughter playing Fredrika), I fret in advance that it will seem like homework, and find, once the lights have dimmed, that I have an exhilarating time watching it. I underestimated Hugh's work shamefully when I first read it. After living with it through numerous productions for more than thirty-five years, I've come to the conclusion that it is one of the half dozen best books ever written for a musical.

On opening night in Boston, Dr. van Loewen wired Hal that the rights to *Ring Round the Moon* were now available. We began, belatedly, to suspect that perhaps M. Anouilh had never even heard of our proposition (the "Dr." alone should have been a dead giveaway). Hal, being the gent that he is, refrained from replying as he would have liked to. He simply answered that we were no longer interested.

---

* The sad truth is that musicals are the only public art form reviewed mostly by ignoramuses. Books are reviewed by writers, the visual arts by disappointed, if knowledgeable, painters and art students, concert music by composers and would-be composers. Plays, at least in this country, are reviewed by people who don't know de Montherlant from de Ghelderode and couldn't care less, whose knowledge is comprised of what they read in *Variety* and gossip columns, and who know nothing, of course, about music. Nor do they think it necessary. Otis Guernsey, Jr., who used to review for *The New York Times* and was the selector of best plays and musicals for the yearly Burns Mantle series of Best Plays, once said to me that music was the one field where a reviewer needed no knowledge. Music, he claimed, was everybody's province and musical knowledge was unnecessary for a critic. His attitude prevails. Musicals continue to be the only art form, popular or otherwise, that is publicly criticized by illiterates.

---

† Actually, there are eleven measures of underscoring in the second act which are not in some form of triple time. I wrote them before I decided on the triple-meter scheme and couldn't let go.

ACT ONE

Before the house lights are down, Mr. Lindquist, a middle-aged man dressed in formal evening clothes, enters in front of the curtain and sits at a spinet at the side of the stage. He removes his gloves, plunks a key and begins to vocalize. He is soon joined by a Mrs. Nordstrom, a Mrs. Anderssen, a Mr. Erlansen and a Mrs. Segstrom, all elegantly dressed. They vocalize with him and, as a Quintet, proceed to sing a medley of songs from the show: a vocal overture.

This was not how *A Little Night Music* originally began. In its first incarnation, the story was to be seen through Fredrika's eyes and began with her practicing Clementi exercises on the spinet and singing to herself.

Numbers (cut)

FREDRIKA
Thirteen . . . Forty-four . . . Twenty-
    seven . . .
Twenty . . . Thirty-four . . . Seventy-
    five . . .

(To the audience)

Grandmother says numbers are
    matters of moment
To people whose moments don't
    matter enough.
Grandmother says numbers are food
    for the foolish
Who tick off the minutiae of life on a
    cuff.
(Grandmother says lots of inscrutable
    stuff.)
Eighteen . . . Forty-eight . . . Twenty-
    seven . . .
Forty . . . Twenty-three . . .
    Seventy . . .

(The Quintet appears)

Twenty . . .

(Henrik appears)

Forty-four . . .

(Desiree appears)

Eighteen . . .

(Anne appears)

QUINTET
Numbers . . .

HENRIK, DESIREE, ANNE
Time . . .

FREDRIKA
Forty . . .

(Frid appears)

Thirty-four . . .

(Carl-Magnus appears)

Twenty-seven . . .

(Charlotte appears)

QUINTET
What are they?

FRID, CARL-MAGNUS,
CHARLOTTE
Time . . .

ANNE
What shall I wear?

CARL-MAGNUS
What about the mail?

CHARLOTTE
Where is my parasol?

HENRIK
How did I fail?

PRINCIPALS
Time . . .

QUINTET
Forty-eight . . .

(Fredrik appears)

PRINCIPALS
Time . . .

QUINTET
Twenty-three . . .

(Petra appears. They all start to dance.)

CHARLOTTE, CARL-MAGNUS
Why were you there?

DESIREE, ANNE
Did you see me weep?

QUINTET
Are you—?

FRID, PETRA
Who shall I sleep with?

FREDRIK, HENRIK,
CHARLOTTE
How shall I sleep?

QUINTET
Is it—?

PRINCIPALS
Time . . .

QUINTET
Thirteen . . .

(Fredrika joins the dance)

PRINCIPALS
Time . . .

QUINTET
Seventy-five . . .

*(Frid brings Madame Armfeldt on
in a wheelchair)*

PRINCIPALS
Questions!

ALL
Time!

PRINCIPALS
Numbers!

ALL
Time!

FREDRIKA
Lessons . . .

FREDRIK
Appointments . . .

13 Know nothing *is green*   40/50 One
                                                      13... 43... 27... Time
18 is lovely *between* green   18   I'm

21 19 is despair
    25
    24 is 24 *is alive*   70
                                                      13... 43... 20... 35,

28 is intolerable

36 is vigor   From 13 to 72 is one
    39
    40 is *a pleasure* is fine *is as good as any*   And everything between

confusing
confused   44 is confusing *Where 43 is a bore, when you're more like forty-four*
amusing   47
amused   48 is too late

72   People are silly

                                                      People are sweet

I look forward to *May* *Will be should*   Only the numbers
I had — (is past)   stick in their heads

    18
13, 48, 27   People think in *terms* organdy dresses
        36
18, 44, 25 and   Cups and saucers
    24   and 3   and
19, 36, 40, 72. And, most important, 13   Nights in hotels

                    And everything in between
           everything
Numbers are wondrous,   Grandmother told me
         us   they
All of them *we*,   Watch the numbers   People *think in* are numbers

  All of them you   Not very edifying,

                            Nevertheless

Grandmother says   Grandmother says fools
                                        defeated
says could Numbers   Fools should be pitied
parable Numbers are people *paramount important*
           Numbers are people
           Grandmother says people
                    fools
           People are sweet

PETRA
Hellos and farewells . . .

CARL-MAGNUS
Photographs . . .

MADAME ARMFELDT
Calendars . . .

DESIREE
Nights in hotels . . .

ALL
Twenty . . . forty-four . . .
Numbers . . . questions . . .
Time . . .
Card games . . . coffee cups . . .
Twenty thousand . . .
What are they?
Time! . . .

This opening had a nice air of mystery to it and served to introduce not only the characters but their ages. When we dropped the notion of seeing everything through Fredrika's eyes, however, the song had to be dropped as well, which is what prompted Hal to suggest the vocal overture as a substitute. The fragmentary notion of the lyric was not entirely abandoned, however, as you will eventually see.

Fredrik arrives home from his office and goes into the bedroom, to find Anne at her dressing table. He moves to kiss her, but she avoids him by chattering about the trivialities of her life and the day's events, which she continues to do throughout the song.

Now

FREDRIK
Now,
As the sweet imbecilities
Tumble so lavishly
Onto her lap . . .
Now,
There are two possibilities:
A, I could ravish her,
B, I could nap . . .

Say
It's the ravishment, then we see

The option
That follows, of course:
A,
The deployment of charm, or B,
The adoption
Of physical force . . .

Now B might arouse her,
But let us assume
I trip on my trouser
Leg crossing the room . . .
Her hair getting tangled,
Her stays getting snapped,
My nerves would be jangled,
My energy sapped . . .

Removing her clothing
Would take me all day
And her subsequent loathing
Would turn me away,
Which eliminates B
And which leaves us with A . . .

Now,
Insofar as approaching it,
What would be festive
But have its effect? . . .
Now,
There are two ways of broaching it:
A, the suggestive
And B, the direct . . .

Say
That I settle on B, to wit,
A charmingly
Lecherous mood . . .
A,
I could put on my nightshirt or sit
Disarmingly,
B, in the nude . . .

That might be effective,
My body's all right,
But not in perspective
And not in the light . . .

I'm bound to be chilly
And feel a buffoon,
But nightshirts are silly
In mid-afternoon . . .

Which leaves the suggestive,
But how to proceed?
Although she gets restive,
Perhaps I could read . . .

In view of her penchant*
For something romantic,

De Sade is too trenchant
And Dickens too frantic,
And Stendhal would ruin
The plan of attack,
As there isn't much blue in
The Red and The Black.

De Maupassant's candor
Would cause her dismay.
The Brontës are grander,
But not very gay.
Her taste is much blander,
I'm sorry to say,
But is Hans Christian Ander-
Sen ever risqué?
Which eliminates A . . .

Now,
With my mental facilities
Partially muddied
And ready to snap . . .
Now,
Though there are possibilities
Still to be studied,
I might as well nap . . .

Bow
Though I must
To adjust
My original plan . . .
How
Shall I sleep
Half as deep
As I usually can? . . .

When now I still want and/or love you,
Now as always,
Now,
Anne . . .

---

* This rhyme proved unexpectedly problematic when the show was performed in London, due to the British penchant for giving certain borrowed foreign words like "penchant" their native pronunciations. Thus, "penchant" is "ponshont" while "trenchant" remains Anglicized, even though its root is equally French. I solved it by changing "penchant" to "fancy" and "trenchant" to "chancy"—or so I thought. I hadn't taken into account that the British pronounce "chance" to rhyme with "wants." Again the rhyme was killed. I thought of other possibilities (such as "liking" / "striking") but nothing that said what I meant. In the end, I asked the British cast to pronounce "penchant" American-style. This may seem like a quirkily exceptional problem, but British linguistic eccentricities (or, looked at from the other side of the Big Pond, American ones) give rise to it more often than you might imagine.

This lyric is another example of the difference between funny and clever. The two elaborately rhymed stanzas about the books Fredrik considers reading to Anne have never gotten even a snicker, nor should they. They are a form of literary masturbation and too clever by half, a phrase British critics are fond of overusing.

Henrik, a repressed seminary student who is fond of playing the cello when he feels melancholy, which is often, wants to sit and talk with Anne, but she lightly dismisses him with "Later, Henrik," an admonition both his father and the maid Petra, who teases him sexually, also use.

Later

HENRIK
(As he plays the cello)
Later . . .
When is later? . . .

All you ever hear is, "Later, Henrik—
Henrik, Later . . ."

"Yes, we know, Henrik,
Oh, Henrik,
Everyone agrees, Henrik,
Please, Henrik!"

You have a thought you're fairly
    bursting with,
A personal discovery or problem,
    and it's
"What's your rush, Henrik?
Shush, Henrik,
Goodness, how you gush, Henrik,
Hush, Henrik!"

You murmur,
"I only—
It's just that—
For God's sake—!"
"Later, Henrik . . ."

"Henrik" . . .
Who is "Henrik"?
"Oh, that lawyer's son, the one who
    mumbles,

Short and boring.
Yes, he's hardly worth ignoring."
And who cares if he's all dammed—

(Looks upward)

I beg your pardon—
Up inside?

As I've often stated,
It's intolerable
Being tolerated.
"Reassure Henrik,
Poor Henrik.
Henrik, you'll endure
Being pure, Henrik."

Though I've been born, I've never
    been!
How can I wait around for later?
I'll be ninety on my deathbed
And the late, or rather later,
Henrik Egerman!

Doesn't anything begin?

Shortly thereafter, Anne is standing over Fredrik as he naps on their bed.

Hermione Gingold as Madame Armfeldt with Judy Kahan as Fredrika

Soon

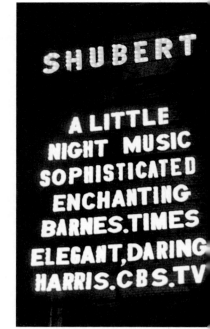

ANNE
Soon, I promise.
Soon I won't shy away,
Dear old—

(Catches herself)

Soon. I want to.
Soon, whatever you say.

Even now,
When you're close and we touch
And you're kissing my brow,
I don't mind it too much.
And you'll have to admit
I'm endearing,
I help keep things humming,
I'm not domineering,
What's one small shortcoming?

And think of how I adore you,
Think of how much you love me.
If I were perfect for you,
Wouldn't you tire of me
Soon,
All too soon,
Dear old—?
Soon—

HENRIK
"Later" . . .

ANNE
I promise.

HENRIK
When is "Later"?

ANNE	HENRIK
Soon	"Later, Henrik, later."
I won't shy	All you ever hear is,
Away,	"Yes, we know,
	Henrik,
	Oh Henrik,
	Everyone agrees,
	Henrik,

ANNE	HENRIK	FREDRIK
Dear		
Old . . .	Please, Henrik!"	
Soon.		*(In his sleep)*
		Now,
		As the
	"Later" . . .	Sweet imbecilities
I want to.	When is "later"?	
	All you ever hear is	Trip on my
Soon,		Trouser leg,
	"Later,	Stendhal
Whatever you	Henrik,	
	Later."	
	As I've often	Eliminates
Say.	Stated:	"A," But
	When?	When?
Even	Maybe	Maybe
Now,	Soon,	Later.
When you're		
Close and we	Soon,	
Touch,	I'll be	
	Ninety and	
And you're		When I'm
Kissing my	Dead.	Kissing your
Brow,		Brow and I'm
		Stroking your
I don't mind it too	I don't mind it too	Head,
Much,	Much,	You'll come
		Into my
		Bed.

ANNE	HENRIK	FREDRIK
And you'll	Since I	And you'll
Have to admit I'm	Have to admit I	Have to admit I've
Endearing, I	Find peering	Been hearing
Help keep things	Through life's gray	All those tremulous
Humming,	Windows impatiently	Cries
I'm not	Not	Patiently, not
Domineering,	Very cheering.	
What's		Interfering
One small short-	Do I fear	With those tremulous
Coming?	Death? Let it	Thighs.
And	Come to me	Come to me
Think of how	Now,	Soon,
I adore you,		
Think of how	Now,	Soon,
Much you love me.		
If I were perfect	Now,	Soon,
For you,		
Wouldn't you	Now.	Soon.
Tire of me		
Later?	Come to me	Come to me
	Soon. If I'm	Soon,
We will,	Dead, I can	
Later.	Wait.	Straight to me,
	How can I	Never mind how.
We will . . .	Live until	Darling.
Soon,	Later?	Now
		I still want
		And/or
	Later . . .	Love you.
Soon,		
		Now as
	Later . . .	Always,
Soon.		
		Now,
		Desirée

FREDRIK

Desiree . . .

As Anne reacts, startled, Fredrika appears and begins practicing her scales on the spinet.

Veronica Page as Anne Egerman (London, 1975)

Joss Ackland as Fredrik Egerman (London, 1975)

The Glamorous Life

FREDRIKA
Ordinary mothers lead ordinary lives,
Keep the house and sweep the parlor,
Cook the meals and look exhausted.
Ordinary mothers, like ordinary
      wives,
Fry the eggs and dry the sheets and
Try to deal with facts.
Mine acts.

(She reads a letter from her mother)

DESIREE
Darling, I miss you a lot,
But, darling, this has to be short,
As Mother is getting a plaque
From the Halsingborg Arts Council
Amateur Theatre Group.

Whether it's funny or not,
I'll give you a fuller report
The minute they carry me back
From the Halsingborg Arts Council
Amateur Theatre Group . . .
Love you . . .

QUINTET
Unpack the luggage, la la la
Pack up the luggage, la la la
Unpack the luggage, la la la
Hi-ho, the glamorous life!

Ice in the basin, la la la
Cracks in the plaster, la la la
Mice in the hallway, la la la
Hi-ho, the glamorous life!

Run for the carriage, la la la
Wolf down the sandwich, la la la
Which town is this one? la la la
Hi-ho, the glamorous life!

MADAME ARMFELDT
Ordinary daughters ameliorate
      their lot,
Use their charms and choose their
      futures,
Breed their children, heed their
      mothers.
Ordinary daughters, which mine I
      fear, is not,
Tend each asset, spend it wisely
While it still endures.
Mine tours.

(She reads a letter from her daughter)

DESIREE
Mother, forgive the delay,
My schedule is driving me wild.
But, Mother, I really must run,
I'm performing in Rottvik
And don't ask where is it, please.

How are you feeling today,
And are you corrupting the child?
Don't.
Mother, the minute I'm done
With performing in Rottvik,
I'll come for a visit
And argue.

QUINTET
Mayors with speeches, la la la
Children with posies, la la la
Half-empty houses, la la la
Hi-ho, the glamorous life!

Cultural lunches, la la la
Dead floral tributes, la la la
Ancient admirers, la la la
Hi-ho, the glamorous life!

FREDRIKA
Mother's romantic,
      la la la!

MADAME ARMFELDT
Mother's misguided,
      la la la!

DESIREE
Mother's surviving, la la la!
Leading the glamorous life!

(Looking in a mirror)

Cracks in the plaster, la la la!
Youngish admirers, la la la!
Which one was that one? la la la!
Hi-ho, the glamorous life!

DESIREE, QUINTET
Bring up the curtain, la la la!
Bring down the curtain, la la la!
Bring up the curtain, la la la!
Hi-ho, the glamorous—

DESIREE
(Wearily)
Life.

Fredrik takes Anne to the local theater to see a touring company, whose star is Desiree. When Desiree, onstage, spots him sitting in his box, their eyes lock and the action freezes. The Quintet appears, unseen and unheard by the principals.

Remember?

QUINTET
(Individually)
The old deserted beach that we
      walked—
Remember?
The café in the park where we
      talked—
Remember?
The tenor on the boat that we
      chartered,
Belching "The Bartered Bride"—
Ah, how we laughed,
Ah, how we cried.
Ah, how you promised,
And ah, how I lied.

That dilapidated inn—
Remember, darling?
The proprietress' grin,
Also her glare.
Yellow gingham on the bed—
Remember, darling?
And the canopy in red,
Needing repair?

I *think* you were there . . .

Anne, catching the look between the ex-lovers, becomes upset and Fredrik is forced to take her home. Once she is there and calm, he tells her that he feels like taking a stroll. As he leaves the house, the Quintet appears again.

QUINTET
The local village dance on the
      green—
Remember?
The lady with the large tambourine—
Remember?

The one who played the harp in her
      boa
Thought she was so a-

Dept.
Ah, how we laughed,
Ah, how we wept.
Ah, how we polka'd and ah,
How we slept.

How we kissed and how we clung—
Remember, darling?
We were foolish, we were young—
More than we knew.
Yellow gingham on the bed,
Remember, darling?
And the canopy in red,
Or was it blue?

The funny little games that we played—
Remember?
The unexpected knock of the maid—
Remember?
The wine that made us both rather
    merry
And, oh, so very
Frank.
Ah, how we laughed,
Ah, how we drank.
You acquiesced and the rest
Is a blank.

What we did with your perfume—
Remember, darling?
The condition of the room
When we were through . . .
Our inventions were unique—
Remember, darling?
I was limping for a week,
You caught the flu.

I'm *sure* it was—
You . . .

This is the lyric equivalent of a trompe l'oeil painting—it fools the mind not through the eye but through the ear. It is certainly possible that Desiree and Fredrik's long-ago affair involved the incidents mentioned in the song, but the climactic lines "I think you were there" and "I'm *sure* it was you" imply two promiscuous people, which they decidedly are not. Desiree may never have been married, but she is a believer in long relationships, and Fredrik is too conservative to have been with many women between marriages. Luckily, the audience is misled by the smooth phrasing, the flirtatious images and the smattering of truth in the specifics of the incidents into not listening to what the song is actually saying—as have all the actors, directors, songwriters, critics and correspondents who have been involved in or commented on the show. Not one has ever questioned me about it, to my embarrassed relief. The fact is that I simply became so enthralled with the brittle easy-to-write quality of the song that I ignored logic for laughs. I haven't often done that, but whenever I hear this example or one of the others (which I shall not name but leave to the interested reader to discover), I shudder with a mixture of pleasure and shame.

Fredrik goes to visit Desiree in her digs. Increasingly aroused by her warmth and the direction of the conversation, he tries to delay the inevitable by talking about his wife. Desiree is amused—for a while.

You Must Meet My Wife

FREDRIK
She lightens my sadness,
She livens my days.
She bursts with a kind of madness
My well-ordered ways.
My happiest mistake,
The ache of my life—
You must meet my wife.

She bubbles with pleasure,
She glows with surprise,
Disrupts my accustomed leisure
And ruffles my ties.
I don't know even know
Quite how it began.
You must meet my wife, my Anne.

One thousand whims to which I
    give in,
Since her smallest tear turns me
    ashen.
I never dreamed that I could live in
So completely demented,
Contented
A fashion.

So sunlike, so winning,
So unlike a wife.
I do think that I'm beginning
To show signs of life.
Don't ask me how at my age
One still can grow—
If you met my wife,
You'd know.

DESIREE
Dear Fredrik. I'm just longing to meet her. Sometime.

FREDRIK
She sparkles.

DESIREE
How pleasant.

FREDRIK
She twinkles.

DESIREE
How nice.

FREDRIK
Her youth is a sort of present—

DESIREE
Whatever the price.

FREDRIK
The incandescent—what? The—

DESIREE
(Holding up her cigarette)
Light?

FREDRIK
—Of my life!
You must meet my wife.

DESIREE
Yes, I must, I really must. Now—

FREDRIK
She flutters.

DESIREE
How charming.

FREDRIK
She twitters.

DESIREE
My word!

FREDRIK
She floats.

DESIREE
Isn't that alarming?
What is she, a bird?

FREDRIK
She makes me feel I'm—what?

DESIREE
A very old man?

FREDRIK
Yes—no!

DESIREE
No.

FREDRIK
But—

DESIREE
I must meet your Gertrude.

FREDRIK
My Anne.

DESIREE
Sorry—Anne.

FREDRIK
She loves my voice, my walk, my
    moustache,
The cigar, in fact, that I'm smoking.
She'll watch me puff until it's just ash,
Then she'll save the cigar butt.

DESIREE
Bizarre, but
You're joking.

FREDRIK
She dotes on—

DESIREE
Your dimple.

FREDRIK
My snoring.

DESIREE
How dear.

FREDRIK
The point is, she's really simple.

DESIREE
Yes, that much seems clear.

FREDRIK
She gives me funny names.

DESIREE
Like—?

FREDRIK
"Old Dry-As-Dust."

DESIREE
Wouldn't she just?

FREDRIK
You must meet my wife.

DESIREE
If I must—yes, I must.

FREDRIK
A sea of whims that I submerge in,
Yet so lovable in repentance.
Unfortunately, still a virgin,
But you can't force a flower—

DESIREE
Don't finish that sentence!
She's monstrous!

FREDRIK
She's frightened.

DESIREE
Unfeeling!

FREDRIK
Unversed.
She'd strike you as unenlightened.

DESIREE
No, I'd strike her first.

FREDRIK
Her reticence, her apprehension—

DESIREE
Her crust!

FREDRIK
No!

DESIREE
Yes!

FREDRIK
No!

DESIREE
Fredrik . . .

FREDRIK
You must meet my wife.

DESIREE
Let me get my hat
And my knife.

FREDRIK
What was that?

DESIREE
I must meet your wife.

FREDRIK	DESIREE
Yes, you must.	Yes, I must.

*Fredrik and Desiree go into Desiree's
bedroom to resume where they left off
fourteen years ago. Madame Armfeldt
comments on the situation.*

Liaisons

MADAME ARMFELDT
At the villa of the Baron De Signac,
Where I spent a somewhat infamous
    year,
At the villa of the Baron De Signac
I had ladies in attendance,
Fire-opal pendants . . .

Liaisons! What's happened to them,
Liaisons today?
Disgraceful! What's become of them?
Some of them
Hardly pay their shoddy way.

What once was a rare Champagne
Is now just an amiable hock,
What once was a villa, at least,
Is "digs."
What once was a gown with train
Is now just a simple little frock,
What once was a sumptuous feast
Is figs.
No, not even figs—
Raisins.
Ah, liaisons!

    Where was I? . . . Oh, yes . . .

At the palace of the Duke of Ferrara,
Who was prematurely deaf but a dear,

At the palace of the Duke of Ferrara,
I acquired some position,
Plus a tiny Titian . . .

Liaisons! What's happened to them,
Liaisons today?
To see them—indiscriminate
Women, it
Pains me more than I can say,
The lack of taste that they display.

Where is style?
Where is skill?
Where is forethought?
Where's discretion of the heart,
Where's passion in the art,
Where's craft?
With a smile
And a will
But with more thought,
I acquired a château
Extravagantly o-
Verstaffed.

Too many people muddle sex
With mere desire,
And when emotion intervenes,
The nets descend.
It should on no account perplex,
Or worse, inspire.
It's but a pleasurable means
To a measurable end.
Why does no one comprehend?
Let us hope this lunacy is just a trend.

Where was I . . . Oh, yes . . .

In the castle of the King of the
    Belgians,
We would visit through a false
    chiffonier,
In the castle of the King of the
    Belgians,
Who, when things got rather touchy,
Deeded me a duchy . . .

Liaisons! What's happened to them,
Liaisons today?
Untidy—take my daughter, I
Taught her, I
Tried my best to point the way.
I even named her Desiree.

In a world where the kings are
    employers,
Where the amateur prevails
And delicacy fails

To pay,
In a world where the princes are
    lawyers,
What can anyone expect
Except to recollect
Liai . . .

(She falls asleep)

I have witnessed a number of memorable auditions in my time, some of them so stunning that we hired the performer virtually on the spot (Pamela Myers for *Company*, Victor Garber and Merle Louise for *Sweeney Todd*, Donna Murphy for *Passion*), others so grotesque that we couldn't believe what we were seeing. Hermione Gingold's audition for Madame Armfeldt covered both bases. Her professional persona had been honed in British revues as an eccentric both in looks and personality, and although she had occasionally played a character straightforwardly, as in the musical movie of *Gigi*, she was always Hermione Gingold. She was camp both on and off the stage, and couldn't have been more wrong for the role of an imperious, elegant ex-courtesan (her physical appearance alone disqualified her). Nevertheless, she insisted on auditioning for us. Hal, ever the gentleman, persuaded Hugh and me to humor her, even though it would be a waste of our time. Considering her insistence on being heard, we were therefore somewhat taken aback when she arrived at the theater not only without an accompanist but without having prepared a song for us to hear. When I murmured deferentially that we knew she could sing but that we needed to hear her vocal range (an excuse to hear whether she could sing or not), she offered to ply us with a music hall song, a cappella. Which she did, charmingly. She then read a couple of scenes with the stage manager—with, unexpectedly, genuine verve and autocratic condescension. Intrigued as we were, we were not prepared for the coup de théâtre which followed. She thanked us for allowing her to audition against our better judgment—not that anyone had told her such a thing,

she had merely assumed we would think her wrong for the part. She then added, "I notice that in the script Madame Armfeldt is seventy-four years old. Coincidentally, gentlemen, so am I. I also noticed that when she dies at the end, the stage direction indicates that her wig slips a bit off her head. Well—" And with that, she lifted off her wig, revealing herself to be completely bald. As the clang of three jaws hitting the floor died away, she thanked us once again and left the stage. We decided to give her the part before she left the theater. Incidentally, she was actually seventy-five.

Desiree and Fredrik's tryst is interrupted by the unexpected arrival of her lover, Carl-Magnus. Fredrik, trying to explain why he is wearing Carl-Magnus's bathrobe, concocts a story about having fallen into Desiree's hip-bath. Desiree supports his story, but Carl-Magnus forces him to leave, dressed only in a nightshirt. Carl-Magnus ponders the situation to himself.

In Praise of Women

CARL-MAGNUS
She wouldn't . . .
Therefore they didn't . . .
So then it wasn't—
Not unless it—
Would she?
She doesn't . . .
God knows she needn't . . .
Therefore it's not.

He'd never . . .
Therefore they haven't . . .
Which makes the question
    absolutely—
Could he?
She daren't . . .
Therefore I mustn't . . .
What utter rot!

Fidelity is more than mere display,
It's what a man expects from life.
Fidelity like mine to Desiree
And Charlotte, my devoted wife.

The papers . . .
He mentioned papers,
Some legal papers,
Which I didn't see there.
Where were they,
The goddamn papers
She had to sign?

What nonsense . . .
He brought her papers,
They were important,
So he had to be there.
I'll kill him!
Why should I bother?
The woman's mine!

Besides, no matter what one might
    infer,
One must have faith to some degree.
The least that I can do is trust in her
The way that Charlotte trusts in me.

Capable, pliable . . .
Women, women . . .
Undemanding and reliable,
Knowing their place.
Insufferable, yes, but gentle.
Their weaknesses are incidental.
A functional but ornamental
Race.

Durable, sensible . . .
Women, women . . .
Very nearly indispensable
Creatures of grace.
God knows the foolishness about
    them,
But if one had to live without them,
The world would surely be a poorer,
If purer,
Place.

The hip-bath . . .
About that hip-bath . . .
How can you slip and trip into a hip-
    bath?
The papers . . .
Where were the papers?
Of course, he might have taken back
    the papers . . .
She wouldn't . . .
Therefore they didn't . . .
The woman's mine!

The song I first wrote for this moment
was a double inner monologue for

Carl-Magnus and Desiree called
"Bang!" During rehearsals, Hal asked
me to replace it with something that
would allow him to change sets during
the song from Desiree's digs to the
breakfast room in Carl-Magnus's
house, where the next scene takes
place. He wanted something specific in
the lyric to motivate the switch, which
is the function of the line "And Charlotte, my devoted wife." On the word
"wife," Desiree's digs rolled off and
Charlotte at her breakfast table rode
on. "Bang!" was the more interesting
song, however, based as it was on a
brilliant speech in Bergman's film,
wherein Carl-Magnus compares making love to making war.

*Carl-Magnus begins unbuttoning his tu-
nic, despite Desiree's protestations.*

Bang! (cut)

CARL-MAGNUS
(To himself)
The war commences,
The enemy awaits
In quivering expectancy.
The poor defenses,
The penetrable gates,
How terrible to be a woman.

The time is here,
The game is there,
The smell of fear,
Like musk, pervades the air.
The bugle sounding,
The pistol steady,
The blood is pounding,
Take aim, and ready—

QUINTET
Bang!

CARL-MAGNUS
Twenty minutes' small talk,
Thirty at the most.

QUINTET
Bang!

CARL-MAGNUS
Two or three
To pour the schnapps.

QUINTET
Bang! Bang! Bang!

CARL-MAGNUS
Half a minute
To propose
The necessary toast,

QUINTET
Bang!

CARL-MAGNUS
The tunic opens,

QUINTET
Bang!

CARL-MAGNUS
The trousers fall.

QUINTET
Bang!

CARL-MAGNUS
The foe is helpless,
Back against the wall.

QUINTET
Bang!

CARL-MAGNUS
An hour and a quarter
Over all,
And—

QUINTET
Bang!

DESIREE
Twenty minutes to arrange those
Bloody awful flowers,
Can I get away with more?

QUINTET
Bang! Bang! Bang!

DESIREE
Then I have to brush my hair,
And that could take me hours.

QUINTET
Bang!

DESIREE
A fit of vapors—

QUINTET
Bang!

DESIREE
No, that's too quaint.

QUINTET
Bang! Bang! Bang!

DESIREE
A racking cough and
Then a graceful faint . . .
A lengthy lecture
On self-restraint . . .

QUINTET
Bang!

CARL-MAGNUS
The battle rages.
Whatever ground I gain
I fortify remorselessly.

QUINTET
Bang! Bang!

CARL-MAGNUS
The foe engages
By shifting the terrain.
How pitiful to be a woman.

Attack,
Retreat,
Lay back,
Reform.

QUINTET
Bang! Bang! Bang! Bang! Bang!

CARL-MAGNUS
Outflank,
Deplete,
Move up
And then
Restorm.

QUINTET
Bang! Bang! Bang! Bang! Bang!

CARL-MAGNUS
The siege succeeding,
The time grows shorter,
She lies there pleading,
I give no quarter . . .

QUINTET
Bang! Bang! Bang! Bang! Bang!

CARL-MAGNUS
Foray at the elbow,
Salvo at the knee!

QUINTET
Bang!

CARL-MAGNUS
Fusillades at breast and thigh!

QUINTET
Bang! Bang! Bang!

CARL-MAGNUS
Then, when she's exhausted—

QUINTET
Bang!

CARL-MAGNUS
A fresh sortie.

QUINTET
Bang! Bang! Bang! Bang!

CARL-MAGNUS
I taste the conquest,
The taste is sweet.
She lays her arms down,
Welcoming defeat.

QUINTET
Bang! Bang! Bang! Bang! Bang!

CARL-MAGNUS
Both sides content,
Secure positions.

QUINTET
Bang! Bang! Bang! Bang! Bang! Bang!
Bang!

CARL-MAGNUS
All passion spent,
Discuss conditions.

QUINTET
Bang! Bang! Bang!

CARL-MAGNUS
How terrible,
How pitiful,
How glorious to be a woman.

QUINTET
Bang! Bang!

DESIREE
He is a peacock,
I keep forgetting.

QUINTET
Bang! Bang! Bang! Bang! Bang!

CARL-MAGNUS
The quarry senses
A momentary pang.

DESIREE
It's all so foolish.
Why am I sweating?

CARL-MAGNUS
The war commences . . .

QUINTET
Bang!

When I began writing the song, I planned that at each "Bang!" Carl-Magnus would undo a button on his heavily buttoned military jacket. I got carried away; no regalia has ever had that many buttons. Luckily for the costume designer, the song never made its way out of rehearsals.

Another song that never emerged from rehearsals was the one which established Charlotte at her breakfast table. Here she is, angrily buttering her toast.

My Husband the Pig
(cut)

CHARLOTTE
Fop.
Lout.
What am I, a prop
To order about?
Adulterous lowlife!
He seems to assume I have no life
Of my own.
Well, he isn't alone!

I lie on the shelf at my station
To bolster his self-adulation.

I have no objection
To passing inspection,
But who can contend with an endless
    erection
That falls on its knees when it sees its
    reflection?

My husband the pig,
The swaggering bore
I'll do anything for,
What a pig!
The air of disdain is appalling,
The level of decency nil.
If he thinks that I'll always come
    crawling,
Ha! I will.

My husband the pig.
I worship the ground
That he kicks me around
On, the pig.

A stunted affront to humanity,
A vat of gelatinous vanity,
The stamp of my rampant insanity:
My husband the—Ugh!

There's a clot in the cream
And a fly in the jam
And I think that I'm going to
    scream . . .
Yes, I am!
But would anyone here give a damn?
No.
Ah, well,

Every day a little death,
In the parlor, in the bed,
In the curtains, in the silver,
In the buttons, in the bread.
Every day a little sting
In the heart and in the head.
Every move and every breath,
And you hardly feel a thing,
Brings a perfect little death.

Every day a little death,
On the lips and in the eyes,
In the murmurs, in the pauses,
In the gestures, in the sighs.
Every day a little dies
In the looks and in the lies,
And you hardly feel a thing . . .

Ugh!
There's a leaf in the cup
And a crack in the pot,

And I think I'm about to throw up,
But I'm not,
'Cause I have to go out, and for what?

A pat on the hand and I'm suet.
I don't understand why I do it.
While I'm in abstention
In every dimension,
His horse and his whores
And his wars
Get attention,
And I decompose
Like a rose
With a pension!

My husband the pig.
I loathe and deplore
Every bone I adore,
He's a pig!

He throws me a crumb to be cruel
And then expects humble delight.
Does he think a duet is a duel?
Ha! He's right!

My husband the pig!
My swain is a swine
Or, to further refine
It, a pig!
It's ghastly and vastly ironical,
A cynical, clinical chronicle:
"The woman who married a
    monocle."
My husband the pig!
Ugh!

Another one of those lyrics which
reads better than it sings. At the rapid
clip of the music, the song became a
tongue-twister of the wrong kind:
instead of marveling at the singer's
agility and the songwriter's deftness,
the listener could only wince at the
singer's discomfort and the songwriter's gluey verbiage. I cut the song
after the first rehearsal, but one section was salvageable and at Hal's suggestion I expanded it and inserted it
into the next scene.

*At Carl-Magnus's insistence, Charlotte
visits Anne to inform her of Fredrik's midnight foray. As she does so, she begins to
break down, but quickly pulls herself
together and describes her married life.*

Every Day
a Little Death

CHARLOTTE
Every day a little death,
In the parlor, in the bed,
In the curtains, in the silver,
In the buttons, in the bread.
Every day a little sting
In the heart and in the head.
Every move and every breath,
And you hardly feel a thing,
Brings a perfect little death.

He smiles sweetly, strokes my hair,
Says he misses me.
I would murder him right there,
But first I die.

He talks softly of his wars
And his horses and his whores.
I think love's a dirty business!

ANNE
So do I! So do I . . .

CHARLOTTE
I'm before him on my knees
And he kisses me.
He assumes I'll lose my reason,
And I do.
Men are stupid, men are vain,
Love's disgusting, love's insane,
A humiliating business!

ANNE
Oh, how true!

CHARLOTTE
Ah, well . . .

Every day a little death—

ANNE
Every day a little death—

CHARLOTTE
In the parlor, in the bed—

ANNE
On the lips and in the eyes—

CHARLOTTE   ANNE
In the curtains,   In the murmurs,
In the silver,   In the pauses,

In the buttons,
In the bread.
Every day a
Little sting

In the gestures,
In the sighs.

Every day a little
dies

In the heart
And in the head.

In the looks
And in the lies.

CHARLOTTE
Every move and every breath—

BOTH
And you hardly feel a thing,
Brings a perfect little death.

Hal was so enamored of this song that
for the film version he asked me to
write an extra chorus for Charlotte to
sing in her carriage on the way to visit
Anne. I protested that there was nothing for her to say that she wasn't going
to say in the subsequent scene, but
battered by his enthusiasm, I rewrote
the second section of the song:

Every Day
a Little Death
(film version)

CHARLOTTE
Give the lapdog a command
And she crawls for him,
For the little understand-
Ing she is owed.
See her beg for her reward.
Is her master getting bored?
Love's a miserable business.

(To the coachman)

Mind the road!

She waits patiently for days
In the halls for him
With the memories of his prais-
Es in her ear,
And then only to be told
That the coffee's getting cold.
It's a nauseating business—

Oh, we're here.
Ah, well . . .

To ameliorate the repetition that was
about to take place, I inserted Charlotte's asides to the coachman and to
herself. To no avail—when three minutes later the song resurfaced in
Anne's drawing room, it was an anticlimax at best.

*At Desiree's request, Madame Armfeldt
invites the Egerman family to her country
château for the weekend.*

A Weekend
in the Country

(Anne's room)

PETRA
Look, Ma'am, an invitation—
Here, Ma'am, delivered by hand.
And, Ma'am, I notice the station-
Ery's engraved and very grand.

ANNE
Petra, how too exciting!
Just when I need it!
Petra, such elegant writing,
So chic you hardly can read it.
What do you think?
Who can it be?
Even the ink—
No, here, let me.

(Opens the envelope, reads)

"Your presence—"
Just think of it, Petra!
"Is kindly—"
It's at a château!
"Requested—"
Et cetera, et cetera . . .
"Madame Leonora Armf—"
Oh, no!

A weekend in the country!

PETRA
We're invited?

ANNE
What a horrible plot!
A weekend in the country!

PETRA
I'm excited.

ANNE
No, you're not!

PETRA
A weekend in the country!
Just imagine!

ANNE
It's completely depraved.

PETRA
A weekend in the country!

ANNE
It's insulting!

PETRA
It's engraved.

ANNE
It's that woman,
It's that Armfeldt.

PETRA
Oh, the actress.

ANNE
No, the ghoul!
She may hope to
Make her charm felt,
But she's mad if she thinks I would be
    such a fool
As to weekend in the country!

PETRA
How insulting!

ANNE
And I've nothing to wear.

BOTH
A weekend in the country!

ANNE
(Hands the invitation back)

Here!
The last place I'm going is there!

(Fredrik's study)

Dominant on 24?

I I

Guess what — an invitation
Guess how —
This weekend — it's at a château
Is kindly requested, etc.

(22) wait there   III   But it's vicious
                                         Is delicious

                might be —
                If it's properly planned
                might be
                Understand!?

IV — 26 — That's one for you.   (61) They'd...

Ch-Wife: Uninvited, uninvited, uninvited, We should stay in Town!

Pste: A weekend (7x) Away from Town.

Fredrik: Are you sure you want to go? (2x) Are you sure you want to go away + leave
                                                        Go and leave town

Anne: A weekend (7x) Away from Town!

C-M: Charlotte, we're going 4x — Down!

H: Shallow, worldly people going, shallow people going out of Town.

PETRA
(To Fredrik)
Guess what, an invitation!

ANNE
Guess who, begins with an "A."
Armfeldt—is that a relation
To the decrepit Desiree?

PETRA
Guess when we're asked to go, sir—
See, sir, the date there?
Guess where—a fancy château, sir!

ANNE
Guess, too, who's lying in wait there,
Setting her traps,
Fixing her face—

FREDRIK
Darling,
Perhaps a change of pace . . .

ANNE
Oh, no!

FREDRIK
A weekend in the country
Would be charming,
And the air would be fresh.

ANNE
A weekend
With that woman . . .

FREDRIK
In the country!

ANNE
In the flesh!

FREDRIK
I've some business
With her mother.

PETRA
See, it's business!

ANNE
Oh, no doubt,
But the business with her mother
Would be hardly the business I'd
worry about.

FREDRIK, PETRA
Just a weekend in the country—

FREDRIK
Smelling jasmine—

ANNE
Watching little things grow.

FREDRIK, PETRA
A weekend in the country—

ANNE
Go!

FREDRIK
My darling, we'll simply say no.

ANNE
Oh.

(Charlotte and Anne having lunch)

ANNE
A weekend!

CHARLOTTE
How very amusing.

ANNE
A weekend!

CHARLOTTE
But also inept.

ANNE
A weekend!
Of course, we're refusing.

CHARLOTTE
Au contraire, you must accept.

ANNE
Oh, no!

CHARLOTTE
A weekend in the country—

ANNE
But it's frightful!

CHARLOTTE
No, you don't understand.
A weekend in the country
Is delightful
If it's planned.

Wear your hair down and a flower,
Don't use makeup,

Dress in white.
She'll grow older by the hour
And be hopelessly shattered by
    Saturday night.
Spend a weekend in the country.

ANNE
We'll accept it!

CHARLOTTE
I'd a feeling you would.

BOTH
A weekend in the country!

ANNE
Yes, it's only polite that we should.

CHARLOTTE
Good.

(The Malcolms' house)

CARL-MAGNUS
Well?

CHARLOTTE
I've an intriguing little social item.

CARL-MAGNUS
What?

CHARLOTTE
Out at the Armfeldt family manse.

CARL-MAGNUS
Well, what?

CHARLOTTE
Merely a weekend.
Still, I thought it might am-
Use you to know
Who's invited to go,
This time with his pants.

CARL-MAGNUS
You don't mean—!

CHARLOTTE
I'll give you three guesses.

CARL-MAGNUS
She wouldn't!

CHARLOTTE
Reduce it to two.

CARL-MAGNUS
It can't be—!

CHARLOTTE
It nevertheless is—

CARL-MAGNUS
Egerman!

CHARLOTTE
Right! Score one for you.

CARL-MAGNUS
Aha!

CHARLOTTE
Aha!

CARL-MAGNUS
(Slyly)
Aha!

CHARLOTTE
(Nervously)
Aha . . .

CARL-MAGNUS
A weekend in the country—
We should try it.

CHARLOTTE
How I wish we'd been asked.

CARL-MAGNUS
A weekend in the country,
Peace and quiet—

CHARLOTTE
We'll go masked.

CARL-MAGNUS
A weekend in the country—

CHARLOTTE
Uninvited—
They'll consider it odd.

CARL-MAGNUS
A weekend in the country—
I'm delighted!

CHARLOTTE
Oh, my God.

CARL-MAGNUS
And the shooting should be pleasant

If the weather's not too rough.
Happy Birthday, it's your present.

CHARLOTTE
But—

CARL-MAGNUS
You haven't been getting out nearly
enough,
And a weekend in the country—

CHARLOTTE
It's perverted!

CARL-MAGNUS
Pack my quiver and bow.

CHARLOTTE, CARL-MAGNUS
A weekend in the country!

CARL-MAGNUS
At exactly two thirty, we go.

CHARLOTTE
We can't.

CARL-MAGNUS
We shall.

CHARLOTTE
We shan't.

CARL-MAGNUS
I'm getting the car
And we're motoring down.

CHARLOTTE
Yes, I'm certain you are,
And I'm staying in town.

(Both households are seen
simultaneously)

CARL-MAGNUS	ANNE
Go and pack my suits!	We'll Go.

CHARLOTTE	PETRA
I won't!	Oh, good!

CARL-MAGNUS	ANNE
My boots! Pack everything I own That shoots.	We should. Pack Everything White.

CHARLOTTE	PETRA
No!	Ma'am, It's wonderful News.

CARL-MAGNUS	FREDRIK
Charlotte!	Are you sure it's All right?

CHARLOTTE	ANNE
I'm thinking it out.	We'd be rude to Refuse.

CARL-MAGNUS	FREDRIK
Charlotte!	Then we're off!

CHARLOTTE	PETRA
There's no need to Shout.	We are?

CARL-MAGNUS	FREDRIK
Charlotte!	We'll take the car.

CHARLOTTE	ALL THREE
All right, then!	We'll pack Champagne And caviar!

ALL
We're off on our way,
What a beautiful day
For a weekend in the country.
How amusing,
How delightfully droll.
A weekend in the country,
While we're losing
Our control.

A weekend in the country,
How enchanting
On the manicured lawns.
A weekend in the country
With the panting
And the yawns.

With the crickets and the pheasants
And the orchards and the hay,
With the servants and the peasants,
We'll be laying our plans
While we're playing croquet

For a weekend in the country,
So inactive that one has to lie down.
A weekend in the country where—

HENRIK
A weekend in the country,
The bees in their hives,
The shallow, worldly figures,
The frivolous lives.

The devil's companions
Know not whom they serve.
It might be instructive
To observe.

CARL-MAGNUS	FREDRIK	HENRIK
		A
Charlotte!	We're off!	Weekend

PETRA
We are?

CHARLOTTE	FREDRIK/ANNE	
I'm	We'll	
Thinking it out.	Take the car.	In the

CARL-MAGNUS	PETRA	
	We'll	Country,
Charlotte!	Bring champagne	The

CHARLOTTE		
There's	And	
No need to shout!	Caviar.	Bees in

CHARLOTTE, CARL-MAGNUS, PETRA, FREDRIK, ANNE
We're off and away;   Their hives.
What a beautiful day!

ALL, PLUS QUINTET

With riotous laughter   We'll be laying our plans
We quietly suffer   While we're playing croquet
The season in town,
Which is reason enough for   For a weekend in the country,
                                          So inactive that one has to lie down.
A weekend in the country!   A weekend in the country,
How amusing,   Where we're
How delightfully droll.   Twice as upset as in
A weekend in the country,   Twice as upset as in
While we're losing our control.   Twice as upset as in
                                          Twice as upset as in
A weekend in the country,   Town!
How enchanting
On the manicured lawns.
A weekend in the country,
With the panting
And the yawns.

With the crickets and the pheasants
And the orchards and the hay,
With the servants and the peasants,

about the reactions to Madame Armfeldt's invitation, preparing the audience for Act Two, in which all the parties would assemble at the château. It was my first experience at writing an extended number which was a small play in itself, involving action which takes place over a period of time. "Simple" in *Anyone Can Whistle* had also been an extended number embedded in the main plot, but it had no new incidents of its own, only a situation. I was worried that Hal wouldn't be able to change the sets as swiftly as I needed, but I gave him the plot—the schedule of events—and he showed me in the rehearsal hall how, with the use of screens, he could transport the characters from place to place almost instantaneously. Armed with this, I wrote freely and quickly. Although it was my first attempt to tell a story with motivations and complications within song form (as opposed to *recitative*), and I had such a good, if exhausting, time writing it that I did it again subsequently whenever I got the chance ("Chrysanthemum Tea" in *Pacific Overtures*, for example, and "God, That's Good!" in *Sweeney Todd*, as well as a number of songs in *Passion*).

For the movie version, I had no restraints, since the camera could cut from location to location in the blink of an eye* and the cuts could be punctuated dramatically with beats of music. I wrote a shot-by-shot breakdown of the sequence, which, to my delight, Hal followed meticulously (except for one section where I elected to use a split screen). Because the producer not unreasonably wanted the number shortened, it necessitated rewriting two choruses in the last third of the song, as follows:

This was one of five songs written during the five-week rehearsal period, which is as fast as I've ever written, especially considering that they included such a long and intricate piece. With no finale for the first act, Hal suggested that I write a mini-operetta

---

* When I was a clapper boy on the movie *Beat the Devil*, John Huston explained to me that cutting in film was nothing more than eye-blinking.

A Weekend
in the Country
(film version)

ALL
A weekend in the country,
Taking rambles,
Having leisurely chats.
A weekend in the country,
With the brambles
And the gnats.

A weekend in the country,
Full of craning
To see grouse in their nests.
A weekend in the country,
Entertaining
Other guests.

MADAME ARMFELDT
I'll receive them in the red room
And impress them with a feast,
Then retire to my bedroom
Where I'll manage to stay until
    Monday at least.

ALL
A weekend in the country,
Rising early
To go out and lie down.
A weekend in the country where . . .

And:

ALL
A weekend in the country!
A refresher
For the body and mind.
A weekend in the country,
With the pressure
Far behind.

A weekend in the country,
Gently gliding
Over manicured lawns.
A weekend in the country,
Gently hiding
All the yawns.

With the pheasants and the thickets
And the peasants mowing hay,
In the presence of the crickets,
We'll be laying our plans
While we're playing croquet

On a weekend in the country,
With umbrellas to avoid getting
    brown.
A weekend in the country
Where we're
Twice as upset as in
Twice as upset as in
Twice as upset as in
Town!

ACT TWO

*Before the curtain rises in front of
Madame Armfeldt's château, the Quintet
strolls on, singing about the dubious
charms of the endless daylight in Sweden's midsummer.*

Night Waltz I

MRS. ANDERSSEN
The sun sits low,
Diffusing its usual glow.
Five o'clock . . .
Twilight . . .
Vespers sound,
And it's six o'clock . . .
Twilight
All around . . .

ALL
But the sun sits low,
As low as it's going to go.

MR. ERLANSEN
Eight o'clock . . .

MR. LINDQUIST
Twilight . . .

WOMEN
How enthralling!

MR. ERLANSEN
It's nine o'clock . . .

MR. LINDQUIST
Twilight . . .

WOMEN
Slowly crawling
Towards

MR. ERLANSEN
Ten o'clock . . .

MR. LINDQUIST
Twilight . . .

WOMEN
Crickets calling . . .

ALL
The vespers ring,
The nightingale's waiting to sing.
The rest of us wait on a string.
Perpetual sunset
Is rather an unset-
Tling thing.

*(Madame Armfeldt, Desiree and
Fredrika are revealed on the lawn of the
château, being served Champagne by a
cadre of liveried servants)*

QUINTET
The sun won't set.
It's fruitless to hope or to fret.
It's dark as it's going to get.
The hands on the clock turn,
But don't sing a nocturne
Just yet.

*(The guests arrive: the Egerman family
with Petra and, unexpectedly, the
Malcolms. They all go into the house to
dress for dinner)*

Night Waltz II

MRS. NORDSTROM
The sun sits low
And the vespers ring.

MR. ERLANSEN
And the shadows grow
And the crickets sing,
And it's—

MRS. NORDSTROM
Look! Is that the moon?

MR. ERLANSEN
Yes.
What a lovely afternoon.

MRS. NORDSTROM
Yes.

MR. ERLANSEN
The evening air
Doesn't feel quite right

MRS, NORDSTROM
In the not-quite glare
Of the non-quite night,
And it's—
Wait! Is that a star?

MR. ERLANSEN
No.
Just the glow of a cigar.

MRS. NORDSTROM
Oh.

*(Anne and Charlotte plot to undermine
Fredrik's romantic attachment
to Desiree)*

MR. LINDQUIST
The atmosphere's becoming heady,
The ambience thrilling,

MRS. SEGSTROM
The spirit unsteady,
The flesh far too willing.

MR. LINDQUIST
To be perpetually ready
Is far from fulfilling.

MRS. SEGSTROM
But wait, the sun is dipping.

MR. LINDQUIST
Where? You're right. It's dropping.
Look! At last it's slipping.

MRS. SEGSTROM
Sorry, my mistake, it's stopping.

ALL
The light is pink
And the air is still,
And the sun is slinking
Behind the hill.
And when it finally sets,
As finally it must,
When finally it lets
The moon and stars adjust,
When finally we greet the dark
And we're breathing amen . . .

MRS. ANDERSSEN
Surprise of surprises,
It instantly rises
Again.

There was a third "Night Waltz,"
which I'm sorry we had to cut. but the
point had been made, and it was time
to get on with the story. It was sung
a cappella.

Night Waltz III (cut)

QUINTET
Crickets chuckling,
Twilight thickening,
Morals buckling,
Pulses quickening . . .
Not quite night yet,
But it might yet . . .

Sunlight trickling,
Daylight blackening,
Passions tickling,
Virtue slackening . . .
Not quite night out,
Put that light out.

In the thickets
Crickets thickening,
Night won't stick, it's
Slightly sickening.
Not quite light,
But not quite night.

*While waiting for dinner to be an-
nounced, Fredrik and Carl-Magnus find
themselves alone with each other on the
terrace outside the house.*

It Would Have Been Wonderful

FREDRIK
(To himself)
I should never have gone to the
     theater.
Then I'd never have come to the
     country.

If I never had come to the country,
Matters might have stayed as they
     were.

CARL-MAGNUS
(Stiffly, to Fredrik)
Sir . . .

FREDRIK
(Stiffly, to Carl-Magnus)
Sir . . .

(To himself)

If she'd only been faded,
If she'd only been fat,
If she'd only been jaded
And bursting with chat,
If she'd only been perfectly awful,
It would have been wonderful.
If . . . If . . .

If she'd been all a-twitter
Or elusively cold,
If she'd only been bitter,
Or better,
Looked passably old,
If she'd been covered with glitter
Or even been covered with mold,
It would have been wonderful.

But the woman was perfection,
To my deepest dismay.
Well, not quite perfection,
I'm sorry to say.
If the woman were perfection,
She would go away,
And that would be wonderful.

Sir . . .

CARL-MAGNUS
Sir . . .

(To himself)

If she'd only looked flustered
Or admitted the worst,
If she only had blustered
Or simpered or cursed,
If she weren't so awfully perfect,
It would have been wonderful.
If . . . If . . .

If she'd tried to be clever,
If she'd started to flinch,

If she'd cried or whatever
A woman would do in a pinch,
If I'd been certain she never
Again could be trusted an inch,
It would have been wonderful.

But the woman was perfection,
Not an action denied,
The kind of perfection
I cannot abide.
If the woman were perfection,
She'd have simply lied,
Which would have been wonderful.

FREDRIK
If she'd only been vicious . . .

CARL-MAGNUS
If she'd acted abused . . .

FREDRIK
Or a bit too delicious . . .

CARL-MAGNUS
Or been even slightly confused . . .

FREDRIK
If she had only been sulky,

CARL-MAGNUS
Or bristling,

FREDRIK
Or bulky,

CARL-MAGNUS
Or bruised,

BOTH
It would have been wonderful . . .

CARL-MAGNUS
If . . .

FREDRIK
If . . .
If she'd only been willful . . .

CARL-MAGNUS
If she only had fled . . .

FREDRIK
Or a little less skillful . . .

CARL-MAGNUS
Insulted, insisting . . .

FREDRIK
In bed . . .

CARL-MAGNUS
If she had only been fearful,

FREDRIK
Or married,

CARL-MAGNUS
Or tearful,

FREDRIK
Or dead,

BOTH
It would have been wonderful.

But the woman was perfection,
And the prospects are grim—
That lovely perfection
That nothing can dim.
Yes, the woman was perfection,
So I'm here with him . . .

CARL-MAGNUS
Sir . . .

FREDRIK
Sir . . .

BOTH
It would have been wonderful.

At this point in the first draft of the show, Anne and Henrik were seen simultaneously dressing for dinner in their rooms. The sound of Fredrika practicing her scales gave rise to the melody they sang.

Two Fairy Tales

(cut)

ANNE
Once upon a time—

HENRIK
Once upon a time—

ANNE
There lived a princess—

HENRIK
There lived a knight—

ANNE
Who was exceedingly beloved—

HENRIK
Who was devout—

ANNE
Who had a kingdom—

HENRIK
In a kingdom—

ANNE
Which was perfect—

HENRIK
Which was wretched—

ANNE
Which was carpeted with jewels.

HENRIK
Which was under someone's curse.

ANNE
She was beset—

BOTH
On every side—

HENRIK
It was beset—

ANNE
With handsome princes—

HENRIK
With giant trolls—

ANNE
And lesser nobles—

HENRIK
And with dragons—

ANNE
Bearing gifts and begging marriage.

HENRIK
Bringing famine.

ANNE
She would spurn them—

HENRIK
He would pray—

ANNE
And they would kill themselves in
    duels.

HENRIK
And it constantly got worse.
Of course, the knight was much
    inspired—

ANNE
But the princess soon grew tired—

HENRIK
By the misery at hand.

ANNE
Of all the fires she had fanned.

HENRIK
And as time went on—

ANNE
As time went on—

HENRIK
He thought—

ANNE
She thought,
"I must wed someone—

HENRIK
"I must do something—

BOTH
To alleviate the sorrow in the land."

ANNE
Now there were three—

HENRIK
There were three—

ANNE
Princes—

HENRIK
Dragons—

ANNE
In particular, named
Virtue—

HENRIK
Falsehood—

ANNE
Kindness—

HENRIK
Greed—

ANNE
And Excellence.

HENRIK
And Lust.

ANNE
But she could not—

HENRIK
He could not—

ANNE
Choose—

HENRIK
Refuse the call.

ANNE
At all.

HENRIK
He bade his wife—

ANNE
She bade the three appear.

HENRIK
Farewell, for go he must.
Then to the west—

ANNE
She got her wizard to suggest—

HENRIK
The knight set off upon his quest.

ANNE
A sort of test—

HENRIK
He bore his crest—

ANNE
At her behest.

HENRIK
As if possessed.

ANNE
The princely suitors did their best—

HENRIK
Nor did he rest.

ANNE
And who'd have guessed?

HENRIK
He was obsessed.

ANNE
All three were test-
Ed and they passed.

HENRIK
He found a priest—

ANNE
She was depressed—

HENRIK
He made a fast
And was confessed.

ANNE
To say the least.

HENRIK
He never ceased—

ANNE
But she got dressed—

HENRIK
Until at last
He had laid waste—

ANNE
And served a feast,
Where she was faced—

HENRIK
And turned to dust—

ANNE
With princes—

HENRIK
The Dragons—

ANNE
Virtue—

HENRIK
Falsehood—

ANNE
Kindness—

HENRIK
Greed—

ANNE
And Excellence.

HENRIK
And Lust.

ANNE
After many years—

HENRIK
After many years—

ANNE
The King, her father—

HENRIK
The noble knight—

ANNE
Who'd been abroad in search of
truth—

HENRIK
Who'd lost an arm—

ANNE
Returned to find—

HENRIK
Returned to find—

ANNE
The kingdom wretched—

HENRIK
The kingdom perfect—

ANNE
All activity suspended.

HENRIK
All activity resumed.

BOTH
To his dismay he also found—

ANNE
His daughter mad—

HENRIK
His wife had died—

ANNE
With indecision.

HENRIK
With the waiting,

ANNE
She had lapsed into a coma—

HENRIK
And his children—

ANNE
While her suitors—

HENRIK
Left alone—

ANNE
Had grown
Restless and offended.

HENRIK
Had been starving and were doomed.

ANNE
And so the King, to ease her sorrow—

HENRIK
So the court upon the morrow—

ANNE
Passed a curious decree—

HENRIK
Proclaimed a holiday to be.

ANNE
That she could marry all three suitors.

HENRIK
And the day was named for him.

ANNE
Did she feel guilty?

HENRIK
Did he feel guilty?

ANNE
No!

HENRIK
Oh, yes!

BOTH
And it was wonderful to see!

ANNE
So she lived—

HENRIK
So he lived—
Not for long—

ANNE
Ever after—

HENRIK
Ever watchful for—

ANNE
With Virtue—

HENRIK
Falsehood—

ANNE
Kindness—

HENRIK
Greed—

ANNE
And Excellence.

HENRIK
And Lust.

ANNE
That's a tale—

HENRIK
That's a tale—

ANNE	HENRIK
Which was read me	Which was read me
By my father—	By my mother—

BOTH
And there's
Probably a moral
To be pointedly discussed,
But it's always been my favorite,
And I read it when I'm gloomy,
And though fairy tales are foolish,
That's a fairy tale to trust.

**The song was cut for that perennial,
and best, reason: it interrupted the
flow of the story.**

*As the guests are ushered into the dining
room and seated at the table, the three
women in the Quintet comment, in ca-
nonic form.*

Perpetual Anticipation   Send in the Clowns

MRS. NORDSTROM

Perpetual anticipation
Is good for the soul
But it's bad for
The heart.
It's very good for
Practicing self-control.
It's very good for
Morals, but
Bad for morale.
It's very
Bad.
It can lead to
Going quite
Mad. It's very
Good for reserve and
Learning to
Do what one
Should. It's very
Good.
Perpetual anticipation's a
Delicate art:
Playing a role,
Aching to start,
Keeping control
While falling apart.
Perpetual anticipation
Is
Good for the
Soul but it's
Bad for the
Heart.

MRS. SEGSTROM

Perpetual anticipation
Is good for the soul
But it's
Bad for
The heart.
It's very good for
Practicing
Self-control.
It's very good for
Morals but
Bad for morale.
It's too unnerving.
It's very
Good, though, to
Have things to
Contemplate.

Perpetual anticipation's a
Delicate art:
Aching to start,
Keeping control
While falling apart.

Perpetual anticipation
Is
Good but it's
Bad for the
Heart.

MRS. ANDERSSEN

Perpetual anticipation
Is good
For the soul
But it's
Bad for the
Heart.
It's very good, though,
Learning to wait.

Perpetual anticipation's a
Delicate art:
Keeping control
While falling apart.

Perpetual anticipation
Is
Bad for the
Heart.

DESIREE

Isn't it rich?
Are we a pair?
Me here at last on the ground,
You in mid-air.
Send in the clowns.

Isn't it bliss?
Don't you approve?
One who keeps tearing around,
One who can't move.
Where are the clowns?
Send in the clowns.

Just when I'd stopped opening doors,
Finally knowing the one that I wanted
    was yours,
Making my entrance again with my
    usual flair,
Sure of my lines,
No one is there.

Don't you love farce?
My fault, I fear.
I thought that you'd want what I
    want.
Sorry, my dear.
But where are the clowns?
Quick, send in the clowns.
Don't bother, they're here.

(Fredrik apologizes ruefully and leaves)

Isn't it rich?
Isn't it queer,
Losing my timing this late
In my career?
And where are the clowns?
There ought to be clowns.
Well, maybe next year . . .

The refrain line I originally intended was:

Perpetual anticipation is good for the
    soul,
But it's bad for the skin.

I rarely change a lyric idea simply because of a collaborator's taste, but Hal disliked the line so intensely that I gave in. I'm sorry I did; the wry tone would have been just weird enough to enliven the mysteriousness of the moment.

Fredrik tells Desiree that he can't resume their affair, as he is too smitten with his childlike wife. She responds.

When we were casting Desiree, we knew we needed someone in early middle age, charming and seductive enough to make Fredrik think of cheating on, and perhaps even leaving, his beautiful and very young wife. She also had to be an actress capable of playing light comedy (Lonsdale, Pinero, Behrman or even in his less laborious moments, Coward), of which there were few practitioners still working on the stage, the tradition of light comedy having been all but replaced by the more forceful situation comedies of the Neil Simon school. With all those qualities necessary, we could hardly expect that whomever we cast would also be a strong singer, so I wrote the score to lean heavily on the voices of the other characters. In the event, we hired Glynis Johns, perhaps the only major British stage actress not associated with Shakespeare, and to our delighted surprise, she had a small but silvery voice that was musical and smokily pure. (I was a sucker for smoky female sounds, my favorite movie stars being Jean Arthur and Margaret Sullavan, although their voices were husky, whereas Glynis's was on the nasal side.) The song in this scene was supposed to be Fredrik's, since the action is his, the passive reaction being Desiree's, and I started to write one. But by design Desiree had only two songs in the first act, neither one a solo, and none in the second. During rehearsals, Hal called me to say that he thought this scene might be the ideal place for a solo for her and that he had directed it so that the thrust of the action came from her rather than from Fredrik. I went skeptically to see a rehearsal, and he had indeed accomplished what he had promised: the scene was now Desiree's.

I had tailored songs before to the talents and limitations of particular performers ("Everything's Coming Up Roses" for Merman, "The Ladies Who Lunch" for Stritch), so writing one for Glynis was not difficult. Her chief limitation was an inability to sustain a note; the breathiness that I loved was, ironically, her liability as a singer. The solution was to write short breathy phrases for her, which suggested to me that they should be questions rather than statements. Once I'd reached that conclusion, the song wrote effortlessly; I finished the first chorus that evening, played it for Hugh and Hal the following morning, got their approval and wrote the second chorus that night. The song sat so well in Glynis's voice that at the recording session, even though she'd never recorded a song

before, she did it perfectly in one take. I've heard it sung since by many fine singers (I'm happy to say), but to me her version is still the most satisfying.

Then again, when it comes to my own songs, I almost always prefer the original to every other stage and recording artist. I use "prefer" because it's a matter of emotion rather than judgment. The first performance of a song I've never heard before, whether my own or someone else's, tends to be not only the definitive one but also the one I want to live with. Deeply moving as Judi Dench's cello-voice performance of this song was in the British Royal National Theatre revival of the show, I'll always hear Glynis's flute. Barbara Cook singing "In Buddy's Eyes" is art-song quality of the highest order, but it's Dorothy Collins, who sang it in *Follies*, whom I hear when I think of it. Lee Remick was an actress first and a singer second, but her version of "Anyone Can Whistle" is the one I would take to the proverbial desert island. The notion that first love is the best can pertain not just to human relationships.

Why so many fine (and not so fine) singers have recorded "Send in the Clowns" is a mystery to me. Not that I don't think the song is eminently worth singing, but why this ballad of all the ones I've written? For two years after *A Little Night Music* opened, the only even faintly known vocalist who took an interest in it was Bobby Short, a singer and piano player who performed it in nightclubs, where it made no impression on even that tiny and dwindling audience. Then Judy Collins recorded it in England, where it incomprehensibly became a hit, after which Frank Sinatra's recording made it an even bigger one, and soon enough virtually everybody in the pop field climbed on the bandwagon. To this date, there are more than five hundred separate recordings of the song, and new ones pop up every month. It even won a Grammy Award as Song of the Year in 1975, amid rock and pop contenders—a song from a musical, no less. (It's the last one that did.) Granted, nobody knows what makes a hit. Once upon a time it was

the song, not the singer; then with the pop revolution and the rise of vocalists and groups who sang their own material it became the singer, not the song. Still, just as Cole Porter's name on a song didn't guarantee its success, neither did Frank Sinatra's or any other recording artist's, including the hottest groups today. The success of "Send in the Clowns" is still a mystery to me.

One of those fine singers who recorded it was Barbra Streisand, a performer who examines the lyrics she sings very carefully, and who questioned the dramatic connection between the two choruses (that is, the moment leading to the stanza that begins with the second iteration of "Isn't it rich?"). Without Fredrik's apology and departure in between, there is indeed an emotional gap, so when she asked me to write something that would accomplish the transition, it seemed a logical request rather than the whim of a diva. This is what I wrote:

What a surprise!
Who could foresee
I'd come to feel about you
What you felt about me?
Why only now when I see
That you've drifted away?
What a surprise . . .
What a cliché . . .

Frid, a butler of Madame Armfeldt's, invites Petra, the Egerman's maid, into the woods after dinner.

Silly People (cut)

FRID
Lie here with me on the grass.
Let the wind be our words
As the night smiles down.
Don't they know, don't they?
No, they don't, do they?
Silly people, silly people,
Silly people . . .

Voices glide by, let them pass.
Let them float in their words

Till they slowly drown.
Don't they know, don't they,
What they want?
Silly, silly people,
Patient and polite,
Crying in their teacups,
Shying from the night.

When now it smiles,
It smiles for lovers.
When next it smiles,
It smiles for fools.
The last it smiles
It smiles for them,
The others,
The rememberers,
The truly silly people.

Them . . .
And us . . .
And all . . .

Lie then with me, closer still.
You can float in my arms
Till we gently drown.
Don't they know, don't they,
What it means, dying?
Silly people, silly people . . .

Float and flow,
And down we go
To drown.

"Silly People" was cut in Boston because the audience neither knew nor cared about who Frid was and, as in the case of so many other songs in this volume, it impeded the flow of the story. This frequent problem is unfortunately not so apparent while a show is being written as one might expect. Often, it's only when the piece has been staged, particularly when it has been staged in front of an audience, that redundancies, superfluities, needless diversions and as other items Not Wanted on Voyage stand out with neon clarity. I have a pretty good internal censor which prevents bad songs from either being finished or escaping from my study, but wrong songs are another matter. Wrong songs take just as much time to write as right songs, and are frequently good ones, but they are often impossible to spot as wrong until you see them in performance. And

what a disappointment they are, *especially* when they're good.

One point in the lyric worth noting: the unfortunate juxtaposition of "lovers" and "others." When a musical parallel seems to call for a rhyme and either none is available or it would neaten the structure too much, the solution is to use two words which sonically have nothing to do with each other so that the ear doesn't register them as a near-miss. That had been (for me, anyhow) a problem with "Together Wherever We Go" in *Gypsy*, where at the end of the chorus "Together" and "Wherever" were sung slowly, sounding as if they *should* rhyme. In that case, the fogginess of the near-rhyme was partly mitigated by the two words coming together in the title, so that it seemed part of the fabric of the lyric. Here, the word "others" was the only word that I wanted to use, and I couldn't avoid the juxtaposition. Much as I like this song, the sound of "others" still makes the word a wrong choice.

After making love, with Frid asleep on the grass, Petra puts on her clothes and ruminates about her future.

The Miller's Son

PETRA
I shall marry the miller's son
Pin my hat on a nice piece of
    property.
Friday nights, for a bit of fun,
We'll go dancing.
Meanwhile . . .

It's a wink and a wiggle
And a giggle on the grass
And I'll trip the light fandango,
A pinch and a diddle
In the middle of what pass-
Es by.

It's a very short road
From the pinch and the punch
To the paunch and the pouch
And the pension.
It's a very short road

To the ten-thousandth lunch
And the belch and the grouch
And the sigh.

In the meanwhile,
There are mouths to be kissed
Before mouths to be fed,
And a lot in between
In the meanwhile.
And a girl ought to celebrate
What passes by.

Or I shall marry the businessman:
Five fat babies and lots of security.
Friday nights, if we think we can,
We'll go dancing.
Meanwhile . . .

It's a push and a fumble
And a tumble in the sheets
And I'll foot the Highland Fancy,
A dip in the butter
And a flutter with what meets
My eye.

It's a very short fetch
From the push and the whoop
To the squint and the stoop
And the mumble.
It's not much of a stretch
To the cribs and the croup
And the bosoms that droop
And go dry.

In the meanwhile,
There are mouths to be kissed
Before mouths to be fed,
And there's many a tryst
And there's many a bed
To be sampled and seen
In the meanwhile.
And a girl has to celebrate
What passes by.

Or I shall marry the Prince of Wales:
Pearls and servants and dressing for
    festivals.
Friday nights, with him all in tails,
We'll have dancing.
Meanwhile . . .

It's a rip in the bustle
And a rustle in the hay
And I'll pitch the Quick Fantastic,
With flings of confetti
And my petticoats away
Up high.

It's a very short way
From the fling that's for fun
To the thigh pressing un-
Der the table.
It's a very short day
Till you're stuck with just one
Or it has to be done
On the sly.

In the meanwhile,
There are mouths to be kissed
Before mouths to be fed,
And there's many a tryst
And there's many a bed.
There's a lot I'll have missed,
But I'll not have been dead
When I die!
And a person should celebrate
Everything passing by.

And I shall marry the miller's son.

Eventually, Anne and Henrik run off together, Charlotte and Carl-Magnus resolve their marriage, at least temporarily, and Fredrik and Desiree are reunited. Fredrik is lying prone on the lawn, having passed out due to plot complications; Desiree is kneeling next to him.

Send in the Clowns
(Reprise)

DESIREE
Isn't it rich?

FREDRIK
Are we a pair?
You here at last on the ground.

DESIREE
You in mid-air.
Was that a farce?

FREDRIK
My fault, I fear.

DESIREE
Me as a merry-go-round.

FREDRIK
Me as King Lear.
Make way for the clowns.

DESIREE
Applause for the clowns.

BOTH
They're finally here.

Five of the shows in this collection have been made into movies, only one of which found a satisfactory cinematic transposition: Tim Burton and John Logan's adaptation of *Sweeney Todd*. The others (*West Side Story, Gypsy, A Funny Thing Happened on the Way to the Forum* and *A Little Night Music*) used cinematic techniques such as rapid editing and cross-cutting—Richard Lester's version of *Forum* the most conspicuous of them—but they were essentially stage productions "opened up" in terms of setting and spectacle. The least successful in every way was *A Little Night Music*, and for good reason: it's at heart a leisurely and static show, two qualities movies find hard to deal with. A song like "You Must Meet My Wife" can last four minutes on a stage and hold an audience's attention through the emotional byplay of the lyric, by turns sweet and sour, but on the screen that byplay can be accomplished in two close-ups: Fredrik's rapture and Desiree's clear-eyed reaction. As a movie buff, I knew in advance that the film couldn't work without radical rethinking and tried to persuade Hal and Hugh not to attempt it, but to no avail. Hal in particular was determined that it could make an elegant and glamorous musical of the sort not seen since the days of Ernst Lubitsch and Rouben Mamoulian. In any event, it would have needed performers with silkier skills and a director whose heart was in the project. Hal's enthusiasm dissolved quickly when he started filming. After I'd returned home from London and Vienna, where we had prerecorded the score, he wrote me a letter in despair from Bavaria, where he was shooting, to say that with all the practical troubles that putting on a stage musical presented, in the theater he felt in control of what he was doing and not at the mercy of technicians and financiers. The loss of his usual fervent inventiveness showed on the screen: the movie was a sad and listless affair, and a waste of everyone's time.

As for the adaptation, the chief problem in the score was to find an equivalent for the Quintet, who served both narrative and commentary functions in the show, but who would have been a clumsily abstract presence in the movie. (This was the reason that Tim Burton cut the choral commentary in the film of *Sweeney Todd*, a wise choice.) The two numbers that were most affected by this change were the vocal Overture, which had set both style and content for the piece, and "The Glamorous Life." Here are my two solutions:

The film began with a theatrical performance of the show, which dissolved into reality, like Laurence Olivier's Henry V. *The opening number involved the same waltz that begins the show, the principals dancing and exchanging partners with one another, presaging the romantic complications to follow, but in the film they sang as they danced.*

Love Takes Time

PRINCIPALS
Love takes time,
Entirely too much, but sublime.
Frightening, love is,
Full of quicksand.
Enlightening, love is,
Full of tricks and

It does take time,
Which really is rather a crime.
Curious, love is,
Self-tormenting.
Embarrassing, love is,
Unrelenting.
A labyrinth, love is.
Just resenting

The time love takes
Compounds the confusion it makes.
One muddles the facts with the fakes.
And love is a lecture

On how to correct your
Mistakes.

(Individually)

What shall I wear?
Where is my parasol?
Do I compare?

(Overlapping)

Have I missed it?
Will I ever?
Did he notice?
What will they say?
Should I care?
How does one start it up again?
Why can't we stay just the way—?
Will I ever?
Was I ever?
Can I ever?

MADAME ARMFELDT
I have no questions.

OTHERS
Love comes first.
It matters the most at its worst.
You always feel underrehearsed.
One sets the conditions,
Then finds the positions reversed.

The time love takes
Awakens the heart that it breaks.
Consider the new friends it makes.
Yes, love is a lecture
On how to correct your
Mistakes.

(Individually, overlapping)

What shall I wear?
Where is my parasol?
Do I compare?
Would she dare?
Have I missed it?
Will I ever?
Did he notice?
What will they say?
Why should I bother?
Why should I care?
How can I start it?
Why can't we stay just the way—?
Will I ever—? Did I ever—? Can I
    ever—?

How shall I sleep? What am I doing?
Am I too cold?
Where shall we go? Where were you?
Are you so jealous?
Will she ever—? When does it start?
Where is my present?
Would she ever—? Did she ever?
Am I invited? Why did you stop?
What if I fail? How will I know? Was I
    too eager?

MADAME ARMFELDT
I have no time.

OTHERS
(Fading into the distance)
Who needs a haystack? How shall I
    cope?
Whom shall I ask?
Why did she smile? Will she
    remember?
Would you ever—?
Why are we laughing? What will he
    want?
Are you ever—? Do you ever—?
What does she want? Why are they
    laughing?
When will I learn?
Am I too late? Is it love? Is he
    unhappy?
Why did I say that? Is there time?
Am I too late? Have I the right?
What are the chances?
Will he remember? Will it be soon?
Am I too late?
What shall I wear? When do we start?
Should I approach her?
Is she alone? How to proceed?
Where is my parasol? . . .

As you can see, I finally was able to
utilize the idea of the first song I had
written for the show ("Numbers"),
proving that nothing is lost if you keep
your memory sharp and your archives
in order.

    The other song written for the
movie was an alternate version of
"The Glamorous Life," this one told
from Fredrika's point of view.

*The song begins with Fredrika practicing
scales at the spinet.*

The Glamorous Life
(film version)

FREDRIKA
Ordinary mothers lead ordinary lives:
Keep the house and sweep the parlor,
Mend the clothes and tend the
    children.
Ordinary mothers, like ordinary
    wives,
Make the beds and bake the pies
And wither on the vine—
Not mine.

*(She reads a postcard from her mother,
who is touring in a stock production of
Camille. During the following, we see
Desiree performing and taking bows in
front of provincial audiences, in ratty
dressing rooms, being received by local
dignitaries, traveling by rail to town
after town, exhausted,
always in chaos.)*

FREDRIKA (VOICE-OVER)
Dying by inches
Every night—
What a glamorous life!
Brought on by winches
To recite—
What a glamorous life!

Ordinary mothers never
Get the flowers
And ordinary mothers never
Know the joys,
But ordinary mothers couldn't
Cough for hours,
Maintaining their poise.

Sandwiches only,
But she eats
What she wants when she wants.
Sometimes it's lonely,
But she meets
Many handsome *gallants*.

Ordinary mothers don't live out of
    cases,
But ordinary mothers don't go
    different places,
Which ordinary mothers can't do,
Being mothers all day.
Mine's away in a play,
And she's realer than they . . .

What if her brooch is
Only glass
And her costumes unravel?
What if her coach is
Second class?
She at least gets to travel.

And sometime this summer, meaning
 soon,
She'll be traveling to me!
Sometime this summer, maybe June,
I'm the new place she'll see!

Ordinary daughters may think
Life is better
With ordinary mothers near them
When they choose,
But ordinary daughters seldom
Get a letter
Enclosing reviews!

Gay and resilient,
With applause—
What a glamorous life!
Speeches are brilliant,
If they're Shaw's—
What a glamorous life!

Ordinary mothers needn't meet
 committees,
But ordinary mothers don't get keys
 to cities.
No, ordinary mothers merely see their
 children all year,
Which is lovely, I hear,
But it does interfere
With the glamorous—

*(Cutting back to Fredrika, we see
Madame Armfeldt riding around her
estate in a liveried pony cart)*

I am the princess, guarded by
 dragons,
Snorting and grumbling and
 rumbling in wagons.
She's in her kingdom, wearing
 disguises,
Living a life that is full of surprises.
And sometime this summer,
She'll come galloping over the green!
Sometime this summer,
To the rescue, my mother the queen!

*(We cut back to Desiree and her play,
which has arrived in the town where the
Egermans live; Fredrik sees the poster for
Woman of the World.)*

FREDRIKA (VOICE-OVER)
(cont'd)

Ordinary mothers thrive on
Being private,
But ordinary mothers somehow
Can survive it,
And ordinary mothers never
Know they're just standing still,
With the kettles to fill,
While they're missing the thrill
Of the glamorous life!

When I was in my twenties, I made a number of short films with a Cine Kodak Special 16mm camera. I knew (and know) nothing about lighting and had no pictorial sense, but I loved editing. The film of *A Little Night Music* gave me my first professional chances. I worked out "The Glamorous Life" shot by shot as I wrote it, but the sequence was scheduled for the end of shooting and the producer ran out of money, so only its barest bones remain. The one other song for which I had a chance to write a detailed scenario was "A Weekend in the Country"; luckily, it was scheduled near the start of production, so it was filmed pretty much the way I laid it out. I like the puzzle aspect of writing songs specifically for film and TV, and had sporadic chances to do so again in *Evening Primrose* and *Dick Tracy*, but the greatest pleasure was to come with *Singing Out Loud*, a movie musical I wrote with William Goldman and which remains unproduced—which of course, may be part of the reason I like it so much.

The high point of my association with *A Little Night Music* occurred a year after we opened. I received a letter from Ingmar Bergman asking me to collaborate with him on an English-speaking film version of *The Merry Widow*. Not only did he want me to write lyrics for Lehár's score, he wanted me to help him with the script, as English was a second language for him. He sent me his first draft with profuse apologies for his English and, as you might expect, his language was more articulate, more elegant, more pointed and more surprising than the work of many screenwriters who claim English as their native tongue. I de-

murred that he needed no help on the script, but that I could do something with the lyrics, which I felt sure were not his. They were conventional in thought and stodgy in diction and were placed badly in the story. But he had done wonders with the familiar story, filling it with unexpected turns and changes of tone. He said he would like to come to New York to meet me, and I replied that I would be delighted but that I first wanted him to see *A Little Night Music*, which was still running on Broadway. I didn't want us to start a collaboration on the wrong foot, the foot being his horror at what we had done to his beautiful movie.

We met in his suite at the Sherry-Netherland hotel. I was seated by his assistant on a small sofa in the parlor and when he emerged from the bedroom and shook my hand with both of his, fixing me with a warm but probing eye and murmuring how pleased he was to meet me, I was hooked. His magnetism was so powerful that I would gladly have flung myself out the window and onto a Fifth Avenue bus if he had asked me. But business first. "Mr. Bergman, before we can even begin to talk about *The Merry Widow*, I have to know what you thought of the show, and please don't hesitate to tell me whatever you feel, as I have a very thick skin and I know our version is lightweight and doesn't begin to convey the depths of your movie and last night's performance was a little slow and Len Cariou had a cold and—" I'm sure I went babbling on a good deal longer, but he graciously cut me off. "No, no, Mr. Sondheim, please. I enjoyed the evening very much. Your piece has nothing to do with my movie, it merely has the same story." I thought: only someone with that understanding and generosity would realize, much less say, such a thing. And then came the kicker. "After all," he added, "we all eat from the same cake." I may have paraphrased his earlier sentences, but that last one is memorable and exact.

He continued, "I must admit I thought I was hallucinating for the first fifteen minutes. The actress playing Anne looked exactly like the girl on which I based the character." He followed this with (and again, I quote exactly): "As for that Hermione Gingold, she does tend to fuck the audience, doesn't she?" With that acute observation, I was ready to sign a contract on the spot, but, disappointingly, the film never went into production—Bergman couldn't get it financed.

Hal Prince has often said publicly, with some disdain, that our collaboration with Hugh on *A Little Night Music* was "all about having a hit." I disagree. Certainly, we both wanted a commercial success after the financial failure of *Follies*, but I think that Hal's lack of enthusiasm stems from two sources: first, the show wasn't daringly different enough, as *Company* and *Follies* had been, and second, *A Little Night Music* was a writer's piece rather than a director's—it lacked the chances for invention and spectacle called for by other musicals which he had directed. Nevertheless, despite his demurrer, I do think he had a good time bringing out the elegance and lightness of the show. It was an exercise in style, something both Hal and I like to do, and, with Hugh, we did it well.

Because of its operetta-like nature, *A Little Night Music* has had a life in opera houses. Its first three revivals in New York, in fact, were not on Broadway but at New York City Opera, where it fell under the purview of music critics, many of whom do not take well to this crossover from frivolous to serious art. One such reviewer was Peter G. Davis, the critic for *New York* magazine, who savaged the score roundly, claiming that Bergman would be disgusted by what I had done to his lovely movie. When I wrote him, asking him if he would be surprised to learn that Bergman had liked the show so much that he had asked me to collaborate with him, I suspect it will shock no one to learn that he didn't respond.

Yale Repertory Theatre

presents a comedy written in 405 B.C. by

Aristophanes

entitled

THE FROGS

freely adapted in 1974 A.D. by
Burt Shevelove

with music and lyrics by
Stephen Sondheim

The music has been orchestrated and supervised by
Jonathan Tunick

and the orchestra and chorus are directed by
Don Jennings

The scenery has been designed by
Michael H. Yeargan

the costumes by
Jeanne Button

and the lighting by
Carol M. Waaser

The words of William Shakespeare and Bernard Shaw have
been selected and arranged from their works by
Michael Feingold

The production has been choreographed by
Carmen de Lavallade

and staged by
Burt Shevelove

10. The Frogs (1974, revised in 2004)

Book by Burt Shevelove (1974)

Additional material by Nathan Lane (2004)

Based on The Frogs *by Aristophanes*

The Notion

The time is the present, the place is Ancient Greece. Dionysos, god of wine and drama, is in despair at the state of the world and decides that what it needs is a great dramatist to rouse mankind from its moral torpor. The writer he is passionate about is George Bernard Shaw, and he takes as his mission a journey to the Underworld to bring Shaw back from the dead and have him write more great plays on earth.

General Comments

The Groves of Academe are a dangerous place for producing theater. The inhabitants are isolated enough from reality that they can mistake pretension for depth and incompetence for art. I speak of the faculties, of course, the directors, producers and dramaturges, not the students, whose attraction to pretentiousness can be attributed to the fact that their tastes are still being formed and whose amateurishness can be chalked up to lack of experience. I speak in this particular case of the Yale Repertory Theatre in 1974, home to one of the few deeply unpleasant professional experiences I've had, largely because it was so unprofessional. The occasion was the first production of *The Frogs* (Burt's and mine, not Aristophanes'). The participants—performers, musicians, designers, students, most of the technicians—all did their jobs efficiently and sometimes even imagina-

tively, but to little avail: the producer was that worst of both worlds, the academic amateur. The result was a calamity, by which I mean not merely a failure of intent but a mess which, at the producer's insistence, was presented to a paying audience before it was ready to be seen. Even *A Funny Thing Happened on the Way to the Forum,* which almost closed out of town, had Jerome Robbins riding in on a white horse at the last minute to save it. No such luck with our other ancient comedy.

My connection with it can be traced to the presentation of a benefit in 1973 for both the American Musical and Dramatic Academy and the National Hemophilia Foundation: show business makes strange bedfellows, though if you think about it, there is a connection. In any case, three weeks before the event was to occur, I discovered that one of the presenters—another amateur, although not an academic—intended to demonstrate his creative powers by incorporating two dozen disparate songs from nine different shows into a book musical, with me as the central character. This instance of a producer with more ambition than ability should have prepared me for what was to come a year later, but, having obligated myself to the benefit and not wanting to deprive a lot of people with theatrical ambitions or blood disorders, I placed an emergency call to Burt Shevelove, who lived in London and whom I knew to be a first-rate organizer of such evenings. In the spirit of friendship, he agreed to come to New York and take charge, which he did, with two results: the benefit was a triumph, and I owed him a favor.

Less than a year later, he phoned me to call the favor in. He had been asked by the man running the Yale Repertory Theatre to revive a production of *The Frogs* in the spectacular version Burt had devised and directed in 1941, when he had been hired as supervisor of the Yale Dramatic Association. The show had been written (book, music and lyrics) by undergraduates and presented in and around the Olympic-size exhibition pool in the Payne Whitney Gymnasium at Yale. Burt assured me it would be fun for us to do: he would rewrite the book, and I would write half a dozen songs for it. Time was of the essence, he added, as we'd have only six weeks to concoct the thing, followed by four weeks of rehearsals plus a few previews in which to do more rewriting. After three shows in three years under commercial pressure, I thought it would be a lark: I fancied that Burt and I could wallow in Aristophanes' bawdry with no fear of offending Broadway tastes, we'd have the let's-put-on-a-show-by-Friday excitement of backstage musicals and I would have a chance to fiddle with the ritual and structural aspects of Greek comedy without fear of letting down investors or being criticized for "cerebral" songwriting. "All in the interest of education," I thought, and it wouldn't be reviewed—what a happy way to pay off a favor. So I said yes.

There was a pause on the other end of the phone, and then in a casual murmur (at least he tried to make it sound casual) Burt added that the person running the Yale Rep and overseeing the production would be Robert Brustein, a man respected by many, especially academics, as an astute critic,* essayist, translator, director, teacher and general pontificator about the theater. I replied that it was most unlikely that Brustein would want me, in view of the fact that as a critic he had been less than enthusiastic about my work. Burt was too smart for me to escape so easily: he cheerfully informed me that he had already taken it up with Brustein, and Brustein was delighted with the idea. To publicly denigrate someone's work and then invite him to write for you struck me as both arrogant and impractical—bad feeling doesn't make for good work most of the time, despite the relationship between Gilbert and Sullivan—but I still owed Burt one. Besides which, I kept telling myself, it was only college theater. Indeed, as I'd expected, the moment I met Brustein his condescension was palpable and I told Burt that I'd go ahead with the piece only on the condition that I never had to be in a meeting with Brustein. I knew about Brustein's arrogance; what I underestimated was his ambition.

The show, like its predecessor in 1941, was presented in and around the pool at the gym. The audience was seated on three sides, the stage proper being the fourth, and the orchestra was perched on bleachers above and to the side of the pool. Playgoers were greeted on entering by the sight of Charon, the River Styx ferryman, asleep in

a rowboat at one end of the pool, his eight-foot-long beard trailing in the water. The show featured a large cast, one of the perks of academe: eleven principals, six supernumeraries, twenty-two singers, eight dancers, twelve musicians and twenty-one Frogs, the latter all members of the medal-winning Yale swim team. A formidable group to manage and not a job for amateurs. Nevertheless, there were no dramatic catastrophes during the weeks of rehearsals, just a slow erosion of organization and confidence. Apart from the myriad minor problems of costume, scenery and lighting arising from a minuscule budget (efficiency would have helped), the major one was that of plotting rehearsal time and space for so many disparate forces, making certain that each element would be thoroughly ready to blend with every other element while at the same time working around class schedules and swimming practice. Scheduling matters were further complicated by Brustein having had the scenery built without fireproofing material, despite warnings from the technical staff that the Fire Department would come down heavily on us if they found out. Find out they did: the set had to be fireproofed at the last minute and we couldn't get into the gym for two of the three days prior to the opening. The result was chaos. We had been scheduled to have two dress rehearsals; we had none.

One hilarious, though dangerous, consequence was that no one foresaw the puddles of water that would form on the sides of the pool after the title number, which was a violent aquacade. The rest of the evening became a series of scenes and songs performed as a slow, slippery, tentative ballet of avoidance. Luckily, there were no bone-snapping pratfalls, but the pace of the show was hardly helped. And this was on opening night. With every department unprepared, we assumed that Brustein, the man at the helm, would postpone the opening so that we could run through the show at least once before a paying audience appeared, but, as I said, we hadn't reckoned with his ambition: without informing us, he had invited the New York critics to the opening, and they couldn't change their schedules. With a shock, I realized the major purpose of the exercise, the reason behind Brustein's inviting Burt to revive the piece and approving of me—whose work he loathed—to write the songs. Burt was much in demand at the time, having just written and directed the smash hit revival of *No, No, Nanette,* and I had had a number of successes and prestigious failures, and Mr. Brustein wanted Broadway's attention.

There are three dangerous classes of people in academic theater, and they sometimes overlap: department heads who want to be directors, directors who think they know how to improve plays, and dramaturges who know everything about plays and nothing about playwriting— that is, everything about the page and nothing about the stage. Brustein was a formidable combination of all three, but at least he didn't try to "improve" the piece, as many

---

*A surprising valuation, if his review of *A Funny Thing Happened on the Way to the Forum* in *The New Republic* is any example: every instance of brilliant staging he attributed to George Abbott was the work of Jerome Robbins. In fairness, not being able to differentiate among the contributions of actors, directors and choreographers is common to most reviewers, not just Brustein. But most reviewers don't apply their ignorance to producing.

of his counterparts in the Grove are wont to do. Musicals, not being "serious" theater in their eyes, are a prime target of improvement, especially those which have been commercial failures. Nothing attracts theorists and pontificators like the chance to improve "flops." They don't change *Oklahoma!* or *My Fair Lady* much (although I wouldn't put it past them to do a little cutting and rerouting of scenes and numbers), but shows like *Company,* which was a very moderate hit, or *Merrily We Roll Along,* which closed in two weeks, are regarded as wounded animals in need of ministrations. Thus, one university production of *Merrily We Roll Along,* a show that unfolds backward in time, was played in reverse; one of *Company* ended with Bobby shooting himself; a completist version of *A Little Night Music* restored all the cut numbers, thus turning a leisurely show into a soporific one. The list is long and continuing.* This kind of arrogance is not exclusive to academe, of course: it is rife in regional theaters, many of which operate with the same cavalier attitude toward plays and musicals that universities do, allowing, even encouraging, their directors to "improve" the work. These directors are just as cocooned as the academics; in their serenity they think they know how to fix the Little Shows That Couldn't, and they relentlessly do so, cutting and rearranging with great pride. It makes them feel creative, as if they were writers. A lot of unwitting audiences have gone home from these evenings misled into thinking that what they've seen is the work of the authors whose names are printed in the program. I've often wondered how any of these directors would feel if an author restaged their work, maybe recast a couple of roles, changed the look of the scenery a bit, relit a few moments, restaged some of the action and so forth, and then signed the director's name to it in big bold letters on the front of the program (directors always demand big billing). Actually, I haven't wondered; I know.

As for *The Frogs,* despite its botched birth, it was received rather kindly by both press and public, and it improved considerably during its second and final week, when Burt and I had a chance to tinker with the writing as well as the reverberant acoustics which made the orchestra sound as if it had been piped in from a neighboring tunnel, and Burt had a chance to pull the troops together. Neither of us spoke publicly about the ineptitude of the production process; we finished our work, licked our wounds, packed up our things and went home, only to find that Mr. Brustein had written an

article for *The New York Times,* commenting on the difficulty of revivifying the classics while having to deal with "Broadway" types like Burt and me. He justified this judgment with the observation that we had invited a dozen or so friends to come to the opening and had hired a van to bring them, which he found very "Broadway"—an odd statement from the man who had invited all the New York critics. This, of course, was meant to cement his reputation as a Cerberus of the arts while publicly lamenting the necessity of a partnership with the grubby forces of commercialism and simultaneously getting his name in the papers again.

Universities and schools are the most important bastion of keeping theater alive today, though less and less each year—the arts programs are always the first to be cut in any institutional budget reappraisals. Theater serves education just as much as education serves theater, in that it supplies both a playful (pun intended) window to the arts and a means of emphasizing community in creative activity. The shared experience of a cast of performers and an audience of strangers mutually experiencing a story, a laugh, a surprise, occasionally even a catharsis, and knowing unconsciously that the performance they're seeing is a unique one never to be duplicated exactly again, has implications beyond the auditorium walls. I love education, and teachers have saved my life emotionally and intellectually on more than one occasion, but the teaching of art, especially theater, tends to be hidebound and stultifying as scholarship and dangerously fulfilling to the teacher's ego as an exercise in aesthetics. Arts education handily fosters little fiefdoms like Brustein's that function as ego-builders and often serve primarily to make their practitioners feel like playwrights or producers or directors or critics—which occasionally they have been or become. If my experience at Yale is any example, they also want to be stars.

In 2000, Nathan Lane played Dionysos in a concert version of the show under the auspices of the Library of Congress and became intrigued by the notion of transforming the piece into a full-length musical. To this end, he expanded the book, persuaded me to write additional songs and brought in Susan Stroman to supervise, direct and choreograph the production. It was presented at Lincoln Center in 2004 and, although it had many funny and effective moments in both dialogue and staging, it suffered from inflation. In Aristophanes' and Burt's hands, it had been an hour and a half long; it should have stayed that way.

---

*Such depredations are illegal, of course, but the depredators know that by the time the authors find out what they've done, the productions can't be stopped—because they've closed. This is the one good thing about these ventures: the shows have short runs.

ACT ONE

Dinoysos and his slave, Xanthias, enter in front of the curtain and pray to the gods.

Prologos:* Invocation and Instructions to the Audience (1974, 2004)

DIONYSOS
(To the heavens)
Gods of the theater, smile on us.[†]

XANTHIAS
You who sit up there stern in
    judgment,
Smile on us.

DIONYSOS
You who look down on actors . . .

XANTHIAS
. . . And who doesn't?

BOTH
Bless this yearly festival and smile
    on us.

DIONYSOS
We offer you song and dance.

XANTHIAS
We offer you rites and revels.

BOTH
We offer you grace and beauty.
Smile on us for this while.

DIONYSOS
(To the audience)
Gods of the theater, smile on us.

XANTHIAS
You who sit out there stern in
    judgment,
Smile on us.

DIONYSOS
We offer you song and dance.

XANTHIAS
We offer you gods and heroes.
We offer you rites and revels.
We offer you paeans and pageants.
We offer you jokes and insults.
Bacchanales and social comment.

BOTH
Bless our play and smile.

DIONYSOS
Yes, but first,
Some do's and don'ts,
Mostly don'ts:

Please don't cough,
It tends to throw the actors off.
Have some respect for Aristophanes
And please,
Don't cough.

Please don't swim—
The theater is a temple, not a gym.
Apart from being perilous to life and
    limb,
We may be in the middle of a sacred
    hymn,
So please,
Don't swim.[‡]

If you see flaws, please,[§]
No loud guffaws, please,
Only because, please,
There are politer ways.

As for applause, please,
When there's a pause, please,
Although we welcome praise,
The echo sometimes lasts for days . . .

CHORUS
Days . . . Days . . . Days . . . Days . . .
    Days . . .

*(Dionysos starts to continue,
but the echo repeats)*

Days . . . Days . . . Days . . . Days . . .
    Days . . .

(Dionysos waits, then resumes)

DIONYSOS
Don't take notes
To show us all you know the famous
    quotes.
And when you disapprove, don't clear
    your throats
Or throw your crumpled programs,
    coins and coats,
Or anything that splatters, stains, or
    floats,**
And please,
No grass.
This is a classic, not a class.[††]

If we should get rhetorical,
Please don't curse.
Wait till it's allegorical,
And in verse!

---

*See the commentary at the end of the song.

[†]If this Invocation seems familiar, it's because you read it in the chapter about *A Funny Thing Happened on the Way to the Forum* as part of the song "Forget War."

[‡]When performed on dry land and not at a university, the lyric is adjusted:

> *Please don't squeak.*
> *We haven't oiled the seats all week.*
> *You wouldn't want to miss a single word of Greek,*
> *It's hard enough for us to hear each other speak—*
> *So please,*
> *Don't squeak.*

[§]For the 2004 production, I brought this section up to date:

> DIONYSOS
> *If you see flaws, please,*
> *Don't drop your jaws, please.*
> *No loud guffaws, please,*
> *When actors enter late.*

> XANTHIAS
> *When there's a pause, please,*
> *Lots of applause, please.*
> *And we'd appreciate*
> *You turning off your cell phones while we wait . . .*

**dry-land lyric:

> *Or tell your neighbor scintillating anecdotes . . .*

[††]dry-land theater (vs. school) lyric:

> *Don't go "Oh,"*
> *Each time you see an actor that you know.*
> *And if you have to use the lounge below,*
> *Don't wait until we're halfway through the show,*
> *Especially if you're sitting in the middle of the row.*

> XANTHIAS
> *And please, no chow—*

> BOTH
> *Unwrap those candy wrappers now.*

If we should get satirical,
Don't take it wrong.
And if, by a sudden miracle,
A tune should appear that's lyrical,
Don't hum along.

When we are waxing humorous,
Please don't wane.
The jokes are obscure but
   numerous—
We'll explain.

When we are waxing serious,
Try not to laugh.
It starts when we get imperious,
And if you're in doubt, don't
   query us,
We'll signal you when we're serious
(It's in the second half).

CHORUS
(Echoing)
Half . . . Half . . . Half . . . Half . . .

DIONYSOS
But first . . .
Please, don't strip.

It's hot but it's a pleasure trip.
The author might have been
   Euripides,
So please,
Don't strip.*

Don't say "What?"
To every line you think you
   haven't got.
And if you're in a snit
Because you've missed the plot,
(Of which I must admit
There's not an awful lot),
Still don't
Say, "What?"

XANTHIAS
   What?

*(Dionysos shoots him a look, then
continues to the audience)*

DIONYSOS
Do not intrude, please,
When someone's nude, please.
She's there for mood, please,
And mustn't be embraced.†

If we are crude, please,
Don't sit and brood, please.
Let's not be too straitlaced—
The author's reputation isn't based
On taste.

So please don't fart,
There's very little air and this is art.
And should we get offensive, don't
   lose heart,
Pretend it's just the playwright being
   smart.
Eventually we'll get to the catharsis,
   then depart.

And now . . .
But first—

*(A sound of thunder—the gods are
getting impatient. Dionysos looks up,
terrified, then sings meekly.)*

DIONYSOS
We start.

Traditional Greek comedy had a fairly
rigid set of structural conventions,
which I paraphrased dutifully for the
songs of the 1974 production. The
first of them, the *Prologos*, functions
much as you might expect, as a pref-
ace introducing the protagonist. Aris-
tophanic prologues were full of verbal
and sometimes vulgar humor. Other
structural pillars will be footnoted as
we travel along.

---

*Dionysos, accompanied by a reluctant
Xanthias, sets out for the Underworld,
the Chorus providing an overview of their
journey.*

I Love to Travel
(1974, extended 2004)

CHORUS
Walk walk trudge trudge
Slog slog travel travel
March march trudge trudge
Slog slog travel travel
Lumber lumber plod plod
Shuffle shuffle talk . . .

*(Dionysos and Xanthias stop and chat
for a moment, then resume walking)*

Walk walk trudge plod
Tramp slog stretch . . .

*(Dionysos and Xanthias stop and stretch
elaborately, then resume walking)*

CHORUS
March march trudge plod
Tramp slog stumble stumble
Trek trek trudge plod
Tramp slog grumble grumble . . .

DIONYSOS
I love to travel—

CHORUS
Walk trudge sweat . . .

DIONYSOS
—Don't you?

CHORUS
Plod tramp sweat . . .

DIONYSOS
I love a change of pace,
I love a change of space.
I love to see a place
That's absolutely new.

CHORUS
Sweat . . .

DIONYSOS
I love to travel—

---

*Alternately:

   *Please don't leave,
   It only makes the actors grieve.
   We may have something better up our sleeve,
   So please,
   Don't leave.*

†Alternately:

   *Do not throw food, please,
   Till we conclude, please.
   Do not allude, please,
   To "talent gone to waste."*

CHORUS

Bump . . .

DIONYSOS

Don't you?

CHORUS

Limp . . .

DIONYSOS

Of course you do.

CHORUS

Pant Pant Puff Puff
Drip Drip Dawdle Dawdle . . .

DIONYSOS

I love to travel,
It's true.
I love a change of venue,
A change of menu,
The feeling when you
Meet with something strange.

CHORUS

Slog . . .

DIONYSOS

I love to travel.

CHORUS

Slog . . .

DIONYSOS

I love a challenge.

CHORUS

Slog . . .

DIONYSOS

I love change.

CHORUS

Puff puff drip drip
Slip fall
Kvetch . . .

*(They stop again, while Xanthias
complains, then resume walking)*

CHORUS

Mud dirt thorns vines
Sand rock gravel gravel . . .

XANTHIAS

I hate to travel.
I hate to even leave the house.

I hate the change of air,
I hate the getting there.
I hate to pack and all of that,
I hate to change my habitat,
I hate to not know where I'm going,
Then to not know where I'm at.
I hate the—

CHORUS

Swamp slush rain fog
Gnats wasps snakes mosquitoes . . .

XANTHIAS

Who needs to travel?
I say to leave the world alone.
It may unravel,
But it's the mess we've always known.

All right, okay, it isn't perfect,
Still it's perfectly okay.
And if it's gonna go to hell,
Then let it.
Why should I as well?
Forget it.
First I had the grippe,

*(He starts to buck-and-wing his
way offstage)*

Then trouble with my hip,
Now I have blisters on my lip,
This trip is giving me the pip—

DIONYSOS
(As Xanthias reaches the wing)
You can stop rhyming right there.

(They resume walking)

CHORUS

Trek trek jog jog
Limp limp climb . . .

DIONYSOS
(A bit dismayed)
Climb?

CHORUS

Pant pant puff puff
Wheeze grunt complain
Pant pant puff puff
Wheze grunt grunt curse
Stagger stagger lurch lurch
Stagger stagger
Squoosh . . .

DIONYSOS

Squoosh?

(Looks at the sole of his sandal)

Yuk.

CHORUS

March march trudge trudge
Slog slog travel travel . . .

DIONYSOS

I love to travel—

XANTHIAS

Who needs to travel?

DIONYSOS

You, too.

XANTHIAS

I do?

DIONYSOS

Don't you just love a change?
You've gotta love a change,
You've gotta love it or I'll turn you
     into something very strange . . .

(A beat, as Xanthias takes this in)

BOTH

I love to travel!

DIONYSOS

What joy!

XANTHIAS

Oh, boy!

DIONYSOS

If it's exotic,
It's erotic,
And that's all I have to say.
I love to travel!
Don't you?

XANTHIAS

I do!

DIONYSOS

Okay!

*Dionysos and Xanthias arrive at the
House of Herakles (Hercules), a giant of a
man, dressed in the skin of a lion he has
killed. He gives Dionysos advice on how
to handle himself in the Underworld.*

Dress Big (2004)

HERAKLES
You gotta dress big,
Dress bold,
Dress large.
You gotta look forceful
And resourceful
And in charge.

You wanna dress mean,
Not clean—
Aggressive.

(Flexes his muscles)

DIONYSOS
Very impressive.

HERAKLES
Gotta dress massive,
Not passive.

DIONYSOS
Very imprassive.

HERAKLES
Gotta dress fierce
And raw
And hairy,
More than just prominent,
Predominantly
Scary.

It's not the real you, I guarantee you,
That'll see you
Through this gig.
It's the rig,
You dig?
Dress big!

It isn't enough
To be
A god.
You gotta convey it
With a deity's
Façade.
A god should look godlike,
With a bod like—
Well, like mine.

DIONYSOS
You're the meaning of divine.

HERAKLES
So then that's who you'll be.

DIONYSOS
What's who I'll be?

HERAKLES
You'll pretend to be me.

(Starts removing his lion skin)

DIONYSOS
Not in a million years.

HERAKLES
You flaunt a few furs,
You drape a few skins,
You hang a few pelts.

DIONYSOS
(Helpfully, gesturing to his outfit)
I have this in sable—

HERAKLES
Takes more than a mink
To make people think
You're somebody else.

You gotta wear everything you've
    killed,
Which oughta help cover up your
    build.

(Holding the lion skin up)

Just let 'em see this, boy, they'll be
    chilled.
Not to say thrilled . . .

*(He hands Dionysos the lion skin;
Dionysos keeps straightening the skin,
adjusting the drape, wetting his finger to
wipe out the blood spots, etc., while
Herakles keeps trying to make it look
more barbaric.)*

HERAKLES
You gotta look messy,
Not saucy,
Less dressy.
More bossy.
Be mussy,
Not glossy.

(Dionysos smoothes out a wrinkle)

Too fussy.

(Dionysos tilts the head forward rakishly)

Too Fosse.

(He adjusts the head)

You don't walk, you stride.
You don't amble, you don't sidle.
You remind them you're an idol.
You don't talk, you growl.
You don't mutter things, you roar 'em.
As for matters of decorum,
Ignore 'em.

You gotta act big
And loud
And rough.

DIONYSOS
You sure that's enough?

HERAKLES
As long as you swear a lot
And wear a lot
Of stuff.

DIONYSOS
(Not very convincingly)
Damn. Fooey.

HERAKLES
You gotta speak firmer—

DIONYSOS
*(Lowering his voice and stamping
his foot)*
Damn! Fooey!

HERAKLES
Don't murmur—

DIONYSOS
(Growing in volume)
Damn! Fooey!

HERAKLES
Don't mumble—

(Growling)
Rumble—

(Dionysos roars like a lion)

HERAKLES
By George, he's got it!

HERAKLES, XANTHIAS
(To Dionysos)
I think you've got it!

DIONYSOS
(Menacingly, to Herakles)
You talkin' to me? You talkin' to me?!

(He punches Herakles square in
the stomach)

HERAKLES
That's it, now glower—

DIONYSOS
Butt out!

HERAKLES
—To show your power.

DIONYSOS
So's your old man!

HERAKLES
Watch how they cower
As your power
Starts to flower.

DIONYSOS
Stick it in your ear!

HERAKLES
What you'll discover
Is that people think the cover
Is the book.
It's all in the look.

(Dionysos looks menacingly out at the
audience and breathes heavily)

HERAKLES
You gotta start acting like an oak,
Not like a twig!

DIONYSOS
(Thunderously amplified)
Blow it out your ass!

HERAKLES
Walk tall!
Stand proud!
Look fierce!
Talk loud,
Dress big!

Dionysos and Xanthias come to the River
Styx. Charon, the ferryman, waits in his
boat. He rings a bell.

All Aboard! (2004)

CHARON
All aboard!
Hades express!
Nonstop,
Just a short hop
To the bottomless pit—
This is it!

All aboard!
Club Dead
Straight ahead!
Bring your shroud,
No coffins allowed—
There's too big a crowd.

But if you're a stiff,
Then get in the skiff
And we're off to perdition.
And wait till you see perdition:

You think you know dank?
Hoo, boy.
You think you know dismal?
Sheesh, forget it.
Talk about dark,
Talk about dreary,
What you think is dreary
Is what we call cheery
Down here on the River Styx.

All aboard!
No delay,
Long as you're D.O.A.

If you fell off of the perch,
If you bought the farm,
Kicked the bucket,
Bit the dust,
All aboard!
You're going down
To that toddling town—
And I do mean *down* . . .

*During the voyage, Dionysos reminisces
to Xanthias about his wife.*

Ariadne (2004)

DIONYSOS
She was young, she was wild,
Ariadne . . .
She was shy, like a child,
Had this sort of dimple when she
smiled,
Lips as soft as petals,
Hair the color of the sun,
Breasts—

XANTHIAS
I get your point.

DIONYSOS
—And eyes that looked at me as if I
were a god!
Which I am.

Being young, feeling odd,
I mean, when you're married to a god,
Mingling with the likes of
Zeus and Hera, Aphrodite
And Apollo, not to mention
Demeter, that bitch—

XANTHIAS
I get your point.

DIONYSOS
So I gave her a crown
On the day we were wed.
"If you look like a goddess,
You'll feel like a goddess,"
I said.
"Ariadne! . . ."

And the years filled with joy
And my heart filled with pride,
Just to know Ariadne was there at my
side.
Then she died.
Being mortal, she died . . .

She was young, she was shy,
Ariadne . . .
She was young, as was I,
Surely, she was much too young
to die.
So I flung her crown high into
the sky,
In a rage,
With a cry:
"Ariadne! . . . Ariadne! . . ."

And its jewels broke free
And they never came down,
But they stayed there as stars
In the shape of a crown.

And they're there every night
As a sign of our love,
And it fills me with joy
And it fills me with pain.
It reminds me of how much I miss
   her and want her
And wish every day she were here.

(Looking up)

There are no stars in Hell.
Just as well . . .

Ariadne . . . Ariadne . . . Ariadne . . .

The ferry trip is interrupted by the Frogs,
who try to overturn the boat and abort
Dionysos's mission, nearly drowning him
in the process.

Parados:* The Frogs

(1974, 2004)

CHORUS
Brek-kek-kek-kek!

DIONYSOS
What's that?

CHARON
That?

CHORUS
Brek-kek-kek-kek!

DIONYSOS
That!

CHARON
Oh, that . . . That's frogs.

CHORUS
Whaddaya think it is, mice?
Well, dummy, think twice!
Brek-kek-kek-kek-kek-kek!
Ko-ax! Ko-ax!

What have eyes that pop?
What have skins that glisten?
What have feet that plop?
Elephants?
No, listen:

Brek-kek-kek-kek-kek-kek-kek-
   kek-kek!†
Ko-ax!
Rib-et rib-et!
Brek-kek-kek-kek-kek-kek-kek-
   kek-kek!
Right!

Frogs!
We're the frogs,
The adorable frogs!
Not your hoity-toity intellectuals,
Not your hippy-dippy homosexuals,
Just your easygoing, simple,
Warmhearted, cold-blooded
Frogs
Of the pond
And the fronds we never go beyond.
When you rearrange a single frond,
We respond
With a

Brek-kek-kek-kek! Brek-kek-kek-kek!
Whaddaya care the world's a wreck?
Leave 'em alone, send 'em a check,
Sit in the sun and what the heck,
Whaddaya wanna break your neck
For? What for?
Big deal!
Big bore!

Forget your troubles,‡
Wallow with us,

---

†The lyric has been abridged slightly, to avoid
repetitions which are effective when sung but
tedious when read. Also, and again for reading purposes, I have incorporated some
verses from the 2004 version.

‡The lyrics in this section overlap in choral
chaos.

Squat and take a mud bath!
What's it get you,
Making a fuss?
Just another bloodbath!
Aw!
Boo-hoo!
Oh, pshaw!
What's new?
We seen it,
We heard it,
We been there,
We know it already.
Row, row, row your boat
Gently down the stream,
Merrily, merrily, merrily, merrily,
Life is but a scream.

You and he, you sweat and strain,
Bodies all achin' an' racked wid pain.
Tote dat barge an' lift dat crud!
You gets a little drunk an' you lands
   in mud!

Who cares
If the sky
Cares to fall
In the swamp?

Bull-frog! Bull-frog!
Squat squat squat!
E-li—!
Whaddaya get, stirring the pot?
Wouldn't you rather blink and squat?
Everything's gonna stay afloat,
As long as you don't rock the boat.

Be-de-de-beep, be-de-de-beep,
Leave it alone and go to sleep.
Leave it alone, you're in too deep.
You gotta look before you leap.
And nothing and nobody knows how
   to leap more!
And who in the world are you saving
   the world for?

For the frogs!
For the frogs!
For the bumps on the logs!
Not for fancy-pants humanitarians,
Not for chatty platitudinarians,
But for easygoing, simple, jocular,
Ocular
Frogs,
Who can thrive
Just by staying friendly and alive.
When there's any trouble, we survive,

---

*The *parados* is the song sung by the Chorus
on its first entrance. The Chorus presents
itself in the character chosen for it by the poet
(Wasps, Birds, Frogs, Women of Athens, Initi-
ates, etc.).

Frogs!

We're the frogs!

We're the crème de la crème

Of the frogs

Not your phony intellectuals

Not your radical homosexuals

Just your easy-going unaffectuals

Not your high-falutin elocutionists

Not your ... revolutionists

Don't get mad

Why not dive and go ...

We just dive
And go

Breb-bleb-bleb-bleb!
Breb-bleb-bleb-bleb-bleb-bleb-bleb-
    bleb-bleb!
Blo-ax!
Blib-et!

What have arms that flail?
What have teeth that glisten?
What have hopes that fail?
Elephants?
No, listen!
Listen! Listen! Listen:

Brek-kek-kek-kek-kek-kek-kek-
    kek-kek!
Ko-ax! Rib-et rib-et!

Stay with the frogs.
With the frogs,
With the wits of the bogs!
Not your hippy-dippy
    insurrectionists,
Not your hasty pasty-faced
    perfectionists,
With the easygoing, simple,
    rollicking,
Frolicking
Frogs
In the reeds.
Leave the world alone and count the
    weeds.
While the world may not know what
    it needs,
It proceeds,
And in time
Will be
Sublime:
All bogs
And weeds
And frogs,
And beautiful slime.

Brek-kek-kek-kek-kek-kek-
Kek-kek-kek-kek-kek-kek!
Ko-ax!

This song may seem inordinately long, but it accompanied a ten-minute aquatic ballet in which the Frogs unsuccessfully tried to wreck Charon's boat and eventually slunk back into their watery homes, defeated. As a

large-scale choral piece, it was also something of a mess, due partly to the hyperreverberant qualities of the gymnasium, but its imperfections were thankfully drowned out by the happy splashing of the Yale swimming team. In the 2004 production, which took place on terra firma, the Frogs additionally tried to change Dionysos into one of their own. And the song sounded a lot better.

Having landed safely, Dionysos, disguised as Herakles and still accompanied by Xanthias, searches for the palace of Pluto, king of the Underworld. He comes upon a group of Dionysos-worshippers in a sacred grove and stops delightedly to eavesdrop.

Hymnos:* Hymn to Dionysos (1974, 2004)

DIONYSIANS

Dionysos,
We are come to praise you
For the wondrous blessing, the taste
    of wine.
Evoe!
Alalai! Alalai!
Evoe!
Alalalalalalalai!

Out of wine comes truth,
Out of truth the vision clears,
And with vision soon appears
A grand design.
From the grand design
We can understand the world.
And when you understand the world,
You need a lot more wine!

Dionysos,
We are come to join you
In a shout of joy at the only shrine
Where you come benighted and leave
    benign.

---

*A *hymnos* is a song of praise or joy to heroes or gods.

For that endless blessing, the taste of
    wine,
Evoe!
Alalai! Alalai!
Evoe!
Alalalalalalai!

Wine makes the passions sing,
Wine leads the feet to dance,
Wine answers every question.
Pour the wine!
Wine takes away the sting,
Wine gives the heart its chance,
Wine aids the indigestion.
Pour the wine!

See the curmudgeon smile,
Hear the insomniac snore,
Look at the coward roar,
All from wine.
Pour the wine!
Wine lends a sense of style,
Wine gets the spirit to soar,
Wine makes you thirsty—pour
More wine!

Wine helps the edges blur,
Wine lets the mind escape,
Wine settles all dissension.
Pour the wine!
Wine makes the blood to stir,
Wine leads to friendly rape,
Wine eases tension—
What an invention
Is wine!
Pour the wine!
Glory be to wine!

Dionysos,
We are come to praise you
For the hazy vision that sees
    through all,
For the happy fog that dissolves
    recall,
For the sudden hug and the lively
    brawl,
For the false resolve and the gift of
    gall,
For the edge that blurs,
For the blood that stirs—

Dionysos,
We are come to praise you
Every afternoon by the fading light,
To exalt your name in the sacred rite
Which begins at five and goes on all
    night.

THE FROGS

A NEW MUSICAL

a comedy written in 405 b.c. by
ARISTOPHANES

freely adapted by
BURT SHEVELOVE

even more freely adapted by
NATHAN LANE

music & lyrics
STEPHEN SONDHEIM

direction & choreography
SUSAN STROMAN

Lincoln Center Theater *in association with* **Bob Boyett** *presents* **THE FROGS** *a comedy written in 405 b.c. by* **Aristophanes** *freely adapted by* **Burt Shevelove** *even more freely adapted by* **Nathan Lane** *music & lyrics* **Stephen Sondheim** *with (in alphabetical order)* **Ryan Ball Roger Bart Peter Bartlett James Brown III John Byner Daniel Davis Bryn Dowling Rebecca Eichenberger Meg Gillentine Eric Michael Gillett Pia C. Glenn Timothy Gulan Tyler Hanes Francesca Harper Rod Harrelson Jessica Howard Naomi Kakuk Kenway Hon Wai K. Kua Nathan Lane Luke Longacre David Lowenstein Joanne Manning Burke Moses Mia Price Michael Siberry Kathy Voytko Steve Wilson Jay Brian Winnick** *set design* **Giles Cadle** *costume design* **William Ivey Long** *lighting design* **Ken Posner** *sound design* **Scott Lehrer** *dance music arrangements* **Glen Kelly** *aerial design* **AntiGravity®** *special effects* **Gregory Meeh** *puppet design* **Martin P. Robinson** *casting* **Tara Rubin Casting** *associate director & choreographer* **Tara Young** *stage manager* **Thom Widmann** *orchestrations* **Jonathan Tunick** *musical direction* **Paul Gemignani** *direction & choreography* **Susan Stroman**

LINCOLN CENTER THEATER

Evoe!
Alalai! Alalai!
Evoe!
Alalalalalai!
Evoe! Evoe! Evoe!
Alalai!

*After a number of misadventures,
Dionysos and Xanthias reach the Palace
of Pluto, where Pluto makes a grand
entrance, complete with Torchbearers,
Attendants and Chorus Girls, and greets
Dionysos enthusiastically.*

Paean:* Hades (2004)

PLUTO

Everybody dumps on Hades,
People yelling, "Go to Hell!"
Well,
Let me tell you, life in Hades
Is just swell!

It's got flash! It's got flair!
It's got spectacle to spare!
People come from everywhere,
Like it or not—
Mostly not.
Then they see what we've got
And they like it a lot.
Hell is hot.

I mean,
You never gain weight,
You're never out-of-date,
You never get balder, older,
You never have to fret about Fate,
It's all too late—
I mean, you're dead.

You're not afraid of time rushing by.
Not afraid of oceans running dry,
All because you're not afraid to die,
Once you're dead.

And you get to live in Hades,
Where it's always two a.m.,
Where it's party till you drop
And never stop,

---

*The *paean* is a song of praise or thanks to a
deity. Here Pluto delivers it to himself.

Because there's nothing we condemn.
Where whatever you regret
You just forget,
Or better yet,
Forgive.
Where you're not afraid to die,
And when you're not afraid to die,
Then you're not afraid to live!

And you're living here in Hades,
And I mean you're living well.
Everybody comes to Hades.
Everybody goes to Hell.

Up there, lots of sun,
Down here, fire and gloom.
Up there, not a lot of fun,
Down here, va-va-voom!
Up there, gotta get a grip.
Down here, one long acid trip.
R.I.P. down here means "Let 'er rip!"
Hell is hot,
Hell is happening,
Hell is cool!

Up there, that's just life.
Down here, this is living,
An endless party that no one's giving,
But everybody's invited.

Once you settle down in Hades,
You can leave the world behind.
Here where everyone is gay—
No, not that way—
No, I mean *gay*—
Oh, never mind.

Everyone's afraid of Hades,
So they never misbehave.
If they got a glimpse of Hades,
They'd be racing to the grave.

Here no one has a need anymore
To commit a murder, wage a war.
Who're you going to murder, and
  what for?
They're all like dead.

ALL

Deceased,
Kaput, defunct, released . . .

PLUTO

And we're flying high in Hades,
Where it's always two a.m.,
Where it's party till you drop
And never stop,
Because there's nothing we condemn!

GIRLS

For the mortal human race
Who need their space,
This is the place
To be.

PLUTO

'Cause you're not afraid of death,
And when you're not afraid of death,
Then you're ready for *la vie!*

GIRLS

Day is night when you're in Hades.

PLUTO

That's the thing that gives it zing!
How about a hand for Hades?

GIRLS

Ooh ooh ooh ooh ooh ooh . . .

PLUTO

I just love being king.

ALL

Hail to Pluto!

*In 1974 the paean was another song
entirely, and sung by the Chorus:*

Paean: Evoe!
For the Dead (1974)

CHORUS

They do an awful lot of dancing, the
  dead.
It's very comforting, perpetual
Serenity and such.
It's very comforting, and yet you will
Put up with just so much.
So there's an awful lot of dancing
  instead,
Down here among the dead.

They give an awful lot of banquets,
  the dead.
You turn around, another table is
  spread.
And if you don't become habituated
Quickly, it's a bore.
You're always eating something which
  you ate

The Bacchanal before.
And what's the remedy for being
   overfed?
One guess, among the dead.

They do an awful lot of laughing, the
   dead.
There's always just that little smidgin
   of dread.
Most any person in a panic dotes
On everlasting noise,
So they tell everlasting anecdotes
Which everyone enjoys,
Since no one listens to what anyone
   has said,
Down here among the dead.

They do an awful lot of drinking, the
   dead.
They have a truly endless evening
   ahead.
The time is always right and fitting
   when
You pour another round,
Because it's nighttime unremitting
   when
You're sitting underground.

What with the dancing and the eating
And the laughing and the drinking,
There's no problem in retreating
From the awkwardness of thinking
And that ever-present smidgin of
   dread,
Down here among the dead.

Like up there, among the dead.

*Pluto invites Dionysos to banquet with
him and meet all the famous dead playwrights, Shaw and Shakespeare among
them. Once they have disappeared into
the Banquet Hall, the Dionysians enter.*

Parabasis:*
It's Only a Play
(1974, 2004)

DIONYSIANS (Individually)
Good fellow . . .
Good man, Dionysos.
Don't worry.
Relax.
He'll do it for you.
Besides,
No cause for alarm.

ALL
It's only a play.

DIONYSIANS (Individually)
It doesn't really matter.
Don't worry, relax.
What can one person do?
After all, you're only human,
And it's all been said before.
And you've got enough to think
   about.
Besides . . .

ALL
It's only a play.

DIONYSIANS (Individually)
And there's time,
There's plenty of time—
There always is time.
You've got all the time in the world.
You know, time has a way of healing
   all things.
Things fix themselves.
Don't worry, relax.
Why not wait and see what
   happens?

ALL
It's only a play.

DIONYSIANS (Individually)
Good fellow . . .
Good man, Herakles.
Don't worry.
Relax.
He could do it for you.
Too bad.

---

*The *parabasis* is a scene in which the Chorus
directly addresses the audience while all of
the actors are offstage. Although still partly in
character, they speak for the playwright.

He doesn't exist.
He never was real.
He's only a myth.

ALL
It's only a play.

DIONYSIANS (Individually)
Let the leaders raise your voices for
   you.
Let the critics make your choices for
   you.
Somewhere somebody rejoices for
   you—
The dead.
And a leader's useful to curse,
And the state of things could be
   worse.
And besides . . .

ALL
It's only a play.

DIONYSIANS
Well, words are merely chatter,
And easy to say.
It doesn't really matter,
It's only a play.

It's only so much natter
Which somebody wrote.
And the world's still afloat,
So it's hardly a note
For today.
Anyway . . .

The earth's a little fatter,
But still pretty green.
And life's a little flatter,
But what does that mean?

It really doesn't matter
What somebody writes.
You can turn off the lights
And on alternate nights,
You can pray.
Don't worry.
Relax.
On with the play.

*Dionysos enters from the Banquet Hall in
a state of wild excitement.*

Shaw (2004)

DIONYSOS

I knew that I could do it!
I knew it, I knew it!
I knew they'd all pooh-pooh it,
And indeed they did.

I knew if I stuck to it,
I'd somehow get through it.
At times I thought, "Oh, screw it!"
But proceed I did,
And oh, you kid—!

I just met Shaw!
I got to meet Shaw!
There isn't any doubt
The man's without
A single flaw!

I talked to Shaw,
I said to him, "Shaw,
The world is in a crisis."
He said, "Listen, Dionysos,
What you need is Shaw.
I'll go with you," says Shaw.
"I happen to be free,
And who could be
A bigger draw?"

That instant generosity,
That's Shaw!
The verbal virtuosity,
That's Shaw!
The righteous animosity,
That mind with such velocity—
All right, there's the pomposity,
But that's just Shaw—
And maybe some verbosity,
But still you'll be
In awe.

And here comes Shaw!

(Shaw enters, surrounded by worshippers)

DIONYSOS

He has no use for piety
Or bromides or propriety.
He'll show us our society
In ways we never saw.
The world will soon be dancing "The
Shaw."

SHAVIANS
(Illustrating the dance)

First you think.
Then you comment.
Then you think.
Then you discuss.
Then you read.
Then you make a quip.

SHAW

All great truths begin as
blasphemies.

SHAVIANS

That's how you dance "The Shaw."

DIONYSOS

Isn't he amazing?
Isn't he adorable?

(To the Shavians)

Couldn't you die?
Well, you already have.
Still—

SHAVIANS

Words can dance,
Thoughts can dance,
Syllables can samba.
Sentences can waltz around in your
mind.
Epigrams can leap and bound,
Simply from the way they sound—

SHAW

Patriotism is the conviction that this
country is superior to all other countries because you were born in it.

DIONYSOS

Even when he's not profound,
He's so refined!

SHAW

If all economists were laid end to
end they would not reach a conclusion.

SHAVIANS

Shaw is here to stay,
Shaw is for today.
Take him off the shelf.

DIONYSOS

Everything he writes
Dazzles and delights—
He told me so himself.

I'll show them Shaw!
I want to share Shaw!
I'm sure of Shaw!
You can't shush Shaw.
You can't shake Shaw.

SHAVIANS

Such sanity, humanity,
Who cares about the vanity?
His work is just so literate,
It leaves you all atwitter, it's
Got gravity and levity,
That's why it's got longevity.

DIONYSOS

A little short on brevity—
Is that against the law?

DIONYSOS, SHAVIANS

We still need Shaw!
I'm (he's) bringing back Shaw!
The world will have an orgy
Of Georgie
Shaw!

This song is followed by the agon, the core of traditional Greek comedy. It is a contest, usually a debate, culminating in the decisive defeat of one of the parties. In Aristophanes' play, the debate is between Euripides and Aeschylus, Euripides claiming that his characters are more true to life and logical, and Aeschylus claiming that his are heroic and models for the future. In Burt's version, the contenders are Shaw and Shakespeare, who represent clarity of thought vs. poetic imagination and who argue only in excerpts from their plays. In each case, Dionysos has to choose which playwright to revive and take back to earth. In the first instance, he chooses Aeschylus because he feels that the world needs the heroic size of his work; in the latter, he chooses Shakespeare because it needs poetry more than conscience. If the play were written today, the antagonists might be Arthur Miller and Tennessee Williams, which could make for an interesting argument.*

Just before the agon begins, Charon reappears with his boat, ringing his bell, ready to take the winner back to earth.

---

*Shakespeare wins, his final entry being the song "Fear No More" from *Cymbeline*. I do not reprint the lyric here out of sheer self-preservation. Suffice it to say that I collaborated with Shakespeare.

All Aboard! (Reprise) (2004)

CHARON

All aboard!
Hades express!
Last bell
For the real hell,
Where you've had it at birth—
Good ol' earth.

Boy, if you think you know doom,
If you think you've seen dismal,
Wait till you're back
Where it's really abysmal,
Where hearts are heavy and heads are
    bowed
And each silver lining conceals a
    cloud,
Where men are men and sheep are
    nervous—
At your service—

All aboard!

After the agon, Dionysos prepares to take Shakespeare back to earth. The Dionysians bid them farewell as Charon rows them home.

Exodos:* The Sound of Poets (1974, 2004)

DIONYSIANS

Dionysos,
Bring the sound of poets
In a blaze of words to a heedless
    earth.
Evoe!
Alalai! Alalai!
Evoe!
Alalalalalalai!

Dionysos,
Bring the taste of wisdom
In a feast of words to a hungry earth.
Evoe!
Alalai! Alalai!

_____
*Just what you might expect.
_____

Evoe!
Alalalalalalai!

Dionysos,
Bring a sense of purpose,
Bring the taste of words,
Bring the sound of wit,
Bring the feel of passion,
Bring the glow of thought
To the darkening earth.
Evoe!
Alalai! Alalai!
Evoe!
Alalalalalalai!

CHARON
The frogs are quiet tonight.

CHORUS
Brek-kek-kek-kek . . .
Brek-kek-kek-kek . . .
Ribet . . . Ribet . . .
Ko-ax . . .

For the 2004 revival, I added a brief Epilogue:

Standing on the stage with Shakespeare, Dionysos has been exhorting the audience not to be Frogs but to take action against what is wrong with the world.

Final Instructions to the Audience (2004)

DIONYSOS

No, please, don't nod,
Agreeing with me just 'cause I'm a
    god.
Have some respect for Aristophanes
And please, don't nod.

Don't just shrug,
Content to be a conscientious slug.
It's fine to feel contented, safe and
    snug,
But soon enough contented turns to
    smug.
Don't shovel what's uncomfortable
    underneath the rug.
Speak up! Get sore!
Do something more than just deplore.

CHORUS

Now to conclude, please,
If we've been crude, please,
We can be booed, please—
It shows you were awake.
Don't sit and brood, please.
Learn to be rude, please.

DIONYSOS

There's just too much at stake,
And now is simply not the time to
    take
A break.

CHORUS

So shake
Your ass!

DIONYSOS

I know, I know, that sounds a little
    crass.
But, citizens of Athens,
If you're smart,
Don't sit around while Athens
Falls apart.

CHORUS

Good citizens of Athens,
Let us not lose heart!
And now—
And now—
And now—
And now—

DIONYSOS
(Quietly, speaking)
And now—

ALL
We start.

BLACKOUT

I have commented very little on the lyrics for *The Frogs* because the experience of writing them (in the initial version) was primarily—wait for it—an academic one. It was an exercise: it offered me a chance to harangue an audience, to use a chorus a cappella to make sound effects, to write massed choral music, and to indulge in vulgarity, adolescent humor and moral preachment, just like Aristophanes. It was more instructive for me, I suspect, than for you who are reading about it. Nor is there much to be said about the additional lyrics for the revival of the show. They were written to suit the requests of the star and director, a process I had encountered before; they were tailored for a commercial, albeit nonprofit production (the two are not as dissimilar as you might think, particularly in New York). Although the 2004 production was professional, it did have its problems, but at least they were professional problems: problems of writing, staging, performance and ego. And the egos of the professional theater are nothing compared to those lurking in the Groves of Academe.

The Frogs *(1974)*

PACIFIC OVERTURES

11. Pacific Overtures (1976)

Book by John Weidman

The Notion

A chronicle of Japanese history, beginning with the 1853 incursion of American warships, under the command of Commodore Matthew Calbraith Perry, into Japanese waters in order to open up trade with a nation that had been closed to foreigners for centuries. In particular, it concerns the relationship during the next fifteen years between Kayama, a minor samurai relegated to order the ships to leave, and Manjiro, a Japanese fisherman recently returned from the United States.

General Comments

Writing *Pacific Overtures* reinforced something I'd begun to learn and am learning still: of my three guiding principles—Less Is More, Content Dictates Form, God Is in the Details—the first is the hardest to put into practice. The struggle against discursiveness never ends and is too often unsuccessful, even for writers who know better. The famous Hemingway dictum that what you leave out is as important as what you leave in is one I suspect that most writers wish they had never learned. Tolstoy, Melville, Proust and numerous all-inclusive others would probably disagree; for lyric writers concision is unavoidable, if for no other reason than that the presence of music can not only supply what's unwritten but resonate beyond it. Still, it's a precept hard to follow, since it takes so much of the fun out of writing by putting the brakes on flamboyant cleverness, ostentatious imagery, decorative elaboration, overly insistent emphasis and rhythmically repetitive lists like this one. Novelists, essayists and journalists have the room to indulge themselves in such pleasures, but lyric writers do not: lyrics are an unforgivingly compact form. If you think of a theater lyric as a short story, as I do, then every line has the weight of a paragraph. A good lyric, even a patter song, cannot afford unnecessary words, redundancies or needless flourishes. The price of such extravagance is diffusion—nothing blunts a strong emotion or a good punch line as effectively as too many words.

If a lyric is protracted or digressive, either it should be the modus operandi of a garrulous character like Mrs. Lovett in *Sweeney Todd,* or it should arise from an emotional reason, such as Amy's hysteria in *Company,* Buddy's vaudeville despair in *Follies* or George's tense self-justification at the party in *Sunday in the Park with George,* an urge which often gives rise to loquacity. Frustrated befuddlement (Fredrik at the beginning of *A Little Night Music*) and anger (Charley's explosion in *Merrily We Roll Along*) are other motivations. There are many possible grounds for a song to pile up words, but without at least one of them it becomes a piece about the lyric writer rather than the lyric. In the days before Rodgers and Hammerstein subsumed the giddiness of lyrics that were playful for their own sake, glisten alone could justify a song and verbosity could be a virtue (Cole Porter's "Let's Not Talk About Love"). Now it needs justification; otherwise—there's no getting away from it—Less Is More.

I first learned about this principle from studying composition with Milton Babbitt. An experimental and avant-garde composer, he was a closet songwriter, an admirer of Kern and Arlen as much as Mozart and Schoenberg. The first hour of each of our weekly sessions would be devoted to analyzing a song like "All the Things You Are," the next three to the Jupiter Symphony, always concentrating on the tautness of the structures, the leanness and frugality of the musical ideas. My first epiphany in regard to Less Is More, the one that had the

most impact and has lasted longest in my mind, was an analysis Milton gave of a Bach fugue, in which he demonstrated how Bach had taken a four-note theme and built out of it a "cathedral," as he eloquently put it. I learned then that the best art, or at least the kind that I like best, usually involves making the most out of the least (though not always, as for example *Ulysses,* which makes a great deal out of a lot and which I love).

The second epiphany arrived when, thirty-three years after Babbitt and Bach, I encountered a threefold Japanese screen at a Metropolitan Museum exhibition. Each panel was about six feet high and two feet across. The left panel—a third of the total surface space—was blank, completely white; the middle one was the same, except for the end of a small tree branch snaking its way shyly from the right-hand border toward the middle of the whiteness; the panel on the right from which the branch grew was filled with a luxuriant tree, extravagantly plumaged birds nested in the branches. It was like a sudden explosion; it seemed to grow as I looked at it. Even if read from right to left, as the Japanese do, it was an explosion followed by its aftermath. The effect was magical—largely because, as with so much Japanese art, what was omitted was as important as what was there. In fact, it was the emptiness of almost two thirds of the total screen which made the other third so powerful. I found myself actually *moved* by an idea I had so long merely acknowledged. I had heard "Less Is More" propounded in its bite-size axiomatic form innumerable times over the years and had watched it operating triumphantly in work like E. B. White's and Nathanael West's, but it was *Pacific Overtures* and an immersion in Japanese culture that breached the blood-brain barrier for me and changed my intellectual appreciation into an emotional one. Writing the songs became nothing less than learning on the job.

The literary equivalent of that screen is a haiku, the type of Japanese poetry most familiar to Westerners. Strict in form, it consists of three lines: the first of five syllables, the second of seven and the third of five again. Here are a couple of typical ones:

White chrysanthemums,
Making all else about them
Reflected riches

When the waterpot
Burst that silent night with cold . . .
My eyes split open

What do they mean? Nothing—nothing explicit, that is. A haiku is a wisp of a poem, often just a sketch of a scene, compressed and airy at the same time, and never explicit. It sometimes comprises a single extended image, sometimes two apparently unrelated ones, making no specific connection between them, only an ineffable one. The juxtaposition conveys a feeling of things unexpressed but necessary, which the reader can fill in with his own imagination: not unlike all poetry perhaps, but the brevity of the haiku is what distinguishes it. Because it seemed to me emblematic of the Japanese nature it became a model of intention for me as I wrote the songs. I tried to infuse the lyrics with the evocative simplicity of haiku (although there are only two proper examples of the form in the score), especially in the first act, which takes place before the United States has established a foothold and started to infiltrate Japanese culture.

Another reason that Less Is More is a difficult principle to adhere to is that unless you can avoid the traps of banality and vagueness, Less Is Less. The distinction between simple and simplistic is something of a cliché, but no less valid for that; there is a thin dividing line between economy of means and penury of ideas. Hammerstein's lyrics, especially those he wrote with Rodgers, are shining examples of this difference, "Oh, What a Beautiful Morning" of the former, "Climb Every Mountain" the latter. (It is both these qualities in Hammerstein's work that irritate those who compare him unfavorably with Lorenz Hart.) Irving Berlin is the master of Less Is More ("White Christmas," "How Deep Is the Ocean?"), but the lyrics that demonstrate evocative simplicity most potently are DuBose Heyward's for *Porgy and Bess.* Songs like "Summertime" and "My Man's Gone Now" are not merely transparent like Berlin's, they resonate with great power, and that power comes from their illusion of simplicity. They are simple but dense.

I'd written lean lyrics before, but with *Pacific Overtures* I tried to make that leanness a style. Following John Weidman's example in his dialogue, I restricted myself as much as I could to an unadorned, basic vocabulary until the song "Please Hello," which opens Act Two and accompanies the entrance of ambassadors from foreign countries demanding rights and commodities and introducing long words with Latinate roots. I hoped the contrast would lend the other songs a slightly stilted, archaic feel, to convey the out-of-touch isolation of the country. Content Dictates Style, as well as Form.

ACT ONE

Japan. By the Western calendar, 1853. The Reciter, who narrates the events of the story as well as occasionally taking part in them, describes the daily life. As he sings, the populace—a cross-section of Japanese society—forms around him.

The Advantages of Floating in the Middle of the Sea

RECITER
In the middle of the world we float,
In the middle of the sea.
The realities remain remote
In the middle of the sea.

Kings are burning somewhere,
Wheels are turning somewhere,
Trains are being run,
Wars are being won,
Things are being done
Somewhere out there.
Not here.
Here we paint screens.
Yes!
The arrangement of the screens:

We sit inside the screens
And contemplate the view
That's painted on the screens
More beautiful than true.
Beyond the screens
That glide aside
Are further screens
That open wide
With scenes of screens like the ones
    that glide.

And no one presses in,
And no one glances out,
And kings are burning somewhere.

ALL
Not here!

As the hurricanes have come, they've
    passed
In the middle of the sea.
The advantages are made to last
In the middle of the sea.

Gods are crumbling somewhere,
Machines are rumbling somewhere,
Ways are being found,
Watches being wound,
Prophets being crowned
Somewhere out there.
Not here.
Here we plant rice.

RECITER
Yes!
The arrangement of the rice:

The farmer plants the rice.
The priest exalts the rice.
The Lord collects the rice.
The merchant buys the rice.
The craftsman makes the sword
And sells it to the Lord
And buys at twice the former price
What he counts on his Lord to protect
    with his sword:

ALL
The rice!

RECITER
They eat the rice and then
The day begins again.

ALL
And gods are crumbling
    somewhere—
Not here!

The disturbances are worlds away
In the middle of the sea.
And tomorrow will be like today
In the middle of the sea.

Blood is flowing somewhere,
Ideas are growing somewhere,
Trails are being blazed,
Voices being raised,
Women being praised
Somewhere out there.
Not here.
Here we trade bows.

RECITER
Yes!
The arrangement of the bows:

First for the Emperor,
Descendant of the Sun-goddess
    Amaterasu!

All-knowing and all-powerful!
Ruler absolute!
One year old.

Second for the Shogun,
Protector of the kingdom,
Keeper of the peace.
Seldom seen.

Then for the Lords of the South,
Vassals to the Shogun,
Loyal to their master . . .
Not for long.

And kings are burning somewhere.

ALL
Not here!

The advantages go on and on
In the middle of the sea.
As the centuries have come, they've
    gone
In the middle of the sea.

Days arise to be replaced,
Lines are drawn and lines erased.
Life and death are but verses in a
    poem.
Out there blood flows.
Who knows?

Here we paint screens,
Plant the rice,
Arrange the flowers,
View the moon,
Exchange the gifts,
Plant the rice,
Arrange tomorrow like today to float,
Slide the screens,
Exchange the poems,
Stir the tea,
Exchange the bows,
Plant the rice,
Arrange tomorrow to be like today,
To float.

The viewing of the moon,
The planting of the rice,
The stirring of the tea,
The painting of the screens.
We float.

(Overlapping)

The viewing of the moon,
The stirring of the tea,

The planting of the rice,
The folding of the fans.
The weaving of the mats.
We float.

The placing of the stones,
The painting of the sliding screens,
The viewing of the moon,
The wrapping of the gifts,
The planting of the rice,
The sliding of the painted screens,
The catching of the fish.
We float.

The weaving of the mats,
The painting of the screens . . .
The stirring of the tea . . .
We float . . .
We float . . .

RECITER
We float.

The first version of this song was called simply "We Float" and, although it covered pretty much the same territory—establishing the time, the place, the customs and the class system, as most opening numbers are wont to do—it additionally suggested the pared-down, haiku-like style of the lyrics to come. It was less "Western" in feeling:

We Float (cut)

RECITER
Winds blow and waves break,
And see:
The island floats.
Winds blow and waves break,
And we,
We float.
Kings are burning somewhere
Out there,
Not here.
We float.

Winds blow and towers go down.
We float.
Waves rise and centuries drown.

We float.
Gods are crumbling somewhere,
Machines are rumbling somewhere,
Not here.
We float.

We paint screens.
There are screens
To provide pleasant scenes
And to hide further screens.

We paint screens,
Which can slide.
Some have scenes
Ten feet wide
Of screens.

And we sit inside
As the watches tick,
And the trails are tried
And the air is thick
With doubt.
Not here.
We float.

CHORUS
Winds blow with fury.
They pass.
The island floats.
Windows are paper,
Not glass.
We float.
Kings are burning somewhere,
Great wheels are turning
    somewhere . . .

And so forth. This was the song we opened with in Boston, the first of our two tryout towns, but it was too long and filled with needless dance interludes, so we decided to replace it, and by the time the show got to Washington I had written "The Advantages . . ." The Reciter's opening couplet at that time was

The advantages of being set
In the middle of the sea.
Some advantages of being set
In the middle of the sea:

I wanted to begin the score with a topic sentence rather than a personalized statement, partly to establish the Reciter as a teacher/guide, but also to sug-

gest the dry objectivity of the Japanese approach to the world. Hal was uncomfortable with my setting this tone at the top of the opening number, just as he had been with the sour tone of "Happily Ever After," the closing number in *Company*, and once again persuaded me to change it. In the case of *Company*, I think he was right; in this case I should have stuck to my guns.

The Shogun and his Councilors, hearing rumors of approaching warships from America, hastily promote Kayama, a young samurai "of little consequence," to the position of Prefect of Police for the city of Uraga, where the ships are expected to arrive. His mission is to tell the foreigners that they are breaking the Japanese law which states that no foreign ships are allowed, and they must go away. He returns home and gives the news of this hopeless assignment to his wife, Tamate. A distant bell announces the imminent arrival of the ships. Tamate does a mournful dance as Kayama dresses to receive the foreigners. As she does so, two Observers appear, one singing about her, the other singing her thoughts.

There Is No Other Way

FIRST OBSERVER
The eye sees, the thought flies.
The eye tells, the thought denies.

SECOND OBSERVER
I will prepare for your returning.
(Is there no other way?)

FIRST OBSERVER
The word falls, the heart cries.
The heart knows the word's disguise.

SECOND OBSERVER
I shall expect you then at evening.
(Is there no other way?)

FIRST OBSERVER
The bird sings, the wind sighs,
The air stirs, the bird shies.
A storm approaches.

SECOND OBSERVER
(There must be other ways . . .)

FIRST OBSERVER
The leaf shakes, the wings rise.
The song stops, the bird flies.
The storm approaches.

SECOND OBSERVER
I will have supper waiting.

FIRST OBSERVER
The song stops, the bird flies.
The mind stirs, the heart replies,
"There is no other way."

SECOND OBSERVER
I will prepare for your return.
I shall expect you then at evening.

FIRST OBSERVER
The word stops, the heart dies.
The wind counts the lost goodbyes.

SECOND OBSERVER
There is no other way.
There is no other way.

Initially, this song comprised three prayers, one by Tamate, one by Kayama, and one by the Councilors:

Prayer (cut)

TAMATE
God of Fortune,
Take my meager gift.
Let him come home swiftly,
In favor,
Daikoku.
Show me a sign.

God of Fortune,
Brush my husband's sleeve:
Let his Lords receive him
With favor,
Daikoku.
Show me a sign.
Let me see a sign.

Let me see a spider in the morning,
Let me dream a river overflowed.

Let me see a spider on the ceiling in
   the morning
Or a ribbon pointing northward in
   the road.
Show me a sign.

I have hung a sandal facing inward,
Drawing him home.
Let me have a gesture.
Show me a sign.
Daikoku!

KAYAMA
God of Wisdom,
Hear my useless prayer.
Are you even there
For an answer,
Jorojin?
Show me a sign.

God of Riddles,
Tell me what to do.
Or will even you
Have no answer,
Jorojin?
I know the sign,
If there is a sign:

I will see a spider in the evening,
I will dream of rivers running dry.
I shall see a spider on the ceiling in
   the evening
Or a funeral procession passing by.
I know the signs.
Point me to a door that can be
   opened.
Is there a door?
Let me have a gesture.
Show me a sign,
Jorojin.

(I have omitted the Councilors' prayer, which was incorporated into "Chrysanthemum Tea," a song sung later in Act One.)

Being a reader who gets impatient easily, especially with textbook styles, I let John Weidman do the period research on the show and reduce it for me to easily digested nuggets of information—not that he had to research much, as he had majored in East Asian history at Harvard. He also gave me a Japanese daybook of the period, each page of which dealt with a different custom, means of transporta-

tion, kind of food, building, tool, etc. Like *Daily Life in Ancient Rome*, the research book I had used for *A Funny Thing Happened on the Way to the Forum*, this was a guide to daily life in nineteenth-century Japan. We wanted to be authentic in quotidian details in order to counterbalance our more free-wheeling manipulation and compression of the actual events. Studying the book, I was particularly taken with the bizarre superstitions of the day, images that would not only be startling to use at the top of the show and would help yank the audience into an unknown world, but would also give me license to make up my own exotic images later without (I hoped) the self-conscious aspirations toward "poetry" that had hamstrung me in *West Side Story* lyrics such as "Tonight." All of the "lucky" signs I used in "Prayer" and subsequently in "Chrysanthemum Tea" are authentic historical idiosyncrasies.

"Prayer" was the first song I wrote for the show and was my attempt to find and establish a style for the piece, lyrically and musically. It was the first song replaced, as well, but like the theme on which Elgar's "Enigma" Variations is based, it is the invisible, or more accurately inaudible, presence which pervades the score, the seed from which much of the rest of the music grew. When I auditioned "Prayer" for John and Hal and eventually others, I gave it the proper twangy exotic sound of the samisen—the Japanese version of a mandolin—by peppering the piano strings with thumbtacks and pieces of paper, transforming the soft-hammer sound into something more like the harsh plucked tones of a harpsichord. Everyone was duly impressed at my inventiveness—everyone except those who knew the music of John Cage.

The clanging of the bell gets louder. A fisherman appears, wildly excited.

Backstage at the 1985 Off-Broadway revival

Four Black Dragons

FISHERMAN
I was standing on the beach
Near the cliffs
At Oshima.
I was spreading out the nets
For the morning sun.
It was early in July
And the day was getting hot,
And I stopped to wipe my eyes,
And by accident I turned
And looked out to sea . . .

And there came,
Breaking through the mist,
Roaring through the sea,
Four black dragons,
Spitting fire.
And I ran,
Cursing through the fields,
Calling the alarm,
Shouting to the world,
"Four black dragons,
Spitting fire!"

And the earth trembled,
And the sky cracked,
And I thought it was the end of the
    world.

(A thief appears)

THIEF
I was rifling through the house
Of some priests
In Uraga.
It was only after dawn,
They were sleeping still.
I had finished with the silks,
I was hunting for the gold,
When I heard them getting up,
So I bolted through a door
Which looked out to sea . . .

FISHERMAN
And there came . . .

THIEF
And there came . . .

FISHERMAN
Breaking through the mist . . .

THIEF
Boiling through the mist . . .

FISHERMAN
Roaring through the sea . . .

THIEF
Rising from the sea . . .

FISHERMAN
Four black dragons . . .

THIEF
Four volcanoes . . .

FISHERMAN
Spitting fire . . .

THIEF
Spitting fire!
And I ran . . .

FISHERMAN
And I ran . . .

THIEF
Cursing down the halls . . .

FISHERMAN
Cursing through the fields . . .

THIEF
Shouting to the priests . . .

FISHERMAN
Shouting to the world . . .

BOTH
"Notify the gods!"

THIEF	FISHERMAN
Four volcanoes,	Four black dragons,
Spitting fire!	Spitting fire!

(Panic-stricken townspeople appear)

RECITER
And the feet pattered
As the men came down to stare,
And the women started screaming
Like the gulls.
Hai! Hai!

And they crowded into temples
And they flapped about the square—
Hai!
Like the gulls.
Hai!

TOWNSPEOPLE
Hai! Hai!
Four black dragons,
Spitting fire!

RECITER
Then the hooves clattered
And the warriors were there,
Driving quickly through the panic
Like the gulls.
Hai! Hai!

And the swords were things of beauty
As they glided through the air—
Hai!
Like the gulls.
Hai!

TOWNSPEOPLE
Hai! Hai!
Four black dragons,
Spitting fire!

TOWNSPEOPLE	THIEF, FISHERMAN
And the sun darkened	I had seen
And the sea bubbled	Dragons before,
And the earth trembled	Never so many,
And the sky cracked	Never like these!

ALL
And I thought it was the end
Of the world!

RECITER
And it was.

I am very fond of that last line.

With Kayama's mission having accomplished nothing and the Americans waiting in the harbor for a reply to their request to come ashore, the weak-willed Shogun, overwhelmed by the emergency confronting him, has taken to his bed. As he smokes, eats and drinks himself into oblivion, he is surrounded by his Court: his Physician, his Priests, his Soothsayer, his Sumo Wrestlers, his male Companion, his Wife, and his formidable Mother.

Chrysanthemum Tea

MOTHER
(Trying to get the Shogun's attention)
My lord . . .

(He pays no attention)

My lord . . .
Noble lord . . .

It's the day of the Rat, my lord.
There are four days remaining,
And I see you're entertaining,
But we should have a chat, my lord.

To begin, if I may, my lord,
I've no wish to remind you
But you'll notice just behind you
There are ships in the bay,
They've been sitting there all day
With a letter to convey
And they haven't gone away,
And there's every indication
That they're planning to stay, my
    lord . . .
My lord . . .

(The Physician offers him tea)

Have some tea, my lord,
Some chrysanthemum tea.
It's an herb
That's superb
For disturbances at sea.
Is the Shogun feeling better?
Good! Now what about this letter?
Is it wise to delay, my lord?
With the days disappearing,
Might we benefit from hearing
What the soothsayers say, my lord?

SOOTHSAYER
(Consults a chart)
Wood star . . .
Water star . . .
All celestial omens are—
Excellent.

(Tosses various objects onto the floor)

Deer bones . . .
Turtle shells . . .
Each configuration spells—
Victory!

(Goes into a trance)

Ahhhhhh—

(Whirls and points)

A spider on the wall—
Signifies success!

(Shrugs)

Whose success I cannot guess—

(Attempting to recover quickly)

Unless . . .

*(The Shogun snaps his fingers and has
    him thrown out; time passes)*

MOTHER
It's the day of the Ox, my lord.
With but three days remaining
And today already waning,
I've a few further shocks, my lord.

To begin, let me say
At the risk of repetition,
There are ships in the bay,
And they didn't ask permission,
But they sit there all day
In contemptuous array
With a letter to convey
And they haven't gone away
And there's every indication
That they still plan to stay,
And you look a little gray, my lord . . .
My lord . . .

Have some tea, my lord,
Some chrysanthemum tea,
While we plan,
If we can,
What our answer ought to be.
If the tea the Shogun drank will
Serve to keep the Shogun tranquil,
I suggest, if I may, my lord,
We consult the Confucians—
They have mystical solutions.
There are none wise as they, my lord.

PRIESTS
Night waters do not break the moon.
That merely is illusion.
The moon is sacred.

No foreign ships can break our laws.
That also is illusion.
Our laws are sacred.

It follows there can be no ships.
They must be an illusion.
Japan is sacred.

*(But the ships remain, and the priests are
    thrown out; time passes; the Shogun
    grows visibly weaker)*

MOTHER
It's the day of the Tiger, my lord.
Only two days remaining,
And I'm tired of explaining
There are ships in the bay
With a letter to convey.
They're on permanent display,
And we must take some position
Or the Southern coalition
Will be soon holding sway, my lord,
And we'll all have to pay, my lord . . .

(Feebly, the Shogun tries to answer)

Have you something to say, my lord?

Have some tea, my lord,
Some chrysanthemum tea.
It's a tangled situation,
As your father would agree.
And it mightn't be so tangled
If you hadn't had him strangled—
But I fear that I stray, my lord.
I've a nagging suspicion
That in view of your condition,
What we should do is pray, my
    lord . . .

SAMURAI COMPANION
Blow, wind,
Great wind.
Great Kamikaze,
Wind of the gods.

OTHERS
Blow, wind!
Smite them down!
Make the invaders dance and drown!

Blow, wind!
Build the waves!
Hurl the infection
Out of the ocean,
Blow, wind!
Blow, wind!
Blow, wind!

*(But the ships remain; time passes; the
    Shogun seems near death)*

MOTHER
It's the day of the Rabbit, my lord.
There's but one day remaining,
And beside the fact it's raining,
There are ships in the bay
Which are sitting there today
Just exactly where they sat
On the day of the Rat—
Oh, and speaking of that, my lord . . .

(The Shogun falls back on his bed)

My lord—?

*(The Shogun seems to die; the Mother
and the Physician pray over the body)*

PHYSICIAN
The blossom falls on the mountain.
The mountain falls on the blossom.
All things fall . . .

(The Shogun twitches)

Sometimes . . .

MOTHER
(Resuming her harangue)
As I started to say:
From that first disturbing day,
When I gave consideration
To this letter they convey,
I decided if there weren't
Any Shogun to receive it,
It would act as a deterrent
Since they'd have no place to leave it,
And they might go away, my lord . . .
Do you see what I say, my lord?
My lord—?

*(As the Physician offers him more tea,
the Shogun pushes it away in realization)*

In the tea, my lord,
The chrysanthemum tea—
An informal variation
On the normal recipe.
Though I know my plan had merit,
It's been slow in execution.
If there's one thing you inherit,
It's your father's constitution,
And you're taking so long, my
   lord . . .

(As the Shogun sinks)

Do you think I was wrong, my lord?

(He tries to say something)

No, you must let me speak:
When the Shogun is weak,
Then the tea must be strong, my
   lord . . .

(He falls back again)

My lord—?

(He dies)

MOTHER, PHYSICIAN
The blossom falls on the mountain.
The mountain falls on the blossom.
All things—

(She checks the body)

Fall.

This is an intricately plotted song, like
"A Weekend in the Country" in *A Little Night Music*, "God, That's Good!"
in *Sweeney Todd*, "Opening Doors" in
Merrily We Roll Along and others. It is
my favorite kind of song to write, since
it appeals to my fondness for puzzle-
solving, not only verbally but dramatically. To tell a story which occurs over
a period of time and which contains
actual incident, but in song form—as
opposed to *recitative*, which is the way
most composers not only of musicals
but of operas handle it—is just difficult
enough to be fun.* As with the opening number, this song was a Washington replacement. The original version
contained no conspiracy and no murder (nor did history, this being the
most extreme liberty we took with the
actuality of events). It was essentially
a Jewish mother song. Here it is in a
much-abridged version, as it was full
of stage business which consisted
largely of variations on the Shogun's
moaning distress and his mother's
fussing and fluttering about.

_____

*Furthermore, the order of the days is accu-
rate according to the Japanese calendar.

_____

Chrysanthemum Tea
(original version)

SHOGUN
Ohhh . . . Ohhh . . . Ohhh . . .
Na—na—
Ohhh . . .
Na—na—

MOTHER
*(Variously, to the Physicians, Servants,
   Priests, Musicians and Wife)*
Fix the Shogun's pillow . . .
Brew the Shogun's tea . . .
Chop the Shogun's ginger . . .
Play for the Shogun!
Pray for the Shogun!

Look, the Shogun falters . . .
No, the Shogun rallies . . .
Quick! The Shogun shakes!

FIRST PHYSICIAN
The fever breaks.

MOTHER
The Shogun wakes.

SECOND PHYSICIAN
Elevate the Shogun.

(Hands a cup of tea to the Mother)

Chrysanthemum tea.

MOTHER
(Coaxing the Shogun)
Just poured—
Chrysanthemum tea,
Your adored—

MOTHER, PHYSICIANS
—Chrysanthemum tea,
My lord!

*(The Shogun slurps tea throughout the
   following)*

MOTHER
Good! The Shogun brightens!

FIRST PHYSICIAN
Let the Shogun breathe.

COUNCILOR
Is the Shogun calmer?

(The Shogun goes into near-convulsions)

MOTHER
Who upset the Shogun?
You upset the Shogun!

COUNCILOR
I regret the Shogun
Got upset.

FIRST PHYSICIAN
Now you've wet the Shogun!

MOTHER
Don't forget, the Shogun's
Shogun yet!

SECOND PHYSICIAN
Shall we let
The Shogun sweat?

MOTHER
Wait! The Shogun gestures—
Feel the Shogun's cheeks.

FIRST PHYSICIAN
The fever peaks.

MOTHER
The Shogun speaks.

SHOGUN
H-h-have they gone yet?

COUNCILOR
No, my lord.

(The Shogun shrieks in terror)

MOTHER
Play something!
Pray something!

PRIESTS
The blossom falls on the mountain.
The mountain—

MOTHER
(Simultaneously, to the Shogun)
Say something!

(To the Physicians)

Fix something!
Brew something!
Mix something!
Do something!

FIRST PHYSICIAN
(To the Second Physician)
Let me have a leech.

MOTHER
(Trying to feed the Shogun)
Chrysanthemum tea—don't drip—

MOTHER, PHYSICIANS
Chrysanthemum tea—sip, sip.
Chrysanthemum—

(The Shogun seems to die)

PRIESTS
The blossom falls on the mountain.
The mountain falls on the blossom.
All things fall.

*(The Shogun twitches; he burrows into
his pillows and hides)*

MOTHER
Light the Shogun's incense.
Fill the Shogun's pipe.
Mop the Shogun's forehead.

(Looking down)

Where is the Shogun?

*(Seeing a movement under
the comforter)*

There is the Shogun!
Quick! The Shogun pales!

(The Shogun cries out)

The Shogun wails!

(He cries out again)

FIRST PHYSICIAN
The Shogun fails . . .

SECOND PHYSICIAN
(To a servant)
Flagellate the Shogun.

MOTHER
Chrysanthemum tea!

FIRST PHYSICIAN
(To the servant)
More force!

MOTHER
Chrysanthemum tea!

SECOND PHYSICIAN
(To the servant)
Like a horse.

MOTHER
Chrysanthemum tea!

PHYSICIANS
Of course.

MOTHER
There, the Shogun's quiet.
See, the Shogun waves!
Change the Shogun's pillow.

*(The servant obediently whips the pillow
away; the Shogun's head hits the floor
with a dull thud)*

Did you drop the Shogun?
Never drop a Shogun!

FIRST PHYSICIAN
Someone prop the Shogun
Up right there!

MOTHER
Someone mop the Shogun!

SECOND PHYSICIAN
Better stop, the Shogun
Should have air.

COUNCILOR
(To the first physician)
Should we crop the Shogun's
Hair?

MOTHER
Fetch the Shogun's panda.
Rub the Shogun's ankles.
Look! The Shogun spits!

FIRST PHYSICIAN
The fever quits.

MOTHER
The Shogun sits.

(To the Court Musicians)

Strum something.
Hum something,
Drum something.

MOTHER, PRIESTS
Chrysanthemum tea—

MOTHER
Hot and thick.

MOTHER, PRIESTS
Chrysanthemum tea—

MOTHER
He's sick . . .

(The Shogun falls back, unconscious)

MOTHER
Look! The Shogun's red—!

COUNCILOR
Have the Shogun bled!

FIRST PHYSICIAN
Tilt the Shogun's bed!

SECOND PHYSICIAN
Lift the Shogun's head!

COUNCILOR
Wait, the Shogun's dead.

(Everyone stops and looks; the mother starts wailing)

PRIESTS
The blossom falls on the mountain.
The mountain falls on the blossom.
All things—

(Checking the body)

—Fall.

(The mother looks on impassively as the others sing softly)

PHYSICIANS, PRIESTS, COUNCILOR
Rest the Shogun's spirit
Till the Shogun's next life.

(The mother fans herself slowly)

MOTHER
Get another Shogun.

(Speedily, but with organized delicacy, they fold up the trays, the bed and the Shogun and leave the stage)

As with many songs which have too little to say, once the premise was stated, there was nothing to add, so I tried, as I had tried before in previous shows, to distract the listener from the repetitious emptiness by opening my bag of pyrotechnical dazzlements—in this case, rhymes. It was minimally effective, which is one reason the song was replaced. I include the lyric here not only in the interests of completeness and to present an exemplary instance of overrhyming but also because, as in the case of "Four Black Dragons," I'm extremely fond of the last line.

Kayama offers the Shogun's court a plan that will allow Commodore Perry to come ashore and deliver a letter from President Fillmore demanding rights to open trade, while at the same time, at least superficially, maintaining the country's sovereignty. The Court is so delighted that they make him permanent governor of the City of Uraga. The plan had been suggested to Kayama by Manjiro, a young fisherman, one of the few Japanese who had been to the United States, and who has been condemned to death for trying to return to his homeland. Kayama asks that Manjiro's life be spared and that he be assigned to Kayama's service. The Court agrees, and Kayama hurries home with Manjiro in tow to tell his wife, Tamate, the good news. To pass the time on the long journey, the men decide to exchange poems, which they make up as they go along.

Poems

KAYAMA
Rain glistening
On the silver birch,
Like my lady's tears . . .
Your turn.

MANJIRO
Rain gathering,
Winding into streams,
Like the roads to Boston . . .
Your turn.

KAYAMA
Haze hovering,
Like the whisper of the silk
As my lady kneels . . .
Your turn.

MANJIRO
Haze glittering,
Like an echo of the lamps
In the streets of Boston . . .
Your turn.

KAYAMA
Moon,
I love her like the moon,
Making jewels of the grass
Where my lady walks,
My lady wife . . .

MANJIRO
Moon,
I love her like the moon,
Washing yesterday away,
As my lady does,
America . . .
Your turn.

KAYAMA
Wind murmuring.
Is she murmuring for me
Through her field of dreams? . . .
Your turn.

MANJIRO
Wind muttering.
Is she quarreling with me?
Does she want me home? . . .
Your turn.

KAYAMA
I am no nightingale,
But she hears the song
I can sing to her,
My lady wife . . .

MANJIRO
I am no nightingale,
But my song of her
Could outsing the sea . . .
America . . .

KAYAMA
Dawn flickering,
Tracing shadows of the pines
On my lady sleeping . . .
Your turn.

MANJIRO

Dawn brightening
As she opens up her eyes,
But it's I who come awake . . .
Your turn.

KAYAMA

You go.

MANJIRO

Your turn.

BOTH

Leaves,
I love her like the leaves,
Changing green to pink to gold,
And the change is everything.

Sun,
I see her like the sun
In the center of a pool,
Sending ripples to the shore,
Till my journey's end.

MANJIRO

Your turn.

KAYAMA

Rain . . .

MANJIRO

Haze . . .

KAYAMA

Moon . . .

MANJIRO

Wind . . .

KAYAMA

Nightingale . . .

MANJIRO

Dawn . . .

KAYAMA

Leaves . . .

MANJIRO

Sun . . .

BOTH

End.

**The poems in this lyric are imitation
haiku; they have the feeling but not**
the correct syllabic counts, unlike the
proper haiku in the next song.

*Upon reaching home, Kayama discovers
that Tamate, fearing that he would be in
disgrace for not having carried out his
mission, has committed suicide. As he
howls in mourning, a garish, middle-aged
Madam enters, urging on four very
young, awkward and reluctant girls to
welcome the arriving Americans. She
addresses the audience.*

Welcome to Kanagawa

MADAM

I own a small commercial venture
With a modest clientele
In Kanagawa.

GIRLS

I think I see one over there,
Behind the trees!

MADAM

Sh!

It's been my family's for centur-
Ies and doing very well—
For Kanagawa.

GIRLS

I hear they're covered all with hair,
Like some disease.

MADAM

Sh!

GIRLS

Except their knees.

MADAM

Sh!

The arrival of these giants
Out of the blue,
Bringing panic to my clients,
Alters my view.
With so many of them fleeing,
Conferring, decreeing,
I find myself agreeing
With the ancient haiku:

RECITER

The nest-building bird,
Seeing the tree without twigs,
Looks for new forests.

MADAM

Exactly.

Welcome to Kanagawa.

GIRLS
(*Loudly*)

Welcome to Kanagawa!

MADAM

No . . .

(*Seductively*)

Welcome to Kanagawa.

GIRLS

Oh . . .

(*Seductively*)

Welcome to Kanagawa.

MADAM

So.

With all my flowers disappearing
In alarm,
I've been reduced to commandeering
From the farm.
But with appropriate veneering,
Even green wood has its charm.

GIRLS

Yo-ho! Yo-ho!

MADAM

Yo-ho!

(*The girls whip out fans with
pornographic drawings on them; the
Madam points to each drawing
instructively*)

That you'll have to bend for—
Can you see why?
That you'll need a friend for—
Still, you might try.

That you do through the kimono—
Not very much.
That you use glue, then you—

No, no, no, no,
Those you don't touch!

ALL
Welcome to Kanagawa,
Music and food for twenty yen—
Music and food—

MADAM
And maybe then—

ALL
Welcome!

GIRLS
Welcome to Kanagawa!

MADAM
Low . . .

GIRLS
(Lowering their voices)
Welcome to Kanagawa.

MADAM
So.

You must neither be too wary
Nor too bold,
As there's no telling with barbari-
Ans, I'm told,
Because not only are they hairy,
But extremely uncontrolled.

GIRLS
Yo-ho!

MADAM
Yo-ho!

(Pointing to the fans)

That you mustn't wash for,
Not till you're done.
That you use a squash for—
Or pumpkins are fun.

That you do slow-
Ly and gently—
Don't take a chance.

That they don't know
About, evidently—
Get an advance.

ALL
Welcome to Kanagawa!
Music and food and company!
Music and food—

MADAM
And for a fee—

ALL
Welcome!

MADAM
When a country is in trouble,
Choices are few.
And apart from charging double,
What can you do?
With my clients off defending,
And strangers descending,
I find myself depending
On the ancient haiku:

RECITER
The bird from the sea,
Not knowing pine from bamboo,
Roosts on anything.

MADAM
Exactly.

GIRLS
Welcome to Kanagawa!

MADAM
Flow!

GIRLS
Welcome to Kanagawa!

MADAM
Glow!

GIRLS
Welcome to Kanagawa!

MADAM
Grow!

GIRLS
(Triumphantly)
Welcome to Kanagawa!

MADAM
Go!

GIRLS
(Exiting)
Welcome to Kanagawa! Yo-ho!
Welcome to Kanagawa! Yo-ho!

This is the most annoyingly problematic song I've ever written. With each revival of *Pacific Overtures* I rewrite it and with each revival it fails to be funny; not the sections in which the Madam justifies herself, which strike the right note of edgy satirical humor that I intended, but the pornographic ones which lie there like lumps of dough, no matter how gracefully or amusingly staged. During the same year that I wrote "Welcome to Kanagawa," I wrote a decent dirty song called "I Never Do Anything Twice" for the movie *The Seven-Per-Cent Solution*, so it can't be a matter of prurience or loss of technique. Perhaps it's the coyness of tone, the very thing I counted on to be humorous, that kills the jokes. Perhaps the idea shouldn't be verbalized, but merely suggested in dance: Japanese pornography is nothing if not humorlessly explicit. In any event, I'm open to suggestions.

By the way, the Reciter's haikus here, although formally correct, are, like the ones in "Poems," imitation, but for the opposite reason: they have the proper syllabification, but not the feeling: the metaphors are too blatant.

Commodore Perry and his escorts come ashore and meet with the Japanese Councilors in a treaty house which, as in Kayama's plan, has been temporarily erected to receive them and which will be destroyed the minute they leave, so that their feet will never have touched sacred Japanese soil. Under the floorboards a samurai warrior crouches, ready to spring up and kill the Americans should anything go wrong. The Reciter deplores the fact that no one knows what was said behind the closed shutters on that historic day. An Old Man enters.

OM Pardon me. I was there.   When they came & when they went —

(Well, you see)

R You were where?   I was part of the event

OM At the treaty house.   I was someone in a tree!

R At the treaty house?   I was younger then!

OM There was a tree...

R Which was where?   B: Tell him what I see.

OM Very near.

R Over here?

OM Maybe over there,

But there were trees then everywhere —

May I show you?

R If you please.

There were trees then everywhere —

But you were there...

And I was there!   Hidden in the
                                         Hiding in a tree

I will
May I   Let me show you.

If you please.

I was younger then.

I was good at climbing trees.

I was younger then.

I saw everything!

I was hidden all the time.

It was easier to climb.

I was younger then.
On that very day
It was years ago.   I was just a boy

I was good at climbing trees.

I saw everything!

what's essential
"inconsequential"

!

(Carrying a briefcase)

Pardon me. I was there.
You were where? At the [trusty] house
In the [really] house? There was In a tree
Which was near Near? Very near? Over here?
(Maybe)(over)there — well, there were trees
Everywhere. I can show you —
If you please. I was there. ↑
So you did. Yes I did. Behind a tree?
Yes, of course, behind a tree.

No! No! In a tree! Both: In In the a tree!

(stupidly) I was nine at the time. Only nine +
I could climb a the tree
Like this boy? Like the boy.
Just about the [size] age of this/boy
Just about his size.

And [just] what did you see?

B: Tell him, what do I see?
And I saw, and I heard
And you heard from behind a tree? No!
No! I did! I hid
Behind the tree. No! No!
But you could see. No! No!
Behind the tree. In In! So di!
In the tree. R: In the tree
In the tree.
I couldn't hear — I could
But I could see — at, good!
I could see.

I saw it all. I recall
Every detail and the details are what
Essence
Matters;

Not the building but the beam
Not the sentence but the word
And I heard — and you heard?
From a tree? Well, I could see

So I climbed the tree.
I was nine at the time.
I could climb a tree.

May I show you?
I was younger then
Only nine or so

I saw everything
I recall it all
I saw everything
I was hardly more than nine.
I was younger then, you see I can
Only nine then, you see nine!
I was seven at the time. Nine.
It was easier to climb
I was good at climbing trees.
May I show you? If you please
I was only but a child
I was just a little boy
Tell him, what do I see?

Ah, indeed I forgot
Forgive me
So sorry
Now you know everything

OM I was there. You were where?. At the house. In the house? In a tree
which was near. Which was here? Maybe there. There were
trees everywhere. If you please. I'll explain. That's the spot —
no it's not. Please explain. I will try.
No, that's fine. I was nine. And I hid. So you did.
In the tree, I could see through the leaves. In between the eaves
and the roof. Like a mouse. Right into the house.
So. I climbed the tree... I was nine. I could climb a tree

(Boy for Chorus) I am in a tree

W: I am here, too, I am also here. And this's me.
OM I was there. B I am there W I am here.
I could see. I can see. I can hear.

OM It's the details that count. Outsiders see details, insiders aren't objective
I noticed everything, didn't miss a thing. That remarkable day.
Everything effects everything — if I hadn't been there, it might
have been different, who's to say? I was part.
Like the flower, like the candy, like the squeak, like the cough.
R: Wait! Wait!

B. Tell him what I see.

Someone in a Tree

OLD MAN
Pardon me, I was there.

RECITER
You were where?

OLD MAN
At the treaty house.

RECITER
At the treaty house?

OLD MAN
There was a tree . . .

RECITER
Which was where?

OLD MAN
Very near.

RECITER
Over here?

OLD MAN
Maybe over there,
But there were trees then,
    everywhere.
May I show you?

RECITER
If you please.

OLD MAN
There were trees
Then, everywhere.

RECITER
But you were there.

OLD MAN
And I was there!
Let me show you.

RECITER
If you please.

OLD MAN
(Trying to climb the tree)
I was younger then . . .
I was good at climbing trees . . .
I was younger then . . .
I saw everything! . . .
I was hidden all the time . . .
It was easier to climb . . .
I was younger then . . .
I saw everything! . . .
Where they came and where they
    went . . .

I was part of the event.
I was someone in a tree!

I was younger then . . .

*(A young boy tumbles on and scrambles
up the tree)*

BOY
Tell him what I see!

OLD MAN
I am in a tree.
I am ten.
I am in a tree.

BOY
I was younger then.

OLD MAN
In between the eaves I can see—

(To the boy)

Tell me what I see.

(To the Reciter)

I was only ten.

BOY
I see men and matting.
Some are old, some chatting.

OLD MAN
If it happened, I was there!

BOTH
I saw (see) everything!

OLD MAN
I was someone in a tree.

BOY
Tell him what I see!

OLD MAN
Some of them have gold on their
    coats.

BOY
One of them has gold—
He was younger then.

OLD MAN
Someone crawls around, passing
    notes—

BOY
Someone very old—

OLD MAN
He was only ten.

BOY
And there's someone in a tree—

OLD MAN
—Or the day is incomplete.

BOTH
Without someone in a tree,
Nothing happened here.

OLD MAN
I am hiding in a tree.

BOY
I'm a fragment of the day.

BOTH
If I weren't, who's to say
Things would happen here the way
That they happened here?

OLD MAN
I was there then.

BOY
I am here still.
It's the fragment, not the day.

OLD MAN
It's the pebble, not the stream.

BOTH
It's the ripple, not the sea.
Not the building but the beam,
Not the garden but the stone,
Not the treaty house,
Someone in a tree.

(The warrior pokes his head up)

WARRIOR
Pardon me, I am here.
If you please, I am also here—

OLD MAN
They kept drinking cups of tea.

BOY
They kept sitting on the floor.

BOY, OLD MAN
They drank many cups of tea—
No, we told him that before.

WARRIOR
If you please, I am here.

RECITER
You are where?

WARRIOR
In the treaty house.

RECITER
In the treaty house?

WARRIOR
Or very near.

RECITER
Can you hear?

WARRIOR
I'm below.

RECITER
So I notice.

WARRIOR
Underneath the floor,
And so I can't see anything.
I can hear them,
But I can't see anything.

RECITER
But you can hear?

WARRIOR
But I can hear.
Shall I listen?

RECITER
If you please.

WARRIOR
I can hear them now . . .
I shall try to shift my knees . . .
I can hear them now . . .
I hear everything . . .
I'm the part that's underneath,
With my sword inside my sheath . . .
I can hear them now . . .
One is over me . . .
If they knock, then I appear!
I'm a part of what I hear.
I'm the fragment underneath.
I can hear them now!

RECITER, OLD MAN, BOY
Tell us what you hear!

WARRIOR
First I hear a creak and a thump.
Now I hear a clink.
Then they talk a bit . . .
Many times they shout when they speak.
Other times they think.
Or they argue it . . .

I hear floorboards groaning . . .
Angry growls . . . Much droning . . .

Since I hear them, they are there,
As they argue it.
I'm the listener underneath.

BOY
Someone reads a list
From a box.

WARRIOR
Someone talks of laws.

OLD MAN
Then they fan a bit.

BOY
Someone bangs a fist.

WARRIOR
Someone knocks.

OLD MAN
Now there was a pause.

ALL
Then they argue it:

WARRIOR
"But we want . . ."
"No, you can't
And we won't . . ."
"But we need it,
And we want . . ."
"Will you grant—?"
"If you don't . . ."
"We concede it . . ."

OLD MAN	WARRIOR	BOY
And they	I can	
Sat through the	Hear	
Night and they		
Lit yellow tapers.	Them.	
I was	I'm a	And they
There	Fragment of the	Chat and they
	Day.	Fight and they
		Sit signing
Then.		Papers.
If I	If I	I am
		There
Weren't, who's to	Weren't, who's to	
Say	Say	Still.
		If I
Things would	Things would	Weren't, who's to
Happen here	Happen here	Say
The way	The way	That they're
That they're	That they're	Happening?
Happening?	Happening?	

ALL

It's the fragment, not the day.
It's the pebble, not the stream.
It's the ripple, not the sea
That is happening.
Not the building but the beam,
Not the garden but the stone,
Only cups of tea
And history
And someone in a tree!

When I'm asked to name my favorite song of those I've written, an understandable but unanswerable request, I often proffer this one. I like the swing and relentlessness of the music and the poetic Orientalism of the lyric, but what I love is its ambition, its attempt to collapse past, present and future into one packaged song form. That ambitious invention was John Weidman's. The song is a distillation of a five-page scene he wrote, too long to include here. I have often taken dialogue passages from book writers and musicalized them, examples of which will surface in volume two in the chapters on *Sunday in the Park with George* and *Evening Primrose.* Suffice it to say that this song comes the closest to the heart of *Pacific Overtures:* historical narrative as written by a Japanese who's seen a lot of American musicals.

ACT TWO

Admirals from five different countries—the United States, Great Britain, the Netherlands, Russia and France—arrive and descend on Lord Abe, First Councilor to the Shogun, demanding that he sign treaties with them, granting each of them various trading rights.

Please Hello

AMERICAN ADMIRAL
Please hello, America back,
Commodore Perry send hello.
Also comes memorial plaque
President Fillmore wish bestow.

Emperor read our letter? If no,
Commodore Perry very sad.
Emperor like our letter? If so,
Commodore Perry very merry,
President Fillmore still more glad.

Last time we visit, too short.
This time we visit for slow.
Last time we come, come with
    warships,
Now with more ships—
Say hello!
This time request use of port,
Port for commercial intention,
Harbor with ample dimension.

ABE
But you can't—

AMERICAN ADMIRAL
Only one
Little port
For a freighter.

ABE
But you can't—

AMERICAN ADMIRAL
Just for fun,
Be a sport.

ABE
Maybe later—

AMERICAN ADMIRAL
But we bring many recent invention:
Kerosene
And cement
And a grain
Elevator,
A machine
You can rent
Called a "train"—

ABE
Maybe later—

AMERICAN ADMIRAL
Also cannon to shoot
Big loud salute,
Like so:

(He gestures toward the sea; an enormous explosion offshore)

Say hello!

(Another explosion)

Treaty meet approval? If no,
Commodore Perry very fierce.

(Indicating treaty)

Disregard confusion below—
President Fillmore now name Pierce.

(Abe signs the treaty)

Good! At last agreement is made,
Letter will let us come again.
First result of mutual trade:
Commodore getting letter letting,
Councilor getting fancy pen!
Goodbye.

ABE
Goodbye.

AMERICAN ADMIRAL
Goodbye.

ABE
Goodbye.

AMERICAN ADMIRAL
Please goodbye.

(The British Admiral enters)

BRITISH ADMIRAL
Hello!

AMERICAN ADMIRAL
Goodbye.

BRITISH ADMIRAL
Hello, please!

AMERICAN ADMIRAL
Goodbye.

BRITISH ADMIRAL
Please
Hello, I come with
Letters from
Her Majesty Victoria
Who, learning how
You're trading now,
Sang "Hallelujah, Gloria!"
And sent me to
Convey to you
Her positive euphoria
As well as lit-
Tle gifts from Brit-
Ain's various emporia.

(He offers Abe a tin of tea)

RECITER

The man has come with letters from
Her Majesty Victoria
As well as little gifts from Brit-
Ain's various emporia.

ABE

Tea?

BRITISH ADMIRAL

For drink.

ABE

I see.
I thank you—

BRITISH ADMIRAL

I think
Her letters do

Contain a few
Proposals to your Emperor
Which if, of course,
He won't endorse,
Will put her in a temper or,
More happily,
Should he agree,
Will serve to keep her placid, or
At least till I
Am followed by
A permanent ambassador.

RECITER

A treaty port
And from the court
A permanent ambassador.

A treaty port
And from the court
A permanent ambassador.
A treaty port

And from the court
A permanent ambassador
And more . . .

BRITISH ADMIRAL

Her Majesty
Considers the
Arrangements to be tentative
Until we ship
A proper dip-
Lomatic representative.
We don't foresee
That you will be
The least bit argumentative,
So please ignore
The man-of-war
We brought as a preventative.

(He gestures toward the sea; an offshore explosion, bigger than the Americans')

W. S. GILBERT
An Unacquired Taste

Terence Rattigan said of Noël Coward: "The best of his kind since W. S. Gilbert." I'm not sure what genre "his kind" implies, but I would guess that it refers to Coward's penchant for rapid patter or, to put it less kindly, verbosity. Gilbert's lyrics are sometimes clever and inventive, they have energy and charm, and they bore me to distraction—literally. When I go to Gilbert and Sullivan operettas, which is not often, during most of the songs my mind soon wanders, first to their imperfections and the ostentation with which the lyrics draw attention to themselves, then to my guilt at not being appreciative enough, then to the costumes and makeup, then to counting the number of people in the cast. Although I admire Gilbert's skill at rapid verbal patter to some extent, in large doses (that is to say, a whole score) his charm wears tedious on me.

As far as I'm concerned, Rattigan was right in his comparison of Gilbert and Coward. As with Coward, I have rarely found a Gilbert lyric funny (see "I Am the Very Model of a Modern Major General"). It baffles me when I hear an audience laugh at a Gilbert and Sullivan song; such enjoyment requires a taste for archness that eludes me. The only thing I've ever found funny in their operettas is the sight of middle-aged actors playing cartoonish characters in cartoonish costumes with stylized attitudes and rouged cheeks. And as with Coward, the patter lyrics strike me as more like typing than writing, to use Truman Capote's famous distinction. As with Coward, I suffer the effort expended on the strenuous list songs and cringe at the bloodless quaintness of the ballads, although to be fair, Gilbert was writing in accordance with the sentiments of his time. But if Coward is the master of blather, Gilbert is the master of prattle.

The most attractive thing about Gilbert and Sullivan is their energy, the energy of extremely sophisticated schoolboys making fun of authority, something I can identify with (it describes *Anyone Can Whistle*). Perhaps I'd like their work better if I knew more about the contemporary targets of their satire, if I knew, for example, the model for Sir Joseph Porter. Perhaps I'd feel different about them if I liked Sullivan's work more, but I have a limited attention span for what strikes me as decorative music, the kind whose chief virtue is surface sparkle and restrained lyricism—which, I blush to say, also includes a

good deal of music written before the Romantic era. Perhaps I could get into their groove if I took greater pleasure in music by composers I accept as great, like Haydn and Handel. Perhaps.

I never fail to be startled by the fervor of their fans. Leonard Bernstein was one. He knew every word and note that they wrote and would quote them voluminously at the drop of a title. My guess is that his love for their work was one of the things that fueled his writing *Candide*. His score and Richard Wilbur's lyrics, however, are not only superior to G & S, they constitute the most scintillating set of songs yet written for the musical theater. I suspect that the basis of Gilbert and Sullivan's continuing popularity, such as it is, is that the square and stodgy rhythms, along with the general predictability and formal dexterity of the lyrics, give many people the same comfortable feeling of familiarity that Agatha Christie mysteries do. The importance of what Gilbert and Sullivan accomplished, as Hammerstein did later, was to make an amalgam of sources into a new entity: in their case, the topically satiric operetta.

RECITER
Yes, please ignore the man-of-war
That's anchored rather near to shore.
It's nothing but a metaphor
That acts as a preventative.

BRITISH ADMIRAL
All clear?
Just so.
Sign here.

(Abe signs)

AMERICAN ADMIRAL
Hello, hello, objection resent!
President Pierce say "Moment's
    pause."
British get ambassador sent,
President Pierce get extra clause!

(The Dutch Admiral enters)

DUTCH ADMIRAL
Wait! Please hello!
Don't forget the Dutch!
Like to keep in touch.
Thank you very much.

Tell them to go,
Button up the lips.
What do little Nips
Want with battleships?

Hold everything,
We gonna bring
Chocolate!
Wouldn' you like to lease
A beautiful little piece
Of chocolate?
Listen, that's not to mention
Wonderful—pay attention!—
Windmills
Und tulips.
Und wouldn' you like a wooden
    shoe?

There—can you read?
Good! We will need
Two ports,
One of them not too rocky—
How about Nagasaki?
Two ports,
One of them for the cocoa—
What do you call it?—Yoko-
Hama! Ja!
Und Nagasaki! Ja!
Sign here!

*(He gestures; an offshore explosion bigger
than the British one. Abe signs)*

AMERICAN ADMIRAL
Wait please, objection again!
Dutch getting too many seaports.
President now wanting three ports—

BRITISH ADMIRAL
(Overlapping)
Great Britain wish-
Es her position
Clear and indisputable.
We're not amused
At being used
And therefore stand immutable.
And though you Japs
Are foxy chaps
And damnably inscrutable—

*(The Russian Admiral enters, wearing an
ornate greatcoat)*

RUSSIAN ADMIRAL
Please hello . . .

DUTCH ADMIRAL
Wait! Please hello!
Comes the monkey wrench!
Smell that awful stench—
Probably the French.

AMERICAN ADMIRAL
(Overlapping)
Also insist giving free ports—

BRITISH ADMIRAL
(Overlapping)
Reviewing it
From where we sit,
The facts are irrefutable—

RUSSIAN ADMIRAL
Please hello . . .

DUTCH ADMIRAL
Ach, nein, of course,
My mistake, the Czar.
Smell the caviar—
Leave the door ajar.

AMERICAN ADMIRAL
(Overlapping)
Also want annual reports—

BRITISH ADMIRAL
(Overlapping)
And thus, in short,

A single port
Is patently unsuitable!

RUSSIAN ADMIRAL
Please hello,
Is bringing Czar's request,
Braving snow
With letter to protest.
Since we know
You trading with the West,
You might at least
(Don't touch the coat!)
Start looking East
Or closer West—
Well, farther North—
Are we the fourth?
I feel depressed.
(Don't touch the coat!)

Coming next
Is extraterritoriality.
Noting text
Say "extraterritoriality."
You perplexed
By "extraterritoriality"?
Just noting clause
(Don't touch the coat!)
Which say your laws
Do not apply
(Don't touch the coat!)
When we drop by,
Not getting shot,
No matter what—
A minor scrape,
A major rape,
And we escape
(Don't touch the cape!)
That's what is extraterritoriality.

Fair is fair—
You wish perhaps to vote?
What we care
You liking what we wrote?
Sitting there
Is finest fleet afloat.
Observing boat?

*(He gestures; an explosion even bigger
than the Dutch one)*

Don't touch the coat.
Just sign the note.

(Abe signs)

BRITISH ADMIRAL

The British feel
These latest dealings
Verge on immorality.
The element
Of precedent
Imperils our neutrality.
We're rather vexed,
Your giving ext-
Raterritoriality.
We must insist
You offer this
To every nationality!

DUTCH ADMIRAL
(Overlapping)

We want the same
What the Russkies claim!
Why you let them came?
Dirty rotten shame!

AMERICAN ADMIRAL
(Overlapping)

U.S.A. extremely upset!
President Pierce say solid "No!"

(The French Admiral enters, dancing)

FRENCH ADMIRAL

'Allo!—
Please 'allo!
Please 'allo
'Allo! 'Allo! 'Allo!

I bring word,
I bring word
From Napoleon ze Third.
'E 'ad 'eard what 'ave occurred 'ere
From ze little bird!

Undeterred,
We conferred,
Though we felt zat we'd been slurred,
And ze verdict was he spurred me
    'ere to
Bring ze word!
Would you like to know ze word
From Napoleon ze Third?

It's détente! Oui, détente!
Zat's ze only thing we want!
Just détente! Oooh, détente!
No agreement could be more fair!
Signing pacts,
Passing acts,
Zere's no time for making warfare
When you're always busy

Making wiz ze
Mutual détente!

A détente! A détente
Is ze only thing we wish!
Same as zem, except additional
Ze rights to fish!
You'll be paid, you'll be paid,
And we'll 'ave ze big parade
If we somehow can persuade
You to accept our aid.
It is not to be afraid . . .

(Gestures; the biggest explosion yet)

As we merely wish to trade . . .

(Another; Abe signs the treaty)

A détente! Oui, détente!
Zat's ze only thing we want!
Leave ze grain,
Leave ze train,
Put Champagne among your imports!
Tell each man
Zat Japan
Can't be bothered giving him ports
While she's in a tizzy,
Dizzy
Wiz ze
Mutual détente!

ABE

It is late,
And I fear—
Well,
You see,
There's a famine.
Could you wait
For a year?
We'll agree
To examine
It, but we've
Had a quake
And a flood
And a famine . . .
Please believe
We will take
It to study,
Examine it . . .

FRENCH ADMIRAL
(Simultaneously)

Just détente! Oooh détente!
No agreement could be more fair!
Signing pacts,

Passing acts,
Zere's no time for making warfare.
Why discuss,
Make ze fuss,
Since ze West belong to us?
And ze East
We have leased
For ze French administration.
If you force
In ze Norce,
Zen we burn ze Dutch legation.

DUTCH ADMIRAL
(Simultaneously)

Wait! Please hello!
Don't forget the Dutch!
We want just as much
Fishing rights and such!
Tell them to go,
Otherwise we post
Battleships at most
Ports along the coast.
You can have the West,
We will take the rest.

BRITISH ADMIRAL
(Simultaneously)

One moment, please,
I think that these
Assure us exclusivity
For Western ports
And other sorts
Of maritime activity,
And if you mean
To intervene,
As is the Dutch proclivity,
We'll blow you nits
To little bits
With suitable festivity.

AMERICAN ADMIRAL
(Simultaneously)

Wait please, hello, West is ours.
Wait please, the East is the best coast.
We'll trade you two on the West
    coast.

RUSSIAN ADMIRAL
(Simultaneously)

Please hello, no seaports on the West.
United States too near to Czar,
Is tempting fates, is go too far—
(Don't touch the coat!)

ALL ADMIRALS

Ah, détentes!
Ah, détentes!

They're what everybody wants!
You should want
A détente—
Makes a nation like a brother!
We'll be here
Every year
To protect you from each other
And to see you aren't
Signing foreign
Treaties and détentes!

Please hello!
We must go,
But our intercourse will grow
Through détente,
As détente
Brings complete cooperation.
By the way,
May we say
We adore your little nation,
And with heavy cannon
Wish you an un-
Ending please hello!!!

*(There follows a profusion of
cannon roars)*

The conceit of the show, postulating
it as one written by a Japanese playwright exposed to American musical
theater, spawned one of Weidman's
most inventive ideas: the Japanese
would speak elegant, formalized
King's English, whereas all the foreigners would speak a pidgin form of
their native language. Thus the verbal
style of "Please Hello." I also would
like to point out with suitable pride
that the lyric is historically accurate as
an account not only of the succession
of arrivals but of the specifics of each
country's demands. The music, unsurprisingly, is a series of pastiches:
Sousa march, Gilbert and Sullivan patter, Dutch clog dance, Russian dirge
and French can-can.

In the interests of thumbing my
nose at Gilbert, I summoned up a
meticulous series of inner rhymes
without distorting syntax, syntax
distortion being a feature excused
by his fans as part of his style, but
something which I deplore, as I
deplore it in Hart, Gershwin and
Coward.

*On one side of the stage, Kayama, as
Governor of Uraga, sits behind a low
table, writing an official letter; Manjiro,
on the other side, performs the ritual tea
ceremony. During the course of the song,
which takes place over a period of fifteen
years, Kayama becomes more prosperous
and more politically powerful, continuing
to write as his table becomes a desk and
his clothes and furnishings more Western-
ized; at the same time Manjiro slowly fin-
ishes the ceremony and dons a samurai's
robes in preparation for sword practice.*

A Bowler Hat

RECITER
A letter from Kayama Yesaemon to
the Shogun.

(Reading as Kayama writes)

My Lord Abe. It is my privilege to
inform you of the current state of
our relationship with foreigners
here in Uraga.

*(Kayama removes a bowler hat from the
box under his table and examines it)*

RECITER
As you have doubtless learned from
servants far more worthy than myself, there are now two hundred Westerners among us. Five times as many
as a year ago—when they first came.

KAYAMA
It's called a bowler hat.
I have no wife.
The swallow flying through the sky
Is not as swift as I
Am, flying through my life.
You pour the milk before the tea.
The Dutch ambassador is no fool.
I must remember that.

*(His writing brush is replaced with
a steel pen)*

RECITER
Three years ago we set aside one dis-
trict of the town for Westerners, and
yet we are still unable to provide

them with residences which they
consider suitable. For this I humbly
ask your indulgence.

KAYAMA
I wear a bowler hat.
They send me wine.
The house is far too grand.
I've bought a new umbrella stand.
Today I visited the church beside the
    shrine.
I'm learning English from a book.
Most exciting.
It's called a bowler hat.

*(As the Reciter reads, Kayama's table is
replaced by a more Western one. He is
given a chair.)*

RECITER
Of all the Westerners with whom I
have to deal, the merchants are the
most worrisome. They import goods
we do not need and export those we
cannot do without. Last month they
bought and shipped to Shanghai so
much flour that the price here
almost tripled. The noodlemakers
were affected most severely and
threatened to set fire to the Western
warehouses. I found it necessary to
restrain them.

*(Kayama takes a watch from his pocket
and checks the time)*

KAYAMA
It's called a pocket watch.
I have a wife.
No eagle flies against the sky
As eagerly as I
Have flown against my life.
One smokes American cigars.
The Dutch ambassador was most rude.
I will remember that.

*(A nineteenth-century tea service is
placed on his table and he pours himself
a cup of tea)*

RECITER
Although the Westerners have been
in residence for upwards of six years
now, our samurai still mistake their
foreign manners for disrespect. To
avoid unpleasant incidents, I have
required all samurai to remove their
swords before entering the city.

KAYAMA

I wind my pocket watch.
We serve white wine.
The house is far too small.
I killed a spider on the wall.
One of the servants thought it was a
    lucky sign.
I read Spinoza every day.

(With French pronunciation)

Formidable.
Where is my bowler hat?

*(His table is replaced by a desk and
revolving chair)*

RECITER

I will not bother you with details of
the rowdy sailors and adventurers
who plague our port. As you know,
provisions of the treaties which
you signed eight years ago make it
impossible for us to deal with
them. But fortunately, the behavior
of the foreign consuls and ambassadors themselves has been above
reproach. They have built themselves a club, complete with bar and
billiards room. And only gentlemen
may enter.

*(Kayama slowly spins around in his
chair; he now sports a monocle)*

KAYAMA

It's called a monocle.
I've left my wife.
No bird exploring in the sky
Explores as well as I
The corners of my life.
One must keep moving with the
    times.
The Dutch ambassador is a fool.
He wears a bowler hat.

*(A French oil painting is hung on the
screen behind him)*

RECITER

My lord, here in Uraga we have
reached an understanding with the
Westerners. Of course I wish them
gone, but while they remain I shall
try to turn their presence into an
advantage rather than a burden. Last
week I joined them in a fox hunt.

KAYAMA
(Putting on glasses)

They call them spectacles.
I drink much wine.
I take imported pills.
I have a house up in the hills
I've hired British architects to
    redesign.
One must accommodate the times
As one lives them.
One must remember that.

*(A servant enters and holds up a
diplomat's coat for him to wear)*

It's called a cutaway . . .

When we first discussed this scene, I
asked John to go home (we worked at
my house) and write Kayama's letter,
which I would turn into a song. But
after reading the crystalline formality
of the prose, I decided that rhyming
it would ruin it and that it would be
better to include it as written in the
body of a lyric which gave an impres-
sionistic picture of Kayama's development over the years: a succession of
images that would evoke the changes
in both him and Japan—a lyrical
scrapbook. It was a smart decision.
The combination of prose, lyric and
Hal's elegant minimal staging made
for a memorable theatrical moment,
compressing fifteen extraordinary
years into five extraordinary minutes.

*Three British Cockney sailors see a young
Japanese girl in a garden and attempt to
woo her.*

Pretty Lady

THIRD SAILOR

Pretty lady in the pretty garden,
    can'tcher stay?
Pretty lady, we got leave and we got
    paid today.
Pretty lady with a flower,
Give a lonely sailor 'alf an hour.
Pretty lady, can you understand a
    word I say?
Don't go away.

FIRST SAILOR

Pretty lady, you're the cleanest thing I
    seen all year.

THIRD SAILOR

I sailed the world for you.

FIRST SAILOR

Pretty lady, you're enough to make me
    glad I'm here.

SECOND SAILOR
(Simultaneously)

Pretty lady, could I hear you laugh?
I ain't heard a lady laugh for I don't
    know how long.
I'll sing a song for you,
Tell you tales of adventuring, strange
    and fantastical.
Pretty lady, I ain't never been away
    from home.

SECOND SAILOR

Pretty lady, beg your pardon,
Won'tcher walk me through your
    pretty garden?

THIRD SAILOR
(Simultaneously)

Pretty lady, I'm a million miles from
    Stepney Green.
You are the softest thing I've ever
    seen.
Stay with me please, I been away so
    long.
Don't be afraid . . .
Hey, no, listen, pretty lady, beg your
    pardon,
Won'tcher walk me through your
    pretty garden?

FIRST SAILOR
(Simultaneously)

Pretty lady, how about it?
Don'tcher know how long I been
    without it?
Pretty lady in the garden, wotcher
    say?
Can'tcher stay? . . .
Hey, wait, don't go yet.
Pretty lady with the pretty bow,
Please don't go, it's early.
Won'tcher walk me through your
    pretty garden?

ALL

Pretty lady, look, I'm on my knees,
Pretty please.

SECOND SAILOR
Pretty lady, in the pretty garden,
won'tcher stay?

SECOND, THIRD SAILORS
Pretty lady, we got leave and we got
paid today.

FIRST SAILOR
Pretty lady with a flower,

ALL SAILORS
Give a lonely sailor 'alf an hour!

FIRST SAILOR
Pretty lady in the pretty garden,
won'tcher stay?

SECOND SAILOR
(Overlapping)
Pretty lady in the pretty garden,
won'tcher stay?

THIRD SAILOR
(Overlapping)
Pretty lady in the pretty garden,
wotcher say?

FIRST SAILOR
Why can'tcher stay?

SECOND SAILOR
I sailed the world for you!

THIRD SAILOR
Don't go away.

*The impact of the Western incursions
reaches a tipping point, the Tokugawa
Shogunate collapses and the Emperor
Meiji brings Japan into the twentieth century. The Chorus, a cross-section of contemporary Japanese society, echoing the
opening number, sings.*

Next

CHORUS
Streams are flowing.
See what's coming
Next!
Winds are blowing.
See what's coming,
See what's going
Next!

Roads are turning,
Journey with them.
A little learning—
Next!
Waters churning,
Lightning flashes.
Kings are burning,
Sift the ashes—
Next!

Tower tumbles,
Tower rises—
Next!
Tower crumbles,
Man revises.
Motor rumbles,
Civilizes.
More surprises—
Next!

Streams are roaring,
Overspilling—
Next!
Old is boring,
New is thrilling,
Keep exploring—
Next!

First the thunder—
Just a murmur,
A little blunder—
Next!
Then the wonder,
See how pretty—
(Going under,
What a pity!)
Next!

Streams are flying,
Use the motion—
Next!
Streams are drying,
Mix a potion!
Streams are dying,
Try the ocean!
Brilliant notion—
Next!

Never mind the small disaster.
Who's the stronger, who's the faster?
Let the pupil show the master—
Next!
Next!

RECITER
Nippon. The Floating Kingdom.
There was a time when foreigners
were not welcome here. But that was
long ago. One hundred and thirty
years.

(Pause)
Welcome to Japan.

CHORUS
Brilliant notions,
Still improving!
Make the motions,
Keep it moving—
Next!
Next!
Next!
Next!

Lyric writing in general would be a
lot easier in Italian, a language with a
plethora of words ending in singable
and easily rhymed open vowel sounds,
but sometimes the English language
serves a lyricist well. "Next" is the perfect word for a song which deals with
the apocalyptic effect of Western cultures, especially contemporary Western cultures blasting open a serene,
self-contained society that had existed
snugly and smugly for centuries.
"Next!" is an onomatopoeic blast if
there ever was one. How much less effective this blast would have been if its
refrain had been "Successivo!" or
"Volgended!" or "Suivant!" How lucky
to have an explosive word like "Next!"
which sums up the violence of the intrusion sonically and contrasts with
the gentle mellifluousness of trans-
lated haiku so vividly. Then again,
English has always been the language
whose sound I like best. Except for
Russian.

Sweeney Todd

The Demon Barber of Fleet Street

A MUSICAL THRILLER

12. Sweeney Todd, the Demon Barber of Fleet Street (1979)

Book by Hugh Wheeler

Based on the play Sweeney Todd, the Demon Barber of Fleet Street *by Christopher Bond*

The Notion

England in 1849. Sweeney Todd, a barber unjustly convicted and sent to an Australian prison, escapes and returns to London, determined to avenge himself on Judge Turpin, the man who convicted him. He allies himself with his former landlady, Nellie Lovett, but his plans to kill the Judge go awry and in his frustration he sets out to avenge himself on the world.

General Comments

The music that dominated my childhood was neither show music nor classical repertoire, although my father played Broadway tunes (by ear) and I took piano lessons for two years. I was thus exposed to Gershwin via "The Man I Love" and Rodgers via "Blue Moon" simultaneously with Beethoven via "Für Elise" and Rimsky-Korsakov via "The Flight of the Bumblebee." It was movie music, however, that mesmerized me—by which I mean background music, not songs. At the age of ten I was more a fan of Korngold than of Kern, more of Steiner than of Strauss—Richard, that is. (I was too unschooled to know that Steiner *was* Richard Strauss.) I liked theater, but I *loved* movies, and movies of every kind: dramas, comedies, short subjects and especially trailers—everything in fact except musicals, which with the exception of *The Wizard of Oz* I either tolerated if I enjoyed the songs or was bored by if I didn't. My particular favorites were romantic melodramas and suspense pieces like *Casablanca* and the Hitchcock movies of the period, movies in which the music was as important to the storytelling as the actors were. For me, the apotheosis of these melodramas was *Hangover Square*, an Edwardian thriller about a sweet-natured, gifted composer who, when he hears a certain high-pitched sound, clicks into a schizophrenic state and becomes a serial killer. The music was by Bernard Herrmann and it was (and is) an astonishing score, not just for the mood of suspense it maintains but for the fact that the climax of the story is a concert at which the composer premieres his avant-garde piano concerto, has a mental breakdown, goes berserk, sets fire to the concert hall and still manages to finish playing the piece before dying in the flames. (Since everyone else has fled the hall, including the orchestra players, Herrmann is forced to end the concerto with a lengthy piano solo, making it perhaps the only concerto in history to do so.) At the age of fifteen I believed every word of it, intensely enough to encourage me to sit through the movie a second time so that, with the music blaring from the soundtrack, I could memorize the first page of the concerto's score, which appeared on the screen for just a few seconds after one of the murders. When I got home that night, I played it over and over until I was sure I had it right and it was imprinted into my DNA. I can play it still.

At this same time I was falling under the influence of Oscar Hammerstein and becoming increasingly interested in theater songs, but it wasn't until thirty years later that these two passions coincided. It happened in 1973, when in London I chanced to see Christopher Bond's version of the nineteenth-century British potboiler

Sweeney Todd, the Demon Barber of Fleet Street. Although it was played primarily as a comedy, with pub songs interspersed between scenes, it immediately struck me as material for a musical horror story, one which would not be sung-through but which would be held together by ceaseless underscoring that would keep an audience in suspense and maybe even scare the hell out of them. It would, in fact, be my tribute to Bernard Herrmann and *Hangover Square.* Given my antipathy toward opera—impatience with it, really—I was determined that the piece would be constructed mainly of song forms: something between a musical and a ballad opera, like *Carmen,* only with less *recitative,* if any. The problem lay in how to make the flamboyance of the outrageous story believable to a contemporary audience; I trusted that a steady stream of moody, churning background music would do the trick, just as it had for Hitchcock's films, many of which Herrmann had scored.

The lyrics presented a different problem. Bond is, or at least was at the time, a playwright much interested in the British class system and to this end his characters were sharply delineated by their language: Judge Turpin, the aristocrat of the bunch, spoke in measured cadences, Sweeney and the young lovers in proper and slightly flowery King's English, and the others in either Cockney or working-class argot. It was the others who worried me. Writing anything in contemporary American English, be it artificial, colloquial or slang, doesn't give me pause—it's part of my everyday experience. But period language, even American period language, stops me short: I could never have written *Oklahoma!* or *Carousel.* To begin with, period language limits your vocabulary unless you research it—and, as I've said before, I'm a lazy reader. Moreover, to my ear period language as written by contemporaries is rarely convincing; it usually comes across as quaint or false, and almost always as self-conscious.

Having taken the project on, I hoped that I'd be able to manage the argot by limiting myself to the British colloquialisms Bond had used, mingled with the few I knew. There weren't enough, however, to allow for variety of image, variety of humor and, most important, variety of rhyme. Dutifully, however, I did turn to research: Eric Partridge's *A Dictionary of Slang and Unconventional English,* from which I hoped to collect all the Victorian words and terms I could find. But how can you look up an entry when all you know is the definition? In a dictionary, the word comes before the definition, so how do you look up the slang word whose definition is "sexy"? That's the job of a thesaurus, which deals in synonyms rather than definitions. What I needed was a British slang thesaurus, and such a thing doesn't exist. I decided I'd have to invent some language, much as Arthur Laurents had done for *West Side Story.* This was particularly necessary for the songs of the Beggar Woman, a minor but important character, who tries to sell herself to passersby in bawdy Cockney. Invent I did, and nobody who read or heard the lyrics caught me until, glowing with too much self-satisfaction, I had the mistaken nerve to show the script to Peter Shaffer, a playwright who had once fooled his own British countrymen, critics and audiences alike, with faux Shakespearean dialogue. Needless to say, he spotted every word I'd made up. Shortly thereafter I was lucky enough to meet David Land, a British producer who had been born in Cockney territory. After a few minutes' conversation, he had given me enough terms to keep a men's smoker going for hours.

Sweeney Todd has been called by people who care about categories everything from an opera to a song cycle. When pressed, I have referred to it as a dark operetta, but just as all baggage comes with labels, so do all labels come with baggage. "Opera" implies endless stentorian singing; "operetta" implies gleeful choirs of peasants dancing in the town square; "opéra bouffe" implies hilarious (in intent, at least) complications of mistaken identity; "musical comedy" implies showbiz pizzazz and blindingly bright energy; "musical play" implies musical comedy that isn't funny. For me, an opera is something that is performed in an opera house in front of an opera audience. The ambience, along with the audience's expectation, is what flavors the evening. When *Porgy and Bess* was performed on Broadway, it was a musical; when it was performed at Glyndebourne and Covent Garden, it was an opera. When *Carmen* is at an opera house, it is an opera, *comique* or not; when it was presented on Broadway, transmuted into *Carmen Jones,* it had *less* dialogue than the original, but it was a musical. Opera is defined by the eye and ear of the beholder. So where does that leave *Sweeney?*

"Dark operetta" is the closest I can come, but that's as much a misnomer as any of the others. What *Sweeney Todd* really is is a movie for the stage.

ACT ONE

The entire Company enters, except for Sweeney and Mrs. Lovett.

The Ballad of Sweeney Todd

A MAN
Attend the tale of Sweeney Todd.
His skin was pale and his eye was
    odd.
He shaved the faces of gentlemen
Who never thereafter were heard of
    again.
He trod a path that few have trod,
Did Sweeney Todd,
The Demon Barber of Fleet Street.

ANOTHER MAN
He kept a shop in London town,
Of fancy clients and good renown.
And what if none of their souls were
    saved?
They went to their maker impeccably
    shaved
By Sweeney,
By Sweeney Todd,
The Demon Barber of Fleet Street.

COMPANY
Swing your razor wide, Sweeney!
Hold it to the skies!
Freely flows the blood of those
Who moralize!

His needs were few, his room was bare:
A lavabo and a fancy chair,
A mug of suds and a leather strop,
An apron, a towel, a pail and a mop.
For neatness he deserved a nod,
Did Sweeney Todd,
The Demon Barber of Fleet Street.

Inconspicuous Sweeney was,
Quick and quiet and clean 'e was.
Back of his smile, under his word,
Sweeney heard music that nobody
    heard.

Sweeney pondered and Sweeney
    planned,

Like a perfect machine 'e planned.
Sweeney was smooth, Sweeney was
    subtle,
Sweeney would blink and rats would
    scuttle.
Inconspicuous Sweeney was,
Quick and quiet and clean 'e was,
Like a perfect machine 'e was,
Was Sweeney!
Sweeney! Sweeney! Sweeeeeneeeeey!

(Sweeney Todd appears)

TODD, COMPANY
Attend the tale of Sweeney Todd.
He served a dark and a vengeful god.

TODD
What happened then—well, that's the
    play,
And he wouldn't want us to give it
    away,
Not Sweeney,

TODD, COMPANY
Not Sweeney Todd,
The Demon Barber of Fleet Street.

If ever there was an example of "God is in the details," it's the line that opens this show: "Attend the tale of Sweeney Todd." Detail 1: the use of "attend" to mean "listen to" is just archaic enough to tell the audience that this will be a period piece. Detail 2: the idea of a "tale" suggests that the audience not take the story realistically but as a fable, and opens them up to accept the bizarrerie of the events which follow; it also promises a story that will unfold like a folk ballad, foreshadowing the numerous choruses of the song that will pop up during the course of the evening. Detail 3: the alliteration on the first, second and fourth accented beats of "At*t*end the *t*ale of Sweeney *T*odd" is not only a microcosm of the AABA form of the song itself, but in its very formality gives the line a sinister feeling, especially with the sepulchral accompaniment that rumbles underneath it.

If all of that seems like the kind of academic hyperanalysis which regularly shows up in studies of literary forms, I can assure you that even if the audience is not consciously aware of such specific details, they are affected by them. Hammerstein, in the Introduction to his book *Lyrics*, wrote:

> A year or so ago, on the cover of the *New York Herald Tribune Sunday Magazine*, I saw a picture of the Statue of Liberty. It was a picture taken from a helicopter and it showed the top of the statue's head. I was amazed at the detail there. The sculptor had done a painstaking job with the lady's coiffure, and yet he must have been pretty sure that the only eyes that would ever see this detail would be the uncritical eyes of seagulls. He could not have dreamt that any man would ever fly over this head and take a picture of it. He was artist enough, however, to finish off this part of the statue with as much care as he had devoted to her face and her arms and the torch and everything that people can see as they sail up the bay. He was right. When you are creating a work of art, or any other kind of work, finish the job off perfectly. You never know when a helicopter, or some other instrument not at the moment invented, may come along and find you out.

His point is well taken and well made, although if I'd known it at the time, I could have suggested to him that the sculptor might have had another reason for his painstaking attention to the top of her head: the disassembled statue was lying on the ground in the middle of Paris for all to see for months before it was assembled and shipped to America.

Hammerstein also claimed that the opening number is the most important song in a musical because it establishes tone, character, information and everything in between. If that's true (and it is), I would add that for the same reason the first line of any song is the most important line in it, which in turn means that the first line of the opening number is crucial to an audience's acceptance of everything which follows. It was a lucky moment for me, therefore, when "Attend the tale of Sweeney Todd" swam into my consciousness. As Tennessee Williams wrote, "Sometimes there's God so quickly."

Todd, a sullen man seething with anger, and Anthony, an eager young sailor, arrive at the London docks after a long sea voyage.

No Place Like London

ANTHONY
I have sailed the world, beheld its
    wonders
From the Dardanelles
To the mountains of Peru,
But there's no place like London!
I feel home again.

I could hear the city bells
Ring whatever I would do.
No, there's no place—

TODD
(Grimly, overlapping)
No, there's no place like London.

ANTHONY
Mr. Todd, sir?

TODD
You are young.
Life has been kind to you.
You will learn.

(A beggar woman appears out of the shadows)

BEGGAR WOMAN
Alms! Alms!
For a miserable woman
On a miserable chilly morning . . .

(Anthony gives her a coin)

Thank yer, sir, thank yer . . .

(Suddenly leering in a mad way)

'Ow would you like a little muff, dear,
A little jig jig,
A little bounce around the bush?
Wouldn't you like to push me
    parsley?
It looks to me, dear,
Like you got plenty there to push.

(She grabs at him. He pushes her away. She turns instantly to Todd, who turns away from her)

BEGGAR WOMAN
Alms! Alms!
For a pitiful woman
Who's got wanderin' wits—
Hey, don't I know you, mister?

TODD
Must you glare at me, woman? Off with you! Off, I say!

BEGGAR WOMAN
(Leering)
Then 'ow would you like to split me muff, mister?
We'll go jig jig,
A little—

(Todd gestures as if to strike her. She scuttles away)

BEGGAR WOMAN
(Into the distance)
Alms! Alms!
For a desperate woman . . .

This is the lyric I referred to earlier as the cause of my research into Cockney, my subsequent decision to make words up and my eventual meeting with a genuine East Ender. The result is an amalgam of pure invention, authentic Cockney, American slang and universal poetry. The scorecard:

1. "Muff." Authentic Cockney all right, but also authentic American, and I wanted a word that sounded specifically Dickensian. I invented the word "squiff," which can still be heard on the original recording. By the time the vocal score was ready to go to press, however, I had met Mr.

Land, my Cockney expert, who told me he couldn't think of another one-syllable term which would be both authentic and common. So I reverted to "muff," although I have to say that I miss the archaic sound, spurious though it may be, of "squiff."
2. "Jig jig." This isn't Cockney either, it's American (in England it was "jig-a-jig"), but the implications of the sounds are universal.
3. "Bounce around the bush." Pure invention, although "bush" is immediately recognizable in the United States.
4. "Push me parsley." The "parsley" is authentic, the "push" is not, but I needed the setup for the "push" rhyme at the end of the next line, which is the intended punch. "Push me parsley" had been "Push me crumpet" in the original version because I had heard "a bit of crumpet" in innumerable British films about the working class and thought it had a sexual connotation. I had confused class with dialect. I asked my expert for a two-syllable equivalent and he came up with a number of them, the most humorously elegant being "parsley."
5. "Split me muff." Authentic Cockney. I had written "Fish me squiff." The authentic is better.

To spare the sensibilities of school administrations, I wrote a bowdlerized version for school and squeamish regional productions:

'Ow would you like a little kiss, dear?
I'll be your girlfriend—
You won't do better on the docks.
Wouldn't you like to take me dancin'
And be my boyfriend
And buy me lots of pretty frocks?

Todd thanks Anthony for having rescued him from a life raft in the middle of the ocean and bids him farewell. Anthony affirms his friendship and offers Todd money should he need it, which Todd fiercely refuses. Anthony is taken aback and Todd tries to explain his outburst.

T: Get away!   widge

Alms! Alms! Alms!   Something for the pot, mister
For a poor ~~unfortunate~~ witless woman   For a woman wot's witless
Through no fault of her own, sir   Ooh! Pretty sailor boy!
A poor creature wot's lost her wits   But I know what you want
And given to fits.

Just A couple of bits   Ooh! Cor!
Alms! Alms!
For a miserable /   For a woman wot's /
Woman on a miracle   Lost her wits, for a mis'rable
Chilly morning   Woman on a chilly morning

                  3   Thankee, mister
How would you like a little   Thankee, sir,   Pardon me, Mr. High &
  Squink, honey   Thankee, hey   Mighty, your Lordship —
        sailor   sir   Hey! ...

You're a good & bunky lad, sailor   Tell me, sailor, is it

Ooh, you got such lovely   Taw, if your
                                     Fingers and feet are big
Fingers there, sailor boy —   Fingers are big,
Wot you got below?   Then your

                                     How'd ja like a little
                                     scruffy boy
Judging from those fingers   crumpet   a little
Those long   Quince paste, a little
Plenty there to push   Bounce around the brick

To push the crumpet   I can give you it to soft & warm
I'd guess bet there's plenty there to push   Wot, boy

Why don't we push around the crumpet   Wouldn't you like to push me crumpet?
For just an hour?   You're long enough, boy

whots
a gruff

a Dowdy
chiddle

Hey (Ahoy)! Sailor boy

Give me a poke
I'll tell you a joke
back on the ship lays asleep abed
And you'll be aboard by morning

Ahoy

Hey, pretty sailor boy,
Got the itch, 'ave you?

It's knees you want

Whatcha want that for?

Hey! Hey! Sailor Boy
you'll be abed by sunrise

Is it a twitch that which you want?

Hey!
whoops! Sailor boy,
Is it a twitch you want

Give us a   it   till sunrise
'Til after I'd made your gun rise

Whether got on your mind,
sailor boy, sailor boy?

Hey, sailor boy -
Lookin' for some fun?
Whatcha looking for?

sealegs
I'll send you home on three legs

your pocket
I'll give you a place to lock it

Pick (on) a girl wot is willing
Wedge it with one wot's willing
another shilling

(I'll) want
Keep it snugly harbored
I'd wedge it in good
I see
In case it lists to starboard
you be the sport
I'll be the port

How's the part

Hey! (A)Hey! Sailor boy!
wot is Tell you when to dock it —

Instead of in your pocket.

31
THANK-EE, SIR, THANK-EE.
'OW WOULD YOU LIKE A LIT-TLE
SQUIFF, DEAR, A LIT-TLE
34
JUG JUG, A LIT-TLE
BOUNCE A-ROUND THE BUSH?
WOULD-N'T YOU LIKE TO PUSH ME
cresc.
37
CRUM-PET? YOU LOOKS TO
ME, DEAR, LIKE YOU GOT
LOTS OF IT TO PUSH.

The Barber and His Wife

TODD

There's a hole in the world
Like a great black pit
And the vermin of the world
Inhabit it,
And its morals aren't worth
What a pig could spit,
And it goes by the name of London.

At the top of the hole
Sit the privileged few,
Making mock of the vermin
In the lower zoo,
Turning beauty into filth and greed.
I too
Have sailed the world and seen its
    wonders,
For the cruelty of men
Is as wondrous as Peru,
But there's no place like London!

There was a barber and his wife,
And she was beautiful.
A foolish barber and his wife.
She was his reason and his life,
And she was beautiful.
And she was virtuous.
And he was—
Naïve.

There was another man who saw
That she was beautiful,
A pious vulture of the law
Who with a gesture of his claw
Removed the barber from his plate.
Then there was nothing but to wait
And she would fall,
So soft,
So young,
So lost,
And oh, so beautiful!

ANTHONY
And the lady, sir—did she—
    succumb?

TODD
Oh, that was many years ago . . .
I doubt if anyone would know.

*(They part. Todd mutters to himself
as he exits)*

TODD

There's a hole in the world
Like a great black pit
And it's filled with people
Who are filled with shit,
And the vermin of the world
Inhabit it . . .

*Todd arrives at Mrs. Lovett's Pie Shop.
She is rolling out dough and flicking flies
and roaches off the counter. She notices
Todd entering and shrieks.*

The Worst Pies in London

MRS. LOVETT
A customer!

(Todd, alarmed, starts out)

Wait! What's yer rush? What's yer
    hurry?
You gave me such a—

(Wipes her hands on her apron)

Fright. I thought you was a ghost.
Half a minute, can'tcher?
Sit! Sit ye down!
Sit!

(Forces Todd into a chair)

All I meant is that I
Haven't seen a customer for weeks.

Did you come here for a pie, sir?
Do forgive me if me head's a little
    vague—
Ugh!

(Plucks something off a pie)

What is that?
But you'd think we had the plague—

(Drops it on the floor, stamps on it)

From the way that people—

(Flicks something else off the pie)

Keep avoiding—

(Spots it moving on the counter)

No, you don't!

(Smacks it with her hand)

Heaven knows I try, sir!

(Looks at her hand)

Yich!

(Wipes her hand on the counter)

But there's no one comes in even to
    inhale—
Tsk!

*(Blows a bit of dust off the pie, hands
it to Todd)*

Right you are, sir. Would you like a
    drop of ale?

(Todd nods)

Mind you, I can't hardly blame
    them—
These are probably the worst pies in
    London.
I know why nobody cares to take
    them—
I *should* know,
I make them,
But good? No,
The worst pies in London—
Even that's polite.
The worst pies in London—
If you doubt it, take a bite.

(He does)

Is that just disgusting?
You have to concede it.
It's nothing but crusting—
Here, drink this, you'll need it.

(Gives him the ale)

The worst pies in London—

(Resumes pounding dough)

And no wonder, with the price of
    meat
What it is

(Grunts)

When you get it.
Never

(Grunt)

Thought I'd live to see the day
Men'd think it was a treat
Finding poor

(Grunt)

Animals

(Grunt)

Wot are dying in the street.
Mrs. Mooney has a pie shop,
Does a business, but I notice
   something weird—
Lately, all her neighbors' cats have
   disappeared.
Have to hand it to her—

(Grunt)

Wot I calls

(Grunt)

Enterprise,

(Grunt)

Popping pussies into pies.
Wouldn't do in my shop—
Just the thought of it's enough to
   make you sick.
And I'm telling you them pussy cats is
   quick!
No denying times is hard, sir—
Even harder than
The worst pies in London.
Only lard and nothing more—

(As Todd gamely tries another mouthful)

Is that just revolting?
All greasy and gritty,
It looks like it's molting,
And tastes like—
Well, pity
A woman alone
With limited wind
And the worst pies in London!

(Sighs heavily)

Ah, sir,
Times is hard. Times is hard.

"The Worst Pies in London" illustrates as well as any song in this book the second principle of my mantra: Content Dictates Form. Mrs. Lovett is not only a chatterbox, she is a glitteringly disorganized one. She switches moods mid-thought and thought mid-subject. She is cheery one moment, complaining the next, and can instantaneously alternate her attention between pie and customer. Her garrulousness causes her to seem irritating but harmless, which makes the eventual revelation of her villainy, for she is indeed the true villain of the piece, more surprising. The mercurial, eruptive quality of her scatterbrained chatter calls for an irregular song form, something that feels closer to rapid recitative than to song. Patterned metrical approaches and evenly periodic rhymes, the staples of most musical-theater songs, would not bespeak an aimless, unpredictable mind like Mrs. Lovett's: therefore a song with arbitrary metric patterns in both music and lyric, rhymes which pop up sporadically, along with sentences interrupted by grunts of effort, killing of bugs and whacks of a rolling pin— but still a song. *Sweeney Todd* is a traditional musical, no matter how eccentric the subject matter, built of traditional songs and scenes; there had to be some recognizable form to Mrs. Lovett's loquaciousness, so that the audience would feel they were on firm ground. The way to handle this was to compose the first half of the song as a seemingly incoherent monologue and then to repeat it with variations, the only line heard more than once being "The worst pies in London." When the audience hears that phrase the second time, the apparent formlessness of the song drops away and they feel at home. Finally, not rhyming the last word leaves Mrs. Lovett the unfocused character she seems to be.

The content of a song is less about information than about character. Amy, the nervous bride who sings "Getting Married Today" in *Company* is, like Mrs. Lovett, a chatterbox, but she is a focused one: she has only one subject on her mind, her impending

marriage. The different forms of the two songs reflect the different characters of the two women, even though their surface characteristics are similar—not just so that the audience can get to know them, but so that the actresses can play them more convincingly.

Todd indicates a room above the shop and wonders why Mrs. Lovett doesn't rent it out if she's so hard up for money. She replies that no one will go near it because of something that happened up there years ago, "Something not very nice." As Mrs. Lovett sings, the events in the song are reenacted behind her.

Poor Thing

MRS. LOVETT
There was a barber and his wife,
And he was beautiful,
A proper artist with a knife,
But they transported him for life.
And he was beautiful . . .

   Barker, his name was—Benjamin
   Barker.

He had this wife, you see,
Pretty little thing.
Silly little nit
Had her chance for the moon on a
   string—
Poor thing. Poor thing.

There were these two, you see,
Wanted her like mad,
One of 'em a Judge,
T'other one his Beadle.
Every day they'd nudge
And they'd wheedle.
But she wouldn't budge
From her needle.
Too bad,
Pure thing.

So they merely shipped the poor
   blighter off south, they did,
Leaving her with nothing but grief
   and a year-old kid.

Did she use her head even then? Oh,
  no, God forbid!
Poor fool.
Ah, but there was worse yet to come,
Poor thing.

        Johanna, that was the baby's
        name . . . Pretty little Johanna . . .

Well, Beadle calls on her, all polite,
Poor thing, poor thing.
The Judge, he tells her, is all contrite,
He blames himself for her dreadful
  plight,
She must come straight to his house
  tonight!
Poor thing, poor thing.

Of course, when she goes there,
Poor thing, poor thing,
They're havin' this ball all in masks.
There's no one she knows there,
Poor dear, poor thing.
She wanders tormented and drinks,
Poor thing.
The Judge has repented, she thinks,
Poor thing.
"Oh, where is Judge Turpin?" she asks.

He was there, all right—
Only not so contrite!

        (The Judge rapes Lucy, Todd's wife)

She wasn't no match for such craft,
  you see,
And everyone thought it so droll.
They figured she had to be daft,
  you see,
So all of 'em stood there and laughed,
  you see.
Poor soul!
Poor thing!

**Content Dictates Form again. Mrs.
Lovett is chattering away as she did
before, but this time with a purpose: she thinks she has recognized
Sweeney as Benjamin Barker, her ten-
ant of fifteen years ago, and is driving
him into a fury of remembrance. Instead of the meandering of her first
song, this one takes on a calculated
regularity of rhythm and rhyme that,
like Poe's relentless tell-tale heart,
drives Todd to the breaking point.**

*In a rage, Todd reveals himself to be
Barker and demands to know where
Lucy and his daughter, Johanna, are.
Mrs. Lovett tells him that Lucy, after
being raped, poisoned herself and that the
judge, Judge Turpin, brought Johanna up
as his ward. Exploding with fury, Todd
vows revenge on Turpin and his beadle,
Beadle Bamford, as well. With no money,
though, how can he even afford to live,
much less avenge himself? Mrs. Lovett
suggests that he resume barbering. She
has saved his box of razors and now presents them to him. He handles them as if
they were sacred objects and sings softly.*

My Friends

TODD
These are my friends,
See how they glisten.
See this one shine,
How he smiles in the light,
My friend, my faithful friend.

Speak to me, friend.
Whisper, I'll listen.
I know, I know,
You've been locked out of sight
All these years—
Like me, my friend.

Well, I've come home
To find you waiting.
Home,
And we're together,
And we'll do wonders,
Won't we?

TODD	MRS. LOVETT
You there, my friend.	

Come, let me
  hold you.
	I'm your friend
	  too, Mr. Todd.
	If you only knew,
	  Mr. Todd—

Now, with a sigh	Ooh, Mr. Todd,
You grow warm	You're warm
In my hand,	In my hand.
My friend,	You've come home.
My clever friend.	Always had a fondness for you, I did.

Rest now, my
  friends.

Soon I'll unfold
  you.
	Never
	  you fear, Mr.
	  Todd.

Soon you'll
  know splendors
	You can move in
	  here, Mr. Todd.

You never have
  dreamed
	Splendors you
	  never have
	  dreamed

All your days,	All your days
My lucky friends.	Will be yours.
Till now your shine	I'm your friend.
Was merely silver.	Don't they shine beautiful?
Friends,	Silver's good enough for me,
You shall drip rubies,	Mr. T . . .
You'll soon drip precious	
Rubies . . .	

TODD
(Holding a razor aloft)
My right arm is complete again!*

The Ballad of
Sweeney Todd (Part II)

COMPANY
Lift your razor high, Sweeney!
Hear it singing, "Yes!"
Sink it in the rosy skin
Of righteousness.

His voice was soft, his manner mild.
He seldom laughed but he often
  smiled.
He'd seen how civilized men behave.
He never forgot and he never forgave,
Not Sweeney,
Not Sweeney Todd,
The Demon Barber of Fleet Street . . .

*Johanna stands on the balcony of Judge
Turpin's house, gazing at the caged birds
of a bird seller below.*

---

*As luck would have it, both Len Cariou,
who played Sweeney, and George Hearn, his
replacement, were left-handed. In both cases
I had to remove the "right," which effectively
takes the power out of the line.

Green Finch and Linnet Bird

JOHANNA
Green finch and linnet bird,
Nightingale, blackbird,
How is it you sing?
How can you jubilate,
Sitting in cages,
Never taking wing?

Outside the sky waits,
Beckoning, beckoning,
Just beyond the bars.
How can you remain,
Staring at the rain,
Maddened by the stars?
How is it you sing
Anything?
How is it you sing?

Green finch and linnet bird,
Nightingale, blackbird,
How is it you sing?
Whence comes this melody
    constantly flowing?
Is it rejoicing or merely halloing?
Are you discussing
Or fussing
Or simply dreaming?
Are you crowing?
Are you screaming?

Ringdove and robinet,
Is it for wages,
Singing to be sold?
Have you decided it's
Safer in cages,
Singing when you're told?

My cage has many rooms,
Damask and dark.
Nothing there sings,
Not even my lark.
Larks never will, you know,
When they're captive.
Teach me to be more adaptive.

Green finch and linnet bird,
Nightingale, blackbird,
Teach me how to sing.
If I cannot fly,
Let me sing.

*Anthony has entered the street and looks
up at Johanna, transfixed.*

Ah, Miss

ANTHONY
I have sailed the world,
Beheld its wonders,
From the pearls of Spain
To the rubies of Tibet,
But not even in London
Have I seen such a wonder . . .

Lady, look at me look at me miss oh
Look at me please oh
Favor me favor me with your glance.
Ah, miss,
What do you what do you see off
There in those trees oh
Won't you give won't you give me a
    chance?

Who would sail to Spain
For all its wonders,
When in Kearney's Lane
Lies the greatest wonder yet?

Ah, miss,
Look at you look at you pale and
Ivory-skinned oh
Look at you looking so sad so queer.
Promise
Not to retreat to the darkness
Back of your window,
Not till you not till you look down
    here.
Look at

ANTHONY	JOHANNA
Me!	Green finch and linnet bird,
Look at	Nightingale, blackbird,
Me!	Teach me how to sing.
	If I cannot fly,
Look at me . . .	Let me sing . . .

"Kearney's Lane" is not in London,
nor is it anywhere else as far as I
know. Unimportant as choosing the
name of a place may seem, it presented the kind of problem which only
obsessively meticulous lyric writers
(as all good ones are) have to face: the
way that music dictates inflection. For
the location of Johanna's balcony I

wanted to repeat the same three-note
melodic phrase I had used for the
word "Dardanelles," the name of the
islands that had been the other cause
of Anthony's "wonder" in "No Place
Like London." All I had to find was a
three-syllable address that connoted
the elegance of a British magistrate's
house, as "Beekman Place" would to
American ears. The choices, I thought,
would be innumerable: "Chatham
Street," say—all I had to do was go
through a map of London. But the arc
of that particular musical phrase comprises three ascending notes which
emphasize the third one because it's
the highest. To my frustration, I soon
realized that "Street" in any address
carries the weakest emphasis and is
almost always inflected downward:
it's *Chatham* Street, not Chatham
Street, just as it is *Bleecker* Street,
not Bleecker *Street*. Perhaps nobody
in the audience would notice this in-
fraction, but I would—and so, perhaps,
might the performer.

It hardly seemed an insurmount-
able obstacle. There were always Roads
and Squares and Mewses and Lanes,
all of which, luckily and peculiarly, sat
on upward inflections: Fulham *Road*,
not *Fulham* Road; Eaton *Square*, not
Eaton Square, Chelsea *Mews*, not
Chelsea Mews, Chancery *Lane*, not
Chancery Lane. These were always the
inflections, unless there was a reason
for changing the emphasis, and in this
instance there was none. But "road"
sounds middle class, not where a
powerful autocrat would live, and to
American ears a "square" would imply
commerce, or at least a lack of privacy.
A "mews" connotes something more
akin to a cozy cottage than an impos-
ing judicial mansion, although it at
least implies exclusivity, but "Lane"
seemed right: it sounded picturesquely
private rather than exclusive. I combed
my map for an appropriate two-
syllable London lane. "Maiden Lane"
suggested the extreme wealth of diamond mine owners rather than the
moderate wealth of judges, and I
couldn't find any others: there aren't
many Lanes in London, whatever their
syllabic content. So I invented one.

The third principle of my mantra is "God is in the details." There are those who claim that it's not God but the Devil. Both are true of "Kearney's Lane." The God of it is that "Kearney's" scanned properly and the sudden harsh sound of the "K" prevented the line from being monotonously mellifluous; the Devil is that it sounded a bit Irish and therefore smelled of inauthenticity, although I'm certain that there are many London thoroughfares whose names derive from the little island to the left. "Kearney's Lane" went unnoticed, but it's a near-miss; I should perhaps have had more patience and a larger map.

The above takes longer to read than it took me to think through when I was writing the lyric. The point is that although knowing exactly what you want can narrow your search, it can also make a satisfactory destination more difficult to find. Once you know exactly what you need, you get fussy, and sometimes fixing a detail to satisfy that particular God can take a very long time.

Johanna's and Anthony's eyes meet, but the Beggar Woman interrupts, asking for alms. She warns Anthony to stay away from Judge Turpin and his ward, then suddenly leers at his crotch.

BEGGAR WOMAN
Hey! Hoy! Sailor boy!
Want it snugly harbored?
Open me gate, but dock it straight,
I see it lists to starboard.*

Anthony buys a caged bird for Johanna and she comes down tremulously to receive it. Their hands touch.

Johanna

ANTHONY
I feel you,
Johanna,
I feel you.
I was half convinced I'd waken,
Satisfied enough to dream you.
Happily, I was mistaken,
Johanna!
I'll steal you,
Johanna,
I'll steal you . . .

---

*Needless to say, this verse does not exist in the scripts sent to (most) schools.

(Judge Turpin returns home unexpectedly and, furious at Johanna's leaving the house, warns Anthony never to come near her again. He then exits into the house with Johanna, leaving Anthony alone on the street.)

ANTHONY
I'll steal you,
Johanna,
I'll steal you!
Do they think that walls can hide you?
Even now I'm at your window.
I am in the dark beside you,
Buried sweetly in your yellow hair.

I feel you,
Johanna,
And one day
I'll steal you.
Till I'm with you then,
I'm with you there,
Sweetly buried in your yellow hair . . .

St. Dunstan's Marketplace, centered on a gaudily painted caravan emblazoned with "Signor Adolfo Pirelli—Haircutter–Barber–Tooth Puller to His Royal Majesty the King of Naples" and under this "Banish Baldness with Pirelli's Miracle Elixir." Todd and Mrs. Lovett are in the crowd which is being summoned by Tobias, a boy who comes out of the caravan beating a small drum.

Pirelli's Miracle Elixir

TOBIAS

Ladies and gentlemen!
May I have your attention, perlease?
Do you wake every morning in shame
    and despair
To discover your pillow is covered
    with hair
Wot ought not to be there?

Well, ladies and gentlemen,
From now on you can waken at ease.
You need never again have a worry
    or care,
I will show you a miracle marvelous
    rare.
Gentlemen, you are about to see
    something

Wot rose from the dead—!
On the top of my head.

Scarcely a month ago, gentlemen,
I was struck with a 'orrible
Dermatologic disease.
Though the finest physicians in
    London were called,
I awakened one morning amazed and
    appalled
To discover with dread that my head
    was as bald
As a novice's knees.
I was dying of shame
Till a gentleman came,
An illustrious barber, Pirelli by name.
He give me a liquid as precious as
    gold,
I rubbed it in daily like wot I was
    told,
And behold!

(He whips off his cap, revealing mountains of hair cascading to his shoulders)

Only thirty days old!

'Twas Pirelli's
Miracle Elixir,
That's wot did the trick, sir,
True, sir, true.

Was it quick, sir?
Did it in a tick, sir,
Just like an elixir
Ought to do!

How about a bottle, mister?
Only costs a penny, guaranteed.

CROWD
(Lines overlapping each other)
1ST MAN: Penny buys a bottle, I
    don't know . . .
2ND MAN: You don't need—
1ST MAN: Ah, let's go!
TOBIAS: Go ahead and tug, sir.
3RD MAN: Penny for a bottle, is it?
TOBIAS: Go ahead, sir, harder . . .

TOBIAS
Does Pirelli's
Stimulate the growth, sir?
You can have my oath, sir,

Julia McKenzie as Mrs. Lovett and Denis Quilley as Sweeney Todd (Royal National Theatre, London, 1993)

'Tis unique.
Rub a minute—
Stimulatin', i'n' it?
Soon you'll have to thin it
Once a week!

Penny buys a bottle, guaranteed!

CROWD
(Lines overlapping each other)
1ST MAN: Penny buys a bottle,
    might as well . . .
3RD MAN: Wotcher think?
2ND WOMAN: Go ahead and try
    it, wot the hell . . .
TOBIAS: How about a sample?
    Have you ever smelled a cleaner
    smell?
1ST WOMAN: Isn't it a crime they
    let these urchins clog the pavement?
4TH MAN: Penny buys a bottle,
    does it?
TOBIAS: That's enough, sir, ample.

TOBIAS
Gently dab it.
Gets to be a habit.
Soon there'll be enough, sir,
Somebody can grab it.
See that chap with
Hair like Shelley's?
You can tell 'e's
Used Pirelli's!

CROWD
(Lines overlapping each other)
1ST MAN: Let me have a bottle.
2ND MAN: Make that two.
3RD WOMAN: Come to think of it,
    I could get some for Harry . . .
4TH WOMAN: Nothing works on
    Harry, dear. Bye-bye.
TOBIAS: Go ahead and feel, mum.
Absolutely real, mum . . .
2ND MAN: How about a beer?
1ST MAN: You know a pub?
2ND MAN: There's one close by.
1ST WOMAN: You got all the hair
    you need now.
3RD MAN: That's no lie.
4TH MAN: Pass it by.
2ND WOMAN: I'm just passing by.

TODD
(Loudly)
Pardon me, ma'am, what's that awful
    stench?

MRS. LOVETT
(Even more loudly)
Are we standing near an open trench?

TODD
Must be standing near an open
    trench!

TOBIAS
Buy Pirelli's Miracle Elixir:
Anything wot's slick, sir,
Soon sprouts curls.
Try Pirelli's—
When they see how thick, sir,
You can have your pick, sir,
Of the girls!

Want to buy a bottle, missus?

CROWD
(Lines overlapping each other)
TODD: What is this?
MRS. LOVETT: What is this?
1ST MAN: Propagates the hair, sir.
4TH MAN: I'll take one!
TODD: Smells like piss.
MRS. LOVETT: Smells like—phew!
2ND MAN: He says it smells like
    piss.
TODD: Looks like piss.
MRS. LOVETT: Wouldn't touch it
    if I was you, dear.
2ND MAN: Wotcher think?
TODD: This is piss. Piss with ink.
5TH MAN,
2ND WOMAN: Says it smells like
    piss or something.
TOBIAS: Penny for a bottle . . .
Have you ever smelled a cleaner
    smell?
How about a sample? . . .
How about a sample, mister?
1ST WOMAN: Give us back our
    money!
2ND WOMAN: Give us back our
    money!
1ST WOMAN: Did you ever—?
Give us back our money!
3RD WOMAN: Glad I didn't buy
    one, I can tell you!
4TH WOMAN: If you think that
    piss can fool a lady,
You're mistaken!
MRS. LOVETT: Give 'em back
    their money!
3RD WOMAN: Give 'em back their
    money, I say!

Give 'em back their money!
TOBIAS: Never mind that madman,
    mister . . .
Never mind the madman . . .

TODD, MRS. LOVETT
Where is this Pirelli?

CROWD
Where is this Pirelli?
What about my money, laddie?
Yes, what about my money?
Hand it back!
We don't want no piss, boy!
Give it here . . .

TOBIAS
Let Pirelli's
Activate your roots, sir—

TODD
Keep it off your boots, sir—
Eats right through.

CROWD
Go and get Pirelli!

TOBIAS
Yes, get Pirelli's!
Use a bottle of it!
Ladies seem to love it—

MRS. LOVETT
Flies do, too!

CROWD
Hand the bloody money over!
Hand the bloody money over!

TOBIAS
(Frantically)
See Pirelli's
Miracle Elixir
Grow a little wick, sir,
Then some fuzz.
The Pirelli's
Soon'll make it thick, sir,
Like a good elixir
Always does!

Trust Pirelli's!
If your hair is sick, sir,
Fix it in the nick, sir,
Don't look grim.
Just Pirelli's

Miracle Elixir,
That'll do the trick, sir—

1ST MAN
What about the money?

TOBIAS
If you've got a kick, sir—

CROWD
What about the money?
Where is this Pirelli?
Go and get Pirelli!
What about our money?

TOBIAS
Tell it to the mixer
Of the Miracle Elixir!
If you've got a kick, sir—!

(Gestures toward the caravan)

Talk to him!

One of the more thrilling things about traditional musical theater is the sound of a full chorus singing full harmonies full-throatedly. One of the more unconvincing things about it is that as a crowd, whether of peasants, soldiers, convicts, reporters, cocktail party attendees or any other general congregations, they all sing the same lyric; that is to say, they apparently all have exactly the same thought at the same time. Most people in most audiences accept this convention (their own uniformity being a mirror of what they're looking at), but although I happily accept a great many theater conventions, this one irritates me. Do all the settlers in *Oklahoma!* who claim that "Every night my honey lamb and I / Sit alone and talk / And watch a hawk / Makin' lazy circles in the sky" really do so? Does everybody have a companion? And do they all bird-watch *every night*? Life may have been simple in those days, but surely there were other ways of getting their minds off the droughts and dust storms. What about the picnickers in *Carousel*? Did every one of them have a real nice clambake? Wasn't there anyone who had indigestion or a rot-

ten time? Do all the Seabees in *South Pacific* think there is nothing like a dame? What about the misogynists in the group? Or if there are no misogynists, are there no homosexuals? If I pick on Rodgers and Hammerstein's shows as examples, it's only because their choruses are among the most effective and their shows are revived so many times that the examples will be familiar. Virtually every show features monolithic choruses.

Ironically, it was Hammerstein himself who opened the door to a certain kind of musical comedy realism; he should be held at least partly accountable for the change in sensibility. He made it possible, even necessary, to take characters in a musical seriously, and so I for one can't believe in a homogeneous multitude, unless of course that is the point. I could more easily accept the members of a large group singing exactly like one another if they were in a musical about the Stepford Wives or about partisan politicians, or if there were a satirical point, as in the "Ascot Gavotte" of *My Fair Lady*. In *West Side Story*, when either the Jets or the Sharks sang together, I tried to keep the lyric generic enough so that it was a thought they all shared at the moment. Some of the kids may have been frightened at the prospect of a rumble, others eager, but determination was common to all, which allowed songs like the "Jet Song" and the "Quintet" to pass under the radar, at least for me. And in "Simple" in *Anyone Can Whistle*, the chorus sings separate thoughts until Hapgood molds them into a group of like-minded people, the unison lyrics illustrating their loss of individuality.

The tradition of the chorus as one voice persists even today, but surely no two people in a crowd being exhorted by a seller of what is essentially snake oil have the same degree of sales resistance. Thus the overlapping voices in the lyric above. Every single chorus member is characterized as an individual and the director can decide how to treat each one specifically; at the very least he has something he can say to each of the performers which may

help them distinguish themselves from their fellow spectators. (When the chorus is presented as a Greek Chorus, however, commenting on the action or telling the story directly to the audience, as in the case of "The Ballad of Sweeney Todd," it's both justifiable and necessary that they all sing the same lyric.)

The problem of writing for choruses like this is that what you gain in the realism of individuality you lose in concerted choral power, and therefore you have to find a line, or preferably lines, that they can all sing without violating the principle. In "Pirelli's Miracle Elixir," for example, "Give us back the money" and "Where is this Pirelli?" tie the garbled counterpoint of the simultaneously different musical lines together and allow for a joyful noise, which is not only expected but welcome.

Tobias opens the curtains of the caravan, revealing Pirelli, an excessively flamboyant Italian with a glittering suit and a glittering smile. Holding an ornate razor in one hand and a wicked-looking tooth-extractor in the other, he bows and poses.

The Contest

PIRELLI
I am Adolfo Pirelli,
Da king of da barbers, da barber of
    kings,
E buon giorno, good day.
I blow you a kiss!

And I, da so-famous Pirelli,
I wish-a to know-a
Who has-a da nerve-a to say
My elixir is piss!
Who says this?

(Todd answers and challenges him for five pounds to a shaving contest, with Beadle Bamford serving as the judge. Todd and Pirelli each pick a man from the crowd, seat him in a chair and begin to stir up lather.)

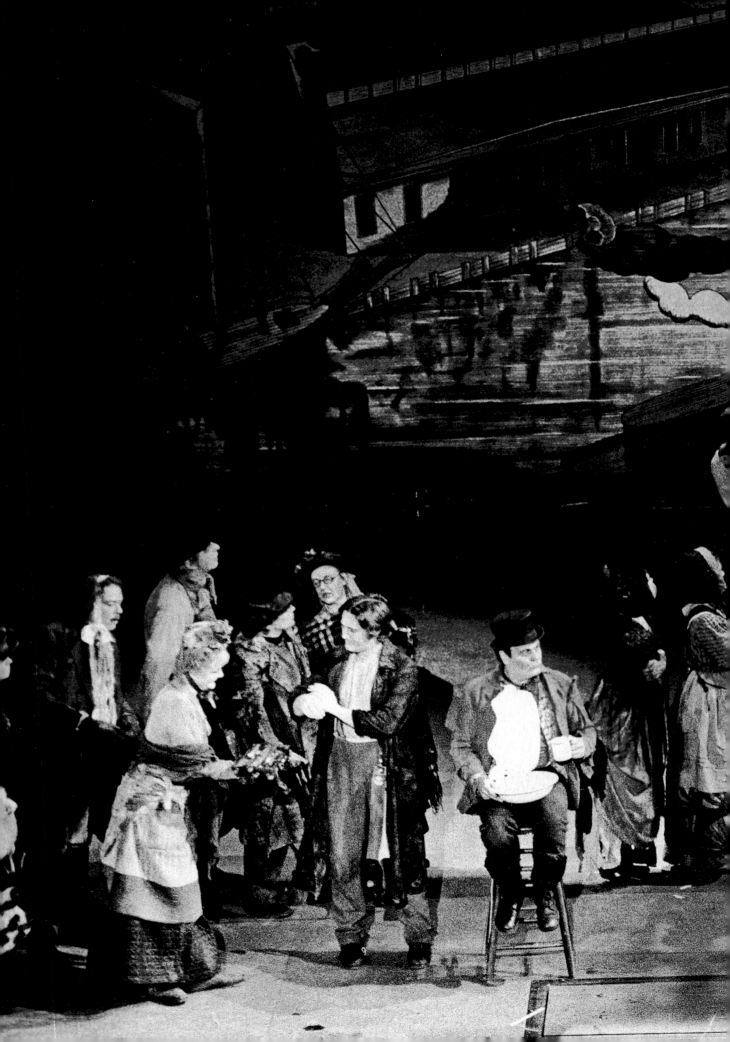

PIRELLI

Now, signorini, signori,
We mix-a da lather,
But first-a you gather
Around, signorini, signori,
You looking a man
Who have had-a da glory
To shave-a da Pope!
Mr. Sweeney whoever—

(Accidentally splashing lather all over the man's face)

I beg-a you pardon—'ll
Probably say it was only a cardinal—
Nope!
It was-a da Pope!

To shave-a da face,
To pull-a da toot',
Require da grace
And not-a da brute,
For if-a you slip,
You nick da skin,
You clip-a da chin,
You rip-a da lip a bit
And dat's-a da trut'!

To shave-a da face
Or even a part
Widout it-a smart
Require da heart.
It take-a da art—
I show you a chart
I study-a starting in my yout'!

(Pulls down an elaborate medical chart)

To cut-a da hair,
To trim-a da beard,
To make-a da bristle
Clean like a whistle,
Dis is from early infancy
Da talent give to me
By God!

It take-a da skill,
It take-a da brains,
It take-a da will
To take-a da pains,
It take-a da pace,
It take-a da grace—

(As he keeps shaving elaborately, Todd, with a couple of quick whisking motions, shaves his man clean)

BEADLE BAMFORD
The winner is Todd!

In the original production, the contest continued with a competition to see who could extract a tooth more quickly and painlessly. Todd selects a man from the crowd with an aching tooth but Pirelli, with no customers volunteering, forces Tobias to be the object of his ministrations. Once again, Pirelli addresses the crowd grandiloquently as he works, while Tobias squirms in the chair with increasing distress.

PIRELLI
Perhaps, signorini, signori,
You like-a I tell-a
Da famous-a story
Of Queen Isabella,
Da queen of-a Polan'
Whose toot' was-a swollen.
I pull it so nice from her mout'
That-a though to begin she's-a
    screaming-a murder,
She's later-a swoon-a wid bliss an' was
    heard-a
To shout:
"Pull all of 'em out!"

To pull-a da toot'
Widout-a da skill
Can damage da root—

(To Tobias)

Now hold-a da still!

(To the crowd)

An' if-a you slip
You grip a bit,
You hit da pit of it
Or chip-a da tip
And have-a to fill!

To pull-a da toot'
Widout-a da grace,
You leave-a da space
All over da place.
You try to erase
Widout-a da trace . . .
Sometimes is da case
You even-a kill.

To hold-a da clamp
Widout-a da cramp,
Wid all dat saliva,
It could-a drive-a
You crazy—

(To Tobias)

Don' mutter,
Or back-a you go to da gutter!

(To the crowd)

My touch is as light as a butter-a-
Cup!

I take-a da pains,
I learn-a da art,
I use-a da brains,
I give-a da heart,
I have-a da grace,
I win-a da race—!

(He is still tugging at Tobias's tooth, the boy screaming with pain, when Todd quickly and easily extracts the tooth from his man's mouth. The beadle blows his whistle and indicates Todd as the winner.)

PIRELLI
I give-a da up.

The reason for cutting the tooth-pulling sequence was connected with the cutting of the Judge's song (see below).

Pirelli reluctantly and suspiciously pays Todd the five pounds. Todd invites the Beadle to come and get a free shave at what Mrs. Lovett refers to as "Sweeney Todd's Tonsorial Parlor," directly over her pie shop in Fleet Street. The Company turns to the audience.

The Ballad of Sweeney Todd (Part II)

COMPANY
Sweeney pondered and Sweeney
  planned.
Like a perfect machine 'e planned,
Barbing the hook, baiting the trap,
Setting it out for the Beadle to snap.

Slyly courted 'im, Sweeney did,
Set a sort of a scene, 'e did.
Laying the trail, showing the traces,
Letting it lead to higher places . . .
Sweeney . . .

Judge Turpin, in his judicial robes, sits in his parlor, a Bible in his hands. Johanna, wearing a diaphanous gown, sits in an adjoining room, sewing.

Johanna

JUDGE TURPIN
Mea culpa, mea culpa,
Mea maxima culpa,
Mea maxima maxima culpa.
God, deliver me! Release me!
Forgive me! Restrain me! Pervade me!

(He peers through the keyhole of the door into Johanna's room)

Johanna, Johanna,
So suddenly a woman,
The light behind your window,
It penetrates your gown . . .
Johanna, Johanna,
The sun, I see the sun through your—

(Ashamed, he stops peering)

No!
God!
Deliver me!

(Sinks to his knees)

Deliver me!

(Starts tearing off his robes)

Down!
Down.
Down . . .

(Now naked to the waist, he picks up a scourge from the table)

Johanna, Johanna,
I watch you from the shadows.
You sigh before your window
And gaze upon the town . . .
Your lips part, Johanna,
So young and soft and beautiful—

(Whips himself)

God!

(Whipping himself again and again)

Deliver me!
Filth!
Leave me!

Johanna!
Johanna!
I treasured you in innocence
And loved you like a daughter.
You mock me, Johanna,
You tempt me with your innocence,
You tempt me with those quivering—

(Whips himself)

No!

(Again and again)

God!
Deliver me!
It will—
Stop—
Now! It will—
Stop—
Right—
Now.
Right—
Now.
Right—
Now . . .

(Calm again, having kneed his way over to the door, he peers through the keyhole)

Johanna, Johanna,
I cannot keep you longer.

The world is at your window,
You want to fly away.
You stir me, Johanna,
So suddenly a woman,
I cannot watch you one more day—!

(Whipping himself into a frenzy)

God!
Deliver me!
God!
Deliver me!
God!
Deliver—

(Climaxes)

God!

(Panting, he calms down. When he is in control again, he starts to dress.)

Johanna, Johanna,
I'll keep you here forever,
I'll wed you on the morrow.
Johanna, Johanna,
The world will never touch you,
I'll wed you on the morrow!

As years pass, Johanna,
You'll tend me in my solitude,
No longer as a daughter,
As a woman.

Johanna, Johanna,
I'll hold you here forever then,
You'll keep away from windows and
You'll
Deliver me,
Johanna,
From this
Hot
Red
Devil
With your
Soft
White
Cool
Virgin
Palms . . .

Just as I had hoped with "Gee, Officer Krupke" to be the first songwriter in Broadway history to use "Fuck you" in a lyric, so I had hoped here to be the first to have a character reach an orgasm in the middle of a song. Once again I was disappointed—the song was cut during previews, for two reasons. The first was a surprising (to me) prudishness on the part of Hal Prince, who directed the show and who is a man of fearless courage when it comes to taking theatrical risks. He refused to see the humor (to me) in the number. That wouldn't have been enough cause for me to cut it, however. The second and more important reason was that the shape and pace of the show in preview performances seemed to be exactly right except for a sag in the middle of the first act. When Hugh Wheeler and I examined the arc of the evening carefully, we realized that we had made a mistake in storytelling: for the first twenty minutes, the story had been about Sweeney, but just when the audience was getting involved in it, the focus switched for twenty minutes to the young lovers, the market-place (which, although Todd and Mrs. Lovett are present, is essentially about Tobias and Pirelli) and then to the Judge, before we renewed concentration on our main characters. The solution was to cut the tooth-pulling sequence and the Judge's song, although that left the Judge as the only character in the story not to be introduced musically. Nevertheless, the excisions worked by tautening the act. I was so bothered by the lack of a defining moment for the Judge, however, that I restored the song for the original cast album. Years later, when the show was presented by New York City Opera, I restored it for the stage, too, and a strange thing happened: even though it was the same production that Hal had directed fifteen years earlier, a sea change had somehow occurred and the act no longer sagged. The show had mysteriously found its shape and had elasticized itself somehow to allow, in fact to welcome, the Judge's song into its pace and texture. It's the only time I've ever known such a thing to happen. By contrast, in 2008 Trevor Nunn, directing a production of *A Little Night Music* in London, urged me to restore "Silly People" to the score. Not wanting to stand in the way of a director's cre-ative ferment, I reluctantly agreed. The song held the show up just as it had in 1973 and it soon went back into the trunk.

Todd has set himself up in a meagerly furnished "tonsorial parlor" over Mrs. Lovett's pie shop and is pacing impatiently, waiting for a visit from the Beadle. Mrs. Lovett tries to calm him down.

Wait

MRS. LOVETT

Easy now.
Hush, love, hush.
Don't distress yourself,
What's your rush?
Keep your thoughts
Nice and lush.
Wait.

Hush, love, hush.
Think it through.
Once it bubbles,
Then what's to do?
Watch it close.
Let it brew.
Wait.

I've been thinking, flowers—
Maybe daisies—
To brighten up the room.
Don't you think some flowers,
Pretty daisies,
Might relieve the gloom?
Ah, wait, love, wait.

Slow, love, slow.
Time's so fast.
Now goes quickly—
See, now it's past!
Soon will come.
Soon will last.
Wait.

Don't you know,
Silly man,
Half the fun is to
Plan the plan?
All good things come to
Those who can
Wait.

Gillyflowers, maybe,
'Stead of daisies . . .
I don't know, though . . .
What do you think?

The Beadle doesn't arrive, but Pirelli does, revealing himself as an Irishman with a fake persona. He once worked for Todd when Todd was Benjamin Barker and now recognizes him as an escaped convict. Reverting sarcastically to his phony Italian accent, he demands half of Todd's wages, threatening to expose him.

PIRELLI

You t'ink-a you smart,
You foolish-a boy.
Tomorrow you start
In my-a employ!
You unner-a-stan'?
You like-a my plan—?

(Todd strangles him into unconsciousness and slits his throat, dumping the body into a trunk in the room. Three tenors appear.)

The Ballad of Sweeney Todd (Part III)

TENORS

His hands were quick, his fingers
    strong.
It stung a little but not for long.
And those who thought him a simple
    clod
Were soon reconsidering under the
    sod,
Consigned there with a friendly prod
From Sweeney Todd,
The Demon Barber of Fleet Street.

See your razor gleam, Sweeney,
Feel how well it fits
As it floats
Across the throats
Of hypocrites . . .

Anthony has slipped into Johanna's room in the Judge's house while the Judge is in court.

Kiss Me

JOHANNA
He means to marry me Monday.
What shall I do? I'd rather die.

ANTHONY
I have a plan—

JOHANNA
I'll swallow poison on Sunday,
That's what I'll do, I'll get some lye.

ANTHONY
I have a plan—

JOHANNA
Oh, dear, was that a noise?

ANTHONY
A plan—

JOHANNA
I think I heard a noise.

ANTHONY
A plan!

JOHANNA
It couldn't be,
He's in court,
He's in court today,
Still, that was a noise,
Wasn't that a noise?
You must have heard that—

ANTHONY
Kiss me.

JOHANNA
Oh, sir . . .

ANTHONY
Ah, miss . . .

JOHANNA
Oh, sir . . .
If he should marry me Monday,
What shall I do? I'll die of grief.

ANTHONY
We fly tonight—

JOHANNA
'Tis Friday, virtually Sunday,
What can we do with time so brief?

ANTHONY
We fly tonight—

JOHANNA
Behind the curtain—quick!

ANTHONY
Tonight—

JOHANNA
I think I heard a click.

ANTHONY
Tonight!

JOHANNA	ANTHONY
It was a gate.	
It's the gate!	
We don't have a gate.	It's not a gate.
Still there was a—	There's
wait!	no gate,
There's another click!	You don't have
	a gate.
You must have heard	If you'd only
that—	listen, miss,
	and

ANTHONY
Kiss me!

JOHANNA
Tonight?

ANTHONY
Kiss me.

JOHANNA
You mean tonight?

ANTHONY
The plan is made.

JOHANNA
Oh, sir!

ANTHONY
So kiss me.

JOHANNA
I feel a fright.

ANTHONY
Be not afraid.

JOHANNA	ANTHONY
Sir, I did	Tonight I'll
Love you even as I	Steal

Saw you, even as it	You,
Did not matter that I	Johanna,
Did not know your	I'll steal
name . . .	you . . .

ANTHONY
It's me you'll marry on Monday,
That's what you'll do!

JOHANNA
And gladly, sir.

ANTHONY
St. Dunstan's, noon.

JOHANNA
I knew I'd be with you one day,
Even not knowing who you were.

JOHANNA	ANTHONY
I feared you'd	Ah, miss,
never come,	
That you'd be	Marry me, marry
called away,	me,
	Miss,
That you'd been	Oh, marry me
killed,	Monday!
Had the plague,	Favor me, favor
	me
Were in debtor's	With your hand.
jail,	
Trampled by a	Promise,
horse,	
Gone to sea	Marry me, marry
again,	me,
	Oh, marry me
	please,
Arrested by the—	Monday—

JOHANNA
Kiss me!

ANTHONY
Of course.

JOHANNA
Quickly!

ANTHONY
You're sure?

JOHANNA
Kiss me!

ANTHONY

I shall!

JOHANNA

Kiss me!
Oh, sir . . .

Unbeknownst to the lovers, the Judge is on his way home early from court, accompanied by the Beadle. He announces that he is determined to make Johanna accept his proposal of marriage. The Beadle, with utmost deference, suggests that the Judge might spruce himself up a bit before confronting her.

Ladies in Their Sensitivities

BEADLE

Excuse me, my lord.
May I request, my lord,
Permission, my lord, to speak?
Forgive me if I suggest, my lord,
You're looking less than your best, my
    lord,
There's powder upon your vest, my
    lord,
And stubble upon your cheek.
And ladies, my lord, are weak.

Ladies in their sensitivities, my lord,
Have a fragile sensibility.
When a girl's emergent,
Probably it's urgent
You defer to her gent-
Ility, my lord.

Personal disorder cannot be ignored,
Given their genteel proclivities.
Meaning no offense, it
Happens they resents it,
Ladies in their sensit-
Ivities, my lord.

Fret not, though, my lord,
I know a place, my lord,
A barber, my lord, of skill.
Thus armed with a shaven face, my
    lord,
Some eau de cologne to brace my
    lord,

And musk to enhance the chase, my
    lord,
You'll dazzle the girl until
She bows to your every will.

JUDGE TURPIN

Perhaps you're right. Take me to
him.

BEADLE

The name is Todd . . .

ANTHONY

We'd best not wait until Monday.

JOHANNA	BEADLE
Sir, I concur,	
And fully, too.	Sweeney
	Todd . . .

ANTHONY

It isn't right.
We'd best be married on Sunday.

JOHANNA

Saturday, sir,
Would also do.

ANTHONY

Or else tonight.

JOHANNA

I think I heard a noise.

ANTHONY

Fear not.

JOHANNA

I mean another noise!

ANTHONY

Like what?

JOHANNA	ANTHONY
Oh, never mind,	
Just a noise,	
Just another noise,	You mustn't
	mind,
Something in the	It's a noise,
street,	
I'm a silly little	Just another
	noise,
Ninnynoddle—	Something in
	the street,
	You silly—
Kiss me!	Kiss me!
Oh, sir . . .	

ANTHONY

We'll go to Paris on Monday.

JOHANNA

What shall I wear?
I daren't pack!

ANTHONY

We'll take a train . . .

JOHANNA

With you beside me on Sunday,
What will I care
What things I lack?

ANTHONY

Then sail to Spain . . .

JOHANNA	ANTHONY
I'll take my reticule.	
I need a reticule.	Why take
	your
	reticule?
You mustn't think	We'll buy a
	reticule.
Me a fool,	I'd never
	think
But my reticule	You a fool,
Never leaves my side,	But a
	reticule—
It's the only thing	Leave it all
	aside
My mother gave me—	And begin
	again and—
Kiss me!	Kiss me!
Kiss me!	I know a
	place where
	we can go
	Tonight.
We'll go there,	Kiss me!
Kiss me!	
We have a place	We have a
	place
Where we can	Where we
	can
Go . . .	Go tonight.

BEADLE
(Simultaneously with the above)
The name is Todd.

JUDGE TURPIN

Todd?

BEADLE

Todd. Sweeney Todd.

JUDGE TURPIN
Todd . . .

BEADLE
Todd.

JOHANNA
I loved you
Even as I saw
you,
Even as it does not
Matter that I still
Don't know your
name, sir,
Even as I saw you,
Even as it does not
Matter that I still
Don't know your
name . . .

ANTHONY
I loved you
Even as I saw
you,
Even as it did
not
Matter that I
did not
know your
name . . .

Johanna . . .
Johanna . . .
Johanna . . .

BEADLE
(Simultaneously)
Todd . . . Sweeney Todd.
Sweeney Todd.

JUDGE TURPIN
Sweeney Todd.

ANTHONY
Anthony!

JUDGE TURPIN
Todd . . .

BEADLE
Todd.

JOHANNA
Anthony . . .

JUDGE TURPIN
Todd, eh?

JOHANNA
I'll marry Anthony
Sunday,
That's what I'll do,

No matter what!
I knew you'd come
For me one day,

Only afraid
That you'd forgot.

ANTHONY
You'll marry
Anthony Sunday,
That's what you'll
do,
No matter what!
I knew I'd come
For you
One day,
Only afraid
That you'd
forgot.

BEADLE
(Simultaneously)
Ladies in their sensitivities, my lord—

JUDGE TURPIN
Pray lead the way.

BEADLE
Have a fragile sensibility . . .

JUDGE TURPIN
Just as you say.

JOHANNA
I feared you'd
Never come,
That you'd been
called away,
That you'd been
Killed,
Had the plague,
Were in debtor's jail,
Trampled by a
horse,
Gone to sea again,

Arrested by the . . .

ANTHONY
Marry me,
Marry me, miss,
You'll marry me
Sunday,
Favor me,
Favor me
With your hand.
Promise,
Marry me,
Marry me,
That you'll marry
me—
Enough of all
this . . .

BEADLE
(Simultaneously)
When a girl's emergent,
Probably it's urgent . . .
Ladies in their sensitivities . . .

JUDGE TURPIN
Todd.

JOHANNA
Oh, sir . . .

ANTHONY
Ah, miss . . .

JOHANNA
Oh, sir . . .
Oh, sir . . .
Oh, sir . . .
Oh, sir . . .
Oh, sir . . .
Oh, sir . . .

ANTHONY

Ah, miss . . .
Ah, miss . . .
Ah, miss . . .
Ah, miss . . .
Ah, miss . . .

Judge Turpin arrives at Sweeney's tonsorial parlor and settles himself in the small wooden barber's chair, humming contentedly. Todd inquires affably as to the source of his contentment.

Pretty Women

JUDGE TURPIN
You see, sir, a man infatuate with love,
Her ardent and eager slave.
So fetch the pomade and pumice
stone
And lend me a more seductive tone,
A sprinkling, perhaps, of French
cologne,
But first, sir, I think—a shave.

TODD
(Muttering)
The closest I ever gave.

(Todd whistles cheerfully. The Judge inquires as to the source of his merriment.)

TODD
'Tis your delight, sir, catching fire
From one man to the next.

JUDGE TURPIN
'Tis true, sir, love can still inspire
The blood to pound, the heart leap
higher.

BOTH
What more, what more can man
require—?

JUDGE TURPIN
Than love, sir?

TODD
More than love, sir.

JUDGE TURPIN
What, sir?

TODD
Women.

JUDGE TURPIN
Ah, yes, women.

TODD
Pretty women.

(Todd lathers the Judge's face, then turns to his razor)

TODD
Now then, my friend,
Now to your purpose.

Patience, enjoy it.
Revenge can't be taken in haste.

JUDGE TURPIN
Make haste, and if we wed,
You'll be commended, sir.

TODD
My lord . . .
And who, may it be said,
Is your intended, sir?

JUDGE TURPIN
My ward.
    And pretty as a rosebud.

TODD
(Muttering)
Pretty as her mother?

JUDGE TURPIN
What? What was that?

TODD
Oh, nothing, sir. Nothing. May we
proceed?

Pretty women . . .
Fascinating . . .
Sipping coffee,
Dancing . . .
Pretty women
Are a wonder.
Pretty women . . .

Sitting in the window or
Standing on the stair,
Something in them
Cheers the air.

Pretty women . . .

JUDGE TURPIN
Silhouetted . . .

TODD
Stay within you . . .

JUDGE TURPIN
Glancing . . .

TODD
Stay forever . . .

JUDGE TURPIN
Breathing lightly . . .

TODD
Pretty women . . .

BOTH
Pretty women!
Blowing out their candles or
Combing out their hair . . .

JUDGE TURPIN   TODD
Then they leave . . .
Even when they   Even when
  leave you   they leave,
And vanish,   They still
  they somehow
Can still remain   Are
There with you,   There.
There with you.   They're there.

BOTH
Ah, pretty women . . .

TODD
At their mirrors . . .

JUDGE TURPIN
In their gardens . . .

TODD
Letter-writing . . .

JUDGE TURPIN
Flower-picking . . .

TODD
Weather-watching . . .

BOTH
How they make a man sing!
Proof of heaven
As you're living—
Pretty women, sir!

JUDGE TURPIN TODD
Pretty women, yes! Pretty women,
                here's to
Pretty women, sir! Pretty women,
                all the
Pretty women!   Pretty women . . .
Pretty women, sir . . .

(Todd is about to cut Judge Turpin's
throat when Anthony suddenly bursts
in to announce that he and Johanna
plan to elope)

In accordance with musical-theater convention, especially opera, a chance to sing excuses everything, even dramatic logic. For example, if Sweeney is so intent on killing Judge Turpin, why does he spend three minutes singing a duet with his victim before dispatching him? I don't accept this convention any more than I do that of having a chorus of disparate people sing with one point of view. Sweeney's warbling away till Anthony enters allows the Judge to escape and has to be justified. That is the reason for "Wait," the apparent purpose of which seems to be to calm Sweeney down, the real purpose being to establish his motive to "wait" on the proverbial grounds that revenge is a dish best served cold, and that he enjoys playing with the Judge the way a cat does with a mouse. "Wait" is a song that doesn't seem necessary to the score or the action when it occurs but is essential in establishing this moment, and this moment is one I had planned from the day I began writing the show. One of two moments, actually: a song during which the audience expects Todd to murder someone and he doesn't, and another when they don't expect it and he does (which occurs in Act Two). If Mrs. Lovett had merely *told* Todd to savor his revenge, it wouldn't have had the same impact on him (as well as the audience) that singing it for two minutes does, and the suspense of the scene wouldn't have been as believable. It's the kind of believability that opera lovers don't need. Suspending disbelief is of course a requirement for anyone entering a theater, particularly a theater with a musical, but we all have limits, among the most annoying for me (along with prolonged death scenes) being the one in which a threat is made and not carried out post-haste because the threatener keeps talking. Or singing.

The Judge leaps up from his chair, vowing to hide Johanna where Anthony will never find her, and slams out in a rage. Todd angrily orders Anthony to leave and Mrs. Lovett runs upstairs to see what the commotion is.

Epiphany

TODD
I had him!
His throat was bare
Beneath my hand—!

MRS. LOVETT
(Trying to pacify him)
There, there, dear. Don't fret.

TODD
No, I had him!
His throat was there,
And he'll never come again!

MRS. LOVETT
Easy now.
Hush, love, hush.
I keep telling you—

TODD
When?

MRS. LOVETT
What's your rush?

TODD
Why did I wait?
You told me to wait!
Now he'll never come again!

There's a hole in the world
Like a great black pit
And it's filled with people
Who are filled with shit
And the vermin of the world
Inhabit it—
But not for long!

They all deserve to die!
Tell you why, Mrs. Lovett,
Tell you why:
Because in all of the whole human
    race, Mrs. Lovett,
There are two kinds of men and only
    two:
There's the one staying put
In his proper place
And the one with his foot
In the other one's face.
Look at me, Mrs. Lovett,
Look at you!

No, we all deserve to die!
Even you, Mrs. Lovett,

Even I.
Because the lives of the wicked
    should be made brief.
For the rest of us, death will be a
    relief.
We all deserve to die!

(Keening)

And I'll never see Johanna,
No, I'll never hug my girl to me—
Finished!

(Turning to the audience)

All right! You, sir,
How about a shave?
Come and visit
Your good friend Sweeney!
You, sir, too, sir,
Welcome to the grave.
I will have vengeance,
I will have salvation!

Who, sir? You, sir?
No one's in the chair—
Come on, come on,
Sweeney's waiting!
I want you bleeders!
You, sir—anybody!
Gentlemen, now don't be shy!

Not one man, no,
Nor ten men,
Nor a hundred
Can assuage me—
I will have you!

And I will get him back
Even as he gloats.
In the meantime I'll practice
On less honorable throats.
And my Lucy lies in ashes
And I'll never see my girl again,
But the work waits,
I'm alive at last
And I'm full of joy!

This was the crux of Bond's play: a
man is transformed instantaneously
from someone who kills only for specific and justifiable reasons into a mass
murderer. Bond glossed over it in a
three-line interchange:

TODD
A second chance may come. It must, it
shall! Until it does, I'll pass the time in
practice on less honored throats.

MRS. LOVETT
I don't understand you. You let that
Judge escape one minute, and the next
you're on about slicing up any Tom,
Dick or Harry. This revenge business
don't blow half hot and cold, it don't.

TODD
Revenge? Oh, no! The work's its own
reward. For now I find I have a taste
for blood, and all the world's my meat.

In the less overheated modesty of
his play, that may have satisfied the
actor and the audience, but in a full-
blooded (no pun intended) musical,
it was nowhere near enough. Hugh
(Wheeler) suggested that some kind
of religious overtone might intensify
Todd's conversion into a mass murderer (hence the title) but I thought
a schizophrenic breakdown would be
more spectacular for the actor and
give more variety to the song. I could,
and did, alternate between fixed,
rhythmic, rhymed sections to represent Todd's organized determination to
be a Sword of Justice, and free-flowing
unrhymed passages to mirror his disorganized grief, in the middle of which
he could break the fourth wall and
make direct contact with the world
outside the stage, a truly mad gesture.
All well and good, except for what
might seem like an unimportant problem, but isn't: Should he get a hand at
the end of the song? In the case of
"Rose's Turn" in *Gypsy,* Oscar had
persuaded me that it was in the best
interest of the show to make room for
applause. Here, Hal persuaded me
that it was in the best interest of the
actor. It was, but it allowed the audience a breather and dissipated the
tension that I hoped would increase
the humor of the next number, as
tension always does. The applause did
its job, but I included an alternate
ending in the published score, one
which ends in an unresolved disso-
nance and deprives the actor of his
encomium, but makes what follows
explosively funny.

Todd and Mrs. Lovett discuss how to get rid of Pirelli's body. Mrs. Lovett comes up with an idea.

A Little Priest

MRS. LOVETT
Seems a downright shame . . .

TODD
Shame?

MRS. LOVETT
Seems an awful waste . . .
Such a nice plump frame
Wot's-his-name
Has . . .
Had . . .
Has . . .
Nor it can't be traced.

Business needs a lift,
Debts to be erased.
Think of it as thrift,
As a gift . . .
If you get my drift . . .
No?
Seems an awful waste.

I mean,
With the price of meat what it is,
When you get it,
If you get it—

TODD
Ah!

MRS. LOVETT
Good, you got it.

Take, for instance,
Mrs. Mooney and her pie shop:
Business never better, using only
    pussy cats and toast.
And a pussy's good for maybe six or
    seven at the most.
And I'm sure they can't compare as far
    as taste . . .

TODD   MRS LOVETT
Mrs. Lovett,
What a charming
    notion,

Eminently practical   Well, it
    and yet   does seem a
Appropriate, as   Waste . . .
    always.
Mrs. Lovett, how
    I've lived
Without you all   It's an idea . . .
    these years
I'll never know!   Think about it . . .
How delectable!   Lots of other
                           gentlemen'll
Also undetectable.   Soon be coming
                           for a shave,
                       Won't they?
                       Think of
How choice!   All them
How rare!   Pies!

TODD
For what's the sound of the world out
    there?

MRS. LOVETT
What, Mr. Todd, what, Mr. Todd,
What is that sound?

TODD
Those crunching noises pervading
    the air?

MRS. LOVETT
Yes, Mr. Todd, yes, Mr. Todd,
Yes, all around.

TODD
It's man devouring man, my dear—

BOTH
And who are we to deny it in
    here?

TODD
These are desperate times, Mrs.
    Lovett, and desperate measures are
    called for.

MRS. LOVETT
(Proffering an imaginary meat pie)
Here we are, hot from the oven.

TODD
What is that?

MRS. LOVETT
It's priest.
Have a little priest.

TODD
Is it really good?

MRS. LOVETT
Sir, it's too good, at least.
Then again, they don't commit sins of
    the flesh,
So it's pretty fresh.

TODD
Awful lot of fat.

MRS. LOVETT
Only where it sat.

TODD
Haven't you got poet
Or something like that?

MRS. LOVETT
No, you see the trouble with poet
Is how do you know it's
Deceased?
Try the priest.

TODD
(Pretending to taste it)
Heavenly. Not as hearty as bishop,
    perhaps, but not as bland as curate,
    either.

MRS. LOVETT
And good for business—always
    leaves you wanting more. Trouble
    is, we only get it in Sundays . . .

Lawyer's rather nice.

TODD
If it's for a price.

MRS. LOVETT
Order something else, though, to
    follow,
Since no one should swallow
It twice.

TODD
Anything that's lean.

MRS. LOVETT
Well, then, if you're British and loyal,
You might enjoy Royal
Marine.
Anyway, it's clean.
Though, of course, it tastes of
    wherever it's been.

TODD
Is that squire
On the fire?

"A Little Priest" (Angela Lansbury and Len Cariou, 1979)

when you think of
After all, what goes on transpires in the markets, in the law courts, in
the corridors of power — why not at the table, too.

(1) T These are desperate times, Mrs. Lovett, & desperate measures
        are called for.

(2) T (tasting it)
        Heaven!
        (snorts with glee)
   ML Well, you're one price it's the most pious

        (T giggles; ML presents another pie)

(3) T I thought it was
        No, if it were rancid, it'd be journalist.
   ML Then it must be journalist. They never retain the heat, you know.
        student. Student always spoils away. can't don't

(2) T Perfect. Not quite a stand is accurate Not as handy as bishops, perhaps but too
        verges on too
        either. (ML snorts with glee) number
   ML And it's good for business — always leaves you wanting more. Trouble is,
        we only get 'em in Sundays.
        (T roars with laughter giggles)

(5) ML If you don't mind a bit of gristle, is summer's nourishing
    T   This isn't iron-monger. It's piccolo player
   ML How can you tell?
    T It's piping hot.
        Naughty, naughty

(4) ML: Butcher? T: Something subtler. ML: Potter? T: (feels it) Hotter.
        Locksmith? I give up.

We're expecting   Beadle any day now   It's Monday, it's all that we've got,
      Beadle in   On mondays you take what you get.
We ought to be getting some Beadle in soon.

priest
let
taste

      Have you tried some
      How about the priest   Have you tried the priest
      Try a little priest   Try a bit of priest
      I can guarantee   I can guarantee
'Twill be   But it's a C of E   They it's C of E   It's C of E
      At the very least   But it's rather nice.   At least

lord
peer
duke
page

                                  I can guarantee
      I can guarantee   C of E
      It to be   At the least
      C of E

constable
bailiff
sheriff

                                 I always have a price though it always
                                    nice   smells
                             Lawyer's rather good — tastes like a tart
                                  of the house   a little too rich
                             Specially today judge
                             Better stick to priest

cleric
clergy
                 is it good?
apprentice Is it really good? It's relic   What's it then today?
deficit   is there
too good It's so good it's angelic   What you got today
too good   not in its nature
drummer It's one of the ways of (the)   Let me see, today
plumber
scribe butler (You'll) pardon the phrase - of the beast.   Special on the clerk
cook butler
page sailor Why not try the clerk
foot tailor Sort of for a lark?   How about a change
actor farmer   Though it's rather strange
tailor driver   sweep
crier gigolo If you want it cheap   flavor
mason grocer And you like it dark It does you a favor If you like it lean,
student potter   How about a Dean?
quack rector Man who run the banks Actor—overdone Never can be carved
smith squire But the only place   Haven't you got priest
thief stoker   Or something that's stewed?
tutor broker They have used in the shanks
valet tinker   Though it makes a wonderful fillet
vendor waiter never will serve unemployed
                                    The minute you kill it,
              the head   It's spoiled
peddler costumer Which has always been dead.

MRS. LOVETT
Mercy, no, sir,
Look closer,
You'll notice it's grocer.

TODD
Looks thicker,
More like vicar.

MRS. LOVETT
No, it has to be grocer—it's green.

TODD
The history of the world, my love . . .

MRS. LOVETT
Save a lot of graves,
Do a lot of relatives favors . . .

TODD
Is those below serving those up
above.

MRS. LOVETT
Everybody shaves,
So there should be plenty of
flavors . . .

TODD
How gratifying for once to know—

BOTH
(Indicates the room upstairs)
That those above will serve those
down below!

MRS. LOVETT
Now, let me see . . .
We've got tinker.

TODD
Something pinker.

MRS. LOVETT
Tailor?

TODD
(Pondering)
Something—paler.

MRS. LOVETT
Butler?

TODD
Something—subtler.

MRS. LOVETT
Potter?

TODD
Something—hotter.

MRS. LOVETT
Locksmith?

(Todd is stumped)

Lovely bit of clerk.*

TODD
Maybe for a lark . . .

MRS. LOVETT
Then again, there's sweep
If you want it cheap
And you like it dark.

Try the financier—
Peak of his career.

TODD
That looks pretty rank.

MRS. LOVETT
Well, he drank.
It's a bank
Cashier.

Last one really sold.†
Wasn't quite so old.

TODD
Have you any beadle?

MRS. LOVETT
Next week, so I'm told.
Beadle isn't bad till you smell it
And notice how well it's
Been greased.
Stick to priest.

(Offering him another imaginary pie)

Now, this might be a bit stringy, but
then, of course, it's fiddle player.

TODD
This isn't fiddle player. It's piccolo
player.

---

*In Britain, this word is pronounced "clark."
†This couplet has always dissatisfied me,
chiefly because of the word "really," which is
both unnecessary and clumsy. Reading it over
thirty years later, it strikes me that the line
should be: "Last one that we sold / Wasn't
quite so old."

MRS. LOVETT
How can you tell?

TODD
It's piping hot.

MRS. LOVETT
Then blow on it first!

TODD
The history of the world, my sweet—

MRS. LOVETT
Oh, Mr. Todd, ooh, Mr. Todd,
What does it tell?

TODD
Is who gets eaten and who gets to eat.

MRS. LOVETT
And, Mr. Todd, too, Mr. Todd,
Who gets to sell.

TODD
But fortunately, it's also clear—

BOTH
That (But) everybody
Goes down well with beer.

MRS. LOVETT
Since marine doesn't appeal to you,
how about Rear Admiral?

TODD
Too salty. I prefer General.

MRS. LOVETT
With or without his privates?
"With" is extra.

TODD
(As she proffers another pie)
What is that?

MRS. LOVETT
It's fop.
Finest in the shop.
And we have some shepherd's pie
peppered
With actual shepherd
On top.
And I've just begun.
Here's the politician: so oily
It's served with a doily—

(As Sweeney shakes his head)

Not one?

TODD

Put it on a bun.

(As she looks at him quizzically)

Well, you never know if it's going
     to run.

MRS. LOVETT

Try the friar.
Fried, it's drier.

TODD

No, the clergy is really
Too coarse and too mealy.

MRS. LOVETT

Then actor—
That's compacter.

TODD

Yes, and always arrives overdone.
I'll come again when you
Have judge on the menu . . .

MRS. LOVETT

Wait! True, we don't have judge—
yet—but would you settle for the
next best thing?

TODD

What's that?

MRS. LOVETT

(Handing him a meat cleaver, as she
takes up a rolling pin)
Executioner.

TODD

Have charity toward the world, my
     pet.

MRS. LOVETT

Yes, yes, I know, my love.

TODD

We'll take the customers that we can
     get.

MRS. LOVETT

High-born and low, my love.

TODD

We'll not discriminate great from
     small.

No, we'll serve anyone—
Meaning anyone—*

BOTH

And to anyone
At all!

Again, Christopher Bond had reduced
this moment to its essence: the two
conspirators concoct their bizarre notion and Todd sums it up in one line.

TODD

Your pies shall be the wonder of the
town. For every customer who
comes up here shall serve the ones
below.

(They both start to giggle, then fall into
each other's arms laughing helplessly.
The Curtain falls.)

Not the most dynamic first act curtain
for a musical, I realized, but what was
there to sing about? I looked again at
the stage direction and started to wonder what they might be laughing helplessly about; it didn't take long to
come up with the notion of their imagining the consistency of the pies. A list
song, indeed, made up of numerous
professions and social positions, each
little verse dealing with a different
one. In order to keep the pattern
going (and pattern recognition is essential to comic list songs—look at
"Let's Do It" and "Adelaide's Lament"
for two outstanding examples) I'd have
to find a few other one-syllable professions or social positions such as
"clerk" and "fop" which could spin off
enough triple rhymes. As with the
search for "Kearney's Lane," easy
enough, I thought, but I had overestimated again. Apart from the ones I actually used, all I could come up with
were dean, smith, thief, scribe and
cook for the professions and page,
groom, peer, lord, duke and earl for

the social positions. I can't believe
there aren't dozens more, but I spent a
significant number of hours trying to
find them. And how many rhymes are
there for "smith" and "duke"? Even
"cook" and "groom" have their limitations. Two-syllable professions are
plentiful: doctor, dentist, mason,
plumber, porter, valet, etc., and they
didn't have to rhyme (as in "Lawyer's
rather nice"). I did find a way of using
a few of them, but once I'd set up
short lines and an increasingly intricate rhyme scheme to avoid monotony, I was stuck. All of which is a
defensive explanation of the occasional clumsiness and flatness of the
jokes, as in the "financier" and "politician" sections. (Moreover, as a sharp-
eared friend of mine pointed out, in
England politicians don't "run" for office, they "stand." And a "bun" is a
sweet bun, not a hamburger roll.)

Until 2007 I had always been bothered by the way I filled out the last
quatrain: "Meaning anyone" is a
stocking-stuffer, an unnecessary inten-
sifier clearly present for the sole purpose of padding the quatrain into
shape. It wasn't until pondering
changes for the movie of Sweeney
Todd that it occurred to me to make a
virtue of repetition instead of hiding it,
and so the pair of conspirators sang:

TODD

We'll not discriminate great from
     small.
No, we'll serve anyone—!

MRS. LOVETT

We'll serve anyone—!

BOTH

And to anyone
At all!

Oscar, a lyricist who took great delight
in repetition as a means of intensifica-
tion, would have approved, I think.

*A meaningless line to fill an empty space,
and another which, thirty years' later, I know
how to improve. It should be a solo for Mrs.
Lovett, repeating Sweeney's words to the audience: "We'll serve anyone—."

ACT TWO

Tobias is drumming up trade for Mrs. Lovett's pie shop, which now has a garden with tables in front of it. Above the shop, Sweeney is pacing, waiting for his new chair to arrive.

God, That's Good!

TOBIAS
Ladies and gentlemen,
May I have your attention, perlease?
Are your nostrils aquiver and tingling
  as well
At that delicate, luscious, ambrosial
  smell?
Yes, they are, I can tell.

Well, ladies and gentlemen,
That aroma enriching the breeze
Is like nothing compared to its
  succulent source,
As the gourmets among you will tell
  you, of course.

Ladies and gentlemen,
You can't imagine the rapture in
  store—
Just inside of this door!

There you'll sample
Mrs. Lovett's meat pies,
Savory and sweet pies,
As you'll see.
You who eat pies,
Mrs. Lovett's meat pies
Conjure up the treat pies
Used to be!

(The garden is revealed, packed with customers eating and drinking as Mrs. Lovett, fancily dressed, takes orders and collects money, assisted by Tobias. The Beggar Woman hangs about in the shadows. The following lines overlap.)

1ST MAN: Over here, boy, how
  about some ale?
2ND MAN: Let me have another,
  laddie!
1ST WOMAN: Tell me, are they
  flavorsome?
2ND WOMAN: They are.
3RD WOMAN: Isn't this delicious?
TOBIAS: Right away.
4TH MAN: Could we have some
  service over here, boy?
4TH WOMAN: Could we have
  some service, waiter?
3RD MAN: Could we have some
  service?
2ND, 3RD WOMAN: Yes, they
  are.

1ST MAN: God, that's good!
2ND MAN: What about that pie,
  boy?
1ST WOMAN: Tell me, are they
  spicy?
2ND WOMAN: God, that's good!

5TH WOMAN: How much are you
  charging?
TOBIAS: Thruppence.
3RD WOMAN: Yes, what about the
  pie, boy?
4TH WOMAN: I never tasted
  anything so . . .
1ST, 5TH WOMAN: Thruppence?
5TH MAN: Thruppence for a meat
  pie?
1ST, 2ND MEN: Where's the ale I
  asked you for, boy?
TOBIAS: Ladies and gentlemen—!

MRS. LOVETT
Toby!

TOBIAS
Coming!

(To a customer)

'Scuse me . . .

MRS. LOVETT
Ale there!

"God, That's Good!" (Julia McKenzie)

TOBIAS
Right, mum!

MRS. LOVETT
Quick, now!

CUSTOMERS
God, that's good!

MRS. LOVETT
(Making her way from customer to customer)
Nice to see you, dearie,
How have you been keeping?
Cor, me bones is weary!
Toby, one for the gentleman—!

(To a customer)

Hear the birdies cheeping—
Helps to keep it cheery . . .
Toby!

(Referring to the Beggar Woman)

Throw the old woman out!

CUSTOMERS
God, that's good!

MRS. LOVETT
(To another customer)
What's your pleasure, dearie? . . .
No, we don't cut slices . . .
Cor, me eyes is bleary! . . .
Toby—!

(Referring to a drunken customer)

None for the gentleman!

(To another customer)

I could up me prices—
I'm a little leery . . .
Business couldn't be better, though—

CUSTOMERS
God, that's good!

MRS. LOVETT
Knock on wood.

TODD
(Whispering out the window)
Psst!

MRS. LOVETT
(To a customer)
Excuse me . . .

TODD
Psst!

MRS. LOVETT
(To Tobias)
Dear, see to the customers.

TODD
Psst!

MRS. LOVETT
Yes, what, love?
Quick, though, the trade is brisk.

TODD
But it's six o'clock!

MRS. LOVETT
So it's six o'clock.

TODD
It was due to arrive
At a quarter to five—

MRS. LOVETT	TODD
And it's probably already	And it's six o'clock!
Down the block!	
It'll be here, it'll be here!	I've been waiting all day!
Have a beaker of beer	
And stop worrying, dear.	But it should have been here
Now, now . . .	By now!

CUSTOMERS
More hot pies!

MRS. LOVETT	TODD
Gawd!	
Will you wait there, Coolly?	You'll come back When it comes?
'Cos my customers truly	
Are getting unruly.	

MRS. LOVETT
(To a customer)
And what's your pleasure, dearie?
Oops! I beg your pardon!
Just me hands is smeary—
Toby!

(Referring to a man who is trying to skip out without paying)

Run for the gentleman!

(To another customer)

Don't you love a garden?
Always makes me teary . . .
Must be one of them foreigners—

CUSTOMERS
God, that's good that is delicious!

MRS. LOVETT
(To another customer)
What's my secret?
Frankly, dear—forgive my candor—
Family secret,
All to do with herbs.
Things like being
Careful with your coriander,
That's what makes the gravy grander!

CUSTOMERS
More hot pies!
More hot!
More pies!

TODD
Psst!

MRS. LOVETT
Excuse me . . .

TODD
Psst!

MRS. LOVETT
Dear, see to the customers.

TODD
Psst!

MRS. LOVETT
Yes, what, love?
Quick, though, the trade is brisk.

TODD
But it's here!

MRS. LOVETT
It's where?

TODD
Coming up the stair!

(He points to a crate being delivered)

MRS. LOVETT	TODD
I'll get rid of this lot	
As they're still	
pretty hot	
And then I'll be	It's about
there!	to be opened,
	Or don't you
	care?
No, I'll *be* there!	
I will *be* there!	But we have to
	prepare!
But they'll never	
be sold	
If I let 'em get cold—!	

(During the following, Todd uncrates an elegant barber chair)

MRS. LOVETT
(To a customer)

Oh, and
Incidentally, dearie,
You know Mrs. Mooney?
Sales've been so dreary—
Toby—!
Poor thing is penniless.

(To Tobias, referring to the Beggar Woman)

What about that loony?

(To the customer)

Lookin' sort of beery . . .
Oh, well, got her comeuppance—
And that'll be thruppence—
And so she should!

CUSTOMERS
(Overlapping)

God, that's good that is de have you
Licious ever tasted smell such
Oh my God what more that's pies good!

(Mrs. Lovett ascends the stairs to Todd's parlor and they both look at the chair)

TODD, MRS. LOVETT
Oooohhh! Oooohhh!

TODD	MRS. LOVETT
Is that a chair fit	
for a king,	
A wondrous neat	It's gorgeous!
And most particular	
chair?	It's gorgeous!
You tell me where	
there is a seat	
Can half compare	It's perfect!
With this particular	
thing!	It's gorgeous!
I have a few	
Minor adjustments	You make your
	few
To make—	Minor
	adjustments.
They'll take	
A moment.	You take your
	time,
I'll call you . . .	I'll go see to the
(Embraces the chair)	Customers.
I have another	
friend . . .	

(Todd starts tinkering with the mechanics of the chair as Mrs. Lovett returns to the garden)

TOBIAS	MRS. LOVETT
Is that a pie fit	
for a king,	
A wondrous sweet	It's gorgeous!
And most	
delectable thing?	It's gorgeous!
You see, ma'am, why	
There is no meat	
Pie can compete	It's perfect!
With this	
delectable	It's gorgeous!
Pie!	

CUSTOMERS
(Simultaneously with the above)
Yum! Yum! Yum!

TOBIAS, MRS. LOVETT	CUSTOMERS
The crust all velvety	Yum! Yum!
and wavy,	
That glaze, those	Yum! Yum!
crimps . . .	
And then the thick,	Yum! Yum!
succulent gravy . . .	
One whiff, one	Yum! Yum!
glimpse . . .	

TODD
And now to test
This best of barber chairs . . .

MRS. LOVETT	TOBIAS	CUSTOMERS
So rich,		Yum!
So thick	So tender,	Yum!
It makes you sick . . .	That you	
	Surrender.	Yum! Yum!

"God, That's Good!" (Angela Lansbury)

TODD
It's time . . .
It's time . . .

(To Mrs. Lovett)

Psst!

MRS. LOVETT
Excuse me . . .

TODD
Psst!

MRS. LOVETT
Dear, see to the customers.

TODD
Psst!

MRS. LOVETT
Yes, what, love?

TODD
Quick, now!

MRS. LOVETT
Me heart's aflutter—!

TODD	MRS. LOVETT
When I pound the floor,	
It's a signal to show	When you pound the floor,
That I'm ready to go,	Yes, you told me, I know,
When I pound the floor!	You'll be ready to go
Will you trust me?	When you pound the floor—
I just want to be sure.	Will you trust me?
When I'm certain	I'll be waiting below
That you're In place,	For the whistle to blow . . .

TODD
I'll pound three times.

(Knocks on the floor three times)

Three times.

(Does it again; she nods impatiently)

And then you . . .

(She knocks the air twice)

Three times—!

(She knocks the wall heavily and wearily)

If you—

(She knocks again, nodding and rolling her eyes)

Exactly.

CUSTOMERS
More hot pies!

MRS. LOVETT
Gawd!

CUSTOMERS
More hot!

MRS. LOVETT
(To the customers)
Right!

CUSTOMERS
More pies!

TODD
Psst!

CUSTOMERS
More!

MRS. LOVETT
(In a frenzy with all the demands)
Wait!

(Mrs. Lovett descends to the cellar. Todd puts a pile of books on the seat of his barber chair and pulls a lever. A trapdoor opens below the chair, the chair tilts downward and the books fall through a chute into the cellar as the chair rights itself. Mrs. Lovett pounds the chute triumphantly—three times—then returns to the customers.)

CUSTOMERS
More hot pies!
More hot! More pies!
More! Hot! Pies!

MRS. LOVETT, TOBIAS
Eat them slow and
Feel the crust, how thin I (she) rolled it!
Eat them slow, 'cause
Every one's a prize!
Eat them slow, 'cos
That's the lot and now we've sold it!
Come again tomorrow—!

MRS. LOVETT
(Spotting a man approaching, as Tobias is hanging up a SOLD OUT sign)
Hold it—

CUSTOMERS
More hot pies!

MRS. LOVETT
(As the man starts up the stairs)
Bless my eyes—!

(Todd beckons the man up)

MRS. LOVETT
Fresh supplies!

MRS. LOVETT	TOBIAS
How about it, dearie?	Is that a pie
Be here in a twinkling!	Fit for a king,
Just confirms my theory—	A wondrous sweet
Toby—!	And most Delectable Thing?
God watches over us.	You see, ma'am,
Didn't have an inkling . . .	Why There is no meat
Positively eerie . . .	Pie—

MRS. LOVETT
Toby!
Throw the old woman out!

CUSTOMERS
God that's good that is de have you
Licious ever tasted smell such
Oh my God what perfect more that's
Pies such flavor
God, that's good!!!

As in the case of "Pirelli's Miracle Elixir," rather than having simply a Chorus of Customers, I characterized each of them individually in the lyric—the demanding one, the envious one, the freeloader, the drunk, etc.—so that the actress playing Mrs. Lovett would have different colors to play, everything from flattery to annoyance, rather than merely repeating general greetings differentiated only by a variety of rhymes. It also gave each of the chorus members—in most musicals mere clones of one another with little to do but sing and dance as items in a conglomeration—something to act even if only in pantomime. I had planned them to be seated at little tables, as in a beer garden, with Mrs. Lovett skipping in and out between them, but Hal had the stunning notion of putting them all (eighteen, no fewer) at one large communal table, infusing the scene with a Breughel-like frenzy of chomping and swilling. And singing. My only unsolvable lyric problem turned out to be the seemingly innocuous "Knock on wood." The British expression is "Touch wood," but I needed three syllables to match the rhythm and rhyme of "God, that's good." As with other instances in this collection, I'm open to suggestions.

Anthony is searching the streets of London for Johanna.

Johanna

ANTHONY
I feel you, Johanna,
I feel you.
Do they think that walls can hide
    you?
Even now I'm at your window.
I am in the dark beside you,
Buried sweetly in your yellow hair,
Johanna . . .

(As Anthony continues his search, Todd ushers a customer into his parlor, seats him in the chair and proceeds to lather the man's face)

TODD
(To himself, as if in a trance)
And are you beautiful and pale,
With yellow hair, like her?
I'd want you beautiful and pale,
The way I've dreamed you were,
Johanna . . .

ANTHONY
Johanna . . .

TODD
And if you're beautiful, what then,
With yellow hair, like wheat?
I think we shall not meet again—

(He slashes the man's throat)

My little dove, my sweet
Johanna . . .

ANTHONY
I'll steal you,
Johanna . . .

TODD
Goodbye, Johanna.
You're gone, and yet you're mine.
I'm fine, Johanna,
I'm fine!

(He pulls the lever and the customer disappears down the chute)

ANTHONY
Johanna . . .

(Night falls. While Mrs. Lovett, in a white nightdress, tosses bloody objects into the bake oven in the cellar and black smoke rises from the chimney, the Beggar Woman appears among the passersby, coughing and spitting.)

BEGGAR WOMAN
Smoke! Smoke!
Sign of the devil! Sign of the devil!
City on fire!
Witch! Witch!
Smell it, sir! An evil smell!
Every night at the vespers bell,
Smoke that comes from the mouth of
    hell!
City on fire!
City on fire!
Mischief! Mischief!
Mischief . . .

(Another day. Another customer.)

TODD
And if I never hear your voice,
My turtledove, my dear,
I still have reason to rejoice:
The way ahead is clear,
Johanna . . .

JOHANNA'S VOICE
I'll marry Anthony Sunday . . .
Anthony Sunday . . .

ANTHONY
I feel you . . .

TODD
And in the darkness when I'm blind
With what I can't forget—

ANTHONY
Johanna . . .

TODD
It's always morning in my mind,
My little lamb, my pet,
Johanna . . .

JOHANNA'S VOICE
I knew you'd come for me one
    day . . .
Come for me . . . one day . . .

TODD   ANTHONY
You stay, Johanna—   Johanna . . .

(Todd slashes the customer's throat)

TODD
The way I've dreamed you are.
Oh, look, Johanna—
A star!

(He sends the customer down the chute)

ANTHONY
Buried sweetly in your yellow hair . . .

TODD
A shooting star!

(He sends the customer's hat down the chute. Night falls.)

BEGGAR WOMAN
There! There!
Somebody, somebody, look up there!
Didn't I tell you? Smell that air!
City on fire!

(To a passerby)

Quick, sir! Run and tell!
Warn 'em all of the witch's spell!
There it is, there it is, the unholy
   smell!
Tell it to the Beadle and the police as
   well!
Tell 'em! Tell 'em!
Help!!! Fiend!!!
City on fire!!!
City on fire . . .

Mischief . . . Mischief . . . Mischief . . .
Fiend . . .
Alms . . . alms . . .

(Another day and another customer, but this one brings his wife and child, so Todd, though disappointed, merely shaves him)

TODD
And though I'll think of you, I guess,
Until the day I die,
I think I miss you less and less
As every day goes by,
Johanna . . .

ANTHONY
Johanna . . .

JOHANNA'S VOICE
With you beside me on Sunday,
Married on Sunday . . .

TODD
And you'll be beautiful and pale,
And look too much like her.
If only angels could prevail,
We'd be the way we were,
Johanna . . .

ANTHONY
I feel you . . .
Johanna . . .

JOHANNA'S VOICE
Married on Sunday . . .
Married on Sunday . . .

TODD
Wake up, Johanna!
Another bright red day!
We learn, Johanna,
To say
Goodbye . . .

ANTHONY
I'll steal you . . .

One of the pleasures I had in writing this lyric (and there are not many to be had in lyric writing) was that it allowed me to include three entirely different songs called "Johanna" in the score. Another was that I got to fulfill the second of the murder ploys I mentioned earlier in connection with "Pretty Women": there the audience expected a killing and didn't get one— here, lulled by the long-lined placid melody and plaintive lyric, they were properly discombobulated when in mid-phrase Sweeney slit the throat of an ordinary man and blood gushed all over the victim, the chair, the barber and occasionally members of the orchestra. A third pleasure was that I was once again able to indulge myself in writing a song which dramatizes a story that takes place over a period of days or weeks, like "Chrysanthemum Tea." Writing songs like these not only appeals to my instinct for intricate plotting, it makes me feel like a playwright, even if the plays are only six or seven minutes long.

In Mrs. Lovett's parlor, Todd sits brooding while she gleefully counts the takings from her dining establishment.

By the Sea

MRS. LOVETT
Ooh, Mr. Todd,

(Kisses him)

I'm so happy

(Kisses him again)

I could eat you up, I really could!
You know what I'd like to do, Mr.
   Todd,

(Again)

What I dream,

(And again)

If the business stays as good,
Where I'd really like to go?
In a year or so . . .
Don't you want to know?

TODD
Of course.

MRS. LOVETT
Do you really want to know?

TODD
Yes, yes, I do, I do.

MRS. LOVETT
By the sea, Mr. Todd,
That's the life I covet.
By the sea, Mr. Todd,
Ooh, I know you'd love it!
You and me,
Mr. T.,
We could be
Alone
In a house wot we'd almost own
Down by the sea . . .

TODD
Anything you say . . .

MRS. LOVETT
Wouldn't that be smashing?

With the sea at our gate,
We'll have kippered herring
Wot have swum to us straight

From the Straits of Bering.
Every night in the kip
When we're through our kippers,
I'll be there slippin' off your slippers

By the sea . . .
With the fishies splashing,
By the sea . . .
Wouldn't that be smashing?
Down by the sea . . .

TODD
Anything you say,
Anything you say.

MRS. LOVETT
I can see us waking,
The breakers breaking,
The seagulls squawking
Hoo! Hoo!
I do me baking,
Then I go walking
With you—hoo . . .

(Waves to imaginary strollers)

Yoo-hoo . . .

I'll warm me bones
On the esplanade,
Have tea and scones
With me gay young blade.
Then I'll knit a sweater
While you write a letter,
Unless we got better
To do—hoo . . .

TODD
Anything you say . . .

MRS. LOVETT
Think how snug it'll be
Underneath our flannel
When it's just you and me
And the English Channel.
In our cozy retreat,
Kept all neat and tidy,
We'll have chums over every Friday,
By the sea . . .

TODD
Anything you say . . .

MRS. LOVETT
Don't you love the weather
By the sea?

We'll grow old together
By the seaside,
Hoo! Hoo!
By the beautiful sea!

It'll be so quiet
That who'll come by it
Except a seagull?
Hoo! hoo!
We shouldn't try it,
Though, till it's legal
For two—hoo!

But a seaside wedding
Could be devised,
Me rumpled bedding
Legitimized.
Me eyelids'll flutter,
I'll turn into butter,
The moment I mutter,
"I do—hoo!"

By the sea, in our nest,
We could share our kippers
With the odd paying guest
From the weekend trippers,
Have a nice sunny suite
For the guest to rest in—
Now and then, you could do the
   guest in—

By the sea,
Married nice and proper.
By the sea—
Bring along your chopper*
To the seaside,
Hoo! Hoo!
By the beautiful sea!

Anthony enters, bringing the news that he has located Johanna, who has been sent by Judge Turpin to an insane asylum. Since hair for wigs is often obtained from asylum inmates, Todd hatches a scheme whereby Anthony will be disguised as a wigmaker and, with a pistol, rescue Johanna. He starts to teach Anthony the fine points of hair colors.

---

*When Sweeney Todd was premiered in England, I discovered that by happy coincidence "chopper" is British slang for penis, making Mrs. Lovett a sly punster indeed.

Wigmaker/Letter Sequence

TODD
There's tawny and there's golden
   saffron,
There's flaxen and there's blonde . . .

ANTHONY
There's tawny and there's golden
   saffron,
There's flaxen and there's blonde . . .

TODD	ANTHONY
Good.	
There's coarse and fine,	
There's straight and curly,	
There's gray, there's white,	There's coarse and fine,
There's ash, there's pearly,	There's straight and curly,
There's corn-yellow,	There's gray, there's white,
Buff and ochre and	There's ash, there's pearly,
Straw and apricot . . .	There's corn-yellow . . .

(They leave the parlor. A quintet from
   the Company appears)

QUINTET
Sweeney'd waited too long before—
"Ah, but never again," he swore.
Fortune arrived. "Sweeney!" it sang.
Sweeney was ready and Sweeney
   sprang.

Sweeney's problems went up in
   smoke,
All resolved with a single stroke.
Sweeney was sharp, Sweeney was
   burning,
Sweeney began the engines turning.

(The following lines overlap)

Sweeney's problems went up in
   smoke,
All resolved
And completely solved
With a single stroke
By Sweeney!
Sweeney didn't wait,

Not Sweeney!
Set the bait,
Did Sweeney!
Sweeney! Sweeney! Sweeney!

(Anthony and Sweeney reappear)

ANTHONY   TODD
With finer textures,
Ash looks fairer,
Which makes it rare,   Good.
But flaxen's rarer—
                     No! No!
Yes, yes, I know—   The flaxen's
                     cheaper . . .
Cheaper, not rarer . . .

(Todd sends Anthony off and sits down at a desk to write a letter. The quintet voices his thoughts as well as what he writes.)

QUINTET
(Variously)
Most Honorable Judge Turpin—
Most Honorable—
Honorable!
I venture thus to write you this
Urgent note to warn you that the
Hot-blooded—
Young—
Sailor has abducted your ward
    Johanna—
(Johanna! Johanna!)—
From the institution
Where you so wisely confined her.

But hoping to earn your favor,
I have persuaded the boy to lodge her
    here tonight
At my tonsorial parlor in Fleet Street.
If you want her again in your arms,
Hurry
After the night falls.
She will be waiting.
Waiting . . .

Your obedient humble servant,
Sweeney Todd.

This may look more like recitative than a lyric, but it's a song, and the stage directions that accompany it are longer than the lyric itself. As with "The Worst Pies in London," every line is punctuated with details of action incorporated into the music: each dip of Sweeney's pen, each hesitation as he thinks of how to lure the Judge, every chuckle and murmur and sigh. It's much more interesting on the stage than on the page and was more fun to write than any other song in the score. Choreographing action with music is always a joy, as I've learned the few times I've written background scores for movies.

Tobias has become devoted to Mrs. Lovett and suspects Sweeney of being up to no good. He voices his suspicions to her and promises to protect her.

Not While I'm Around

TOBIAS
Nothing's gonna harm you,
Not while I'm around.
Nothing's gonna harm you,
No, sir,
Not while I'm around.

Demons are prowling
Everywhere
Nowadays.
I'll send them howling,
I don't care—
I got ways.

No one's gonna hurt you,
No one's gonna dare.
Others can desert you—
Not to worry,
Whistle, I'll be there.

Demons'll charm you
With a smile
For a while,
But in time
Nothing can harm you,
Not while I'm
Around.

Not to worry, not to worry,
I may not be smart but I ain't dumb.
I can do it,
Put me to it,
Show me something I can overcome.
Not to worry, mum.

Being close and being clever
Ain't like being true.
I don't need to, I won't never
Hide a thing from you,
Like some.

(Mrs. Lovett offers Tobias a bonbon, which she extracts from a purse that Tobias recognizes as having belonged to Pirelli. She claims that it was a present from Todd, but she can see that Tobias's suspicions are confirmed. Alarmed, she tries to quiet him.)

MRS. LOVETT
Nothing's gonna harm you,
Not while I'm around!
Nothing's gonna harm you, Toby,
Not while I'm around.

TOBIAS
Two quid was in it,
Two or three—
    The guv'nor giving up his purse—
    with two quid?

Not for a minute!
Don't you see? . . .

(She finally gets him to calm down. He hugs her.)

Demons'll charm you
With a smile
For a while,
But in time
Nothing's gonna harm you,
Not while I'm
Around!

Mrs. Lovett, panicky about Tobias's suspicions, takes him down to the cellar on the pretext of teaching him how to bake the pies, and locks him in. Upstairs, the Beadle arrives at the shop and seats himself at the harmonium in the parlor, thumbing through a book of songs on the easel, accompanying himself as he sings from it.

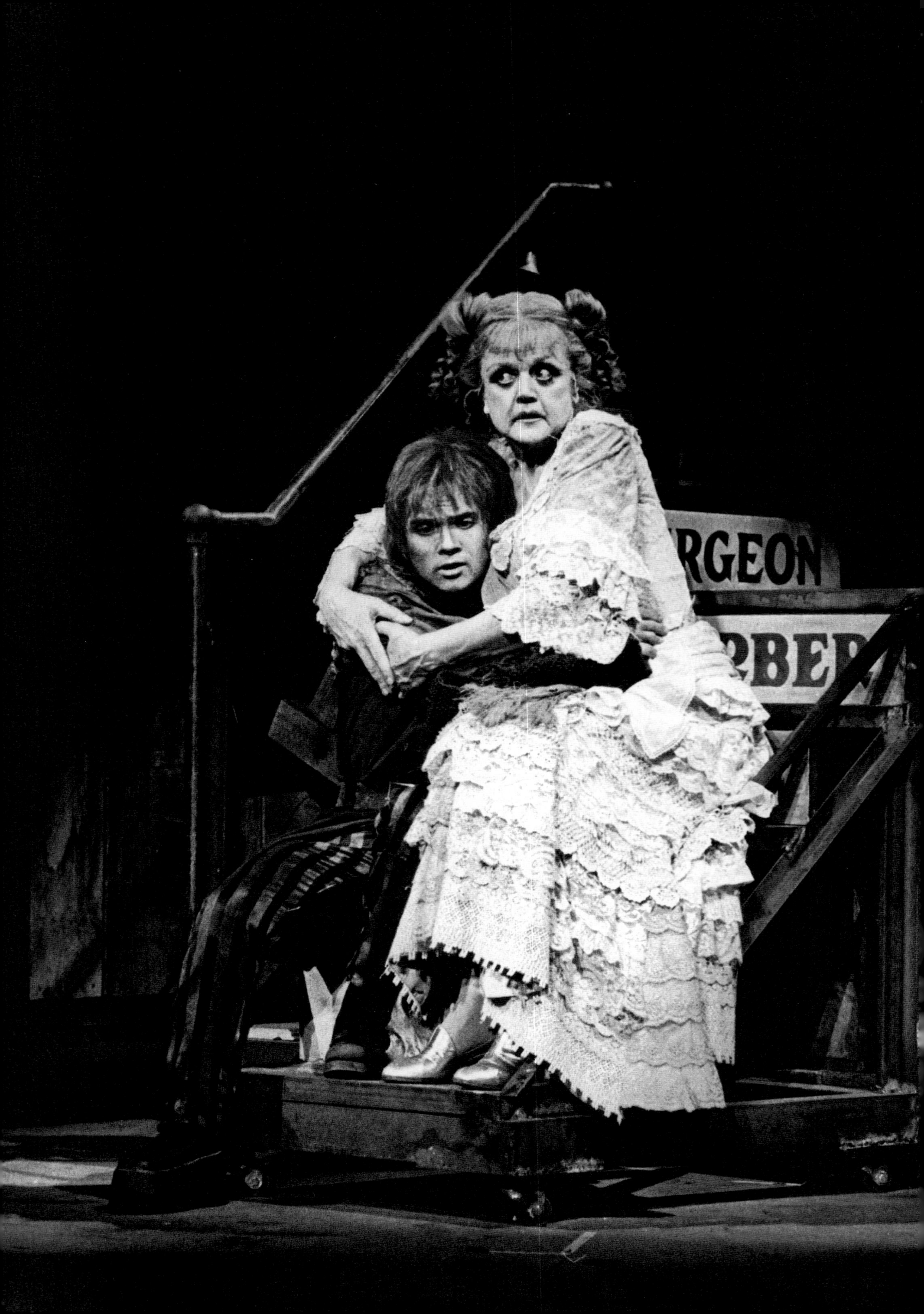
RGEON
RBER

Parlor Songs

BEADLE

Sweet Polly Plunkett lay in the grass,
Turned her eyes heavenward, sighing,
"I am a lass who alas loves a lad
Who alas has a lass in Canterbury.
'Tis a row dow diddle dow day,
'Tis a row dow diddle dow dee . . ."

Sweet Polly Plunkett saw her life pass,
Flew down the city road, crying,
"I am a lass who alas loves a lad
Who alas has a lass loves another lad
Who once I had
In Canterbury.
'Tis a row dow diddle dow day,
'Tis a row dow diddle dow dee . . ."

(Hearing the Beadle's voice, Mrs. Lovett rushes upstairs to find that he has come to investigate complaints of mysterious smells coming from her bakehouse. Mrs. Lovett claims that she doesn't have the key to it, that only Todd has, and tries to persuade the Beadle to leave and return another time. The Beadle insists on staying, and cajoles her into joining him in another song, which she does to placate him. During this one, however, Tobias, unaware that he has been locked in, hears their voices and joins them.)

BEADLE
(With Mrs. Lovett and Tobias occasionally joining in)
If one bell rings in the Tower of Bray,
Ding dong! Your true love will stay.
Ding dong! One bell today
In the Tower of Bray . . .
Ding dong!

But if two bells ring in the Tower of Bray,
Ding dong, ding dong! your true love will stray.
Ding dong, ding dong! Two bells today
In the Tower of Bray!
Ding dong, ding dong!

If three bells ring in the Tower of Bray,
Ding dong, ding dong, ding dong!
Your love's gone away.
Ding dong, ding dong, ding dong!
Three bells today
In the Tower of Bray . . .
Ding dong, ding dong, ding dong!

If four bells ring in the Tower of Bray—

MRS. LOVETT
(Wearily)
Just how many bells are there?

BEADLE
Twelve.

—Ding dong, ding dong, ding dong, ding dong,
Then lovers must pray!
Ding dong, ding dong, ding dong, ding dong,
Four bells today
In the Tower of Bray . . .
Ding dong, ding dong, ding dong, ding dong!

My one regret about the score of *Sweeney Todd* is that I missed an opportunity to musicalize this scene as Bond had written it, a scene in which Mrs. Lovett tries to poison the Beadle. It was both hilarious and tense, involving as it did the time-ripened routine of switching glasses. "The Tower of Bray" was written for this purpose—a counting lyric that Mrs. Lovett could use as a drinking song, encouraging the Beadle to knock one back with each verse. She never gets past the first one, however, because the Beadle insists she join him, and she almost poisons herself when she gets distracted by Tobias's voice rising from the cellar. It would have made a nice chaotic trio, but I never got around to it. Still, the moment did allow me the chance to write a couple of twee English folk ballads, poking fun at a genre which is faintly silly without any help from me.

(Todd returns. The Beadle asks to investigate the bakehouse, but Todd suggests that first he might like a shave, a pomade and a facial rub with bay rum— all free, of course, which makes it irresistible to the Beadle. He goes upstairs with Todd. Meanwhile, in the cellar, Tobias discovers human parts in the meat and is appropriately horrified. He tries to leave, only to find that Mrs. Lovett has locked him in. Simultaneously, the Beadle's bloody body emerges from the chute and Tobias runs hysterically into the dark reaches of the cellar. Upstairs, Mrs. Lovett corrals Todd into going to the cellar to look for the boy and dispose of him. Members of the Company appear.)

The Ballad of Sweeney Todd (Part IV)

COMPANY
(Variously)
The engine roared, the motor hissed,
And who could see how the road would twist?
In Sweeney's ledger the entries matched:
A Beadle arrived and a Beadle dispatched
To satisfy the hungry god
Of Sweeney Todd,
The Demon Barber of Fleet . . .
Sweeney! . . .
Street . . .
Sweeney!
Sweeney! Sweeney! Sweeeeeeney!

The cries of "Sweeney!" become the cries of lunatics in Fogg's Asylum for the Mentally Deranged, among them Johanna. Anthony, disguised as a wigmaker, threatens to shoot Fogg unless he releases her. When Fogg resists and Anthony is too soft-hearted to shoot, Johanna grabs the pistol from him and does it herself. With Fogg dead, the lunatics break out of the asylum, screaming and dispersing themselves throughout London while Anthony and Johanna flee to Todd's barbershop.

Opposite: *"Not While I'm Around"*

City on Fire

LUNATICS
City on fire!
Rats in the grass
And the lunatics yelling in the streets!
It's the end of the world! Yes!
City on fire!
Hunchbacks dancing!
Stirrings in the ground
And the whirring of giant wings!
Watch out! Look!
Blotting out the moonlight,
Thick black rain falling on the
City on fire!
City on fire!
City on fire!

JOHANNA
Will we be married on Sunday?
That's what you promised,
Married on Sunday!
That was last August . . .
Kiss me!

LUNATICS
City on fire!
Rats in the streets
And the lunatics yelling at the moon!
It's the end of the world! Yes!
City on fire!
Hunchbacks kissing!
Stirrings in the graves
And the screaming of giant winds!
Watch out! Look!
Crawling on the chimneys,
Great black crows screeching at the
City on fire!
City on fire!
City on Fire!

(Mrs. Lovett and Todd are searching through the cellar for Tobias)

MRS. LOVETT
Toby!
Where are you, love?

TODD
Toby!
Where are you, lad?

MRS. LOVETT
Nothing's gonna harm you . . .

TODD
Toby!

MRS. LOVETT
Not while I'm around . . .

TODD
Toby!

MRS. LOVETT
Where are you hiding?
Nothing's gonna harm you,
Darling . . .

TODD
Nothing to be afraid of, boy . . .

MRS. LOVETT
Not while I'm around.

TODD
Toby . . .

MRS. LOVETT
Demons are prowling everywhere
Nowadays . . .

TODD
Toby . . .

LUNATICS
City on fire!
Rats in the streets
And the lunatics yelling at the moon!
It's the end of the world! Yes!

(The Beggar Woman has been waiting in the shadows for the Beadle to emerge from Mrs. Lovett's parlor)

BEGGAR WOMAN
Beadle . . . Beadle! . . .
No good hiding, I saw you!
Are you in there still,
Beadle? . . . Beadle? . . .
Get her, but watch it!
She's a wicked one, she'll deceive you
With her fancy gowns
And her fancy airs
And her—

(Suddenly shrieking)

Mischief! Mischief!
Devil's work!

(Plaintively)

Where are you, Beadle?
Beadle . . .

LUNATICS
City on fire! . . .

The Beggar Woman sneaks into Todd's barbershop, sees the chest in which Todd dumped Pirelli's body, and starts keening a lullaby to an imaginary baby whom she rocks in her arms.

Beggar Woman's Lullaby

BEGGAR WOMAN
And why should you weep then, my
jo, my jing?
Your father's at tea with the Swedish
king.
He'll bring you the moon on a silver
string.
Ohh . . .
Ohh . . .

Quickly to sleep then, my jo, my jing,
He'll bring you a shoe and a wedding
ring.
Sing here again, home again, come
again spring.

He'll be coming soon now
To kiss you, my jo, my jing,
Bringing you the moon
And a shoe and a wedding ring.
He'll be coming here again,
Home again . . .

This was written for the London production, and the reason has to do more with murder mysteries than with musicals.

When the Beggar Woman turns out to be Sweeney's wife in the last scene, it's supposed to be a surprise. It's Christopher Bond's invention, of course, not part of the traditional version, and it certainly surprised me. I thought I could enhance it by planting a musical clue along the way: during

"Poor Thing," Lucy gets raped while a minuet is playing at the masked ball, and the melody of this minuet recurs throughout the evening as the melody of the demented Beggar Woman's street solicitations. To my dismay, I found that some members of the audience, whether clued in by the music or not, were way ahead of this twist from the beginning and found it, if anything, an anticlimax, whereas others figured it out when Sweeney kills the Beggar Woman at the end of this scene, others not until the moment at the end of the show when Sweeney realizes who she is (the ideal moment), and others not at all. Even after the show had been reviewed and had played a substantial number of performances, even after the recording had been released, there was no unanimity of recognition. I didn't take a poll, but the signal from the audience was clear: the collective intake of breath at the moment of Sweeney's realization in the cellar during the last scene varied seismically from night to night. Ideally, I wanted everyone in the theater to be stunned at the same time, but the Beggar Woman's function in the plot became apparent to too many people too soon.

I propounded the problem to Peter Shaffer, a playwright who not only knows his Cockney slang but knows how to plot, too, having written murder mysteries with his brother Anthony, author of *Sleuth*. He suggested that I not hold off the information till the last scene but release it earlier, at the moment when the Beggar Woman enters Todd's room looking for the Beadle. I therefore wrote this lullaby to her imagined baby, staged as an exact echo of the (unheard) lullaby she sings during the pantomime at the beginning of "Poor Thing." In that way the entire audience, except for the few who had cottoned on to the revelation from the start of the show, would be surprised at the same time. More important, this advance knowledge would make Sweeney's unwitting murder of his own wife not merely a momentarily shocking action but a tragic one. Instead of the authors'

being a step ahead of the audience, the audience would be a step ahead of Sweeney. So I wrote it, we put it in the London production, and the results were exactly the same: some of the audience were way ahead of the plot, others caught on gradually and others not at all. There are aspects of theatrical plotting I will never understand, fortunately in *Sweeney Todd* it doesn't matter. Sweeney's reaction to the revelation is what counts, and everybody in the audience gets that at the same time.

Sweeney bursts into the room and tries to shoo the Beggar Woman away, to no avail. He sees through the window the Judge arriving and hastily kills the Beggar Woman, sending her body to the cellar just in time. The Judge enters, asking for Johanna.

Final Sequence

TODD
I think I hear her now.

JUDGE TURPIN
Oh, excellent, my friend!

TODD
Is that her dainty footstep on the stair?

JUDGE TURPIN
I hear nothing.

TODD
Yes, isn't that her shadow on the wall?

JUDGE TURPIN
Where?

TODD
There!
Primping,
Making herself even prettier than usual—

JUDGE TURPIN
Even prettier . . .

TODD
If possible.

JUDGE TURPIN
Ohhhhhh,
Pretty women!

TODD
Pretty women, yes . . .

JUDGE TURPIN
Quickly, sir, a splash of bay rum!

TODD
Sit, sir, sit.

(The Judge sits in the chair)

JUDGE TURPIN
Johanna, Johanna . . .

TODD
Pretty women . . .

JUDGE TURPIN
Hurry, man!

TODD
Pretty women
Are a wonder . . .

JUDGE TURPIN
You're in a merry mood again today,
Mr. Todd.

TODD
Pretty women!

JUDGE TURPIN	TODD
What we do for	
Pretty women!	Pretty women!
Blowing out	Blowing out their
their candles	candles
Or combing out	Or combing out
their hair—	their hair,
Then they leave—	
Even when they	Even when they
leave you	leave,
And vanish, they	They still
somehow	
Can still remain	Are there,
There with you,	They're there . . .
there . . .	

JUDGE TURPIN
How seldom it is one meets a fellow spirit!

TODD
With fellow tastes in women, at
least.

JUDGE TURPIN
What? What's that?

TODD
The years no doubt have changed
me, sir. But then, I suppose, the face
of a barber—the face of a prisoner
in the dock—is not particularly
memorable.

JUDGE TURPIN
(With horrified realization)
Benjamin Barker!

TODD
Benjamin Barker!!!

(Todd kills the Judge and sends him to
the cellar. Exhausted, he falls to his knees
and picks up his razor.)

TODD
Rest now, my friend,
Rest now forever.
Sleep now the untroubled
Sleep of the angels . . .

(Todd hears Mrs. Lovett screaming from
the cellar and rushes down to her)

COMPANY
Lift your razor high, Sweeney!
Hear it singing, "Yes!"
Sink it in the rosy skin
Of righteousness!

(In the cellar the Judge, still alive, is
clinging to Mrs. Lovett's skirts but dies as
Todd enters. The light from the ovens
illuminates the Beggar Woman's face and
reveals her to be Lucy. Todd cries out in
anguish, cradles Lucy's head and accuses
Mrs. Lovett of lying to him when she told
him that Lucy had committed suicide.)

MRS. LOVETT
No, no, not lied at all,
No, I never lied.

TODD
Lucy . . .

MRS. LOVETT
Said she took the poison—she did!
Never said that she died,
Poor thing!
She lived—

TODD
I've come home again . . .

MRS. LOVETT
But it left her weak in the head.
All she did for months was just lie
there in bed—

TODD
Lucy . . .

MRS. LOVETT
Should've been in hospital,
Wound up in Bedlam instead,
Poor thing!

TODD
Oh, my God . . .

MRS. LOVETT
Better you should think she was
dead.
Yes, I lied 'cause I love you!

TODD
Lucy . . .

MRS. LOVETT
I'd be twice the wife she was!
I love you!

TODD
What have I done? . . .

MRS. LOVETT
Could that thing have cared for you
like me?

TODD
(Rising)
Mrs. Lovett,
You're a bloody wonder,
Eminently practical and yet
Appropriate as always.
As you've said repeatedly,
There's little point in dwelling on the
past.

MRS. LOVETT   TODD
Do you mean it?   No, come here,
                                     my love . . .
Everything I did,
I swear I thought
Was only for the   Not a thing to
   best.   fear,
Believe me!   My love . . .
Can we   What's dead
Still be   Is dead.
Married?

TODD
The history of the world, my pet—

MRS. LOVETT
Oh, Mr. Todd,
Ooh, Mr. Todd,
Leave it to me . . .

TODD
—Is learn forgiveness and try to
forget.

MRS. LOVETT
By the sea, Mr. Todd,
We'll be comfy-cozy,
By the sea, Mr. Todd,
Where there's no one nosy . . .

TODD
And life is for the alive, my dear,
So let's keep living it—!

BOTH
Just keep living it,
Really living it—!

(He flings her into the oven and
slams the door behind him.
Slowly, he moves back to the
Beggar Woman and kneels,
cradling her again.)

TODD
There was a barber and his wife,
And she was beautiful.
A foolish barber and his wife.
She was his reason and his life.
And she was beautiful.
And she was virtuous.
And he was—
Naïve.

(Tobias appears from the shadows,
completely insane. He picks up
Todd's razor.)

TOBIAS

Pat-a-cake, pat-a-cake, baker man.
Bake me a cake—
No, no, bake me a pie
To delight my eye,
And I will sigh
If the crust be high . . .

Pat him and prick him
And mark him with a B,
And put him in the oven for baby and
    me!

He slits Todd's throat. Todd dies. Anthony and Johanna enter with policemen as Tobias, in a trance, grinds the meat. The characters become members of the Company once again, as at the beginning of the play, and address the audience.

The Ballad of Sweeney Todd (Finale)

TOBIAS

Attend the tale of Sweeney Todd.
His skin was pale and his eye was
    odd.

JOHANNA, ANTHONY

He shaved the faces of gentlemen
Who never thereafter were heard of
    again.

POLICEMEN

He trod a path that few have trod,

POLICEMEN, JOHANNA, ANTHONY

Did Sweeney Todd,

ALL

The Demon Barber of Fleet Street.

BEGGAR WOMAN

He kept a shop in London Town,
Of fancy clients and good renown.

JUDGE TURPIN

And what if none of their souls were
    saved?
They went to their maker impeccably
    shaved

BEGGAR WOMAN, JUDGE, POLICEMEN

By Sweeney,
By Sweeney Todd,

ALL

The Demon Barber of Fleet Street.

PIRELLI, BEADLE

Swing your razor wide, Sweeney!
Hold it to the skies!
Freely flows the blood of those
Who moralize!

COMPANY

His needs are few, his room is bare.
He hardly uses his fancy chair.
The more he bleeds, the more he
    lives.
He never forgets and he never
    forgives.
Perhaps today you gave a nod
To Sweeney Todd,
The Demon Barber of Fleet Street.

WOMEN

Sweeney wishes the world away,
Sweeney's weeping for yesterday,
Hugging the blade, waiting the years,
Hearing the music that nobody hears.
Sweeney waits in the parlor hall,
Sweeney leans on the office wall,

MEN

No one can help, nothing can hide
    you—
Isn't that Sweeney there beside you?

COMPANY

Sweeney wishes the world away,
Sweeney's weeping for yesterday,
Is Sweeney!
There he is, it's Sweeney!
Sweeney! Sweeney!

(Variously, each looking at one audience member but pointing to another)

There! There! There! There!
There! There! There!

(Todd appears)

ALL

(Pointing to Todd)

There!

TODD, COMPANY

Attend the tale of Sweeney Todd!
He served a dark and a hungry god!

(Mrs. Lovett appears)

TODD

To seek revenge may lead to hell,

MRS. LOVETT

But everyone does it, if seldom as
    well*

TODD, MRS. LOVETT

As Sweeney,

COMPANY

As Sweeney Todd,
The Demon Barber of Fleet—
Street!

Most of the musicals I've been connected with have been received at first with extreme reactions, both good and bad, the barometer leaning toward the negative, the exceptions being *West Side Story, Gypsy, A Funny Thing Happened on the Way to the Forum* and *A Little Night Music.* Time has mediated things considerably. None, however, elicited the extravagant accolades and contemptuous rage that *Sweeney Todd* did, the latter coming mostly from the less literate among the newspaper reviewers and the most intellectual among the magazine reviewers. The bizarre subject matter may have accounted for some of it, as the newsprint was filled with cries of "repellent," "sick," "loathsome" and the like. The most egregious example of critical resentment was probably that of John Lahr, who panned the show scathingly in *Harper's Magazine.* It was part of an essay propounding the thesis that I represented the death of the American musical, having taken all the joy and spontaneity out of this

---

*The original couplet, which I replaced a couple of weeks into the run, was both forced and irrelevant:

> *To kill for love is such a thrill*
> *You don't even notice you lose what you kill,*
> *Like Sweeney . . .*

beloved, exuberant American art form and infused it with an impotent sourness (Walter Kerr of *The New York Times* had also been beating that drum for a long while). This assessment would have been his right to make had he seen the show, but he hadn't. He had merely read an early rehearsal script, although he didn't indicate that to the reader. I protested to the editor, who added an explanatory demurrer as a footnote to the review. I then wrote Lahr himself a letter, saying that although it was his privilege to give a show both barrels of his contempt, I thought he ought to see it first. Unlike Peter G. Davis in the case of *A Little Night Music*, Lahr responded. The note was succinct, not to say dismissive of such a trivial objection. "I guess you're right," he replied.

That cured me. I rarely read critics anymore, except for those in *The New York Times*, who directly affect the box office (and not all that much). When I look back at the ones I've encountered over the years, however, I have the dismaying thought that if, as the saying goes, a man is best measured by the size of his enemies, I'm in a lot of trouble.

Sweeney Todd was a resounding commercial failure both on Broadway and in the West End, the latter reception a particularly disheartening one to me, since I had written the show as my love letter to London, a city I treasure above all except for New York. But over the years, considering the number of performances it's had in stock, schools and opera houses, it has turned out to be one of the most popular shows in my canon of collaborations, alongside *West Side Story*, *A Funny Thing Happened on the Way to the Forum* and *Into the Woods*—four shows which prove that if you give an audience a good story, especially an extravagant one, they'll accept it with pleasure, no matter how bizarre and idiosyncratic it may be.

Edmund Lyndeck as Judge Turpin and George Hearn as Sweeney Todd singing "Pretty Women" (1980)
Opposite: Ken Jennings as Tobias and George Hearn as Sweeney Todd in the final scene (1980)

Lord Grade, Martin Starger, Robert Fryer
and
Harold Prince
present

MERRILY WE ROLL ALONG
a new musical comedy

Music and Lyrics by
Stephen Sondheim
Book by
George Furth
From the Play by
George S. Kaufman and Moss Hart

with
James Weissenbach
Ann Morrison
Lonny Price

Set Designed by	Costumes Designed by	Lighting Designed by
Eugene Lee	**Judith Dolan**	**David Hersey**
Orchestrations by	Musical Director	
Jonathan Tunick	**Paul Gemignani**	
Make-up and Hair by	Sound Design by	Casting by
Richard Allen	**Jack Mann**	**Joanna Merlin**

Choreography by
Ron Field
Associate Producers
Ruth Mitchell and Howard Haines

Production Directed by
Harold Prince

Music Publisher
Tommy Valando
Original Cast Album on **RCA** Records and Tapes

MERRILY
WE ROLL
ALONG

a new musical comedy

13. Merrily We Roll Along (1981, revised in 1985)

Book by George Furth

Based on the play Merrily We Roll Along *by*

   George S. Kaufman and Moss Hart

The Notion

Franklin Shepard, a successful songwriter and movie producer in his forties, reviews his life, both professional and personal, especially his relationships with his best friends, Mary Flynn and Charley Kringas (his songwriting collaborator), and his two wives, Beth and Gussie. The action moves backward in time from 1981 to 1957.

General Comments

In that apocryphal period known as the Golden Age of Musicals, the thirty-two-bar song* was the mainstay of every show score and of most popular hits. There were exceptions and variations, of course, particularly in songs by Harold Arlen and Cole Porter, such as "Blues in the Night" and "Begin the Beguine," but there weren't many. Gershwin's experiments were confined to his opera *Porgy and Bess* and his parodies of operetta in *Of Thee I Sing* and *Let 'Em Eat Cake*. Kern's experiments were chiefly har-

monic rather than structural, while Rodgers pretty much stuck to the template until he collaborated with Hammerstein, the great experimenter. It was that team (again) who broke the mold, or at least diminished its value, most influentially with two moments in *Carousel*: the "Soliloquy," which pioneered the plot-and-character-defining internal monologue song ("I've Grown Accustomed to Her Face" in *My Fair Lady,* "Rose's Turn" in *Gypsy*), and the bench scene, with its fragments of songs leading to "If I Loved You," which opened up fresh possibilities of blending song and dialogue. Both instances were nothing more than extensions of techniques traditional in opera but comparatively new to musical comedy. As in *Oklahoma!* and subsequently *South Pacific,* these were not out-of-nowhere innovations, but because the shows were such enormous popular successes they not only seemed startling, they led the way to sophisticated improvements and experimentation that, happily, are still taking place today. Even so, a great deal of contemporary pop and rock and especially country music sticks to the conventional AABA and ABAB structures, the kinds which make listeners feel comfortable, no matter what the actual number of bars or what small variations of the A's and B's there may be. The audience knows when to expect the tune to repeat, the line to end, the main recurrent phrase ("hook" in pop terms) to reappear; the form is immediately recognizable. Ever since *Oklahoma!,* however, musical theater has been slowly but constantly blurring the boundaries between opera, traditional musical comedy and art song recital, as Adam Guettel's 1996 *Floyd Collins,* an exemplary amalgamation of them, demonstrates.

  Merrily We Roll Along was written in 1980, but the story, which is about the souring of ideals and the erosion of friendships, concerns two songwriters who came to their maturity in the 1950s, when traditional song forms still ruled the stage; it seemed appropriate, therefore, that it should be told as much as possible in a

---

*"Thirty-two-bar song" is a generic term for a song built in four stanzas of equivalent lengths, the most common being eight measures ("bars"). These are presented in a sequential form of AABA or ABAB, where A and B each signify a stanza and there is sometimes a slight variation in the last one to bring the song to a conclusion. The "A" section is often referred to as the "refrain," the "B" section as the "release." Examples of AABA would be "Ol' Man River" and "Send in the Clowns"; examples of ABAB would be "White Christmas" and "Anchors Aweigh."

With (clockwise) Harold Prince, George Furth, Ron Field and Jonathan Tunick at rehearsal

series of thirty-two-bar songs. I knew this would make the score sound anachronistic; in fact, I hoped it would. The scores of *Company* and *Follies* had been constructed largely of thirty-two-bar songs, but one show was a revue and the other a collection of pastiches; both genres feature conventional song structures. Here I was trying to tell a story that would involve a 1981 audience on an emotional level with characters who were, if not exactly three-dimensional, at least two-and-a-half, but who would be expressing themselves through stultified song forms. We had tried to do the same thing in *Gypsy*, but it was easier then: to a 1959 audience, the *Gypsy* songs read as contemporary and acceptable in the still-thriving Rodgers and Hammerstein storytelling tradition. By 1981 the musical and theatrical language of Broadway had evolved considerably, but I hoped to write the score of *Merrily We Roll Along* as if I still believed in those conventional forms as enthusiastically as I had twenty-five years earlier, before I and my generation had stretched them almost out of recognition. As with the score of *Follies*, I didn't want to appear as if I were commenting on them or satirizing them. In truth, like the characters in the show, I was trying to roll myself back to my exuberant early days, to recapture the combination of sophistication and idealism that I'd shared with Hal Prince, Mary Rodgers, Jerry Bock and Sheldon Harnick, John Kander and Fred Ebb, and the rest of us show business supplicants, all stripped back to our innocence.

If the songs were to be conventional, telling the story backwards suggested something unconventional: the possibility of reversing the usual presentation of them. In standard musicals, custom dictated that songs would have reprises, but until Hammerstein came along, they were reprised for the sole purpose of plugging as potential hits, this being in the days when hit songs came from the stage, a source which died out during the pop revolution of the 1960s. Hammerstein tried to make reprises an integral part of the stories he told: the tune, and even the lyric, might be the same, but the situation would be changed, lending the reprise poignancy or triumph or, rarely in Hammerstein's case but often in the hands of his followers, irony. The structure of *Merrily We Roll Along* suggested to me that the reprises could come first: the songs that had been important in the lives of the characters when they were younger would have different resonances as they aged; thus, for example, "Not a Day Goes By," a love song sung by a hopeful young couple getting married, becomes a bitter tirade from the wife when they get a divorce, but the bitter version is sung first in the musical's topsy-turvy chronology. This notion also gave rise to an unconventional use of melodic material: what were vocal lines in their early lives could become accompaniments for other songs in their later lives, undercurrents of memory, but the audience would hear the accompaniments first. All of this was not intended to be unconventional for its own sake or solely

for my delight in manipulating musical ideas in puzzle fashion, but a method of holding the score together as more than just a disparate group of songs, which was characteristic of musicals based on the standard thirty-two-bar template. As always, Content Dictated Form.

In addition, the show gave me the chance to revert to the sharp urban feeling of the songs in *Company* and *Follies*, the kind of "smart" lyric style typical of so many theater songs of the preceding decades that, at its best, restricted by its thirty-two-bar straitjacket, had the precision and concentration of a sonnet. The simplicity of such a form might make it seem easy to write, but it isn't, and it's harder still to tell a story in a sequence of such rigid patterns. The constraints of repeated refrain lines and frugal concision in all but the patter songs in *Merrily We Roll Along* was in uncomfortable contrast to the free and easy flow of the arioso writing which had characterized *Sweeney Todd*. That challenge, of course, is what exhilarated me. Of all the shows I've worked on, *Merrily We Roll Along* was, with the possible exception of *A Funny Thing Happened on the Way to the Forum* (and for similar reasons), the most difficult score to write. With *Forum*, however, I didn't have to worry about holding the score together—the piece didn't require cohesion, only variety. Indeed, the score of *Merrily* turned out to be what I wanted it to be, and eventually the show did, too. In its initial incarnation it was deplored by the critics and ignored by the public, and it took a number of revisions over the years for George Furth and me to make it the show we had hoped for. The turning point took place in La Jolla in 1985 in a production supervised and directed by James Lapine. He suggested some structural changes, particularly in Act One (explained below), which were crucial. Encouraged, George and I kept tinkering until, in 1992, for a production in Leicester, England, we finally succeeded in fixing the show to our satisfaction, and when years later it was produced in London, others agreed: it won the Laurence Olivier Award as Best Musical of the Year.

Whatever the flaws the show may have had to begin with, the original production compounded the felonies. Hal and I had conceived the treatment of the Kaufman-Hart play as a vehicle for young performers. In 1934 the play had been cast with actors in their twenties and thirties who played slightly older than themselves at the start and slightly younger at the finish. What we envisioned was a cautionary tale in which actors in their late teens and early twenties would begin disguised as middle-aged sophisticates and gradually become their innocent young selves as the evening progressed. Unfortunately, we got caught in a paradox we should have foreseen: actors that young, no matter how talented, rarely have the experience or skills to play anything but themselves, and in this case even that caused them difficulties. (The singular exception was a remarkable performer named Jason Alexander, who at twenty-one seemed like an old pro: it was as if he had been born middle-aged.) The last twenty minutes of the show, when the cast reverted to their true ages, was undeniably touching, but the rest of the evening had an amateur feeling—which, ironically, had been what we wanted. If the show had played in an off-Broadway house at off-Broadway prices, it would have stood a better chance of fulfilling our intentions; as it was, at Broadway's Alvin Theatre and at Broadway prices, it turned the audiences off. The theatergoers who didn't leave at intermission did a lot of squirming, and with reason: they felt cheated. There were severe problems with the sets and costumes as well, the former being cluttered and charmless, the latter so confusing that Hal threw them all out at dress rehearsal and replaced them with T-shirts lettered with a description of each wearer's relationship to Frank: "Best Friend," "Ex-Wife," etc. I rather liked it; the paying audience did not.

The month of previews took place in New York, the era of out-of-town tryouts having passed because of the expenses of traveling on the road. It was a painful month, spent under the gimlet eyes of theatrical vultures (show buffs, rival producers, gossip columnists and the like), a month that saw George and me frantically rewriting, Hal busily restaging, the leading actor and choreographer being replaced—in short, all the showbiz chaos which I had seen and thought I'd envied in movies like *42nd Street, Footlight Parade* and the Mickey Rooney–

Judy Garland musicals, but which even during the disastrous out-of-town tryout of *Forum* I had never really encountered. Worse, we fell victim to the age-old illusion that blinds all rewriters: by the time opening night arrived, we thought we'd fixed the show. What we had done was bettered it, not fixed it, and the critics and theatrical "community" (a myth if ever there was one) were merciless. Part of the reason for the virulent overreaction, I suspect, was that at this time Hal and I were resented as having become successful despite our maverick ventures. We had done eccentric shows and yet were not living in garrets. In the commercial theater this was not only an anomaly, it was an irritation. If we'd been teaching or working at odd jobs to stave off starvation, or if we'd been getting rich by sticking to formulaic musicals and thus easy targets for snickering condescension, it might have been acceptable. But to have done shows like *Follies, Pacific Overtures* and *Sweeney Todd* and still be living well was not our best revenge, it was theirs. The unfortunate side effect was that although *Merrily* eventually survived, our partnership, echoing Frank and Charley's in the piece itself, did not. We reunited twenty years later for *Bounce*, but the glory days were over. Nevertheless—I speak for myself, but I suspect Hal would agree—that month of fervent hysterical activity was the most fun that I've ever had on a single show. It was what I had always expected the theater to be like.

Between Harold Prince and conductor Paul Gemignani at rehearsal

ACT ONE

Prologue: As the orchestra starts to play, slides are projected onto a scrim at the front of the stage, slides which tell us the story we are about to see—photos of Franklin Shepard, Charley Kringas and Mary Flynn each at the age of eight, then at their individual high schools and colleges, followed by a variety of moments such as the three of them posing for humorous pictures in amusement palace booths, their initial successes as writers, Frank's marriages and scandalous divorce, reviews of their shows, Variety articles, gossip columns, newspaper accounts of the breakup of Frank and Charley's partnership, Frank's career as a movie producer, Charley's Pulitzer Prize as a playwright, etc. During this, the other members of the company appear behind and in front of the scrim and sing. The slides culminate with one that is a huge formal invitation, reading:

You Are Cordially Invited
To a Party at the Home of
Franklin Shepard
To Celebrate the Premiere
of His Latest Picture,
Darkness Before Dawn.

Merrily
We Roll Along

COMPANY
(Variously)
Yesterday is done.
See the pretty countryside.
Merrily we roll along, roll along,
Bursting with dreams.

Traveling's the fun,
Flashing by the countryside,
Everybody merrily, merrily
Catching at dreams,
Rolling along . . .
Rolling along . . .
Rolling along . . .

GROUP I
Dreams don't die,
So keep an eye on your dream—

GROUP II
And before you know where you are,
There you are.

GROUP I
Time goes by
And hopes go dry,
But you still can try
For your dream.

GROUP I	GROUP II
Tend your dream . . .	How does it happen?
Dreams take time . . .	When does it disappear?
Time goes by . . .	How can you get so far Off the track? Why don't you turn around And go back?
Bend your dream	How does it happen? Where is the moment?
With the road . . .	How can you miss it? Isn't it clear? How can you let it Slip out of gear?

ALL
How did you ever get there from here?

GROUP I	GROUP II
You roll . . .	How does it happen? How does it happen? When does it disappear?
You just roll . . .	Isn't it always clear?
Everybody roll . . .	How does it start to go?

ALL
Does it slip away slow,
So you never even notice it's happening?

CHARLEY
How did you get to be here?

OTHERS
What was the moment?

MARY
How did you get to be here?

MARY, CHARLEY
Pick yourself a road.
Get to know the countryside.
Soon enough you're merrily,

ALL
Merrily
Practicing dreams.
Dreams that will explode,
Waking up the countryside,
Making you feel merrily merrily
What can go wrong,
Rolling along?

ALL
Some roads are soft
And some are bumpy,
Some roads you really fly.
Some rides are rough
And leave you jumpy.
Why make it tough
By getting grumpy?
Plenty of roads to try.

GROUP I	GROUP II
Some roads are soft	One
And some are bumpy,	Trip, all you get is
Some roads you really Fly.	One quick ride,
Some rides are rough	Look around a bit.
And leave you jumpy.	One quick ride
Why make it tough	Through the
By getting grumpy?	Countryside.
Plenty of roads to try.	Stay on the track.
Some roads you really Fly.	Never look back.

Never look back.
Never look back.
Never look back!
Never look back!
Never look—

ALL
How did you get to be here?
What was the moment?
How did you get to be here?

Bending with the road,
Gliding through the countryside,
Merrily we roll along,
Roll along,
Catching at dreams,

Dreams that will explode,
Waking up the countryside.
Everybody merrily merrily
Sing 'em your song,
Rolling along!
Rolling along!
Rolling along!
Rolling a—

(And we are at Frank's party)

This is not how the first version of the
show, the one produced on Broadway
in 1981, began. In that version:

*Prologue. 1981. The graduation exercises
at Lake Forest High School, where Frank
and Charley had been classmates. As the
Curtain rises, we hear the last fragment
of the school song, "The Hills of Tomorrow," which they had written. We will not
hear the full version until the end of the
show.*

STUDENTS
. . . Behold! Begin!
There are worlds to win!
May we come to trust
The dreams we must
Fulfill!

*Frank, now middle-aged, has returned
to give the commencement address. His
speech is filled with sour self-pity and
disillusion. The students will have none of
it and voice their disapproval, singing
"Merrily We Roll Along," at the end of
which they throw off their graduation
robes and reveal themselves as early
middle-aged Hollywood swingers, partygoers at Frank's house, chattering to each
other.*

Rich and Happy (1981)

TERRY (A movie executive)
So we bought this little
condominium . . .

KATE (A gossip columnist)
So we found this little Chinese
gardener . . .

JEROME (Frank's lawyer)
It's a clear case of studio politics . . .

PHOTOGRAPHER
We were stuck on the freeway till half
past six . . .

TERRY
So we bought this little
condominium . . .

FOUR GUESTS
(Individually)
Great . . .
Smog . . .
Points . . .

(Everyone takes a snort of cocaine)

ALL
Party!

FRANK
Life is swinging,
Skies are blue and bells are ringing.
Every day I wake up singing,
"Look at me, I'm rich and happy!"

Days are sunny,
Working hard for lots of money,
Filled with people smart and funny,
Filled with people rich and happy!

Who says, "Lonely at the top"?
I say, "Let it never stop!"
It's my time coming through,
All my dreams coming true:
Gorgeous house, gorgeous wife,
Who wants any more from life?

Skies are beaming,
Future bright and prospects gleaming.
Best of all, I don't stop dreaming
Just because I'm rich
And famous

And therefore
Happy, too!

ALL
Party!

GUEST
Well, you must admit the movie's
terrible . . .

ANOTHER GUEST
I imagine Frank is feeling terrible . . .

MARY
These are the movers,
These are the shapers,
These are the people
That fill the papers.

ALL
Terrible . . .

MARY
These are the friends of Frank . . .

ALL
Wasn't it just terrible?

MARY
They all have Frank to thank.

ALL
When you see a movie that bad,
What on earth can you say?

(To Frank)
Congratulations!

FRANK
Thanks.

MARY
These are the movers,
These are the shapers,
These are the people
That give you vapors . . .

FRANK
(To Mary)
Twenty years ago who'd have guessed,
Who'd have guessed
I'd be standing here,
Playing host to the very best,
All the powers that be?

ALL
Terrible . . .

FRANK
Everybody I see . . .

ALL
Wasn't it just—

FRANK
And look who's one of them—me!

GROUP I
Terrible . . .

GROUP II
Beautiful, Frank!

(To one another)

Wasn't it just terrible?

GROUP I
Beautiful, Frank!

ALL
(Except Mary and Frank)
When a movie's that bad,
What on earth can anyone say?
Party!

ALL
(Except Mary)

Life is swinging,
Skies are blue and bells are ringing.
Every day I wake up singing,
"Look at me, I'm rich and happy!"
Days go zipping,
Sitting by the pool and tripping.

MARY
Everybody's flip or flipping.
Everybody's rich—

ALL
And happy!

FRANK
Who says all our dreams get burned?
Every bit of this was earned.
It's our time coming through,
All our dreams coming true,
All our days full of beans—

ALL
This must be what happy means!

Skies are beaming,
Future bright and prospects
     gleaming!
Best of all, we don't stop dreaming
Just because we're rich—

FRANK
And famous—

ALL
And suntanned—

FRANK
And influential—

ALL
And on the covers of magazines
And in the columns and on the
     screens
And giving interviews,
Being photographed,
Making all the important scenes,
And at the parties cutting capers,
And on the talk shows and in the
     papers
And unbelievably
Happy, too!

The critical moment in the rehabilita-
tion of *Merrily We Roll Along* occurred
in 1985, four years after its initial run.
It was a production in La Jolla, California, directed by James Lapine,
who, being both a writer and director,
firmly suggested that casting young
but experienced adults rather than talented but inexperienced teenagers was
only part of the solution: in order to
accommodate the change in casting,
the writing would have to be reexam-
ined as well. Furthermore, as Hammerstein's dictum would have it,
the opening number would have to
establish the tone for the rest of the
evening. "Rich and Happy" had been
(deliberately) a kid's idea of a Hollywood party. This is the song that replaced it:

That Frank (1985)

TYLER **(A tycoon)**
I said, "Frank, this picture is a
     watershed . . ."

TERRY **(A movie executive)**
I said, "Frank, one day you'll run my
     studio . . ."

SCOTTY **(An agent)**
I told Frank we should pass on the
     record deal . . .

DORY **(An art dealer)**
I said, "Frank, at a million, it's still a
     steal . . ."

TYLER
(Turning to someone else)
I said, "Frank, this picture is a
     watershed . . ."

MARY
Know what I'm having?

REUBEN **(Frank's protégé)**
What?

MARY
Not much fun.

REUBEN
Oh.

FRANK
(Entering, raising his glass)
Party!

GROUP I
That Frank—

JEROME
Another big smash—

GROUP II
That Frank—

TERRY
It's really great trash!*

_____

*In later productions, I changed these four
lines to:

   GROUP I
   That Frank—
      JEROME
   The guy is too much!
   GROUP II
   That Frank—
      TERRY
   The platinum touch.

_____

SCOTTY
He has taste, he has talent—

TERRY
Is he the best?

TYLER
Plus a fine head for business.

KATE **(A TV interviewer)**
The man is blessed.

COMPANY
That Frank!

GROUP I
That Frank—

REUBEN
What do you do?

JEROME
He's full of advice.

MARY
I drink.

GROUP II
That Frank—

REUBEN
No, what do you really do?

COMPANY
And God, is he nice.

MARY
I *really* drink.

KATE
What a friend—

MEG **(A starlet)**
What a host—

RICH GUEST
And his work is great.

TERRY
Has a wife who is gorgeous—

MEN
A son who's straight.

COMPANY
He's the type you could easily learn to hate,

That Frank!

The man has had his share of woe,*
But look at him, you'd never know!
It's his time,
Coming through—

MEG
He is hot—

JEROME
He is due—

TERRY
He is now—

SCOTTY
He is new—

COMPANY
Everybody's dream come true!*

GROUP II
That smile—

GROUP I
He's hot but he's cool.

GROUP II
What style—

MEG
And what a great pool!

GROUP I
If you had no idea what charisma meant—

GROUP II
And you just can't be jealous, he's such a gent—

---

*In later productions, I changed the lyrics between asterisks to:

COMPANY (CONT'D)

Who says lonely at the top?
I say, "Let it never stop!"
It's our time
Coming through,
All our dreams
Coming true.
Working hard,
Getting rich,
Being happy—
There's a switch!

COMPANY
He's the kind of a man that you can't resent,
That Frank!

TYLER
I said, "Frank, you're coming down to Mexico . . ."

JEROME
I think Frank is moving back to Paramount . . .

MARY
(To audience)
These are the movers,
These are the shapers,
These are the people
That fill the papers.

GROUP I
Mexico . . .

MARY
These are the friends of Frank.

GROUP II
Moving back to Paramount . . .

MARY
Each one a perfect blank.

COMPANY
When you see a movie that successful,
What can you say?

(To Frank)

Congratulations!

FRANK
Thank you!

MARY
These are the movers,
These are the shapers,
These are the people
That give you vapors . . .

FRANK
(To Mary)
Twenty years ago, who'd have guessed,
Who'd have guessed
We'd be standing here?

God, we would have been so
impressed!
Now we're here with the most—

(Listens mockingly)

GROUP I
Mexico . . .

FRANK
—Brilliant minds on the coast.

GROUP II
Moving back to Paramount . . .

FRANK
(Self-deprecating)
And notice who is their host.

GROUP I
Mexico . . .

GROUP II
Beautiful, Frank!

GROUP I
Acapulco, Mexico . . .

GROUP II
Beautiful, Frank!

COMPANY
When you've made a movie that
successful,
Where do you go?

FRANK
Uh—Paramount . . .

(Mary is drunk and causes a loud,
embarrassing scene with Frank. He
manages to calm her down.)

COMPANY
Poor Frank—
He handled that well.

GROUP II
That Frank—

JEROME
He's loyal as hell.

COMPANY
He's polite and considerate, rain or
shine.

MARY
(Brightly, to anybody listening)
It began when I tasted communion
wine—

COMPANY
That Frank!

*We all have had our share of woe,
But look at us, you'd never know.
It's our time, coming through,
All our dreams, right on cue.
Nothing more
Left to plan—
No one feels it
Deeper than*

COMPANY

That Frank!
You'd think he'd relax.
Not Frank—
He's laying new tracks.
If you had no idea what charisma
meant—
And you just can't be jealous, he's
such a gent—
He's the kind of a man could be
President,
That Frank!
That Frank!
That Frank!

"That Frank" not only introduced the
show with adult performers, it allowed
me, in the final rhyme, to make a
point connecting the substance of
what we were writing about to the
time in which we were writing it: the
Reagan era, one built on expedience
disguised as affability.

*Frank's wife Gussie, an aging movie star,
enters and accuses him of having an*

<hr>

*In later productions, I changed the lyric
between asterisks to:

FRANK
Who says, "Mustn't go too far?"
I say, "Look at where we are."
It's our time
Coming through,
I say, "Good—
Me and you."
I say, "Roll!"
I say, "Ride!"
I say, "Hey, there's food inside!"

*affair with Meg. He admits it, and an
argument ensues, culminating in Gussie's
throwing iodine into Meg's eyes, an
ambulance being called, and Frank's
evening—and life—falling apart. The
Company faces front and sings.*

First Transition†

SOLO VOICES
How did you get to be here?
What was the moment?
How did you get to be here?

GROUP I
Dreams don't die,
So keep an eye on your dream,
Or before you know where you are,
There you are.

GROUP II
Roads may wind
And you may find
What you've left behind
Is your dream.

SOLO VOICES
Tend your dream . . .
How does it happen? . . .
Dreams take time . . .
Once it was all so clear . . .
Time goes by . . .
How do you get so far off the track?
Why don't you turn around and go
back? . . .

(Voices overlapping)

Bend your dream—
How does it happen?
Where is the moment?—
With the road . . .
—When did the road behind disappear?
Where did you let things slip out of
gear?
How did you ever get to be here?

<hr>

†During these Transitions, we again see projections of slides from the Prologue, matching
and illustrating each time and event in Frank's
life.

GROUP
Nineteen seventy-six . . . Nineteen
seventy-five . . .

In the rehearsal draft of the original
show, the Transitions between scenes
involved specific references to the
times involved. Thus, for example:

First Transition (1981)
(cut)

COMPANY
Dreams don't die,
And you're as young as your dreams.
Time goes by
And dreams go dry,
But you don't give up on your
    dreams . . .

Nineteen seventy-nine . . . Nineteen
    seventy-eight . . . Nineteen
    seventy-seven . . .
New winds are blowing,
New streams are flowing—
Just don't eat the fish.

Have a baby now if you wish—
They can start one right in a dish.

Garbage is growing,
Some of it glowing,
Some of it falling into the sea.
Turn up the Bee Gees on the CB.
Watch how your Congress works on
    TV . . .

Hot tubs
And sex clubs
And deep rubs
And overdubs,
Oil spills
And oil bills
And no frills
And Wilbur Mills,
Gas queues
And Chrysler's blues,
Running shoes
And Howard Hughes . . .

Nineteen seventy-six . . .
Jimmy's elected,
Concorde connected,
Disco is dead and won't disappear.
Who are these Arabs, why are they
    here?
Quick, give a Bicentennial cheer!

 Nineteen seventy-five . . .

Kaufman and Hart had wanted to
write about the deterioration of American idealism and the rise of capitalist
greed in what they called "the heedless years" which followed the end of
World War I until the Depression. In
fact, their original title for the play was
Wind Up an Era. In our transposition,
we were writing about a generation's
idealistic expectations for the future,
symbolized by the launch of *Sputnik*,
and their deterioration into compromise and deceit, exemplified by Nixon
and Watergate and culminating in the
Me Decade, as the 1970s came to be
labeled. The "Transitions" were written to accomplish this: the lyrics were
snapshots of the passing years. Many
readers of this book may not understand some of the specific references,
but the tone ought to be apparent. We
had to cut these potted-history interludes during rehearsals because they
cluttered up the story with unnecessary information. As the show took
shape, it became clear that the "Transitions" should reflect Frank's history,
not the country's. I was sorry to see
them go; I like to show off with lyrics
which rhyme historical events, such as
those in "I'm Still Here" and "Please

Harold Prince showing the set to the company

Hello." I did get to implement my fondness for that kind of topicality later on in Act Two, however, with "Bobby and Jackie and Jack."

In the 1981 version, the next scene takes place at the Polo Lounge of the Beverly Hills Hotel. Mary is seated at a table, waiting for Charley to arrive. Gussie rushes in, attempting to avoid her ex-husband, Joe Josephson, who is down on his luck, and parks herself at Mary's table.

Darling! (1981) (cut)

GUSSIE
Darling!
Deliver me, darling!
If I can just park here a sec,
You can have my cook.

(Indicating the entrance, as Mary looks baffled)

It's so dark near the checkroom,
I didn't look . . .

(Looking back to the entrance)

Good, he didn't come in.

Darling,
You saw him? Poor darling,
Poor Joe,
It's a shame watching some-
One you love go "plunge."
All the same, he's become
El eternal sponge–
You're so thin!

(Looking at the entrance again)

No, he isn't coming in.

Oh, I know what I owe him:
God, just everything—

(Spotting somebody)

Eek, who's that?—
Well, not quite everything.
I'm happy to know him—
God, isn't everyone?

(Sotto voce)

He lives at the track,
And he's always on my back . . .

Darling,
Forgive me for snarling,
But go and have lunch in a place
And your life is in danger.

(Glances at her watch)

Look at that! I must race—
Darling, don't be a stranger.
You're a peach,
We're at the beach,
And darling, as I said—

(Makes a kissing noise)

Call
And we'll all
Break bread.

(She gets up to leave, but Joe enters. She looks at him in great surprise.)

Joe!
Is it Joe?
It could be anyone,
You're so thin–
Well, not just anyone.
But where did it go?
I eat protein like anything!
You must tell me how,
Only, pussy, not right now . . .

(As Joe tries to borrow money from her, she tells him that a reporter is waiting to interview her on the patio)

Darling!
Forgive me but, darling,
She's there with her quill.
I should sprint
Or she'll be in a swivet
And she'll kill me in print—
Well, that's life and we live it!
Keep the weight off
And I hate you
'Cause I feel so fat!

(Kisses the air in front of his face)

Love you, Joe,
But then you know *that.*

(Joe leaves and Kate enters. She and Gussie spot each other and rush together excitedly.)

GUSSIE
Darling!

KATE
Darling!

BOTH
(Big air-kiss)
Mwanh!
I'm grossly late.

GUSSIE
Darling!

KATE
Darling!

BOTH
But then you don't know who I met,
Lurking right outside,
Looking so sympathet-
Ic I had to hide.

(Rearing back)

What, you too?

(Appraising each other)

Darling, you're so thin!!

This song was cut before rehearsals because "Rich and Happy" seemed to have sufficiently established the kids' idea of Hollywood sophisticates. Not only was the song cut, so, eventually, was the scene, which was incorporated into the subsequent one for the 1985 revision:

1973. A TV studio. Charley is being made up to appear on an interview show with Frank, who is late in arriving. Charley is impatient and resentful, his partnership with Frank having soured because of Gussie's ambitiousness, but Mary has persuaded him to use this occasion both to announce their next show in public and as a chance to ease the tensions between them. Charley, fed up with Frank's habitual tardiness, gets up to leave the studio. Mary stops him with a pleading gesture.

Like It Was

MARY
Hey, old friend,
What do you say, old friend?
Make it okay, old friend,
Give the old friendship a break.
Why so grim?
We're going on forever.
You, me, him,
Too many lives are at stake.

Friends this long
Has to mean something's strong,
So if our old friend's wrong,
Shouldn't an old friend come
    through?
It's us, old friend—
What's to discuss, old friend?
Here's to us,
Who's like us—?

*(She lifts her pinkie, waits for him to grab
it with his, which he does, after a beat)*

CHARLEY
Damn few.

MARY
Charley,
Why can't it be like it was?
I liked it the way that it was.
Charley,
You and me, we were nicer then.

We were nice,
Kids and cities and trees were nice,
Everything . . .
I don't know who we are anymore,
And I'm starting not to care.

Look at us, Charley,
Nothing's the way that it was.
I want it the way that it was.
Help me stop remembering then.

Don't you remember?
It was good, it was really good.
Help me out, Charley,
Make it like it was.

Charley,
Nothing's the way that it was.
I want it the way that it was.
God knows, things were easier then.

Trouble is, Charley,
That's what everyone does:
Blames the way it is
On the way it was.
On the way it never ever was . . .

The "Old Friends" section of "Like It Was" is the first instance in the show of the reverse reprise that I mentioned earlier. In traditional musicals, this section would have been a reprise of the full song "Old Friends," a song which isn't sung until the next scene, which takes place five years earlier. Got that? Some of the audience didn't, I'm afraid. This verse is a reference to a past we haven't seen yet, the point being that as people age, each encounter with the past is the richer for memories. Metaphorically, the old tunes linger, even if in fragmented forms, and if you tell a story backwards in order to make such a point (among others), the music and lyrics should not merely reflect but embody it.

Frank finally arrives at the TV studio, effusively upbeat, and Charley greets him warily. His wariness is an accurate response: a moment before the TV cameras roll on them Kate, the interviewer, deliberately lets slip the fact that, unbeknownst to Charley, Frank has made a deal to produce movies, further postponing their working on the show that Charley has been patiently waiting to write with him. Charley is humiliated, angry and unnerved when the interview suddenly begins.

David Garrison as Charley, Victor Garber as Frank and Becky Ann Baker as Mary in the Arena Stage revival (1990)

Franklin Shepard, Inc.

KATE
(To Frank)
Now how do you two work
together?

CHARLEY
Can I answer that?

(Beat)
How do we work together?

(He looks to Frank, who smiles and
nods encouragingly)

Sure.

He goes . . .

(Mimes playing an elaborate arpeggio)

And I go . . .

(Mimes typing, in similar
elaborate fashion)

And soon we're humming along—
Hmmm-hmmm-hmmm . . .
And that's called writing a song—
Hmmm-hmmm-hmmm . . .
Then he goes—

(Plays another arpeggio)

And I go—

(Types)

And the phone goes—
Drrrrring!
And he goes—

(Mimicking Frank into an
imaginary phone)

"Mutter mutter mutter mutter yes,
    Jerome.
Mutter no, Jerome.
Mutter mutter mutter mutter—"

(To Kate)

That's his lawyer, Jerome—

(Back into the "phone")

"Mutter mutter mutter mutter mutter
    do it, Jerome.

(Hangs up, turns back to himself)

Sorry, Charley . . ."

(Plays the arpeggio, as himself)

So I go—

(Types)

And he goes—

(Arpeggio)

And I go—

(Types)

And soon we're tapping away—
Hmmm-hmmm-hmmm . . .

(Mimicking an intercom)

Bzzz!
"Sorry, Charley . . ."
Bzzz!

(To Kate)

It's the secretary—
Bzzz!
On the intercom—

(As Frank)

"Yes, Miss Bzzz . . ."

(Nasal, as the secretary)

"It's a messenger."

(As Frank)

"Thanks, Miss Bzzz,
Will you tell him to wait?
Will you order the car?
Will you call up the bank?
Will you wire the coast?
Will you—"
Drrrrring!
"Sorry, Charley . .

(Into the "phone" again)

Mutter mutter mutter mutter sell the
    stock,
Mutter buy the rights,
Mutter mutter mutter mutter
    mutter—"
Bzzz!

(Into "phone")

"Let me put you on hold . . ."
Bzzz!
"Yes, Miss Bzzz . . ."
"It's the interview . . ."
"Thanks, Miss Bzzz,
Will you tell him to wait?
Will you wire the car?
Will you order the coast?
Will you send up the bank? . . ."

And the telephones blink
And the stocks get sold
And the rest of us he keeps on "hold,"
And he's into making movies,
And he's now a corporation.
Right?

So I play at home
With my wife and kids,
And I wait to hear the movie bids,
And I've got a little sailboat,
And I'm into meditation.
Right?

He flies off to California,
I discuss him with my shrink.
That's the story of the way we work,
Me and Franklin Shepard, Inc.

KATE
Now, when you do work together,
I've always been curious, which
generally comes first—the words or
the music?

CHARLEY
Generally, the contract.

KATE
It sounds like you think making
money's a bad thing for an artist.

CHARLEY
Money? Did I say money?

No, I like money a lot—
Hmmm-hmmm-hmmm . . .
I mean it's better than not—
Hmmm-hmmm-hmmm . . .
But when it's—

*(Grunts like a pig and starts grabbing
imaginary money)*

Money—

(Grunt, grunt)

Money—

*(Snorts, gathering money like a manic,
drooling octopus)*

When you're into—

(Snort)

Money—

(Lightly)

And you should be—

*(Plays an imaginary arpeggio, then
gestures to Frank)*

Listen, Frank does the money thing
very well, and you know what?
There are people who do it better.
And Frank does the music thing
very well. And you know what? *No
one does it better.*

Still, the telephones blink
And the buzzers buzz
And I really don't know what he does,
But he makes a ton of money,
And a lot of it for me—
Right?

So I think "Okay"
And I start a play,
And he somehow knows,
'Cause right away
It's Drrrrring!

(Into "phone" again, as Frank)

"Hiya, buddy,
Wanna write a show?
Got a great idea,
We'll own all the rights

With a two-week out
And a turnaround
On the guarantee
Plus a gross percent
Of the billing clause—"

And there I am in California,
Talking deals and turning pink,
Back in business and I mean just that,
Back with Franklin Shepard, Inc.

Very sneaky how it happens,
Much more sneaky than you think.
Start with nothing but a song to sing,
Next you're Franklin Shepard—

*(He breaks off and describes in dialogue
how much his friendship and collaboration with Frank mean to him)*

Nothing permanent has happened,
Just a temporary kink.
Friendship's something you don't
  really lose . . .

. . . Very sneaky how it happens,
Every day you're on the brink.
First the prizes, then the interviews—

(Looks around, realizing where he is)

Oh, my God, I think it's happened!
Stop me quick before I sink.
One more triumph that I can't
  refuse—

(Into the camera)

In case you didn't notice, this is my
first time on TV—and my last.

(To Kate)

No, here's the point, whatever
  happens,
Then we'll all go have a drink.

(Gestures toward Frank)

That's the guy I love, the fella who's
Inside

(Into "phone")

"Mutter mutter mutter mutter quick,
  Jerome,
Get the President,

There's a crazy man
On my TV screen!"

(To camera)

Inside
Bzzz! Bzzz! Drrrrring!
Inside
Franklin Shepard—
Just write him care of Any Bank,
  U.S.A.—
Inc.!

In compiling this book, I've observed a
number of things about the songs I've
written, not the least of which is that
in addition to my attraction to the easy
pleasures of historical list songs such
as the "Transitions," I seem to have a
penchant for nervous breakdowns:
"Rose's Turn," "Getting Married
Today," "Epiphany" and now
"Franklin Shepard, Inc." Part of the
explanation, of course, is that I'm attracted to volatile characters because
they're the stuff of drama, and when
they explode in song, it allows the
songwriter to veer off unexpectedly in
many directions, echoing the disorder
in the character's mind. Each of the
above songs bubbles with changes of
pace and form, alternating between
tight rhyming and free verse, percus-
sive and lyrical music—in other words,
surprise, the lifeblood of theater. And
they come with a bonus: such songs
are meat for actors.

*As a result of "Franklin Shepard, Inc."
Frank and Charley come to blows. The
Company sings a shortened version of the
generic "Transition." The original one:*

Second Transition (1981)
(cut)

COMPANY
(In small groups)
Some roads are bumpy,
Off the track a bit—
Bump!
What was that?

With Harold Prince at rehearsal

An unpaid bill.
Oh.
Bump!
Every time you—
Bump!
—Sit back a bit,
Bump! Disappointment.
Bump! Disillusion.
Bump! Feeling—
Bump!—complete confusion.
Bump! Bump! What was that?
The wrong conclusion.
Oh.
That one's the one that can kill.

Nineteen seventy-three . . .
Bump! Local hero—
Bump!—name of Spiro—
Bump!—has so many major
    concerns—
Bump! Bump!—he forgot to file his
    returns.

'Seventy-two . . .
Someone at the Watergate
Bump!—is discovered working late.
Bump! Bang!

'Seventy-one . . .
Lots of cussing—
Bump!—at the busing.
Bump! Mr. Ellsberg gives us the poop.
Bump! Bump!
Bon Vivant is—

(Someone makes a choking noise)

—In the soup.

(Wistful solo)

Tasted great . . .

Nineteen seventy . . .
Bang!
What was that one?
Kent State . . .

Nineteen sixty-nine . . .
Boom!
If it isn't Vietnam,
It's Chappaquiddick.
Bump! Splash!
It's Charlie Manson.
Bump! Thud!

Altamont!
Bump! Bang!
Weathermen!
Rattle! Crash!
Hurricane Camille!

ALL
Nineteen sixty-eight! . . .

The Transition leads us to the empty, ultra-sleek apartment on Central Park West that Frank has acquired. He has just returned from an ocean voyage on his rich friend Tyler's yacht, to be greeted joyfully by Mary and Charley. Frank excitedly informs Charley that they have had an offer to do a Hollywood musical of one of their shows. Charley is furious; Frank had promised him that as soon as the voyage was over they would get back to work on Take a Left, *the Broadway show they had started to write. Frank protests that the divorce from his wife Beth has wiped him out financially. They argue. As their voices escalate, Mary intervenes.*

Old Friends

MARY

Hey!!

*(Quietly, charmingly, she lifts a
pinkie finger)*

Here's to us—

FRANK
*(After a pause, grabbing her pinkie
with his)*
Who's like us?

CHARLEY
*(After a pause, grudgingly doing
the same)*
Damn few.

FRANK
(To Charley)
Hey, old friend,
Are you okay, old friend?
What do you say, old friend,
Are we or are we unique?

Time goes by,
Everything else keeps changing.
You and I,
We get continued next week.

Most friends fade
Or they don't make the grade.
New ones are quickly made
And in a pinch, sure, they'll do.
But us, old friend,
What's to discuss, old friend?
Here's to us—
Who's like us?
Damn few!

CHARLEY
(Relaxing, his arm around Frank)
So, old friend,
Fill me in slow, old friend—
Start from hello, old friend,
I want the when, where, and how.
Old friends
Do tend to become old habit—
Never knew
How much I missed you till now.

ALL THREE
Most friends fade
Or they don't make the grade,

New ones are quickly made,
Some of them worth something, too.
But us, old friends—
What's to discuss, old friends?

FRANK
Tell you something:
Good friends point out your lies,
Whereas old friends live and let live.

MARY
Good friends like and advise,
Whereas old friends love and forgive.

FRANK
And old friends let you go your own
way—

CHARLEY
(Pointedly)
Help you find your own way—

MARY
(To Charley)
Let you off when you're wrong—

FRANK
If you're wrong—

CHARLEY
When you're wrong—

MARY
Right or wrong, the point is:
Old friends shouldn't care if you're
wrong.

FRANK
Should, but not for too long.

CHARLEY
(Edgily)
What's too long?

FRANK
If you're wrong—

CHARLEY
When you're wrong—

MARY
The thing is:
Old friends do leave their brands on
you,
But old friends shouldn't compete.

FRANK
Old friends don't make demands on
you—

CHARLEY
Should make demands on you—

FRANK
Well, don't make demands you can't
meet.

CHARLEY
Well, what's the
Point of demands you *can* meet?

MARY
Well, there's a time for demands,
Whether you meet them or not—

*(They argue vociferously for a moment,
then stop and look at one another)*

ALL
Hey, old friends,
How do we stay old friends?
Who is to say, old friends,
How an old friendship survives?
One day chums,
Having a laugh a minute,
One day comes
And they're a part of your lives.

New friends pour
Through the revolving door—
Maybe there's one that's more,
If you find one, that'll do.
But us, old friends,
What's to discuss, old friends?

FRANK
Here's to us!

CHARLEY
Who's like us? . . .

MARY
Two old friends—
Fewer won't do, old friends—
Gotta have two old friends
Helping you balance along.
One upbraids you
For your faults and fancies,
One persuades you
That the other one's wrong.

ALL
Most friends fade
Or they don't make the grade,
New ones are quickly made,
Perfect as long as they're new.
But us, old friends,

What's to discuss, old friends?
Here's to us!
Who's like us?
Damn few!

Gussie arrives with her husband Joe Josephson in tow, stopping by on their way to see a show. She is a Broadway star, he a Broadway producer. She and Frank have been having an affair, of which everyone in the room is aware. Frank, Charley and Mary are on their way to celebrate Frank's return at the Downtown Club, the place where their careers began, but Gussie whispers to Frank that she is desperate to leave Joe and begs him to stay where he is and wait for her call. Frank reluctantly agrees to do so, and when Gussie and Joe leave, he tells Mary and Charley that they should go ahead and he will meet them later. They exit, dismayed at his postponement of their reunion. Frank goes to the only piece of furniture in the apartment—his piano—and starts to noodle at the keyboard.

Growing Up (1985)

FRANK

Thanks, old friends . . .
Keep reminding me . . .
Frank's old friends
Always seem to come through.
Frank will, too . . .

So, old friends,
Now it's time to start growing up.
Taking charge,
Seeing things as they are.
Facing facts,
Not escaping them,
Still with dreams,
Just reshaping them,
Growing up . . .

Charley is a hothead,
Charley won't budge.
Charley is a friend.

Charley is a screamer,
Charley won't bend.
Charley's in your corner.

Mary is a dreamer,
Mary's a friend.
Mary is a nudge.

Mary is a purist,
Charley's a judge.
Charley is a dropout,
Everything's a "copout."

Why is it old friends
Don't want old friends to change?
Every road has a turning,
That's the way you keep learning.

So, old friends,
Don't you see we can have it all,
Moving on,
Getting out of the past?
Solving dreams,
Not just trusting them,
Taking dreams,
Readjusting them,
Growing up,
Growing up . . .

Trying things,
Being flexible,
Bending with the road,
Adding dreams
When the others don't last.
Growing up,
Understanding that growing never
    ends,
Like old dreams—
Some old dreams—
Like old friends.

(Gussie returns and announces that she has packed her things and left Joe. Frank is upset at the precipitousness of her decision.)

GUSSIE

Life is knowing what you want,
    darling.
That's the only thing to know.
As I told you moons ago, darling,
Nothing wrong with wanting . . .

Nothing wrong with wanting me,
    darling.
Also nothing wrong with not,
Though it's only fair that
You should be aware that
I want you a lot.

Growing up
Means admitting
The things you want the most.
Can't pursue
Every possible line.
Folding tents,
Making choices,
Ignoring all
Other voices,
Including mine . . .
You're divine . . .

You decide on what you want,
    darling,
Not on what you think you should.
Not on what you want to want,
    darling,
Not from force of habit.
Once it's clearly understood, darling,
Better go and grab it.
Things can slip away for good,
    darling,
What is it you really—?

(Frank follows Gussie into the bedroom as the lights dim)

The overriding problem in every version of *Merrily We Roll Along* is that Frank, the central figure, is entirely unsympathetic for the first half hour of the show. He is arrogant, an adulterer, a betrayer of his best friend and the cause of near-suicidal alcoholism in the woman who loves him unrequitedly. As the story unfolds we get to know him better and like him more as we see his vulnerabilities and the reasons for all the wrong choices he has made. Even in 1934, however, despite mostly excellent reviews, a lavish production, a cast of ninety-one (on the stage of one of the smallest Broadway theaters, the Music Box) and the authorship of Kaufman and Hart, the hottest playwriting team then in the commercial theater, the audiences didn't come. Herman Mankiewicz (brother of Joseph and co-screenwriter of *Citizen Kane*) summed up the situation succinctly: "Here's this wealthy playwright [in the play the central character was a playwright] who has had repeated successes and earned enormous sums of money, has mistresses as well as a family, an expensive town house, a luxuri-

ous beach house and a yacht. The problem is: How did the poor son of a bitch get into this jam?"

I happen to like stories about un-sympathetic characters, because I trust the author to tell me why they interest *him*. That was the purpose of "Growing Up," a song suggested by an observation of James Lapine's: after two scenes of Frank at his corruptible worst, it was not enough that we should see him being sentimental with his friends, we should have a progress report on his moral state, preferably in song. We should see him torn between decisions—making, as he always does, the wrong one. Having Gussie bolster his indecision with a corrupting decision of her own made the point, and it allowed the audience to feel affection for Frank an hour earlier than they had in 1981. Which still may not be early enough for some.

The Company sings another Transition. The original one:

Third Transition (1981)

(cut)

COMPANY
(Variously)
I keep telling people black is
    beautiful . . .
Just remind them all it's tax
    deductible . . .
We were there with you, suffering all
    the way.
Must have been really hell—would it
    make a play?
I keep telling people black is
    beautiful . . .
Peace! . . .
Peace! . . .
Nineteen sixty-six . . .

The steps of a courthouse, where Frank's first wife, Beth, is suing him for divorce on the grounds of infidelity. He confronts her as she emerges from the courthouse and begs her to stay with him, insisting that she still loves him. She replies angrily.

Not a Day Goes By

BETH
Not a day goes by,
Not a single day
But you're somewhere a part of my
    life,
And it looks like you'll stay.

As the days go by,
I keep thinking, when does it end?
Where's the day I'll have started
    forgetting?

(With increasing fury)

But I just go on
Thinking and sweating
And cursing and crying
And turning and reaching
And waking and dying
And no,
Not a day goes by,
Not a blessed day
But you're still somehow part of my
    life,
And you won't go away.

So there's hell to pay,
And until I die,

I'll die day after day
After day after day
After day after day
After day,
Till the days go by!
Till the days go by!
Till the days go by!

This is another reverse reprise, but unlike the fragmented one at the beginning of "Like It Was," it's a complete
and emotional one: a full chorus of a
furious song that prefigures a raptur-
ous version in Act Two. In any other
musical, the reprise would be the disil-
lusionment; here it is the promise.

*Frank is in a near-suicidal state of
despair at losing his wife and the custody
of his son. Mary and Charley and the rest
of his friends urge him to get away for a
while.*

Now You Know (1985)

SCOTTY
So you've made a mistake,
So you're singing the blues,
So you'll take some time, go visit
    some places—

MARY
You've got to be somewhere
Where there's nothing to remind you,
Right?

TYLER
What you need is a break.
I'll arrange a nice cruise,
You'll relax a bit and see some new
    faces—

CHARLEY, MARY
You've got to do something,
But just never look behind you.

CHARLEY, MARY, TYLER
Right?

SCOTTY, KATE
Best thing that ever could have
    happened—

FRANK
(*Pleasant, dead*)
Right.

JOE
So you'll sit in the sun,
You'll come back with a tan,
Then we'll do that show you've
    always been talking.

SCOTTY
The side is retired,
So we start another inning—
Right?

DORY
On a boat is such fun—

JEROME
You'll come back a changed man—

TYLER
I've had lots of guests and no one's
    squawking—

CHARLEY, MARY
Feels like an ending,
But it's really a beginning,
Right?

KATE
Best thing that ever could have
    happened,
I say, best thing that ever could have
    happened—

SCOTTY, DORY
(*overlapping*)
It was all getting much too
    complicated—

FRANK
(*Edgily*)
Right!

MARY
(*Stepping forward impatiently*)
All right, now you know:
Life is crummy.
Well, now you know.

I mean, big surprise:
People love you and tell you lies.
Bricks can tumble from clear blue
    skies.
Put your dimple down,
Now you know.

Okay, there you go—
That's the sum of it.
Now you know.

It's called flowers wilt,
It's called apples rot,
It's called thieves get rich and saints
    get shot,
It's called God don't answer prayers
    a lot.
Okay, now you know.

Okay, now you know,
Now forget it.
Don't fall apart at the seams.
It's called letting go your illusions,
And don't confuse them with dreams.
If the going's slow,
Don't regret it,
And don't let's go to extremes.

It's called what's your choice?
It's called count to ten.
It's called burn your bridges, start
    again.
You should burn them every now and
    then
Or you'll never grow!

Because now you grow.
That's the killer is,
Now you grow.

You're right, nothing's fair,
And it's all a plot,
And tomorrow doesn't look too hot—
Right, you better look at what you've
    got:

(*Pause, as Frank doesn't respond*)

Over here, hello?

(*As he looks at her, smiling for the first
time*)

Okay, now you know.
Right?

SCOTTY
So you'll find a new gal,
So you'll write a new play—
In a month or two, you're going to
    thank us.

MARY
You may have missed one road,

But there's plenty more to follow,
Right?

TYLER
We'll go through the canal,
Up the coast to L.A.,
You'll come see the place I'm building
    in Trancas—

CHARLEY
You hang around here, pal,
And you're only gonna wallow.
Right?

ALL
Right!

KATE, SCOTTY
Best thing that ever could have
    happened!

MARY
I mean, you'll come back,
I mean, what's the fuss?

CHARLEY
I mean, sea and sun and comfort
    plus—

CHARLEY, MARY
I mean, after all, you've still got us—

ALL
(Overlapping one another)
Best thing that ever could have
    happened!
It was all getting much too
    complicated—
Best thing that ever could have
    happened!

FRANK
Right!
You've gotta let go,
Gotta do it from scratch,
Take a long deep breath,
Go back to your sources,
A little vacation,
Which is all about forgetting—
Right?

ALL
Right!

FRANK
Right!

(To Charley)

Then we'll do a new show—
No, we'll do a whole batch,
Maybe one that's all about divorces!
I mean, a divorce court—
What a fascinating setting!
Right?

ALL
Right!

FRANK
Right!

ALL
(Variously, overlapping)
Best thing that ever could have
    happened . . .
I say, best thing that ever could have
    happened . . .
It's your time, your time . . .
Yesterday is done,
See the pretty countryside,
Soon enough you're merrily merrily
Rolling along . . .

So you'll sit in the sun,
You'll come back with a tan,
In a month or two
You're going to thank us . . .
It's your time . . .

(In unison)

What's your choice?
It's called count to ten.
It's called burn your bridges, start
    again.
You should burn them every now and
    then
Or you'll never grow!

Because now you grow.
Life's a killer, so now you grow.

MARY
You're right, nothing's fair,
And it's all a plot,
And tomorrow doesn't look too hot—

ALL
Right, you better look at what you've
    got:

SCOTTY
Me.

TYLER
Me.

MARY
Me.

DORY, JEROME
Us.

CHARLEY
Over here, hello?

SCOTTY, KATE
Over here, hello?

JOE
Me.

ALL
Us!

MARY, CHARLEY
Over here, hello?

(The joyful babble grows louder and
louder. Tyler reenters with two yachting
caps and blue sea-blazers which Frank
and he put on.)

ALL
Right! Right! Right! Right!
Right! Right! Right! Right!
All right, now you know!
Now you know!
Now you know!

(A loud boat horn sounds as Frank and
Tyler board a yacht and the crowd waves
them off)

END OF ACT ONE

The 1981 version of the show had a
somewhat different set of characters
for Frank's friends, so the song required a somewhat different set of
lyrics:

Now You Know (1981)

JOE
So we'll do a new show,
So you'll meet a new dame,
So you'll take some time for personal
    pleasure.

CHARLEY
There gotta be endings
Or there wouldn't be beginnings—
Right?

PRESS AGENT
You got talent to blow
And you're making a name,
And that song you wrote's a national
    treasure.

HIS LAWYER
You're looking at losses
When you should be counting
    winnings.

OTHERS
Right!

CHARLEY
Best thing that ever could have
    happened—

FRANK
(Pleasant, dead)
    Right.

INTERIOR DECORATOR
So you'll get a new flat
And you'll have a few flings,
Start a whole new life and learn to
    adore it.

GOSSIP COLUMNIST
If you want to have weddings,
Then you gotta have divorces—

(As Frank shoots her a look)

No?

MOVIE STAR
Though it's sad and all that,
You get over these things
And you come out somehow better
    for it.

HIS LAWYER
Just because you change horses
Doesn't mean you're changing
    courses.

MARY
Right!

OTHERS
(Overlapping)
Best thing that ever could have
    happened—
One more thing not to think about—
It was all getting much too
    complicated—

FRANK
(Edgily)
    Right!

(Mary steps forward and sings her solo
chorus, after which the friends resume)

MOVIE STAR
It's a month at the most—

PRESS AGENT
Sure, you'll spin a few wheels—

INTERIOR DECORATOR
But you don't look back—

GOSSIP COLUMNIST
Just leave all the pieces.

GROUP I
When you haven't got one choice,
Might as well enjoy the other.

GROUP II
Right!

MOVIE STAR
You'll come out to the Coast—

HIS LAWYER
We can set a few deals,
And I'm talking strictly major
    releases.

GROUP I
An exit from one place
Is an entrance to another.

GROUP I
Right!

CHARLEY
Best thing that ever could have
    happened!

MARY
(Overlapping)
I mean, socks have holes,
I mean, roads have bumps,

They make meatheads champs and
    nice guys chumps.
I mean, even Cream of Wheat has
    lumps!

ALL
(Variously, overlapping)
Best thing that ever could have
    happened—
It was all getting much too
    complicated anyhow—
Best thing that ever could have
    happened!

FRANK
(Cheerful and determined, to Joe)
Right, we'll do a new show—!

(To Charley)

No, we'll do a whole batch!

(To Mary)

And it's over with, I'll cut the
    connection—

(To everyone)

Gotta have endings,
Or there wouldn't be beginnings.

ALL
Right!

CHARLEY
When you're flattened this low
And you're starting from scratch,
You can only go in one direction!

MARY, CHARLEY
The side is retired,
But there still are lots of innings,
Right?

ALL
Best thing that ever could have
    happened—
I say, best thing that ever could have
    happened—!

—and the song and action continued as
in the 1985 production.

1964. Gussie, in a sexy evening gown, is pacing an empty stage.

Gussie's Opening Number (1985)

GUSSIE

He's only a boy . . .
Why do I think he loves me?
Maybe he loves what I can do for
    him.
Maybe he thinks that I'll come
    through for him.
Maybe the moon is cheese!

And yet maybe,
Maybe,
Something real is happening here.
But baby,
You're a baby,
And the man that I'm married to
    needs me near . . .

Okay, the moon is cheese!
And I love the guy I shouldn't,
And I don't the one I should.
Ah, but love is blind,
And I go for the kind
That I finally find
Is no good . . .

(Although Gussie seems to have been singing about Frank, she suddenly starts to belt out the lyric and strut around the stage, joined by a couple of Chorus Boys. We realize that we're watching her perform in a show.)

GUSSIE

It started out like a song.
It started quiet and slow, with no
    surprise,
And then one morning I woke to
    realize
We had a good thing going . . .

The lights fade on her and we are in an alley outside the stage door of the Alvin Theatre in New York. It is 1964, and the opening night of Frank and Charley's first Broadway show, Musical Husbands. Frank, Charley, Mary, a very pregnant Beth, and Joe, who has produced the show, are waiting nervously as the performance ends to see what the audience's reaction is. Joe opens the stage door, and an enormous ovation sounds from inside the theater.

It's a Hit!

JOE

Listen to that!
Will you listen to that!

FRANK

Do you know what that means?
Let me tell you what that means—
Wait, no—
Anyone who even thinks it,
Don't say it,
You'll jinx it . . .

CHARLEY

Listen to that!

JOE

Did you listen to that?

FRANK

Does that make you feel proud?
Well, feel more than just proud—
Okay, wait,
I'll tempt fate,
And I'll say it out loud:
That, unless
I miss my guess,
Is—I can't stand it!
Listen—! Yes,
That's the sound of

A hit!
It's a hit!
Gang, I think this is it!
No more writing clever little shows
For those basement saloons,
No more proclamations from the pros
That you "can't hum the tunes"—

CHARLEY

No more sneaking in at intermission
To the plays you wish you could
    afford—

MARY

Or producers having you audition
Whenever they're bored—

CHARLEY

And who'll say right away
As you play the first chord:
    "I think it's very, very—what is the
    word? Interesting. And if it wasn't
    my investors' money, I would do it
    in a minute."

(He cups his hand to his mouth as if to call the next songwriter)

"Next!"

(Ovation)

ALL

We're a hit!
We're a hit!

JOE

You're ahead,
You should quit.

FRANK

No more coaching those sopranos
With voices like bees—

CHARLEY

No more secondhand pianos
With six broken keys—

MARY

No more agents giving you opinions
As they turn you over to their
    minions—

ALL

Just for these
Guarantees
We should please
Thank the Lord!

It's a hit!
It's a hit!

BETH

Will my folks have a fit!
After all of that baloney
They made me go through,
All that "Honey, not that he's a phony,
But what does he do?"
Will their faces be stony
When they see on their Sony

Someone handing the phony
The Tony Award!

FRANK

"I would like to begin by thanking
all the hundreds of people who have
turned down every show I have ever
written so that I could win for this
one.

(Ovation)

Thank you!"

ALL

It's a hit!

JOE

Hold it, folks,
There's still the reviews left.
Both the *Trib* and the *News* left
Early,
Surly—
Not a good sign.
Also, even if there's a chance, folks,
Let's not forget the advance, folks,
Not a
Lotta
Cash, folks.

CHARLEY

Also, even if it's a smash, folks,
Doesn't that mean we sell out?

JOE

Well, I hope we sell out!

CHARLEY

What I mean is "sell out"—
Well, you know:
Success is like failure,
It's how you perceive it.
It's what you do with it,
Not how you achieve it,
And I can't believe it's a hit!
It's a hit!
It's a hit!

ALL

It's a—

(Joe opens the door to the biggest
ovation yet)

FRANK

Listen to that!
Will you listen to that?
Tell me,

Is that a noise,
Or is that a noise?
That is a noise
I've been waiting
The whole of my life to hear!

BETH

Listen to that!
Did you listen to that?
That is the loveliest noise
For a bread-winning wife to hear!

FRANK
(Overlapping)

I—can't—stand—it!

MARY
(Overlapping)

Listen to that!
That's obscene!

ALL
(Overlapping)

Listen to that!
Will you listen to that?
I can't stand it!
Did you listen to that!
Listen to that!

That's the sound of an audience
Losing its mind!
It's the Pope on his balcony,
Blessing mankind!

JOE

Folks, it's *Funny Girl, Fiddler*
And *Dolly* combined!

ALL

It's a hit!
It's a hit!
It's a palpable hit!

FRANK, CHARLEY

If it only even runs a minute,
At least it's a wedge.
It's the theater and we're really in it,
Not just on the edge!

JOE

If your spirits ever need improving,
You can drop in any night for free!

FRANK
(Looking at Charley)

But the thing that's positively
moving—

CHARLEY
(To Frank)

You could have fooled me—

FRANK, CHARLEY

—Is we're still old friends!
Nothing can kill old friends!

FRANK, CHARLEY, MARY

Where there's a will, old friends
Don't need success to survive!

TRIO PLUS BETH

And us, old friends,
What's to discuss, old friends?

ALL

We've got a surefire genuine
Walk-away blockbuster
Lines down to Broadway
Boffola sensational
Box office lalapalooza gargantuan—!

(Two playgoers, leaving, pass by)

WOMAN

You liked it?

MAN
(Shrugs)

Eh . . .

ALL
(Undeterred)

It's a hit!

*Mary and Charley leave to take Beth to
the hospital to have her baby, while Frank
remains behind to listen to the applause.
The Company sings a Transition.*

The original Transition:

Fourth Transition (1981)
(cut)

COMPANY

Western Berliners
Rise from their dinners,
Go for a stroll and—whoops, there's a
    wall!
Meanwhile, the Bay of Pigs has a
    squall.

Let's join the Peace Corps and go to
Nepal . . .

**And that was a brief rewrite of the
original original version:**

Bump!
Cuba has missiles.
Washington bristles.
There go the good cigars.
Someone named Nader frets about
    cars.
Enter the British waving guitars . . .
Bump!
Ole Mississippi's
Swarming with hippies.
Gasoline's up to thirty cents per.
Valium helps to keep things a blur.
Meantime, it's friendly out at Big Sur.
Bump!
What was that? A grassy knoll.
Bang!
Hold it steady, we're losing
    control . . .

As is apparent, *Merrily We Roll Along*
**allowed me to indulge myself in an
orgy of history.**

*1962. A cocktail party at Joe and Gussie's
apartment. It is jammed with important
people from every stratum of New York
life.*

The Blob/
Growing Up

GUESTS **(In groups)**

Have you seen—?
How was it—?
You're not serious!
Do you mean—?
That does it!
You're not serious!

Darling!
We bought the most—!
Darling!
We had the best—!
Did you read—?
It'll never—!

We saw the first—!
What they need—!
Did you ever—!
Was that the worst—?

Darling!
We saw the most—!
Darling!
We had the most—!
Best—!
It's the first—!
It's the finest—!
It's the latest—!
It's the least—!
It's the worst—!
It's the absolutely lowest—!
It's the greatest—!
It's the single—!
It's the only—!
It's the perfect—!
It's the—!

Hi!
Dreadful!
Fabulous!

*(Frank and Charley enter, with Beth.
They have been invited by Joe, who has
heard their songs and who, they hope,
will option their political musical,* Take a
Left. *They gawk at the guests.)*

GUESTS

Darling!
We saw the new—!
Darling!
We had the most—
Bad—
Was it good?
It's the biggest—!
He's a genius!
Well, he can't—
But he used to—
It's the dumbest—
She's a genius!
It's the—!

GUSSIE
(To Frank)

Meet the Blob,
The bodies you read about.
The ones who know everyone
That everyone knows.

GUESTS **(In groups)**

Hi!
Dreadful!
Fabulous!

GUSSIE

Meet the Blob.
Not many and yet—

GUESTS

Oh.
Right . . .

GUSSIE

You never see one.

GUESTS

What?
No!

GUSSIE

They come as a set.

GUESTS

Who—?
Him?

GUSSIE

And we're in their debt.

GUESTS

But what did *you* think?

GUSSIE

'Cause honeybunch,
They write the books
And put on the shows
And run the saloons
And design the clothes.
They keep us natives on our toes.

GUESTS

Albee!
Warhol!
Kurosawa!

GUSSIE

Then they read the books
And go to the shows
And swamp the saloons,
Wearing all the clothes—
What you might call a glut.
But
They're the most important people
In the most important city
In the most important country
In the you-know-what!

GUESTS

Heavy!
Miltown!
Gestalt!

Gussie takes Frank into the conservatory and tells him that Joe doesn't want to produce Take a Left, *but wants him and Charley to write the score for a big, brassy show that she and Joe are cooking up. Frank is disappointed, but Gussie tells him to grab any chance he can to get ahead.*

Growing Up (reprise) (1985)

GUSSIE
Life is knowing what you want,
   darling,
That's the thing you have to know.
You'll get everything you want,
   darling,
Have a little patience.
Climbing mountains can be slow,
   darling,
Take it easy as you climb.
I'd say you're a winner,
Also a beginner—
One step at a time.

(More intimately)

Growing up,
It's what they call growing up.

It's when we're all starting out
And starting to sway.

Growing up,
You hate the delay,
But after today
You'll be on your way.
So what do you say—?
Hm?

(Reluctantly, Frank agrees. He and Gussie rejoin the party in the living room.)

GUESTS
It's the best it's the first
It's the finest it's the latest
It's the least it's the worst
It's the absolutely lowest
It's the greatest it's the single
It's the only it's the perfect
It's the one it's the true—

Gussie interrupts them to announce that Frank and Charley are going to perform a song from a show they've written but which will now be in a new show that Joe will produce and she will star in. The guests quiet down, and Charley sings while Frank plays the piano.

Good Thing Going

CHARLEY
It started out like a song.
We started quiet and slow,
With no surprise.
And then one morning I woke
To realize
We had a good thing going.

It's not that nothing went wrong:
Some angry moments, of course,
But just a few,
And only moments, no more,
Because we knew
We had this good thing going.

And if I wanted too much,
Was that such
A mistake
At the time?
You never wanted enough—
All right, tough,
I don't make
That a crime.

And while it's going along,
You take for granted some love
Will wear away.
We took for granted a lot,

With George Furth at the Leicester, England, production (1992)

I felt no wonder

It started out like a song
Beginning Continued quiet It grew so It hummed   Developed   The kind you're learning
It started easy   flowed
And slow   grew slowly   It built so   The kind that's limiting   Before
With no surprise   Gently
Slowly   And grows   You know it's there
Until the morning   And slowed
I woke

To realize
We
I had a good thing going

It's not that nothing went wrong
Some angry moments,   An angry moment   Some small confusions
Of course
Oh sure,   Would flare
But hardly hell
Nor did I bother to listen
with fools
To friends
They
Who couldn't tell

I had this GTG   Wo

I may have
What if I loved her too much   wanted you
Was that such a mistake at the time?
She didn't love me enough —   want   She loved me not quite enough
well
But
All right, tough, but a break, not a crime.   tough   just

While it was
While it's been   'Cause while you're going along   And say it's   When it's been going so long,   you're
I took
You to to for granted some love will wear away   would
Until the morning   You to be for granted   You never think that   forget
I woke
You woke   And wake   Then Top earth   Then
One day And have   And wake   Then wake   You wake   That's why
And have to say   One day to say   Another day   One day and say   One day you say   say the day
Again   Again
But still I say   I'll say + say
I said + say

                              FRANK

```
       WE
       IT STARTED OUT LIKE A SONG,              like
 ✓   (DEVELOPED) EASY         It grew so easy    So slow and sexy
     AND SLOW,
                              avick
     WITH NO SURPRISE,
AND THEN UNTIL ~~THE~~ MORNING
     I WOKE        ONE
     TO REALIZE!
     I HAD A GOOD THING GOING.            We


     IT'S NOT THAT NOTHING WENT WRONG:        There are angry moments
     SOME ANGRY MOMENTS,       e                And well
    (OF COURSE,)                    AWKWARD     To struggle through
     BUT HARDLY HELL. BUT JUST A FEW  THAT LEFT
     NOR DID I BOTHER  NO ANGRY MOMENTS  A SCAR OR TWO      Those
     WITH FRIENDS   COULD LAST          lesten   But angry moments  The moments never
     WHO COULDN'T TELL  BECAUSE I KNOW   To      Would pass   Could last
     I HAD THIS GOOD THING GOING.        They                Because I know
```

```
I may have  WHAT IF I LOVED YOU~~HER~~ TOO MUCH,     you
            WAS THAT SUCH
            A MISTAKE
            AT THE TIME?
          YOU~~SHE~~ DIDN'T LOVE ME ENOUGH --     you (never) loved me not quite enough
All right. WELL, THAT'S TOUGH, All right, tough
           BUT A BREAK,  I don't make      Did I break    But why make
           NOT A CRIME.  not It a crime.
                                          And 'Cause when the good stuff is strong
Save And   'CAUSE WHILE IT'S GOING ALONG,    you're   When you've been going so long
           YOU TAKE FOR GRANTED
           SOME LOVE
           WILL WEAR AWAY.
        WE I TOOK FOR GRANTED     WE
Too long  (TOO MUCH,)  A LOT    So much      THAT LOVE  You take for granted
But     AND (AND) STILL I SAY:  AND NOW WE SAY  WOULD SAVE  And will
                                It should      THE DAY   One day to say
```

```
        WE
        I HAD NO WAY OF KNOWING
        IT WOULD~~N~~'T JUST GO ON.
        WE
        I HAD A GOOD THING GOING
        GOING
        GONE.
```

                              It could
                              (We should) have kept on growing
                              Instead of just kept on.

                              We had a G.T.G.

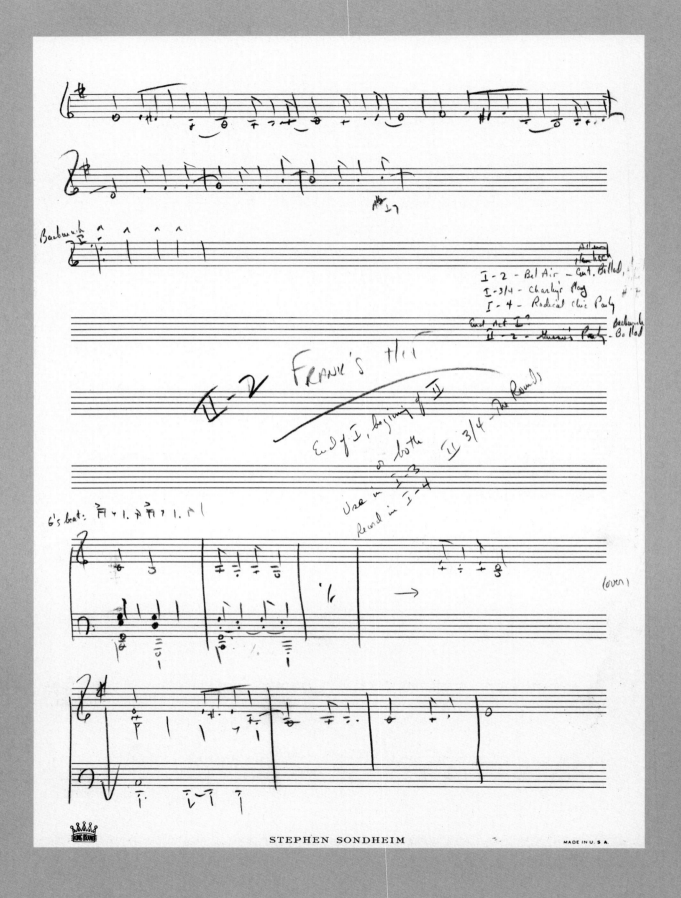

STEPHEN SONDHEIM

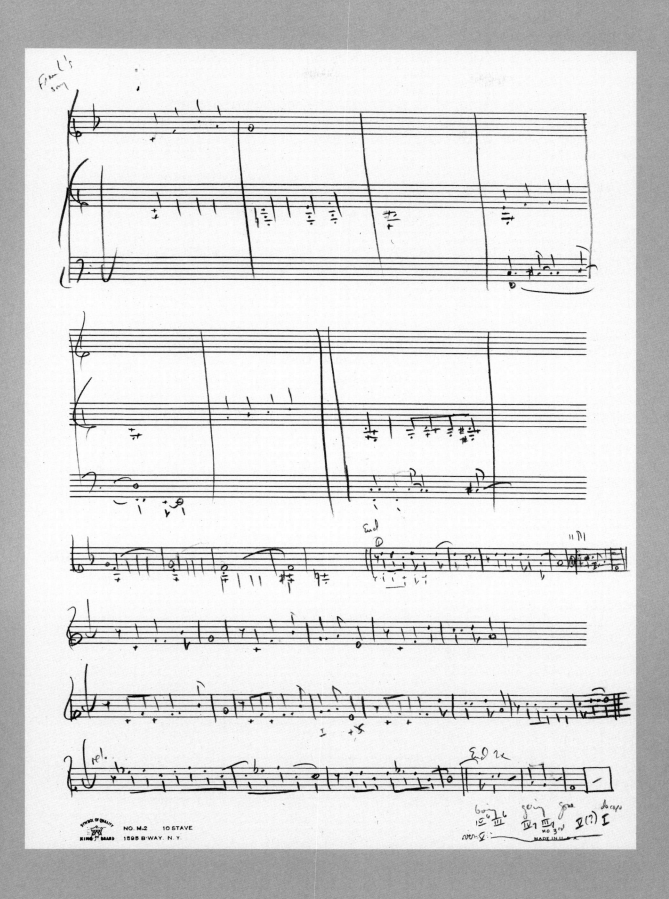

But still I say:
It could have kept on growing,
Instead of just kept on.
We had a good thing going,
Going,
Gone.

Frank and Charley are pressed by Gussie to repeat their performance; Charley resists but Frank welcomes the chance. As they start to sing, the guests resume their "Blob" chatter and the scene ends in cacophonous chaos.

Since, as the time-honored shibboleth has it, writers should write what they know, it's only natural that playgoers, along with moviegoers and in fact all fans of narrative fiction, are tempted to look for autobiographical hints about an author's emotional life in his work. I have been identified publicly with Bobby in *Company*, Ben in *Follies*, Sweeney in *Sweeney Todd* and, most particularly, George in *Sunday in the Park with George*. All authors, of course, identify with their characters or they wouldn't be able to write them convincingly, but they parcel out the elements of their own personalities to *all* of their characters, or at least I do. Of course, there's a part of me in Bobby, but there are also parts of me in *Company*'s Joanne and Amy, just as there are not only in George but in his lover Dot. Moreover, as I've said before, I don't create these characters, the book writer does. What I do is inhabit them as best I can.

The only song I've written which is an immediate expression of a personal internal experience is "Finishing the Hat" from *Sunday in the Park with George*. Every other song comes from nothing more than my identification with the characters who sing them, not my identification with myself. There are two songs, however, which are drawn directly from external life experiences, both of them in this show: one is embodied in the song, or rather the situation, above, the other in the song, or rather the situation, below ("Opening Doors"). In my heyday as a young songwriter, I played many requests at many parties through the short attention span of the requesters and suffered many opinions of producers and directors who felt that their credentials demanded that they have something critical to say. I have spent a good deal of my professional life with the Joe Josephsons of the theater.* All young songwriters have to, and my heart goes out to them.

A Transition takes us back to 1960 and we are in the Downtown Club, a small nightclub where Frank, Charley and Beth, accompanied by their pianist Ted, are concluding their performance before a small audience, which happens to include Joe Josephson and his secretary, Gussie Carnegie.

Thank You for Coming (1981) (cut)

BETH, FRANK, CHARLEY, TED
We're awfully glad that you came!
We're awfully glad you were with us
    for the nonce!
Now tell your waiter what everybody
    wants—
Thank you for coming.

To say goodbye is a shame.
We'd say hello but we said that at the
    start,
So all we'll say is good night and,
    from the heart,
Thank you for slumming.

The show, we knew,
Might tweak a toe or two.
And if you thought our taste was
    rank,

---

*They come in all shapes, sizes of reputations and genders. One of my favorites was George Abbott, whose ear was not the most easily pleased. He was our first choice as a producer for *West Side Story* but even though he had worked with Robbins and Bernstein in *On The Town*, he turned us down on the grounds that the score had "too mush Stravinsky" in it. I eventually had the chance to immortalize the moment, as you'll see.

That's why the show's called "Frankly
    Frank."

So please remember the name,
And if you liked us, then while we
    have your ear,
Would you go home and tell everyone
    we're here?
Make us a trend!

Good night—

             TED
From Ted—

             BETH
And Beth—

             FRANK
And Frank—

             ALL
    (Gesturing toward Charley)
And friend!
The end.

This number was replaced when we decided that we needed something more substantial to demonstrate Frank and Charley's talents. The replacement:

Bobby and Jackie and Jack

             CHARLEY
Nineteen sixty . . .

             BETH
It's nineteen sixty . . .

             FRANK
And gosh, what a swell year it's been!

             ALL THREE
So many blessings,
Such wonders it has brought,
You hardly know where to begin:
There's Xerox
And lasers,
The twist and the "pill,"
A city in Brazil—

BETH
That no one wants to fill.

ALL THREE
Khrushchev stopped screaming
And Librium came in.

CHARLEY
And Nixon didn't win.

ALL THREE
Goodbye then to Ike and the brass,
To years that were cozy but crass.

FRANK
It's true Ike was icky,

CHARLEY
But better him than Dicky—

ALL
Now meet the first first family with
    class
En masse.

CHARLEY
There's Bobby—

BETH
And Jackie—

FRANK
And Jack—

TRIO
And myriads more in the back:
There's Ethel and Teddy and Pat
    alone—

CHARLEY
Plus Eunice—

BETH
And Peter—

FRANK
And Jean—

PIANIST
And Joan—

CHARLEY
And what's-his-name—?

BETH
Stephen—

FRANK
And hold the phone—
The one in the army—

BETH, CHARLEY
The one in the army?

FRANK
Captain . . . Major . . .

CHARLEY
Sargent!

FRANK
That's it!

TRIO
So many cards in the pack.
You want to know how to keep track?
Well, one is good-looking and young
    and rich
While one is good-looking and young
    and rich.
The rest are good-looking and young
    and rich—
There isn't a lot that they lack,
Not Bobby and Jackie and Jack
And Ethel and Ted and Eunice and
    Pat and Joan and Steve and Peter
    and Jean and Sarge—
There's probably dozens of others at
    large,
God knows—
And Joe and Rose.

(They put on Kennedy wigs)

TRIO
We're bringing back style to the
    White House.

BETH
I'm painting it cream for a start.

TRIO
We're making it into a cultural
    lighthouse—

CHARLEY
For glamour—

BETH
And beauty—

FRANK
And art:

BETH
Evenings of the Budapest playing
    Vivaldi
And Munch doing bits of Ravel.
I'll get Leontyne Price to sing her
Medley from "Meistersinger,"
Margot Fonteyn to dance "Giselle."

CHARLEY
Together?

BETH
Won't it be perfectly swell?

FRANK
We'll have Bernstein play next on
The Bechstein piano—

CHARLEY
And Auden read poems and stuff.

BETH
And Galina Vishneyskaya,
The Russian soprano—
Just pronouncing her name is
    refreshing enough.

TRIO
We're bringing back style to the
    White House,
With casual culture the rule.

FRANK
Let's have Tebaldi—

CHARLEY
She makes a guy feel good.

BETH
And Oleg Cassini—
Well, I think he's real good.

CHARLEY
And how about Heifetz?

BETH
And Callas!

FRANK
And Gielgud!

TRIO
And later when everything's cool,
We'll push them all into the pool!

CHARLEY
With Bobby—

BETH
And Jackie—

FRANK
And Jack—

TRIO
The White House is under attack.

FRANK
Eight years is the limit, but eight
  will do.

CHARLEY
By then there'll be Bobby—

PIANIST
—and Teddy, too.

BETH
Or Peter or Stephen—

FRANK, CHARLEY, TED
(To Beth)
—or even you.

BETH
Ooh!
And then there's the Colonel—

FRANK, CHARLEY
Colonel?

BETH
Major—?

FRANK, CHARLEY
Major?

BETH
You know—!

FRANK
Sargent.

BETH
Yes . . .

TRIO
Dozens to take up the slack,
If anything goes out of whack.

FRANK
And some day elections will be
  unknown—

BETH
'Cause each of our kids will ascend
  the throne—

CHARLEY
And their kids have more kids with
  kids of their own—

FRANK
It's sort of a family knack—

TRIO
Till most of the nation's
Made up of relations
Of Bobby and Jackie and Jack
And Ethel and Ted and Eunice and
    Pat and Joan and Steve and Peter
    and Jean and Sarge
And Joe and Rose and rows and rows
And rows and rows and rows and
    rows . . .
The decade is starting anew,

(Crossing fingers)

And maybe the country is, too.

Mr. and Mrs. Spencer, Beth's parents, are
in the audience because on this night
Frank and Beth are going to be married
at the club. (Unbeknownst to them, she
has told Frank that she is pregnant, which
she isn't.) The Spencers disapprove
wholeheartedly, but Beth is defiant. She
and Frank repair to the makeshift dressing room in the basement to change
clothes for the wedding, where they have
to speak in whispers in order not to be
heard upstairs.

Honey (1981)* (cut)

BETH	FRANK
Honey . . .	
(Whispers)	Sh! Not so loud . . .
It's gonna be	
fine.	
	(Whispers)
	I think we'll
	make it.

---

*Cut before previews, for length.

It's bound to feel	
funny	
At first—	At first . . . I
	know . . .
Hang on to	But hang on
the line.	
	And you'll never
	regret it,
	I promise . . .
We're gonna be	
Happy—	
(Getting louder)	Right . . .
—And rich,	
	You bet . . .
And openly love it.	
	I just wish I
	had more
We'll hardly know	I could give
	you . . .
Which of the two	
is which,	
We'll have so	(Getting louder)
much of it.	
	It's not just the
	baby—
Sh!	
	(Whispers)
	I hope you know
	that.
Honey . . .	
(Whispers)	No, all I meant
	was
It's gonna turn out	It'll turn out
For the best.	For the best . . .
I know, 'cause I've	
Never been so	
depressed,	
And so glad of	
my luck.	
	Your luck?
	My luck! . . .
Honey, trust	
me . . .	That's
	understood . . .
But remember,	
It's just me.	(Holding her)
(Louder)	God, you feel
	good . . .
Then, honey,	
Everyone in the world	
Can go milk a duck!	

FRANK, BETH

Honey—

BETH

Mmhm . . .

FRANK

We beat it this far.

BETH

I surely love you . . .

FRANK

We're gonna be different than all the
    rest—

BETH

We already are.

FRANK

We're gonna be happy *and* sad—

BETH

And changing and growing.

FRANK

The prospect of driving your parents
    mad
Will help us keep going.

BETH

It's not just your talent,
I hope you know that . . .

FRANK

Honey—

FRANK	BETH
It's gonna	God, we' re so
	crazy, but it'll
Turn out for	Turn out for the
the best.	best.

BETH

I hope so, I've never been so
    depressed
Or so high on the vine.

FRANK

Long as everything comes out of
    love . . .

BETH

Honey—

BOTH

Trust me,
But remember, it's just me,

And, honey—
It's gonna be fine.

*Frank and Beth return upstairs and are
married, with Charley as best man. Mary
sits aside at a table. Frank and Beth sing
to each other, Mary to herself.*

Not a Day Goes By
(reprise)

BETH

Not a day goes by . . .

MARY

Not a single day . . .

MARY, BETH

But you're somewhere a part of my
  life
And it looks like you'll stay.

FRANK, MARY

As the days go by,
I keep thinking, when does it end?

BETH

That it can't get much better much
    longer.
But it only gets better and stronger
And deeper and nearer—

FRANK, BETH

And simpler and freer
And richer and clearer . . .

ALL THREE

And no,
Not a day goes by—

MARY

Not a blessed day—

BETH, MARY

But you somewhere come into my life
And you don't go away.

ALL THREE

And I have to say
If you do, I'll die.

FRANK, BETH

I want day after day
After day after day after—

MARY

(Overlapping)
I'll die day after day after—

ALL THREE

Day after day after day after day
After day,
Till the days go by . . .

FRANK, BETH

Till the days go by . . .

MARY

Till the days go by . . .

*The Company sings a Transition, a frag-
ment of the First, which takes us back
to the years 1958–1959. Frank and
Charley are in their apartment, Frank
working at a piano, Charley busy at a
typewriter. Mary is in her apartment,
also at a typewriter, typing slowly and
sporadically.*

Opening Doors

FRANK

How's it going?

CHARLEY

Good. You?

FRANK

Fair.

CHARLEY

Yeah, tell me.

(The phone rings, Frank answers)

FRANK

Chinese laundry.

MARY

Hi.

FRANK
(To Charley)

Mary.

CHARLEY

Say hello.

Bells + carriage return   Eating — scraping of hands

M — hunt + peck   Mumble + hum as they read their own

Pulling sheets out of typewriter, + crumpling   stuff

Humming   X-ing out

C | One typewriter — stop, smoke — A major vamp

F | Piano — tinkle in quarters or 8ths

(C repeat?)M | One typewriter — stop, coffee — A major or variation

C | (overlap) — stop

F | Piano — stop

C | — goes

M | goes

F | Vamps — goes — Fight

Work — F + C	F's song
Chat — F + C	Something they can hum	Working
Work — M, F, C	Chat	Chatter
Chat — "	Opening Doors	Performing says/Producers
Opening Doors	Chat — C getting married (But we got an audition)	Opening Doors
Work	Something They Can Hum	Events: C marries F/Both; M/pfair
Chat	Chat — I got us a booking — we'll rehearse	The Little Rock Follies

Sounds / + Talk | Typewriters + Piano — F finding the tune

How's it going?

Sounds | T + C (add Mary) ... F finding the harmony ... then just sent back

/8 Vamp | I got an audition, a nibble, a meeting, an interview — they want a resume ... I just sent out the play

Chorus | We're Opening Doors

Sounds | F finding the vamp + rhythm, whistling

(Talk)

(Sounds)   got up

Vamp | I finished the lyric — F + C trying lyric — F corrects him

F+C Song | — interrupted

Prod. Chorus | You Gotta Give 'Em

Chat VI — We'll do a revue (though what about the (a) book?)
Auditions for pianist — 1st 8 of "We're glad that you're here." Pick Ted, also plays
                                                                   in next 8
Auditions for girl — 2nd 8 — 3 girls — Thank you, you're hired.
I'm Beth, I'm Frank — interns. — we open next week
(Chat VII) (finish chorus, segue into
   OD

Wrk	F, C
"/4 Chat I	F, C — How's it going? Write the book, Mary
Wrk	M, F, C —
Chat II	— Activities for 2nd 8 — contacts are made, people making things I finished the play
Opening Doors	(lyric or an up statement at start of 2nd 8) .... pianist .... start an affair
Chat III	I'm getting a reading, an option, a nibble, rejection, having a meeting, interview
OD	
Wrk	in F with audience every body going, F. singing, whistling (sim (tunes?))
"/4 Chat IV	I finished the lyric (tighted up a little) — starts to sing
Sing	Starts, F correct tune, C tries (corrects) lyric
Sing	F, C
Prod.	many producers? Something they can hum — echo w/ M? — release (chorus?) of F's song
"/8 Chat V	Stuff brought up 6/8 They're dropping the option (C getting married? or in VII?)
Opening Doors	They're slamming the doors trying to sketch out a dime We're making our own — action all over? lasting longer
Chat VI	— C getting married — But we got an audition — Right after the problem I ought a try rock
(sing?) → Prod.	Something they can follow — action all over?
Chat VII	Break out 6/8. I got an idea. same sketches We'll write a revue. I got us a booking. (to M) And you write the jokes. We'll get us a cast, we'll hold some auditions C: I'm gonna get married
+ Sing	3 girls (or 4) auditioning, one each 8. F picks B. Same Ending — Thank you.
Chat	F + B (+ Ted? — rehearsal pianist) (Slow — rubato) (original per line)
Opening D	reprise I All 4 (+ Ted?) — And it's about time! sung
Activities I	F as reh. pianist, writing on the side (syncopated motif — still dissolute bwit — rehearse to Chat C with agent, M with editor — both gossipy + rising
II	F coaching singer (scales); C with reading, M with chess editor
IV	M at Confidential — research? No such luck — F phones M?

*whistle
cadas*

There's not a tune you can hum.

There's not a tune you go bum-bum-bum-di-dum

What's wrong with writing me *(melody)*   What's wrong with tunes that go

Throw the folks a crumb   Go home with us some

I know what I mean, boys   Buy 'em

You never know where the   Throw me a melody

Next note's coming from

You gotta   Why don't you throw 'em a crumb? *(can't)* *us*   I know, according to some,

         Okay, you think that I'm dumb *(say)*

start   You're slow to close
goes

What's wrong with givin' 'em
You gotta give 'em some tunes to tap their toes

Where is the   Give 'em some melody.

What's wrong with letting 'em *(something)*

Tap their toes a bit   You don't hear Shostakovich *(of the)*

don't like buying   They'll never pay $10.00   writing no hit shows

For Prokofiev

You let me   I'll do it soon as   put it on   The problem is that *Prokofiev*
I'll let you know when   you never heard of Shavinsky. *(why)*
writes   Stravinsky has a hit   Writing shows   Don't have hits *(hits)*

But Shostakovich   That's why Stravinsky ain't *(you hope)*
                 Writing no more shows *(Broadway)*

And you expect 'em *(his)*
To hum a phrase like that? *(go out hummin')*
    pick their way through that

has
Who wants to "live in NY?   screaming
Who wants the worry,
The pace, the dirt, the heat?
Who wants the garbage
Cans clanging in the street
Suddenly I do.

They're always popping a cork:
scurvy Hall   The cops, the cabbies,   supers
Murray   The sales girls up at Saks
You gotta have a
Real taste for maniacs.
Suddenly I do.

Who wants to dance at the Stork?
Who wants to live in NY?
I always loved the dirt, the heat
                    the noise
                                      Well, ever since I met you, I
         But since I met you,   But now there's you and I haven't
It doesn't I haven't —   And um
              never   But since I
        JJ: Listen, boys   Now But I'm in love with a girl from

MARY

I think I got a job.

FRANK

Where?

MARY

True Romances.

FRANK

Posing?

MARY

Thank you. Writing captions.

FRANK

What about the book?

MARY

What about the book?

FRANK

Nothing, are you working on the
book?

MARY

Yes . . .

FRANK

Good.

MARY

No . . .

FRANK

Mary—

MARY

Right, I know, yes, me and Balzac . . .

*(They work furiously, only to slump
over in frustrated despair. They meet
center stage.)*

CHARLEY

I finished the one-act.

FRANK

I got an audition—

MARY

I started the story.

FRANK

Rehearsal pianist.

CHARLEY

So where are we eating?

MARY

I'm moving to *Playboy.*

FRANK

The publisher called me.

CHARLEY

I'm doing a rewrite.

MARY

My parents are coming.

FRANK

I saw *My Fair Lady.*

CHARLEY

I rewrote the rewrite.

FRANK

I sort of enjoyed it.

MARY

I threw out the story.

CHARLEY

I'm meeting an agent.

ALL

We'll all get together on Sunday.
We're opening doors,
Singing, "Here we are!"
We're filling up days on a dime.
That faraway shore's
Looking not too far.
We're following every star—
There's not enough time!

*(The stage becomes alive with activity:
Charley being interviewed by an agent,
Frank playing the same bars of music
over and over while dancers rehearse,
Mary meeting a musician on a subway.
The three come together once again.)*

FRANK

I called a producer.

CHARLEY

I sent off the one-act.

MARY

I started the story.

FRANK

He said to come see him.

CHARLEY

I dropped out of college.

MARY

I met this musician.

FRANK

I'm playing a nightclub.

CHARLEY

They're doing my one-act!

MARY

I'm working for *Redbook.*

FRANK

I rewrote the ballad.

MARY

I finished the story.

CHARLEY

We started rehearsals.

MARY

I threw out the story
And then the musician.
I'm moving to *Popular Science.*

ALL

We're opening doors,
Singing, "Look who's here!"
Beginning to sail on a dime.
That faraway shore's
Getting very near!
We haven't a thing to fear—
We haven't got time!

*(They throw themselves simultaneously
into activity as music continues underneath. Charley and Mary type fero-
ciously while Frank whistles and hums
as he tries out different vamps for his
tune. After a bit, he hits a chord triumphantly, turns, and looks over at
Charley, as Mary picks up her phone
and starts to dial.)*

FRANK

How's it coming?

CHARLEY

Good. You?

FRANK

Done.

CHARLEY

One minute . . .

(The phone rings, Frank answers)

FRANK
Hamburg Heaven.

MARY
Hi.

FRANK
(To Charley)
Mary.

CHARLEY
Say hello.

MARY
I got another job.

FRANK
Where?

MARY
"Chic."

FRANK
What's that?

MARY
A brand new concept:
Pop-up pictures.

FRANK
What about the book?

MARY
What about the book?

FRANK
Did you give the publisher the book?

MARY
Yes . . .

FRANK
Good.

MARY
No . . .

FRANK
Mary—

MARY
Look, I never—

CHARLEY
(Ripping the paper out of the typewriter)
Finished!

FRANK
(Into phone)
Let me call you back.

MARY
Right.

(Hangs up)

CHARLEY
(Hands the paper to Frank)
This is just a draft.

FRANK
Right.

CHARLEY
Probably it stinks.

FRANK
Right.

CHARLEY
I haven't had the time to do a
    polish—

FRANK
Will you sing!

CHARLEY
Right.

(Sings, as Frank accompanies him)

Who wants to live in New York?
Who wants the worry, the noise, the
    dirt, the heat?
Who wants the garbage cans clanging
    in the street?
Suddenly I do!

(During the above, Joe Josephson has
    appeared and started to listen
    judiciously: Frank and Charley are
    auditioning for him.)

They're always popping their cork—
    I'll fix that line—

The cops, the cabbies, the salesgirls
    up at Saks.
You gotta have a real taste for
    maniacs—
Suddenly I do!

JOE
(Interrupting them)
That's great! That's swell!

The other stuff as well.
It isn't every day I hear a score this
    strong,
But fellas, if I may,
There's only one thing wrong:

(Singing to Frank's tune)

There's not a tune you can hum.
There's not a tune you go bum-bum-
    bum-di-dum—
You need a tune to go bum-bum-
    bum-di-dum—
Give me a melody!

Why can't you throw 'em a crumb?
What's wrong with letting 'em tap
    their toes a bit?
I'll let you know when Stravinsky has
    a hit—
Give me some melody!

Oh, sure, I know,
It's not that kind of show.
But can't you have a score
That's sort of in between?
Look, play a little more,
I'll show you what I mean . . .

CHARLEY
(Overselling)
Who wants to live in New York?
I always hated the dirt, the heat, the
    noise.
But ever since I met you, I—

JOE
Listen, boys,
Maybe it's me,
But that's just not a hum-mm-mm-
    mm-mm-mm-mm-mable melody!

Write more, work hard—
Leave your name with the girl.
Less avant-garde—
Leave your name with the girl.
Just write a plain old melodee-dee-
    dee-dee-dee-dee . . .

(He is humming "Some Enchanted
    Evening"—incorrectly)

Dee-dee-dee-dee-dee-dee . . .

(He exits. Frank, Charley and Mary
    meet dejectedly.)

CHARLEY
They're stopping rehearsals.
They ran out of money . . .

MARY
We lasted one issue.
My book was rejected . . .

FRANK
The nightclub was raided.
I have to start coaching . . .

MARY
My parents are coming.

CHARLEY
They screwed up the laundry.

FRANK
My wallet was stolen.

MARY
I saw the musician.

CHARLEY
We're being evicted.

MARY
I'm having a breakdown.

ALL
We'll all get together on Sunday.

They're slamming the doors,
Singing, "Go away!"
It's less of a sail than a climb.
That faraway shore's
Farther every day.
We're learning to ricochet.
We still have a lot to say . . .

FRANK
You know what we'll do?

CHARLEY
What?

FRANK
We'll do a revue.

CHARLEY
What?

MARY
What?

FRANK
We'll do a revue of our own!

MARY
What?

CHARLEY
Where?

MARY
Why?

CHARLEY
When?

FRANK
Not just songs but stories, scenes,
Piano pieces, mime—

CHARLEY
Yeah!

MARY
(Pantomiming a sign)
"Frankly Frank!" . . .

FRANK
A showcase of our own!

CHARLEY
Where?

FRANK
The club's reopening.

MARY
We'll write a lot of new stuff—

CHARLEY
Rewrite old stuff—

FRANK
What about the girl?

CHARLEY
What about the girl?

FRANK
Only that we're gonna need a girl.

CHARLEY
Well, Mary—

MARY
Thanks, I don't perform except at
    dinner.

(Two girls have entered and hold
rehearsal copies of music, ready to
audition. The first girl starts, singing
shrilly and off-key as Frank plays.)

FIRST GIRL
Who wants to live in New York?
Who wants the worry, the noise, the
    dirt, the heat?
Who wants the garbage cans
    clanging—

I can sing higher!

FRANK
(Polite dismissal)
Thank you for coming. Next eight,
    please.

SECOND GIRL (BETH)
They're always popping their cork—

FRANK
Up a tone.

BETH
(Sings a tone higher)
The cops, the cabbies, the salesgirls
    up at Saks—

FRANK
Up a tone.

BETH
(Again)
You gotta have a real taste for
    maniacs—

FRANK
Thank you. You're hired.

BETH
(Offers her hand)
I'm Beth.

FRANK
I'm Frank.

BETH
I really thought I stank.

MARY
I'm Mary.

CHARLEY
(Offers his hand)
Charley.

FRANK
By the way,
I'm told we open Saturday.

OTHERS
What?!

MARY
You're not serious!

CHARLEY
Nobody's ready!

FRANK
Apparently somebody canceled a
    booking.

CHARLEY
The songs aren't finished!

MARY
And what about costumes?

BETH
And how do I learn all these
numbers?

*(They all sing the following lines
simultaneously)*

FRANK
I'll bring you the copies of everything
Later this evening.

BETH
Okay, but I'll have to have all of the
music
And Saturday I've got to sing at a
wedding.
Oh, God, is there dancing, 'cause I'm
not a dancer . . .

CHARLEY
Not to mention I still haven't
Finished the Synanon song or the
Kennedy number . . .

FRANK
You don't have to, we'll segue the
End of it into the dance we cut
out . . .

CHARLEY
And what'll we do about getting
publicity,
Run around town putting stickers on
windows?

MARY
And have we decided or not on the
restaurant sketch?
I need two or three days at the least to
replace it . . .

FRANK
No, we'll use it but not with the long
introduction . . .

ALL
(Together)
We'll worry about it on Sunday!

We're opening doors,
Singing, "Here we are!"
We're filling up days on a dime.
That faraway shore's looking not
too far.

We're following every star—
There's not enough time!

We're banging on doors,
Shouting, "Here again!"
We're risking it all on a dime.
That faraway shore's looking near
again,
The only thing left is when,
We know we should count to ten—
We haven't got time!
We haven't got time!

Although the details may vary, that song
describes what the struggle was like for
me and my generation of Broadway
songwriters. I'm sure it must often have
seemed frustrating at the time, but in
retrospect it strikes me as the most exhilarating period of my professional life.

*The Company sings a Transition which
takes us back to 1957. We are on the
rooftop of a tenement in New York City
at dawn. Frank, fresh out of the army,
has just moved in with Charley, who is
writing a play. They are waiting for a
glimpse of Sputnik, which has just been
launched, and are eagerly contemplating
their future.*

Our Time

COMPANY
Something is stirring,
Shifting ground.
It's just begun.
Edges are blurring
All around,
And yesterday is done.

Feel the flow,
Hear what's happening:
We're what's happening.
Don't you know?
We're the movers and we're the
shapers.
We're the names in tomorrow's
papers.
Up to us, man, to show 'em.

It's our time, breathe it in:
Worlds to change and worlds to win.

Our turn coming through,
Me and you, man,
Me and you!

*(Frank and Charley meet Mary for the
first time. She lives a floor below them
and has also come up to the roof to catch
a sight of Sputnik.)*

FRANK
Feel how it quivers,
On the brink . . .

CHARLEY
What?

FRANK
Everything!
Gives you the shivers,
Makes you think
There's so much stuff to sing!

And you and me,
We'll be singing it like the birds,
Me with music and you the words,
Tell 'em things they don't know!

BOTH
Up to us, pal, to show 'em . . .

Our time, breathe it in:
Worlds to change and worlds to win.
Our turn, we're what's new,
Me and you, pal, me and you!

Feel the flow,
Hear what's happening:
We're what's happening!
Long ago
All we had was that funny feeling,
Saying some day we'd send 'em
reeling,
Now it looks like we can!

CHARLEY
Some day just began . . .

BOTH
It's our heads on the block.
Give us room and start the clock.
Our time coming through!
Me and you, pal,
Me and you!
Me and you!

*(The other tenants, all young and
hopeful, come up to the roof)*

Dare to be different   emblem pennant   Let your motto be ^say   horizon
Brave the winds   flag   standard   We will seize the day   prospect
                            mark   streamers   It's our turn
                            print   beacon light   we will renew the world and in so doing, ourselves
                            seal   In light that shines
                            stamp   up to us

Behold the hills of tomorrow
Beneath a
Behold the limitless sky
                                              way runs
Though the risk(s) be great   The road is straight
There are worlds that wait   To the worlds that wait
And the road in view   And the vistas new
That summons   And fling your banners
Which beckons you   Which beckon you
                                     High
To try.
                                              knightly noble + free
Beyond the hills of tomorrow   mountains wait to be climbed
    valleys fertile & green   Lie valleys
Lie kingdoms yet to be won.   Are vistas wondrous to see
    that wondrous
On the farthest range   Beyond the rise
There are worlds to change   Even better skies
                                              that each
And the road runs true   And beyond the rise
                                     Lie
To point you to   Are better skies
                                              these
The sun.   Than these   To see
                                     far filled proud sure pure
                                              true
Beyond the hills of tomorrow   Behold our hearts
    other hills   our
Lie mountains noble and free green   As the journey starts
Though the road be strange   make a footprint plan
In that wondrous range   Do the best we can
                                              float your emblem
There are worlds to change   To keep our banners high.
                                 each
And beyond that rise   Behold the way
    Can   That we
Even better skies   We will seize the day
    be sure
To see.   Wait for him who tries
                                                   our eyes gaze
                                              waits long
                                              reaches
Beyond the range   Behold the view   Before us stretches
Lie   where the road runs true
Is a world to change Of a world that's new Lie Stretch a hundred ways

                         Begin the climb
                                             Prepare
Before we start   On the road of time   Beware the way

                                          That the heart can stay

Let us make a plan
To keep our banners high

(left margin word lists:)
between
before
begin
believe
because
become

beyond begrudge
behind
below
beneath
beset
beside
besiege bemused
beyond
below
beside
be to be
becomes   no trust
betray
beware

talisman
beyond oar
I can   cursor
more
than
scan
span

are wait stand

tread
thread
spread
sped
said   the
instead can
led

Beyond the range
Lie
Is a world to change

FRANK, MARY, CHARLEY
Something is stirring,
Shifting ground.
It's just begun.
Edges are blurring
All around,
And yesterday is done.

COMPANY
Feel the flow,
Hear what's happening:
We're what's happening.
Don't you know?
We're the movers and we're the
    shapers.
We're the names in tomorrow's
    papers.
Up to us now to show 'em.

It's our time, breathe it in:
Worlds to change and worlds to win.
Our turn coming through,
Me and you, pal,
Me and you!

FRANK, MARY, CHARLEY
Years from now,
We'll remember and we'll come back,
Buy the rooftop and hang a plaque:
"This is where we began
Being what we can."

ALL
It's our heads on the block.
Give us room and start the clock.
Our dream coming true,
Me and you, pal,
Me and you!
Me and you!
Me and you!
Me and you!
Me and you!
Me and you!
Me and you!
Me and you!

*(Frank, Mary and Charley interlock
their pinkies: their sign of friendship.
Frank places his hand over all three.*

*They smile at one another lovingly as the
Curtain falls.)*

In the 1981 version, the last scene
took us back to the Commencement
Address that began the story. Young
Frank is finishing his valedictorian address, but it is the older Frank who
speaks, having relived his life. The
young Frank then turns and conducts
the students in the Commencement
song that he and Charley have written.
We recognize the tune as the seed of
"Good Thing Going," the song that
launched their careers.

The Hills of Tomorrow (1981)

STUDENTS
Behold the hills of tomorrow!
Behold the limitless sky!
Fling wide the gates
To a world that waits!
As our journey starts,
Behold! Our hearts
Are high!

Between the hills of tomorrow,
At times the road may seem strange.
The hills are deep,
And the way is steep,
But for those who dare
The world is there
To change!

Then raise the torch and seize the day!
Behold! Our banners fly to mark the
    way!
Standards billowing, unsullied,
    proud!
Visions bright, voices loud!

Beyond the hills of tomorrow
Are skies more beautiful still!

INTERMISSION

Behold! Begin!
There are worlds to win!
May we come to trust
The dreams we must
Fulfill!

*(The two Franks smile at each other as
the Curtain falls)*

Two realizations about the show have
occurred to me as I was writing this
chapter, and I'm surprised that they
hadn't before. The first is that *Merrily
We Roll Along* is nothing more nor
less than an updated version of *Allegro*. Instead of the story of an idealistic, corrupted and disillusioned doctor,
we have an idealistic, corrupted and
disillusioned composer, both of them
helped to their doom by grasping, ambitious wives, each betraying their best
friends. The only, and crucial, difference is that Hammerstein redeems his
hero, whereas Kaufman, Hart, Furth
and Sondheim leave him sinking into
the hell he has created. Still, both tales
have a happy ending, ours because it
is told backward. Perhaps that's why
the idea for the show, even though it
was Hal's, appealed to me in the first
place—I was trying to fix *Allegro*.

The second realization is that I
once had a Franklin Shepard moment
myself. It was when I agreed to write
Do I Hear a Waltz? I took the job out
of expedience and greed, and although
I didn't pay for it as heavily as Frank
does, it taught me a lesson—I never
again wrote anything that wasn't for
love. And it had a silver lining: the experience helped me write *Merrily We
Roll Along*. It was a show I adored
and a deep disappointment in its first
outing, and it marked an important
period in my professional life.

But then I met James Lapine.

Acknowledgments

To my editors Peter Gethers and Christina Malach, for their patient and relentless prodding;

To Iris Weinstein, who designed the book with more elegance than it required;

To Frank Rich and Mike Nichols, for being so persistently encouraging about what I was writing that I had to finish it;

To Anna Quindlen, for showering a neophyte with sage advice, the most important of which was "Punctuation is everything."

To Peter Jones, for tireless research, collation and scanning, as well as a number of perceptions which I've commandeered as my own;

To Mark Eden Horowitz of the Library of Congress, for emending memory and texts;

To Steven Clar, for scrupulous and critical oversight (now and for the past twenty-two years);

To the writers of the liner notes in the recordings of the shows, without which winnowing down plot synopses would have been a lot more tedious;

To Jack Feldman in particular, for his extravagant enthusiasm accompanied by meticulously detailed corrections and timidly argued suggestions, all of which not only saved me time but spared me the humiliation of misquotation, misstatement and misidentification.

Finally, to Addie and Willie and especially Jeffrey, for everything else.

Appendix: Original Broadway Productions

West Side Story

OPENING	September 26, 1957
CLOSING	June 27, 1959
TOTAL PERFORMANCES	732

Produced by Robert E. Griffith and Harold S. Prince
Produced by arrangement with Roger L. Stevens
Book by Arthur Laurents
Conceived by Jerome Robbins
Music by Leonard Bernstein
Lyrics by Stephen Sondheim
Directed by Jerome Robbins
Choreographed by Jerome Robbins
Co-choreographer: Peter Gennaro

OPENING NIGHT CAST

	THE JETS
Mickey Calin	RIFF
Larry Kert	TONY
Eddie Roll	ACTION
Tony Mordente	A-RAB
David Winters	BABY JOHN
Grover Dale	SNOWBOY
Martin Charnin	BIG DEAL
Hank Brunjes	DIESEL
Tommy Abbott	GEE-TAR
Frank Green	MOUTH PIECE
Lowell Harris	TIGER
	THEIR GIRLS
Wilma Curley	GRAZIELLA
Carole D'Andrea	VELMA
Nanette Rosen	MINNE
Marilyn D'Honau	CLARICE
Julie Oser	PAULINE
Lee Becker	ANYBODYS
	THE SHARKS
Ken Le Roy	BERNARDO
Carol Lawrence	MARIA
Chita Rivera	ANITA
Jamie Sanchez	CHINO
George Marcy	PEPE
Noel Schwartz	INDIO
Al De Sio	LUIS
Gene Gavin	ANXIOUS
Ronnie Lee	NIBBLES
Jay Norman	JUANO
Erne Castaldo	TORO
Jack Murray	MOOSE

	THEIR GIRLS
Marilyn Cooper	ROSALIA
Reri Grist	CONSUELA
Carmen Guiterrez	TERESITA
Elizabeth Taylor	FRANCISCA
Lynn Ross	ESTELLA
Liane Plane	MARGUERITA
	THE ADULTS
Art Smith	DOC
Arch Johnson	SCHRANK
William Bramley	KRUPKE
John Harkins	GLADHAND

Gypsy

OPENING	May 21, 1959
CLOSING	March 25, 1961
TOTAL PERFORMANCES	702

Produced by David Merrick and Leland Hayward
Book by Arthur Laurents
Based on the memoirs of Gypsy Rose Lee
Music by Jule Styne
Lyrics by Stephen Sondheim
Musical Director: Milton Rosenstock
Music orchestrated by Sid Ramin and Robert Ginzler
Dance arrangements by John Kander and Betty Walberg
Additional Dance music by Betty Walberg
Directed by Jerome Robbins
Choreographed by Jerome Robbins

OPENING NIGHT CAST

Ethel Merman	ROSE
Sandra Church	LOUISE
Jack Klugman	HERBIE
Kathryn Albertson	SHOWGIRL
Marvin Arnold	FARM BOY
John Borden	ARNOLD (AND HIS GUITAR)
Lane Bradbury	JUNE
Bobby Brownell	NEWSBOY
Patsy Bruder	MARJORIE MAY
Gene Castle	NEWSBOY
Ricky Coll	FARM BOY
Marilyn Cooper	AGNES
Steve Curry	NEWSBOY
Faith Dane	MAZEPPA
Imelda De Martin	GAIL

Marilyn D'Honau	DOLORES
Don Emmons	FARM BOY
Chotzi Foley	ELECTRA
Erving Harmon	POP
Billy Harris	NEWSBOY
Maria Karnilova	TESSIE TURA
Gloria Kristy	SHOWGIRL
Jody Lane	BALLOON GIRL
Merle Letowt	THELMA
Loney Lewis	KRINGELEIN; CIGAR
Barbara London	SHOWGIRL
Mort Marshall	UNCLE JOCKO; MR. GOLDSTONE
Jacqueline Mayro	BABY JUNE
Denise McLaglen	SHOWGIRL
Karen Moore	BABY LOUISE
Peg Murray	MISS CRATCHITT
Theda Nelson	SHOWGIRL
Michael Parks	L.A.; FARM BOY
Joan Petlack	EDNA MAE
Richard Porter	PASTEY
Marsha Rivers	MAID
Joe Silver	WEBER; PHIL
Willy Sumner	GEORGE; COW
Carroll Jo Towers	SHOWGIRL
Ian Tucker	ANGIE; FARM BOY
Marie Wallace	SHOWGIRL
Paul Wallace	TULSA; FARM BOY
David Winters	YONKERS; FARM BOY
George Zima	BOUGERON-COCHON; COW

A Funny Thing Happened on the Way to the Forum

OPENING	May 8, 1962
CLOSING	August 29, 1964
TOTAL PERFORMANCES	964

Produced by Harold Prince
Book by Burt Shevelove and Larry Gelbart
Music by Stephen Sondheim
Lyrics by Stephen Sondheim
Based on the plays of Plautus
Music orchestrated by Irwin Kostal and Sid Ramin
Musical Director: Harold Hastings
Dance arrangements by Hal Schaefer
Additional dance music by Betty Walberg
Assistant to Harold Hastings: Arthur Wagner
Directed by George Abbott
Choreographed by Jack Cole
Uncredited staging and choreography by Jerome Robbins

OPENING NIGHT CAST

Zero Mostel	PROLOGUS; PSEUDOLUS
David Burns	SENEX
John Carradine	LYCUS
Brian Davies	HERO
Jack Gilford	HYSTERIUM
Ron Holgate	MILES GLORIOSUS
Ruth Kobart	DOMINA
Preshy Marker	PHILIA
Raymond Walburn	ERRONIUS
Judy Alexander	GEMINAE
Lucienne Bridou	PANACEA
David Evans	PROTEAN
Lisa James	GEMINAE
Roberta Keith	TINTINABULA
Gloria Kristy	GYMNASIA
Eddie Phillips	PROTEAN
George Reeder	PROTEAN
Myrna White	VIBRATA

Anyone Can Whistle

OPENING	April 4, 1964
CLOSING	April 11, 1964
TOTAL PERFORMANCES	9

Produced by Kermit Bloomgarden and Diana Krasny
Book by Arthur Laurents
Music by Stephen Sondheim
Lyrics by Stephen Sondheim
Music orchestrated by Don Walker
Musical Director: Herbert Greene
Vocal arrangements by Herbert Greene
Dance arrangements by Betty Walberg
Directed by Arthur Laurents
Choreographed by Herbert Ross

OPENING NIGHT CAST

Harry Guardino	J. BOWDEN HAPGOOD
Angela Lansbury	CORA HOOVER HOOPER
Lee Remick	FAY APPLE
Sterling Clark	ONE OF THE BOYS; COOKIE, NURSE, DEPUTY, TOWNSPERSON, PILGRIM, TOURIST
Georgia Creighton	OSGOOD; COOKIE, NURSE, DEPUTY, TOWNSPERSON, PILGRIM, TOURIST
Gabriel Dell	COMPTROLLER SCHUB
Don Doherty	DR. DETMOLD
Eugene Edwards	COOKIE, NURSE, DEPUTY, TOWNSPERSON, PILGRIM, TOURIST
Dick Ensslen	COOKIE, NURSE, DEPUTY, TOWNSPERSON, PILGRIM, TOURIST
Harvey Evans	JOHN; ONE OF THE BOYS, COOKIE, NURSE, DEPUTY, TOWNSPERSON, PILGRIM, TOURIST
James Frawley	CHIEF MAGRUDER
Janet Hayes	JUNE; COOKIE, NURSE, DEPUTY, TOWNSPERSON, PILGRIM, TOURIST
Alan Johnson	TELEGRAPH BOY; COOKIE, NURSE, DEPUTY, TOWNSPERSON, PILGRIM, TOURIST
Larry Roquemore	GEORGE; ONE OF THE BOYS; COOKIE, NURSE, DEPUTY, TOWNSPERSON, PILGRIM, TOURIST
Jeff Killion	SANDWICH MAN; COOKIE, NURSE, DEPUTY, TOWNSPERSON, PILGRIM, TOURIST
Peg Murray	MRS. SCHROEDER
Tucker Smith	ONE OF THE BOYS; COOKIE, NURSE, DEPUTY, TOWNSPERSON, PILGRIM, TOURIST
Arnold Soboloff	TREASURER COOLEY
Jeanne Tanzy	BABY JOAN
Eleonore Treiber	OLD LADY; COOKIE, NURSE, DEPUTY, TOWNSPERSON, PILGRIM, TOURIST
Lester Wilson	MARTIN; COOKIE, NURSE, DEPUTY, TOWNSPERSON, PILGRIM, TOURIST
Susan Borree	COOKIE, NURSE, DEPUTY, TOWNSPERSON, PILGRIM, TOURIST
Loren Hightower	
Bettye Jenkins	
Patricia Kelly	
Barbara Lang	
Paula Lloyd	
Barbara Monte	
Jack Murray	
Odette Phillips	
William Reilly	
Hanne Marie Reiner	
Donald Stewart	

Do I Hear a Waltz?

OPENING	March 18, 1965
CLOSING	September 25, 1965
TOTAL PERFORMANCES	220

Produced by Richard Rodgers
Produced by special arrangement with AML Enterprises, Inc.
Book by Arthur Laurents
Music by Richard Rodgers
Lyrics by Stephen Sondheim
Based on the play *The Time of the Cuckoo* by Arthur Laurents
Music orchestrated by Ralph Burns
Musical Director: Frederick Dvonch
Dance arrangements by Richard De Benidictis
Directed by John Dexter
Choreographed by Herbert Ross

OPENING NIGHT CAST

Elizabeth Allen	LEONA SAMISH
Sergio Franchi	RENATO DI ROSSI
Carol Bruce	SIGNORA FIORA
Stuart Damon	EDDIE YAEGER
Fleury D'Antonakis	GIOVANNA
James Dybas	VITO
Jack Manning	MR. MCILHENNY
Julienne Marie	JENNIFER YAEGER
Madeleine Sherwood	MRS. MCILHENNY
Christopher Votos	MAURO
Helon Blount	MRS. VICTORIA HASLAM
Michael Lamont	MAN ON BRIDGE; SINGER
Darrell Askey	SINGER
Syndee Balaber	
Bill Berrian	
Rudy Challenger	
Pat Kelly	
Liz Lamkin	
James Luisi	
Jack Murray	
Carl Nicholas	
Candida Pilla	
Casper Roos	
Bernice Saunders	
Liza Stuart	
Bob Bishop	DANCER
Wayne De Rammelaere	
Steve Jacobs	
Sandy Leeds	
Joe Nelson	
Janice Peta	
Walter Stratton	
Nancy Van Rijn	
Mary Zahn	
Jere Admire	DANCER; SINGER

Company

OPENING	April 26, 1970
CLOSING	January 1, 1972
TOTAL PERFORMANCES	705

Produced by Harold Prince
Produced in association with Ruth Mitchell
Music by Stephen Sondheim
Lyrics by Stephen Sondheim
Book by George Furth
Musical Director: Harold Hastings
Music orchestrated by Jonathan Tunick
Dance arrangements by Wally Harper
Directed by Harold Prince
Musical Staging by Michael Bennett
Associate Choreographer: Bob Avian

OPENING NIGHT CAST

Barbara Barrie	SARAH
Charles Braswell	LARRY
Susan Browning	APRIL
George Coe	DAVID

John Cunningham	PETER
Steve Elmore	PAUL
Beth Howland	AMY
Dean Jones	ROBERT
Charles Kimbrough	HARRY
Merle Louise	SUSAN
Donna McKechnie	KATHY
Pamela Myers	MARTA
Teri Ralston	JENNY
Elaine Stritch	JOANNE
Marilyn Saunders	MEMBER OF THE VOCAL MINORITY
Dona D. Vaughn	
Cathy Corkill	
Carol Gelfand	

Standbys: Sandra Deel (*Joanne*), Jessica James (*Joanne*), Larry Kert (*Robert*).

Follies

OPENING	April 4, 1971
CLOSING	July 1, 1972
TOTAL PERFORMANCES	522

Produced by Harold Prince
Produced in association with Ruth Mitchell
Book by James Goldman
Music by Stephen Sondheim
Lyrics by Stephen Sondheim
Musical Director: Harold Hastings
Music orchestrated by Jonathan Tunick
Dance arrangements by John Berkman
Choral arrangements by Harold Hastings
Assistant Musical Director: Paul Cianci
Directed by Harold Prince and Michael Bennett
Choreographed by Michael Bennett
Associate Choreographer: Bob Avian

OPENING NIGHT CAST

Dorothy Collins	SALLY DURANT PLUMMER
John McMartin	BENJAMIN STONE
Gene Nelson	BUDDY PLUMMER
Alexis Smith	PHYLLIS ROGERS STONE
Yvonne De Carlo	CARLOTTA CAMPION
Roy Barry	SINGER AND DANCER
Michael Bartlett	ROSCOE
Helon Blount	DEE DEE WEST
Steven Boockvor	SINGER AND DANCER
Suzanne Briggs	SHOWGIRL
Trudy Carson	SHOWGIRL
Ethel Barrymore Colt	CHRISTINE CRANE
Kathie Dalton	SHOWGIRL
Graciela Daniele	YOUNG VANESSA; SINGER AND DANCER
Fifi D'Orsay	SOLANGE LAFITTE
Harvey Evans	YOUNG BUDDY
Victor Griffin	VINCENT
John Grigas	CHAUFFEUR
Mary Jane Houdina	YOUNG HATTIE; SINGER AND DANCER
Justine Johnston	HEIDI SCHILLER
Fred Kelly	WILLY WHEELER
Dick Latessa	MAJOR-DOMO
Sonja Levkova	SANDRA DONOVAN
Victoria Mallory	YOUNG HEIDI
John J. Martin	MAX DEEMS
Ursula Maschmeyer	SHOWGIRL
Mary McCarty	STELLA DEEMS
Michael Misita	YOUNG VINCENT; SINGER AND DANCER
Arnold Moss	DIMITRI WEISMANN
Ralph Nelson	KEVIN; SINGER AND DANCER
Linda Perkins	SHOWGIRL
Kurt Peterson	YOUNG BEN
Marti Rolph	YOUNG SALLY
Virginia Sandifur	YOUNG PHYLLIS
Ethel Shutta	HATTIE WALKER

Sheila Smith	MEREDITH LANE
Marcie Stringer	EMILY WHITMAN
Margot Travers	SHOWGIRL
Jayne Turner	VANESSA
Peter Walker	CHET RICHARDS
Donald Weissmuller	SINGER AND DANCER
Charles Welch	THEODORE WHITMAN
Rita O'Connor	SINGER AND DANCER
Julie Pars	
Joseph Nelson	
Suzanne Rogers	
Kenneth Urmston	

A Little Night Music

OPENING	February 25, 1973
CLOSING	August 3, 1974
TOTAL PERFORMANCES	601

Produced by Harold Prince
Produced in association with Ruth Mitchell
Music by Stephen Sondheim
Lyrics by Stephen Sondheim
Book by Hugh Wheeler
Suggested by the film *Smiles of a Summer Night* by Ingmar Bergman
Music orchestrated by Jonathan Tunick
Musical Director: Harold Hastings
Assistant to Mr. Hastings: Arthur Wagner
Directed by Harold Prince
Choreographed by Patricia Birch

OPENING NIGHT CAST

Len Cariou	FREDERIK EGERMAN
Hermione Gingold	MADAME ARMFELDT
Glynis Johns	DESIREE ARMFELDT
George Lee Andrews	FRID
D'Jamin Bartlett	PETRA
Despo	MALLA
Patricia Elliott	COUNTESS CHARLOTTE MALCOLM
Beth Fowler	MRS. SEGSTROM
Laurence Guittard	COUNT CARL-MAGNUS MALCOLM
Judy Kahan	FREDRIKA ARMFELDT
Mark Lambert	HENRIK EGERMAN
Barbara Lang	MRS. ANDERSSEN
Victoria Mallory	ANNE EGERMAN
Teri Ralston	MRS. NORDSTROM
Benjamin Rayson	MR. LINDQUIST
Gene Varrone	MR. ERLANSON
Will Sharpe Marshall	BERTRAND
Sherry Mathis	OSA

The Frogs

OPENING	July 22, 2004
CLOSING	October 10, 2004
TOTAL PERFORMANCES	92

Produced by Lincoln Center Theater (André Bishop: Artistic Director; Bernard Gersten: Executive Producer)
Produced in association with Bob Boyett
LCT Musical Theater Associate Producer: Ira Weitzman
A comedy written in 405 B.C. by Aristophanes, *The Frogs*, freely adapted by Burt Shevelove
The Frogs even more freely adapted by Nathan Lane
Music by Stephen Sondheim
Lyrics by Stephen Sondheim
Lyrics for "Fear No More" from *Cymbeline* by William Shakespeare
Music orchestrated by Jonathan Tunick
Musical Director: Paul Gemignani
Dance arrangements by Glen Kelly
Associate Musical Director: Annbritt du Chateau

Directed by Susan Stroman
Choreographed by Susan Stroman
Associate Director: Tara Young
Associate Choreographer: Tara Young
Assistant Director: Scott Bishop

OPENING NIGHT CAST

Roger Bart	XANTHIAS
Peter Bartlett	PLUTO
John Byner	CHARON / AEKOS
Daniel Davis	GEORGE BERNARD SHAW
Bryn Dowling	ENSEMBLE; HANDMAIDEN CHARISMA; ONE OF PLUTO'S HELLRAISERS
Rebecca Eichenberger	ENSEMBLE; SHAVIAN
Meg Gillentine	ENSEMBLE; ONE OF THREE GRACES; ONE OF PLUTO'S HELLRAISERS; SHAVIAN
Pia C. Glenn	ENSEMBLE; VIRILLA
Tyler Hanes	ENSEMBLE; SHAVIAN
Francesca Harper	ENSEMBLE; ONE OF PLUTO'S HELLRAISERS; SHAVIAN; ONE OF THREE GRACES; ONE OF PLUTO'S HELLRAISERS
Naomi Kakuk	ENSEMBLE; ONE OF THREE GRACES; ONE OF PLUTO'S HELLRAISERS
Nathan Lane	DIONYSOS
Luke Longacre	ENSEMBLE; FIRE BELLY BOUNCING FROG
David Lowenstein	ENSEMBLE; SHAVIAN
Burke Moses	HERAKLES
Michael Siberry	WILLIAM SHAKESPEARE
Kathy Voytko	ENSEMBLE; ARIADNE
Jay Brian Winnick	ENSEMBLE; SHAVIAN
Ryan L. Ball	ENSEMBLE; FIRE BELLY BOUNCING FROG
Rod Harrelson	ENSEMBLE
Jessica Howard	
Steve Wilson	
Kenway Hon Wai K. Kua	

Pacific Overtures

OPENING	January 11, 1976
CLOSING	June 27, 1976
TOTAL PERFORMANCES	193

Produced by Harold Prince
Produced in association with Ruth Mitchell
Music by Stephen Sondheim
Lyrics by Stephen Sondheim
Book by John Weidman
Additional material by Hugh Wheeler
Music orchestrated by Jonathan Tunick
Musical Director: Paul Gemignani
Dance music by Danny Troob
Directed by Harold Prince
Choreographed by Patricia Birch

OPENING NIGHT CAST

Mako	RECITER; SHOGUN; JONATHAN GOBLE
Soon-Teck Oh	TAMATE; SAMURAI; STORYTELLER; SWORDSMAN
Isao Sato	KAYAMA
Yuki Shimoda	ABE, FIRST COUNCILOR
Sab Shimono	MANJIRO
Ernest Abuba	SAMURAI; ADAMS; NOBLE
James Dybas	SECOND COUNCILOR; OLD MAN; FRENCH ADMIRAL
Timm Fujii	SON; PRIEST; GIRL; NOBLE; BRITISH SAILOR; PROSCENIUM SERVANT, SAILOR AND TOWNSPERSON
Haruki Fujimoto	SERVANT; COMMODORE MATTHEW CALBRAITH PERRY
Joey Ginza	PROSCENIUM SERVANT, SAILOR AND TOWNSPERSON
Larry Hama	WILLIAMS; LORD OF THE SOUTH
Ernest Harada	PHYSICIAN; MADAM; BRITISH ADMIRAL
Alvin Ing	SHOGUN'S MOTHER; OBSERVER; MERCHANT; AMERICAN ADMIRAL
Susan Kikuchi	PROSCENIUM SERVANT, SAILOR AND TOWNSPERSON

Patrick Kinser-Lau   SHOGUN'S COMPANION; GIRL;
DUTCH ADMIRAL;BRITISH SAILOR;
PROSCENIUM SERVANT, SAILOR
AND TOWNSPERSON
Jae Woo Lee   FISHERMAN; SUMO WRESTLER; LORD OF THE SOUTH
Freddy Mao   THIRD COUNCILOR; SAMURAI'S DAUGHTER
Tom Matsusaka   IMPERIAL PRIEST
Freda Foh Shen   SHOGUN'S WIFE; PROSCENIUM SERVANT,
SAILOR AND TOWNSPERSON
Mark Hsu Syers   SAMURAI; THIEF; SOOTHSAYER; WARRIOR;
RUSSIAN ADMIRAL; BRITISH SAILOR; PROSCENIUM
SERVANT, SAILOR AND TOWNSPERSON
Ricardo Tobia   OBSERVER; PROSCENIUM SERVANT,
SAILOR AND TOWNSPERSON
Gedde Watanabe   PRIEST; GIRL; BOY; PROSCENIUM SERVANT,
SAILOR AND TOWNSPERSON
Leslie Watanabe   GIRL; PROSCENIUM SERVANT, SAILOR
AND TOWNSPERSON
Conrad Yama   GRANDMOTHER; SUMO WRESTLER;
JAPANESE MERCHANT
Fusako Yoshida   MUSICIAN—SHAMISEN
Kevin Maung   PROSCENIUM SERVANT, SAILOR AND TOWNSPERSON
Kim Miyori
Dingo Secretario
Diane Lam
Kenneth S. Eiland
Tony Marinyo

Sweeney Todd, the Demon Barber of Fleet Street

OPENING   March 1, 1979
CLOSING   June 29, 1980
TOTAL PERFORMANCES   557

Produced by Richard Barr, Charles Woodward, Robert Fryer, Mary
Lea Johnson and Martin Richards
Produced in association with Dean Manos and Judy Manos
Associate Producer: Marc Howard
Music by Stephen Sondheim
Lyrics by Stephen Sondheim
Book by Hugh Wheeler
Based on a version of Sweeney Todd by Christopher Bond
Music orchestrated by Jonathan Tunick
Musical Director: Paul Gemignani
Assistant Musical Director: Les Scott
Directed by Harold Prince
Dance and movement by Larry Fuller

OPENING NIGHT CAST

Len Cariou   SWEENEY TODD
Angela Lansbury   MRS. LOVETT
Victor Garber   ANTHONY HOPE
Ken Jennings   TOBIAS RAGG
Merle Louise   BEGGAR WOMAN
Edmund Lyndeck   JUDGE TURPIN
Sarah Rice   JOHANNA
Joaquin Romaguera   PIRELLI
Jack Eric Williams   THE BEADLE
Robert Ousley   JONAS FOGG; MEMBER OF THE COMPANY
Duane Bodin   MEMBER OF THE COMPANY
Walter Charles
Carole Doscher

Nancy Eaton
Mary-Pat Green
Cris Groenendaal
Skip Harris
Marthe Ihde
Betsy Joslyn
Nancy Killmer
Frank Kopyc
Spain Logue
Craig Lucas
Pamela McLernon
Duane Morris
Richard Warren Pugh
Maggie Task

Merrily We Roll Along

OPENING   November 16, 1981
CLOSING   November 28, 1981
TOTAL PERFORMANCES   16

Produced by Lord Lew Grade, Martin Starger, Robert Fryer and
Harold Prince
Associate Producer: Ruth Mitchell and Howard Haines
Music by Stephen Sondheim
Lyrics by Stephen Sondheim
Book by George Furth
From the play by George S. Kaufman and Moss Hart
Music orchestrated by Jonathan Tunick
Musical Director: Paul Gemignani
Directed by Harold Prince
Choreographed by Larry Fuller
Assistant Choreographer: Janie Gleason

OPENING NIGHT CAST

Jason Alexander   JOE
Marianna Allen   GIRL AUDITIONING
James Bonkovsky   GEORGE
David Cady   JEROME
Liz Callaway   NIGHTCLUB WAITRESS
Donna Marie Elio   TERRY
Giancarlo Esposito   VALEDICTORIAN
Terry Finn   GUSSIE
Geoffrey Horne   FRANKLIN SHEPARD (at age 43)
Paul Hyams   MR. SPENCER
Steven Jacob   PHOTOGRAPHER
Mary Johansen   MRS. SPENCER
Sally Klein   BETH
David Loud   TED
Marc Moritz   ALEX
Ann Morrison   MARY FLYNN
Tonya Pinkins   GWEN WILSON
Abby Pogrebin   EVELYN
Lonny Price   CHARLEY KRINGAS
Daisy Prince   MEG
Forest D. Ray   RU
Clark Sayre   SOUNDMAN
Tom Shea   BARTENDER
David Shine   LES
Gary Stevens   WAITER
Jim Walton   FRANKLIN SHEPARD
Maryrose Wood   MS. GORDON

Index of Songs

Subject Index

Page numbers in *italics* refer to illustrations.

Broadway musicals, xvii, xxi
  academic productions of, 285–7
  acts in, 106–7, 120
  backstage, 286, 382
  bare stage, 166
  book, xxii, 28, 112, 166, 285
  "buzz" about, 82
  casting of, 22, 82, 180, 263
  chamber, 4, 149
  character-driven, 6, 7–8, 55–7, 99,
    200
  concept, 4, 166
  curtain times of, 135
  cutting of songs from, 28, 31–5, 42–3,
    60, 61, 65, 68–9, 74, 86–7, 350
  dance as essential element in, 25, 166
  experimental, 80, 142, 165–7
  farce, 66, 79–109
  illegal tampering with, 287
  "integrated," 166
  intellectual bias against, 287
  irony in, 166
  movie, 99, 180, 231, 282, 331, 382
  nightclub, 166
  opening numbers in, 83, 333–4, 385
  opera house performances of, 283, 332,
    350
  out-of-town tryouts for, 28–30, 34, 48,
    49–50, 60, 81, 82, 86, 382
  period, 330–77
  piano rehearsals of, 60, 62, 81, 82
  plotless, 166, 199–200
  popular songs from, 106–7, 381
  pre-production auditions and readings
    of, 81–2, 111
  pre-production "development" of, 112
  production of, 21–2, 29–30, 82, 166
  prominence of directors in, 112
  published scores of, 355
  raising money for, 22, 82
  rewriting and fixing of, 82, 86, 87
  rock and pop, 57
  romantic, 166, 251
  running times of, 120
  satirical, 166, 176
  scenes in, xxi–xxii, 28
  singing and dancing choruses in, 4, 80,
    166, 219, 237, 345
  "sophisticated," 212
  Sondheim seen as presiding over "death
    of," 375–6
  as star vehicles, 55, 56, 193, 220–1,
    237, 278
  television, 64, 252, 282
  theatrical convention in, 345, 354
  through-composed, 253
  through-sung, 253, 332
  ticket prices of, 165, 382
  title credits for, 112
  "Why," 143, 162
Broadway songs, xxi, 331
  abridged versions of, 311–13
  action, 167
  advancing the plot with, 79, 167, 271
  "book," 221
  character-driven, 7–8, 105, 106–7, 200,
    392

  collage of, 77
  comment, 175
  "eleven-o'clock," 135
  experimenting with melody, harmony
    and form in, 80, 142, 165–7, 339,
    379
  as homages, 222, 228, 241
  "hook" in, 379
  hummable, 86–7
  lead-ins to, 60
  list, 63, 83, 100, 101, 145, 175, 209,
    212, 230, 324, 361, 392
  love, 26–7, 28, 37–40, 212, 228, 230,
    381
  "mechanical," 142
  message, 211
  meter in, 28
  novelty, 207
  one-joke, 80, 145, 220
  pastiche, 200, 207, 209–11, 219, 221,
    222, 228, 230, 232, 235, 238, 327,
    381
  patter, 177, 184–5, 212, 229, 230, 324,
    327
  period, 200, 209, 230, 233, 327,
    333–77
  recycling of, 61, 64
  "release" in, 60, 230, 379n
  reprise of, 13–14, 100, 106–7, 147,
    280, 300, 381
  as short plays, xxii, 79, 80, 271, 303
  showstopping, 77, 149, 162, 180, 193,
    220, 221
  telling a story with, 142, 271, 303
  thematic connections in, 167
  throwaway, 220
  urban feeling in, 381
  as vehicles for specific stars, 55, 56,
    193, 220–1, 278
  verses and choruses of, 102n, 106, 153,
    161, 209, 222, 230, 232
  "wrong," 279
  see also song form; specific songs
Brooklyn Dodgers, 4
Brown, Lew, xiii, 200, 211
Brown, Nacio Herb, xii, 200, 231
Browning, Robert, 161
Bruce, Carol, 147
Brustein, Robert, 286–7
Burgess, Anthony, x, xix
burlesque, 57, 62, 74
Burthen Music, 232
Burton, Tim, 280
By George, 25

Cabaret, xixn, 166
Cabin in the Sky, 99
Cage, John, 307
Cahn, Sammy, xii, 64
Caldwell, Anne, xiii, 222
Camelot, xii, 17
camp, 176, 212, 263
can-can, 327
Candide, x, xi, xix, 51, 176, 324
Capote, Truman, x, xix, xx, 22, 324
Cariou, Len, 282, 340
Carmelina, 17

Carmen (Bizet), 332
Carmen Jones, 332
Carnelia, Craig, xi, xxvi
Carousel, x, 5, 36, 79, 142, 143, 165, 202,
  332, 345, 379
Casablanca (film), 331
Cat on a Hot Tin Roof (Williams), 51
Chaplin, Charlie, 107
Charley's Aunt (Thomas), 80
Chavalier, Maurice, 14
Chekhov, Anton, 196
Chichester Psalms (Bernstein), 34
Chopin, Frédéric, 200
choreography, 173
  chorus line, 219
  narrative function of, 166
  see also ballet; dance
choruses
  choreography for, 219
  Greek, 165, 293n, 298n, 345
  individualized, 166, 345, 366
  overlapping voices in, 345, 383–4
  singing and dancing, 4, 80, 166, 219,
    237, 345
  see also Broadway songs, verses and
    choruses of
Chorus Line, A, 219
Christie, Agatha, 324
Church, Sandra, 56
Cincinnati Conservatory, 180
Citizen Kane (film), 77, 395
Climb High, 3
clog dance, 327
Coleman, Cy, xii, 222
Collins, Dorothy, 238, 278
Collins, Judy, 278
Colvan, Zeke, 112n
Columbia Records, 51
Comden, Betty, ix, xii, 26
comedy
  film, 331
  Greek, 285–6, 287, 299
  light, 277–8
  situation, 278
  see also farce
"Comment" (Parker), xviii, xxvii
Company, 3, 82, 164–97, 283, 287, 303,
  339, 381, 408
  Act One of, 168–85
  Act Two of, 186–96
  casting of, 180, 263
  choreography in, 173
  finale of, 195–6, 306
  form of, 3, 165–6
  musicals influenced by, 167
  1995 Roundabout Theater production
    of, 186
  1996 London production of, 166
  opening number of, 167–73
  orchestra in, 166
  original 1970 production of, 166, 186
  out-of-town tryouts of, 180, 184, 196
  premise of, 165–6
  rehearsals of, 180, 185
  sets of, 166, 173
  songs cut from, 185, 195–6
  source of, 165

George School, 25
George White's Scandals, xii
Gershwin, George, xi, xx, 28, 64, 176, 200, 222, 235, 241, 331, 379
Gershwin, Ira, xi, xx, 6, 17, 37, 53, 55, 80, 99, 153, 175, 176, 200, 212, 222, 233, 234, 235, 241
ghost lights, 77
Gianni Schicchi (Puccini), 80
Gigi, 14, 263
Gilbert, W. S., xiii, 17, 37, 63, 142, 200, 212, 286
Gingold, Hermione, 14, *257,* 263, 283
Girl Crazy, xi
Girl Who Came to Supper, The, 112
Glyndebourne Festival Opera, 332
Golden Age of Musicals (1925–1960), xix, 13*n,* 81, 99, 200, 232, 379
Goldman, James, v, 4, 79, 80, 100, 199–200, 203, 220–1, 243, 252
Goldman, William, 282
Goldoni, Carlo, 80
Good News, xii
Gould, Morton, xii, 222
Grammy Awards, 278
Grant, Cary, 129
Greatest Story Ever Told, The (film), x
Greek Chorus, 165, 293*n,* 298*n,* 345
Green, Adolph, ix, xii, 26
Green Grow the Lilacs (Riggs), 143
Greenwillow, 6, 222
Grieg, Edvard, 247
Griffith, Robert, 30
Guardino, Harry, *133*
Guernsey, Otis, Jr., 253*n*
Guettel, Adam, 379
Guys and Dolls, xi, 6
Gypsy, 8, 48*n,* 54–77, *56,* 80, 99, 116*n,* 141, 142, 193, 200, 279, 355, 375, 379, 381
  book of, 55
  film version of, 280
  opening night of, *57,* 64
  out-of-town tryouts of, 60, 77*n*
  rehearsals of, 75–7
  songs cut from, 60, 61, 65, 68–9, 74, 77*n*

haiku, 304, 306, 316
Hallelujah, Baby!, xii
Hamilton, Margaret, 252
Hamlet (Shakespeare), xxi, 112
Hammerstein, Dorothy, 37
Hammerstein, Oscar, II, x, 6, 112*n,* 129, 200, 202, 333, 421
  death of, 3, 141
  Harbach as mentor of, 36, 228
  Kern and, 37, 222
  lyrics of, xvii–xx, xxv–xxvii, 5, 26, 36–7, 79, 99, 106–7, 148, 153, 203, 212, 222, 232–3, 304, 324
  nature imagery of, 26, 36–7, 212, 222
  Rodgers and, xx, 4, 7–8, 17, 36–7, 55, 142–3, 155, 165, 222, 232–3, 252, 304, 345, 379, 381
  as Sondheim's mentor, xv, xix*n,* xxii, 3, 26, 28, 36, 37, 55, 56, 77, 79, 80, 83, 87, 99, 141–2, 165, 212, 222, 233, 331, 385

Handel, George Frederick, 324
Hangover Square (film), 331, 332
Hans Christian Anderson (film), 6
Happy Breed, This (film), 229
Harbach, Otto, xiii, 36, 200, 228
Harburg, E. Y., xii, xx, xxvii, 6, 17, 22, 37, 55, 63, 99, 100, 153, 176, 200, 203, 212, 220, 222, 228, 233, 235
Hard Day's Night, A (film), 92
Harnick, Sheldon, xi, xix*n,* 48, 153, 203, 381
Harper's, 375
Hart, Lorenz, x, xx, 5, 6, 17, 37, 55, 80, 99, 166, 200, 203, 211, 228, 235
  careless lyric writing of, 153, 176, 327
  homosexuality of, 155, 212
  Rodgers and, xviii, 36, 131, 153, 155, 212, 222, 232–3, 304
Hart, Moss, 112, 166, 379, 381, 388, 395, 421
Harvard University, 307
Havoc, June, 55
Haydn, Joseph, 324
Hearn, George, 340
Hemingway, Ernest, 200, 303
Henderson, Ray, xii, 200, 211
Henry V (film), 280
Herbert, Victor, 200, 238
Herman, Jerry, 153
Herrmann, Bernard, 331–2
Heyward, DuBose, ix, x, xix, xx, 17, 37, 176, 304
High Button Shoes, 81
High Tor (Anderson), 3
Hitchcock, Alfred, 56, 331, 332
Hit Parade, 106
H.M.S. Pinafore, xiii
Hofmannsthal, Hugo von, xx
Holden, Stephen, xxi
Hold Everything!, xiii
Hold on to Your Hats, xiii
Holman, Libby, 55
homosexuality, 143, 155, 212
Hope, Bob, 55
Hot Spot, 165
House of Flowers, x, xii, xix, 22
Howland, Beth, *181*
How to Succeed in Business Without Really Trying, 6
huapango, 41
Hughes, Langston, x, xix
Huston, John, 271*n*

I Can Get It for You Wholesale, 111
Idiot's Delight (Sherwood), 17
I Married an Angel, 153
Imperial Theatre, 199
Into the Woods, xxii, 376
Invitation au Chateau, L' (Anouilh), 251
In Which We Serve (film), 229
Iroquois Hotel, 29
Isherwood, Christopher, 166
Is There Life After High School?, xi

Japanese culture, 304, 307, 316
Johns, Glynis, 278
Jones, Dean, *181*

jukebox musicals, xxi
June Moon, xxiii
Jupiter Symphony (Mozart), 303

Kahan, Judy, *257*
Kallman, Chester, xix
Kander, John, xi, xix*n,* 381
Kaufman, George S., 3, 112, 379, 381, 388, 395, 421
Kazan, Elia, 112
Kazan, Lainie, 222
Keats, John, xviii*n*
Keeler, Ruby, 180
Kelly, George, 112
Kern, Jerome, x, xvii, 28, 37, 200, 232, 234, 241, 303, 331, 379
  Hammerstein and, 37, 222
Kerr, Walter, 37
King and I, The, x, 36, 148
Kiss Me Kate, xi, 4, 149, 212
Kitt, Eartha, 222
Kleine Nachtmusik, Eine (Mozart), 252*n*
Knickerbocker Holiday, x
Korngold, Erich, 331
Kostal, Irwin, 49

Lächeln einer Sommernacht, Das, 252*n*
Lady, Be Good, xi, 75
Lady in the Dark, xi
Lahr, John, 375–6
Land, David, 332, 334
Lane, Burton, xiii, 22, 200, 222, 232
Lane, Nathan, 285, 287
Lansbury, Angela, 56, 111, *117,* 130, 135, 238, *357, 364*
Lapine, James, v, 4, 112*n,* 120, 385, 396, 421
Lascoe, Henry, 111
Lasker-Schüler, Else, 28
La Touche, John, ix, 17
Laurence Olivier Award, 381
Laurents, Arthur, v, 4, 25–7, 33, 40, 41, 43, 50, 52, 116*n,* 153, 221, 332
  directing of, 111–12, 141
  plays of, 141, 143, 162
  Sondheim's collaboration with, v, 55–7, 61–2, 66, 68, 77, 80, 111–12, 120, 141–3, 148, 155, 186
Lean, David, 141
Leave It to Me, 212
Lee, Gypsy Rose, 55, 71, 74
Lehár, Franz, 282
Leicester, 381, *403*
Leigh, Carolyn, ix, xiii, 222
Lerner, Alan Jay, xii, 14, 17, 153, 222
Lester, Richard, 92, 280
Let 'Em Eat Cake, 379
Library of Congress, 287
Lieberson, Goddard, 51
Liebling, William, 4*n*
Life Begins at 8:40, xii, 176
light comedy, 277–8
light verse, xviii, 80
Liliom (Molnár), 143
Lincoln Center, 287
Little Night Music, A, 82, 153, 162, 166, 250–83, 311, 375, 376
  Act One of, 154–72

Illustration Credits

A Note About the Author

Stephen Sondheim wrote the music and lyrics for *A Funny Thing Happened on the Way to the Forum* (1962), *Anyone Can Whistle* (1964), *Company* (1970), *Follies* (1971), *A Little Night Music* (1973), *The Frogs* (1974), *Pacific Overtures* (1976), *Sweeney Todd, The Demon Barber of Fleet Street* (1979), *Merrily We Roll Along* (1981), *Sunday in the Park with George* (1984), *Into the Woods* (1987), *Assassins* (1991), *Passion* (1994) and *Bounce* (2003), as well as lyrics for *West Side Story* (1957), *Gypsy* (1959), *Do I Hear a Waltz?* (1964) and additional lyrics for *Candide* (1974). *Side by Side by Sondheim* (1976), *Marry Me a Little* (1980), *You're Gonna Love Tomorrow* (1983), *Putting It Together* (1993, 1999), *Moving On* (2000) and *Sondheim on Sondheim* (2010) are anthologies of his work as composer and lyricist. For films, he composed the scores of *Stavisky* (1974) and co-composed *Reds* (1981) as well as songs for *Dick Tracy* (1990). He also wrote the songs for the television production *Evening Primrose* (1966), co-authored the film *The Last of Sheila* (1973) and the play *Getting Away with Murder* (1996) and provided incidental music for the plays *The Girls of Summer* (1956), *Invitation to a March* (1960), *Twigs* (1971) and *The Enclave* (1973). *Saturday Night* (1954), his first professional musical, finally had its New York premiere in 1999. He has received the Tony Award for Best Original Score (Music/Lyrics) for *Company, Follies, A Little Night Music, Into the Woods* and *Passion*, all of which won the New York Drama Critics' Circle Award for Best Musical, as did *Pacific Overtures* and *Sunday in the Park with George*. In total, his works have accumulated more than sixty individual and collaborative Tony Awards. "Sooner or Later" from the film *Dick Tracy* won the Academy Award for Best Song. Mr. Sondheim received the Pulitzer Prize for Drama in 1985 for *Sunday in the Park with George.*

In 1983 he was elected to the American Academy of Arts and Letters, which awarded him the Gold Medal in Music in 2006. In 1990 he was appointed the first Visiting Professor of Contemporary Theatre at Oxford University and was the recipient of the Kennedy Center Honors in 1993. Mr. Sondheim is on the council of the Dramatists Guild of America, the national association of playwrights, composers and lyricists, having served as its president from 1973 to 1981. In 1981 he founded Young Playwrights, Inc., to develop and promote the work of American playwrights aged eighteen years and younger.

A Note on the Type

The text of this book was set in Berkeley Oldstyle, a typeface designed by Tony Stan based on a face originally developed by Frederick Goudy in 1938 for the University of California Press at Berkeley.

Composed by North Market Street Graphics, Lancaster, Pennylvania

Printed and bound by Quad/Graphics, Taunton, Massachusetts

Designed by Iris Weinstein